DENMARK VESEY'S GARDEN

ALSO BY ETHAN J. KYTLE

Romantic Reformers and the Antislavery
Struggle in the Civil War Era

ALSO BY BLAIN ROBERTS

Pageants, Parlors, and Pretty Women:
Race and Beauty in the Twentieth-Century South

DENMARK VESEY'S GARDEN

Slavery and Memory in the Cradle of the Confederacy

* * * *

ETHAN J. KYTLE

and

BLAIN ROBERTS

THE NEW PRESS

25 YEARS

NEW YORK
LONDON

Portions of the following article are reprinted with the permission of the *Journal of Southern History*: Blain Roberts and Ethan J. Kytle, "Looking the Thing in the Face: Slavery, Race, and the Commemorative Landscape in Charleston, South Carolina, 1865–2010," *Journal of Southern History* 78 (August 2012): 639–684.

Portions of the following chapter are reprinted with the permission of the University Press of Florida: Ethan J. Kytle and Blain Roberts, "Is It Okay to Talk about Slaves? Segregating the Past in Historic Charleston," in *Destination Dixie: Tourism in Southern History*, ed. Karen L. Cox (Gainesville: University Press of Florida, 2012), 137–159.

Published in the United States by The New Press, New York, 2018
Distributed by Two Rivers Distribution

LIBRARY OF CONGRESS CATALOGING-IN-PUBLICATION DATA

Names: Kytle, Ethan J., author. | Roberts, Blain, author.
Title: Denmark Vesey's garden : slavery and memory in the cradle
  of the Confederacy / Ethan J. Kytle and Blain Roberts.
Description: New York ; London : The New Press, [2018] | Includes
  bibliographical references and index.
Identifiers: LCCN 2017041546 | ISBN 9781620973653 (hc : alk. paper)
Subjects: LCSH: Slavery—South Carolina—Charleston—History. |
  Memory—Social aspects—South Carolina—Charleston. | Vesey, Denmark,
  approximately 1767-1822. | Charleston (S.C.)—History—Slave Insurrection,
  1822. | Emanuel AME Church (Charleston, S.C.)
Classification: LCC F279.C457 K97 2018 | DDC 975.7/91503092—dc23 LC record available at https://lccn.loc
.gov/2017041546

The New Press publishes books that promote and enrich public discussion and understanding of the issues vital to our democracy and to a more equitable world. These books are made possible by the enthusiasm of our readers; the support of a committed group of donors, large and small; the collaboration of our many partners in the independent media and the not-for-profit sector; booksellers, who often hand-sell New Press books; librarians; and above all by our authors.

www.thenewpress.com

Cartography by Nick Trotter
Book design by Lovedog Studio
Composition by Westchester Publishing Services
This book was set in Garamond Premier Pro and Craw Modern

Printed in the United States of America

10 9 8 7 6 5 4 3 2 1

For Eloise and Hazel

"Here [in Charleston] is a subtle flavor of Old World things, a little hush in the whirl of American doing. Between her guardian rivers and looking across the sea toward Africa sits this little Old Lady (her cheek teasingly tinged to every tantalizing shade of the darker blood) with her shoulder ever toward the street and her little laced and rusty fan beside her cheek, while long verandas of her soul stretch down the backyard into slavery."

—W.E.B. Du Bois, 1917

Contents

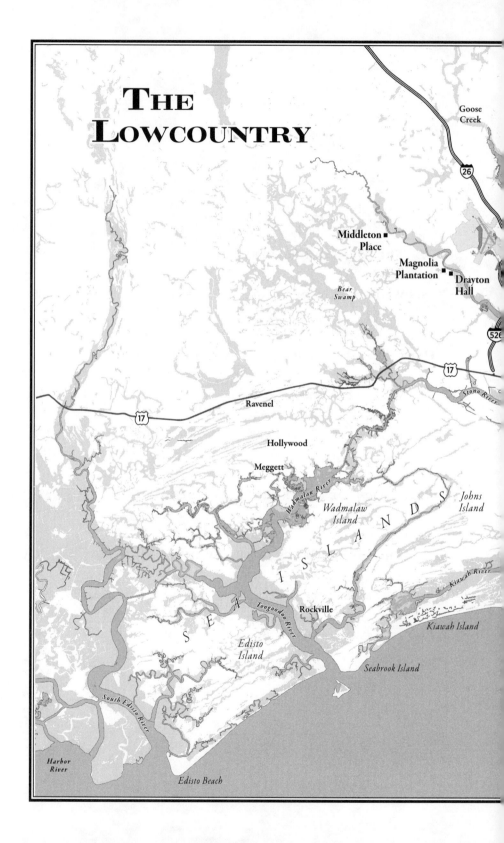

THE LOWCOUNTRY

Goose Creek

26

Middleton Place

Magnolia Plantation

Drayton Hall

Bear Swamp

526

17

Stono River

Ravenel

17

Hollywood

Meggett

Wadmalaw River

Wadmalaw Island

Johns Island

S E A

I S L A N D S

Kiawah River

Rockville

Kiawah Island

Edisto Island

Toogoodoo River

Seabrook Island

South Edisto River

Harbor River

Edisto Beach

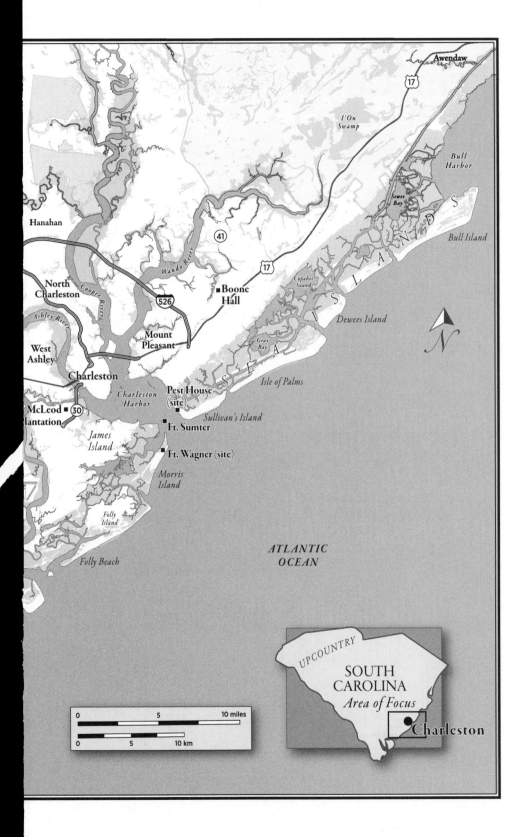

Awendaw

17

I'On
Swamp

Bull
Harbor

Sewee
Bay

S
L
A
N
D
S

Bull Island

Hanahan

41

17

Copahee
Sound

Dewees Island

Wando River

Boone
Hall

N

North
Charleston

Cooper River

526

Mount
Pleasant

Gray
Bay

SEA

ISLANDS

Ashley River

West
Ashley

Charleston

Charleston
Harbor

Pest House
(site)

Isle of Palms

McLeod
Plantation

30

Ft. Sumter

Sullivan's Island

James
Island

Ft. Wagner (site)

Morris
Island

Folly
Island

ATLANTIC
OCEAN

Folly Beach

| 0 | 5 | 10 miles |
| 0 | 5 | 10 km |

UPCOUNTRY

SOUTH
CAROLINA
Area of Focus

Charleston

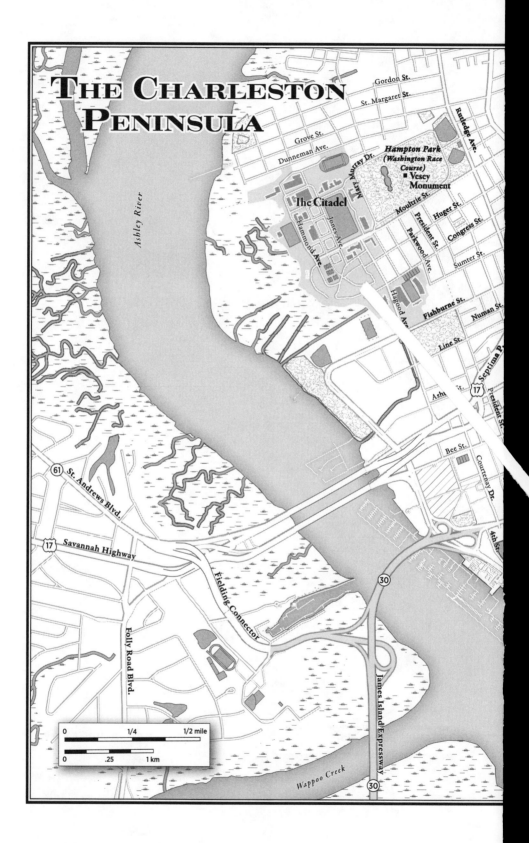

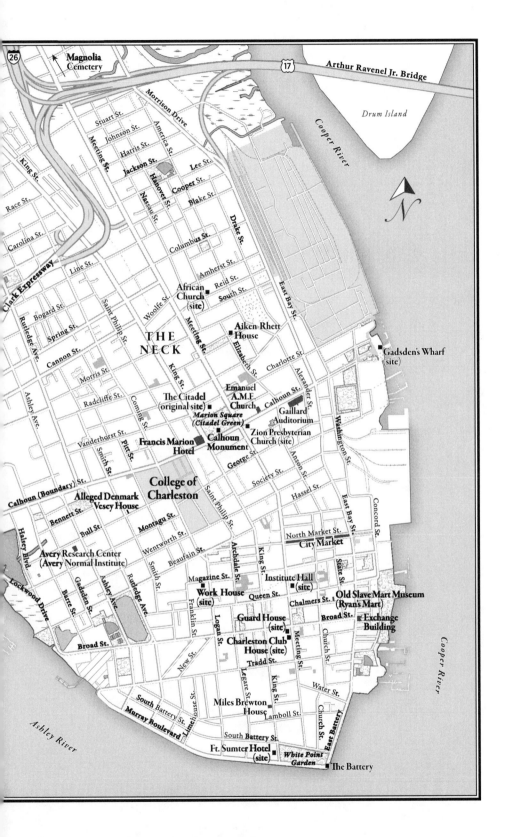

Introduction

On a sweltering June evening in 2015, members of Emanuel African Methodist Episcopal Church in Charleston, South Carolina, welcomed a stranger into their weekly Bible study group. For this gesture of Christian fellowship, most of them received a death sentence. After listening quietly for about forty minutes, the visitor—Dylann Roof, a twenty-one-year-old white supremacist who had driven in from nearby Columbia—opened fire inside the venerable black church, killing nine worshippers. Roof then exited through a side door as calmly as he had entered.

Americans soon learned that Roof's flawed understanding of slavery, among other factors, fueled his racial hatred and his attack. In his online manifesto, he claimed that "historical lies, exaggerations and myths" about how poorly African Americans had been treated under slavery are today being used to justify a black takeover of the United States. Framing himself as a white savior in the tradition of the Ku Klux Klan, he explained during his confession to the FBI that he targeted Charleston because "it's a historic city, and at one time, it had the highest ratio of black people to white people in the whole country, when we had slavery."[1]

In the months before the murders, Roof had made six trips to Charleston and the surrounding area. He later told authorities, "I prepared myself mentally." During each trip, he visited plantations and other locations associated with slavery, including Emanuel A.M.E. Church. Mother Emanuel, as it is affectionately known, is among the oldest black congregations in the South. It was the church of Denmark Vesey, Charleston's most famous—and, to some, infamous—black revolutionary. In 1822, Vesey plotted a massive slave uprising for which he and more than thirty co-conspirators were hastily tried and executed. Before Dylann Roof perpetrated *his* executions two centuries later, he created an archive of his research into Charleston's enslaved past. In Roof's car, investigators found travel brochures and several sheets of paper on which the white supremacist had scrawled the names of black churches, Emanuel A.M.E. among them, as well as the name of Denmark Vesey. On his website, Roof had posted a chilling series of photographs. Some showed him at sites he had toured. Others captured him brandishing the Confederate flag. In all of the images, a menacing Roof stares at the camera, his hatred now all too easy to see.[2]

After the Emanuel massacre, the country looked and felt different. It was as if a veil hiding something disconcerting—an affliction we had been doing our best to ignore—had suddenly been lifted. Behind it sat a toxic mix of beliefs and symbols that, endorsed by some and tolerated by many, came under increased scrutiny. Roof's support for slavery and the Confederacy that waged war to protect it raised troubling questions about how the country has remembered and commemorated its past. Was it acceptable, for instance, that Confederate statues and flags still enjoyed a prominent place in American culture?

Critics insisted it was not. By late June 2015, New Orleans mayor Mitch Landrieu had asked the city council to take down several monuments, including those honoring Confederate generals Robert E. Lee and P.G.T. Beauregard and the Confederate president, Jefferson Davis. In Tennessee, a bipartisan coalition of lawmakers called for the removal of a bust of Nathan Bedford Forrest, a Confederate general and Ku Klux Klan leader. Critics achieved a major victory on July 9, when South Carolina legislators agreed to remove the Confederate battle flag that had flown at the state capitol since the early 1960s. The effort to purge the country of Confederate and proslavery symbols quickly spread beyond the South, as companies such as Amazon, eBay, Walmart, and Sears prohibited the sale of Confederate flags and similar merchandise from their stores and websites.[3]

Protesters in ten southern states vandalized statues that honored the Confederacy and those who fought for it. Unsurprisingly, Charleston itself—the site of the church shootings and the birthplace of the Civil War—was an epicenter of this grassroots graffiti campaign. Four days after the Emanuel massacre, vandals struck the Fort Sumter Memorial

Just days after the Emanuel A.M.E. Church shootings in June 2015, the nearby monument to proslavery statesman John C. Calhoun was vandalized.

in White Point Garden, spray-painting the neoclassical paean to the Confederate defenders of the city with the phrases "Black lives matter" and "This is the problem #racist." Two days later, the towering memorial in Marion Square that honors John C. Calhoun, the South Carolina statesman who famously called southern slavery "a positive good," was similarly defaced. Protesters painted the word "racist" in red near the base of the tribute. They also modified the monument's engraved testament, which reads "Truth Justice and the Constitution," by adding the words "and Slavery."[4]

The backlash came quickly. In the six months after the Emanuel massacre, tens of thousands of Confederate defenders gathered for more than 350 pro-flag rallies, from Fort Lauderdale, Florida, to Spokane, Washington. One of the largest, in Marion County, Florida, was held to show support for the county's decision to return a Confederate flag to its government complex. Legislators in several southern states proposed new laws designed to protect Confederate memorials. One Georgia state representative introduced a bill to restore Confederate Memorial Day and Robert E. Lee's birthday as official state holidays. Accusing detractors of "cultural terrorism," he compared the effort to remove Confederate symbols to ISIS's destruction of mosques and temples. "We're entitled to our heritage," he stated.[5]

The decision to take down Confederate statues provoked real terror in some communities. A contractor hired in New Orleans to remove the city's monuments decided to back out in early 2016 after receiving death threats and finding his car torched by an arsonist. At a 2017 Charlottesville, Virginia, rally in defense of a Robert E. Lee statue slated for removal, a white supremacist plowed his car into a group of counterprotesters, killing one and injuring many. Meanwhile, in Charleston, where the emotional appeal of critics' arguments would seem to have been the most difficult to resist, Confederate and proslavery symbols remained in place. Calls to remove the Calhoun Monument, located just a block away from Emanuel A.M.E. Church, went nowhere.[6]

From the cacophony of voices that weighed in on what to do with these flags and monuments—on whether to keep them or take them down—one thing became clear: Americans do not share a common memory of slavery. Some, like Roof, romanticize the institution or deny its centrality to our history. Others focus on its cruelties as an essential component of our national DNA, one that cannot, and should not, be overlooked.

Denmark Vesey's Garden—the first book to trace the memory of slavery from its abolition in 1865 to the present—offers historical context for this contemporary divide. Since the end of the Civil War more than 150 years ago, generations of whites and blacks in Charleston have forged two competing visions of slavery. On the one hand, former slaveholders, their descendants, and others have promoted a whitewashed memory, one that downplayed or even ignored slavery at times, only to cast it as benevolent and civilizing in other moments. On the other hand, former slaves, their progeny, and some white and black allies have advanced an unvarnished counterpart. They insist that slavery must be recognized and commemorated as a brutal, inhumane institution that has shaped who we are as a nation. The debate sparked in 2015 by the Emanuel massacre, in short, is nothing new.

As the capital of American slavery and a longtime mecca of historical tourism, Charleston provides a better primer for understanding the origins and course of this debate than any other place in the United States. Over the past century and a half, Charleston's black and white residents, as well as its millions of visitors, have been wrestling with memories of our nation's original sin. Since the Civil War, Charleston has been teaching us how—and how not—to remember and memorialize slavery.

* * * *

FOR THE TWO of us, the Emanuel massacre gruesomely punctuated our own decade-long reckoning with the memory of slavery. We had embarked on this journey rather unwittingly in the summer of 2005, when we began the process of relocating to Charleston for jobs at the Citadel and the Avery Research Center for African American History and Culture. One June morning, we drove down from Chapel Hill, where we then lived, on a scouting venture. We wanted to rent an apartment downtown, in the heart of what is known as Historic Charleston, and we hoped to find what many people look for when they move to the city: hardwood floors, high ceilings, and exposed brick. That afternoon, we arrived at the first apartment on our list, which turned out to be the bottom floor of a beautiful antebellum home flanked by spacious verandas and white columns. The owner answered the door and invited us inside the basement apartment, which, updated with gleaming granite countertops and custom window treatments, appeared ready for an *Architectural Digest* photo shoot. As she ushered us through the rooms, we made small talk, asking about the home's construction and its previous owners.

Like many Charlestonians who spend their days surrounded by relics of the past, our prospective landlady had done her research—sort of. The house had been built around 1840 by the Toomers, a wealthy family that included two physicians. Up until the Civil War, she informed us, the apartment we were considering had been the workspace of the servants. "Of the slaves," one of us instinctively replied. The home owner again insisted they were servants. "There's no evidence in the historical records," she explained, "that the Toomers didn't pay them." It was quite a double negative. As we suspected that day and later confirmed, enslaved people in fact lived and worked in the Toomer household.[7]

The apartment was not for us. We found a slightly more ramshackle unit that was a better fit. (By sheer coincidence, our new home was located just half a block from where Denmark Vesey's house had once stood.) But the exchange that June day proved pivotal. Even though we moved to California after only two years in Charleston, we spent the next decade exploring how white residents like the owner of the Toomer house could be oblivious to the role of slavery in their city's history. This book results from our experiences there, from the fact that many of the white Charlestonians we encountered did not want to acknowledge slavery at all, and from the fact that when they did they often mischaracterized it as benign, even beneficial. Put another way, this book stems from our belief that the unvarnished tradition of remembering—which has long competed with the whitewashed tradition, though rarely on equal ground—is superior.

Admittedly, this motivation carries the taint of judgment. Scholars of historical memory tend to focus more on how individuals and groups use memories of the past for particular purposes than on the truthfulness of those memories. They home in, in other words, on the *function* of historical memory rather than on its accuracy. In the pages that follow, we are very much attuned to the function of memory. We explore how Charlestonians invoked and constructed recollections of slavery for political ends—some reactionary, some progressive. We also examine how they filtered the events of their lives through stories of the institution passed down from years or even decades before. Still, this book in an important sense represents a rejection of historical inaccuracy, a rejection of whitewashed memories of slavery. Being clear on this point matters because we should strive to get the past right. But it also matters precisely because of how whitewashed memories have been used in modern America. It does not take a massacre in a black church to see that the way we remember slavery has serious implications for race relations today.[8]

The United States is overdue for an honest conversation about slavery, however much that conversation may be unsettling to the descendants of slaveholders or painful to the descendants of the enslaved. Charleston's long struggle over the memory of slavery can help us understand how that conversation should proceed.

* * * *

CHARLESTON WAS THE capital of American slavery. Nearly half the slaves transported for sale in this country first set foot on North American soil in Charleston or on neighboring Sea Islands. The city also had a vibrant market for slaves traded locally, as well as for those sold down the river to the cotton and sugar plantations of the Deep South.

The enslaved people who toiled in Charleston and the surrounding Low-country made the region's planters among the richest men in America by the end of the eighteenth century, ensuring that they would resist any attempt to limit or abolish slavery. It was South Carolina statesmen who stymied efforts to outlaw the transatlantic slave trade at the Constitutional Convention in 1787 and who led the fight against the antislavery movement in the nineteenth century. By 1860, Charleston had become the hotbed of secessionism, a place dedicated at all costs to maintaining slavery. That defense culminated in the firing on Fort Sumter, the opening salvo of the Civil War. Charleston would never have emerged as the Cradle of the Confederacy, as it has often been called, had it not also been the capital of slavery.[9]

Charleston, moreover, is a city where people have long traveled to learn about America's past. If Philadelphia and Boston serve as the clearest windows into our nation's colonial and Revolutionary-era history, Charleston is the best portal to the antebellum South. It is where the Old South reached its apotheosis and met its demise, a place where the physical reminders of days gone by—antiquated buildings, forts, and plantations—are abundant and well preserved. Since the 1920s, the city has waged a sophisticated campaign to market its historical treasures and frame itself as America's Most Historic City. With just over 100,000 residents, Charleston attracts more than five million visitors a year and has been named the number one small American city for tourists by *Condé Nast* six years in a row. The entire city is a living history museum. No place in America has spent as much time and energy selling memories—most whitewashed, others unvarnished—of its past.[10]

Charleston, then, presents an unrivaled opportunity to study how slavery has been remembered. Indeed, the potency of Charleston as a place of remembrance is no better illustrated than by Dylann Roof himself. Roof set his sights on Charleston because on some level he recognized that it was the capital of American slavery and a mecca of historical tourism. As he prepared himself for the shootings, he played the part of tourist. Roof visited the restored slave cabins at the plantation museums that surround the city, as well as the site of the pest house on Sullivan's Island, where some victims of the transatlantic slave trade were quarantined. He even chose the location of his attack—Emanuel A.M.E., Denmark Vesey's church—with the memory of slavery in mind. After the thwarted slave insurrection and the hanging of Vesey and his co-conspirators, the church was torn down, only to be rebuilt after emancipation. Mother Emanuel emerged from the ashes of the Civil War as the most significant black church in South Carolina. Its most well-known member, meanwhile, haunted the dreams of white Charlestonians for generations.[11]

Charleston also allows us to explore the long history of the memory of slavery. Memories of the "peculiar institution," the southern euphemism for slavery coined in the 1830s by John C. Calhoun, hung over Low-country South Carolina well after emancipation, even when some people attempted to ignore them. Competing recollections of slavery influenced the political debates that roiled Charleston during the 1860s and 1870s, when the city—and the state of South Carolina more generally—was ground zero for the project of Reconstruction. In the decades that followed, Charleston created a tourism industry concerned almost entirely with marketing its history. And within the city and beyond, on the isolated Sea Islands that lay nearby, black remembrances of slavery took root and thrived, surviving the stultifying atmosphere of segregation to become a major source of power during the civil rights movement.[12]

Charleston and the surrounding environs thus enable us to link together a larger narrative usually told only in parts. This extended view yields significant insights. For example, while a whitewashed vision of slavery that softened the institution's cruelties and downplayed its role in causing the Civil War reigned in Charleston for much of the twentieth century, it did not dominate in the aftermath of the conflict. On the contrary, black Charlestonians and their white Republican allies controlled the public memory of slavery in the city in the late 1860s and 1870s. Black memory is sometimes seen as countermemory, but as the case of Charleston shows, white remembrances, not black, existed on the sidelines in the wake of the Civil War.[13]

Charleston, too, offers an unusually clear window into the genealogy of social memory. It reveals how personal memories of the past coalesced into collective, social memory—the aggregation of individual remembrances. Neither white nor black Charlestonians could easily forget slavery, though some certainly tried. By virtue of their intimate ties to slavery and their self-conscious approach to interpreting and preserving their past, individual Charlestonians were prolific memory makers. A small group of white writers and editors, to take one example, promoted a Lost Cause narrative that celebrated the Confederacy and disassociated it from slavery—a narrative they helped spread across the country. To take another, the way in which memory was mapped onto Charleston's public landscape as the city became a tourism hub owed much to one white woman steeped in family remembrances that dated back to the colonial era.[14]

Tracing the genealogy of black social memory is not as easy, particularly after the turn of the twentieth century, when segregation forced the retreat of individual memories into the shelter of homes, schools, and churches. But it is possible, and there are parallels between the histories of white and black memories of slavery in the city. When African American tour guides succeeded in diversifying Charleston's tourism industry in the 1980s, for instance, they, too, drew on stories of slavery handed down from family and friends, forging a newly available collective memory for locals and tourists alike.

Finally, although focused on one Deep South city, the story we tell is a national one with national players. Since 1865, Charlestonians' memory work has been the product of ongoing interaction between locals and outsiders, between the city and the rest of the country. To be sure, Charleston would seem nothing if not a provincial backwater throughout the late nineteenth and much of the twentieth centuries. For one, the city continued to support a recalcitrant southern politics long after the Civil War. It was also isolated, a remote coastal port that was difficult to reach until better roads constructed after World War I facilitated automobile access.

But for many non-natives, Charleston's refusal to join the modern world proved immensely appealing. Some, like Frank Dawson, an Englishman who fought for the Confederacy, made Charleston their adopted home. Moving to the city in 1866, Dawson played a profound role in shaping memories of slavery in his capacity as editor of the *Charleston News and Courier*. Others—like the curious northern tourists who traveled to Charleston to take in its crumbling mansions and scenic plantations—inquired about the history of the peculiar institution in ways that forced local whites to remember it, if on their own terms. One of the most significant efforts to preserve black memories of slavery in Charleston originated with the federal government. The slave narrative program of the Federal Writers' Project resulted from a delicate negotiation between former slaves, local interviewers, and staff at the offices in Charleston, Columbia, and Washington, D.C. While Charleston offered uniquely fertile ground in which memories of slavery could grow, those memories were nurtured by a variety of constituencies, many of whom were not native to the city. As Charleston reminds us, historical memory in the South, and about the South, is not exclusively southern.

This truth has been illustrated time and again since June 2015. Dylann Roof committed the Emanuel massacre in Charleston, and yet the entire nation has since debated how best to remember slavery because the issue has never been—and cannot be—confined within the borders of the South. Since the end of the Civil War, southern memory-making has been American memory-making. The Lost Cause tradition may have been forged in places like Charleston, but its influence extended north and west of the Mason-Dixon Line and persists to this day, even in California's Central Valley, where we now live. Fearful of jeopardizing sales to southern school districts, American publishers have for decades produced middle and high school textbooks that muddy the waters on what caused the Civil War. Despite modern historians' near unanimous agreement that slavery was the central cause of the conflict, these works have taught generations of students that other issues—such as states' rights, tariffs, even the use of public lands—had as much, if not more, to do with sending southern boys off to war as did slavery.[15]

Opinion polls demonstrate the consequences of these lessons. As the United States began the 150th anniversary commemoration of the Civil War in 2011, the Pew Research Center found that 48 percent of Americans believed that the issue of states' rights was the cause of the conflict. Only 38 percent attributed the war primarily to slavery. Among Americans aged thirty and younger, 60 percent stated that states' rights explained the war—the highest among any age group and a worrisome statistic for the future. The enduring misunderstanding of our nation's pivotal conflict is more common in the South, certainly, but it afflicts residents in every region of the country. Other polls reveal that a broad swath of Americans is ignorant of, or indifferent to, the horrors of slavery. According to a *New York Times* analysis of a poll from early 2016, nearly 20 percent of Donald Trump supporters objected to Abraham Lincoln's Emancipation Proclamation, which declared the vast majority of American slaves free. Though tempting, portraying southern proponents of the whitewashed memory of slavery as outliers is mistaken.[16]

Denmark Vesey's Garden, in sum, tells a local story with national relevance. Charleston's long fight over how slavery should be remembered—as an incidental but comforting fairy tale of faithful slaves and doting masters, or as a shocking nightmare that lies at the core of our national identity—provides an unparalleled window into a conversation that involves all Americans. And, as we have seen, it is a conversation that is far from over.

Prelude

Slavery's Capital

"IF THERE BE A TOWN IN THE UNITED STATES, WHICH might be regarded as the citadel and capital of American slavery," wrote New England abolitionist Elihu Burritt in 1851, "that town is Charleston, in South Carolina." Burritt was right. No American city rivaled Charleston in terms of the role that slavery played in its formation and success, nor in the political, economic, and ideological support it provided for the expansion of slavery in the United States. And no American city better illustrates the brutal realities of human bondage, realities that belie the whitewashed image of the peculiar institution crafted by its Old South and latter-day apologists.[1]

Settled by the English in 1670, Charleston was the metropolis of South Carolina—the first British North American colony to hold the dubious honor of being a slave society from its beginning. While older southern colonies, such as Virginia and Maryland, took decades to embrace slavery wholeheartedly, South Carolina's white founders—many of whom came from Barbados, where the institution was essential to the thriving sugar industry—relied upon bound black labor at the outset. Just one year after the colony was founded, a Native American reported that "the settlement grows . . . the castle is getting bigger, [and] many Negroes have come to work." By the middle of the 1670s, one in four Charlestonians was enslaved.[2]

The city's black population surged upward in the eighteenth century. From the early 1700s to the 1850s, African Americans constituted a majority of Charleston residents, making it unlike any other major North American city. In terms of racial composition and hierarchy, Charleston more closely resembled the slave ports of the Caribbean than it did its neighbors to the north. A white minority sat atop the pyramid, while a broad base of slaves formed the bottom. In the middle was the free black community, a small sliver that included a mulatto elite. Often called "browns," this elite group had close ties to planters and counted some slaveholders in its ranks.[3]

At the start of the American Revolution, Charleston had almost 6,000 slaves, more than Boston, New York, and Philadelphia combined. The surrounding Sea Islands and Lowcountry—so named for a flat topography that an early colonist compared to a "Bowling ally"—had an even higher proportion of enslaved residents. Walking the streets of colonial Charleston, which grew into the fourth-largest city in British North America by the mid-eighteenth century, one could hear any number of European and African tongues as well as Gullah, the distinctive hybrid language developed by slaves on isolated, coastal plantations.[4]

In the mind's eye of white Carolinians, the city's black population could seem overwhelming. Some imagined black-to-white ratios of fifteen or even twenty to one. Visitors were also struck by the Lowcountry's distinctive demography. "At my first coming to this Province," a European tourist wrote to the *South Carolina Gazette* in 1772, "I was not a little surprised at the Number of *Black Faces* that every where presented themselves." The anonymous author's surprise only grew when he reached Charleston, which, he suggested, could easily be confused for "Africa, or *Lucifer's Court*." Eighty years later, in the early 1850s, Scandinavian Fredrika Bremer wrote that "Negroes swarm in the streets."[5]

Black faces swarmed those streets because of the region's dependence on white rice. After experimenting with other commodities, including tar, pitch, turpentine, and deerskins, early South Carolina settlers determined that rice was the key to their economic future. Drawing on West African slaves' knowledge of rice cultivation, planters began draining, damming, and irrigating Lowcountry bogs and marshes, which proved well suited to the profitable grain. Building rice plantations without modern machinery, however, was a grueling endeavor, which was only made worse by the heat, humidity, and disease of South Carolina's "funereal lowlands," as one scholar has aptly dubbed them. Still, rice promised remarkable riches to planters who could find the requisite workforce. Unable to entice enough English indentured servants, or to subdue enough Native Americans, to build their burgeoning rice empire, white Carolinians

Smith's Plantation, Beaufort, South Carolina, ca. 1862. Enslaved people greatly outnumbered free people in the Lowcountry.

turned to African forced labor. "Here is no living . . . without" slaves, observed a colonist in 1711.[6]

By the middle of the eighteenth century, the city sitting at the confluence of the Ashley and Cooper rivers was a central node in a thriving British slave trade that brought more than three million Africans to New World colonies between the mid-1600s and early 1800s. Charleston was British North America's leading destination for slaves who were transported from Africa and the West Indies. Between 1670 and 1808, nearly two hundred thousand slaves—approximately half of the bondpeople who disembarked in what became the United States—were imported through the city. Boasting the largest port in the lower South, Charleston enjoyed a veritable monopoly on the slave trade between the Chesapeake and St. Augustine, Florida. Buyers came from more than one hundred miles away to bid on the enslaved men, women, and children who were auctioned off aboard ships in the harbor, in city taverns, and at the wharves that surrounded the peninsula. Slave sales on or near Gadsden's Wharf, which dominated traffic after it opened in 1773, were held six days a week.[7]

Many of these forced migrants and their offspring ended up on sprawling coastal plantations. Their masters often retreated from their countryside estates to urban refuges like Charleston, leaving the backbreaking and at times deadly work of growing rice to their black laborers and overseers. This led to the development of the task system, in which the enslaved had to complete a specific task—say, planting a quarter acre of rice—each day. Once they were finished, whatever portion of the day remained was their own. Planter absenteeism, geographic isolation, and the regular infusion of new slaves contributed to a greater degree of African cultural retention in the Lowcountry than in other North American slave societies. The most obvious example of this phenomenon was the emergence of Gullah—the syncretic language and culture that coastal South Carolina slaves crafted from African and New World elements.[8]

The uncompensated labor of Lowcountry slaves turned South Carolina into "the most opulent and flourishing colony on the British continent of North America," as Robert Pringle, a prominent judge, merchant, and slave trader, put it. By the late eighteenth century, South Carolina was the leading rice supplier for Europe and the Americas, its enslaved workers filling empty bellies from Rotterdam to Rio de Janeiro and the pockets of planters throughout the Lowcountry. Enterprising slaveholders supplemented their incomes by growing indigo, a valuable and complementary crop to rice, which enabled them to more fully use their land and abuse their overtaxed workforce. Meanwhile, the transatlantic slave trade made Charleston merchants, including Henry Laurens, Gabriel Manigault, Miles Brewton, and Robert Pringle, among the wealthiest residents in the original thirteen colonies.[9]

On the eve of the American Revolution, stately homes lined Charleston's unpaved streets. In 1773, Bostonian Josiah Quincy dined at Miles Brewton's new residence, a King Street double house that today is a staple destination on tours of Historic Charleston. It has "the grandest hall I ever beheld," gushed Quincy in his journal. "Azure blue satin window curtains, rich blue paper with gilt . . . most elegant pictures, excessive grand and costly looking glasses etc." While South Carolina also had poor and working-class residents in addition to its enslaved majority, economic analysis confirms local boasts: by the 1770s, slavery had made the Lowcountry one of the wealthiest regions in the world.[10]

Little wonder that white South Carolinians led the fight against the antislavery impulse unleashed by the Revolution. The Enlightenment ideals of liberty and equality, combined with a boycott of commerce with Great Britain, undermined slavery in the late eighteenth century, contributing to its abolition in northern states and the temporary suspension of the foreign slave trade across the fledgling nation, including in South Carolina. But the state's compliance with the Continental embargo on slaves (and everything else) did not reflect fundamental misgivings about slavery or human trafficking. Indeed, South Carolina elites brooked no challenge to their right to buy, sell, or own human beings. When Thomas Jefferson included a passage blaming King George III for the slave trade in a draft of the Declaration of Independence in 1776, South Carolina and Georgia statesmen compelled him to remove it. A decade later, South Carolina's delegation to the 1787 Constitutional Convention in Philadelphia bluffed its way into prolonging the transatlantic slave trade for two decades. "If the Convention thinks that North Carolina, South Carolina, and Georgia will ever agree to the plan, unless their right to import slaves be untouched," declared Charlestonian John Rutledge, "the expectation is vain." Fearful that these southern states—especially South Carolina and Georgia—would not join the new nation if the Constitution empowered the federal government to move immediately against the slave trade, the convention prevented Congress from prohibiting it until 1808.[11]

Rutledge and his fellow South Carolina delegates thus paved the way for the importation of perhaps seventy thousand more African captives through Charleston as well as for the geographic and economic expansion of slavery in the United States—all *after* the American Revolution. Fears of slave insurrection, among other factors, had led South Carolina lawmakers to close the transatlantic slave trade to the state between 1787 until 1802. But after Eli Whitney's cotton gin made short-staple cotton wildly profitable, planters from the northwestern portion of the state, called the Upcountry, began clamoring for slaves. They succeeded in reopening the trade in 1803. Over the next five years, slave ships poured into and out of Charleston, providing enslaved laborers to secondary markets like Georgetown as well as to inland plantations in South Carolina, Georgia, and beyond. As a British visitor observed in 1807, "Thousands of these miserable people are dispersed over the adjoining states, through the port of Charleston, where there is a greater slave-market than, perhaps, was ever known at one place in the West India islands." Combined with Whitney's invention, this great slave market pushed enslaved laborers and the cotton plants they tended steadily westward—from Upcountry South Carolina and Georgia to new states, including Alabama, Mississippi, Louisiana, and, eventually, Texas. Charleston helped make cotton king and the Deep South slave country.[12]

Although the transatlantic slave trade was abolished in 1808, antebellum Charleston served as a vital center of the internal American slave trade through the Civil War. Some two million enslaved people were bought and sold in the United States between 1820 and 1860. The majority of these sales were to local buyers, but more than 600,000 were interstate transactions, many of which resulted in slaves being separated for good from their homes, friends, and family. Few cities—perhaps only Richmond, Virginia—rivaled Charleston as an exporter of enslaved laborers to the emerging Deep South's cotton empire. By the 1850s, the city boasted more than thirty slave-trading firms and many more slave-dealing brokers, auctioneers, and commission agents—euphemisms locals preferred to the more accurate "negro-trader." The sale of Charleston slaves to the Old Southwest was so robust in the years leading up to the Civil War, in fact, that by 1860 white residents outnumbered black for the first time since before the Revolution.[13]

Charleston's domestic slave trade was concentrated in the heart of the city, a stone's throw from City Hall, St. Michael's Church, and the offices of both the *Charleston Courier* and the *Charleston Mercury*. While private sales typically took place in brokers' offices near Adger's Wharf and on Broad, State, and Chalmers streets, most public auctions in the antebellum period were held just north of the Exchange Building, which was home at various times to the city hall, the custom house, and the post office. Outside this well-trafficked East Bay location, humdrum municipal and commercial routines intersected with the most tragic of transactions: the sale of human flesh. New England missionary Jeremiah Evarts witnessed one such spectacle on March 13, 1818, when 105 slaves of the recently deceased Colonel John Glaze were auctioned off to the highest bidder. As the men, women, and children took turns mounting a large table to be examined by the crowd, they appeared to Evarts to be "exceedingly disconsolate, much as if they were led to execution." Awaiting their fate at the auction block, the human chattel sat on a razor's

British artist Eyre Crowe's sketch of a slave sale outside the Exchange Building, published in the Illustrated London News, *November 29, 1856.*

edge: Would their new master be kind or cruel? Would they be sold away from their loved ones? Some sales brought relief, even glimmers of joy. Others left the enslaved venting their "grief, rage, indignation, and despair" through "tears and broken sentences." Three decades later, in 1853, a European visitor wrote that watching a slave sale outside the Exchange made his "hair stand on end." Grown men wept like infants as they were separated from their wives. Children clung in vain to their mothers' dresses.[14]

The visibility of these heart-wrenching scenes caused much consternation in Charleston, for they exposed slavery's unseemly underbelly to anyone who came to town. In the late 1830s and early 1840s, city officials passed multiple ordinances to regulate the trade, including a measure that prohibited the sale of slaves in public spaces. Yet slave brokers routinely ignored this prohibition without consequence, and in 1848 they convinced the city council to repeal it. Still, worries about the open sale of slaves persisted. So, too, did the traffic jams produced by crowds that regularly spilled over into East Bay Street during auctions at the Exchange. In 1856, Charleston passed an ordinance that outlawed the public sale of slaves, among other commodities, in the area around the

Exchange Building. The new interdiction sparked strong opposition from the mayor, who worried that it was a concession to *"mawkish and false sentiment as to the publicity of slave sales."* A group of slave traders, led by Louis DeSaussure, Alonzo J. White, and Ziba B. Oakes, denounced the measure as an impolitic admission that would give "strength to the opponents of slavery" and "create among some portions of the community a doubt as to the moral right of slavery itself." Yet the law was maintained, and starting July 1, 1856, slave auctions took place behind closed doors in nearby slave-trading offices and marts, the most prominent of which was a large complex between Queen and Chalmers streets called Ryan's Mart.[15]

Charleston was more than just a hub of human trafficking. It was also the epicenter of social and cultural life for South Carolina planters, whether they grew rice in the Lowcountry or cotton in the Upcountry. The closest thing in the United States to European nobility, these elite slaveholders were preoccupied with manners and ancestral pedigree, flaunting their wealth despite the misery around them. Each January, planter families and their domestic slaves descended on Charleston for a season of balls, concerts, and horse races that lasted through March. Extravagant parties, many held just blocks away from the slave auctions at the Exchange and Ryan's Mart, provided diversion during the winter social season. In 1851, Emma Clara Pringle Alston entertained two hundred guests, who dined on four turkeys, four hams, sixty partridges, ten quarts of oysters, and dozens of cakes, creams, and jellies. These migrating entourages returned to their Charleston homes again during the summer months, trading the malarial swampland for the port city's cooling sea breezes.[16]

Few Charlestonians could match Emma Alston's lavish offerings or the enslaved manpower that made them possible. But the widespread dispersal of slaveholding in the city—three out of every four white families owned at least one slave in the mid-1800s—meant that most white residents had a slave to wait on, or earn money for, them. It also meant, however, that most white residents interacted on a daily basis with someone who had every reason to despise them or even wish them dead.[17]

The fear of slave insurrection plagued the Old South and gave nightmares to white residents of Lowcountry South Carolina, with its black majority. Local authorities responded by cracking down after slave revolts, whether realized, imagined, or foiled at the last minute. The bloody 1739 Stono Rebellion, which began southwest of Charleston, was frighteningly real. More than sixty people (white and black) died, and as a result the state passed new laws that limited manumission and called for greater surveillance and stricter discipline of the enslaved.[18]

Eighty years later, in 1822, news that another slave uprising was in the works again rocked Charleston. The mastermind behind this plot was Denmark Vesey, a black carpenter and former slave who had purchased his freedom with winnings from the city lottery but was unable to do the same for his family members. Vesey and several of his co-conspirators were class leaders at the recently established African Church, the African Methodist Episcopal congregation that became Mother Emanuel after the Civil War. More than four thousand African Americans worshipped at the large church built at the corner of Reid and Hanover streets in the Hampstead neighborhood, or at several missionary branches. Charleston officials viewed this independent African Church as a threat to their authority and repeatedly harassed its members. Infuriated by these attacks and unwilling to live any longer under this repressive regime, Vesey and his colleagues formulated a plan for a large-scale insurrection. On July 14, Bastille Day, slaves and free blacks from across Charleston and the surrounding plantations were to rise up, attack white masters, and then set sail for freedom in Haiti. But the rebellion was foiled before it could be carried out, and local authorities arrested 131 slaves and free blacks, torturing many of them. Ultimately, Charleston executed Vesey and thirty-four co-conspirators and sold a similar number, including Vesey's son Sandy, outside the United States.[19]

In the aftermath of the affair, white South Carolinians tore down the African Church's house of worship, curtailed the few liberties afforded free blacks, and tightened slave supervision. To bolster the City Guard that policed Charleston, the state appropriated funds to support a permanent Municipal Guard of 150 men and authorized the construction of "a Citadel" that would house the new guardsmen and their weapons. In 1830, the Citadel, which sat between Meeting and King streets on the northern outskirts of town, opened its doors. Manned first by a detachment of U.S. soldiers and later by members of the state militia, this well-fortified brick structure became home to the cadets of the South Carolina Military Academy in 1843.[20]

The Work House, where slaves were imprisoned and tortured, in 1886. Damaged by a massive earthquake that year, the building was torn down in 1887.

The Citadel was just one part of the city's elaborate architecture of racial control. At the corner of Meeting and Broad streets, across from City Hall and St. Michael's Church, sat the Guard House. After it was remodeled in the late 1830s, this hulking building featured enormous Doric colonnades that projected out into a sidewalk at the very center of the city. The Guard House was the headquarters of the City Guard, whose daily patrols were, like the Guard House itself, an ever-present reminder to slaves that they were being watched. Farther up the peninsula, the Picquet Guard House at the Citadel Green, the parade ground adjacent to the Citadel, served as the headquarters for the guardsmen who monitored northern neighborhoods.[21]

Near the center of the city, on Wentworth Street between Meeting and King streets, was Military Hall, an imposing Gothic structure built in the 1840s in which Charleston's militia companies gathered to meet, drink, feast, and, on occasion, drill. Just a few blocks away from Military Hall, on the corner of Magazine and Mazyck streets, was the even more ominous Work House, where many of those accused in the Vesey conspiracy trials had been tortured. Standing just to the east of the District Jail, the Work House was a house of corrections for slaves. Once located in an old sugar refinery, the Sugar House, as the Work House was popularly known by the nineteenth century, held enslaved people arrested by the City Guard as well as those sent by their masters to get "a bit of sugar" for a small fee. After visiting Charleston in the 1850s, antislavery reporter James Redpath compared the Work House to "a feudal castle in its external form." But "in its internal management," Redpath added, the Work House resembled "the infamous Bastille or the Spanish Inquisition." It "is destined to be levelled [sic] to the earth amid the savage yells of insurgent negroes and the shrieks of widowed ladies," he predicted. The building was outfitted with whipping posts and a treadmill that used human steps to grind corn, an instrument of torture that kept twenty-four black men and women plodding eight hours a day on two enormous wheels. With its victims' arms shackled to an overhead rail and a driver who whipped those who fell behind with a cowhide, the Work House treadmill inspired greater fear than a flogging.[22]

Private citizens supplemented Charleston's racial architecture. Planters surrounded their property with high walls and other barriers designed to keep human property in and trespassers out. A former slave recalled that the owner of one mansion placed broken bottles atop the surrounding wall so as "to inflict mortal injury on any who attempted to climb into the inclosure [sic]." Others topped fences and walls with systems of defensive metal spikes called *chevaux-de-frise*. While strolling down lower Meeting Street in November 1818, New England minister Abiel Abbot noticed several luxurious homes that "were fortified by lofty iron railings & a horizontal bar of great strength, stuck close with sharp spikes of a foot in length." A few years later, *chevaux-de-frise* were added to the fence in front of the Miles Brewton House that had so impressed Josiah Quincy.[23]

In the decades after Vesey's failed revolt, the City Guard monitored Charleston on foot and horseback, day and night. By the 1850s, the City Guard had grown to more than 250 men. Visitors often remarked on its ubiquitous presence, as well as on the strict observance of the city's nightly curfew. "Among my first impressions of Charleston," wrote a northerner in the early 1830s, was "the sense of insecurity on the part of its inhabitants. . . . The police were in military uniform, and one of these seeming soldiers was stationed in the porch of each church during the time of service. At evening, close following a sweet chime from

St. Michael's, resounded the drum-beat, signal to the black population that they must no longer be found abroad." The city extended the reach of its police force in the early 1850s, when it annexed the Charleston Neck. This poor neighborhood north of Calhoun Street, which was the residence of many free blacks as well as a number of slaves who lived apart from their owners, already had its own police force and guard-house, which included a workhouse outfitted with a treadmill. Chang-ing the name of the Charleston Neck to the Upper Wards, the city coun-cil consolidated the Neck guard with its own and assumed management of the newly dubbed Upper Wards Guard House.[24]

Charleston also tracked slaves who were hired out by their masters by imposing the nation's only slave badge system. Dating back to the earliest days of the colony, the practice of slave hiring enabled masters to earn wages from their human property, whether they were domestics, un-skilled laborers, or skilled craftsmen, while conceding to the enslaved greater autonomy over their working and living arrangements. Some slaves were even permitted to hire themselves out, a frowned upon but not uncommon practice. To better monitor hired-out laborers, Charleston officials passed laws that required hired-out slaves (and for a brief time free blacks) to carry a ticket or, more often, a metal badge issued by the city. Hired-out slaves were expected to wear their badges in a visible place or, in the case of house servants, be able to present them upon demand.[25]

Defending slavery necessitated more than just keeping a watchful eye on the city's enslaved population; it also required a resolute effort to miti-gate external threats. After the Vesey conspiracy, South Carolina passed the Negro Seamen Act, which called for any free black sailors on ships that docked in Charleston Harbor to be imprisoned for the duration of their stay, lest they corrupt enslaved residents with subversive ideas. A decade later, South Carolina supporters of Vice President John C. Calhoun's theory of nullification came close to sparking armed conflict with the federal government in an effort to forestall future challenges to slavery. Nominally, the Nullification Crisis concerned the tariffs of 1828 and 1832, both of which the state's cotton and especially rice planters found onerous. At its base, however, the South Carolina Nullification Conven-tion's decision to declare the two tariffs unconstitutional and unenforce-able in the state after February 1, 1833, was an attempt to check federal power that might eventually be aimed directly at slavery.[26]

"I consider the Tariff, but as the occasion, rather than the real cause of the present unhappy state of things," Calhoun had admitted to a northern friend in 1830. "The truth can no longer be disguised, that the peculiar domestick institutions of the Southern States, and the consequent direction which that and her soil and climate have given to her industry, has placed them in regard to taxation and appropriation in opposite relation to the majority of the Union." If slaveholding states did not have the power to nullify federal laws, they would be forced to either rebel against federal authority "or submit to have . . . their domestick institutions exhausted . . . and themselves & children reduced to wretchedness." The nullifiers' gambit failed after other southern states refused to rally alongside South Carolina. Yet the Nullification Crisis did help to unify the state behind Calhoun and his even more extremist allies, undercutting the voices of Unionism and moderation when it came to slavery.[27]

Two years later, white Charlestonians led the South in its radical response to an equally radical movement that was burgeoning up north. Rejecting the moderate solutions of previous generations of abolitionists—gradual emancipation, African colonization, compensation for slaveholders—a biracial coalition of northern reformers led by William Lloyd Garrison set out in the early 1830s to convince the nation that a sin like slavery must be abandoned immediately and without any thought to recompense for masters. Garrison's American Anti-Slavery Society printed one million antislavery tracts, many of which they mailed to prominent whites in the South. When a shipment of these pamphlets arrived in Charleston on July 29, 1835, members of a vigilante group called the Lynch Men broke into the post office and seized them. The following evening, several thousand Charlestonians gathered at the Citadel Green to watch the Lynch Men burn the tracts as well as effigies of Garrison and other prominent abolitionists in an enormous bonfire. In the week that followed, Charleston officials responded as if the city were under siege. They appointed a special committee that suspended free black schools, redoubled City Guard patrols, and made sure that no "incendiary" mail was delivered. Eventually, President Andrew Jackson and his postmaster general effectively sanctioned Charleston's response, implementing a policy that permitted southern postmasters to refuse to deliver abolitionist mail—arguably "the largest peacetime violation of civil liberty in U.S. history," according to historian Daniel Walker Howe.[28]

In July 1835, a white mob raided the Charleston post office and stole abolitionist pamphlets, which they torched in a bonfire on the Citadel Green.

Charlestonians did not stop there. As northern antislavery critiques grew louder in the late 1830s and 1840s, elite residents curtailed their practice of sending their sons to New England universities, where they might be "*tainted* with Abolitionism." By this point, the city's myriad newspapers and periodicals dared not print a negative word about slavery. "Among all these publications, whether quarterly, monthly, weekly, or daily," declared a British travel writer in 1842, "there is not one that ever ventures to speak of slavery as an institution to be condemned, or even regretted. They are all either indulgent towards, or openly advocates of, this state of bondage." A decade later, Robert Bunch, the newly arrived British consul in Charleston, reported back to his superior in London that "it is most difficult for anyone not on the spot to form an adequate idea of the extreme sensitiveness and captious irritability of all classes of this community on the subject of Slavery." It was "the very blood of their veins."[29]

With slavery coursing through the bodies of their constituents, South Carolina statesmen did everything they could to inoculate against the abolitionist contagion. In response to a flood of antislavery petitions to Congress in the mid-1830s, James Henry Hammond, a congressman and planter from the Upcountry, formulated a "gag rule" by which the House of Representatives declined to receive any petition that addressed slavery. Hammond's Upcountry ally John C. Calhoun proposed a similar measure in the Senate. In the end, both the House and the Senate adopted modified versions of the South Carolinians' gag rules, which prevented the discussion of antislavery petitions in Congress for nearly a decade.[30]

Calhoun and Hammond saw no reason to apologize for slavery as southern politicians, including George Washington, Thomas Jefferson, and James Madison, had done for decades. Instead, they trumpeted slavery as a benevolent system that should be celebrated. "Every plantation is a little community, with the master at its head, who concentrates in himself the united interests of capital and labor, of which he is the common representative," declared Calhoun in 1838. Seven years later, in a public letter addressed to British abolitionist Thomas Clarkson, Hammond wrote, "Our patriarchal scheme of domestic servitude is indeed well calculated to awaken the higher and finer feelings of our nature."[31]

South Carolina politicians were not alone in promoting this paternalist ethos. Several influential Charleston clergymen had been saying much the same thing since the 1820s. In the months after the Vesey affair, Richard Furman, pastor of Charleston Baptist Church and a longtime slaveholder, dashed off a proslavery letter, which was then adopted by the South Carolina Baptist convention and published as a pamphlet. Furman posited the master as "the guardian and even father of his slaves," adding that when treated justly the enslaved became part of a master's "family (the whole, forming under him a little community) and the care of ordering it, and of providing for its welfare, devolves on him." Reverend Frederick Dalcho, of St. Michael's Church, concurred. Guided by their Christian faith, South Carolina's masters approached their black flock with kindness and humanity, he insisted in an 1823 book.[32]

As John C. Calhoun brought this paternalist vision to the national stage in the 1830s, he stressed that southern slavery not only "secured the peace and happiness" of master and slave but also proved to be "the most safe and stable basis for free institutions in the world." The struggle to protect the peculiar institution, Calhoun maintained in 1836, was the South's "Thermopylae." John C. Calhoun died fourteen years later, a decade before the South made its final stand in the name of slavery.

Fittingly, the South's most vocal champion of slavery was buried in Charleston. And fittingly, when the South's Thermopylae came to pass in the form of a full-blown war in 1861, it began in Charleston.[33]

* * * *

IN THE YEARS leading up to the Civil War, white Charlestonians echoed Calhoun's benevolent take on slavery. In the process, they transformed the capital of American slavery into the Cradle of the Confederacy. After Harriet Beecher Stowe published her blockbuster antislavery novel, *Uncle Tom's Cabin*, in 1852, city residents scrambled to dispute it. Stowe's book was a frequent topic of conversation—and target of vitriol—among the intelligentsia who gathered at John Russell's King Street bookshop. The same year *Uncle Tom's Cabin* appeared, a Charleston publisher released *The Pro-Slavery Argument, as Maintained by the Most Distinguished Writers of the Southern States.* Featuring essays by several prominent proslavery voices, including Charleston poet and novelist William Gilmore Simms, the collection sought to counter Stowe's negative portrait of life in the plantation South. Local lawyer Edward J. Pringle challenged *Uncle Tom's Cabin* in a pamphlet he published in 1852, which characterized slavery as a humanitarian institution in which abuses were rare, especially when compared to those suffered by the poor in the industrial North. Four years later, Charleston officials declared that the whole city shared these sentiments. "This community entertains no morbid or fanatical sentiment on the subject of slavery," maintained a city council committee. "The discussions of the last twenty years have lead [*sic*] it to clear and decided opinions as to its complete consistency with moral principle, and with the highest order of civilization."[34]

The South Carolinian who assumed the mantle of defending that moral and civilizing institution from John C. Calhoun was Robert Barnwell Rhett Sr. In the 1830s, the Beaufort-born politician and newspaperman had been a stronger supporter of nullification than even Calhoun himself. Two decades later, in the wake of Calhoun's death, Rhett urged South Carolina to secede from the Union after the passage of the Compromise of 1850—a stance that earned him the hearts of the state's proslavery legislators, who rewarded Rhett with Calhoun's Senate seat that December. Thereafter, he was South Carolina's leading proponent of slavery, southern interests, and secession—or a "fire-eater," as such men came to be called. Rhett beat the drum for immediate secession in Congress until he resigned in 1852 and in the pages of the *Charleston Mercury*, which he and his son Robert Barnwell Rhett Jr. purchased in 1857.[35]

Goaded on by fire-eaters like Rhett, Charleston—like much of the South—was approaching a war footing by the late 1850s. After John Brown's failed attempt to spark a slave insurrection at Harpers Ferry, Virginia, in October 1859, British consul Robert Bunch wrote, "I do not exaggerate in designating the present state of affairs in the Southern country as a reign of terror." From the consular office on East Bay Street, he reported to London that "persons are torn away from their residences and pursuits, sometimes 'tarred and feathered,' 'ridden upon rails,' or cruelly whipped; letters are opened at the post offices; discussion upon slavery is entirely prohibited under penalty of expulsion, with or without violence, from the country." In the wake of Harpers Ferry, white Charlestonians formed a new vigilance society, the Committee of Safety, which pledged to police the community more vigorously than its predecessors had. The committee will not "be deterred by nervous gentlemen or Abolition sympathies from ferreting out these friends and disciples of 'Old John Brown,'" said one of its members. When the Democratic National Convention met in Charleston the following April, city residents openly intimidated South Carolina's cautious delegates, strong-arming them into walking out of the convention in response to its moderate party platform. "If they had not retired," wrote Robert Barnwell Rhett Sr., "they would have been mobbed, I believe."[36]

Soon the city tightened its grip on the free black population. In August 1860, Charleston officials started going door to door, forcing blacks—even members of the brown elite—to provide proof of their status or face enslavement. Four months later, free black tailor James Drayton Johnson admitted that, like many in his community, he was contemplating leaving the city. "Our situation is not only unfortunate but deplorable & it is better to make a sacrifice now than wait to be sacrificed," Johnson told his brother-in-law.[37]

South Carolina fire-eaters were equally vigilant in declaring that if Abraham Lincoln—the presidential nominee of the antislavery Republican Party—were to be elected in 1860, the state would immediately secede. Charleston merchant Robert N. Gourdin and a number of wealthy

Lowcountry planters formed the 1860 Association, which unleashed a storm of propaganda to awaken hesitant whites to the dangers posed by a Lincoln administration. In a matter of months, the 1860 Association printed more than 150,000 pamphlets with menacing titles like *The Doom of Slavery in the Union* that focused white southerners squarely on the future of the system that kept most black southerners in chains. Worried that the South's nonslaveholding majority might not be willing to join a revolution in the name of human bondage, these fire-eaters emphasized how the institution served as a bulwark against white servility. "No white man at the South serves another as a body servant, to clean his boots, wait on his table," Charleston-born editor James D.B. DeBow reminded nonslaveholders. "His blood revolts against this." A Republican victory put this racial hierarchy, so important to poor and middling whites, at risk.[38]

Other pamphlets aimed to boil the blood of slaveholders and nonslaveholders alike. Lincoln's election, wrote Edisto Island planter John Townsend, portended "emancipation . . . then poverty, political equality with their former slaves, insurrection, war of extermination between the two races, and death." Charleston's leading fire-eater newspaper joined the chorus too. "Should the dark hour come, we must be the chief sufferers," warned a self-proclaimed Southern-Rights Lady in the Rhetts' *Charleston Mercury.* "Enemies in our midst, abolition fiends inciting them to crimes the most appalling . . . *we* degraded beneath the level of brutes." The purity of southern ladies hung in the balance.[39]

A paramilitary outburst cast a long shadow over the elections that fall. Armed groups drilled in front of convention halls from Charleston to the Upcountry. Unionists were assaulted in the streets. "Not a suspicious person, or event, escapes their notice," wrote a correspondent to the *Mercury* of new committees of safety and vigilance created in Barnwell, South Carolina.[40]

These efforts worked. Secessionists swept the October legislative election. After Lincoln's victory the following month, the only political choice was between immediate secession and leaving the Union in concert with other southern states. And, when South Carolinians went to the polls in early December to elect delegates to a secession convention, they chose a slate overwhelmingly committed to the immediate course. A unanimous vote was all but ensured as the delegates—90 percent of whom were slaveholders—convened in the state capital of Columbia on December 17. Later that day, the secessionists' triumph was symbolically sealed when the convention was moved to Charleston because of a small-pox outbreak. On December 20, 1860, the secession convention voted 169–0 to leave the Union. That evening the delegates gathered at Institute Hall on Meeting Street, where they signed the Ordinance of Secession before a crowd of 3,000.[41]

South Carolina secessionists were quite clear about their motivations. Four days after they voted to break with the Union, convention delegates explained their decision in a "Declaration of Immediate Causes." Lincoln's election, they reasoned, represented the culmination of "an increasing hostility on the part of the non-slaveholding States to the Institution of Slavery," jeopardizing their property, their culture, and their lives. In the words of one delegate, "The true question for us is, how shall we sustain African slavery in South Carolina from a series of annoying attacks, attended by incidental consequences that I shrink from depicting, and finally from utter abolition? That is the problem before us—the naked and true point." However real abolitionists' threats, in fact, were, sustaining slavery was certainly the naked point for South Carolina secessionists. Ignoring Lincoln's protestations that he had no intention—nor, to his mind, constitutional authority—to touch slavery in states in which it was already established, they believed that, as the *Charleston Mercury* put the matter, "the issue before the country is the extinction of slavery."[42]

South Carolinians did not plan to go it alone. "The Southern States," explained William Gilmore Simms, "are welded together by the one grand cohesive institution of slavery." But having watched southern states fail to rally to their side in the Nullification Crisis three decades earlier, South Carolina fire-eaters made sure to cover their bases. In early January, the secession convention selected seven commissioners to spread the gospel of secession to other southern states. These secession commissioners stressed time and again that Lincoln's election foretold the imminent destruction of slavery and the apocalyptic future that would follow.[43]

When six other Deep South states joined South Carolina to form the Confederate States of America in February 1861, representatives of the new nation made it clear that slavery was the cause that motivated them. Forty-nine of the fifty delegates who met in Montgomery, Alabama, to create the Confederacy were slaveholders. Not surprisingly, they drafted a constitution that explicitly prohibited laws that might undermine "the right of property in negro slaves." The "cornerstone" of this new government, declared the Confederate vice president Alexander Stephens on March 21, rests "upon the great truth that the negro is not equal to the white man; that slavery, subordination to the superior race, is his natural and moral condition."[44]

Weeks later, with thousands of Confederate soldiers camped around Charleston Harbor, the fight to secure southern slavery seemed nearly complete. At the center of the harbor sat Fort Sumter, one of the few federal forts in Confederate territory still in the United States' hands. Fort Sumter had been under siege since U.S. major Robert Anderson and his small garrison had decamped there the previous December. By April, Anderson's men were nearly out of food. Rather than surrender the fort, President Abraham Lincoln, who had assumed office in March, sent a ship to resupply it with nonmilitary provisions. This decision prompted Confederate commander P.G.T. Beauregard, acting under orders from the Confederate president Jefferson Davis, to demand the immediate surrender of Fort Sumter or face attack.[45]

The first shot came at 4:30 a.m. on April 12, 1861. Mist lingered over the water that morning as Confederate troops opened fire from spots across Charleston Harbor. Mary Boykin Chesnut, who was staying in the splendid Mills House on Meeting Street, rushed to the roof to "see the shells bursting." A few blocks away, along the Battery, Charleston's wealthiest residents also crowded onto rooftops. Sitting on carpets, chairs, and tables that their slaves had spent the night arranging, they watched the fireworks while they sipped drinks and dined from picnic baskets. A light rain fell throughout the day, but this did not dampen the spirits of the crowds or the intensity of the attack. By April 13, Fort Sumter was on fire. Realizing that he could not hold out much longer, Anderson signaled that he would surrender. Charleston rejoiced. Late into the night, church bells tolled and bonfires burned, marking a victory that had been won without the loss of a single life.[46]

* * * *

WHITE CHARLESTONIANS ANTICIPATED that the swift and bloodless victory over the Union force guarding Fort Sumter would, like the creation of the Confederacy itself, help guarantee the survival of their most cherished institution. They could not have been more wrong. Instead, it launched four years of war that ultimately spelled the end of slavery. In converting their hometown into the Cradle of the Confederacy—the place where the idea of southern secession was born, where the first vote for secession from the Union was registered, and where the Civil War began—Charleston's fire-eaters helped speed slavery's demise.

Some observers detected signs of trouble for white southerners and their slaveholding republic at the very outset of the conflict. Arriving in Charleston two days after Major Robert Anderson's surrender, Irish reporter William Howard Russell saw militiamen parading through the streets in song. Others crowded into restaurants and taverns to brag about Sumter: "Never was such a victory; never such brave lads; never such a fight."[47]

Yet Russell thought the rebels overconfident, especially in light of the enemy in their midst. As Russell passed the Guard House one night, a friend pointed out "the armed sentries pacing up and down before the porch," their weapons gleaming. "Further on, a squad of mounted horsemen, heavily armed, turned up a by-street, and with jingling spurs and sabres disappeared in the dust and darkness." This slave patrol scoured the countryside in search of runaways. With the curfew bell ringing in his ears, Russell had little patience for planter claims about "the excellencies of the domestic institution."[48]

The underlying problems noted by Russell soon began to take their toll on Charleston's slaveholders. Although they had launched a war to save slavery, the conflict cracked the foundations of the mental and physical citadels they had spent the last few decades constructing. Since Denmark Vesey's failed 1822 uprising, the city had "seemed to be in a permanent state of siege," in the words of one observer. Fears of slave insurrection intensified once the Civil War began. After the Union Army occupied the Sea Islands to the south in late 1861, many planters fled to Charleston with at least some of their slaves, swelling the city's black population. Rumors of revolt abounded. When slave refugees accidently started a fire that roared through the center of the city in December 1861, destroying more than five hundred homes, elites suspected arson.[49]

White residents kept up a brave face in public, publishing newspaper articles emphasizing slaves' fidelity. Privately, however, many Charlestonians said something different. "This war has taught us the perfect impossibility of placing the least confidence in any Negro," wrote rice planter Louis Manigault in his journal. Mary Boykin Chesnut worried that beneath her slaves' apparent indifference to the course of the war they harbored insurrectionary thoughts. "Are they stolidly stupid or wiser than we are," she wondered, "silent and strong, biding their time?"[50]

By the middle of the war, slaves in Charleston and on nearby plantations began to assert themselves like never before. Some declined to follow their masters to Upcountry plantations; others aided federal soldiers in the area. After Benjamin M. Holmes refused to flee with his owners in 1862, he was sold to a slave trader, who deposited him in a jail in Charleston's slave-trading district. The literate slave managed to get a copy of Lincoln's Emancipation Proclamation, which he read to his fellow prisoners. The president's liberating words did not stop Holmes from being sold to a man who took him to Chattanooga. When Union forces occupied the Tennessee city, however, Holmes seized his freedom, signing on as valet to a Union commander.[51]

Countless slaves ran away. Just as he sat down to dinner in his Charleston home on March 3, 1862, John Berkley Grimball received word that roughly eighty of the enslaved men, women, and children living on one of his plantations had fled during the night. The most celebrated escape occurred two months later. In the early morning hours of May 13, Robert Smalls, a slave who served as the wheelman of the Confederate supply boat the *Planter*, slipped out of Charleston Harbor with the rest of the enslaved crew and nearly a dozen other bondpeople, including his wife and two children. Smalls then turned the *Planter* over to Union forces, wryly telling one officer that he thought it "might be of some use to Uncle Abe." The following spring, the former slave, by then a Union pilot, sailed back toward Charleston as part of a major naval assault.[52]

Local slave owners responded by meting out extreme punishment. Whippings became more severe, and some masters resorted to shooting disobedient slaves. Meanwhile, city officials passed new ordinances that outlawed slaves from fishing in parts of the harbor vulnerable to the Union fleet and compelled anyone going in or out of Charleston to carry a passport.[53]

Born a slave in Charleston, Archibald Grimké ran away during the Civil War and later became a prominent lawyer and NAACP leader.

For some slaves, harsher discipline and closer supervision only reinforced a desire to escape. Archibald Grimké, the enslaved son of a planter and a mulatto nurse and the nephew of prominent abolitionist sisters Angelina and Sarah Grimké, was one. As a young boy, Archibald had experienced the partial freedom of Charleston's free black community, residing with his mother, rather than with his father/master, and enjoying unusual social and educational opportunities. Early in the conflict, he was ordered to move into the home of his new owner and half brother Montague Grimké, who had inherited Archibald, and perform the duties of a family servant. When the thirteen-year-old slave failed to build a fire that suited his half brother's taste, Montague beat Archibald and then sent him to the infamous Work House, where he was flogged. Soon after, Archibald ran away, disguising himself as a girl to make his way to the home of a free black drayman, where he spent the next two years in hiding.[54]

As black Charlestonians chipped away at slavery from within, the Union Army and Navy pounded Charleston from without. After failing to take the city in the spring and summer of 1863, Union forces inaugurated what became the longest siege in American history. For more than five hundred days, artillery shells rained down on Charleston, destroying much of the lower peninsula. The Citadel, the College of Charleston, and most hotels and restaurants closed, while other businesses relocated their offices to northern sections of the city. South of Market Street, Charleston looked like a ghost town, as many of its wealthy residents had fled to inland plantations. Union prisoner of war Willard Glazier observed in the fall of 1864 that the lower peninsula—now referred to as the Burnt District—was inhabited only by black Charlestonians, who bolted every time the shelling started, only to return shortly after. The siege was breaking down every rule in slavery's capital. "Before the siege the poor negroes could only gain admission by the back entrance, where with hat in hand they awaited the orders of 'Massa,'" wrote Glazier. But now they entered Charleston's ornate mansions through the front door and took up residence once inside.[55]

The Union Army would join them in a matter of months. Having burned his way through the heart of Georgia the previous fall, General William Tecumseh Sherman marched his men north into South Carolina in early 1865. Though fearful that Sherman aimed to take the city he called "the Hellhole of Secession," some white Charlestonians tried to put on a brave face and conduct business as usual. The *Charleston Mercury* continued to publish advertisements for the private sale and public auction of slaves. The latter took place on the corner of King and Ann streets, beyond the range of Union artillery. On January 19, 1865, in what may have been the final time human beings were offered up to the highest bidder in Charleston, T.A. Whitney sold thirty "PRIME NEGROES," including several field hands, two house girls, and a one-year-old.[56]

Several weeks later, P.G.T. Beauregard decided to evacuate the city before Sherman's army cut off his supply line. By mid-February, Confederate forces and the few remaining wealthy residents had packed up and left, the former setting fire to cotton supplies and munitions on their way out of town. Nearly four years after the Civil War began, the slaves who called Charleston home were at long last free. The capital of American slavery was no more.[57]

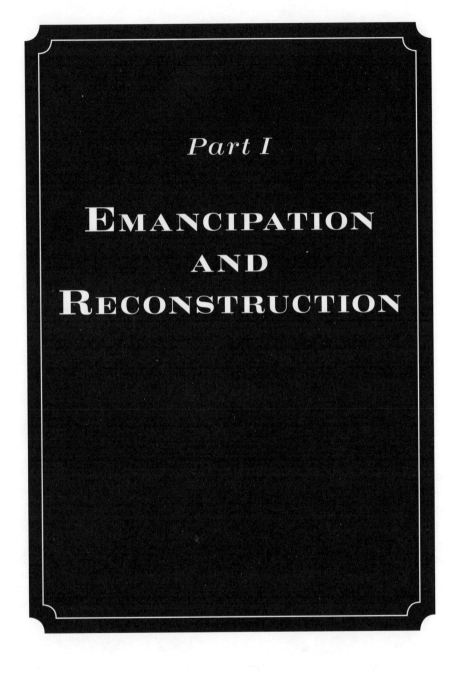

Part I

EMANCIPATION AND RECONSTRUCTION

1

The Year of
Jubilee

NEARLY TWO DOZEN FIRES BURNED OUT OF CONTROL
across Charleston on Saturday, February 18, 1865, as the Union Army
moved into the Cradle of the Confederacy. The brutal 545-day siege had
reduced much of the city to rubble, leaving gaping holes in buildings
across the lower peninsula. Witnesses compared Charleston to the ruins
at Pompeii.

But the city quickly came alive as the Union soldiers advanced into
Charleston—and not just because they helped to put out the flames.
Thousands of former slaves thrilled at the sight of their liberators, most
of whom were members of the 21st United States Colored Troops. "As
boat after boat landed, on the morning of the 18th, our troops were
received with cheers, prayers, cries, and countless benedictions by the
negroes," wrote Kane O'Donnell, correspondent for the *Philadelphia Press*.
"The colored soldiers were hugged and kissed by the women of their
race, and clasped in the arms of brothers." Just hours after the liberation
of the city, hundreds of men, women, and children welcomed a company
of the black 54th Massachusetts Infantry, which marched across the
Citadel Green. "Shawls, aprons, hats, everything was waved," observed
northern minister C.H. Corey. "Old men wept. The young women danced,
and jumped, and cried, and laughed."[1]

Three days later, on February 21, the Massachusetts 55th Regiment arrived, singing "John Brown's Body" to the African American crowds
that cheered them on. "Imagine, if you can," wrote *New-York Tribune*
correspondent James Redpath, "this stirring song chanted with the most
rapturous, most exultant emphasis, by a regiment of negro troops, who

After a lengthy Union siege, much of Charleston was in ruins when the Union Army occupied the city in 1865.

have been lying in sight of Charleston for nearly two years—as they trod with tumultuous delight along the streets of this pro-Slavery city." Some of the men in the 55th had once walked Charleston streets as slaves. But now they proudly marched through Charleston as free men, American soldiers, and saviors of the nation. Freedpeople assembled again on February 27 to receive the rest of the Massachusetts 54th. "On the day we entered that rebellious city, the streets were thronged," commented John H.W.N. Collins, a black sergeant. "I saw an old colored woman with a crutch,—for she could not walk without one, having served all her life in bondage,—who, on seeing us, got so happy, that she threw down her crutch, and shouted that the year of Jubilee had come."[2]

Over the next several months, as the Civil War ground to a halt, local freedmen and -women and the occupying Union force came together time and again to mark Union victory and the end of the peculiar institution with parades, commemorations, and other public demonstrations. Collectively, they transformed Charleston from the birthplace of secession into the burial ground for slavery. Although the city had been practically burned to the ground, revelry reigned. In this opening stage of the long

On February 21, 1865, the Massachusetts 55th marched into the city singing "John Brown's Body" to the delight of the black citizenry. From Harper's Weekly, *March 18, 1865.*

struggle over the memory of slavery, former slaves and their allies held the upper hand.

* * * *

THROUGHOUT THE SPRING and summer of 1865, freedpeople flocked to Charleston. Some had lived all their lives in the Piedmont, Upcountry, or the surrounding Sea Islands; others were returning home after being removed to the interior by their masters. Believing that "freedom was free-er" in towns and cities than on isolated plantations, these former bondpeople made Charleston an African American–majority city once more.[3]

As was true across the South, Charleston's freedpeople set about rebuilding their lives and reconstructing their families as best they could. Once-trusted servants wasted little time in demonstrating where their true allegiance lay. Less than two weeks after the city fell, one thousand black Charlestonians joined the Union Army, a brisk pace that kept up through April under the stewardship of Major Martin R. Delany, the first black officer commissioned at that rank. Among the new recruits was fifteen-year-old Archibald Grimké, who emerged from the shadows to serve as an officer's boy.[4]

These new volunteers joined with more seasoned Union soldiers and the rest of the city's black population to mark the death of slavery with a yearlong wake. From impromptu gatherings to elaborately planned affairs, these "festivals of freedom"—as the black abolitionist William C. Nell once dubbed such pageants—helped put slavery at the center of Civil War commemoration.[5]

Perhaps the most memorable festival of freedom that spring occurred on Tuesday, March 21, when between four thousand and ten thousand people gathered at the Citadel Green. It was a scene laden with irony. For decades the park had served as a parade ground for the adjacent South Carolina Military Academy, also known as the Citadel. But now the square where white cadets charged with protecting the city against slave insurrection had conducted public exercises became the gathering point for a parade of black Union soldiers and countless African Americans. According to *New-York Tribune* reporter James Redpath, the assembled viewed the procession as "a celebration of their deliverance from bondage and ostracism; a jubilee of freedom, a hosannah to their deliverers."

The parade, which stretched more than two miles long, started at about 1 p.m. under rainy skies. It took several hours to wind its way down King Street to the Battery at the base of the peninsula and then back to the Citadel Green. Led by dignitaries on horseback and a marching band, the procession also included tradesmen, fire companies, and nearly two thousand recently enrolled schoolchildren. A company of boys marched behind a banner reading "We know no masters but ourselves." They were followed by "A Car of Liberty," which carried fifteen young women representing the fifteen slave states. Clad in white dresses—outfits no doubt chosen to evoke the purity and virtue once associated exclusively with white womanhood—they refuted the lowly status assigned to black women, enslaved or free. The 21st U.S. Colored Troops participated in the procession, too. With armed black men marching through town, southern white nightmares appeared to be coming true.

As if to put the lie to planter mythology about unruly blacks in need of discipline, Unionist accounts highlighted the order of the African American parade. Even the schoolchildren, with no experience and just one hour's training, "kept in line, closed up, and were under perfect control," reported James Redpath. The lone exception to this rule came with the students' rendition of "John Brown's Body," which they sang throughout the march. Although they had been instructed to omit the verse, "We'll hang Jeff. Davis on a sour apple tree!" they belted it out again and again.

The most striking feature of the freedpeople's procession was a large mule-drawn cart bearing a sign that read, "A number of negroes for sale." The cart also carried an auction block and four African Americans—one man, two women, and a child—all of whom had been sold at some point in their lives. The man playing the role of auctioneer cried out to the crowd along the parade route, *"How much am I offered for this good cook? . . . Who bids?"* Behind the mock auction cart trailed a simulated slave coffle comprising some sixty men "tied to a rope—in imitation of the gangs who used often to be led through these streets on their way from Virginia to the sugar-fields of Louisiana."[6]

The participants in this carnivalesque bit of street theater meant to ridicule the chattel system that had victimized millions of black southerners, and the show did, in fact, produce "much merriment," according to one observer. Yet, as Redpath wrote, "old women burst into tears as they saw this tableau, and forgetting that it was a mimic scene, shouted wildly: *'Give me back my children! Give me back my children!'"* Just a couple of months removed from the final slave sale in Charleston—a mock auction of a different sort, with the slave system crumbling around it—the tableau may well have touched a still-raw nerve. Or, perhaps their emotional display was a calculated move intended to remind those watching the parade—and those who would read about it from afar—that although slavery was over, the pain of what it had cost them endured. Following the auction cart and slave coffle came a more unambiguously humorous element of the tableau: a hearse carrying a coffin labeled "Slavery," which elicited laughter from the audience.

This mock funeral harkened back to the raucous funeral rites performed by the enslaved in many southern cities as well as to a broader American tradition that dated back to the 1700s. During the Revolution, patriots marched through the streets with caskets, testifying to their anger at the actions of British authorities. More recently, in 1854, Boston abolitionists protesting the rendition of runaway slave Anthony

Burns had suspended a large black coffin, with the word "Liberty" painted on it in white, along the route by which Burns was marched back into bondage under armed guard. Now, the tables were turned, and the funeral march was for slavery, not freedom. Scrawled in chalk on the hearse were the inscriptions "Slavery Is Dead," "Who Owns Him," "No One," and "Sumter Dug His Grave on the 13th of April, 1861." A long train of female mourners dressed in black followed behind the coffin, their smiling faces the only tell of their true sentiments.[7]

"Charleston never before witnessed such a spectacle," concluded the *New York Times* correspondent of the day's events. "Of course, this innovation was by no means pleasant to the old residents, but they had sense enough to keep their thoughts to themselves. The only expressions of dislike I heard uttered proceeded from a knot of young ladies standing on a balcony, who declared the whole affair was 'shameful,' 'disgraceful.'"[8]

Surrounded by black soldiers and their former slaves, the few whites who remained in Charleston were too chastened to protest. Although a handful of Confederates insisted that their cause was not yet lost, most locals scrambled to demonstrate their allegiance to the United States by taking the loyalty oath. Northerners marveled at the new climate in Charleston. "I have given utterance to my most radical sentiments to try their temper, and have not even succeeded in making any one threaten me by word, look or gesture," noted *Boston Daily Journal* correspondent Charles Coffin in late February. "William Lloyd Garrison or Wendell Phillips or Henry Ward Beecher can speak their minds in the open air . . . without fear of molestation."[9]

Three weeks later, Garrison and Beecher would do just that. The abolitionists traveled south to Charleston along with hundreds of allies for the first government-sponsored festival of freedom, held on April 14, 1865, which was, coincidentally, Good Friday. Four years earlier to the day, Major Robert Anderson had lowered the American flag, surrendering the federal installation at Fort Sumter to Confederate General P.G.T. Beauregard and inaugurating four years of war. Now, just days after Robert E. Lee and his Army of Northern Virginia had yielded to Ulysses S. Grant at Appomattox Court House, signaling an end to the Civil War, Anderson returned to raise the very same flag in the very same place. Many Americans viewed Charleston as the Cradle of the Confederacy. Hereafter, predicted one northern minister, the city would be known as "at once its cradle and its grave."[10]

President Abraham Lincoln and his cabinet understood the symbolic significance of the occasion. While the flag-raising ceremony itself signaled political and military victory, they made sure to include individuals who would underscore the revolutionary social changes wrought by the conflict. Secretary of War Edwin M. Stanton asked Henry Ward Beecher, a renowned orator and vocal critic of slavery, to give the ceremony's keynote address. A good portion of Beecher's Brooklyn congregation joined him on the venture. Stanton also invited William Lloyd Garrison—the most famous abolitionist in America, a man who had once publicly burned the Constitution—and British abolitionist George Thompson to attend the ceremony as official guests of the government. Several other prominent opponents of slavery joined Beecher, Garrison, and Thompson, including black reformer and army major Martin R. Delany, newspapermen Theodore Tilton and Joshua Leavitt, and Senator Henry Wilson of Massachusetts. Among the homegrown abolitionists were Robert Smalls, the former slave who had dramatically seized his freedom by commandeering the Confederate ship the *Planter* in Charleston three years earlier, and Robert Vesey, son of Denmark Vesey.[11]

At ten o'clock in the morning on April 14, boats began ferrying people—northern and southern, soldier and civilian, white and black, all now free—out to Fort Sumter. Some made the short journey in steamships, while a number of the freedpeople ventured into the water in flats and dugouts, hoping that they might be picked up by a larger vessel, perhaps the legendary *Planter*. Still captained by Smalls, the ship ferried ex-slaves to Fort Sumter under an overcast sky.[12]

Like Charleston, the tiny man-made island at the mouth of the harbor was a bombed-out shell of its former self. "Fort Sumter is a Coliseum of ruins," Theodore Tilton wrote. "Battered, shapeless, overthrown, it stands in its brokenness a fit monument of the broken rebellion." More than three thousand people, including members of a black regiment commanded by Beecher's brother James, filled the fort, some spilling out onto its crumbing walls.

The ceremony opened with a song, a short prayer, and recitations of several psalms as well as Major Anderson's 1861 dispatch of surrender.

On April 14, 1865, thousands of people gathered at Fort Sumter for a flag-raising ceremony that commemorated the end of the Civil War.

Then, after saying a few words, Anderson and a dozen men, including George Thompson, lifted the enormous flag that had been taken down four years before. As "the old smoke-stained, shot-pierced flag" rose, so, too, did everyone in the fort. Waving hats and handkerchiefs, the spectators erupted with shouts, laughter, and tears when the flag reached its peak. "It was the most exciting moment in my life when the flag went up," wrote Brooklyn pastor Theodore Cuyler.

Beecher approached his keynote address, which followed soon after, in a spirit of Christian forgiveness. He pulled no punches, however, in assigning blame for the war—"the ambitious, educated, plotting political leaders of the South"—or in praising its radical results. "The soil has drunk blood, and is glutted," he admitted, but the time had come "to rejoice and give thanks." In unfolding the flag at Fort Sumter, the assembled were restoring the peace and sovereignty of the nation. "No more war! No more accursed secession! No more slavery, that spawned them both!" Beecher intoned to great applause.[13]

That evening, Major General Quincy A. Gillmore hosted a banquet at the Charleston Hotel. After dinner, the guests offered up a series of toasts. Abraham Lincoln was on the mind of many that night. Perhaps most moving were the words of Garrison, a longtime critic of the president. "Of one thing I feel sure," announced the editor, "either he has become a Garrisonian Abolitionist or I have become a Lincoln Emancipationist." Whatever the case, Garrison concluded that Lincoln's "brave heart beats for human freedom everywhere." Little did he or anyone else in Charleston know that the president's brave heart would not beat much longer. For that same night, as abolitionists and federal officers in the Charleston Hotel cheered the maintenance of the Union and the end of slavery, Lincoln's assassin John Wilkes Booth made it clear that for some Confederates the war was not over.[14]

Charleston still had its fair share of unreconstructed rebels, too. Writing from her residence on South Bay Street on April 14, Maria Middleton Doar fumed over the "crowds of Negro women accompanied by men in uniform parading on the battery" while they waited for the flag to be raised at Fort Sumter. "There is to be a ball tonight at Cousin W[illiam Middleton]'s house," she told a cousin. "Would you believe that some Charleston ladies are going[?]" Doar was happy to report that "<u>most</u> of those who have been insulted by invitations have indignantly refused."[15]

Outside the city, Confederate sympathizers also stewed. In May, Emma Holmes, an elite young woman who had moved from Charleston to Camden midway through the war, wrote in her diary that the word from home was that a "grand Union glorification" had taken place on Good Friday. Among the fooleries of the day, she complained, were the flag-raising ceremony, a parade of the city's black residents, and a "'promiscuous' ball" held at the Middleton residence—the same ball that troubled Maria Middleton Doar. Holmes found a measure of satisfaction in reports out of Charleston that "the really respectable class of free negroes, whom we used to employ as tailors, boot makers . . . etc., won't associate at all with the 'parvenue free.'"[16]

Other white southerners traded stories—some true, many false or exaggerated—of the theft and destruction of private property, plots of black insurrection, and worse. Perhaps prompted by the Slavery Is Dead procession on March 21, a Newberry, South Carolina, newspaper reported on April 6 that a group of black Charlestonians had recently put up slave trader John S. Riggs at a mock auction. The following week, Emma LeConte, of Columbia, seethed in her diary that Charleston recently "had a most absurd procession described in glowing colors and celebrating the Death of Slavery." It was a world turned upside down. "Abolitionists delivered addresses on the superiority of the black race over white. . . . Also, 'As Christ died for the human race, so John Brown died for the negroes,' etc., etc." Emancipation aroused white southerners' deepest fears. "Abolition seems to be in full black" in Charleston, reported the *Columbia Phoenix* on March 21. "From the rumors which reach us, miscegenation is soon likely to follow."[17]

* * * *

OPPONENTS OF SLAVERY rejoiced over the news of Charleston's festivals of freedom. In Columbia, the newly liberated asked for "permission to follow the example of Charleston negroes and bury slavery with pomp and ceremony." Up north, hundreds of thousands of Americans read the moving columns on the city's emancipation published in newspapers such as the *New-York Tribune*, the *Boston Daily Journal*, and the *Philadelphia Press*. Much of this coverage also featured reporters' firsthand accounts of their search for the remains of Charleston's slave regime. Inspired by such stories, scores of northerners made pilgrimages to the former capital of American slavery, touring its holy sites—the slave-trading district, the Work House, the Citadel, the offices of the *Charleston Mercury*—and often picking up a keepsake or two to take back home.[18]

These excursions reflected the popularity of memento collecting in the nineteenth century, when middle-class Americans traveled to historical sites to gather relics that they believed would help them forge a deeper connection with the nation's past. This phenomenon reached its apex during the Civil War. Soldiers and civilians in both the North and the South saved objects that reminded them of the conflict, from fragments of battle-scarred trees to bullets that had pierced loved ones.[19]

In early April, abolitionist Theodore Tilton visited the place many believed was the ideological epicenter of both slavery and the Civil War: the gravesite of John C. Calhoun. No fan of Calhoun, Tilton was nonetheless disturbed to find that relic seekers had desecrated the statesman's tomb. The New York editor chose a less destructive method to acquire his memento of Charleston, plucking some clover growing near the ruins of Institute Hall, where the Ordinance of Secession had been signed in 1860. James Redpath, for his part, grabbed a keepsake from the *Charleston Mercury* offices. When the antislavery reporter had visited the battered newspaper headquarters in late February, he found some printer's type that editor Robert B. Rhett Jr. had set up for its final issue. Redpath absconded with it "for posterity."[20]

Redpath also joined with a number of other northern visitors who pillaged Charleston's slave-trading district for what he called "relics of barbarism." After Charleston had outlawed public slave sales outside the Exchange Building, most auctions had been conducted in the buildings and offices clustered on Chalmers and State streets. Charles Coffin recorded a detailed account of his visit to Ryan's Mart, the most prominent of such venues. The *Boston Daily Journal* correspondent entered the Chalmers Street complex through an iron gate, above which sat the word "Mart" in gilt letters. Behind the gate, he found a sizable hall, with an auction table running the length of the structure and ending at a locked door. With the help of a freedman, Coffin broke through the wooden door, gaining entry to the rest of the complex. At one end of the yard, which was walled in on all sides, was the four-story brick prison known as Ryan's Jail. Next to the hall was a small room—"the place where women were subjected to the lascivious gaze of brutal men."

Coffin focused his gaze on "the steps, up which thousands of men, women and children have walked to their places on the table, to be knocked off to the highest bidder." The journalist decided to take the steps back with him to New England. "Perhaps," he reasoned, "Gov. Andrew, or Wendell Phillips, or Wm. Lloyd Garrison . . . would like to make a speech from those steps." Coffin also secured two locks and the gilt letters from the front of Ryan's Mart. Other accounts suggested that Coffin and his colleagues acquired a slave-market bell, manacles, and the correspondence of local slave dealers. These abolitionist raiders did not sweep Charleston's slave markets clean, however. Among the items they left behind was a slave trader's desk on which someone had inscribed antislavery messages from William Lloyd Garrison and John Brown.[21]

Many slavery relics did find their way into the hands of northern reformers. Wendell Phillips was reported to have received a slave-market bell as a gift from a Massachusetts man, most likely James Redpath. *Philadelphia Press* correspondent Kane O'Donnell gathered papers from several slave marts. His newspaper subsequently published excerpts from these documents, which included correspondence between Charleston slave dealers and prominent public figures, such as former governor

James Henry Hammond and the Confederacy's first two secretaries of the treasury, Christopher Memminger and George Trenholm.[22]

A few weeks after he toured the slave-trading district, on March 9, 1865, Charles Coffin officially presented some relics to the Eleventh Ward Freedmen's Aid Society at the Boston Music Hall before a large audience. In a striking display, the auction block steps from Ryan's Mart were placed on the very stage from which antislavery minister Theodore Parker once rained invective down upon slaveholders in his Sunday sermons. The lock to the slave pen was placed on the Music Hall's desk, and the gilt letters "Mart" were suspended from the organ. Coffin regaled the crowd with stories about the Charleston slave trade, reading from a broker's papers.

Later, fulfilling the wish Coffin had expressed when he salvaged the auction block steps, William Lloyd Garrison mounted them in order to put "the accursed thing under his feet." Standing atop the steps—portals into the enslaved past—the abolitionist editor sought to enhance his connection to the people for whom he had fought so long. The Music Hall crowd erupted in thunderous applause, waving white handkerchiefs in celebration, before Garrison offered a lengthy lecture. Over the next few weeks, Garrison, George Thompson, and other antislavery colleagues re-created this scene at Freedmen's Aid Society meetings in Lowell and Leicester.[23]

One month after Garrison mounted the auction block steps in Boston, he and Thompson set sail for Charleston for the April 14 flag-raising ceremony at Fort Sumter. While in Charleston, Garrison and many of his antislavery colleagues combed the city in search of slave sites. Although northern teacher Laura Towne's sightseeing was limited by seasickness, she made sure to see the Work House. Still standing amidst the burned-out shells of homes and businesses in the lower part of the peninsula, the Gothic building looked "like a giant in his lair." Towne wanted to confirm that the building she found was, indeed, the despised Sugar House, so she asked an elderly black woman standing nearby. "Dat's it," she responded, "but it's all played out now."[24]

Other visitors that weekend followed the path blazed by Coffin and Redpath. After describing the tiny dens that held the enslaved on their way to the auction block as "dark, filthy, and horrible" in the *Independent*, for instance, Brooklyn minister H.M. Gallaher noted the too-good-to-be-true name of one of the city's slave-auction firms: Clinckscales and Boozer. "Well," Gallaher concluded sarcastically, "they will clink no more the dollar that has blood upon it, and booze no longer on the money that made mad a slave mother."[25]

Henry Ward Beecher strolled through Charleston on Saturday morning, April 15, the day after the Fort Sumter flag raising, seeing reminders of slavery—and its demise—all over town. At one point, he called on former governor William Aiken Jr., who lived in an imposing home not far from the Citadel Green. Aiken had owned close to one thousand slaves before the war. Beecher hoped to talk about the future with Aiken, a prominent Unionist, but the governor seemed drawn incessantly back to one point: "The President ought not to have issued his Proclamation." Aiken spoke of his relationship with his slaves in *"couleur de rose."* The governor's tales were familiar. "There is a liturgy on this subject," wrote Beecher. "You may take a thousand Southerners at Saratoga and Newport, and they will all repeat the same story of their care and nurture of the slaves, and of the addiction of the slaves to them." The next day, Beecher spoke directly to Aiken's former slaves, who gave him an altogether different impression. "We shall never know what slavery is," he concluded, "until the slaves tell us."[26]

Later that morning, Beecher joined George Thompson, Henry Wilson, Theodore Tilton, and Garrison on a visit to John C. Calhoun's tomb. "All this great crop of war," maintained Beecher, "is from the dragon-toothed doctrines that were sowed by the hands of that dangerous man." In what one eyewitness described as being among the most striking scenes of the extraordinary weekend, Garrison put his hand on the simple marble slab, which was inscribed with just a single name: Calhoun. "Down into a deeper grave than this slavery has gone," he said, "and for it there is no resurrection." The abolitionists stood in silence as Garrison's pithy obituary hung in the air before walking the short distance over to the Citadel Green. Thirty years earlier, white Charlestonians had gathered on that parade ground to burn antislavery tracts and an effigy of Garrison in a large bonfire. But on April 15, 1865, the Citadel Green played host to thousands of black Charlestonians who were listening to the words of Martin R. Delany.[27]

That afternoon, a vast crowd packed into Zion Presbyterian Church, adjacent to the green on the corner of Calhoun and Meeting streets, to listen to speeches by Garrison, Thompson, and Henry Wilson, among others. At the start of the program, an ex-slave named Samuel Dickerson came forward with his two small daughters, each of whom carried a bouquet of flowers. Dickerson, who would become a lawyer and Republican activist in the decade that followed, welcomed Garrison with moving words. The Massachusetts abolitionist replied that he was incapable of expressing the overwhelming emotions he felt as he listened to Dickerson and looked into the faces of the enormous audience. Reminding them that he had been fighting slavery for nearly four decades, Garrison confessed that he thought this day would never come. "Thank God this day you are free," he proclaimed to great cheers. "And be assured that once free you are free forever." Garrison also read from a record book that someone had recovered from a slave-trading firm, as well as a recent newspaper advertisement for "an active boy about fourteen years old." Looking out at the black masses before him, the abolitionist editor asked, "Have any of you got such a boy to sell?" The crowd began to sway back and forth, scream, cry, and shout "No!"—an uncomfortable response reminiscent of the reaction elicited by the mock slave auction in March. At the close of the meeting, black Charlestonians escorted the abolitionists back to the Charleston Hotel, forming a procession that seemed a mile long.[28]

On Monday, April 17, as Beecher, Garrison, Thompson, and company prepared to leave Charleston, the crowds were even larger. "The streets were full of colored people," wrote Beecher, who noted that Union soldiers, including Garrison's own son George Thompson Garrison, had been busy liberating thousands of slaves from nearby plantations. Though desperately poor, the freedpeople who joined Garrison and his colleagues at the wharf offered whatever tokens of gratitude they could spare. Some carried roses, others honeysuckles. Samuel Dickerson offered another eloquent speech, and black children belted out songs. At ten o'clock in the morning, the abolitionists sailed out of Charleston, watching as Dickerson knelt at the wharf's edge, one arm draped around his daughters and the other holding the American flag.[29]

* * * *

ALL SPRING, BLACK Charlestonians like Dickerson and Unionists in the city celebrated the end of the war and the demise of slavery with demonstrations, large and small. On May 1, 1865, they offered another elaborate tribute—this time to a group that had not only fought but also died for black freedom. On the northern outskirts of town, the remains of 257 Union prisoners of war were buried in unmarked graves. Held in a Confederate prison camp at Washington Race Course, these soldiers had suffered and died in the final year of the war. Union officers, northern reformers, and Charleston's black community determined that their sacrifices should not be forgotten. By creating a suitable cemetery in which to bury the prisoners who had perished there, they sought to put the final nail in the coffin of slavery. In the process, they initiated the national day of remembrance that was originally called Decoration Day and is today marked as Memorial Day.[30]

The Union prisoners' ordeal contrasted sharply with the experiences of those who had frequented the Washington Race Course before the Civil War. Since its opening in the early 1790s, the horse track had been the center of the South Carolina elite's social world. Each winter, the region's planter class gathered in Charleston, mingling at parties and watching the horses run. Even as wealthy southerners lost interest in horse racing by the 1840s in cities like Baltimore, Norfolk, and Richmond, South Carolina elites continued to congregate for—and invest significant meaning in—the Charleston races.[31]

The Civil War, however, brought the yearly festivities at the Washington track to an abrupt halt, and by 1864 the once grand venue was overgrown with grass, the judges' stand looking as if it might fall over at any moment. Confederate forces built a makeshift prison there to hold between six thousand and ten thousand Union captives who in mid-1864 were evacuated from Georgia prisons, including the infamous one at Andersonville. The Charleston prison was not much better. "We had no tents and no shelter whatsoever furnished us," wrote a Connecticut sergeant major of the wretched conditions. All the soldiers had to protect them from the elements were a few blankets, which "were of little use when it rained." And rain it did. That September it seemed to pour day and night, making life at the racecourse even more miserable than usual. Weakened by the horrid conditions that they had endured at Andersonville, many of the prisoners stood little chance. "Men died about as fast, in proportion to their numbers, as at Andersonville," explained one Massachusetts soldier. "Scurvy, diarrhea, and fever swept the prisoners off in vast numbers."[32]

Local whites displayed little compassion for these Union captives. "I am sorry to say that I never heard of a native white doing any thing for the assistance of our prisoners in Charleston," recalled an observer in 1865. Charleston's black community, in contrast, fed the starving men. Some gave bread to the sickly Andersonville prisoners as they were marched into the city, while others brought food out to the racecourse prison, only to be driven away by the rebels. When Henry Ward Beecher visited for the Fort Sumter ceremony, he met four black women who had been whipped for secretly providing food, bandages, and medicine to the Union captives.[33]

As yellow fever swept through Charleston in the fall of 1864, Confederate officials decided to remove the prisoners held at the racecourse to Florence, South Carolina. They left behind hundreds of deceased prisoners, who had been rudely buried in a few rows without any grave markers. The following spring, on March 26, 1865, just days after the Slavery Is Dead parade, James Redpath and several other northern visitors ventured out to the Washington Race Course to see these graves.[34]

As a war correspondent for the *New-York Tribune*, Redpath had come to Charleston with Union troops one month earlier. It was not his first visit. After emigrating from Scotland to the United States in 1849, Redpath had traveled throughout the South secretly interviewing slaves, including in Charleston, and then telling their tales in abolitionist newspapers. He was thrilled not only to be able to report on the liberation of Charleston in the spring of 1865, but also to be offered the position of superintendent of education once there. Redpath swiftly reopened five city schools, enrolling children of all races for the first time. He also helped found a new black orphan asylum, named for Union martyr Robert Gould Shaw, in an East Bay Street mansion.[35]

Not long after he arrived in Charleston, Redpath began hearing tales about the racecourse prison. "The colored population here tell fateful stories of the sufferings of our prisoners, while many of the [ex-Confederate] oath-takers pretend to deny that any cruelties were practiced," he wrote. "But their testimony is like their oath—false and for a purpose." Beyond the memories guarded by Charleston's black citizenry, the only traces of the racecourse prisoners that Redpath and his companions could find when they visited the site in March were small pieces of wood with numbers painted on them. The graveyard, such as it was, sat

In the spring of 1865, black Charlestonians cleaned up and built a fence to protect the Union burial ground at the Washington Race Course.

in an open space not far from the track. Nothing was erected to protect the graves from grazing cattle.[36]

Outraged by this show of disrespect to the Union dead, Redpath and company formed themselves into a committee to raise money to construct a more appropriate gravesite. The committee was headed by Redpath and consisted chiefly of white Union officers, reformers, and ministers, though it included at least one local African American: Robert C. DeLarge, a freeborn black who would later serve in the House of Representatives. They immediately drafted a circular that solicited contributions of ten cents from all loyal South Carolinians in order to "give everyone the privilege and debar none from aiding this noble work." In response to this appeal, approximately five thousand African Americans met at Zion Presbyterian Church, where twenty-eight local black men agreed to build a fence for the racecourse gravesite.[37]

This was not the first time local blacks had sought to commemorate the sacrifices of Union soldiers. In July 1863, Colonel Robert Gould Shaw had led the 54th Massachusetts Infantry on a failed frontal assault of nearby Fort Wagner, leaving Shaw and many of his men dead. Soon after, the surviving members of the Massachusetts regiment, although still unpaid because of a dispute over unequal wages, began to raise a sum of nearly $3,000 for a monument to Shaw and his men. The Sea Island freedpeople contributed to the effort, too. In the end, however, the planned memorial to Shaw and his men, who were buried together in the sands of Morris Island, was abandoned for fears that the shifting ground, both literal and ideological, would put the monument in jeopardy. Instead, at the behest of local donors, the money was used to fund a black school in Charleston, which, like the orphanage, was named for Shaw.[38]

When black Charlestonians built the Martyrs of the Race Course cemetery in April 1865, they picked up where the Sea Island freedpeople had left off. Two new black voluntary associations, the Friends of the Martyrs and the Patriotic Association of Colored Men, cleaned up the grounds and raised the graves of the more than 250 soldiers who had died there. The men also crafted a ten-foot-high, whitewashed fence that surrounded the cemetery, using lumber that they had salvaged from several nearby buildings. General John P. Hatch, Union commander in the city, had offered to secure these materials at government expense, but the black volunteers "would not yield the honor to the Quartermaster's Department." They also painted a "Martyrs of the Race Course" sign "by their own initiation," according to Union physician Henry Marcy and others. All told, Redpath estimated that the black volunteers put in more than two hundred days of work, adding that they "asked and received no material recompense whatever."[39]

Black Charlestonians were responsible not only for building the Martyrs of the Race Course cemetery but also for the success of the Decoration Day ceremony on May 1. African American men, women, and children constituted the bulk of the ten-thousand-person crowd that turned up at the Washington Race Course to celebrate the cemetery's dedication. Local blacks even accounted for the military presence. When General Hatch got wind that a large contingent of black residents was headed out to the racecourse to mark the graves of the deceased prisoners, he decided to send two regiments and a military band to accompany them.[40]

The weather was unusually warm that spring day, the intense sun reminding Esther Hill Hawks of August. A northern physician and educator who worked with Sea Island freedpeople, Hawks joined black schoolchildren from the recently opened Morris Street School as they marched north along King Street toward the Washington Race Course.

In 1822, Denmark Vesey and five fellow insurrectionists, shackled in leg irons, had been paraded past a large crowd on their way to the gallows along a similar route. The children's procession forty-three years later was a remarkable reversal of the city's racial politics—a reminder that the white minority's terrifying rule was over. Although Vesey and his co-conspirators had been intentionally deprived of a proper burial, the same would not be true for the white soldiers who also died for freedom.[41]

Once the parade reached the Martyrs of the Race Course cemetery, the schoolchildren adorned the graves with flowers, and the rest of the procession paid their respects. Then, the parade made its way out of the cemetery, and the gate was shut, leaving just a small group of former slaves to dedicate the space. One white citizen got inside the fence, but he was ordered to leave for having recently "boasted of being a South Carolinian who would not submit to the enfranchisement of the only loyal people here." Those gathered inside then offered prayers, read Bible passages, and sang hymns before joining the rest of the crowd at the judges' stand. Later, the crowd listened to speeches by Union officers and prominent locals and was treated to a formal drill by the soldiers. The festivities lasted well into the evening.[42]

* * * *

AS WEALTHY CHARLESTONIANS made their way back into the city in the summer and fall of 1865, some found their elegant homes in tatters. Cotton broker and Confederate officer Francis J. Porcher learned that his East Battery mansion had recently been "occupied by Charles Macbeth's plantation negroes, with their pigs & poultry." Union soldiers had driven the freedpeople out, but a Yankee who operated a saloon on Broad Street had taken their place. The Porchers hoped to return to the house by November. Henry William DeSaussure advised his father not to return to Charleston at all. "The city is filled up with negro troops insolent & overbearing," he wrote. "It requires great patience and self control to be able to get along."[43]

Some planters were shocked to hear their former slaves criticize them for the first time, while others chafed at what William Middleton called "the utter topsy-turveying of all our institutions." DeSaussure railed that white Charlestonians suffered the indignity of a nightly curfew—once the burden reserved for their slaves. "It is impossible to describe the condition of the city," Henry W. Ravenel wrote fellow Charlestonian Augustin L. Taveau on June 27. "It is so unlike anything we could imagine—Negroes shoving white persons off the walk—Negro women dress in the most outré style, all with veils and parasols for which they have an especial fancy." A couple months earlier, Ravenel had held out hope that "our institution of slavery as it existed before the war with some modifications, may be retained, & amendments to the Constitution defining the Rights of the States [adopted]," but he eventually accepted that slavery was gone for good.[44]

Meanwhile, Taveau published a letter in the *New-York Tribune* highlighting the fundamental challenge that emancipation posed to the planter worldview. "The conduct of the Negro in the late crisis of our affairs has convinced me that we were all laboring under a delusion," he wrote. "Born and raised amid the institution, like a great many others, I believed it was necessary to our welfare, if not to our very existence. I believed that these people were content, happy and attached to their masters." But now, thinking back over the previous few years, Taveau could not help but wonder, "If they were content, happy and attached to their masters, why did they desert him in the moment of his need and flock to an enemy whom they did not know[?]" Lowcountry planter Louis Manigault, who was a family friend of Taveau, agreed, copying Taveau's "correct Remarks" into his journal.[45]

While Charleston planters' cherished fantasies were being turned on their head, their hometown was being turned inside out. Walking the streets of the city in July, Republican Carl Schurz found African American sentinels standing guard at every public building. Whereas it once was a punishable offense to educate black children, they now filled classrooms across Charleston. In the center of the city, Schurz wrote, the Citadel—"a large castle-like building, in which the chivalric youth of South Carolina was educated for the task of perpetuating slavery by force of arms"—was occupied by the black soldiers in the Massachusetts 54th. "This is a world of compensations," concluded Schurz. Although some elite women again shopped on King Street in the morning and walked along the Battery in the evening, others avoided the new reality. As one Charleston lady explained, "We very rarely go out, the streets are so niggery and the Yankees so numerous."[46]

White Charlestonians complained, too, about the outpouring of sympathy for Union soldiers at Washington Race Course. After returning north in mid-June, James Redpath reported that the construction of the Martyrs of the Race Course cemetery "enraged the Rebels." Local whites also lobbied to shut down the Fourth of July celebration planned by the black community. To their dismay, however, Major General Quincy A. Gillmore, commander of the Department of the South, ensured that the holiday was marked. On July 4, 1865, a large group assembled at Zion Presbyterian Church for the city's Fourth of July ceremony. Just as Frederick Douglass had thirteen years earlier in his famous Fifth of July address, the speakers juxtaposed Independence Day ideals with the realities of chattel slavery. The Civil War had altered the meaning of the holiday for black Americans, bursting the "bands of slavery," in the words of one orator, and allowing four million citizens to at last "bask in the sunshine of liberty."[47]

One month later, black Charlestonians convened again, this time on the anniversary of emancipation in Great Britain. Since the 1830s, black communities from Massachusetts to Canada had commemorated the end of slavery in the British Empire on the first day of August. Leaping at the opportunity to celebrate West Indian emancipation for the first time, African Americans in Charleston put on an elaborate banquet, which featured a fine selection of refreshments, as well as a parade of benevolent society members outfitted in handsome regalia.[48]

The city's lengthy jubilee climaxed four months later, on January 1, with a barbecue held on the anniversary of Lincoln's 1863 Emancipation Proclamation. The year 1866 broke cloudy and damp, turning Charleston's streets into mud. "Yet nothing could chill the ardor and enthusiasm of the occasion," observed the *South Carolina Leader*, a new Republican weekly. At ten o'clock in the morning, the procession made its way north from the Battery up to Washington Race Course, where a speaker's stand was set up not far from the Martyrs of the Race Course cemetery. The crowd of perhaps ten thousand was almost entirely black.

The program lasted from twelve until four o'clock and included numerous appeals to not lose sight of all that had changed over the last four years. Reverend Alonzo Webster, a white missionary from Vermont, evoked the harrowing journeys of runaways who were pursued deep into the New England countryside by slavery's hounds. Freedman Samuel

Dickerson said he felt like he was in a dream from which he was scared to be awakened, and General Rufus Saxton underscored the fact that the destruction of slavery had not come easily. Two years earlier, when he met with Beaufort freedpeople on New Year's Day, 1864, "clouds and darkness seemed to hang over our country's cause," said Saxton. Now, not only had the Confederacy surrendered, but the U.S. Constitution had been amended to outlaw slavery once and for all. For the first time on Emancipation Day, he could proudly proclaim that "the United States of America does not recognize the right in man to hold property in human flesh." The crowd listened attentively to the lengthy speeches. Afterward, they were rewarded with a large barbeque. "Not a single disturbance or accident of any kind occurred during the day," concluded the *South Carolina Leader*, "and all went 'merry as a marriage bell.'"[49]

* * * *

THE SUCCESS OF Charleston's first Emancipation Day, like most festivals of freedom over the preceding year, did not mean that former Confederates had come to terms with such demonstrations and all they represented. According to one source, who recounted white reactions to the Emancipation Day celebration, "the citizens generally, and the late nigger drivers in particular, sneered most profoundly at the whole affair." They whispered that "the police were going to interfere and quash the whole matter; but on counting noses, and calculating consequences, the project was prudently abandoned."[50]

Ex-Confederates compensated by complaining. Jacob F. Schirmer, a prominent Charleston native, scribbled in his journal that the freedpeople returned from the Emancipation Day festivities drunk from consuming copious quantities of liquor. And the *Charleston Daily News* parodied the New Year's Day event in a column dripping with sarcasm. It was "a day of jubilee—a JUBILEE JUBILORUM—a one-sided game of chequers, in which the black men were all kings, and the white all privates, except a few, who, having gotten into the enemy's 'back line,' deserted their colors, and were crowned as black kings." The parade consisted of "lordly knights" with "coal-black masks" and "a long row of darkey civilians, wearing each a badge." These were not the "old copper badges, which, in the good old times, or perhaps they may prefer the expression the bad old times—old masters was wont to purchase" for them, "but a badge of honor, a small piece of ribbon, which cost little or nothing, and for which they themselves had paid handsomely." Having traded their slave badges for worthless replacements, snickered the *Daily News* correspondent, they merrily marched on, "indiscriminately mixed up, without regard to size; tall niggers with low hats walked with short niggers with tall hats—some sported umbrellas, some walking canes."

The correspondent was equally galled by what he saw at the Washington Race Course. "The old Jockey Club House, where in days of yore the beauty and fashion of Carolina were wont to congregate now filled with negro men and negro women!" Although little troubled by the words of the black participants, he was sickened by what their white counterparts had to say. "One would-be orator made a speech," wrote the correspondent breathlessly, "in which he first bragged about being a Vermonter, then tried to stir up the negroes by insidious remarks, calculated to make their thoughts revert to the days of their slavery."[51]

Charleston was an altogether different place at the dawn of 1866 than it had been eleven months earlier. Slavery and the Confederacy were dead and buried, and their apologists—outnumbered and outgunned—could do little more than carp about these changes and ridicule those who championed them. In the years that followed, the battle over the memory of slavery would grow more pitched, as whites and blacks confronted the great task before them—how to reconstruct their city, state, and nation.

2

Reconstructing
Charleston in the
Shadow of Slavery

TWO YEARS AFTER CHARLESTON FREEDPEOPLE CONCLUDED
their extended wake for slavery, an astonishing meeting convened in the
city. The purpose: to stamp out the last vestiges of the peculiar institution.
On a windy and rainy January afternoon in 1868, 121 delegates to the
state's constitutional convention gathered in the elegant Charleston Club
House on Meeting Street, just south of Broad. Seventy-two of the men
who came to redraft the South Carolina constitution were African American, and forty-one had once been slaves. For the first time in history, South
Carolina's black majority would have a voice in the state's future.[1]

An hour before the opening session on January 14, black Charlestonians had begun lining the sidewalk across from the Club House. Others
wandered through the building's handsome grounds. When the doors to
the hall opened around noon, the black crowd rushed inside. Few whites
joined them.[2]

While African Americans thrilled at the opportunity to witness history in the making, white South Carolinians fretted about the revolutionary developments under way. "Our Black and Tan members have
gone to Charleston to meet in Convention on tomorrow," wrote a Spartanburg planter in his journal on January 13. "There the negroes are to
make laws to rule white people. For bid it, Fates." The next day, the
Charleston Daily News remarked, "To-day marks the commencement of
a new and sad era in our history. The Carolina of old—with her peace,
her prosperity and her freedom—is, for the present, dead."[3]

Charleston Mercury editor Robert B. Rhett Jr. and his brother Edmund
were struck by the contrast between the gentlemen who had built the

Charleston Club House and the diverse collection that assembled there on that January afternoon. Noting the blustery weather that rattled the windows during much of the first day's proceedings, they ventured that "it would have taken but a slight stretch of a superstitious imagination, to fancy that the ghosts of the departed Carolinians ... had risen from their graves, and come to enter their protest against the awful desecration." To make matters worse, the Rhetts vented, one black delegate had the audacity to dress entirely in gray, an affront to Confederate veterans everywhere.[4]

For Confederate stalwarts like the Rhetts, the memory of slavery cast a long shadow over the 1868 constitutional convention. Predictably, the Charleston brothers played up the antebellum status of the delegates to what they dubbed "the Great Ringed-Streaked and Striped Negro Convention" in their firebrand newspaper, which they had revived in 1866. The *Mercury,* which claimed the largest circulation in the city, ran a monthlong series of mostly critical portraits for its conservative readership. The Rhetts mocked ex-slave delegates' vocabulary, grammar, morals, and behavior, comparing some African American participants to baboons and orangutans.[5]

The convention delegates themselves—almost all of whom counted themselves Republicans—also refracted the gathering through the prism of slavery, albeit from a different angle. On January 15, convention president Albert G. Mackey, a white Unionist physician from Charleston, noted that the meeting was the first constitutional convention in state history untainted by the stain of slavery. Previous conventions had prevented many South Carolinians from exercising "the elective franchise, because slavery, that vile relic of barbarism, had thrown its blighting influence upon the minds of the people." While ex-Confederates denounced the 1868 convention as being representative of everything that had gone wrong over the past few years, Mackey and his fellow Republicans—black and white alike—viewed the 121 delegates as the embodiment of what was possible in a South Carolina that had rid itself of slavery and all that went along with it.[6]

The Civil War may have broken the yoke of bondage, but it could hardly erase the memory of the institution. The wounds of having once been counted as property—of having been beaten, raped, or sold away from loved ones—were still fresh for countless black southerners. So, too, was the sense of betrayal that many white southerners felt when they learned that the enslaved were not the happy, devoted servants they had imagined them to be. The ghosts of the enslaved past were especially haunting in Charleston, where just about every resident had a firsthand familiarity with slavery. Throughout the next decade, as Republicans and Democrats struggled for political supremacy across the city, state, and the rest of the Reconstruction South, these memories—positive and negative, real and imagined—surfaced over and over.

* * * *

BY THE MIDDLE of 1865, most white South Carolinians had made their peace with the reality that they were, as Emma Holmes put it, "a conquered people." Following President Andrew Johnson's directive, Unionists and Confederates took the oath of allegiance, pledging to support not only the United States and its laws but also all wartime proc- lamations regarding emancipation. When a Charleston delegation vis- ited Johnson in Washington, D.C., that summer, the new president told them that though slavery had been destroyed by war, it would be best if it were also ended by law. Hoping to bring military occupation to a swift end, the delegation heeded Johnson's advice. In September, a state consti- tutional convention—the last all-white meeting of its kind—admitted that slavery, having been destroyed by the United States government, would not be reestablished in South Carolina. The following month, in accordance with Johnson's restoration plan, a special session of the state General Assembly ratified the Thirteenth Amendment, which abolished slavery. The institution that had brought great wealth to a few South Carolinians and suffering to so many was over.[7]

Still, in the months that followed, the state's white citizenry worked to limit the social and economic effects of emancipation by passing the Black Codes. These measures gave freedpeople some new rights and lib- erties. They could now make contracts, buy and sell property, and sue or be sued. But the Black Codes, like similar statutes passed across the South, also delineated legal constraints that applied solely to African Americans. South Carolina limited blacks' rights of travel and gun ownership, charged black tradesmen significant license fees, and created a separate district court system for African Americans. Black children as young as two could be apprenticed out to masters, while judicial officers were given the power to whip adult servants and return runaway servants to their employers.[8]

Provisional governor Benjamin F. Perry justified the Black Codes using a paternalistic logic rooted in the culture of the Old South. Positing former slaves as children in need of protection not only from the outside world but also from themselves, he argued that the new laws provided essential safeguards. As Edmund Rhett wrote in October 1865, "the general interest of both the white man and the negro requires that he should be kept . . . as near to the condition of slavery as possible." Slavery was dead and buried, but its specter still hung over South Carolina.[9]

Little wonder, then, that opponents of the Black Codes also turned to remembrances of slavery as they made their case against the offensive measures—and others like them. The *South Carolina Leader*, a Republican newspaper founded in Charleston by several printers from a Pennsylvania regiment, took direct aim at the Black Codes. The new laws, insisted the weekly's white editors on December 16, were little more than an expression of the "average of the justice and humanity which the late slaveholders possess." In the same issue, the paper ran a column from the *Boston Journal* that ridiculed the Black Codes as evidence that South Carolina had given up slavery in name but hoped to retain it in fact. And when planters in Bennettsville, near the North Carolina border, drafted a set of resolutions about contracting with and disciplining freedpeople on the first Monday in December, the *South Carolina Leader* reminded readers of the doleful meaning the day had for black South Carolinians. Before the war, counties had staged sale days on the first Monday of every month, during which town squares were transformed into open markets for the auctioning of all sorts of property, including slaves. But no more. This "is a day which will never again be the occasion of divorcing husband from wife and separating children from parents—a day which never again will witness the sale of 'female domestics guaranteed' to the highest bidder," maintained the *Leader*. Yet the resolutions adopted in Bennettsville, which required freedpeople to gain permission to find a new employer and asserted the right of planters to discipline their workers, were a troubling reminder that planters still fancied themselves "lord[s] of the manor."[10]

Palmetto State planters, however, struggled to reassert their lordly status, at least in the short run. Indeed, just weeks after the General Assembly began passing the Black Codes, General Daniel E. Sickles, the military commander of South Carolina, declared them null and void. Nevertheless, the *South Carolina Leader* determined to keep memories of slavery and the Civil War fresh in the minds of its readers, if only to delegitimize further efforts to circumscribe black rights. In early 1866 the *Leader* began publishing a column called "Secession Gleams," reprinting extracts from southern writing produced during the conflict. The January 6 edition included a sermon that was first delivered in Yorkville, South Carolina, in 1861, in the wake of the Confederate victory at the First Battle of Bull Run. "The eminence of the South," John T. Wightman had proclaimed, "is the result of her domestic slavery, the feature which gives character to her history and which marshals the mighty events now at work for her defence [*sic*] and perpetuity." A week later, the Republican weekly reproduced an 1861 letter written by L.W. Spratt. In it, the South Carolina fire-eater argued that the Confederacy, founded as "a Slave Republic," should "own slavery as the source" of its authority by repealing its ban on the transatlantic slave trade.[11]

Ex-Confederates were less eager to remind South Carolinians about the secessionist past, especially with the Union Army still present in the state. Yet they could hardly forget slavery with the consequences of its demise all around them. More than a year after the end of the war, Charleston remained a wreck—worse than even Richmond or Columbia, according to a *New York Times* correspondent, who described "the tall, towering chimneys, standing alone amid flowering shrubbery, and neglected but beautiful gardens; the broken marble slabs and pieces of statuary that lay amid the waving grass of elegant lawns."[12]

To most former Confederates, the state's political fortunes were equally grim. White South Carolinians fumed over Republicans' refusal to seat southern congressional delegations in Washington, D.C., as well as the passage of the Civil Rights Act, which outlawed discriminatory statutes like the Black Codes. To make matters worse, with the Military Reconstruction Acts of 1867, Republicans in Congress paved the way for black male suffrage in the South. The prospect of living under a "negro constitution" and watching African American men vote and serve in political office led Robert and Edmund Rhett to denounce emancipation, nearly three years after Appomattox. "We did not and do not believe that the negro is fit to be free, and not being fit to be free, we do not believe that he is fit to vote," they announced in the *Charleston Mercury* on April 2, 1868. "We do not believe that all men have, or ever will have, or even ought to have equal rights. We, therefore, believe that slavery was justified—not only justified, but in the highest degree humane."[13]

Many white South Carolinians agreed that slavery had been a righteous institution, but few of them followed the Rhetts in publicly framing emancipation as a mistake. More often, ex-Confederates accepted that slavery was gone for good. In the fall of 1866, Confederate general Wade Hampton III clarified his position on abolition before a group of his former soldiers. Although Hampton objected to the means by which the North had secured the end of slavery—excluding rebel states from the Union until they ratified the Thirteenth Amendment—he consented to the result. "The deed has been done, and, I for one, do honestly declare that I never wish to see it revoked," he stated.[14]

This did not mean, however, that Hampton repudiated slavery itself. On the contrary, the Charleston native—a wealthy planter who had owned hundreds of slaves before the war—regaled the civilizing influence of the peculiar institution on the slave. "Under our paternal care, from a mere handful he grew to be a mighty host," Hampton told his fellow veterans in October 1866. "He came to us a heathen, we made him a Christian. Idle, vicious, savage in his own country; in ours he became industrious, gentle, civilized."[15]

The following March, in response to Congress's decision to extend the vote to southern black men, Hampton pitched this paternalistic message to a group of freedpeople in the state capital. In a speech that was widely covered across the country, he appealed to soon-to-be-enfranchised Columbians on the basis of the benevolent record of slaveholders like him. "I hope that as my past conduct to you has made you look upon me as your friend, so my advice and actions in the future will but confirm you in that belief," Hampton said. "How will you vote?" he then asked his black audience. "Will you choose men who are ignorant of all law—all science of Government, to make your laws and to frame your Government? Will you place in office these strangers who have flocked here to plunder what little is left to us? Or will you trust the men amongst whom you have lived heretofore—amongst whom you must always live?" Having dismissed former slaves and northern carpetbaggers as unfit for government office, Hampton insisted that the third course was the most prudent, for it was in southern whites' interest to ensure that African Americans were prosperous and content.[16]

Charleston's conservative press cheered Hampton's plea. The *Daily News* pronounced his speech to be representative of the convictions of most white southerners. The *Charleston Courier*, which after a short stint as a Unionist paper had returned to local, conservative hands in late 1865, reproduced the general's address in full. Echoing Hampton's sentiments, *Courier* editor and Confederate veteran Thomas Y. Simons insisted that white South Carolinians had readily embraced emancipation once the war ended. Like many of his brethren, Simons doubted the wisdom of giving African American men the ballot. But now he simply hoped every citizen of the state would exercise the vote judiciously. The editor was particularly frustrated by the deep well of moral capital that emancipation provided the Republican Party. "The truth is, that the freedom of the late slaves did not spring from any sentiment of real philanthropy on the part of the North," argued Simons. Instead, Republicans embraced emancipation only when the Union Army became desperate for more recruits. Simons urged black South Carolinians not to be swayed by Republican propaganda but rather to put their trust in "their reliable friends" around them. This particular friend did not remind his readers that before the war he had told the South Carolina legislature that the election of a "Black Republican" to the presidency presented a mortal threat to slavery.[17]

Unsurprisingly, South Carolina Republicans took issue with such appeals. The *Charleston Advocate*, a new Republican weekly, insisted that Wade Hampton and his fellow planters "held the colored man in brutal slavery, and sold him as a dumb brute in the shambles." How "dare they to refer to slavery, and set themselves up as the colored man's best friends in whom he should confide." Francis L. Cardozo, a freeborn black Charlestonian who had left for Scotland as a young man but returned during Reconstruction, also dismissed the idea. "Who advocated and laid down millions of treasure and thousands of lives to maintain this great wrong [of slavery] and oppression to our people?" he asked a large crowd that assembled at Military Hall three days after Hampton's March address. "Who but the Southern whites, who now pretend to be our best friends, and claim our united action with them."[18]

* * * *

JUDGING BY THE election that fall, South Carolina's black majority put little stock in Hampton's and other planters' attempts to curry favor. In late November 1867, ex-slaves turned out en masse to vote for the proposed state constitutional convention, trumping a conservative plan to boycott the election and thereby block the convention by denying it the requisite level of participation. What's more, they elected a slate of delegates that included only a handful of former masters.[19]

Two months later, on January 14, 1868, the South Carolina Constitutional Convention convened at the Charleston Club House. Technically, the Reconstruction Acts required that they draft a document that fully conformed to the U.S. Constitution and gave the vote to both black and white men. But the interracial group of delegates who assembled in Charleston on that rainy day understood their task as something far greater. "It is our duty," announced Beaufort delegate J.J. Wright, a Pennsylvania-born black, "to destroy all the elements of the institution of slavery."[20]

Chief among such elements was South Carolina's uniquely undemocratic political culture. Fears of servile insurrection had undermined political dissent in the state and, as a result, inhibited the establishment of a legitimate two-party system. And while most states in the antebellum period held popular elections for president and governor, South Carolina left those choices (and a host of others) up to its legislature. By means of malapportionment, formidable property qualifications for voting, and even higher qualifications for officeholding, Lowcountry rice planters and Upcountry cotton planters had long dominated the General Assembly.[21]

From the start, convention delegates made it clear that they planned to dismantle South Carolina's undemocratic system rather than reap its benefits. They cut back significantly on the power of the General Assembly and ensured that the state would popularly elect presidential electors as well as the governor. The convention also eliminated property ownership qualifications for serving in the legislature and stipulated that wealth would not be a factor in determining representation in its lower house. Finally, the new constitution provided for universal manhood suffrage.[22]

Richard "Daddy" Cain moved to Charleston in 1865 to help resurrect its African Methodist Episcopal church. He was also a delegate to the 1868 South Carolina Constitutional Convention.

Early on, a few delegates tried to restrict suffrage rights to those who could read and write. Yet several others strenuously objected to this provision, highlighting the blind eye that it turned toward the educational constraints placed upon South Carolina slaves. Literacy restrictions, Virginia-born minister Richard H. Cain told his fellow delegates, were an antebellum holdover inconsistent with the new era of progress. "Daddy" Cain, as his parishioners admiringly called him, had come to Charleston in the spring of 1865 to help reestablish the African Methodist Episcopal congregation, four decades after its church building had been destroyed. A short, charismatic man with a powerful voice, Cain built the new Emanuel A.M.E. Church, whose sanctuary was designed by Denmark Vesey's son Robert, into a large, influential congregation. "In this Constitution," Cain reasoned at the 1868 convention, "we do not wish to leave a jot or title upon which anything can be built to remind our children of their former state of slavery." Such arguments helped convince the convention to vote in near unanimity not to include this remnant of the peculiar institution in the new constitution.[23]

Recollections of slavery shaped convention debates over debtor relief, too. Delegates who wanted to punish slave dealers, for instance, introduced an ordinance to negate all debts incurred through the purchase of slaves.

Some opponents of this measure insisted that contracts from slave sales were the same as any other contracts and should be respected as such. Others made explicitly antislavery arguments against the proposed ordinance. Simeon Corley, a white delegate from Lexington, questioned the legitimacy of a measure that appeared to treat those who sold slaves as more culpable than those who bought them. "Is there any difference between the seller and buyer in a moral sense?" he asked.[24]

Most of Corley's fellow delegates thought there was. "I regard the seller of the slave as the principal, and the buyer as the accessory," pronounced African American delegate Robert Elliott. "A few years ago the popular verdict of this country was passed upon the slave seller and the slave buyer, and both were found guilty of the enormous crime of slavery. The buyer of the slave received his sentence, which was the loss of the slave, and we are now to pass sentence upon the seller. We propose that he shall be punished by the loss of his money." Several of Elliott's allies singled out professional slave traders as particularly unworthy of sympathy. "Many of these men to whom these debts are due, are those who trafficked in slaves and came from all parts of the United States," insisted J.J. Wright. "They came from the Northeast and the West . . . with vessels bringing in a cargo of slaves, sold them to the people of the South, put what money they could in their pockets, and went back where they belonged."[25]

Wright's comments reveal a curious feature of this debate. By placing most of the blame for the peculiar institution on the shoulders of slave traders, supporters of the measure seemed to want to absolve South Carolina, in particular, and the South, more generally, of the sin of slavery. William J. Whipper, a Pennsylvania-born black delegate who also represented Beaufort, went further than Wright in defending his adopted state. "Be it said to the eternal honor of South Carolina, she opposed the institution, and it was not until a renegade dog forced the bone upon her, and made it into dollars and cents, that she consented," concluded Whipper. The black delegate thereby anticipated an argument that in the decades that followed would become a staple of the Lost Cause liturgy.[26]

Other supporters of the ordinance to forgive slave-sale debt focused on the broader message that it would send across the globe. Freeborn Charlestonian Alonzo J. Ransier supported the proposed measure because he could not condone the recognition of human chattel. Daniel H. Chamberlain, a Massachusetts native and future governor of the state, agreed. He viewed the ordinance as the natural by-product of northern victory in the Civil War: "The confederacy fell, and with it fell slavery; with it fell property in man; with it fell every claim and every obligation which rested on the basis of slavery." Shortly after Chamberlain spoke, the convention members overwhelmingly voted to have their state's new constitution invalidate debts contracted for the purchase of slaves.[27]

Memories of slavery also fueled white conservatives' objections to the convention proceedings. "Can there be anything more abhorrent to the feelings of an honorable man," wondered former governor Benjamin F. Perry, "than to see these renegades & adventurers, black & white, from all the northern states coming here associating with our former slaves and the vilest of the white race in order to form organic laws for the gentlemen of South Carolina?" Robert and Edmund Rhett did not think so. They kept up a steady drumbeat against the convention in the pages of the *Charleston Mercury*, ridiculing the proceedings and satirizing its delegates. So offensive was the paper's early coverage that the convention briefly considered banning the *Charleston Mercury*'s reporter from the Charleston Club House.[28]

Seething over the idea that their former field hands and domestics were being allowed to write the state's constitution, the Rhett brothers painted portraits of black delegates that emphasized their enslaved pasts. The *Mercury* described Sumter representative Samuel Lee as "an excellent house servant . . . [who] understands waiting on table, to which he has been trained" and characterized Greenville delegate Wilson Cook as respectable and compliant, despite "his ambition to attend public meetings and make speeches." Even freeborn black delegates evoked slavery for the Rhetts. Their paper represented Pennsylvanian William J. Whipper as "a genuine negro, black and kinky headed, who, in the days of slavery, would have been esteemed a likely fellow for a house servant or a coachman."[29]

Certain memories provided a ray of hope for defenders of the planter class. Of Abbeville's Hutson J. Lomax, the *Mercury* proclaimed: "He was a well behaved servant, and, as he grew up, he was allowed by his master to learn the trade of a carpenter. . . . He was a faithful slave during the late war, and did not appear to undergo any great change in consequence of the 'emancipation' proclamation." But any hope that men like Lomax might demonstrate the same fidelity in freedom as they appeared to have shown in chains did not last long. "The grand purpose of the negro constitution is to set up and establish negro rule in South Carolina," concluded the *Mercury* after the convention closed in March 1868.[30]

Later that year, ex-Confederates watched in horror as the state's black majority ratified the new, racially egalitarian constitution and elected a slew of black and white Republicans to local, state, and national offices. In Charleston, voters chose Gilbert Pillsbury, a Massachusetts abolitionist who had come to the state to work for the Freedmen's Bureau, as mayor and a full slate of Republicans as aldermen. At the state level, white Ohioan Robert K. Scott was elected governor, and Republicans won large majorities in both houses of the General Assembly. Remarkably, 60 percent of the new lower house was black.[31]

As Republicans assumed political power across the state that fall, the South's most infamous conservative newspaper folded once again. Unable to pay its bills, the Rhetts stopped publishing the *Mercury* in October and subsequently printed a broadside bidding farewell to their subscribers. Although distraught about the new regime that had elevated inferior blacks over civilized whites, Robert Barnwell Rhett Sr., who penned the valediction under his son Robert's name, remained defiant. He maintained that the southern people would neither forgive nor forget. "The negro serves a purpose for Southern Independence far greater than his numbers or presence tells against it," he stated. "There is no ground of forgetfulness—no possibility of forgiveness, with these black, moving memorials of our wrongs, polluting our sight."[32]

* * * *

WHILE WHITE CONSERVATIVES like the Rhetts stewed, Republicans enjoyed the fruits of political empowerment. The Union Army occupation of the city between 1865 and 1868 and the Republican Party's control of local and state government for much of the decade that followed ensured that former slaves and their allies had a prominent voice. After a three-year hiatus, Charleston Unionists resumed their Decoration Day ceremonies in 1868, though not at the Martyrs of the Race Course cemetery. The Union burial ground had fallen into disrepair, and eventually the remains of the prisoners who died there were removed to a federal cemetery in Beaufort. The May 30, 1868, ceremony, marked according to the directions of the Grand Army of the Republic (GAR), the North's veterans association, was held at Military Hall. A crowd of fifty or so white Unionists gathered at the Gothic structure on Wentworth Street for the service. The Civil War, insisted New York colonel A.J. Willard, had been the tragic result of the South's "perverted" institution of slavery, which checked the progress of civil rights and universal suffrage.[33]

Black Charlestonians played a bigger role in later Decoration Day services, which were held at Magnolia Cemetery, where some Union dead had been interred. Organized by the Robert Gould Shaw Post No. 1 of the GAR and a committee of Unionist ladies, the May 1869 ceremony boasted a crowd of more than two thousand people, most of whom were African American. The orations that day included a speech by black state representative Alonzo J. Ransier. One year later, a large, mostly African American crowd assembled around a flag-draped stand, upon which sat former Union officers as well as black and white officeholders, including William J. Whipper, who, like Ransier, moved into the legislature after serving as a constitutional convention delegate.[34]

Slavery continued to be a prominent topic at these integrated services. At the 1870 Decoration Day ceremony, General William Gurney, who had relocated from New York to Charleston after the war, underscored the institution's centrality to the Civil War. He acknowledged the sacrifices of soldiers on both sides of the conflict, but Gurney insisted that Union men had given their lives to destroy human bondage, while Confederates had gone to war for an outdated and effete idea. Whipper, too, balanced a tribute to Confederate bravery with a clear statement about the superiority of the Union cause. One side fought "for liberty, which was brought over in the ship which landed its living freight on Plymouth Rock; the other for the maintenance of an oppression which was brought to this country in a low black schooner which sailed upon the James River in 1620."[35]

By the early 1870s, the remains of most Union soldiers in Charleston had been removed to national cemeteries in Beaufort and Florence, undercutting Decoration Day ceremonies in the city. But local African Americans and Unionists still marked the end of slavery on Emancipation Day (January 1), Independence Day (July 4), and three or four other annual freedom festivals, just as they had since 1865.[36]

"South Carolina—The Celebration of Emancipation Day, January 8th in Charleston—Scenes and Incidents of the Parade." *From* Frank Leslie's Illustrated Newspaper, *February 10, 1877.*

The parades accompanying these celebrations followed routes carefully plotted to dramatize freedpeople's newfound status. The Emancipation Day procession on January 2, 1871, for instance, commenced at the Citadel Green, marched north up Meeting Street, west on John Street, and then south along King Street. In a symbolic statement that few could have missed, the route took the armed black procession around not just the Citadel Green, but also the military academy that the defenders of slavery had long called home. The parade then moved south on King Street, east on Hasell Street, and then south again along Meeting, where it passed directly west of the city's slave-trading district. The parade ended at White Point Garden at the Battery, where African Americans had been prohibited from gathering from the 1840s until the end of the Civil War.[37]

Charleston's freedom pageants became larger, more elaborate, and more political in the 1870s. "The entire state government" came to town on Emancipation Day in 1874, sneered the *Charleston News and Courier*, "from the Governor to the thousand and one pages who draw three dollars per diem during the session of the Legislature." By that point, black militia companies from Charleston and neighboring towns were a conspicuous feature on Emancipation Day and the Fourth of July. Each holiday, thousands of Lowcountry African Americans lined up early to watch their armed brethren, many decked out in the dark blue uniforms of the state militia, march in orderly fashion through city streets. These martial displays intertwined past and present. Led by mounted officers, including ex-slaves Robert Smalls and Samuel Dickerson, the black companies were often named for abolitionists and other black heroes. The 1876 Fourth of July parade included the Lincoln Rifle Guard, the Attucks Light Infantry, the Douglass Light Infantry, the Delany Light Infantry, and the Garrison Light Infantry. The sight of former slaves carrying muskets with bayonets and unsheathed swords no doubt inspired pride in the black crowd and fear in the few whites who ventured out to watch. But the processions were also a practical reminder of the military force that kept at bay the white paramilitary groups, including the Ku Klux Klan and hundreds of rifle and sabre clubs, hoping to end Republican rule in the South and return white supremacist Democrats to power.[38]

The parades typically ended at the Battery, where enormous crowds bought peanuts, cakes, fried fish, and sassafras beer from vendors camped out in shady spots in White Point Garden. The scene was especially festive on the Fourth of July. "The whole colored population seemed to have turned out into the open air," reported the *Daily News* on July 5, 1872, "and the gardens were so densely thronged that it was only with the utmost difficulty that locomotion was possible amid the booths, stalls and sightseers."[39]

Still, the black men and women who congregated along the Battery and in White Point Garden on the Fourth—many of whom had come in from the Sea Islands—found space to perform ring dances from dawn to dusk. In form, the dances resembled the ring shout, in which enslaved men and women had danced in a circle, stomping their feet, clapping their hands, and singing in a call-and-response fashion. In substance, these Fourth of July rituals drew on a second enslaved tradition—mocking the formal manners and customs of the planter class in song and dance. Postbellum ring dances provided Charleston's freedpeople a chance to poke fun at elite courtship rituals as they celebrated their emancipation. The rituals also afforded black women, largely excluded from the parades and speakers' platforms, a public role in Charleston's

An 1851 view of the lower peninsula showing the Battery and White Point Garden, which played host to annual Emancipation Day and Fourth of July celebrations after the Civil War.

festivals of freedom. In 1876, the *News and Courier* described the "Too-la-loo," a popular new ring song and dance that became a staple of later commemorations. About two dozen participants—evenly split between men and women—formed a ring, into which one of the female dancers would move while the others began to sing and clap. "Go hunt your lover, Too-la-loo!/Go find your lover, Too-la-loo!" they urged the lady in the center, who eventually chose one man to join her in the ring. While hundreds of revelers danced the Too-la-loo in 1876, hundreds more gathered around the White Point Garden music stand to listen to speeches. Among the most well-attended orations that afternoon, grumbled the *News and Courier*, was the "rambling political harangue" delivered by "Daddy" Cain.[40]

Many of the addresses delivered as a part of prior Fourth of July and Emancipation Day celebrations had been similarly political. Speakers at these events often used references to slavery to promote black and Republican candidates for office. At the 1870 Fourth of July commemoration at White Point Garden, Martin R. Delany warned black Charlestonians not to trust white politicians but rather to support black leaders like him lest they find themselves back in chains. The following year, Samuel Dickerson lauded Republican principles and the party's role in destroying slavery. To the dismay of the *Daily News*, the freedman's Emancipation Day address brought in "much inflammatory matter by a comparison between the present and former condition of the colored people in this state."[41]

Such memories, no doubt, were painful to many South Carolina freedpeople. After black abolitionist Frances Ellen Watkins Harper toured the state in 1867, she wrote, "The South is a sad place, it is so rife with mournful memories and sad revelations of the past. Here you listen to heart-saddening stories of grievous old wrongs, for the shadows of the past have not been fully lifted from the minds of the former victims of slavery." However distressing, Charleston's black community refused to let locals forget about its enslaved past. And if a freedperson wanted a permanent memento, she could pay $2.50 for a "magnificent" copy of the Emancipation Proclamation, which were advertised for sale in the *Charleston Courier*.[42]

* * * *

ALTHOUGH WHITE CHARLESTONIANS were not above making money by helping to hawk emancipationist mementos, they endlessly carped about black festivals of freedom. Nathaniel Russell Middleton told his daughter that the Fourth was "a dreadful day" for white Charlestonians that would "not have been permitted in a civilized community." While white citizens "showed proper respect for the day by the suspension of all business," noted the *Daily News* in 1866, black residents put on an extravagant Fourth of July celebration. "Childlike, he loves a holiday," the paper complained of the typical freedman.[43]

Some members of Charleston's African American elite—concerned about maintaining social distance from former slaves—were also frustrated by such displays. On the eve of Emancipation Day in 1867, the *New York Times* reported that freeborn black Charlestonians "look coldly upon this demonstration of their more recently emancipated brethren, for whom they take no pains to conceal their contempt." But it was white residents who complained the loudest. In 1869, *Charleston Courier* editor Thomas Y. Simons smarted that what had once been a day for the white citizenry to shoot off their rusty muskets and drink mint juleps had become a day for African American revelry. Using a name intended to evoke African Americans' formerly servile status, he wrote that "Cuffee takes the place of the former celebrants of the day.... Cuffee shoulders the time-honored flint muskets of the beats."[44]

Prominent merchant Jacob F. Schirmer was the city's most consistent and vitriolic critic of these black celebrations, though he confined his complaints to his journal. In 1866 Schirmer lamented that the nation's holiday had become "a *nigger* day": "Nigger procession[,] nigger dinner and balls and promenades," and "scarcely a white person seen in the streets." One year later, he called the Fourth "the Day the Niggers now celebrate, and the whites stay home and work." Schirmer struggled to find the words to describe what took place at White Point Garden under the blazing hot sun of July 4, 1872. "All of the African race" seemed to have come out for the festivities.[45]

White Charlestonians also staged commemorations of their own. In the spring of 1866, a group of women determined to shower local Confederates with the same affection that the city's black citizenry had bestowed upon the Union soldiers buried in the Martyrs of the Race Course cemetery one year earlier. To this end, they formed the Ladies' Memorial Association of Charleston (LMAC), which, like similar groups founded in Richmond, Vicksburg, and Augusta, drew its supporters mainly from middle-class and elite circles. The LMAC sponsored the region's first Confederate Decoration Day ceremony, which was held on June 16, 1866, the anniversary of the nearby Battle of Secessionville. It seemed like the Sabbath in Charleston that day, with most stores closing before noon and churches across the city holding services. Confederate graves in the downtown area were decorated with flowers, and, despite heavy rains, men, women, and children packed carriages and train cars for the two-mile ride up to Magnolia Cemetery.

The solemn afternoon ceremonies took place on a makeshift stage erected next to the burial ground. The lead orator for the service was John L. Girardeau, a white Confederate chaplain who before the war had been the minister for Zion Presbyterian Church's large black congregation. "We are here as mourners to-day," he reminded the predominantly female crowd. "Simply retrospective in its character, it has no covert political complexion, and no latent and insidious reference to the future." In contrast to later Confederate Decoration Day ceremonies, this first event largely steered clear of anything that might be perceived as controversial or sectionally divisive.[46]

That fall, the LMAC was joined by the Survivors' Association of Charleston (SAC), one of the nation's first Confederate veterans organizations. The SAC also found support among city bluebloods, including members of the Gaillard, Manigault, and Rutledge families, who proclaimed it their duty to assist impoverished veterans as well as Confederate widows and orphans. Strident ex-Confederates Cornelius Irvine Walker and Edward McCrady Jr. were among the founding members of the SAC, yet the group initially focused its attention on nonpartisan activities, such as encouraging medical assistance to the wounded, securing jobs for the destitute, and documenting individuals who had fought for the Confederacy. In the short run, the Survivors took a back seat when it came to public commemorations, ceding control to their female counterparts in the LMAC, who, following Victorian mores, were assumed to be apolitical and thus no threat to sectional reunion.[47]

For the next several years, the city's Confederate memorial demonstrations were as staid as the original Confederate Decoration Day. The presence of the Union Army, as well as the advent of black political power, kept partisan displays in check. Following General Daniel E. Sickles's December 1866 order that Confederate memorial organizations should confine themselves to charity and memorial services, the LMAC concentrated on establishing the Home for the Mothers, Widows, and Daughters of Confederate Soldiers on Broad Street, installing Confederate headstones, and quietly decorating graves at Magnolia.[48]

In the early 1870s, however, the LMAC began sponsoring more elaborate Decoration Day events, which featured spirited addresses by ex-Confederates. Meanwhile, former rebel soldiers flocked to join veterans organizations, such as the SAC, which gained a wider influence in 1869, when it expanded into the statewide Survivors' Association of South Carolina (SASC). As it grew, the SASC added a second objective to its philanthropic work: honoring "the dead and the principles for which they sacrificed their lives, by collecting and preserving facts for a full and impartial history" of the war. It was the duty of all veterans who survived the war to ensure that the Confederate cause "should not be forgotten, or suffered to be distorted or misrepresented by their enemies," wrote one veteran to Edward McCrady, chairman of the SASC executive committee, in 1871. Under the influence of the SASC and the LMAC,

Charleston took its first steps toward becoming an epicenter of the Lost Cause.[49]

Coined by *Richmond Examiner* editor Edward A. Pollard, who published *The Lost Cause; A New Southern History of the War of the Confederates* in 1866, the term "the Lost Cause" quickly became shorthand for a southern defense of the Confederacy. Like many myths, the Lost Cause comprised a host of arguments and rationalizations, but two of them, which are neatly encapsulated in the phrase itself, loom the largest. First, the Confederate Army had no real chance to win the Civil War. Facing off against a superior force—with greater resources and manpower—Confederate soldiers had waged a valiant, yet ultimately doomed, fight. That the boys in gray had lasted as long as they did was a testament to their bravery, fortitude, and military prowess. Second, the cause for which Confederates fought was, in fact, a cause worth fighting, even dying, for. This second central component implicitly raised a crucial question: had the Confederacy launched a devastating, four-year war to defend slavery?[50]

Before the war, as we have seen, this was no question at all. Southerners announced loudly and proudly that they went to war to preserve an institution they viewed as the foundation of their economy, society, and culture. After the war, however, the answers ex-Confederates gave to the question were not nearly so honest or straightforward. Some white southerners readily admitted that the war had been waged to protect slavery, but many others—worried about losing the moral high ground to proponents of an emancipationist vision of the war—scrambled to distance the Confederacy from the peculiar institution. At times, this meant simply highlighting more easily defensible causes. "We contended for a great principle," Reverend John Bachman told a small group of ladies at the first meeting of the LMAC on May 14, 1866. "The right of self-government; a principle for which our fathers fought and bled."[51]

Other Lost Cause partisans insisted that while slavery played a role in the Civil War, it paled in comparison to more noble goals and principles. At an 1871 Magnolia Cemetery ceremony honoring the return of the remains of South Carolinians who had fallen at Gettysburg, Reverend John L. Girardeau insisted that the preservation of slavery was less important to Confederates than was the maintenance of the "fundamental

principles of government, of social order, of civil or religious liberty."
With an eye as much on the Radical Republican threats of the present
as on the Confederate past, he urged South Carolinians to keep up the
fight that the deceased had started. "Heroes of Gettysburg! Champions
of constitutional rights! Martyrs for regulated liberty! Once again, farewell! . . . Rest ye, here, Soldiers of a defeated—God grant it may not be a
wholly lost—Cause!"[52]

Girardeau's memorial address underscores another reason why Lost
Cause prophets in the late 1860s and 1870s de-emphasized slavery. Immersed in a struggle against Republican rule, they gravitated toward arguments that spoke directly to Reconstruction politics. With slavery
relegated to the dustbin of history, hitching the Lost Cause to contemporary concerns—like states' rights, low taxes, and the protection of
constitutional liberties—seemed an effective way to turn it into a use-
able past.[53]

Putting the Lost Cause to work, however, necessitated a good measure
of willful forgetting. Confederate memorialists proved equal to the task.
"The world has been wickedly taught and foolishly believes that we
resorted to war solely to preserve our institution of African slavery,"
General John S. Preston told a SASC meeting in Columbia in 1870. If
anyone knew what had led to the Civil War, it was Preston, who not only
attended the South Carolina Secession Convention but also served as
the state's official delegate to Virginia's secession convention. The North
and South were antagonistic societies whose differences were fundamentally rooted in slavery and race, he had told the Virginia convention in
February 1861. But a decade later, Preston preached that slavery had not
been the animating cause of secession at all.[54]

In the same vein, South Carolina's leading fire-eater Robert Barnwell
Rhett Sr. had made a career out of urging southern states to secede from
the Union in defense of the peculiar institution. Yet when he sat down to
write his Civil War memoir in the late 1860s and early 1870s, Rhett
minimized the role of slavery in precipitating the secession crisis. He even
censored himself. After pasting into his memoir portions of an 1860 speech,
Rhett crossed out a line in which he maintained that the North's sectional
tyranny was "organized on a hatred of the institution of slavery."[55]

The defensive posture struck by Preston and Rhett highlights an
important point—one that can be obscured by our tendency to reason

backward from later developments. By the early twentieth century, Lost Cause tenets had become widely accepted, and not just in the South. During Reconstruction, however, they functioned as a countermemory rather than as the master narrative, especially in cities like Charleston. Lost Cause proponents there began on the defensive, and, in classic fashion, they started from the local and personal, fashioning a narrative of the Civil War that directly opposed the emancipationist vision of the conflict, which predominated. As Thavolia Glymph has argued, "The Lost Cause movement stands as an explicit rejoinder to the memory-work of black southerners"—and, it should be added, their white Republican allies—"not the other way around."[56]

* * * *

WHILE WHITE SOUTH Carolinians worked to disassociate slavery from the Confederate cause, Republicans in the state invoked memories of the peculiar institution every chance they could get. Thriving on the moral capital provided by emancipation, party leaders reminded South Carolina voters—most of whom were former slaves—that it was Democrats who had supported and fought to maintain slavery, while Republicans had presided over its demise. Just as northern representatives, such as Pennsylvania congressman Thaddeus Stevens, invoked the terrible costs of the Civil War to motivate predominantly white electorates—the "bloody shirt" appeal—South Carolina Republicans deployed memories of human bondage to motivate the state's many black voters. In the Palmetto State, in other words, shaking the shackles of slavery was a more potent rhetorical tool than waving the bloody shirt.[57]

Charleston's Republican newspapers, such as the short-lived *Free Press*, cast their Democratic opponents as "the old states-rights pro-slavery element" and peppered columns on contemporary political issues with references to "the crimes of slavery." Meanwhile, Republican operatives distributed campaign literature that accused the postbellum Democratic Party of having a proslavery agenda. In the months preceding the presidential election of 1868, the *Charleston Daily News* reproduced a campaign document that the paper claimed had been widely circulated across the South. Intended to drum up support for Republican candidate Ulysses S. Grant, the document consisted of a series of questions and answers that painted the Democratic Party as being dominated by

Confederates and slaveholders who hoped to return freedpeople to bondage.[58]

Republicans also stoked memories of slavery at public rallies and in interviews with northern newspapers. When State Executive Committee chair Alonzo Ransier spoke at an 1869 protest, he offered a passionate denunciation of life under slavery. The following year, while campaigning in Spartanburg as the Republican nominee for lieutenant governor, Ransier framed the election as rooted in a lingering divide over the question of human bondage. The 1870 race pitted incumbent governor Robert K. Scott and Ransier against Richard B. Carpenter and his running mate M.C. Butler, who had been nominated by the fusionist Reform Party. Although this new party had pledged its support for black political equality, Ransier viewed it as little more than a proslavery wolf in sheep's clothing. The Republicans, he insisted, were the genuine antislavery article.[59]

By portraying slavery as a partisan issue, Ransier sought both to defame his political rivals and to attract support from some white voters. Slavery not only put black men in chains, he argued, it also prevented poor white men from being able to support their families. Ransier was not the only South Carolina Republican who thought that poor whites could be swayed by shaking the shackles of slavery. The *Free Press* targeted rank-and-file veterans of the Confederate Army during these years. Former rebel soldiers, insisted the Charleston weekly before the April 1868 state election, had "never heard of Republicanism except through a press which caricatures its exponents, misrepresents its ideas, [and] vilifies its practices." The *Free Press* editors, however, believed that a full explication of party doctrine, as well as a reminder of the lowly place nonslaveholding whites had played in the state's antebellum pecking order, would yield Republican converts.[60]

It was not just officeholders like Ransier and Republican newspapers like the *Free Press* that infused recollections of slavery into political debates. Former slaves did, too. During the Charleston mayoral election of 1871, Charleston Democrats tried to build bridges to black voters by highlighting the party's diverse slate, which included Irish, German, and African American candidates. Unconvinced by this argument, black residents displayed a campaign banner that pointedly asked, "We have played together you say, but were we ever whipped together?"[61]

Alonzo J. Ransier was a freeborn black Charlestonian who became lieutenant governor of South Carolina and a U.S. congressman during Reconstruction.

In the meantime, conservative politicians scrambled to avoid being tainted by the brush of slavery. Decrying the nefarious "parrot cry" about the institution, they complained that each new election cycle brought about the same accusations. Just weeks before voters decided the 1870 gubernatorial race, the *Charleston Daily News* denounced the claim spread by Republican incumbent Robert K. Scott and his allies that white conservatives sought to restore slavery. Black South Carolinians were free and would remain so, insisted the paper's editor, Frank Dawson. "Neither this State, nor the whole South," would "restore African Slavery," even if it could.[62]

In 1874, Dawson's newly founded *Charleston News and Courier* published numerous accounts of Republicans telling blacks that they would be re-enslaved if their conservative opponents prevailed. This notion was ludicrous, maintained Dawson, but it was an effective trick nonetheless. After Republicans retained control of the governorship and the General Assembly in elections a few weeks later, the Charleston editor blamed the state's Republican newspapers: "The Scalawag and Carpet-Bag organs in this State continue to fume and fret and to invoke the memories of Slavery and Sumter, to enable them to retain their hold upon the negro."[63]

South Carolina conservatives not only dismissed Republican charges that they had supported or hoped to reintroduce slavery; at times they used their own memories of slavery—however fanciful—to recriminate the Republican Party and its actions. The *Charleston Mercury* pronounced in October 1868, "Whilst Radical emissaries are traversing the South, and striving to excite the black against the white population, on account of the past institution of slavery, it may not be useless to show the part the Northern people took in putting it upon this continent." To this end, Rhett's paper published a table suggesting that New England slave traders had imported far more slaves into Charleston between 1804 and 1808 (when the trade was outlawed by federal law) than had South Carolinians. When Charleston native and Washington College president W.J. Rivers addressed the South Carolina Historical Society eight years later, he focused on the flawed process of Republican-led emancipation. Southerners should not be blamed for the institution, maintained Rivers, who added that they might have voluntarily ended slavery given sufficient time.[64]

A few South Carolina Democrats went further than Rivers, framing their party, or white conservatives more generally, as the real abolitionist force in the state. *Charleston Courier* editor Thomas Y. Simons made a special appeal to black voters to support the Democratic Party on the basis of its emancipatory actions. "By the act of the white people of her own soil, slavery was forever abolished within her limits," he insisted in an August 1868 editorial. Lincoln's Emancipation Proclamation was of questionable legality, but "the white race here, in Convention assembled, removed of their own accord, all doubts, by declaring as a part of the fundamental law, the extinction forever of slavery." Ignoring the Johnson administration's stipulation that South Carolina could not return to the Union unless it ratified the Thirteenth Amendment, Simons concluded that the state's freedpeople *owe their unquestioned freedom and equality before the law* to *their old masters.*[65]

This misinformation campaign reached its zenith during the election of 1876. That year, South Carolina Democrats had high hopes that homegrown hero and gubernatorial candidate Wade Hampton would enable them to break the Republican stranglehold in the state. Democrats in most other former Confederate states had already achieved this feat, combining fraud, harassment, and violence to reassert their political dominance. In 1876, South Carolina was one of only three states that had yet to be "redeemed," a term white southerners employed so as to invest the reassertion of white supremacy with biblical authority. Since blacks in South Carolina enjoyed an electoral advantage of between twenty thousand and thirty thousand votes, Redemption there seemed to necessitate something more than the usual tactics—actually attracting some African American support. Thus, South Carolina Democrats formulated a two-pronged approach. Following Confederate general Martin W. Gary's "Edgefield Plan," thousands of rifle and sabre club members from across the state sought to limit Republican turnout by donning red shirts, arming themselves to the teeth, and terrorizing Republicans. At the same time, Hampton and other leading Democrats sought to win over at least a few black voters with calls for peace, moderation, and equal rights for all.[66]

One of the central planks of the latter strategy involved challenging the Republican Party's antislavery record. On September 27, 1876, the *News and Courier* published an open letter by Democratic ex-governor Benjamin Perry to Hampton's opponent, Republican incumbent Daniel Chamberlain. In this lengthy, front-page epistle, which was entitled "Who Freed the Slaves?" Perry noted that "the colored people have been told over and again by their unprincipled leaders that if they voted for the Democratic party, they would be thrown back into slavery again." Perry took issue with Chamberlain's claim that the Republicans had liberated the enslaved and thus deserved the support of black voters. Instead, like Thomas Y. Simons, Perry credited the planter class for emancipation. "The State Convention of South Carolina, representing all the slaveholders of the State, did almost unanimously, in 1865, abolish slavery, and declare in their constitution that it should never exist again in the State," he insisted. "In this way, and in no other, was slavery abolished in South Carolina."

Next, Perry set his sights on the Republicans' antebellum record on slavery. Conflating the Republican Party in particular with the North in general, Perry offered an indictment of Republican racial attitudes and actions that ran roughshod over the historical record. Despite the fact that the party was not founded until the mid-1850s, he claimed that its members had not only introduced and profited from the African slave trade, but also had "owned slaves themselves and kept them till the population of the Northern States became so dense that slave labor was no longer profitable." Perry balanced such exaggeration and misinformation with well-founded critiques of Republican timidity when it came to embracing an antislavery agenda in the early stages of the war. He failed to contextualize his criticism of Republican failings, however, and entirely ignored the Confederacy's proslavery agenda.[67]

Hampton supporters echoed Perry's points on the campaign trail. So, too, did a handful of former slaves. At a Democratic club meeting in Summerville, for instance, freedman John Gregory publicly declared himself a victim of Republican lies. For eight years, party leaders had "made him believe that to vote with the white men of the State was to assist them in returning slavery upon his race." But now Gregory "realized that this was only the argument of men who wished to retain themselves in office and power."[68]

The disputed nature of the 1876 election—which was marred by ballot stuffing, intimidation, and outright violence, including two bloody riots in Charleston—makes it impossible to determine the effectiveness of this propaganda campaign. Both Republicans and Democrats claimed victory in the races for governor and control of the General Assembly. The outcome of the presidential election, which pitted Republican Rutherford B. Hayes against Democrat Samuel J. Tilden, was also in question when voting closed on November 8, as several southern states, including South Carolina, recorded contested results. In the pivotal race for governor, estimates of blacks who voted for Hampton ranged from 3,000 (according to Chamberlain's camp) to 17,000 (according to Hampton's). Whatever the case, the conservative drumbeat about slavery that fall makes it clear that Democrats believed that certain memories of human bondage—carefully shaped and deployed by party operatives—might bring black voters into their column.[69]

* * * *

WHITE CONSERVATIVES DEVOTED far less time to denouncing shackle shaking after the Bargain of 1877. This backroom deal ended the disputed 1876 presidential election in favor of Republican candidate Hayes and, in the process, brought Reconstruction to a close in South Carolina (and Louisiana). Once President Hayes removed federal troops from the statehouse in April, Chamberlain and his Republican allies were forced to surrender their offices. Hampton and his Red Shirts had redeemed South Carolina. By the end of the year, Democrats would take over not just the state government but also most local municipalities, including Charleston. Through control of election machinery, coercion, and eventually legal disenfranchisement, white conservatives instituted a political monopoly that would last into the 1960s.[70]

Invocations of slavery no longer seemed so politically potent in this new context. An 1880 *News and Courier* column on a Republican rally in Darlington County, for instance, buried the topic in its lengthy list of outlandish and thus benign grievances: "The speeches were about as usual, the main idea being that the Democrats are allied to the Devil; don't furnish public schools; will restore negroes to slavery; will repeal the Thirteenth, Fourteenth and Fifteenth amendments."[71]

White complaints about black festivals of freedom also began to fade as Republican political power dwindled. In 1877, the *News and Courier* praised the Emancipation Day celebration, which had been postponed to January 8 because of the chaos that followed the disputed election, as the best the city had seen. "A noticeable feature of the celebration," held the paper, "was the almost entire absence of anything like politics, which might possibly be accounted for by the absence of the white carpet-bag element which was once a prominent feature in these celebrations." Fifteen years later, in 1892, the *News and Courier* again complimented the Emancipation Day parade staged by black militia companies for being "entirely devoid of any of those unpleasant features which have marred the occasion in the recent past."[72]

Fourth of July commemorations after 1876 were similarly devoid of politics. African Americans continued to celebrate the day by flooding city streets and parks, buying food and drink in White Point Garden, and dancing the Too-la-loo, which became shorthand for black celebration of the holiday. And, remarkably, African American militia companies—which were not disbanded but rather were relegated to ceremonial duties after the return of Democratic rule—also kept parading through downtown Charleston on the Fourth through the late 1890s. Judging by local newspaper coverage, however, the holiday was strictly commemorative and festive after Redemption. In a nod to the leader of the new political order that produced this change, the *News and Courier*'s 1877 column on the celebration was titled "A Hampton Fourth of July."[73]

Slavery remained a topic at such celebrations, but decoupled from Republican politics it no longer seemed so threatening to white Charlestonians. The battle over how to remember slavery, the Civil War, and emancipation would rage on for decades—and, as we shall see in chapter 4, Charleston Lost Causers, including *News and Courier* editor Dawson, played a prominent role in this fight. But things were different after Reconstruction, and nothing symbolized this new context better than a large statue erected a decade after Redemption. In April 1887, on the south side of the Citadel Green, white Charlestonians unveiled a monument to John C. Calhoun—slavery's greatest champion.[74]

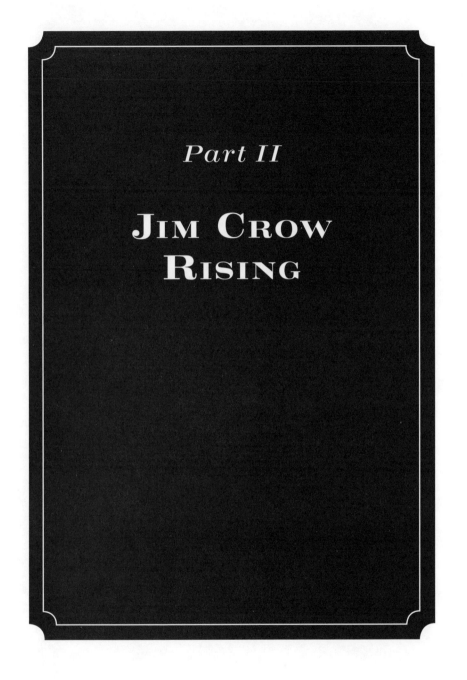

Part II

JIM CROW
RISING

3

Setting Jim Crow
in Stone

JUST AS CONSTRUCTION OF THE BASE OF THE CALHOUN
Monument began in 1886, disaster struck. On the evening of Tuesday,
August 31, a massive earthquake roiled Charleston. As roofs collapsed
and walls crumbled, frantic Charlestonians—many in their bedclothes,
some almost nude—raced into the open air. Fires erupted when the
trembling earth overturned lamps and ruptured gas lines, and after-
shocks rocked the city for twenty-four hours. Eighty-three people ultimately died. Many of those who survived fled to the city's public spaces
that first night—to City Hall Park, on Broad Street; to the Battery,
nearby at the tip of the peninsula; to the College of Charleston campus;
and to the Citadel Green, which locals began calling Marion Square in
the 1880s. Numbering around 40,000, the displaced set up what became
semi-permanent encampments of residents, white and black, unable to
live in their damaged homes.[1]

"It is not a scene to be described by any mortal tongue or pen," wrote
a shell-shocked *News and Courier* reporter. "It is not a scene to be forgotten." While some Charlestonians were lucky enough to return
home within the next few days, thousands remained in the crowded,
increasingly dirty camps. September 9, when a huge rainstorm blew in,
was especially awful. In Marion Square, torrents of water sent refugees
scrambling to find shelter in hastily assembled tents and sheds, to no
avail.[2]

Hundreds of structures were damaged or destroyed, including the
Guard House, Military Hall, and the infamous Work House. Three decades after James Redpath predicted that the terrifying house of corrections would one day be leveled "to the earth amid the savage yells of

insurgent negroes and the shrieks of widowed ladies," the city razed the building.

Amazingly, the earthquake spared the unfinished granite base of the memorial to John C. Calhoun, located on the southern end of Marion Square. And despite all the misery in their midst, stonemasons continued to work on the monument, devoting precious time and energy to a structure that would not save a single soul from the elements. It was fitting: the Calhoun Monument was the culmination of Charleston's lengthy and tenacious crusade to honor South Carolina's favorite son, who had died in 1850. For decades after Calhoun succumbed to tuberculosis, white Charlestonians showed their affection with parades, statues, busts, and then, in 1887, with the bronze monument that would tower over Marion Square. Even in death, Calhoun lived on.[3]

Not everyone relished Calhoun's perpetual presence, however, especially when his imposing likeness was raised just as segregation began to extinguish the dwindling light of Reconstruction. With words and stones, African Americans protested, for their memories of Calhoun challenged whites' unwavering assumption that he should be memorialized. During Jim Crow, fault lines ran deep among Charlestonians, dividing more than the ground beneath their feet.

* * * *

HAILING FROM THE South Carolina Upcountry, John C. Calhoun himself had little love for his state's first city. As a young man, he had attributed a wave of illness that struck Charleston "to the misconduct of the inhabitants," who were cursed "for their intemperance and debaucheries." Yet Charlestonians—even the Lowcountry planters who had more than earned this reputation for decadence—did not feel the same about the dour and humorless figure once described as "the cast iron man." According to Scandinavian writer Fredrika Bremer, locals often joked that "when Calhoun took snuff the whole of Carolina sneezed."[4]

Why were Charlestonians so devoted to a man who held their city in low esteem? It certainly had something to do with his stature. Among the most prominent American statesmen of the nineteenth century, he served as a U.S. congressman, senator, secretary of war, and vice president of the United States over his forty-year political career. Calhoun was the leading figure in the Nullification Crisis, in which the state of

South Carolina politician John C. Calhoun was the South's leading proslavery voice in the 1830s and 1840s.

South Carolina challenged federal supremacy in a dramatic showdown with President Andrew Jackson. On the surface, this crisis was about the tariff, but many South Carolina planters believed something greater was at stake: the slaveholding South's capacity to defend itself from a hostile federal government. The Nullification Crisis reveals a second reason white Charlestonians celebrated Calhoun—he was their culture's most dogged defender.[5]

Calhoun had taken a number of contradictory positions as a politician. He was a vigorous nationalist and later the architect of the theory of nullification, a supporter of Unionism and the Constitution in some moments and the South's loudest voice for secession in others. Where he never wavered, however, was in his commitment to slavery. Reared by a father who owned thirty-one enslaved laborers, Calhoun became the master of two plantations and more than a hundred slaves. He took it for granted that slavery was the foundation of southern society. When northern reformers flooded the nation with antislavery petitions and pamphlets in the mid-1830s, then Senator Calhoun led protests in Washington, D.C. Abolitionism, he insisted, "strikes directly and fatally, not only at our prosperity, but our existence, as a people.... It is a question, that admits of neither concession, nor compromise." Although early American slaveholders such as George Washington and Thomas Jefferson had viewed slavery as, at best, a necessary evil, Calhoun rejected this notion, arguing that it was "a positive good" that benefited both masters and slaves. He maintained that the South had to guard this benevolent institution at all costs. Just weeks before he died in 1850, Calhoun warned that northern agitation on the slavery question might soon force the South "to choose between abolition and secession."[6]

Even before Calhoun's death, Charlestonians sought to honor his legacy. In 1843, cotton merchant Henry Gourdin and a small group of Calhoun supporters commissioned renowned American sculptor Hiram Powers to produce a large sculpture of the statesman. After countless delays, Powers, who lived and worked in Italy, put the sculpture on a ship bound for the United States in April 1850. Yet the wait was not over, for the statue sailed across the Atlantic aboard the *Elizabeth*—a ship that hit a sandbar and sank less than 300 yards from Fire Island, New York. This infamous wreck, which took the lives of eight people, including Transcendentalist writer Margaret Fuller, left Powers's sculpture at the bottom of the ocean. Charlestonians spent three more anxious months as their sunken treasure, stained and damaged by the wreck, was retrieved by divers and then transported to the city, where it was prominently displayed in City Hall.[7]

The Powers statue arrived in Charleston six months after Calhoun was laid to rest in the city. When the senator died on March 31, 1850, the city council commissioned a full-length portrait of Calhoun, also to be featured in City Hall. The *Charleston Courier* and *Charleston Mercury* offered customers copies of Calhoun's final speech printed in either ink or gold, while a bookseller advertised a fresh supply of the "most beautiful" Calhoun portrait available. Locals also ensured that Calhoun would be buried in Charleston rather than at his Fort Hill plantation in the northwestern part of the state.[8]

Calhoun continued to loom large in Charleston in the years that followed. The city celebrated his birthday with extravagant parades and redubbed Boundary Street, which bisected the peninsula and formed the southern boundary of the Citadel Green, Calhoun Street. When former New York senator Nathaniel P. Tallmadge started peddling stories about communicating with Calhoun through two spiritualists in 1853, the *Courier* devoted sizable sections of two issues to the topic. The paper's editor was incredulous, but the chief message that Calhoun delivered from the afterlife—*"I am with you still"*—was no doubt reassuring to its readership.[9]

The city's elaborate funeral for Calhoun in 1850 was the centerpiece of these early memorial activities. When the iron sarcophagus containing the statesman's remains arrived on April 26, it was greeted by the most impressive funeral procession Charleston had ever seen. People from across the state, the region, and even the nation attended the ceremony, while few residents missed the opportunity to celebrate their fallen hero. The two-mile procession included the deceased's family, a delegation from Washington, the governor of South Carolina, and myriad local politicians, militia companies, and fraternal organizations. After the parade, Calhoun's body lay in state in City Hall, where massive crowds paid their respects. The *Courier* took special note of the reception that black and enslaved residents accorded the politician. Reflecting their deep faith in the paternalist ideology championed by Calhoun, city officials permitted everyone—black or white, slave or free—to visit his remains. Black Charlestonians reportedly embraced this opportunity in "considerable numbers."[10]

Yet, while whites viewed the funeral as a somber moment for mourning and reflection, many African Americans were enthused. Fredrika Bremer, who happened to be in town to witness Calhoun's funeral, noted that "during the procession a whole crowd of negroes leaped about the streets, looking quite entertained, as they are by any pomp." Their excitement, she added, had political significance. According to Bremer, blacks at the procession declared, "Calhoun was indeed a wicked man, for he wished that we might remain slaves." Elijah Green, who said that as a young slave boy he had dug Calhoun's grave, agreed, later recalling, "I never did like Calhoun 'cause he hated the Negro; no man was ever hated as much as him by a group of people."[11]

Public displays of disdain did not stop once Calhoun was dead and buried. Soon after Confederate troops abandoned Charleston in early 1865, *New-York Tribune* correspondent James Redpath visited the *Mercury* offices. There, to his surprise, he discovered a black family in what Redpath sarcastically referred to as "the editorial sanctum." Redpath's lack of respect for the fire-eating newspaper matched his scorn for Calhoun, whose bust sat in the office's front room. "Calhoun did more than any one man to make Slavery respectable," he wrote in the *Tribune*. "He used all his great powers to crush the negro." So, Redpath told the woman who showed him the bust, "That man was your great enemy—he did all he could to keep you slaves—you ought to break his bust." Later, when Redpath returned to the front room to get the Calhoun bust, which he thought would make a nice trophy for the *Tribune* headquarters in New York City, he discovered that the freedwoman had destroyed it.[12]

The politician's tomb, which was located at St. Philip's Church cemetery, also suffered in the wake of the war. Portions of the marble slab were broken off, while other parts were marked up with pencil. When Henry Ward Beecher visited the tomb during his visit to Charleston, he was frustrated that "vandal hands were beginning to chip off the marble to bring back pebbles as memorials." Although he blamed Calhoun for the war, the Brooklyn minister saw no point in violating Calhoun's grave. The *New York Times* also condemned the defacement of Calhoun's tomb, urging any future vandals to pay attention to the penciled inscriptions on the grave: "A Massachusetts man and an Abolitionist abhors the violation of this tomb." "Respect ourselves if we do not him who lies beneath this stone."[13]

The original grave of John C. Calhoun, ca. 1865, in St. Philip's Church cemetery.

In fact, nothing worthy of respect, disdain, or anything else lay beneath that stone in 1865. Several years earlier a group of Charleston gentlemen, led by Henry Gourdin and his younger brother, Robert, had secretly moved Calhoun's remains for fear that local blacks—or, worse yet, northern fanatics—might dig them up. Calhoun's casket was not returned until 1871, when Henry Gourdin and a few others placed it in its original tomb in the western half of the cemetery.[14]

Eventually, South Carolina decided to replace the chipped and battered marble slab that marked the Calhoun gravesite. In 1883, the state legislature appropriated $3,000 to erect a more appropriate memorial. The following November, a ten-foot stone sarcophagus was installed atop a brick foundation at St. Philip's. That Calhoun's remains got this new home just as Grover Cleveland—the first successful Democratic candidate since the Civil War—was elected president seemed "a singular coincidence" to *News and Courier* editor Frank Dawson. "At the very moment when the American people have signified their determination that the Federal Government must and shall be cleansed from the corruption with which twenty-four years of continuous Republican rule has encrusted," he wrote, "the bones of the great Calhoun have for the first time found a resting place and memorial stone worthy of his imperishable fame." Viewed this way, the new tomb was a symbolic representation of Redemption—not just of the South, but of the nation as a whole.[15]

Three years later, in 1887, Charleston upped the symbolic ante by erecting the massive monument to Calhoun in Marion Square. As workers labored diligently through the aftermath of the 1886 earthquake, they brought to fruition a project that dated back to the 1850s, when two rival groups of Charlestonians had organized to erect a monument to the revered statesman. After the city council pledged to build a monument to Calhoun in 1850, the all-male Calhoun Monument Association (CMA) and the Ladies' Calhoun Monument Association (LCMA) began competing for the honor of memorializing Calhoun in stone. The superior organizational and fund-raising skills of the LCMA gave it the upper hand. The CMA thought White Point Garden at the Battery was a more appropriate location for the monument, but the LCMA rejected it as "a mere pleasure promenade," preferring the Citadel Green instead.[16]

In choosing the Citadel Green, the LCMA opted for a site that William Gilmore Simms once deemed "the only public square in Charleston that merits the title." But there was also the location's considerable symbolic power. An assemblage of dignitaries had formally received Calhoun's body at the Citadel Green after its journey from Washington, D.C., in 1850. The square, moreover, was home to the Citadel, the arsenal built to police slaves in the wake of the Vesey conspiracy. The ladies hoped that with Calhoun's stern countenance watching over them, Citadel cadets might learn to "emulate the virtues of the great statesman." Finally, the Citadel Green was adjacent to the Neck. This was the neighborhood in which a majority of free African Americans had long lived and which the city had annexed in the months after Calhoun's death in an effort to exert greater control over its inhabitants. Putting the Calhoun Monument in the Citadel Green, as historian Thomas J. Brown has argued, "reinforced this extension of racial authority."[17]

The LCMA laid the cornerstone on June 28, 1858, the anniversary of the battle of Fort Moultrie, a Revolutionary War victory that secessionists held dear. Fire-eater Laurence Keitt delivered the keynote address. When the Civil War broke out in 1861, the project came to a standstill, but the efforts of the organization's treasurer ensured that the dream did not die with the Confederacy. According to the LCMA's official history, Mary A. Snowden, having fled Charleston for Columbia, sewed the group's stocks and bonds into her dress to save them from Sherman's torch. The feat was all the more amazing, the LCMA claimed, because a slave had witnessed Snowden's furtive actions and yet had never revealed the secret. In the LCMA narrative, the ingenuity of Confederate womanhood and the fidelity of the loyal slave combined to ensure the monument's survival.[18]

Similar heroics failed to save another Calhoun memorial. Fearful that the Powers statue, which still stood in City Hall, might succumb to Union artillery after being rescued from its ill-fated voyage across the Atlantic, locals had removed it to Columbia for safekeeping at the start of the Civil War. Yet the star-crossed sculpture was destroyed by the fire that engulfed the state capital in the conflict's final months. Charlestonians could have been forgiven for thinking that Calhoun's memory was cursed when another memorial to the statesman went missing a few years later. Since the 1840s, a stone bust of Calhoun, made by local sculptor Clark Mills, had been on display at City Hall, not far from Powers's statue. In the early years of Reconstruction, however, it disappeared.[19]

The Civil War thus not only opened up a wave of vandalism against Calhoun's tomb; it also cost Charleston its two most prominent Calhoun memorials—the Powers statue and the Mills bust—as well as the bust in the *Charleston Mercury* office destroyed by the freedwoman. By the mid-1870s, the LCMA determined to step into this commemorative breach and complete the monument it had started on the Citadel Green.

The LCMA chose sculptor Albert E. Harnisch, a Philadelphia artist working in Rome, to execute its plan. Harnisch seemed a fine choice to the organization, especially after it received reports from various art critics and friends who had seen his progress in person. Frank Dawson, who spent some time in Rome in 1883 and visited Harnisch's studio while there, vouched for the young man's talent when he returned to Charleston. Although the original antebellum cornerstone appears to have survived the war, the LCMA ordered the construction of a new base in 1884. The work began sometime that year or the next. Then came the August 1886 earthquake. "Strange," the LCMA later observed, that "while the city was almost demolished by that great convulsion of nature, the unfinished base and pedestal of the monument were not in the smallest degree hurt." By February 1887, the completed statue, having arrived in the city several months earlier, was placed atop its pedestal in Marion Square (formerly the Citadel Green). Nearly three decades after the LCMA had begun construction of the monument, Calhoun—perched more than forty feet in the air—finally stood watch over Charleston.[20]

Harnisch's statue depicted Calhoun, cast in bronze, rising from his seat in the Senate, his cloak falling back on his chair and his right index finger upturned and pointed forward, a gesture that signaled the beginning of an address in classical oratory. The large granite base of the statue was to have been surrounded by four allegorical figures, representing Truth, Justice, History, and the Constitution, though only Justice was installed.[21]

The Calhoun Monument made no mention of the politician's strident support of slavery. On this score, it had much in common with the Confederate statues that were raised across the South from the 1870s to the 1930s. From odes to the common soldier to statues of war heroes like "Stonewall" Jackson and Robert E. Lee, Confederate memorials avoided the issue of slavery, highlighting instead the glorious if doomed military

The first Calhoun Monument, including Justice, the only allegorical figure installed, Marion Square, ca. 1892. African Americans mocked and vandalized the monument, which they dubbed "Mr. Calhoun an' he Wife."

struggle that the Confederacy had waged. Charlestonians participated with enthusiasm in this commemorative wave. The Charleston Ladies' Memorial Association erected a monument to the Confederate dead in Magnolia Cemetery in 1882, and, in the years that followed, locals unveiled an obelisk dedicated to the Washington Light Infantry in City Hall Park (which came to be called Washington Square), a monument to General Roswell Sabine Ripley at Magnolia, and a memorial to those who had died aboard early submarines at White Point Garden.[22]

In one sense, the statue of Calhoun, like these memorials, eschewed slavery and did not explicitly address his racial beliefs at all. But, in another sense, the Calhoun Monument dealt directly with slavery, as it differed from Lost Cause memorials in an important way. Calhoun was represented as the South's iconic figure of defiance: standing up, both literally and figuratively, for his region's interests on the Senate floor. The Calhoun Monument thus signaled an attachment to the racial ideology of the Old South in a more direct fashion than most Confederate monuments did, including those erected in Charleston. While none mentioned slavery, the Calhoun Monument alone harkened back to a time before the war, when its precipitating cause occupied the energies of the state's politicians.[23]

Indeed, having died more than a decade before fire rained down on Fort Sumter, Calhoun could not easily be cast in the forgiving light of battlefield heroism. In 1884, just three years before the Calhoun Monument was installed, former slave Archibald Grimké offered a frank evaluation of his fellow South Carolinian's commitment to slavery. Grimké had thrived after leaving Charleston in late 1865. With financial support from his abolitionist aunts, Angelina and Sarah, he had earned a master's degree from Lincoln University and a law degree from Harvard. In the 1880s, he had become active in Republican politics in Boston. Grimké's 1884 speech on Calhoun, which he delivered in Washington, D.C., was, in fact, among the earliest in a public speaking career that lasted well into the twentieth century. "The hand of Calhoun was the master hand that directed the horrible chorus of slavery," he told the audience. Calhoun did anything in his power to advance "this primeval sin."[24]

Fellow Republican and former commander in chief of the Grand Army of the Republic Samuel S. Burdett made a similar point in 1887, just after the Calhoun Monument was unveiled. At a birthday party for Ulysses S. Grant, Burdett departed from his remarks about the Union war hero to criticize leading American statesmen for taking part in the recent dedication ceremony in Charleston. Burdett described Calhoun "as a man who regarded the human race as composed of a few masters with whips in the hands, and a multitude of slaves to do the work of their masters."[25]

The city's evolving residential patterns drove home the statue's association with race and slavery. At the beginning of the nineteenth century, Marion Square sat on the northern periphery of the city. As the population moved up the peninsula over the next several decades, the square became a part of the city's core. By installing a monument to South Carolina's most outspoken proslavery voice in this particular space, in other words, the LCMA proclaimed the centrality of Calhoun—and his defense of slavery and white supremacy—to Charleston, both past and present.

In fact, the long delay in the monument's construction provided a new use for Calhoun's ideology in the present. Three decades after the LCMA's first attempt to honor Calhoun in stone, the completed Calhoun

Monument now invoked slavery to justify segregation. Black Charlestonian Mamie Garvin Fields, who was born in 1888, one year after the monument was erected, interpreted the statue as a message to African Americans about their place in the New South: "I believe white people were talking to us about Jim Crow through that statue." What's more, the statue spoke in a language that the city's black residents could easily understand. In light of the high illiteracy rates that plagued black communities at the time, African American leaders often employed visual and aural, rather than written, methods to reach their followers. White southerners who erected monuments followed a similar strategy. While some African Americans may not have been able to read the segregationist editorials pouring forth from newspapers across South Carolina, they could not miss the visual message the Calhoun Monument announced to them every time they passed by.[26]

Mamie Garvin Fields's suspicion that the Calhoun Monument spoke as much to the New South's emerging racial dynamics as to the Old South's racial order was correct. The statue went up as racial lines began to harden in Charleston, as the expansive possibilities of Reconstruction gave way to the constricting realities of segregation. By the early 1880s, Redeemers had succeeded in removing most black Charlestonians from political office, while the 1882 Eight Box Law disenfranchised tens of thousands of African Americans throughout South Carolina by requiring voters to place ballots in separate boxes labeled for each state-level office, among other restrictive measures. The architect of that law was Edward McCrady, a state representative, Confederate memory stalwart, and former head of the Sumter Guards, one of the rifle clubs that had helped redeem South Carolina in 1876. Seen in this context, the statue marked the new order, both symptom and cause of the changing state of race relations.[27]

* * * *

THE CALHOUN MONUMENT was dedicated at an extravagant ceremony on April 26, 1887. A spring storm brought a cooling breeze that morning, producing bright, sunny, and unseasonably temperate conditions. The crowd matched the occasion and the weather. Some twenty thousand people lined Meeting Street to watch the large parade of dignitaries, civic organizations, military companies, and veterans groups, such as the Survivors' Association of Charleston. "Never, perhaps, since the funeral of the immortal Calhoun," noted Frank Dawson's *News and Courier*, "have the civil societies of Charleston turned out in such large numbers or with such full ranks."

The grand procession marched a mile and a half from the Battery at the base of the peninsula through the center of the city to Marion Square, where the unveiling ceremony took place. There, a crowd of more than fifteen thousand spilled out of the park into the surrounding streets, sidewalks, buildings, and churches. As at Calhoun's funeral nearly forty years before, Charlestonians of all walks of life turned out. "Every window from basement to attic was full of bright, fair faces, and very many others not so fair, looked out from behind the chimney tops or peered over the edges of the roofs," reported the *News and Courier*. Unlike the 1850 funeral, however, there is no evidence that black residents—or anyone else—struck a discordant note during the festivities. The black newspaper the *New York Freeman* noted that the shared suffering of the 1886 earthquake had helped heal the wounds of Charleston's black community. "There is no feeling in the hearts of the colored people towards those who despitefully used them. The war is over with them; they are ready and willing to work for the building up of this common country." A number of leading black Charlestonians even chose to attend the unveiling ceremony.

The Marion Square crowd came together as one, especially once a black band struck up the tune of "Dixie." The enormous group recognized the song instantly and began to cheer. As the band electrified the celebrants, six "baby unveilers" and more than thirty young women—most of whom were descendants of Calhoun—pulled away the flags concealing the statue. Cannon fire and enthusiastic shouts mixed in the air before a deep silence descended over the square. "It seemed for a few moments," the *News and Courier* told its readers, "as if the people felt themselves to be in his presence and expected him to speak to them again in the long-hushed accents of wisdom and warning."[28]

The silence was broken by a brief ode to Calhoun, recited by a local pastor, after which the main speaker of the day, Secretary of the Interior Lucius Quintus Cincinnatus Lamar, took center stage. The Mississippi politician and ex-Confederate general had one foot in Calhoun's world and another in the New South. Before the war, he had been an ardent secessionist and strong supporter of slavery. After Appomattox, Lamar had been a bitter opponent of Reconstruction. As a member of the House of Representatives, he helped undermine federal legislation that aimed to curb white vigilante violence in the South. But Lamar did not carry the stigma other leading Confederates did. In fact, he was known to be a strong supporter of sectional reconciliation, especially after he lauded Republican Charles Sumner in a well-received 1875 eulogy. Cut from the same cloth as Wade Hampton, Lamar had provided a dignified patina that helped mask the violent redemption of his home state of Mississippi. Charleston could not have asked for a better man to honor Calhoun.[29]

Unsurprisingly, Lamar's remarks largely steered clear of divisive issues like secession and slavery, focusing instead on Calhoun's intellectual and political accomplishments and his devotion to the Union. Near the end of the speech, however, Lamar explicitly took up the institution Calhoun had fought so hard to defend. "Slavery is dead—buried in a grave that never gives up its dead," he maintained. "Why reopen it to-day? Let it rest." But Lamar could not let it rest. "If I remain silent upon the subject," he told the crowd, "it will be taken as an admission that there is one part of Mr. Calhoun's life of which it is prudent for his friends to say nothing to the present generation." On the contrary, Lamar contended, Americans today needed to know that in defending the legal status of slavery in the United States, Calhoun was hardly alone. Everyone from Henry Clay to John Quincy Adams to Daniel Webster agreed that the Constitution protected the institution. Calhoun's great gift was in understanding that hostile forces would not stop until they destroyed slavery, even if that meant undermining the Constitution. "His predictions," Lamar observed, "were verified to the letter." Lamar conceded that prevailing sentiments demanded the abolition of slavery and that any attempts to reestablish it were imprudent. Still, Lamar believed that in its day slavery had been a positive institution, especially for the enslaved. Having established Calhoun's virtues as a statesman, thinker, and apologist for the outdated but civilizing institution of slavery, Lamar then surrendered the platform to two ministers who concluded the festivities.[30]

For all the pageantry of the dedication, the Calhoun Monument itself was not universally well received. "The monument meets with as many admirers as detractors," the *New-York Tribune* reported. Noting its considerable $44,000 price tag, the *New York Times* concluded that the Calhoun Monument "might easily have been a more artistic work, and some severe criticisms have been made upon it." Charleston cotton broker Henry S. Holmes was also troubled by the aesthetic failings of the monument. "I remember the unveiling of the monstrosity," he wrote in his diary in 1895. "Great was the disappointment when the hideous bronze figure was disrobed, and ever since it has been a frightful sight to citizens passing over Marion Square." Elsewhere in his journal, Holmes described the statue as a "swindle" and an "abortion."[31]

Some members of the African American community also felt deep contempt for the Calhoun Monument. Not long after the unveiling ceremony, the annual review of black militia companies took place in Marion Square, right behind the Calhoun Monument. Struck by the juxtaposition of black troops marching between the Citadel and the backside of Calhoun, an African American woman shouted out, "Calhoun turn him back on 'em.'"[32]

Most often, black Charlestonians targeted the Calhoun Monument with humor and derision. By early June 1887, African Americans were poking fun at the statue of Justice, which had recently been installed at the base of the memorial. "'De ole man had ee wife wid um now,'" remarked one James Island resident. Or, as the *News and Courier* explained, "The impression prevails generally among the non-reading colored population that the statue of Justice is that of Mrs. Calhoun." Judging from the stories that circulated in numerous newspapers and magazines, as well as among the local citizenry, this idea—and "he wife," the Gullah nickname it spawned—stuck. In 1890, the *Augusta Chronicle* claimed that black Charlestonians believed that Calhoun, with his "finger pointing downwards," was "pintin' at his ma." Henry Holmes wrote that Justice was "a fearful hag whom the street urchins have always called 'he wife.'"[33]

In February 1888, Charlestonians awoke to find the figure of Justice looking "as if it had been on a spree." Someone "had placed a tin kettle in her hand and a cigar in her mouth." Five years later, just after a great hurricane hit the city, the *News and Courier* reported that "old Calhoun" survived "all the terrors of the cyclone," but "not so" with the "bronze female known to the darkies as 'he wife,'" whose face had been turned a "lily complexion" with white paint.[34]

The identity and motives of the vandals in both of these cases is impossible to determine, but black Charlestonians did on occasion use the Calhoun Monument for target practice. In December 1894, an African American boy named Andrew Haig was arrested for shooting a white toddler in the head in Marion Square. Haig told the police that he had not been aiming his tiny pistol at the child, but rather at the female figure that stood at the base of the Calhoun Monument. "I nebber shoot the chile, I shoot at Mr. Calhoun wife, and when I hit 'um he sound like gong," the boy reportedly said.[35]

This informal campaign of ridicule and vandalism climaxed just as the Calhoun Monument met its demise. By the early 1890s, the LCMA had determined to remove the Calhoun Monument, commissioning New York sculptor John Massey Rhind to produce a replacement. The original monument, which the *News and Courier* irreverently dubbed "Mr. Calhoun Number 1," was taken down Thanksgiving Day 1895. In its column marking the holiday, the paper insisted that "all of Charleston had . . . great cause for thanksgiving," for "the men who are engaged in demolishing the dreadful eyesore, the old Calhoun monument, did not take a day off as most other folk did." Some people have "suggested that it be saved up until the death of the sculptor [Harnisch] and then placed over his grave," reported the paper, but "this plan . . . has been abandoned, the punishment being thought too severe." A few days later, Justice was also removed. Unsuccessful in its efforts to find an alternate home for the two bronze statues, as well as another of the allegorical figures that had never been installed, the LCMA sold them as scrap metal.[36]

"Mr. Calhoun Number 2" arrived by steamship on June 7, 1896, followed shortly thereafter by Rhind, who oversaw the first stages of the installation. Three weeks later, the caped likeness of Calhoun—"the largest bronze statue ever cast" in New York, according to the *New York Times*—was placed high atop a fluted column. Reaching more than one hundred feet in the air, the second Calhoun Monument was significantly taller than the first. The base of the monument was adorned with palmetto trees as well as inscriptions to the LCMA's crusade to erect the tribute to Calhoun. It also included reliefs that made gestures to his early stance as a war hawk and later career as a states' rights advocate. Like the original, the new monument did not mention slavery. Mr. Calhoun Number 2 immediately drew large crowds and many admirers, though

THE CALHOUN MONUMENT

Men pose in front of the second, much taller Calhoun Monument, ca. 1901–1902.

the LCMA, chastened after the failure of Mr. Calhoun Number 1, chose not to have an official dedication ceremony.[37]

The association's official explanation for replacing the first monument focused on aesthetic objections to the statue: its imbalance of proportion, Calhoun's anachronistic Prince Albert coat, and his exaggerated right index finger that "amounted to a deformity." The LCMA was equally disappointed by the allegorical figures that were to have been placed around the base of the statue. When the second allegorical figure, History, arrived from Italy, for instance, it was deemed unacceptable and temporarily placed in the courtyard at the Home for the Mothers, Widows, and Daughters of Confederate Soldiers. According to a story that Henry Holmes had heard, the LCMA refused to receive the other two, which remained in Rome. The cotton merchant chalked up the artistic failings of the Calhoun statue and its allegorical companions to their sculptor's mental deficits. "Harnisch is, I hear, in an asylum in Philadelphia," concluded Holmes as the first statue was removed in late 1895. "His mind must have been bad originally and the grotesque creations came from its fevered and distracting workings." Others heard that Harnisch had recently "regained his sanity," only to relapse "into imbecility" upon recalling "Mr. Calhoun and he wife."[38]

But the ridicule and defacement of Mr. Calhoun Number 1 must have been hard for LCMA members to stomach, and even the removal of the statue suggested something more than artistic objections was at stake. After workers placed a rope around the original Calhoun statue and lowered it below "he wife," one black boy climbed up the legs of the statue while asking, "Wha' dey tek Mistah Calhoon down foh?" A companion replied, "He must be tek he down foh straighten out he fingah" while he "skillfully pasted Mr. Calhoun in the eye with a lump of mud," according to the *News and Courier*. When the laborers looked away, a number of black children crawled up the statue's legs "and heaped all sorts of indignities upon him" as well as on his female companion. "She must have pain in she back," said one. Another commented, "She grow fat sence she been dey." The removal of "Missis Calhoon" was to start the following day, an event, the newspaper predicted, that "will undoubtedly be watched by hundreds of the small African citizens for whom 'he wife' has a great power of fascination." The paper's coverage of these events transformed black mockery of the Calhoun Monument into racist parody. Yet this fact should not obscure another facet of these stories. Made the butt of jokes by local blacks, "Mr. Calhoun an' he Wife" represented as much a social and political affront as an aesthetic disaster.[39]

White accounts acknowledge the myriad aesthetic reservations, sprinkling in the occasional reference to "Mr. Calhoun an' he Wife." But black memory places the responsibility for the decision to build a second, significantly taller memorial squarely on the shoulders of African Americans who sought to damage the monument. Mamie Garvin Fields recalled that when she was a girl, Charleston leaders decided "to put up a life-size figure of John C. Calhoun preaching," referring to the first Calhoun Monument. This angered African American residents, who felt that Calhoun constantly reminded them that even if they were no longer enslaved, they still had to stay in their place. So, Fields explained, "we used to carry something with us, if we knew we would be passing that way, in order to deface that statue—scratch up the coat, break the watch chain, try to knock off the nose.... Children and adults beat up John C. Calhoun so badly that the whites had to come back and put him way up high, so we couldn't get to him."[40]

There is no conclusive evidence that black vandalism is what prompted the LCMA to install the taller monument. Still, it is clear that the organization—and Charleston leaders more generally—had deep fears about the first monument's safety. As we have seen, several of the city's tributes to Calhoun suffered at the hands of vandals, so much so that when his new sarcophagus was installed in 1884 the local paper called for measures that would prevent defacement by "thoughtless or evil disposed persons." Moreover, just after the first Calhoun Monument was unveiled in 1887, the *News and Courier* reported that a "Philadelphia crank has written a grossly abusive and ridiculous letter to the Ladies' Calhoun Monument Association." The writer expressed his hope that the Calhoun Monument would be treated like the memorial to British spy Major John André. Erected in New York in 1880 by a railroad magnate, the widely unpopular monument to André (who was executed during the American Revolution) had twice been bombed with dynamite. Hurling "the fiercest anathemas against all Southerners," the "cantankerous crank" from Philadelphia predicted that the Calhoun Monument would also "very soon be blown up or mutilated."[41]

Charleston's newspapers and city officials also regularly expressed worries about the defacement of public statuary and parks, especially Marion Square. On December 2, 1894, the *News and Courier* denounced widespread graffiti in the city as well as "rough usage" of the city's parks. Early the following year—just weeks after black youth Andrew Haig told police that he had been shooting his pistol at the first Calhoun Monument—the commissioners of Marion Square hired a new park keeper to limit "the nuisances and depredations now committed by goats, boys and night prowlers."[42]

In the end, it seems fair to conclude that some combination of black ridicule and vandalism contributed to the decision to replace the first Calhoun Monument with its much larger successor. After all, what could be more embarrassing to LCMA members than to see their Lost Cause shrine defaced by bullets and buckets of paint, or to have it transformed into a joke that invoked howls of laughter from blacks and whites alike? This was no small victory for black Charlestonians. Scholars of Civil War memory have argued that the monuments and statues erected in the decades after the conflict tended to assume "a sort of physical and psychological impermeability," engendering little protest as a result. The Calhoun Monument tells a different story. Though marginalized by Redemption and Jim Crow, local blacks found unconventional means to resist a statue they viewed as a symbol of racial oppression.[43]

And, it is worth noting, they kept up their informal assault well into the twentieth century. As late as 1946, the city's Historical Commission reported the "wanton mutilation by unknown persons" necessitated repairs to the second Calhoun Monument. Municipal sources make no mention of racial motivations, but oral history indicates that some of the vandals attacked the statue because of Calhoun's outspoken stance on slavery. In a 1984 interview, for example, former Avery Normal Institute student Lucille Williams recalled that one of her black classmates had thrown rocks at the monument in the mid-1930s because the antebellum politician "didn't like us."[44]

* * * *

HOWEVER MUCH BLACK distaste for Calhoun contributed to the installation of a new monument in 1896, it is appropriate that the Calhoun statue climbed to its monumental height as race relations plummeted to their nadir. In addition to responding to black defacement and artistic misgivings, white Charlestonians spoke to an increasingly rigid system of Jim Crow with their taller Calhoun memorial. Throughout the 1890s, South Carolina whites labored to ensure that segregation—a haphazard system in the 1870s, inchoate even when the first Calhoun Monument went up in 1887—became more formalized. Led by "Pitchfork Ben" Tillman, governor from 1890 to 1894, this white supremacy campaign scored its greatest victory in 1895 when delegates to a state constitutional convention disenfranchised most of those remaining African Americans who still enjoyed the right to vote. In Charleston, "white only" and "colored" signs blanketed public accommodations by 1900.[45]

Though just a child at the time, Mamie Garvin Fields felt the chill of formal segregation immediately. Having lived in an integrated neighborhood since birth, she noticed that Jim Crow made "friends into enemies overnight," creating a barrier between white and black families who had been on amicable terms. In recalling the institutionalization of segregation in Charleston, Fields focused much of her ire on the Calhoun statues. Both monuments—with their obvious if unstated connection to slavery—were intended to fortify the new barrier and push blacks down to where they supposedly belonged. "Blacks took that statue personally," Fields wrote of the first monument in her memoir. "As you passed by, here was Calhoun looking you in the face and telling you, 'Nigger, you may not be a slave, but I am back to see you stay in your place.'" Whites had then put him up even higher. Out of harm's way, Calhoun could better fulfill his appointed mission—to use the memory of slavery to justify Jim Crow. "Telling you," Fields recalled, "there was a place for 'niggers' and 'niggers' must stay there." As a black newspaper in nearby Savannah argued, the recent success of white supremacists was simply the "logical result" of the philosophy formulated by John C. Calhoun a half century earlier.[46]

4

Cradle of the
Lost Cause

AS WHITE CHARLESTONIANS IMPOSED JIM CROW LAWS
and customs on their hometown, they transformed it from the Cradle
of the Confederacy into a cradle of the Lost Cause. Enthusiasm for all
things Confederate seemed boundless during these years. The city's
earliest Civil War memory organizations, including the Ladies' Calhoun
Monument Association, the Ladies' Memorial Association of Charleston (LMAC), and the Survivors' Association of Charleston (SAC), continued to meet regularly, stage Memorial Day services, sponsor lectures
on the conflict, and install Confederate monuments and memorials.
They were often joined in these activities by local militia groups, including the Sumter Guards, the Washington Light Infantry, the Charleston
Light Dragoons, and, after the Citadel reopened in the early 1880s, its
cadets.[1]

Toward the end of the nineteenth century, white Charlestonians embraced the new wave of Confederate remembrance that swept across the
South. In the summer of 1893, some 150 veteran members of the SAC
resolved to transform the group into Camp Sumter of the United Confederate Veterans (UCV), a national organization created in 1889. The
following November the junior members of the SAC—who as sons of
veterans were prohibited from joining the UCV—formed Camp Moultrie of the newly organized Sons of Confederate Veterans (SCV). That
same month, at the urging of the *Charleston News and Courier*, several
Charleston women formed the fourth chapter of the recently established
United Daughters of the Confederacy (UDC), which became South
Carolina's leading chapter. Over the next decade, Charleston UDC
members opened the Confederate Museum in Market Hall on Meeting

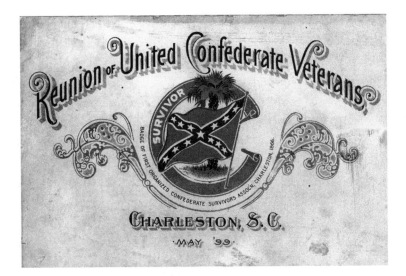

A souvenir program from the 1899 United Confederate Veterans national reunion, held in Charleston.

Street to display war relics and began publishing a monthly ladies magazine, the *Keystone*, which served as the official organ of the Daughters in
southeastern states. Meanwhile, local men founded two additional SCV
camps and three more UCV camps.[2]

In 1899, Charleston played host to the United Confederate Veterans
national convention. Seven thousand veterans crowded into Thomson
Auditorium, hastily erected specifically for the event, to attend the day's
opening meeting. "It is peculiarly fitting, sirs," pronounced one of the
speakers, "that this, your last great Reunion of the nineteenth century,
should be held in historic old Charleston, which is well called the Cradle
of the Confederacy. Here—where the tocsin of war was first sounded—
where so much of the history of that great struggle was enacted, and
where the very atmosphere is instinct with hallowed memories of that war."
Observing the feverish preparations for the reunion, North Carolina
publisher Walter Hines Page wrote that Charlestonians "talk about that
meeting as devout Jews might talk about assembling of all the tribes of
Jerusalem."[3]

Reminders of the city's Confederate sympathies were everywhere.
Statues and memorials to ideological inspirations such as Calhoun, military
leaders such as P.G.T. Beauregard, and the Confederate fallen dotted the

landscape, from White Point Garden at the Battery to Magnolia Cemetery on the northern outskirts of town. After 1901, Charleston even had a tribute to Henry Timrod, the Confederacy's unofficial poet laureate. Not far from the Timrod Memorial in Washington Square lay a more animate memorial to the Confederate cause: the Home for the Mothers, Widows, and Daughters of Confederate Soldiers. Founded in 1867 by LMAC president Mary A. Snowden, her sister, and a handful of other women, the Confederate Home was located on a sizable Broad Street property. Over the next six decades, it provided food and shelter to Confederate mothers, widows, and daughters as well as a private education to young women.[4]

Outsiders were struck by the prevalence of the Confederate flag and near absence of America's banner in Jim Crow Charleston. One northern tourist claimed to have seen some fifty Confederate flags when he visited in 1885. Ohio transplant John Bennett observed that American flags were not displayed in front of city homes until after World War I. Many white Charlestonians, meanwhile, rejected the reconciliationist spirit that took hold of the country, north and south, during this period. Asked in 1889 whether they would be willing to celebrate Confederate Memorial Day on the same day that the northerners observed their own Memorial Day, several directresses of the LMAC rejected the notion. The bitterness and cruelty of the war had been largely forgiven, explained one member, "but we cannot mix up principles and sentiments as such a change in the day would imply."[5]

Unwilling to give up any ground in the struggle over how the Civil War would be remembered, groups like the LMAC made Charleston among the South's most important sites of Confederate veneration. In this crusade, they were helped immeasurably by a small coterie of Charleston journalists, editors, and historians, individuals who helped reshape the Lost Cause from countermemory into master narrative, not just across the South but across much of the country.[6]

* * * *

THE CHIEF VEHICLE for spreading Lost Cause gospel in Jim Crow Charleston was the *Charleston News and Courier*, which between 1873 and 1910 was edited by Frank Dawson and James C. Hemphill. Swept up by the Confederate cause, English-born Dawson had left his native

English-born Frank Dawson, ca. 1888, was a Confederate veteran and editor of the Charleston News and Courier.

country in 1862 to fight with the secessionists, seeing action at Fredericksburg, Gettysburg, and Spotsylvania. Following a brief stint at two Richmond newspapers after the war, he moved to Charleston in late 1866 to become an assistant editor for the *Charleston Mercury.* Dawson only lasted about a year at the struggling newspaper before buying a share first of the *Charleston News* and later the *Charleston Courier,* which the Englishman and his partners combined into the *Charleston News and Courier* in 1873.[7]

Dawson turned the *News and Courier* into one of the South's leading papers. As of 1880, only two New Orleans newspapers enjoyed greater daily readership in the states of the former Confederacy. Under Dawson's stewardship, the *News and Courier* doubled in size and expanded its reach throughout the state by delivering the paper by railroad. "Never in South Carolina's turbulent history has a single paper so dominated the thought of the state," according to historian Robert H. Woody.[8]

The *News and Courier* continued to enjoy the widest daily circulation in South Carolina after James C. Hemphill took charge in 1889. Like so many other Old South apologists of his generation, this Upcountry South Carolinian compensated for being born too late to participate in the Civil War by becoming active in Confederate memory organizations and activities. In 1890, Hemphill was one of the honored guests at the unveiling of the monument to Robert E. Lee in Richmond, Virginia. Eight years later, Hemphill served on the executive committee for the 1899 national UCV reunion.[9]

Broad Street offices of the influential Charleston News and Courier, *champion of the Lost Cause, ca. 1870s–1880s.*

Under both Dawson and Hemphill, the *News and Courier* crafted an idealized picture of the Old South and the noble soldiers who had fought to defend it. To be sure, the editors were not entirely stuck in the past. In the face of an apathetic business class in Charleston, Dawson and Hemphill used the *News and Courier* to trumpet the same sort of economic revitalization that was at the center of Atlantan Henry W. Grady's New South ethos. Yet they also worried that calls for a New South could easily be misconstrued as a critique of the Old South and the Confederacy. "It is not for the sons to apologize for their fathers," wrote Dawson in 1886. "They need no apology . . . . The South fought for the right—for the undying principle of self-government . . . which was as 'eternally right' in 1860 as in 1776." Hemphill was even more outspoken when it came to denouncing Grady's vision for a New South, publishing a column that critiqued the phrase for conveying "the suggestion of an old South, sullen, rancorous, impracticable and reactionary."[10]

With Dawson and Hemphill at the helm, the *News and Courier* did more to downplay slavery as a cause of the Civil War than perhaps any other newspaper in the region. Indeed, judging by a June 1885 article in the Upcountry *Laurensville Herald*, the *News and Courier* had a reputation for its tireless defenses of the Confederacy on precisely this score. Just one month earlier, Frank Dawson had reprinted an account of a postwar interview with Robert E. Lee in which the general said that he had been disturbed by northern claims that "the object of the war had been to secure the perpetuation of slavery." This was "not true," insisted Lee, who "rejoiced that slavery is abolished." Dawson, for his part, added that Lee's sentiments reflected the general consensus across the South, positing that "Grant's army would have made short work of their opponents if they had encountered only those Confederates who were fighting for the perpetuation of slavery." The *Laurensville Herald* took issue with these claims. The North understood that emancipation would follow with Union victory, the paper argued, and the Confederate Army consisted chiefly of slaveholders and their sons.[11]

Unwilling to let this challenge go unmet, Dawson reprinted the *Herald* column and published a lengthy rejoinder that responded to its claims point by point. The Charleston editor excerpted Lincoln, painting a picture of a president who went to war solely to preserve the Union and who, when he finally embraced emancipation, did so not for principled reasons but rather as a military necessity. Turning to the question of the motivations for secession, Dawson declared, "Our position is that slavery was merely the immediate cause, or provocation, of the war, and not the fundamental cause." The conflict was rooted in basic philosophical differences that dated back to the birth of the nation—differences over the scope and power of the federal government. Finally, Dawson sought to debunk the *Laurensville Herald*'s claim that the Confederate war had been fought by slaveholders and their sons by reproducing estimates of the extent of slave ownership among southerners made by secessionist editor James D.B. DeBow. According to the *News and Courier*'s calculations—which relied on numbers that DeBow himself had publicly disavowed in 1860—only one out of every thirty-six Confederate citizens owned a slave and, as of 1864, ten out of every eleven Confederate soldiers were nonslaveholders.[12]

Dawson's position on the relationship between slavery and the Civil War contrasted sharply with that espoused by fellow New South newspaperman Henry W. Grady. The influential editor of the *Atlanta Constitution*, Grady was a tireless promoter of economic revitalization in the

South and sectional reconciliation with the North. Although he believed that slavery was not without its benefits, especially for African Americans, Grady called for an end to sectional hostilities based on a mutual acceptance of the war's righteous outcome. "There have been elaborate efforts made by so-called statesmen to cover up the real cause of the war," declared Grady in 1882, "but there is not a man of common sense in the south to-day who is not aware of the fact that there would have been no war if there had been no slavery."[13]

Dawson would have none of this. Reproducing a critique of Grady originally published by the *Mobile Register*, the Charleston editor chastised the *Atlanta Constitution* "for dragging forward the skeleton of Slavery as the cause of the war." Uncowed, Grady fired back with a series of editorials aimed at both the *Register* and the *News and Courier*—newspapers, he marveled, that questioned the idea that slavery was essential to the coming of the war. "Our esteemed contemporaries assert—or, rather, they intimate, that the war was fought in defense of local self-government," wrote Grady. How is it possible, he wondered, for the South to have lost the war for self-government but nonetheless retained full control of local affairs?[14]

In his response, Dawson admitted that slavery contributed to the conflict and even allowed that had there "been no slavery there would have been no war." But, the Englishman added, it could just as accurately be asserted "that if there had been no United States there would have been no secession." Invoking his own service in the Confederate Army, Dawson also denied that his fellow soldiers had fought for slavery. Grady's insistence that "they were willing to dissolve the Union, and sacrifice their own blood and the blood of their children, for no other or higher reason than to save their negroes and enhance the value of the slaves by establishing a 'Slaveholding Confederacy'" was an insult to "the whole Southern people," concluded Dawson.[15]

As Dawson's exchanges with both Grady and the editor of the *Laurensville Herald* illustrate, the Charleston newspaperman did not suppress dissenting voices when it came to slavery and the Civil War. The same was true of his successor, James Hemphill, who also went out of his way to provide room in the *News and Courier* for other perspectives, if only to hammer home the validity of his own. Five years after he took charge of the paper, Hemphill reproduced portions of a Rhode Island newspaper column that claimed that the Civil War was waged to per-petuate slavery. If this were the case, asked Hemphill, what did the North go to war to accomplish? Highlighting comments by Lincoln and Wil-liam Tecumseh Sherman that suggested that the war had been fought neither to end slavery nor to help African Americans, the editor held that it was difficult to understand why the Confederacy went to war "to defend an institution that was not assailed."[16]

The *News and Courier* was not alone in this fight over the memory of the war. Charleston veterans who had achieved positions of leadership in local historical, educational, and publishing circles lent crucial support. Perhaps the most prominent was Edward McCrady. A Confederate offi-cer who had suffered multiple injuries during the war, McCrady was a long-serving state representative with a thriving law practice. But his heart was in the past. A founding member of the SAC, McCrady wrote several histories of early South Carolina and served as president of the South Carolina Historical Society and vice president of the even more influen-tial American Historical Association. McCrady also regularly addressed reunions of Confederate veterans, and a number of these speeches were reprinted in the *Southern Historical Society Papers*, one of the nation's leading Lost Cause founts.[17]

"We did not fight for slavery," McCrady pronounced before a group of veterans in Williston, South Carolina, on July 14, 1882. "Slavery, a bur-den imposed upon us by former generations of the world, a burden in-creased upon us by the falsely-pretended philanthropic legislation of northern States . . . , was not the *cause* of the war." Instead, McCrady held that slavery was merely "the incidents upon which the differences between the North and the South, and from which differences the war was inevitable from the foundation of our government, did but turn." The real crux of the matter, he concluded, was the right of South Carolinians to control the affairs of their state, especially its race relations, without outside interference.[18]

McCrady's explanation—describing slavery not as the cause of the conflict but rather as incidental—was, as historian David Blight has ob-served, "almost omnipresent in Lost Cause rhetoric." A few years after McCrady framed slavery as incidental, his longtime SAC colleague Cor-nelius Irvine Walker echoed this defense at a Memorial Day gathering held at Magnolia Cemetery. A native Charlestonian from a family with

Charleston attorney and historian Edward McCrady Jr. was a Confederate veteran and Lost Cause prophet.

an established paper and publishing firm, Walker, like McCrady, played a leading role in Confederate resistance and remembrance. He was a founding member of the SAC, worked to redeem South Carolina by forming the Carolina Rifle Club, helped reopen the Citadel, and served as commander of the state division of the UCV and commander in chief of the national UCV. As head of the firm Walker, Evans, & Cogswell, which produced numerous early guidebooks, Walker was also a loud voice in Charleston's publishing and tourism industries. He even authored his own visitor's guide.[19]

When Walker addressed those who had gathered at Magnolia for the twentieth century's first Confederate Memorial Day, on May 10, 1900, he spent much of his time defending the immortal principle of states' rights, which, as he put it, "we all imbibed at our mother's breast." Evoking and contradicting Alexander Stephens's cornerstone metaphor—which held that the Confederacy was founded on the "great truth" of slavery—the Charleston veteran pronounced: "On this rock of States' rights was the secession of the Southern States founded and on it was builded [*sic*] the Southern Confederacy. We were but upholding the principles of our forefathers and those of the original thirteen States." The UCV leader declared that Confederate soldiers did not go to war to prevent the liberation of its slaves but rather to stop Union soldiers from desecrating their homes. In the end, Walker concluded, "slavery . . . was a mere incident of the struggle, not its cause."[20]

* * * *

ONE CURIOUS FEATURE of Lost Cause rhetoric is its conflicted position on slavery. Spokesmen like McCrady and Walker dismissed slavery as incidental to the Confederate struggle, and yet they devoted a great deal of ink to highlighting the centrality of slavery in the Old South. This almost bifurcated conversation forced Confederate enthusiasts to walk a fine line between defending an institution that many people viewed as outdated, if not unjust and inhumane, and renouncing the beliefs and practices of their forebears—which were, after all, central to their own identity. To solve this dilemma, Lost Causers deployed two distinct arguments. Some attempted to absolve the South of responsibility for slavery. Others mounted a full-throated defense of the institution as a civilizing influence. A few made both points simultaneously, despite the seeming incompatibility of these positions—why, after all, would one bother to deny the South's culpability for slavery if one believed it had been a good thing? In every case, however, the project was the same, even if the contradictions remained: reinforcing the moral sanctity of the Lost Cause.

Many Confederate memorialists insisted that slavery was a burden that had been imposed on the South by outsiders. "We of this generation had no part in the establishment of slavery in this country," Edward McCrady told the veterans who gathered in Williston in 1882. Nor did he blame his southern ancestors. McCrady instead pointed his finger at England, from which the South had inherited slavery, and the North, which had transported thousands of slaves from Africa to ports like Charleston and then later cast its enslaved people off on the South through the bogus philanthropy of emancipation. Replete with countless facts and figures to support it, McCrady's disquisition no doubt convinced its sympathetic audience that Rhode Island was chiefly responsible for South Carolina's slave trade.[21]

Dawson and Hemphill likewise took great pains to exonerate the South of any responsibility for the institution of slavery. New Englanders and Englishmen monopolized the slave trade, Dawson insisted on April 19, 1885, while the South's antislavery sentiment "grew stronger and stronger, until it was arrested, and turned back upon itself, so to speak, by the fanatical action of Northern agitators." A few weeks later, Dawson printed a letter to the editor that went one step further. Opposition to slavery, insisted the *News and Courier*'s Camden correspondent, had been so strong in South Carolina in the early nineteenth century that in 1816 a number of planters and other gentlemen from the Upcountry formulated a plan to end both the slave trade and slavery itself. "No more forcible language," he maintained, "was ever used by the Anti-slavery party than was found in that document; sentiments that would have rejoiced the philanthropic heart of Phillips, Garrison, Tappan or Sumner, and others of that ilk."[22]

Robert E. Lee's grandson Robert E. Lee III took this specious line of argument to extraordinary lengths when he visited Charleston in January 1909. He was in town to celebrate his grandfather's birthday, which by then was a state holiday in South Carolina and three other southern states. Southerners never trafficked in slaves, Lee told the large audience sitting in German Artillery Hall (formerly Military Hall), which was located just a few blocks north of Charleston's slave-trading district. Running roughshod over the historical record, he also maintained that the South had tried to solve the problem of slavery only to be defeated by Great Britain and later the New England states. "The Federal Constitution called for emancipation of all slaves in 1800, but the influence of the New England delegates had this date changed to 1820, which later resulted in the Missouri Compromise," he argued. Notwithstanding these nonsensical claims, the local media printed fawning accounts of Lee's speech. The monthly ladies journal the *Keystone*, which was published in Charleston by United Daughters of the Confederacy members Mary B. and Louisa B. Poppenheim, called the address "a wonderful presentation of the subject, epigrammatic and condensed, presenting historic truths in so simple, clear and direct a form that the average intelligence was able to grasp many salient historic points."[23]

When Lost Cause stalwarts were not denying responsibility for slavery, they were vigorously defending its merits. In 1873, for example, Dawson published a column responding to a *New York Evening Post* article that suggested that it was slaves' uncompensated labor that had made possible the luxurious lifestyle of the master class. This gross misrepresentation of southern slavery demanded correction, insisted the *News and Courier* editor. "In exchange for the labor of the working hands, in a family of slaves, the planter gave clothing, shelter and medical attendance to the whole family, young and old; the children, too young to work, were fed and clad, and the like was done for those who were too old to work," he wrote. "This was what the planter paid his slaves, and it is more than most ordinary field hands can make now."[24]

Charleston's Lost Causers also sought to downplay the fear of slave insurrection. In an 1879 speech before the Washington Light Infantry that received front-page coverage in the *News and Courier*, former Citadel professor Hugh S. Thompson offered a sanitized outline of the military academy's origins. The Citadel, he explained, was built as a cost-cutting measure that allowed state officials to save money by substituting cadets for the paid guards who watched over the war munitions stored in Charleston. Glossing over the main reason that Charleston kept a formidable stockpile of weapons—to put down slave rebellions— the future governor of the state spun a reassuring tale to the members of the infantry, many of whom, like Thompson himself, were Citadel graduates.[25]

To be fair, local whites did not entirely dismiss the threat of slave revolts. In 1885, Dawson provided a lengthy account of the 1822 Denmark Vesey conspiracy in a Sunday edition of the *News and Courier*. The article highlighted the ruthlessness of Vesey and his colleagues, insisting that they had planned to pan out through city streets, murdering any white person they found. The larger point drawn from this episode, however, was not that the slave regime was so brutal that even a free black like Vesey was willing to contemplate armed insurrection. Rather, it was that the failed uprising proved the rule of slaveholder benevolence. Conveniently overlooking insurrections such as the Stono Rebellion, which erupted in 1739 just to the south of the city, the paper concluded that Vesey's conspiracy was "the only attempted insurrection of any importance which took place in South Carolina." This article reflected Dawson's belief that slavery, though ultimately a doomed institution, was for black Americans "the best condition in every way that has been devised."[26]

Two decades later, in 1901, James Hemphill similarly refracted the Vesey conspiracy through the lens of slave fidelity, noting that the plot was foiled by faithful slaves whom Vesey had asked for assistance. Hemphill, in fact, was an even more enthusiastic defender of "the good old days of slavery," as he characterized the prewar period, than his predecessor was. A quarter century after emancipation, the editor worried that memories of the sectional crisis were quickly fading. Worse still, "the younger generation are growing up to believe that slavery was unredeemed brutality, inconsistent with civilization, and the least said about it the better."[27]

Like Dawson and Hemphill, many white Charlestonians highlighted the benevolence of antebellum slaveholders by emphasizing the loyalty that slaves had shown when white men marched off to war. "Behind these magnificent troops," insisted Citadel professor J. Colton Lynes in 1905, "were millions of contented slaves, who tilled the fields and furnished them food and forage." In his history of early South Carolina, Edward McCrady contrasted the fidelity slaves had demonstrated during the Civil War with the willingness of their enslaved forebears to assist British invaders during the Revolution. The relationship between masters and the enslaved had improved significantly during the nineteenth century, he held, so much so that when Confederate men left to fight in the Civil War there was not one instance of slave rebellion against the white women and children left behind.[28]

McCrady may have learned this loyal slave narrative from his old College of Charleston history professor Frederick A. Porcher, who taught generations of young men that slavery was a paternalistic institution. Porcher, who preceded McCrady as president of the South Carolina Historical Society, lampooned the idea that slavery was a necessary evil and confessed in his memoirs that he was inclined to accept the theory that enslaved labor provided the most secure foundation for republican institutions. Like McCrady, Porcher believed that the behavior of the enslaved during the Civil War illustrated slave contentment. He stressed to his students that despite the chaos of the conflict and the provocations of Lincoln and the Union Army, the enslaved never endeavored to break the chains of bondage. Remarkably, however, Porcher's insistence on wartime fidelity contradicted his own experiences during the war. When approximately eighty slaves fled Lowcountry planter John Berkley Grimball in March 1862, for example, the professor conducted a letter-writing campaign in an effort to recover the runaways.[29]

By the turn of the twentieth century, the loyal slave trope had become a national phenomenon. Plantation school authors such as Joel Chandler

Harris and Thomas Nelson Page crafted stories, often narrated in dialect by aging ex-slaves, that portrayed the Old South as a place of moonlight-and-magnolia romance and loving bonds between master and servant. Fictional mammies such as Aunt Jemima were used to hawk pancake batter mix, and southern newspapers touted the fidelity of ex-slaves in obituaries and coverage of Confederate reunions. "Uncle William is now bowed with age," reported the *Charleston Evening Post* of one former body servant who attended the 1899 UCV meeting in Charleston. But he "is as devoted to the memories of the Confederacy as any man who has come to the Reunion." Three years earlier, the tiny upstate town of Fort Mill, South Carolina, had even erected a monument to slave fidelity.[30]

Charleston's Confederate memorialists also kept antebellum debates over slavery alive, regularly lambasting abolitionists, including Harriet Beecher Stowe, John Brown, and the Grimké sisters. In the early twentieth century, UDC member Louisa B. Poppenheim wrote Alexander S. Salley, the secretary of the Historical Commission of South Carolina, for information about Charleston-born abolitionists Sarah and Angelina Grimké. Although reared in a prominent planter family, the sisters—who were the white aunts of Archibald Grimké—rejected slavery and their hometown to become prominent northern activists. "Those women," replied Salley, a Charlestonian himself, "were unbalanced mentally, morally, and socially, and the capable historical or literary critic of to-day would anywhere regard it as a case of histeria [*sic*] to see them put down as exponents of the best in the South." Salley encouraged Poppenheim, who with her sister Mary published the *Keystone*, a UDC organ, to "kill the myth if you can and stick a steel pen charged with your brightest sarcasm into its carcass if you cannot kill it."[31]

White Charlestonians were equally disparaging of Harriet Beecher Stowe and *Uncle Tom's Cabin*, which loomed larger in the southern white imagination than perhaps any other book, save the Bible. Stowe's antislavery novel is "entirely lacking in anything like pure literary taste," insisted the *Charleston Courier* in 1869, seventeen years after it was originally released. After the publication of a new edition of *Uncle Tom's Cabin* in 1885, the *News and Courier* urged southerners to read the novel in order to understand how it "caused the South to be placed in a false position in the eyes of the world." A decade later, Charleston-born Mary

Esther Huger raised questions about Uncle Tom's perfect character in a history she penned for her granddaughter. "A Bishop of our Church, after reading the story, said, 'if slavery made men such Christians as Uncle Tom, it was a pity, all men were not slaves,'" Huger wrote.[32]

Nostalgia for the Old South led some Charlestonians to conclude that emancipation had been an unfortunate development. Although Confederate memorialists rarely called for a return to slavery, they often cast the New South in an unflattering light when compared to life before the war. These comparisons had political value. Just as Republican candidates had used unvarnished recollections of slavery as political weapons during Reconstruction, southern whites turned the Lost Cause into a vehicle by which not only to venerate the past but also to critique the present. White remembrances of slavery, in other words, were an effective way to defend Jim Crow laws and practices—measures that Lost Causers believed would curb the problems unleashed by emancipation.[33]

Citadel professor J. Colton Lynes insisted that free black people in the early twentieth century were worse off than their enslaved forebears. "As a rule, those negroes who are old enough to have experience worth remembering do not hesitate to declare that the state of bondage was far happier," he argued. Lynes insisted that now most blacks were surly and prone to criminal activities. Ben Tillman focused his ire on one crime in particular: black-on-white rape. Under the civilizing institution of slavery, this outrage had been unheard of, the South Carolina politician suggested in a 1903 speech. Then, turning to the present, Tillman asked, "What is the situation now? Take your morning paper and read it any day in the year, and there is hardly a day in which our sensibilities are not wrought up and our passions aroused or our pity aroused by some tale of horror and woe." Tillman chose not to speak directly to his preferred method for handling the supposed epidemic of the African "fiend" who, as he put it, lurks around every corner of the South "to see if some helpless white woman can be murdered or brutalized." But few people who read these words could have had any doubt where Tillman—who was known for his lynching pledge—stood on the question.[34]

Pitchfork Ben was not alone in using white memories of slavery to justify lynching. Four years earlier, in the wake of the brutal lynching of Sam Hose—a black laborer accused (likely falsely) of murdering a

Georgia planter and then raping his wife—a writer to the *Charleston Evening Post* attributed such crimes directly to emancipation. "In the days of slavery the crime was unknown," wrote a correspondent calling himself "G." "Women were left unprotected on a plantation of several hundred negroes; and during the war not a white man [was] within miles. These offenders are from a class that have grown up since the days of slavery, and are subject to no control whatever." In the absence of southern slavery and its civilizing effect, "G" concluded, the only answer to beasts like Hose was the lynch mob.[35]

* * * *

BY THE TURN of the century, when Charleston hosted the national UCV convention, local Lost Causers had spent the better part of three decades touting the righteousness of the Confederacy and all for which it had stood. Some northerners, bent on sectional reconciliation, were fooled by this shell game. Union veteran and Massachusetts blue blood Charles Francis Adams Jr., who came to Charleston in late 1902 to lecture to the city's New England Society, was one. Edward McCrady toured him around the city and accompanied him on a harbor cruise. At the New England Society's annual banquet, Adams no doubt pleased his hosts by ignoring sectional differences over slavery, focusing instead on disputes over the question of state versus national sovereignty that extended back to the founding of the nation. In his mind, the Civil War was the inevitable culmination of a constitutional conflict, and, as such, both the Union and the Confederacy had been correct.[36]

Reflecting the reconciliationist temperament of the day, a number of northern and southern newspapers cheered Adams's address. At the same time, however, several northern dailies, including the *New York Evening Post* and the *Springfield Republican*, adamantly dissented. Even Charles Francis Adams had his limits. In the months before Adams's Charleston visit, McCrady had directed his publisher to send the northerner his two volumes on South Carolina during the American Revolution. After perusing the work, Adams raised objections to McCrady's theories about slave loyalty during the Civil War. In particular, Adams questioned McCrady's suggestion that the unwillingness of the enslaved to rise up against their masters reflected the benign nature of antebellum slavery. On the contrary, the former Union officer argued that soldiers like him knew that the enslaved "longed for freedom," for they flocked to federal lines whenever possible.[37]

Before the Civil War, white southerners had decried any unflattering characterization of slavery. Such portraits seemed equally threatening at the dawn of the twentieth century—decades after slavery had ended. There was, for one, a generational crisis, as children were now being born to parents who themselves lacked direct knowledge of slavery or the war. "There is an enemy at your door constantly threatening, constantly aggressive . . . injecting into history the untruths which desecrate the memory of your ancestors, those from whom you claim to be descendants," Major Theodore G. Barker admonished Charleston's original Sons of Confederate Veterans camp in 1895. "It is a solemn work, and one befitting the worthy descendants of such men, to protect in history the truth that has been handed down to you."[38]

The expansion of public education had the potential to make matters worse, since the North was home to most textbook authors and publishers. Would southern children be forced to learn about the Civil War from Union-slanted history textbooks? This fear was so acute in 1890s South Carolina that it appeared to be the only issue—beyond the righteousness of the Lost Cause itself—that could unite the white citizenry, which was deeply divided between supporters of traditional conservatives like Wade Hampton and those of the new, race-baiting governor, Ben Tillman. Although irate over the General Assembly's decision to give Hampton's U.S. Senate seat to a member of the Tillman faction, the pro-Hampton *News and Courier* admitted in 1890 that it agreed "most heartily" with Tillman when it came to the degradation of the Confederacy in textbooks. As Hemphill wrote, "Too frequent reference cannot be made to what Governor Tillman says with so much force in his inaugural address upon the subject of text books for our public schools." Education, in short, became a chief front in the memory battle over the next three decades.[39]

Many white southerners sought to impart the proper lessons within the privacy of their own homes. By the end of the nineteenth century, Charlestonian Mary Esther Huger had become frustrated by her granddaughter's ignorance of the conflict between North and South. "She had never heard any reason given for the civil war, except that the Southerners had Negro slaves, & the Northerners thought they ought to be made free," explained Huger. So she wrote her own narrative of the Civil War. Others made a point of directing their Lost Cause appeals directly to the southern youth. "My young friends who have grown up since the war, educated from the modern histories, (so called,) I commend this especially to you," proclaimed Cornelius Irvine Walker in his 1900 Memorial Day address at Magnolia Cemetery. Walker believed that it was older southerners' duty to preserve the memory of Confederate heroes and martyrs for the benefit of "the younger generation, who should be taught that their fathers fought a good fight, in a pure cause, and fought it well."[40]

At the national level, members of the newly formed United Confederate Veterans and United Daughters of the Confederacy launched a movement to make sure their sons and daughters were not exposed to "long-legged Yankee lies." Responding to the efforts of the Grand Army of the Republic to scrutinize school history textbooks for signs of Confederate sympathies, the UCV and UDC created historical committees that labored to dispel a whole host of northern ideas about, and interpretations of, the war. Sometimes they focused southerners' attention on simple matters of nomenclature. "Never use the word 'civil' in connection with the 'War between the States,'" Mary B. Poppenheim advised her fellow UDC members in 1902, for it erroneously suggested that the United States was a single whole, rather than a confederation of states. Poppenheim preferred "The Confederate War" or, better yet, "The War between the States." In other moments, Confederate heritage groups focused on broader issues like the legality of secession. As always, the place of slavery in the history of the war and the South in general loomed larger than any other concern.[41]

Charlestonians played an outsized role in this memory campaign. Native sons Ellison Capers, known as the Orator Laureate of the Lost Cause, and Stephen D. Lee were leading members of the UCV Historical Committee. Even more influential was Mary B. Poppenheim. Descended from a prosperous planter family, Poppenheim had learned as a child to love the Confederacy. Her father, a veteran of Hampton's Legion, settled his family in Charleston after the Civil War, where he became a successful merchant and active participant in local Confederate groups. Poppenheim inherited his enthusiasm for the region's past, eventually

Charleston native Mary B. Poppenheim served as president-general of the United Daughters of the Confederacy and published the Keystone, *a monthly women's journal that served as the group's organ for the south-eastern states.*

becoming an avid student of American history while at Vassar College in the 1880s. After returning to Charleston, she joined the LMAC and helped to found the city's United Daughters of the Confederacy chapter. One of the earliest women accepted as a member of the South Carolina Historical Society, Poppenheim wrote and edited books and chapters about the Civil War and the UDC. Over the next quarter century, she served as president of South Carolina's UDC division and president-general of the national organization, chairman of the national UDC committee on education, and UDC historian at the local, state, and national levels. Most important, with the help of her sister Louisa, she produced a monthly women's journal, the *Keystone*, from 1899 until 1913. The UDC's official organ in North Carolina, South Carolina, and Virginia, the *Keystone* reached women across the South and as far away as California and Maine. Through her UDC efforts and *Keystone* stewardship, Poppenheim did as much to popularize the cult of the Lost Cause as any person in the early twentieth century.[42]

Poppenheim was one of several Daughters who redirected the UDC toward promoting a southern interpretation of the war in textbooks at its fourth annual meeting, held in Baltimore in 1897. She drew the members' attention to a recent publication, *Southern Statesmen of the Old Régime*, written by a University of the South professor, which offered unflattering portraits of John C. Calhoun and Jefferson Davis. The textbook "tends to prejudice students against these prominent expounders of the doctrine of State's rights," she concluded. The UDC's original 1894 constitution had pledged "to collect and preserve the material for a truthful history of the war between the Confederate States and the United States of America," she reminded the delegates, yet southern minds were in danger of being "poisoned at the very fountain heads of learning." Two years later, in her *Keystone* report on the UDC annual meeting in Richmond, Poppenheim asserted that "no better work can be done by the women of any community than to preserve the facts of history pure and free from prejudice. . . . Truth, at any cost, should be their watchword."[43]

Under Poppenheim's direction, the South Carolina UDC Historical Committee sought to counter northern interpretations by collecting, preserving, and publishing historical manuscripts about the war and encouraging southern historians to write their own accounts of the conflict. As she reported at the state UDC meeting in 1902, the committee also prepared programs of study to be used by individual chapters across the state, including one on the history of American slavery, which proved especially popular. Seven years later, the *Keystone* published outlines of several of its historical programs, which de-emphasized slavery as a cause of the war while also suggesting that emancipation in the South was inevitable. Praising the work of the Historical Committee, state UDC president Harriet S. Burnet held that its efforts were the natural complement to the monuments that Confederate women had been busily erecting across the southern landscape: "Let every woman in the South see to it that the heroism of our beloved South land be not only written in bronze and stone, but let a historical record be made to be read of all men."[44]

In addition to her work on behalf of the Historical Committee, Poppenheim used the *Keystone* to keep UDC members in Virginia, the Carolinas, and elsewhere abreast of other work the group was doing to protect the Confederate legacy. Like the *News and Courier*, the journal functioned as a clearinghouse for Lost Cause events and ideas. In 1904, Poppenheim reported on a new state initiative to supplement what South Carolina children learned about the Civil War in school by organizing auxiliary youth chapters under the guidance of local parent chapters. As older southerners passed away, the UDC had to ensure the next generation was armed with a proper understanding of the conflict. At the local level, the *Keystone* reported, Charleston's UDC chapter maintained the

Confederate Museum, which it actively encouraged school groups to visit, and sponsored an essay contest "to awaken in the children of this generation an interest in the history of the 'Lost Cause.'" The committee that organized the contest, which included Poppenheim, put up $10 in gold as a yearly prize and, unsurprisingly, selected the causes of South Carolina secession as its first subject.[45]

Poppenheim and her UDC colleagues kept careful watch of the textbooks used in the state's public schools as well. In early 1905, the Historical Committee sent every chapter in the state a circular that covered a number of topics, including the textbook question. In addition, the *Keystone* identified appropriate textbooks and histories as well as books that the UCV viewed as biased against the South.[46]

At the annual meeting of the South Carolina division of the UDC, held in Camden in December 1903, Poppenheim focused the Daughters' attention on one objectionable text in particular: Edward Eggleston's *A History of the United States and Its People*. Assigned in numerous southern schools, including those in Charleston, Eggleston's textbook held that slavery caused the Civil War. In the years that followed, Mary, her sister Louisa, and other UDC members led a crusade to remove Eggleston's book, and other unfair histories, from South Carolina classrooms. The Historical Committee circulated lists of acceptable and troubling books to all UDC chapters, and members pressured local school districts and principals to adhere to them.[47]

In late 1905, Poppenheim, who was now president of the state UDC division, cheerfully informed her fellow Daughters that the public schools in Columbia had decided to replace Eggleston's history with a UCV-approved book. The Poppenheim sisters' work eventually paid the same dividends at home. In October 1907, Charleston School Superintendent H.P. Archer announced that the city had exchanged Eggleston's history for Waddy Thompson's *A History of the United States*. The latter textbook subordinated slavery to states' rights as a cause of the war, while succinctly and vaguely concluding that "the underlying cause of the war between the sections was the conflict of Northern and Southern interests."[48]

Several years later, in 1914, Mary B. Poppenheim felt comfortable declaring mission accomplished on at least one front of this memory campaign. Speaking as national chair of the UDC's Committee on Education to an audience in Savannah, Georgia, Poppenheim said that she was frequently asked what she thought about endowing chairs in southern history at southern colleges and universities. Having proclaimed at the 1897 UDC convention that the "fountain heads of learning" were poisoned, she insisted in 1914 that they were now pure. Two decades of UDC work "has borne rich fruits for the harvests of truth," Poppenheim concluded. Now, we "must look elsewhere for the contamination." Three years later, at the twenty-third annual UDC convention in Dallas, Poppenheim was again brimming with optimism. Holding up a recent Yale University Press announcement for the publication of a fifty-volume history of the United States, the chair of education underscored the fact that three of the four men writing the volumes covering the years 1861 to 1865 either had been or were employed at southern colleges and universities.[49]

By this point, state officials in Columbia were lending a hand. Acting upon the request of the South Carolina state superintendent of schools, Mary C. Simms Oliphant updated an 1860 history of the state written by her grandfather, Charleston poet and writer William Gilmore Simms. The state adopted *The Simms History of South Carolina* in 1917, and, over the course of nine editions, it remained an official South Carolina textbook until 1985. For nearly seventy years, countless South Carolinian schoolchildren—black and white, upstate and Lowcountry—learned about the history of their state from one of the Old South's leading proslavery apologists and his descendant.[50]

One measure of the success of this Confederate memory work in South Carolina was the children's catechism produced by the state division of the UDC. In the first three decades of the twentieth century, UDC divisions in North Carolina, South Carolina, and Texas, as well as the national organization, produced catechisms modeled on Christian books of instruction, which laid out the basic tenets of faith in a simple, often question-and-answer format. Most of these catechisms approached slavery through the standard litany of evasions (it was not the cause of the war), excuses (the South was not to blame for it), and mischaracterizations (it was a benevolent system of caring masters and devoted servants). But South Carolina's version, produced by Mrs. St. John Alison Lawton around 1919, entirely ignored the region's history of slavery, the slave trade, and debates about what caused the Civil War. Those subjects and questions, in South Carolina at least, were settled.[51]

* * * *

ON JUNE 5, 1916, just weeks after its fiftieth anniversary celebration, the Ladies' Memorial Association of Charleston, the city's original Confederate memory organization, gathered for its annual meeting at president Videau Legare Beckwith's Church Street home. Beckwith told the group that she had received a letter from Mary B. Poppenheim, who as an LMAC officer was also in attendance that day. In her letter, Poppenheim reported that she had recently stumbled upon an account of the 1865 Martyrs of the Race Course ceremony published in the *Christian Herald*. Although born, raised, and still living in the city, Poppenheim had never heard of the 1865 Decoration Day service, so she asked Beckwith, also a native Charlestonian, what she could find out about the event. "I regret that I was unable to gather any official information in answer to this," Beckwith responded. The fact that two leading Charleston women, both of whom were devoted to Civil War commemoration, knew nothing of their city's first Decoration Day is telling: white Charleston's memory of the war did not extend to the festivals of freedom that took place in 1865. The Lost Cause, like all manifestations of social memory, was a selective approach to the past. It involved forgetting as well as remembering.[52]

Knowledge of the Martyrs of the Race Course ceremony, to be fair, had faded fast in many places. After Ladies' Memorial Associations across the South flocked to Confederate graves in 1866, northern newspapers reminded their readers that this custom was initiated by James Redpath and the black citizens of Charleston. But by 1868, when the Grand Army of the Republic called for its members to honor the federal dead in an annual May ceremony, numerous observers insisted that the northern veterans organization was trying to usurp a tradition begun by white southern women. The debate over the origins of Decoration Day lingered for decades.[53]

Poppenheim, Beckwith, and other early-twentieth-century Confederate memory stalwarts most certainly recalled another memorial service held at the Washington Race Course. On April 11, 1902, Wade Hampton died, bringing the state to a virtual standstill. For many South

Carolinians, the state's Redeemer general rivaled Robert E. Lee as the embodiment of the Lost Cause. In recognition of this native son, Poppenheim and her fellow Daughters hosted a memorial with hundreds of mourners one day after Hampton's death. The services were conducted in a new auditorium, which had been built for the South Carolina Inter-State and West Indian Exposition, a world's fair being held at the Washington Race Course and the surrounding area in 1901 and 1902.[54]

Soon after, South Carolinians started raising money to build a more permanent tribute to Hampton. While many state residents hoped to install a monument to the Confederate hero on the capitol grounds in Columbia, Charlestonians thought that their city was a better location. In the end, however, the Columbia site won out.[55]

White Charlestonians eventually made their peace with the Columbia monument to Hampton, which was installed in 1906, but they also built a memorial of their own, renaming the Washington Race Course in Hampton's honor in 1903. This, in some ways, was the city's final act of Redemption. The site of a black-built tribute to the loyalty of Union soldiers in 1865, the old racetrack became the symbolic home of loyalty to white supremacy. And despite the sizable black population in adjacent neighborhoods, Hampton Park swiftly became a whites-only space.[56]

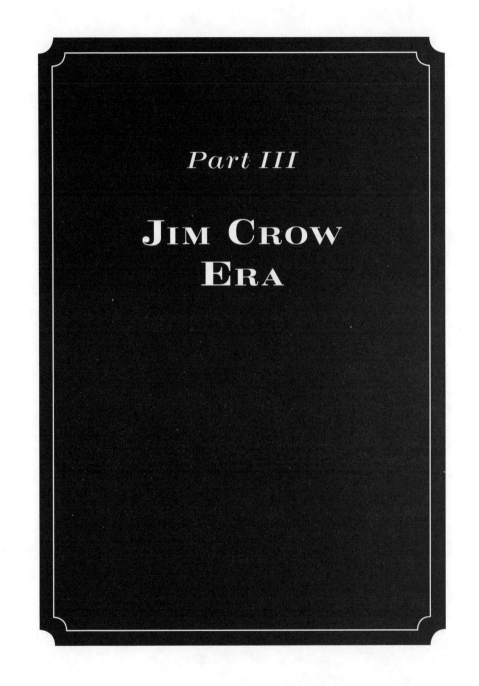

Part III

JIM CROW
ERA

5

Black Memory in the Ivory City

IN THE FALL OF 1901, BLACK CHARLESTONIANS ERUP-
ted in protest over a new statue that had just been installed in the city.
Having hurled insults and rocks at both Calhoun monuments in Marion Square for years, African American residents knew well the pain that
came from seeing an odious image set in stone. But this time the situation must have seemed different: the new statue purported to represent
African Americans, not South Carolina's favorite son. Perhaps their protest of the sculpture, entitled *The Negro Group*, would produce a more
conclusive victory and force white Charlestonians to reconsider the wisdom of putting such statues on display.

The Negro Group had been commissioned by the white directors of
the South Carolina Inter-State and West Indian Exposition, a world's
fair slated to open in December. Held at the Washington Race Course
and the lands adjacent to it just a few years before the course was renamed
in Wade Hampton's honor, the Exposition advertised Charleston's economic potential to willing investors. The 160-acre "Ivory City" comprised
ornate white buildings, sunken gardens, lakes, fountains, plazas, and artwork created especially for the event.[1]

Throughout the autumn, locals—white and black—visited the Exposition grounds, watching laborers put the finishing touches on the buildings and the sculptures that were to be installed. In addition to *The
Negro Group*, there were, among others, statues depicting Native Americans and Huguenot settlers. The first week of October, workers placed
The Negro Group on a pedestal in front of the Negro Building. The low-
slung, Spanish-style structure—located on the margins of the fair, away
from the Court of Palaces that served as the focal point—housed the

Black Charlestonians criticized The Negro Group, *intended as a tribute to African Americans' role in the New South, because it portrayed them as menial laborers.*

Negro Department. A collection of exhibits on agriculture, mechanics, education, and religion, the department highlighted African American accomplishments since emancipation.[2]

Covered in staff, a material made from plaster, cement, and hemp to resemble stone, *The Negro Group* consisted of three figures. In the middle stood a woman balancing a basket of cotton on her head and holding a pitcher of water in her hand. On one side was a kneeling, shirtless man resting on a plow with one hand and leaning on an anvil with the other. Flanking the woman on the other side was a younger man in an artisan's apron strumming a banjo and singing plantation songs. Bradford Lee Gilbert, the white, New York–based architect who designed the Exposition buildings, believed the statue was dignified and predicted that it would be "one of the finest on the grounds."[3]

But many African Americans who saw the statue in the months before the Exposition opened decided that it had to go. Thomas J. Jackson, a member of the Negro Department's African American board, wished the young boy had been portrayed at work or at school, rather than sitting idle and playing the banjo. Jackson criticized the face of the plowman as "equally vicious...in aspect." The two were "the very lowest types of the negro race," he proclaimed, "and in no way does the group represent the progress the colored race has achieved within the past few years."[4]

Thomas E. Miller, another Negro Department board member, explained the objections in a letter to Booker T. Washington in similar terms. Named the figurehead of the Negro Department by the Exposition's white directors, Washington was a renowned black educator and founder of the Tuskegee Institute in Alabama. He had visited the Exposition grounds a few months earlier and had seen *The Negro Group* himself when it was delivered by Gilbert. But Miller, a former U.S. congressman who served as president of the Colored Normal, Industrial, Agricultural, and Mechanical College of South Carolina, reported that the statue had not been well received since then. "The group," Miller wrote to Washington, "is being condemned by every hopeful, aspiring, self respecting Negro of both sexes; and if it remains there it will bring our work into reproach and make the Negro end of this magnificent Exposition a loathsome thing and a byword." Observing from afar, a black newspaper in Cleveland labeled the statue "a burlesque sculpture misrepresenting the race."[5]

The Negro Group offended because it erased African American class divisions. "The colored politics of South Carolina have also their color lines," wrote the *New York Times* in its coverage of the controversy, "being drawn between 'persons of color' and full-blooded Africans." Eager to be recognized as superior to menial laborers, wealthier, better-educated, and often lighter-skinned African Americans—the browns, as they were called in Charleston—saw the statue as an affront, a symbolic check on their status and ambition.[6]

Some critics also felt *The Negro Group* was nothing more than a demeaning portrait of black life *before* emancipation, a throwback to the Old South. Thomas J. Jackson, concerned about how the statue obscured black progress since emancipation, was one. Thomas E. Miller was another. In his letter to Washington, the freeborn black leader admitted that he had had reservations about the statue even before it was installed. Had the choice been his, Miller informed Washington, the statue would never have been put on display. "I did pray that you would have found words with which to make a courteous refusal of the gift," Miller wrote. "Never-the-less," he continued, "if you conclude that the Negro boy with the banjo in hand in the aspect of a blank idiot is a faithful portrayal of yours and mine on the plantations in former days, as your subordinate I will say 'me too' amen." Washington never replied.[7]

Reverend O.D. Robinson, pastor at Mount Zion A.M.E. Church, an offshoot of Emanuel A.M.E. Church, led the opposition to *The Negro Group*, a decision that befit his role as a race man more generally. Robinson used his pulpit as an arena for the discussion of disenfranchisement and other issues facing the black community. At a meeting he spearheaded in October 1901, protesters demanded that *The Negro Group* be removed from the front of the Negro Building. Several black organizations in Charleston supported this plan of action, with some going so far as to threaten the sculpture's destruction if the request were not honored.[8]

The white press, for its part, complained that the black opponents of *The Negro Group* were being ungrateful and unreasonable. The *News and Courier* had little patience with the episode, condemning "the more ignorant of our colored fellow citizens" for criticizing a statue that was not only an aesthetic achievement but also "true to life." A newspaper in Macon, Georgia, decried the "violent protest" against a sculpture that "is said to show high artistic merit."[9]

The white directors of the Exposition bristled at the fuss, too. Unnerved by the gall of what they labeled "the so-called 'new' negroes of Charleston," they complied with the request to remove the statue, transferring it to the main Court of Palaces before the Exposition opened to the public. They moved it, in other words, to a far more visible location, where it would be seen by far more fairgoers. "The result of this wholly unexpected and surprising lack of taste on the part of the negroes," the directors reported, "will be to advertise most widely and to display to far greater advantage [the] splendid typical group."[10]

The skirmish over *The Negro Group*, combined with the Exposition's inadequate facilities for African American patrons, prompted a black boycott of the festivities. After the fair ended in the spring of 1902, James Hemphill, editor of the *News and Courier* and president of the Exposition company, observed that the statue "was bitterly resented by the negroes of the community, who threatened to destroy the group." He noted that moving the statue ensured that it attracted more attention than it might otherwise have garnered, intimating that the disappointing returns of the Negro Department were the result. The low black attendance in Charleston contrasted with earlier expositions in Atlanta and Nashville where, despite stories of discrimination at the fairs, African Americans turned out even on days not set aside exclusively for them. The opponents of *The Negro Group*, in sum, helped undermine the success of the Exposition, a noteworthy achievement in the Jim Crow era.[11]

But white Charlestonians got the last laugh. The city acquired the Exposition statues when it purchased the Washington Race Course, which it soon rechristened to commemorate Wade Hampton. Officials placed *The Negro Group*, among several other statues, on permanent display so as to "attract the interest of lovers of art and add materially to the beauty . . . of the park." Black citizens could take some satisfaction that the staff sculptures could not withstand the elements, despite repeated attempts to repair them. They were removed in 1906. Yet the custom of prohibiting African Americans from Hampton Park, which was surrounded by neighborhoods that were disproportionately black, proved more durable. That practice, like the decision to rename the old racecourse for a Confederate hero, was an unavoidable reminder to black Charlestonians. Shaping the public memory of slavery in Jim Crow Charleston would be no easy task.[12]

* * * *

THOMAS E. MILLER understood the challenges of navigating segregation as well as anyone. He never aired the concerns about *The Negro Group* that he raised in his private correspondence with Booker T. Washington, perhaps with good reason. Miller had begun his political career in South Carolina as a beneficiary and champion of the political gains of Reconstruction, serving as a Republican state representative, state senator, and U.S. congressman. One of only six black delegates to the 1895 state constitutional convention at which blacks were disenfranchised, Miller offered an eloquent, but ultimately ineffective, defense of black rights. By the end of the decade, Miller's optimism and radicalism had largely faded. Living in Orangeburg, where he was president of the Colored Normal, Industrial, Agricultural, and Mechanical College of South Carolina (later South Carolina State), he bemoaned the futility of politics in the segregated South. Like Booker T. Washington, Miller now insisted that blacks should rely on the benevolence of their white neighbors and seek economic advancement through agricultural and mechanical

Former U.S. congressman Thomas E. Miller privately condemned The Negro Group. *Publicly, the African American politician and educator approached the memory of slavery strategically, praising the loyal slave memorial at Fort Mill, South Carolina.*

training. Miller's change of heart must have also stemmed from his institution's dependence upon white patronage. He had to consult the college's white board of trustees about even the smallest of decisions.[13]

Miller knew that if African Americans invoked the memory of slavery in this new climate, they had to do so carefully. Asked to deliver an Emancipation Day address in Beaufort in 1901, Miller quoted the words of Martin W. Gary, a leading secessionist, Confederate general, and mastermind behind the violent Edgefield Plan by which the Red Shirts redeemed South Carolina. Gary had insisted that "the negro is ignorant, but he is loyal to a cause, he is faithful to a trust and there is no body of men found anywhere who will follow a leader with more confidence, love and fidelity than the negro." Miller was grateful for the compliment and underscored Gary's assessment to the African American crowd assembled before him in Beaufort: "Yes, Mr. Chairman, our people have never betrayed a trust, whether at home, in the fields, in the workshops or on the battlefield."[14]

Here was a black statesman and educator invoking the faithful slave—the contented, loyal servant who harbored no resentment about his condition, the trope so central to the Lost Cause—at an Emancipation Day celebration. It was not the only time Miller publicly embraced this ideal. The very next year, on January 1, 1902, Miller gave the Emancipation

Day address in Charleston. His speech did double duty that day. New Year's Day 1902 was also the official opening of the Exposition's Negro Department, which organizers had set aside as Negro Day. In the morning, a parade wound its way through streets teeming with African Americans from the city and surrounding Sea Islands. The procession concluded at the Exposition auditorium, where Miller addressed a crowd that included the white Exposition directors, the Negro Department directors, and a large group of African Americans.[15]

In some ways, Miller's address harkened back to previous Emancipation Day celebrations. He reminded his listeners that before emancipation slaves had dreaded January 1 as the day when families were ripped apart forever. He praised famous opponents of slavery, including William Lloyd Garrison, the Grimké sisters, John Brown, and, most of all, Frederick Douglass and Abraham Lincoln. In other respects, Miller's tone was muted. Echoing Lincoln, he proclaimed that he approached Emancipation Day "with malice towards none" and "love and charity towards all." Confederate soldiers may have fought against the freedom of slaves, but he did not hold that fact against them.[16]

Looming large in his remarks, the faithful slave fit squarely within this conciliatory approach. During the Civil War, on the home front and the battlefield, slaves had never abandoned their masters, Miller insisted. He lingered on the story of one black bondman who, after his Georgia master had been killed, refused to leave the field despite the danger to his own life. Later, the faithful slave carried the officer's body back to camp. To Miller, the tale poignantly highlighted the loyalty that African Americans had rendered not just to their masters but also to the country in which they lived, whether it was the United States or the Confederacy. His only complaint was that Americans were slow to commemorate black sacrifices in stone. The Pension Building in Washington D.C., a structure built in the 1880s to house the U.S. Pension Bureau and memorialize Union soldiers, for example, had been decorated with a frieze that featured no black servicemen.[17]

Miller singled out an important exception to this commemorative neglect: in Fort Mill, South Carolina, a tiny Upcountry hamlet about two hundred miles away, sat the first—and, to that point, the only—faithful slave memorial in the United States. In 1896, five years before the Exposition in Charleston, a Confederate captain and former slave owner named Samuel E. White had erected the monument on the town's green.[18]

Unveiled in May 1896, just one month before the second Calhoun Monument was installed in Charleston, the Fort Mill slave memorial consisted of an obelisk and two panels. The first portrayed a mammy nurturing a white child on the steps of a big house. The second showed a male slave, surrounded by bundles of wheat, holding a sickle while he took a break from his work. An inscription included the name of ten ex-slaves, eight of whom bore the last name White, and praised bondpeople for supporting the Confederate Army and for guarding soldiers' families while they were away at war. The ceremony celebrating the dedication of the slave memorial was a tableau of postbellum racial harmony. Four former slaves removed the drape covering the monument, revealing it to a crowd of thousands, black and white. The highlight of the program was an oration delivered by Polk Miller, a white performer of slave music and folklore. Miller's routine pitted what he called the "uppity," turn-of-the-century African American against the "negro of the good old days gone-by," suggesting emancipation had been an unfortunate development.[19]

Outside South Carolina, critics condemned the Fort Mill monument. The *Milwaukee Sentinel* censured the *News and Courier* for its enthusiastic endorsement of the project after White announced his intentions in 1895. *Sentinel* editors took a sarcastic swipe at the Charleston paper for its willingness to honor blacks in stone while it proposed to disenfranchise them at the upcoming state constitutional convention. The *New-York Tribune* was even more blunt, pointing out that it was inconsistent for southerners to honor deceased blacks with a monument while they lynched live ones. Of course, this inconsistency was more superficial than real. White South Carolinians frequently argued—and no doubt believed—that they lynched blacks because they strayed from the fidelity and docility embodied by the loyal slave ideal. The Fort Mill monument was prescriptive, providing a model of proper black behavior in the New South.[20]

Given the paucity of extant African American newspapers in the state, we do not know what most South Carolina blacks, including those in Charleston, thought about the Fort Mill monument. Glimpses of black opposition appear elsewhere, however. Reverend Caesar A.A. Taylor, a Florida minister, shared his concerns in the *Indianapolis Free-*

man. Although confident that nothing but noble motives had compelled Captain White to act, Taylor believed that the monument would be "a humiliation not alone to the Negroes, but an ever reminding shame" to former slave owners, too.[21]

Thomas E. Miller's admiration for the Fort Mill monument, in contrast, is clear. It was the subject to which his lengthy Emancipation Day address built. As he stood before the large crowd in the Exposition auditorium, Miller concluded his remarks by proclaiming that the Fort Mill obelisk represented a "magnificent testimonial to negro worth, to negro character." He predicted that this touching monument would prove an inspiration: "The whole scene presents a hallowed aspect such as can only be witnessed where fidelity, love, contentment and gratitude are enthroned. Yes, my people, this monument was erected by Capt. White, of Fort Mill, and in time more will follow this one." Miller then quoted four lines of Henry Wadsworth Longfellow—advising his black listeners that they must "Learn to labor and to wait"—and relinquished the podium.[22]

To Thomas E. Miller, the Fort Mill monument was a welcome sign that the white South was eager to include the loyal slave as a part of the commemorative landscape it was so eagerly fashioning at the turn of century. The *News and Courier* suggested his hopes were not unfounded. In 1895, editor James Hemphill endorsed a loyal slave memorial in Richmond based on Captain White's example. A decade later, his paper urged the erection of an imposing shaft honoring faithful slaves somewhere in the South, perhaps in Charleston. In the 1920s, the United Daughters of the Confederacy nearly succeeded in convincing Congress to install a mammy memorial in Washington, D.C.[23]

What should we make of Miller's enthusiasm for the Fort Mill monument and the loyal slave ideal? At first glance, his approbation seems nothing more than a concession to the romanticized vision of slavery, and surely some white listeners interpreted it in this way. But Miller's use of the loyal slave trope must also have been strategic, for it reinforced his broader message of racial conciliation and cooperation. Facing an increasingly hostile racial climate in which southern blacks were disenfranchised, discriminated against, and murdered at the hands of lynch mobs, Miller urged his fellow citizens to let go of their dreams of equality. African Americans could improve their status, but not, as he argued in his address at the Exposition, "by croaking and fault-finding and whining and pining." On the contrary, Miller advised his black audience to embrace hard work, frugality, and "friendship with our white neighbors."[24]

The Fort Mill monument represented an aesthetic manifestation of this political strategy. Like many black leaders of the era, including both Booker T. Washington and W.E.B. Du Bois, Miller preferred the figure of a faithful slave protecting his master on the battlefield and his mistress at home to the bloodthirsty and sexually marauding figure conjured up by lynch mobs and southern authors such as Thomas Dixon. While white southerners invoked the loyal slave to emphasize the proper place of blacks in the segregated New South, Miller used it for his own purposes, arguing that blacks were as true as ever. He focused on the benefits such a representation might confer to African Americans battling against images of black criminality and animalism.[25]

Of course, just a few months before his Emancipation Day speech at the Exposition, Miller had quietly lobbied for the removal of *The Negro Group*, which he judged an offensive vision of slave life in the Old South. Now, he profusely and publicly commended the Fort Mill monument to the loyal slave. On the surface, these positions appear inconsistent. Yet a careful reading of his letter to Booker T. Washington about *The Negro Group* suggests otherwise. "If you conclude," he had written, "that the Negro boy with the banjo in hand in the aspect of a blank idiot is a faithful portrayal of yours and mine on the plantations in former days, as your subordinate I will say 'me too' amen." Miller was not so much troubled by the fact that the statue harkened back to slavery as by the fact that it inaccurately presented the enslaved as banjo-strumming fools. A statue that honored black fidelity was politically useful. One that memorialized black buffoonery was not.[26]

Miller's accommodationist approach, yoked to the memory of the loyal slave, won glowing reviews from white South Carolinians. The *State* in Columbia, for example, praised his 1901 Emancipation Day speech in Beaufort for rejecting fanatical ravings about equality and rights. "The day of the negro agitator," the paper announced, "we hope, is over." When, almost a decade later, Miller dared to violate the bargain he had struck with whites, he discovered the price of disloyalty. In the 1910 South Carolina gubernatorial race, Miller opposed the candidacy of

Coleman L. Blease, a trustee of the Colored Normal, Industrial, Agricultural, and Mechanical College of South Carolina who believed black education was a waste of money. Blease won and, soon after his inauguration, forced Miller to resign the presidency of the college. His "pernicious political activity," Blease declared, demanded it.[27]

* * * *

THOMAS E. MILLER'S turn-of-the-century Emancipation Day addresses highlight the degree to which the ground had narrowed for black leaders in the Jim Crow South. Even on a day set aside for black memories of slavery, Miller found himself drawn to a trope rooted in southern white nostalgia. To publicly dredge up recollections of slavery that implicated whites in perpetuating a cruel and inhumane institution was simply too risky.

In fact, segregation threatened to drive the black past out of the public sphere altogether, a reality with which other leading African Americans struggled. James H. Holloway was a harness maker and member of the prestigious Brown Fellowship Society, an organization created by mixed-race browns who had thrived in the city before the Civil War. To men like Holloway, the Old South was something of a golden age. His grandfather Richard had been a skilled carpenter who owned not only several slaves but also land and houses all over the city. Proud of his family's accomplishments and worried that they would be forgotten in a Jim Crow present that treated all blacks equally poorly, James Holloway compiled a scrapbook that detailed his family's antebellum status and charitable record. "Let us learn from the dominant race to hold sacred every item of historical importance," Holloway advised. He sought out heirlooms from black Charlestonians and helped organize exhibitions that highlighted African American history, including the Negro Exhibit at the 1907 Jamestown Exposition and, perhaps, the Negro Department at the South Carolina Inter-State and West Indian Exposition.[28]

Holloway also sent letters to the editor of the *News and Courier* and the *Evening Post* praising the virtues of Charleston's brown community, urged historians Yates Snowden and Theodore D. Jervey Jr. and filmmaker Freeman Owens to document the lives of the city's free people of color, and raised money to publish a history of the Brown Fellowship Society. In a 1907 letter thanking Jervey for his contributions to this fund, Holloway emphasized free blacks' loyalty to the white community during the Vesey conspiracy. No member of the Brown Fellowship Society could be found in the trial record of the foiled 1822 insurrection, he told the Charleston attorney and historian. "And while our Society held its regular meeting nowhere in the proceedings any mention is made of it," Holloway wrote. "The only sign of unrest was the society transferred its real estate and other funds into U.S. Bonds." With Jervey's permission, Holloway hoped to publicize these facts in an open letter, which he believed would serve as a testament to blacks and whites alike.[29]

As a leader of the Brown Fellowship Society, Holloway was instrumental in changing the group's name to the Century Fellowship Society (better to highlight its longevity and historical significance), restoring and maintaining its Pitt Street cemetery, and building a substantial hall for the organization. Yet neither the Society's hall, which Holloway considered his life's work, nor its cemetery survived the social and economic pressures of Jim Crow. As white Charlestonians transformed their city into a shrine to the past by preserving its historic buildings and homes—a topic explored at length in chapter 6—most physical reminders of black history fell by the wayside.[30]

So, too, did the black militia companies that since Reconstruction had marched through Charleston on Emancipation Day, the Fourth of July, and other occasions. Although Redemption had sapped these units of any practical power, consigning them to symbolic duties, what they symbolized mattered. After all, the early years of Jim Crow were the heyday of Confederate monument building. Black southerners were not able to match the commemorative outburst that saw town after town across the former Confederacy erect tributes to the valor of southern white soldiers. But at least they got to watch African American militiamen parade through cities like Charleston several times a year, walking testaments to their own martial tradition. In the early 1900s, however, South Carolina, like all southern states but Tennessee, disbanded its black militia companies.[31]

By this point, Emancipation Day and Fourth of July celebrations in Charleston were shadows of their former selves. Two decades earlier, white officials had begun driving these black commemorations out of the city's most important public spaces. Rumors that black residents were to be prohibited from celebrating the Fourth of July at White Point

Garden began to circulate immediately after the state was redeemed in 1877. Four years later, in 1881, the city passed an ordinance forbidding the use of the park "for public proceedings, celebrations or festivities of any kind whatsoever."[32]

For the next few years, neither Too-la-loo, as the official black Fourth of July ceremony was called, nor the annual Emancipation Day commemoration was held at its usual home in White Point Garden, but rather at Marion Square. Eventually, most formal Emancipation Day exercises were consigned to private, all-black venues, such as Zion Presbyterian, Morris Brown A.M.E., and Emanuel A.M.E. churches, when they were held at all. The 1902 Emancipation Day celebration, coordinated with the opening of the exposition's Negro Department, was an exception to this new pattern. And, as we have seen, Miller's speech that day aimed to placate a white audience hostile to more radical readings of the day's significance.[33]

The city soon pushed Too-la-loo out of Charleston altogether. In 1883, officials denied the black community the use of the recently renovated Marion Square on the Fourth, offering in its place Hampstead Mall, a park located in a black neighborhood on the northeast edge of Charleston, not far from where the African Church once stood. The crowds at the mall were small that day, observed the *News and Courier*, as many blacks and quite a few whites chose to stroll along the Battery "without the accompaniment of singing, shouting and yelling, that formerly made day and night hideous at that delightful resort." By the evening, rural blacks made their way out to the Hampstead Mall, the paper continued, "and the usual 'Too-la-loo' orgies were soon inaugurated." In 1886, white residents succeeded in removing these so-called orgies from the peninsula. The festivities migrated across the Ashley River to the newly constructed Pleasure Grove in St. Andrew's Parish. Two years later, the *News and Courier* succinctly summarized the "obvious" reason that the black celebration had been banished from Charleston: "watermelon rinds." Too-la-loo never returned to the peninsula, and vendors' practice of setting up tables to sell food along Meeting and King streets on the Fourth was also banned by the early twentieth century.[34]

Black Charlestonians did their best to resist these segregationist efforts. Even though most official Emancipation Day and Fourth of July festivities were held beyond the public gaze by the late 1800s, small

Faced with limited resources, black Charlestonians such as teacher Mamie Garvin Fields (left front) and librarian Susan Dart Butler (right front) labored to preserve and teach African American history.

groups of African American families and friends continued to congregate in White Point Garden on the Fourth. Despite the 1881 ordinance forbidding the use of the park for public celebrations, and despite an unwritten rule that blacks were to stay out of the park altogether, city officials appear to have turned a blind eye to these informal gatherings on the Fourth of July. In 1890, the *News and Courier* observed that on the holiday, which it called "a kind of Mid-summer Emancipation Day," black residents streamed through the streets, adding that the Battery was also packed until late in the evening. Ten years later, on July 5, 1900, the paper observed that blacks again jammed Charleston on the Fourth, taking over White Point Garden for most of the day. Mamie Garvin Fields, who grew up in turn-of-the-twentieth-century Charleston, remembered the area as filled with food, music, and impromptu performances on the Fourth. Children sang "The Battle Hymn of the Republic" and recited the Emancipation Proclamation and other pieces by Abraham Lincoln. Most moving was the reading of Frederick Douglass's antislavery speeches, which, recalled Fields, "many people knew by heart."[35]

Throughout the twentieth century, black residents of Charleston and the surrounding Sea Islands also continued to march through city streets on New Year's Day. One year, the students and teachers from several rural James Island schools built and transported a large float to downtown Charleston for the city's annual Emancipation Day parade, staying up all night at Morris Street School to decorate it.[36]

On occasion, black memories of slavery bubbled to the surface and gained a permanent place in the public record. Ex-slave Archibald Grimké likely drew on stories he had heard growing up in Charleston for an 1899 address on the Denmark Vesey affair at the American Negro Academy in Washington, D.C. An increasingly prominent writer and public speaker, Grimké would go on to help found the NAACP and serve as a president of its Washington, D.C., branch. Grimké hoped his Vesey speech would shed light on an incident largely ignored by white scholars of the day. To that end, he also tried unsuccessfully to place the piece in the *Atlantic*. Two years later, he secured an agreement with the American Negro Academy, which published *Right on the Scaffold, or The Martyrs of 1822*. Although Grimké did not stipulate his sources, his essay included personal details about Vesey—such as his impressive physical strength—that cannot be found in the official court documents and were surely gleaned from black oral sources.[37]

Still, under Jim Crow, such public expressions of black memory—whether they appeared in the streets and squares of Charleston or on the printed page—were few and far between. As was true elsewhere in the segregated South, a countermemory of slavery in the city was really cultivated behind closed doors, in private homes or schools, churches, and similar locations. This was "still social memory," as historian Bruce Baker reminds us, "but it existed, as it had to, well out of sight of the general public, flourishing in just those segregated spaces the Jim Crow system created, where whites were not around to stifle it and shout it down."[38]

Charleston's black churches, for one, sponsored lectures on African American history. In 1905, Boston professor William H. Ferris delivered a lecture entitled "The Ten Greatest Negroes, or Beacon Lights of Negro History" at Mount Zion A.M.E. Church. Black club women actively sought to combat the Lost Cause ideas propagated by groups such as the United Daughters of the Confederacy. Throughout the 1920s and 1930s, members of the Phillis Wheatley Literary and Social Club bought works of African American literature and history, such as *The Negro in Our History*, which they read and discussed at club meetings. They donated money to pioneering black historian Carter G. Woodson, specifically to support the study of black history, and attempted to expand the holdings of local libraries. In 1931, club women requested that the newly established Charleston County Public Library system acquire books by African American authors. Up until that point, the only substitute for a public library that black Charlestonians had was the Dart Hall reading room, a tiny space opened by librarian Susan Dart Butler four years earlier.[39]

African American schools were another important repository of black memory. Until 1920, however, the three public schools for black children in Charleston were staffed almost exclusively by white teachers, who did their best to impart the tenets of the Lost Cause. This was true even at the Shaw School, named for the antislavery Union colonel Robert Gould Shaw and leased to the city in the 1880s by its trustees on the condition that it employ at least some black teachers. The city school commission opposed this stipulation, and by 1900 Shaw employed just two black teachers—the only two in the Charleston public school system. To make matters worse, at least in the minds of black students such as Mamie Garvin Fields, the school's white teachers drilled them in "the Rebel tradition." Students had to memorize "a great many Rebel songs and poems," recalled Fields. "We would sing 'Dixie,' the whole school, in unison, 'I wish I was in de lan' of cotton,' in dialect too. Then they were fond of songs like 'Swanee River,' 'My Old Kentucky Home,' 'Massa's in de Col', Col', Groun'.' This was what they wanted to instill in us." Although a 1919 NAACP protest led by African American artist Edwin Harleston and Thomas E. Miller forced Charleston to begin to staff black schools with black teachers, it would take several more decades for the school board to authorize classes in African American history and literature.[40]

Black educators in the surrounding Sea Islands also confronted daunting obstacles. Having grown up hearing Gullah in their homes, African American students there faced significant language barriers in the classroom, while their instructors had few resources. "Every Negro teacher fought the battle of the book," insisted Mamie Garvin Fields, who did not find any texts at all when she arrived to teach at the school at Society Corner on James Island in 1926. She and her colleagues acquired as many books as they could, despite the fact that the texts were geared toward adults or were simply falling apart. Even educators committed to preserving and imparting knowledge about the black past had difficulty introducing African American history and culture in their classrooms. Fields's fifth-grade history lesson plans, for instance, stuck closely to the narrative provided by Harry F. Estill in *The Beginner's History of Our Country*, a Sons of Confederate Veterans–approved textbook that focused on traditional topics such as Christopher Columbus, John Smith, and Pocahontas. It said next to nothing about the black experience.[41]

Private schools were more successful in teaching African American history, including the history of slavery. In the early twentieth century, Charleston had more than a dozen one- and two-room schools that catered to black students who could pay a small fee. Before enrolling at the Shaw School, Mamie Garvin Fields had attended one such institution, Miss Anna E. Izzard's School, named after and operated by her cousin, whom she called Lala. "It was from her," Fields later wrote, "that I learned about slavery as our relatives had experienced it and what it meant." Lala paired these lessons with a critical reading of the city's public landscape and the historical narrative that whites had begun to inscribe. In blatant disregard of local custom, Lala took her students to White Point Garden, where they pondered a number of queries: "Why were those cannons there and in whose honor?" How did the people who lived along the Battery "get the money to build such great big houses?" At Lala's school, Fields and her classmates were told of how white Charlestonians had accumulated their wealth, and of how they had fought a war to protect the institution that generated it. Countless black Charlestonians learned similar lessons at the other small black schools that proliferated in the city.[42]

The Avery Normal Institute, the most prominent school for African Americans in Charleston, boasted a curriculum that was shaped by northern missionaries with abolitionist leanings as well as by several members of the Phillis Wheatley Club who were teachers there. Studying in classrooms named Lincoln, Sumner, and Grant, Avery students learned about the antislavery movement and black heroes such as Robert Smalls, Toussaint L'Ouverture, and Crispus Attucks. A portrait of Frederick Douglass was one of the few images that hung on the walls.[43]

Those who attended the school in the first half of the twentieth century recalled that Avery teachers worked consciously to bring the black past into the classroom. Leroy Anderson, a 1935 graduate, said

African American schools, such as the Avery Normal Institute, nurtured a countermemory of slavery during Jim Crow with cartoons such as "Lincoln's Legacy," published by the Avery Tiger *in 1948.*

that students were steeped in African American history, studying it every Friday. His good friend J. Michael Graves appreciated Avery because "it was one place where we learned about Negro history." According to Avery student Sadie Green Oglesby, Benjamin F. Cox, the school's principal from 1914 to 1936, "stressed black history and culture in order to make us interested," though she added that he avoided connections between this past and contemporary political issues such as segregation. Cox brought Harlem Renaissance artists and other black speakers to Avery, while the school newspaper, the *Avery Tiger*, included a New Books column that featured titles relevant to black history and culture and published cartoons that celebrated Abraham Lincoln's egalitarian legacy. In 1942, Avery graduate and teacher Alphonso Hoursey advised the American Missionary Association, which governed the school from its 1865 founding through 1947, that black history should be made a formal part of its junior high school social studies curriculum.[44]

Like the Phillis Wheatley Club, Avery students were drawn to historian Carter G. Woodson and his Association for the Study of Negro Life and History (ASNLH), which he founded in 1915. The ASNLH was instrumental in getting African American history off the ground in the early twentieth century through its conferences, publications, research, and public programs. Among the ASNLH's most important public programs was Negro History Week, which replaced Emancipation Day as the central black history celebration in many African American communities after it was introduced in 1926. By the early 1930s, Avery was staging its own Negro History Week program, which devoted a good deal of attention to the subject of slavery. An article in the 1941 *Avery Tiger* advertising Negro History Week recommended books on black abolitionists Sojourner Truth and Harriet Tubman. The 1947 program included a play focusing on Virginia slave insurrectionist Nat Turner.[45]

Avery teachers also kept memories of slavery alive. Cynthia McCottry-Smith remembered that before she enrolled in the 1930s, she had only the barest sense of the black experience in the Old South. Although McCottry-Smith's grandfather Augustus had been born a slave, her "family never talked much about Augustus, or anyone else in our family who was a slave." Given her family's silence, McCottry-Smith counted her time at Avery a revelation. "I couldn't believe some of the history of brutality and indignities the slaves suffered during that period," she recalled in 2008. "We learned that newly freed slaves were happy to be free at Emancipation, but many of them had no direction. Their families, such as they were, had lived on plantations for many generations and they knew nothing else." Gwendolyn A. Simmons, who attended the school before it closed in 1954, likewise was shocked by what she discovered at Avery about the history of slavery. "Grappling with the concept that someone could actually OWN another person, learning about the brutality (physical and emotional) of the system and that most slaves were, by law, denied education was very upsetting to me." She credited her excellent teachers who "were quite knowledgeable about that awful era and could offer a broader, truer picture of slavery than was available in the textbooks."[46]

At the same time, Avery teachers struggled to fully incorporate black history into their lessons. Of the more than three hundred works in the school's circulating library, just a handful spoke directly to black history and culture. In the interwar period, the school's official curriculum included world history, European history, and American history, but not African American history, suggesting that it was up to individual teachers to fill in gaps about the black past. Disappointed by this situation, social studies and history instructor Julia Brogdon, who arrived at Avery in 1943, reached out to her former Atlanta University professor W.E.B. Du Bois. The prominent black scholar sent her plenty of material about African American history to use at Avery.[47]

It was also true that some Avery students had little use for such lessons, preferring to hear about injustices of the Jim Crow present rather than the Old South past. "Although we read about and studied black history at Avery," recalled one 1939 graduate, "I was at that time more concerned about the segregation that existed during my life." Despite her horror at the realities of slavery, Gwendolyn Simmons said that she, too, was more disturbed by her own experiences under Jim Crow.[48]

Slavery could also prove a touchy subject. According to Charlotte De-Berry Tracy, a Massachusetts-born educator who came to the school to teach social studies and math in 1923, she and several colleagues tried to include black history whenever they could, though this sometimes made for awkward moments. While teaching a lesson on the Civil War, for example, Tracy brought up the topic of slavery. Noticing a light-skinned boy who was not listening, she chided the entire class to play close attention since all of them had a slave in the family. The boy responded, "Miss DeBerry, I'm sorry, you didn't have that right. My people never were slaves." Then he added that in fact his grandparents had owned some of his classmates' grandparents. In classrooms filled with the descendants of both slaves and free black slave owners, lessons about slavery could be a reminder of the class divisions that separated working-class black students from their wealthier classmates. Emancipation Day celebrations could prove equally divisive. When Mamie Garvin Fields and other teachers from rural James Island schools decided to have their students produce a float for the annual Emancipation Day parade at some point in the 1920s or 1930s, they were told "that the parade was not for the people out in the country."[49]

Despite such challenges, Avery graduates who went on to become teachers left the school armed with a great deal of knowledge about the black past. Many taught not in Charleston but at black public schools in surrounding counties where, over time, conditions proved more conducive to teaching black history than they had been during Mamie Garvin Fields's early days on James Island. Taking advantage of a lack of white oversight, they infused their curricula with the African American experience and transformed these black schools into critical guardians of black memories. Isadora Richardson, who taught at a Johns Island elementary school in the 1940s, made sure to teach her black students about Harriet Tubman and Frederick Douglass. "She was the best history teacher we ever had. She was the one who taught us about black history," recalled one student. Leroy Anderson, who served as principal of Gresham Meggett High School on James Island from 1953 until 1960, required that students take black history. Like Avery and the Izzard School, the segregated public schools in and around Charleston reflected an irony of the Jim Crow South. Pushed out of the public sphere and ignored by museums, archives, and other traditional repositories of historical memory, black southerners turned to segregated schools to preserve their own stories about the past.[50]

And when schools neglected black history and memory, families and individuals often stepped into the breach. Many black Charlestonians kept careful records of their family's history in Bibles and scrapbooks. Others shared their knowledge about the city's black history whenever they had the opportunity. Pharmacist John A. McFall captured the imagination of children who visited his drugstore and soda fountain on the corner of Smith and Morris streets, lectured at Dart Hall reading room during Negro History Month, and wrote his own history of Lowcountry African Americans. Sonya Fordham, who attended Charleston public schools in the 1950s and 1960s, remembered hearing little about slavery at school, but at home things were different. "My family talked about slavery every Saturday. It was our Saturday thing." Each week, her grandmother took her to the plantation where her family had labored, pointing out the unmarked graves of deceased slave ancestors. "She wanted me to know, because Philip Lucas, who was the patriarch of the family, always told the family to tell the children what happened, to not let the children forget what slavery was."[51]

This was not a new phenomenon. Antebellum slave narratives testify to the fact that illiterate slaves passed down stories of bondage from generation to generation, forging connections to the enslaved past and those who had endured it. To be sure, some black Charlestonians had little interest in passing on such stories after emancipation. Leroy Anderson, for instance, was discouraged by his mother from tracing his family history because her side of the family had much deeper roots in slavery than her husband's. But other individuals and families preserved such memories by telling stories and saving artifacts. Like Fordham, Anderson's Avery classmate Eugene C. Hunt was schooled in the past by his grandmother and her friends.[52]

The prosperous Harleston family kept documents relating to the emancipation of their kin. "One is the Bill of Sale delivered to my Great-great grandmother in 1804 when she bought herself and Flora her little daughter from slavery—brave woman," wrote artist Edwin Harleston to his wife after he discovered these papers. "The other is the deed of emancipation and manumission which she presented to her daughter Flora in 1820 that this daughter might marry then as a 'free person of color' not being owned even by her mother." Edwin Harleston also gave public addresses to commemorate emancipation and its most famous proponents. In 1919, he joined Thomas E. Miller on the program for the Lincoln-Douglass Memorial Meeting of Charleston's NAACP branch. Seven years later, Harleston was the orator for the annual Emancipation Day ceremony, which was held at the Morris Street Baptist Church.[53]

Just as white memories of slavery were often rife with distortions and fabrications, the stories that black Charlestonians told about slavery were not always reliable. In the late 1930s, Dart Hall librarian Susan Dart Butler told African American author and Federal Writers' Project (FWP) employee Augustus Ladson that Denmark Vesey and his co-conspirators had been hanged from a large oak tree situated in the middle of Ashley Avenue. Although apocryphal, this story, and similar ones, attained wide purchase in the twentieth century. When W.E.B. Du Bois wrote in 1931 about a recent trip to Charleston, for instance, he raved that one of the sites he had seen was the large tree where Vesey's colleagues had been hanged. This tale remained popular among black and white Charlestonians, even after the Ashley Oak was removed in 1973.[54]

Former slaves interviewed by Augustus Ladson in the late 1930s as part of the FWP ex-slave narrative initiative also traded specious stories about the legal protections afforded slaves in Charleston. Henry Brown insisted that when an enslaved person fled to the Work House, "he could disown his master an' the State wouldn't le' him take you," while Susan Hamilton suggested that disgruntled slaves could go to the Work House and sell themselves. A few years later, Elijah Green, an elderly freedman who regularly sat in front of Ryan's Mart, the former slave auction complex at 6 Chalmers Street, told a Pennsylvania couple that he had seen thousands of slaves sold from the mart's balcony. This property, which had been turned into the Old Slave Mart Museum in 1938, had in fact been the site of many slave sales in the late 1850s and early 1860s. But historical research confirms that the balcony and second floor were constructed after 1877.[55]

Black memories of slavery were also just as likely to be shaped by personal and familial circumstances as were those of whites. The small group of black Charlestonians whose ancestors had owned slaves remembered the practice as a vehicle for the protection or even liberation of family and friends. A story about the city's black slaveholders, which was published in the *News and Courier* on May 18, 1907, sparked a flurry of letters to the editor and eventually national coverage. Many whites, apparently, had forgotten that a few black Charlestonians had once been slaveholders. Editor James Hemphill and his staff confessed that they had no idea how or why these African American slaveholders came to own slaves, adding, "we were informed yesterday that these colored people bought their slaves just as slaves were purchased by the white people, and that they managed them very much in the same way." Anticipating a staple argument of Confederate apologists today, one intended to absolve white southerners of the sin of slavery, the *News and Courier* then claimed that blacks readily dealt in their "own flesh and blood."[56]

Several prominent African American citizens took issue with this *News and Courier* column. They did not dispute the fact that some black Charlestonians had owned slaves before the Civil War, but rather the claim that they had done so for financial gain. On May 21, James H. Holloway wrote the *News and Courier* that his grandfather Richard— like "the majority of slave owners among the free persons of color" in the city—had bought slaves with benevolence, not profit, in mind. Holloway cited three of Richard's slave purchases, all of which reflected his grandfather's desire to help slaves obtain liberty or to protect them from being sold away from their families. On one level, Holloway's letter resembles the apologia offered up by planters and their kin. It is worth noting, too, that Holloway neglected to acknowledge the fact that when his grandfather died his estate had to sell off several slaves, one to an owner in Key West, Florida. In contrast to most whites in Charleston, however, James Holloway did not use such convenient omissions, nor his grandfather's seemingly benevolent purchases, to whitewash slavery. Instead, he portrayed Richard Holloway as a compassionate man who bought slaves in order to mitigate the negative effects of slavery or speed the emancipation of the enslaved.[57]

A corrective sent by black minister and newspaper editor John L. Dart, Susan Dart Butler's father, took Holloway's implicit critique of slavery one step further. "What I especially desire to call attention to in this letter," wrote Dart, "is the fact that the slave-holding negroes of that day were not such because they loved the unjust traffic in the flesh and blood of their own people nor because they were in sympathy with the oppressive institution of slavery." On the contrary, Charleston's free people of color had humane motives, and through their purchases "many poor and suffering slaves were rescued from cruel and hard taskmasters" and eventually attained their freedom.[58]

Other black Charlestonians had to wrestle with their enslaved forebears' nuanced perspectives on slavery. Growing up in early-twentieth-century Charleston, Marcellus Forrest learned about slavery from his father, Edward A. Forrest, who as a young man was sold away from his Virginia family and brought to the South Carolina city. Unsurprisingly, this sale left a bitter taste in Edward's mouth. After the Civil War, he tried in vain to locate his mother, brothers, and sisters. Yet Edward Forrest fondly remembered John Blake White, the master who had bought and brought him to Charleston, calling him "his friend and benefactor." He also had positive memories of White's two sons, who had secretly taught him to read and write, thereby preparing Edward for his postbellum career as a minister. In the end, however, Edward's love for the Whites did not mean that he loved the institution of slavery. As his son Marcellus put it, Edward was "glad when his freedom had come." He suffered like "so many had suffered . . . from slavery."[59]

Born a few years after Marcellus Forrest, civil rights leader Septima Poinsette Clark grew up listening to her father's stories, too. Unlike most other African Americans who labored on the Georgetown, South Carolina, plantation where he had been enslaved, Peter Poinsette worked not in the rice fields but as a butler. Perhaps reflecting this privileged position, his Old South reminiscences described the inhumanity of slavery without condemning the institution. Poinsette told his daughter of "the practice of some slave owners in the old days . . . who buried dead slaves miles away from the big house at night in order not to interfere with the next day's work." He also remembered that as an older boy he had accompanied his master's children to school, carrying their books while they rode on horseback. Poinsette would then sit outside the school all day while the two white children learned. These experiences did not seem to embitter him toward slavery or his owners, however. Peter would not have supported someone like Denmark Vesey, his daughter explained, for he did not share his deep opposition to the peculiar institution. He recounted tales of slaves being whipped for stealing meat from the smokehouse not with outrage but with amusement, and he took pride in his service as a Confederate manservant during the Civil War.

Septima Clark, for her part, turned her father's tales of the past into a lesson for her own future. Peter's seeming contentment in bondage reinforced in his daughter the idea that civil rights organizing required a great deal of patience. Activists, she concluded, had to learn to build coalitions between people with a range of experiences and perspectives. She also found his silences telling. "I never heard him speak of a father at all," recalled Clark, suggesting that Peter Poinsette may have been, like so many slaves, the product of sexual violence. Some memories of slavery were transmitted without using words at all.[60]

* * * *

IN 1926, FIFTY years after the advent of the Too-la-loo, the *News and Courier* published a nostalgic story about the bygone tradition. "The 'Too-la-loo' has passed, as have so many customs of the older days," observed the paper. Reflecting white historical amnesia about the black tradition, and about the concerted effort to shut it down, this column presented Too-la-loo not as a raucous celebration of liberty but rather as an expression of "the spirit of the negro of the Old South—a spirit that lent color and a certain quaint charm to his actions and which has now all but disappeared as a racial attribute." By the mid-1920s, in other words, white residents were able to lament the dance's demise in much the same way that they lamented the disappearance of the loyal slave. Indeed, one year later, the Plantation Melody Singers, a group of elite Charlestonians who dressed up like former slaves and performed Old South spirituals before enthusiastic white crowds, included a dance called the "Too-la-loo" in one of its shows.[61]

Black Charlestonians no doubt harbored different memories of Too-la-loo as well as of other traditions and practices. Yet like the segregationist policies that undermined the city's freedom festivals, the memory work that white Charlestonians began pursuing in the early twentieth century ensured that the black past remained hidden behind the Jim Crow veil. As local whites increasingly became invested in both historical preservation and tourism, they facilitated an important change. They recast the repositories of historical memory by turning to the vernacular cityscape rather than to symbolic statuary and public spaces. This made it more difficult for blacks to write their history, or any honest accounting of the enslaved past, into the commemorative landscape. It was one thing to protest a statue that honored a proslavery politician or that praised the virtues of old-time "darkeys." It was quite another to dislodge a historical memory that was made manifest everywhere the eye turned, especially in a place that claimed to be America's Most Historic City.[62]

6

America's
Most Historic City

ON FEBRUARY 13, 1906, BOSTON MINISTER GEORGE F.
Durgin sailed out of New York City amidst a rainstorm. Clearer skies
greeted his ship four days later as it steamed into Charleston Harbor on
Saturday morning. Despite the inviting weather, the crew advised the
passengers not to disembark early, as residents got up late. After spending
the day wandering around the sleepy city, it appeared to Durgin as if the
city never awoke at all. The city's drowsy atmosphere was compounded
by its dilapidated appearance. Apart from several public buildings and
one gorgeous residential neighborhood, Charleston seemed entirely neglected by its occupants. "Paint is wanting everywhere; churches need
renovation," Durgin observed. "It looks as though the city had slept right
through the earthquake of twenty years ago, and was waiting patiently
for the resurrection."[1]

Yet if any place deserved to rise from the dead, Durgin suggested, it
was Charleston. There were so many interesting things to see in the old
city. Durgin's first stop was the grave of John C. Calhoun. Too bad that
Calhoun had fatally wed "all his magnificent powers to a doomed and
unrighteous cause," he concluded. Durgin also visited St. Michael's
Church, noting that he followed in the footsteps of George Washington
and Robert E. Lee, as well as what he thought was the city's slave market.
Simultaneously fascinated and troubled by Charleston's many Lost
Cause memorials, he wrote that "there are Confederate monuments,
with Confederate inscriptions and abounding Confederate sentiment."[2]

When Henry James toured Charleston the previous February, he had
been struck by many of the same things as Durgin: St. Michael's Church,
the quiet city streets, its evocation of the past. To the American author,

who had spent decades living overseas, Charleston seemed not so much asleep as empty. Comparing Charleston to a "vacant cage which used in the other time to emit sounds . . . audible as far away as in the listening North," James wondered how, in such a great society, "can *everything* so have gone?" Could it be that slavery had been "the *only* focus of life" and with its abolition no other interest was left? "To say 'yes' seems the only way to account for the degree of vacancy," he reasoned.[3]

Even so, the beautiful, noble old homes captured his imagination. "I had to take refuge here in the fact that everything appeared thoroughly to *antedate*, to refer itself to the larger, the less vitiated past that had closed a quarter of a century or so before the War," James concluded. Charleston's refuge, he implied, lay in its early years. Passed over by the industrial transformations of the New South, Charleston teemed with magnificent old buildings, which despite (and in some ways because of) their state of disrepair evoked a distant, aristocratic past. For northern tourists like Durgin and James, the city beckoned as a window into a foreign world, a stepping-stone back in time.[4]

* * * *

THE TRANSFORMATION OF Charleston into a tourist mecca was a long one, and not, as it may seem to visitors today, an easy development for a city so steeped in history. The seeds of its eventual success were planted in the years after the Civil War, when a full-blown tourism industry began to take off in the South. Before the war, wealthy planters took their families to the springs of Virginia during the summer, and some northerners, primarily journalists, traveled to the South to document the region's issues. These pilgrimages resumed once hostilities had ceased, and by the 1880s the South had gone from a problem to be explained to a destination to be enjoyed. Part of this change had to do with new patterns of travel. Once the provenance of the elite, travel was democratized during the second half of the nineteenth century. Many northern, middle-class families could now afford tourist excursions, and employers increasingly granted paid vacations.

There was also the special allure of the South, which travel writers and resort owners trumpeted in promotional literature. The region offered salutary benefits—warm weather, mineral springs—for the sick and exhausted. For those unhappy that former stomping grounds like Saratoga had been discovered by the masses, southern locales provided exclusivity. Finally, for individuals suffering from the ennui that accompanied life in the standardized, uniform North, the South presented opportunities for unique experiences, chances to encounter distinctive people and places—unusual foliage, an old plantation, or even an aging Confederate veteran.[5]

Charleston was a tourist attraction during these years, but it certainly was not the primary one. Southbound travelers tended to patronize the spas of Virginia and West Virginia or make their way to the mountains of western North Carolina and eastern Tennessee, viewed as a frontier-like retreat from the modern world. Many others chose the eastern coast of Florida, the most popular southern destination in the late nineteenth century. This growing tourist trade all but bypassed Charleston. Most northern visitors to the city did not make it their final destination; Charleston was simply a stopover en route to and from Florida.[6]

In 1873, Massachusetts-born journalist Edward King did visit Charleston. He immediately recognized that the past exerted a great deal of power in the city. In contrast to "our new and smartly painted Northern towns," King wrote, "in Charleston the houses and streets have an air of dignified repose and solidity." Oliver Bell Bunce, a New York journalist writing for *Appleton's Journal*'s "Picturesque America" series, visited Charleston in the early 1870s, too. "It is quite possible," Bunce observed, "the somewhat rude surface and antique color of the brick houses of Charleston would fail to please the taste of Northerners reared amid the supreme newness of our always reconstructing cities."[7]

But Charleston was picturesque to those who knew where to look and how to appreciate it—a project these writers' travelogues helped facilitate—providing just the contrast and novelty many northern travelers sought. Constance Woolson, who described the city for *Harper's* in 1875, delighted in its ancient homes and gardens, which had not "been swept away by the crowding population, the manufactories, the haste and bustle, of the busy North." Woolson, King, and Bunce all waxed rhapsodic about the ruins they stumbled upon, reliquaries of a former civilization or, like the many plantations outside the city, "sorrowful ghosts lamenting the past."[8]

Charleston appealed as a vacation spot the same way a quaint New England village did, as a preindustrial refuge from modern life. According to these writers, the plantations outside of the city existed to enchant. Every spring, Woolson observed, northern tourists, stopping over in Charleston on the way home from Florida, visited Magnolia Plantation, which had burned during the war but whose "bewitchingly lovely" gardens were opened to the public in 1870. Many lost themselves in "the glowing aisles of azaleas." Bunce was also taken with Magnolia. "This place is almost a paradise," he exclaimed, overwhelmed by how the "tropical splendor of bloom" combined with the "overgrown pathways, unweeded beds, and the blackened walls of the homestead" to create a scene of both beauty and desolation.[9]

But race and the vestiges of slavery made Charleston distinct from northern destinations. At Magnolia, where freedmen who lived and worked on the plantation guided visitors through the grounds, Bunce and his party were welcomed by an elderly man "with all the dignity and deportment of the old school." Edward King found that Lowcountry blacks "still maintain their old-time servility toward their former masters" and that whites, when asked if their former slaves had changed much in manners or habits since emancipation, answered with an emphatic, "No!" Ex-slaves exuded an exoticism that proved irresistible to northern white travelers. In both the city and the surrounding countryside, blacks were a spectacle, their sartorial preferences for "gay colors" and "extravagant" and "gaudy" apparel a wonder to these northern eyes. Though it may have been low and degraded, African American character ultimately offered "an endless source of amusement."[10]

From the beginnings of postwar Charleston tourism, then, African Americans were a tourist attraction, like the antiquated churches and plantations that made the area so unique. White visitors saw them— barely removed from an Old South setting, if at all—as a picturesque, even entertaining, aspect of the local scenery. These portraits of blacks functioned like magnolias and Spanish moss, as "a signifier of the Old South" to northern tourists not only craving novelty but also taken with fantasies of white supremacy and black docility. In this way, the remnants of slavery, whether human or architectural, helped foster sectional reconciliation, their aesthetic attributes deflecting from their political content. Oliver Bunce wrote that his outing to the plantations along the Ashley River united his traveling companions—a varied group of northerners, southerners, and Englishmen—in a spirit of amicable camaraderie, defusing the sectional tensions that still smoldered in the 1870s: "The political elements composing the party were as antagonistic as possible; but, regardless of North or South, the Ku-Klux, or the fifteenth amendment, we gathered in peace."[11]

What stands out most about this northern travel literature is the way that it differs from local guidebooks of the same era. The *Charleston City Guide*, issued in 1872, and the *Guide to Charleston*, published in 1875 and again in 1884, barely acknowledged that blacks were a part of the area's past or present at all. These locally produced books also kept the institution of slavery at arm's length, never alluding to its role in making possible Charlestonians' "accumulation of great wealth" or in inciting the Civil War. More generally, these Charleston tourism tracts contained few, if any, of the colorful descriptions of plantations or even contemporary African Americans that northern travel writers provided to their readers. Unlike King, Bunce, and Woolson, in other words, early Charleston tourism writers seemed unaware of the fact that visitors might be drawn to former slaves and plantation ruins as alluring reminders of days gone by. Instead, they simply pointed out the places within the city that tourists should put on their itinerary—from religious sites and government buildings to educational institutions and public parks.[12]

As local guidebooks attest, by the 1870s and 1880s a few Charlestonians, at least, appreciated that some of their city's charms were worth promoting. The natural calamities that brought the Lowcountry to its knees, however, did not make the prospect easy. An 1885 hurricane and the 1886 earthquake caused millions of dollars in damages, funneling scarce resources into rebuilding efforts. Still, enterprising Charlestonians knew an opportunity when they saw one. Frank Dawson, Frederick W. Wagener, and other businessmen organized Gala Week for November 1887, deciding to use the recent disaster to their advantage. This "monster excursion," as Dawson called it, would bring in throngs of tourists to witness the city's post-earthquake progress, to see that it was now "a bright, clean, vigorous city, full of life and activity." He was right. By the middle of Gala Week, hotels were so overcrowded that proprietors turned billiard tables into makeshift beds.[13]

If Charleston was going to attract more tourists, it needed better amenities. In 1888, Frederick W. Wagener led a campaign to build a new hotel at the Battery but failed to raise the necessary funds. Four years later, Governor Ben Tillman's dispensary law went into effect, limiting the sale of alcohol to state-run dispensaries. While Charlestonians ignored the law, drinking at home or in "blind tigers," early versions of speakeasies, the statute proved a thorn in the side of tourism boosters since hotels and restaurants could not satisfy patrons desiring a drink.[14]

Despite these setbacks, enthusiasm for tourism ran high among Charleston's New South boosters, and the end of the nineteenth century gave birth to several major efforts to attract visitors to the city. The Young Men's Business League organized a South Carolina reunion of Confederate veterans in 1898, which in turn inspired a larger campaign to attract the 1899 national meeting of the United Confederate Veterans, considered a resounding success. The 1901–2 South Carolina Inter-State and West Indian Exposition represented a bright spot for tourism as well, though the fair ultimately failed to pay its own bills. Owing to a combination of problems—including local indifference, inclement weather, and black opposition—the Exposition was the first of its kind to be put into receivership.[15]

Henry James's 1905 trip to Charleston—where, as he wrote, "history has been the right great artist"—came on the heels of these events. Like so many northern travelers who had visited Charleston since the end of the Civil War, James was smitten, almost despite himself. Even though the Old South that James glimpsed in Charleston "was the one that had been so utterly in the wrong," he preferred it to the New South, which had "not yet quite found the effective way romantically." Looking around the city, he concluded "that the South is in the predicament of having to be tragic, as it were, in order to beguile."[16]

* * * *

CHARLESTON TOURISM BOOSTERS happily played to this beguilingly tragic aesthetic by showcasing their majestic mansions with peeling paint and unkempt gardens. Most of them recoiled, however, at visitor interest in artifacts and sites that spoke—or at least appeared to speak—to the human tragedy of slavery too directly. Northern tourists, for one, clamored to take home their own slave badges, relics unique to Charleston's antebellum system of urban slavery. Used as early as the 1750s, slave badges—pieces of metal stamped with the year of issue, a

Charleston required slaves hired out by their masters to carry or wear metal slave badges such as these. At the end of the nineteenth century, local merchants began hawking badges, many fake, to tourists.

badge number, and an occupational category—identified Charleston slaves hired out by their owners to work for someone else.[17]

Demand for the now obsolete tags was not an immediate postwar development, as white Charlestonians, and some blacks, at least, appear to have forgotten about their existence. A *News and Courier* article in 1889 reported that "a lot of old brass pass badges which were used by slaves before the war" had been obtained by a stockbroker from an elderly black man, an event that prompted much talk around the city. Six years after the stockbroker's discovery, some collectors in Charleston concluded that the badges might appeal to relic seekers. In 1895, a vendor placed a wanted ad in the *Evening Post*, soliciting Confederate money, Confederate buttons, and slave badges, presumably to sell them as souvenirs.[18]

By the time the Exposition opened in 1901, the tourist market for slave badges—both real and counterfeit—was roaring, a development that did not sit well with some. Daniel Elliott Huger Smith, a Confederate veteran who was a leading member of the South Carolina Historical Society from the 1890s until the early 1930s, denounced this "most ridiculous trade" in which "very ordinary bits of brass" were sold as slave badges at steep prices. "Doubtless many have been dispersed over the North," he ventured, "as curiosities of slavery."[19]

The most detailed report of this activity came from John Bennett, an Ohio-born artist and writer who himself arrived as a tourist in 1898 and never left. Four years earlier, Bennett had vacationed at Salt Sulphur

Springs, West Virginia, where he befriended the Smythe family of Charleston—Augustine, his wife, Louisa, and their daughter, Susan. After a series of illnesses affected his health, Bennett chose to recuperate in Charleston. By 1899, John and Susan were engaged.[20]

Like so many northern visitors, Bennett was taken with the city and its environs. Of Medway, a plantation outside the city where the couple spent time before their wedding, Bennett wrote that it was "the pathos and sadness that hangs over everything in this land that wrings me closest [to] the heart." When, a few months before the couple's April 1902 wedding, Bennett discovered that downtown shops were pedaling slave badges—most of which were counterfeits—to tourists in the city for the Exposition, he was naturally interested. But after talking to a few of these unsuspecting visitors, combing through Augustine's law books, and consulting any number of "the genuine old negro of the genuine old days," Bennett grew indignant. Both the buyers and sellers earned his scorn—the former for their mistaken impressions of the peculiar institution, the latter for catering to such notions with fake artifacts and fake history.[21]

In a *News and Courier* article intended to set the record straight, Bennett's sarcasm was palpable. He took a jab at tourists, who were "full of innocent Northern eagerness to carry home a trophy, some trophy of 'the old, old South' of the days when every morning made a mock of the Fourth of July with the re-echoing and explosive cracks of the 'nigger driver's whip,' when all the swamps were full of runaway slaves." Trinket-shop owners on King Street obliged this curiosity, he wrote, by offering what they claimed to be slave badges but were really nothing more than tags for railroad lockers. Rather than detailing the real purpose of the badges in the hiring-out system, these unscrupulous entrepreneurs told tourists that they were substitutes for brands that allowed owners to claim runaway slaves. Some dealers went so far as to imply that the tags had been affixed to slaves' bodies with safety pins or metal rings.[22]

Bennett lay part of the blame for the misinformation surrounding slave badges at the feet of white Charlestonians, especially the younger generation. It knew nothing of slavery and the Old South and could not refute the tall tales spun by King Street dealers. He also had harsh words for Harriet Beecher Stowe, the South's perennial scapegoat. The average tourist, he complained, was proud of his "precious relic of 'the old regime' so maligned by Harriet Stowe, who must stand to the end responsible for many just such frauds as this," thus proclaiming the faked slave badges—in an extraordinary leap of logic—one of Stowe's many odious legacies.[23]

In addition to the slave badges, local businesses peddled postcards that spoke to slavery and the slave trade. One early-twentieth-century postcard featured a picture of buzzards and a lady in front of the City Market stalls, described as "a part of the Old Slave Market," a common but somewhat confusing term used to describe the open-air sheds. Although slaves had worked in the City Market stalls—hawking meat, fish, and produce—human chattel had not been sold there. Intentionally or not, postcards like this one led some tourists to mistake it for a slave auction site. After exploring the complex in 1906, Illinois-born poet Vachel Lindsay wrote that he felt like he was "being stifled in bloody tiger lilies." On the one hand, Lindsay found "packed in those long stalls the ghosts of a wonderful civilization." On the other hand, "there is a clanking of chains and a rattle of angry skeletons." Visitors in this period could also buy postcards that featured an actual slave market, the former Ryan's Mart at 6 Chalmers Street. A 1920s card of this building—which was referred to interchangeably as the Old Slave Mart and the Old Slave Market in the early twentieth century—proclaimed it "a dilapidated but quaint little structure" that "is all that remains of the once flourishing traffic in slaves."[24]

This postcard was somewhat exceptional, as forthright discussion about the city's slave-trading past was rare. An updated 1911 *Guide to Charleston, S.C.*, which drew on the earlier 1875 and 1884 versions, listed the "Old Slave Market, So-Called" at 6 Chalmers Street in its street-by-street narrative of historic sites. Its very inclusion seems to have been a result of tourist interest. "Many visitors to the city," the text read, "particularly those who have imbibed the traditional prejudices against old time Southern slavery, enquire for the tourists' traditional 'Slave Market.'" "As a matter of fact no such market existed in the city," asserted the guidebook, penned by Confederate memory stalwart Cornelius Irvine Walker. The *Guide to Charleston, S.C.* allowed that slave brokers did, in fact, conduct sales from several buildings in "the neighborhood

Ryan's Mart at 6 Chalmers Street was the city's leading slave-trading site in the late 1850s and early 1860s. To the consternation of some whites, it became a popular tourist destination in the early twentieth century.

of Broad, State and Church Streets," but it nonetheless held that "no general market" for the sale of slaves existed. What's more, Walker held that "most of the Southern owners of slaves never sold them, and the workers on the various plantations passed by inheritance from father to son."[25]

The eagerness of northern tourists to confront the slave past in its less sanitized form surprised and annoyed Walker and some of his fellow residents—though not all, as the thriving business in slave badges and postcards suggests. Tourist interest threatened not only to air their ancestors' dirty laundry in public but also to spoil the feeling of sectional reconciliation many tourist encounters were intended to nurture. Yet controversy sold. Indeed, Civil War prison camps became tourist attractions in the late nineteenth and early twentieth centuries, at least in part because of their divisive nature. In 1899, a group of northern businessmen purchased and moved a Confederate prison from Richmond, Virginia, to their hometown of Chicago, where they operated the Libby War Museum for the next decade. Southerners also capitalized on the commercial potential of Civil War prisons. In the mid-1890s, the residents of Thomasville, Georgia, seized on the town's proximity to the infamous Andersonville Prison as an economic boon. The *Thomasville Review* advertised Andersonville as a "must see" site that was a "Mecca for thousands of tourists each year."[26]

* * * *

NOT ALL CHARLESTON tourists, of course, were white. "The number of excursionists that are brought to Charleston every week would populate a large town," reported the *Indianapolis Freeman*, quoting an unidentified black Charleston newspaper in 1890, which stated that African Americans were among this tourist throng, even though "they cry poor." Where these tourists were from, and what they did and visited once they arrived, is not entirely clear. Did they buy slave badges, real or otherwise? Did they read the same guidebooks as white visitors?[27]

The city was not overly interested in the African American tourism market during these years, but it did attempt to attract black tourists to the Exposition in 1901–2. The effort largely fell flat. As a writer for a black Washington, D.C., newspaper attested, Charleston did not necessarily strike African American visitors as charming. On a trip to the city in the run-up to the Exposition, he was asked by a local if he liked Charleston. "Presumably," he quipped, "the asker of any such question never expects to get a frank and honest expression of opinion from the person to whom it is addressed." To this tourist, Charleston seemed hopelessly hidebound by tradition, a charge he leveled against both white and black residents. He found the deference to tradition off-putting. The "slowness with which they move and the tendency not to do things simply because it is not custom," he complained, "unnerves me and irritates me almost beyond expression."[28]

One wonders if this writer took issue with the area's racial customs, for some travelers certainly did. William D. Crum, assistant commissioner of the Negro Department at the Exposition, observed that poor train facilities prevented many African Americans from other cities and states from attending the world's fair. The *New York Age* heard reports that "all sorts of discriminations were permitted on the Exposition grounds" and concluded that black tourists would have numbered in the thousands had these issues been addressed.[29]

Still, some African Americans ignored the inconveniences of Jim Crow travel—which included the fact that the first hotels catering to black visitors did not open until the second decade of the twentieth century—and put Charleston on their itinerary. One man writing for the *Indianapolis Freeman* in 1905, who signed his essay as simply a "Wanderer," insisted that "historic old Charleston is worth the price of a visit." In stark contrast to the Lost Cause vision pedaled by local chapters of the UDC and UCV, he urged an emancipationist reading of Civil War sites in the area. Fort Sumter, argued the Wanderer, demanded attention. This was so because it "is almost as closely associated with our emancipation as the proclamation itself." He also reminded readers that the harbor in which the fort sat had provided the backdrop for Robert Smalls's daring escape aboard a Confederate supply boat. According to the Wanderer, Charleston Harbor was to be celebrated for its connection to black freedom.[30]

The Wanderer also commented upon the Calhoun Monument, noting that the city had outgrown the statue, "as the greater portion of it is now in the rear of the man in bronze," an accurate assessment of the city's northward population shift. But he intended the observation metaphorically as well: "As the city has outgrown the monument so too this great people are outgrowing many things for which Mr. Calhoun stood." Rather than condemning the statue as a symbol of both slavery and segregation, as local blacks were inclined to do, the Wanderer viewed the memorial as a relic from a bygone era. As proof, he listed black Charlestonians who excelled as teachers, businessmen, ministers, and lawyers. Signing off with a plea for all to promote goodwill between the two races in the city, the Wanderer's optimistic reading of the Calhoun Monument would surely have struck some black residents as naive.[31]

A number of leading African Americans visited Charleston in the early twentieth century, too. In 1906, Archibald Grimké, his brother Francis, and three other well-known black South Carolinians who had moved north came back home. They rode a trolley through the center of the city and visited several historical sites, including Calhoun's tomb. A decade later, just after local black activists founded the Charleston chapter of the NAACP, W.E.B. Du Bois traveled to the city. Mamie Garvin Fields was part of the committee that gave the black scholar and reformer what they thought of as the "grand tour." They drove a car around town, visiting the old Custom House and the Old Slave Mart, among other sites. As Fields later recalled, "Most of those places that we showed off with all our city pride had to do with slavery, which brought our people to South Carolina in the first place." Du Bois, however, was not interested in seeing these vestiges of the Old South. "All you are showing me is what the white people did," he announced at one point. "I want to see what the colored people of Charleston have built." His guides then took him to the black YMCA and YWCA, but Du Bois dismissed them as the outposts of national organizations and chided Fields and her colleagues to do more.[32]

Du Bois was more charitable toward Charleston's black institutions in an editorial he penned for the *Crisis* not long after his trip. "Mighty are the churches of colored Charleston," he proclaimed. And as he reconstructed his visit to the capital of American slavery, Du Bois found that human bondage permeated his memories. "Between her guardian rivers and looking across the sea toward Africa," he wrote of the city, "sits this little Old Lady (her cheek teasingly tinged to every tantalizing shade of the darker blood) with her shoulder ever toward the street and her little laced and rusty fan beside her cheek, while long verandas of her soul stretch down the backyard into slavery." He saw slavery's shadow in black churches such as St. Mark's Episcopal Church, which had been "softened with the souls of fathers and grandfathers who knew Cato of Stono, and Denmark Vesey." While resting "in the quiet reason of Plymouth Church," founded by former slaves after emancipation, Du Bois looked across town "to the white tower of St. Michael's, topping a church of another and seemingly lesser world where a slave once did the deed of a man."[33]

* * * *

THE REAL PUSH to attract white tourists to Charleston came after World War I. The war itself proved instrumental, halting American tourist traffic to Europe and redirecting it toward domestic resorts. The advent of automobile tourism also helped, since formerly inaccessible places—and Charleston, with its minimal rail service, was certainly among them—awaited discovery by the adventurous motorist. But the first task on this front was improving the region's dangerous and at times incomplete roads. Formed in 1921, the South Atlantic Coastal Highway Association spearheaded the good roads effort in the Lowcountry, planning an Atlantic Coast Highway that linked Wilmington, North

Carolina, to Jacksonville, Florida, and that passed through Charleston. The project was completed by the end of the decade, the peninsula now connected to the Sea Islands, beaches, and plantations that surrounded it by bridges over the Ashley and Cooper rivers. Easier travel to outlying plantations was especially important, as many tourists hoped to take in the famous "flower gardens," the common term for area plantations, during their stay in Charleston.[34]

Thomas Stoney, elected mayor in 1923, made tourism a priority from his first days in office. He informed Charlestonians in his inaugural address that he would promote the city as a tourist resort in every possible manner. The next year, he proclaimed Charleston "America's Most Historic City," while at the same time advocating for the modern amenities a thriving tourism industry demanded—paved streets, electric lights, an improved rail station, and, over time, a new airport, a city golf course, and a yacht basin. Charleston welcomed two new luxury hotels in 1924. The first, the Francis Marion, sat at the western edge of Marion Square and stood as a testament to the changing order in Charleston. A group of local investors bought the land and raised the $1,250,000 needed to complete the 312-room structure. The Fort Sumter Hotel, which could accommodate 350 guests, welcomed its first visitors early that summer. Built on the Battery, the spot Frederick Wagener had coveted back in 1888 and deemed holy ground by some, the hotel provided vistas of Charleston Harbor and Fort Sumter.[35]

Private initiatives complemented municipal efforts to turn Charleston into a tourist resort. For the Society for the Preservation of Old Dwellings (SPOD), however, the immediate goal was not to show off the city's treasures, but simply to save them. Organized by a coterie of elite Charlestonians, the SPOD looked around the city with growing alarm. The encroachment of modernity, in addition to years of neglect born of the aristocracy's relative lack of capital, endangered some of Charleston's grandest and most historic homes. In April 1920, Susan Pringle Frost, the group's first president, gathered together twenty-nine women and three men to stop the demolition of the Joseph Manigault House, located not too far from Marion Square. This excellent example of Adam-style architecture, which had been built in 1802–3 for rice planter Joseph Manigault, was to be replaced by automobile garages. The Manigault House was not alone. By the end of the decade, the SPOD had also turned its attention to saving the Heyward-Washington House, which sat next to Cabbage Row—rechristened "Catfish Row" by DuBose Heyward in his 1925 novel *Porgy*.[36]

To rescue these homes and return them to their former glory, the women of the SPOD raised money, donated furniture, and educated the public about the importance of maintaining Charleston's distinctive architectural treasures. In their personal quest to maintain the Miles Brewton House—the residence that had dazzled Bostonian Josiah Quincy back in 1773 and later became the Pringle ancestral home— Susan Pringle Frost and her sisters not only led tours but also raised revenue by renting rooms in the winter to visiting northerners. The lengths to which SPOD members went to salvage homes sometimes strained the limits of good sense. In 1922, Nell Pringle, vice president of the SPOD and Frost's cousin by marriage, convinced her soon-to-be-unemployed husband to assume the debts of the Manigault House, which totaled $40,000, placing a considerable burden upon the family of eight.[37]

This early preservation movement also contributed to the whitening of the peninsula. As was true across the rest of the Jim Crow South, segregation, racial violence, and declining economic prospects drove many black Charlestonians northward in the early twentieth century. By 1930,

A postcard, ca. 1901, of the Miles Brewton House. Preservationist Susan Pringle Frost and her sisters rented out rooms and led tours to raise money to maintain this double house on lower King Street.

both the city and the state of South Carolina had a white majority. Preservationists simultaneously turned the lower portions of the peninsula into white enclaves. Tradd Street, which one Charlestonian complained "was infested with negro dives of the lowest kind whose . . . orgies keep up all night," earned Susan Pringle Frost's ire in the late 1910s and 1920s. She oversaw the restoration of homes on the street and the concurrent removal of black tenants, who were forced to make way for white residents. "Today it is one of the most popular and attractive residential streets in the city," Alston Deas, the first male president of the SPOD, proclaimed in 1928. The SPOD and other preservationists, in short, played a major role in instituting residential segregation in a city that had historically been integrated.[38]

Significantly, too, the SPOD insisted that its work was commensurate with a modern, thriving Charleston. Historic preservation not only protected the city's priceless cultural heritage but also acted as a tourist draw (attracting money to defray the costs of preservation in the process) and fit with the commercial development of the city. "I want to emphasize that members of our society are not opposed to progress," wrote Rosa M. Marks in a letter to the *News and Courier.* "We are most anxious to see industries and everything that would advance a city commercially come to Charleston and we will do every thing to help. But we want them properly located and not at the expense of the beauty and charm of Charleston's distinctiveness." After all, Marks argued, "this distinctiveness annually brings so many visitors to our city." Mayor Stoney shared the preservationists' vision. In 1929, he urged the city council to create the City Planning and Zoning Commission, and under his stewardship Charleston became the first city in the United States to pass a planning and zoning ordinance, which designated twenty-three downtown blocks as the "Old and Historic District." The 1931 ordinance also created the Board of Architectural Review to approve architectural changes to structures in the protected district.[39]

With this act, the city acknowledged the economic value of its old buildings, effectively rejecting those who were skeptical about a future that was too indebted to the past. Although tensions between proponents of preservation and development persisted, the city threw its economic lot in with history. Commodifying Charleston's past represented the most realistic route to economic progress. By 1929–30, the roughly 47,000 tourists who visited contributed $4 million to the local economy, making tourism the city's largest industry. But Charleston had to be on guard. Two other cities took issue with its claim to be America's Most Historic City and hoped to reap their just rewards from the title. Fredericksburg, Virginia, spoke out first, challenging the Charleston Chamber of Commerce to a debate on the issue. Williamsburg then joined the fray, and though it ridiculed the debate as a stunt "beneath [our] dignity," it defended its superior antiquity. "If they want history," one resident announced, "let them come to Williamsburg to get it."[40]

* * * *

NOTWITHSTANDING THE CHALLENGES of its Virginia rivals, plenty of tourists went to Charleston for their history in the interwar period. The stories they heard had been carefully crafted by a group of local whites eager to showcase their city's attractions and reaffirm their vision of the past. The women of the SPOD, for example, believed that the overzealous pursuit of modernity threatened both ancient buildings and white historical memory. If they lost the former, they also lost the latter—"an old order of culture," in Susan Pringle Frost's words. After the SPOD incorporated in 1928 and was reorganized under male leadership, the organization successfully lobbied the state legislature for tax exemptions for two of its houses and acquired federal funding for preservation efforts. By the late 1920s, the private spaces of the white elite were gradually becoming the sites of official public memory, supported by the weight of individual citizens and government institutions alike.[41]

The female members of the SPOD, for their part, hoped to defend a romantic memory of domesticity. As they ushered visitors through the homes they had rescued, these preservationists framed the dwellings as repositories of familial, and feminine, values, regaling tourists with legends of those who had lived there. They also stressed the colonial, revolutionary, and antebellum significance of the homes they guarded. SPOD members did little to connect them to secession, the Civil War, or slavery. Their work—and their particular brand of historical amnesia—played to the Colonial Revival craze of their day. Even locals with family histories that spoke more directly to the sectional crisis, such as Josephine Rhett Bacot, who was the daughter and grand-daughter of antebellum fire-eaters Robert B. Rhett Jr. and Robert B. Rhett Sr., stressed that Charleston was "pre-eminently a Colonial city."[42]

More generally, tourist narratives like the SPOD's reflected the broader desire for sectional reconciliation ushered in by the Spanish-American War and World War I, as well as for a national culture constructed from a shared past. Although Confederate memory groups remained popular in the city, many early-twentieth-century Charlestonians acted as if they, too, were ready to let the war go. On the fiftieth anniversary of the firing on Fort Sumter in 1911, for instance, locals decided not to stage any public commemoration of the event. And tours to Fort Sumter, potentially the most divisive site to northern visitors, promoted reconciliation rather than recalling past antagonisms. Beginning in 1926, cruise boats left twice a day from a pier near the Fort Sumter Hotel, carrying thousands of tourists to the island fort every year by the end of the 1930s. Several small memorials on the grounds—one to Major Robert Anderson, another to Union defenders of the fort—illustrated the site's symbolism of American, rather than Confederate, patriotism. The captain of the boat, a Syrian-born man named Shan Baitary who was a naturalized American citizen, drove home the point. According to one northern travel writer, Baitary finished his tour by "summing up the story of Sumter and expressing satisfaction that we are again a united people under one flag."[43]

Interwar Charlestonians did not entirely elide what they viewed as the unique elements of life in the Lowcountry, nor did they ignore their southern heritage. The SPOD, like similar preservation organizations such as the Society for the Preservation of Spirituals and the short-lived Society for the Preservation of Manners and Customs of the South Carolina Low Country, sought to preserve the region's traditions and culture. Charlestonians were also quick to capitalize on the city's role in the sectional crisis and the Civil War after the publication of *Gone with the Wind* in 1936 and the release of the movie in 1939. In conjunction with the local premiere of the film, the Charleston Museum staged a "Gone with the Wind" exhibition, which ran throughout the winter tourist season. Featuring period dresses, jewelry, and other artifacts, the exhibition was a resounding hit, attracting 23,000 visitors.[44]

Still, the attention the SPOD paid to the city's colonial past, as well as their disinterest in sectionally divisive elements, served to nationalize Charleston's history, better enabling non-Charlestonians to consume and make their own. So, too, did the work of the Historical Commission of Charleston, created by the city council in 1933 to preserve and promote Charleston's history. In 1935, for instance, the commission produced historical dramatizations for radio as a way to advertise Charleston's lively history to listeners near and far. Most of the scripts testified to the commission's deep interest in the city's pirate, colonial, and Revolutionary War history.[45]

On Church Street, where a vibrant row of businesses catering to tourists sprang up during the 1920s, visitors could buy any number of guidebooks and pamphlets to help them learn of the city's history and to determine which sites were worth seeking out. The list of must-sees included many of the same spots tourists had visited since the 1870s, though after 1931 their historical significance was officially affirmed since most of them lay within the protected historic district. A tour designed by the Historical Commission of Charleston took visitors from the Francis Marion Hotel, east along Calhoun past the old Citadel, and down Meeting Street toward the Old Powder Magazine and St. Philip's and the Huguenot churches. After making their way toward to the Battery, they headed back up to Meeting and Broad, passing by various government buildings, and then to Church, Tradd, and Legare streets to view significant Charleston homes. Indicating the influences of the SPOD and other preservationists, visitors were much more likely than before to be pointed toward private residences—like the Heyward/ Washington House, the Miles Brewton House, and the Rutledge, Rhett, Izard, Gibbes, and Elliott homes.[46]

As at the historic homes overseen by preservationists, the literature provided to tourists highlighted the national over the sectional, making little room for the Civil War. And even when the conflict warranted some mention, guidebook writers, like preservationists, ventured no further chronologically, giving the impression that the city's history stopped in 1861. *Picturesque Charleston*, published in 1930, was typical. It celebrated the "varied characteristics of the city's founder stock," describing the English, Caribbean, French, and German origins of its early settlers, Charleston's colorful brushes with piracy, its Revolutionary War skirmishes, and the fact that it was the location of "the first shot of the war between the States." Fast-forwarding through nearly six decades during which apparently nothing of note transpired, *Picturesque Charleston* claimed that today the city was a paradise for "the student of the historic, the searcher after quiet, [and] the sportsman."[47]

The authors of these guidebooks showed their debt to earlier Lost Cause thinkers when it came to slavery, a topic that was not divisive as long as it was presented in a flattering light. A few, like *Picturesque Charleston,* ignored the peculiar institution altogether. Other tourism guidebooks briefly mentioned slavery, if only to deny certain realities about it or defend it. In his 1939 *Charleston: Azaleas and Old Bricks,* Samuel Gaillard Stoney, an elite Charlestonian of Huguenot heritage who was an architect and preservationist, candidly acknowledged that slavery provided "the basis of most of the wealth" in the city. And yet despite its injustices, he insisted that slavery was "suited admirably . . . to the temperament of the Low-Country Negro."[48]

Thomas Petigru Lesesne's 1932 *Landmarks of Charleston*—which remained one of the most popular guides of the city two decades after it was first published—borrowed liberally from Cornelius Irvine Walker's 1911 guidebook in challenging the common description of the Old Slave Mart. Echoing the influential Confederate memory maker, Lesesne questioned the slave-trading history of the Chalmers Street site, calling it the "Mythical Old Slave Market." A descendant of two notable South Carolina families and a longtime *News and Courier* editor, Lesesne explained his objection at length: "Authorities are positive in saying that nowhere in Charleston was there a constituted slave market for the public auctioning of blacks from Africa." Bemoaning that tourists were informed to the contrary, Lesesne also agreed with Walker in concluding that southern slaves "were in better care than were the peasantry in any other part of the world."[49]

* * * *

THE ONE GUIDEBOOK from this period that stood out for the way it addressed slavery was produced, at least in part, by writers who were not native to Charleston. Researched and written by employees of the Federal Writers' Project (FWP), a Works Progress Administration (WPA) program established in 1935, *South Carolina: A Guide to the Palmetto State* placed slavery at the center of the city's and state's history.

Though largely bereft of sites related to the black past, the section on what to see in Charleston listed the Old Slave Mart as one of many places in the city where slaves had been sold. More generally, the guidebook identified slavery as the catalyst for the Civil War and recounted a history of slave insurrections, including Vesey's failed plot, and white efforts to suppress them. A handful of Charlestonians—such as author Herbert Ravenel Sass, who was prone to romantic renderings of slavery in his own writing—served as consultants to the Columbia-based staff. But Louise Jones DuBose, the assistant director of the guide in Columbia and a sociologist by training, pushed her fellow southerners to be open-minded about what went into the guide. Even more influential was the FWP office in Washington, D.C., led by Negro Affairs editor Sterling Brown. A prominent black poet and English professor at Howard University, Brown and his staff closely monitored all state guidebook drafts to make sure that African Americans and their history and culture were neither ignored nor misrepresented.[50]

More remarkable than the WPA's guide was the material assembled by black FWP writers as part of the South Carolina Negro Writers' Project (SCNWP). In 1936, Henry Alsberg, the FWP national director, created the Office of Negro Affairs in order to ensure that African Americans would have a role in researching and writing the WPA state guidebooks. Following Alsberg's instructions, Mabel Montgomery, South Carolina's FWP director, enlisted ten black writers to collect information and draft essays about African American history and culture in South Carolina. These essays were to have been included in the state guide, as well as in a planned Negro Guide, though the latter volume was never published and only a fraction of the research made its way into *South Carolina: A Guide to the Palmetto State*. Still, the draft essays produced by the SCNWP writers, including Charlestonians Mildred Hare, Augustus Ladson, and Robert L. Nelson, outline an alternative approach to the past rooted as much, if not more, in black memory as in white.[51]

More than a dozen of the draft essays explored the history of slavery, emancipation, and Reconstruction. In researching these subjects, the SCNWP authors pushed far beyond traditional (white) source material. Augustus Ladson, for instance, interviewed several black Charlestonians, including Thomas E. Miller, for his history of the Vesey conspiracy. Meanwhile, the essay on slavery in South Carolina referred not only to Edward McCrady's *South Carolina Under Royal Government* but also to the work of pioneering black historians Carter Woodson and W.E.B. Du Bois. Robert L. Nelson likewise balanced the perspective offered by Mary C. Simms Oliphant in her influential textbook *The Simms History of South Carolina* with the insights of Affie Singleton, an eighty-three-year-old former slave.[52]

Overall, the drafts were a far cry from what interwar visitors read when they came to Charleston. Armed with African American sources as well as testimony from ex-slaves and their descendants, the SCNWP writers crafted essays with a fresh and often critical perspective on South Carolina history. One essay, called "Negro Contributions to South Carolina," underscored the horrors of the slave trade: "Slaves were bought and sold at the fairs in markets and at public auction. Family members would be divided, probably not to unite again in life. When love for parent by children and love of children by parent would be expressed in weeping, only whippings followed." Other essays highlighted slaves' quest for education or resistance to bondage. Despite being transported to a foreign land, separated from their family and friends, and distinguished by a skin color that made escape difficult, insisted one piece, "many slaves did run away, suicides were by no means uncommon, and every colony showed the fear of insurrections."[53]

Three essays even offered detailed explications of slave plots and rebellions, including the 1739 Stono Insurrection and Vesey's 1822 conspiracy. And the essay on the Stono uprising went so far as to justify slave rebellion in the name of liberty. "All humanity has the spirit of freedom planted deep within it, and will risk all in the barest hope of gaining it," it began. Later, after highlighting the bloody outcome of the insurrection, the essay concluded that the extent "of the rebellion made it evident that there must have been some substantial cause for this feeling of hatred evinced by so many Negroes toward their masters. The Negro slaves were human, and only a spark was needed to set such tinder into flame."[54]

* * * *

SINCE THE SOUTH Carolina Negro Writers' Project essays remained unpublished, how visitors or tourism officials might have responded to the counternarrative they offered is unclear. It is certainly difficult to

This 1938 tourist brochure, "Charleston Welcomes You," employed the faithful slave trope to advertise "America's Most Historic City."

imagine a white Charlestonian admitting that rebellion was a reasonable response to enslavement. One simply did not say such things, even when prompted by tourists. Instead, most interwar Charleston boosters answered visitor interest in slavery by channeling it in a direction they preferred—by showcasing the loyal slave and his modern-day descendant. In her popular *Street Strolls Around Charleston, South Carolina*, Miriam Bellangee Wilson teased visitors with the possibility that they might see a mammy, or "mauma," as they were called in the Lowcountry—"one of the fast disappearing type of loyal, true, and faithful house servants" with "snow white kinky hair." A later edition of Wilson's guidebook included a sketch of a black man in the guide, "an example," read the caption, "of the fine old type [of] Negro[,] honest, intelligent, trustworthy." Tourist pamphlets like "Charleston Welcomes You" also promised visitors that they would encounter a typical "darkey" during their stay. The cover of this brief guide featured a drawing of the city behind a wrought-iron fence. An elderly black man, hat in hand, stood opening the gate, a tourist's very own loyal servant.[55]

Contemporary black Charlestonians also evoked the primitive and the exotic to out-of-town visitors. Sam Stoney informed readers of *Charleston: Azaleas and Old Bricks* that behind the city's lavish mansions could be found "shanty communities that out-Africa Africa in some of their works and ways." "Charleston Welcomes You" included a photograph of basket weavers and another of flower women, the latter group popularized by local artist Elizabeth O'Neill Verner. From her studio on Atlantic Street, Verner sold her drawings of the women to tourists eager to take home a piece of Charleston's unique culture for themselves. She rendered flower women as features of the landscape, a charming aspect of nature, rather than as individuals. As she wrote in 1925, "one paints [the negro] as readily and fittingly into the landscape as a tree or marsh."[56]

Verner's interest in local blacks was not singular. In fact, she was a member of a small but significant group of white novelists, poets, painters, and singers who put Lowcountry African Americans and their culture at the center of their most significant creations. Headlined by DuBose Heyward, Julia Peterkin, and Josephine Pinckney, these artists sparked what today is known as the Charleston Renaissance. Although overshadowed by the Harlem Renaissance and the Fugitive and Agrarian movements in Nashville, this cultural movement produced important artistic organizations, such as the Poetry Society of South Carolina and the Charleston Etchers' Club, and renowned novels such as Heyward's best-selling *Porgy* and Peterkin's Pulitzer Prize–winning *Scarlet Sister Mary* (1929). These novels, like many of the paintings, poems, and performances created during the Charleston Renaissance, focused squarely on the Lowcountry's racial past and present, though in a manner that was less critical than the more probing works of southern contemporaries such as William Faulkner.[57]

That many Charleston Renaissance artists spent a good deal of time exploring black history and culture is not altogether surprising. After all, the 1920s were, in the words of Langston Hughes, "the period when the Negro was in vogue." African American literature, sculpture, dancing, and especially music seemed both exotic and authentically American to white audiences drawn to jazz and the blues in the speakeasies of Harlem and Chicago. The Charleston Renaissance also reflected the rise of a regionalist artistic movement, which promoted regional folk culture of the American hinterland rather than the mass culture of Hollywood and Madison Avenue. For the artists and writers of the Charleston Renaissance, the ideals of the Old South in the Lowcountry could be resurrected, both to reestablish social order in modern society and to make money. And nothing distinguished the antebellum Lowcountry more

Alice Ravenel Huger Smith's watercolor Sunday Morning at the Great House, *ca. 1935, idealized life on an antebellum rice plantation.*

than the slave culture that had developed on the plantations that surrounded Charleston.[58]

Watercolorist Alice Ravenel Huger Smith, to take one example, created ethereal renderings of life on an antebellum rice plantation based on family memories. Born into a distinguished family in 1876, Smith learned to exalt Charleston's past from her paternal grandmother, Eliza C.M. Huger Smith, and her father, Daniel Elliott Huger Smith, a Confederate veteran and amateur historian. In the mid-1920s, Smith brought these recollections to life with wistful watercolors of Lowcountry plantations and their surroundings. In 1936, she collected thirty of her impressionistic pieces in *A Carolina Rice Plantation of the Fifties.* The book, which also included a historical narrative written by her cousin, Herbert Ravenel Sass, and chapters from her father's unpublished memoirs, sought to re-create and preserve a slice of plantation life in the 1850s for the generations that followed. "I threw the book *back* to the Golden Age before the Confederate War so as to give the right atmosphere because in my day times were hard," Smith later explained.[59]

In contrast to the economic travails of Depression-era South Carolina, her watercolors, awash in the warm glow of her pastel pallet, evoke a genteel and affluent past in which both master and slave enjoyed life on the Carolina rice plantation. Art critics across the country took Smith's rice paintings at face value, calling them "valuable historical documents."

So, too, did the tourists who frequented her studio, which was located on the opposite side of Atlantic Street from Elizabeth O'Neill Verner's. Some came to buy art, while others sought out her shop to enjoy refreshments and to listen to Smith and her father (who made daily visits) spin stories about Charleston's past that were every bit as dreamy as her watercolors.[60]

Charleston Renaissance author DuBose Heyward also looked back to a golden age in his best-selling novel *Porgy*, though his halcyon era was not the 1850s but rather the more recent past, "when men, not yet old, were boys in an ancient, beautiful city that time had forgotten before it destroyed." Heyward came from old planter stock, but his father had died young, leaving his mother, Janie, to raise and support her family as one of several white Gullah impersonators in the city. Janie Heyward's gift for storytelling, knowledge of Gullah, and enthusiasm for local history had a profound influence on DuBose's literary career. He was also shaped by his job as a cotton checker on the docks of Charleston's warehouse district, gaining an intimate look at the tenements, saloons, and bordellos that proliferated there.[61]

He drew on this exposure to working-class life in *Porgy*, which is set in Catfish Row in a dilapidated mansion turned black tenement. The tragic love story of a crippled beggar named Porgy and a drug-addicted prostitute named Bess, Heyward's novel offers sympathetic, multidimensional portraits of its African American characters that contrast sharply with both the faceless slaves in Smith's plantation watercolors and the racist caricatures found in the works of Joel Chandler Harris and Thomas Nelson Page. Yet like the works of Smith, Harris, and Page, *Porgy* played to predominant racial stereotypes. Heyward described blacks living in 1920s Charleston as "exotic as the Congo, and still able to abandon themselves utterly to the wild joy of fantastic play." Evoking the paternalist ethos that Charleston's blue bloods had long proclaimed, and on occasion lived up to, Heyward described Porgy's world as the high tide of beggary: "His plea for help produced the simple reactions of a generous impulse, a movement of the hand, and the gift of a coin, instead of the elaborate and terrifying process of organized philanthropy." And *Porgy*'s tragic conclusion—with the representative New Negro character, Sportin' Life, driven out of Catfish Row, an intoxicated Bess lured to Savannah by stevedores, and Porgy left alone to mourn the loss of his loved one—suggests that the free future did not bode as well for Lowcountry blacks as had their enslaved past.[62]

Heyward echoed this point in a 1931 essay that touched on the Denmark Vesey conspiracy. One fact revealed by the trial record of the foiled 1822 insurrection, Heyward wrote, was that in southern courts of law enslaved people merited better treatment than their liberated descendants, albeit in deference to masters' property rights rather than humanitarian considerations for the bondperson. He and his wife, Dorothy, an Ohio native who co-authored the stage adaptation of *Porgy*, were particularly taken with the Vesey conspiracy. Dorothy eventually wrote a play about the affair that was produced on Broadway in 1948. "The story of Denmark Vesey," she explained, even "as told in the driest reference books, seems to have been dreamed up by a 'true thriller' writer after six martinis." Though Dorothy found Vesey's story intoxicating and displayed greater sympathy toward the "amazing" revolutionary than her fellow white Charlestonians, she placed the internal struggle of George Wilson, one of the slaves who betrayed the plot, at the center of her play. "George cannot sacrifice his master for the freedom of the Negro race," explained a *New York Times* critic after watching the 1948 production. "His personal loyalties take precedence over his racial loyalties. This is the basic conflict of the play." In the end, Dorothy counterbalanced the liberationist themes in her drama with the trope of the faithful slave.[63]

Although Dorothy Heyward's Vesey play did not attract much of an audience, the wild success of her husband's 1925 novel *Porgy* and the subsequent play and opera (the latter was called *Porgy and Bess*) was instrumental in placing the city and its black residents on the tourist itinerary. To many visitors clutching a copy of a guide like Miriam Bellangee Wilson's *Street Strolls*, Cabbage Row—the inspiration for Heyward's Catfish Row—was a site worth seeing. Its imagined inhabitants served as authentic primitives from an earlier age, though some guidebooks, like Wilson's, also pointed out that Cabbage Row had recently been "reclaimed" by whites. By the mid-1930s, locals banked on the fact that Heyward's works would bolster interest in Charleston and bring in deep-pocketed outsiders who would "give the gentry a chance to remove a lot of those 'For Rent' and 'For Sale' signs which grace most of the porticoed residences."[64]

However much *Porgy* was the reason, big spenders did, in fact, come. Some stayed for months on end. Throughout the 1920s and 1930s, families with names like Guggenheim, Roosevelt, Vanderbilt, and du Pont acquired Lowcountry homes and plantations so that they could escape cold and drab northern cities during the winter. Elliman, Huyler, and Mullally, Inc., a real estate firm with an office on Church Street and one in New York City, facilitated these purchases for Yankees wanting their own little slice of Lowcountry romance.[65]

While northern snowbirds lent a hand in this preservationist campaign, they also put some southern traditions at risk. In a 1933 application to the Board of Architectural Review (BAR) for a permit to extend a fence at his Tradd Street home, for instance, C.W. Porter seems to have made reference to "slave quarters" behind the house. In response, architect Albert Simons, who was the most important voice on the BAR, wrote to the city engineer that "Lieutenant Porter might be interested to know that the servants' quarters were never referred to as 'slave quarters' even in slavery times. The term 'slave quarters' is a recent invention of our winter colonists, the general use of which should be discouraged."[66]

White Charlestonians not only taught northerners how to talk about their new properties, they also accommodated the tourist demand for encounters with traditional "darkeys" by incorporating them prominently into the Azalea Festival. Designed to draw thousands of visitors to the city during the lean years of the Depression, this celebration was first held in 1933. In addition to the usual parades, concerts, and pageants (both beauty and historical), for example, festival organizers arranged a street-crying contest for the city's African American vegetable, seafood, and flower peddlers. One of the most popular attractions, a multiday exhibition of blacks husking rice, was staged at the Charleston Museum by Theodore D. Ravenel, who owned a rice plantation on the Combahee River. Each year, Ravenel brought in several African Americans to perform the husking process. In anticipation of the 1937 demonstrations, the *News and Courier* reported that the field hands "will be dressed in their field-working clothes and in all probability they will chant plantation songs as they go about their tasks." They did sing during the shows, and because attendance was so high, the demonstration was extended for an additional week.[67]

This emphasis on the racial "other" typified urban tourism in the United States in the interwar years. Boosters in many American cities presented racial minorities as sights to take in rather than social problems, as many white middle-class travelers might have otherwise seen them. Their presence suggested an unchanging order that obscured contemporary divisions while at the same time making white visitors confident of their own status. San Francisco's guidebook writers highlighted the Chinese presence. By the 1930s, as New Orleans began to cultivate a vibrant tourist industry to counter its Depression-era woes, so-called "darkeys" occupied much the same place in the tourist landscape as they did in Charleston. Dressing as mammies to sell pralines and playing the comical jester in Mardi Gras parades, they blended into the Crescent City scenery as charmingly as azaleas in full bloom.[68]

But even New Orleans—for all its sights and spectacles—could not hold a candle to Charleston when it came to the exploitation of its black residents and their culture. Renowned African explorer Mary L. Jobe Akeley hammered home this point when she attended the 1937 Azalea Festival. Listening to the chanting of Charleston's rice huskers, Akeley told the *News and Courier* that she felt as if she were transported back to Africa. As the paper bragged, "She said she would shut her eyes and imagine herself back in the Congo, among savages more primitive than those she visited on her last trip."[69]

7

The Sounds of Slavery

"THIS IS ONE OF LONDON'S BEASTLIEST AFTERNOONS," complained Philip Hewitt-Myring, an English journalist, in the winter of 1929. "It is bitterly cold outside," he wrote, "and a clammy white fog is pressed hard against the windows and even forceing [sic] its way into the room through crevices that only a London fog could find." On bleak days such as this one, Hewitt-Myring transported himself back in time and across the Atlantic to Charleston, where the year before he had spent three glorious spring weeks. Memories of the "quiet sun-drenched streets," the "lovely old houses," and "Magnolia Gardens . . . at the height of their beauty" cheered him, breaking through the impenetrable fog. What made these images all the more vivid and moving, he added, was that they were "set to music"—"the music of the rise and fall of the Spirituals which has haunted me ever since . . . I first heard it in Charleston."[1]

Hewitt-Myring shared this reverie in a letter to the group that had taught him to appreciate the slave spirituals of Lowcountry South Carolina: the Society for the Preservation of Spirituals. For Hewitt-Myring, the singing troupe—which performed regularly in the 1920s and 1930s—was Charleston's top attraction. As the Walter Hines Page Memorial Traveling Fellow in Journalism, Hewitt-Myring had chronicled his tourist experiences in Charleston for the *News and Courier*. Like English journalist Frank Dawson before him, Philip Hewitt-Myring was smitten with the city. Although 1920s Charleston bustled with tourists—unlike the sleepy city of Dawson's day—it still retained plenty of its Old South charm. In fact, it was Charleston's aged feel and its intimate connection to history that Hewitt-Myring found so alluring. The Society for the Preservation of Spirituals epitomized these qualities. In one of his final dispatches, he told his readers that he would be staying in Charleston for another week, mainly to attend the troupe's upcoming spring concert, though he had already heard the group twice before. Betraying none of the reserve for which his countrymen were known, Hewitt-Myring declared that after each performance he "emerged . . . slightly drunk with the beauty of an entirely new and unforgettable experience." It was impossible to write a series of articles about Charleston "without some reference to so piquant an ingredient in the city's life," he concluded, and so Hewitt-Myring dedicated an entire *News and Courier* column to the group.[2]

Remarkably, this piquant society—whose slave spirituals spiced up Charleston's culture and intoxicated tourists like Hewitt-Myring—was entirely white. Although they sang music composed by the slaves who had toiled in South Carolina's rice and cotton fields, members of the Society for the Preservation of Spirituals descended from the masters and mistresses who owned them. Born too late to have personally known life in the Old South, nearly all of them had been reared on nearby plantations by black maumas. Having left their homes for professional life in Charleston, they waxed romantic not only about the beautiful songs of former slaves but also about the loving bonds that they believed had characterized black and white relations on the antebellum plantation.[3]

The Society for the Preservation of Spirituals viewed performing spirituals and preserving them for posterity as its responsibility. In his lavish praise of the troupe, Hewitt-Myring never questioned this curious act of cultural stewardship. He even went so far as to claim that the white singers understood and performed slave spirituals better than blacks did anyway. The Englishman's love affair with the Society for the Preservation of Spirituals, and with Charleston more generally, was especially passionate and eventually personal. By the end of his trip, the SPS had repaid his kindness, electing him an honorary member, and he went on to marry fellow journalist Eleanor Ball, daughter of William Watts Ball, editor of the *Charleston News and Courier* from 1927 to 1951.[4]

Yet Hewitt-Myring was not alone in his fervor for the city and its spirituals singers. Thousands of other travelers also discovered Charleston in the interwar years, helping to forge the quintessential tourist experience. During their stay in the historic city, visitors were entertained not just by the Society for the Preservation of Spirituals but also by three rival groups that emerged on its coattails: the Plantation Melody Singers, the Southern Home Spirituals, and the Plantation Echoes. Like the Society for the Preservation of Spirituals, the first two troupes consisted of elite whites. The Plantation Echoes, in contrast, was exclusively black, and a handful of members had once been enslaved themselves. Still, the message this black group conveyed through its performances, which were carefully staged by its white director, dovetailed with Charleston's white spirituals troupes.

By the late 1920s, Charleston had become, quite simply, a place worthy "of musical pilgrimage," in the words of *Atlantic Monthly* writer Mark Antony De Wolfe Howe. After a 1930 visit, Howe reported that the Great Depression had sapped the funds necessary for a restoration of the city's physical monuments. So local preservationists had turned their attention to a different sort of commemorative campaign. To Howe's mind, these singers had salvaged songs that seemed "to spring as inevitably from Charleston soil as the porticoed, seaward-looking houses that could be found nowhere else."[5]

Along with several prominent whites who performed as Gullah raconteurs—regaling listeners with tales told in the dialect of Lowcountry slaves—these elites did more than entertain their audiences. They crafted a commemorative soundscape for Jim Crow Charleston.

* * * *

AT THE DAWN of the twentieth century, few locals would have predicted that the sounds of slavery would become all the rage in the interwar period. Indeed, not long after moving to Charleston in 1898, Ohio-born writer and fake slave badge critic John Bennett had tried in vain to find a publisher for a collection of 150 spirituals he had assembled with his new bride, Susan Smythe, and her sister. Reflecting on the popularity of the Society for the Preservation of Spirituals three decades later, Bennett told his children, "Mother and I were many years too soon. We started the interest here however; if that be any credit."[6]

Members of the elite Charleston society into which Bennett had married were indifferent to the history and culture of freedpeople at the turn of the century. The young Yankee transplant, however, was mesmerized by Lowcountry blacks, past and present. Struggling to understand the Gullah dialect he heard on the streets of Charleston, he felt as if he "had

Fascinated with African American culture, Ohio-born John Bennett photographed these black workers at Woodburn Plantation, owned by his wife's family, ca. 1905.

entered a world of which he knew little or nothing . . . and to which he was [to be] forever a stranger and an alien." Unlike so many of his new neighbors, he wanted to understand this world, an impetus in keeping with his relatively liberal racial politics.[7]

While on his 1902 honeymoon at the Smythes' Woodburn Plantation in Pendleton, a summer resort for Charlestonians in the Upcountry, Bennett paid black children to sing spirituals for him. He began working with his wife and sister-in-law to transcribe the lyrics and sound out the music. He also mined his father-in-law's library for works on African and southern history as well as a trunk of dusty documents from the Smythes' Medway Plantation in nearby Berkeley County. Bennett augmented this course of study by making trips to the Charleston Library Society to learn about the African backgrounds of the people who had been transported to the city to be sold at auction. Recording his research in a series of scrapbooks that covered anything he could find on Gullah history, language, and culture, he taught himself to speak the dialect in the process.[8]

Charleston visitors regularly remarked on the distinctive sound of the slave-born tongue, which drew heavily on West African vocabulary and grammar. Like native whites, they tended to dismiss it as broken English. "The lowland negro of South Carolina has a barbaric dialect," wrote New England journalist Edward King in 1875. "The English words seem to tumble all at once from his mouth, and to get sadly mixed whenever he endeavors to speak." But Bennett, who published several pioneering studies of Gullah, concluded that it was much more than just flawed English. "It is the oddest negro patois in America; the most African; unaltered it is one of the oldest; if not the oldest, certainly it is the most archaic, and well worth the scientific and scholarly study which has been given the dialects of the Mississippi Delta, of Haiti, and of Martinique," he wrote in the *South Atlantic Quarterly* in 1909.[9]

Bennett gave public lectures on Gullah music and folklore and, on occasion, performed spirituals while strumming along on a guitar. He tapped Gullah as a source for his fictional work as well. For his 1906 novel, *The Treasure of Peyre Gaillard*, Bennett combined family history, local legend, and his extensive research into Lowcountry slavery. When Booker T. Washington wanted to find out more about Sea Island spirituals, he wrote to Bennett for assistance. The Charleston author responded that he would send Washington a book for the Tuskegee Library.[10]

Though recognized as a Gullah expert in scholarly circles, Bennett never achieved popular acclaim. Society types deemed his work too salacious, as he never shied away from Gullah folktales that dealt with taboo subjects, such as miscegenation. Others dismissed it as too academic. But Bennett did inspire several successors who helped popularize Gullah history, songs, and storytelling. There was, for one, Bennett's nephew by marriage, the architect and preservationist Sam Stoney, who had become interested in the language and culture as a young man listening to Bennett tell his dialect stories. By the late 1920s, Stoney's proficiency in Gullah helped him get a job as dialogue coach for the northern actors cast in the stage version of DuBose Heyward's novel *Porgy*. In the decades that followed, Stoney co-authored a collection of black creation tales, *Black Genesis*, and regularly spoke on and told stories in Gullah at events in Charleston and beyond. Like his uncle, Stoney developed a reputation for his insight into Gullah language and culture.[11]

Even more important was DuBose Heyward, whose novel, play, and opera thrust Gullah onto the national stage. A protégé of John Bennett, DuBose "spoke Gullah like a Gullah," insisted his wife, Dorothy, and much of the dialogue of *Porgy* is rendered in the dialect. Indeed, DuBose joined Sam Stoney as a Gullah tutor for the actors in *Porgy*, which debuted in New York in the fall of 1927. He and Dorothy, with whom he adapted the novel for the stage, also included in the play a number of

Gullah spirituals that had been collected by a group that DuBose had helped to found five years earlier: the Society for the Preservation of Spirituals.[12]

DuBose Heyward's passion for Gullah music and folklore had been shaped not only by Bennett but also by his mother, Janie Screven Du-Bose Heyward, Charleston's most influential Gullah impersonator. Despite her aristocratic pedigree (she descended from the DuBose family and married into the Heywards), Heyward took up professional writing when she was widowed as a young woman and forced to support her children. After publishing *Songs of the Charleston Darkey* in 1912, Janie Heyward began entertaining thousands of people from across the United States, sharing stories of slavery at the very moment that the city began to cultivate its special connection to history and to court tourists in earnest. By the early 1920s, she was Charleston's go-to black raconteur.[13]

The idea that whites understood black culture and could thus perform blackness was hardly new. Blackface minstrels had enthralled white Americans since the early 1800s. By the turn of the century, white writers and raconteurs used black dialect and folktales to entertain audiences north and south, mimicking the slave on stage just as writers of the plantation school did on the page. Specializing in tales of slave mammies, women ranked as the most enthusiastic of these early-twentieth-century storytellers. More than simply entertainers, these slave impersonators cast themselves as serious interpreters of a bygone era. Performing in settings as varied as meetings of the United Daughters of the Confederacy and Chautauqua lectures, private parlors and hotel lobbies, they did important memory work in the service of the Lost Cause.[14]

Janie Heyward was among the most popular, her style and content more pleasing than John Bennett's had ever been. Pundits regularly compared her to the leading lights of plantation-school literature. "What Nelson Page was to Virginia and Joel Chandler Harris was to Georgia in immortalizing this unique dialect and the relationship between master and slave . . . Mrs. Heyward was to South Carolina," pronounced one observer. Like Harris and Page, Heyward's dialect readings, which included her own stories and poems as well as folktales and jokes she collected from local blacks, placed the faithful slave front and center. It was a type she claimed to know from her upbringing on her family's cotton plantations. As she announced in the introduction to one of her shows, "We

Janie Screven DuBose Heyward, mother of Porgy author DuBose Heyward, entertained as a Gullah impersonator in the early twentieth century.

The Philosophy, Humor, Folk-Lore, Weird Superstitions, and Unique Dialect of a Disappearing Type of Negro Arranged in Original Programs Suitable for College, Drawing-Room, and Auditorium Presentation

JANE SCREVEN HEYWARD

in Readings of

Original Poems and Sketches

of the

Carolina Coast Negro

With the Special Permission of the Author
Readings also given of Negro Sketches from The Black Border by
Ambrose E. Gonzales

of the Southland have as our heritage from our Slave holding ancestors, the understanding knowledge of the loving sympathy which existed in the old time between master and man." Left to their own devices, she asserted, slaves had guarded their masters' family and property during the Civil War. The "darkeys" to whom Heyward claimed to give voice thought little of emancipation, sometimes mocking it. Upon seeing a streetcar for the first time, she told her audiences, one Charleston black exclaimed, "My God! Deh Yankee too sma'at! Fus' him is free deh Nigger, An' now look! Him is free deh MULE." In "What Mauma Thinks of Freedom," such jocularity gave way to a plaintive nostalgia for slavery. Mauma proclaimed she had been "happy in de ole time," missing the food, clothing, and shelter she had enjoyed under her generous master. Freedom afforded no such material comforts. Mauma concluded, "I wish Mass Lincoln happy mam/Wherebber he may be;/ But I long foh deh ole, ole days/Befoh deh name ob 'Free.'"[15]

Through her dialect shows, Heyward hoped to "keep the spirit of mutual kindliness alive," and at times she seemed optimistic that it might survive. But each of Heyward's shows was also an act of preservation, an attempt to stop the march of time. The "old time darkey" she portrayed, Heyward observed at the beginning of one show, "has now passed from our civilization, going out with those conditions which produced it." If she could not prevent his passing, at least she could offer stories, which came from her "heart and memory." Audiences could then make them their own.[16]

According to white press accounts, this gift—Heyward's ability to instill her memory of slavery into the hearts and minds of listeners—was invaluable. As a Savannah newspaper remarked after Heyward performed in the city in 1922, few people were privileged enough to have had their own maumas and thus have known slaves' fidelity personally. But, this paper noted, Heyward transported audience members into the past, giving them a glimpse of what they had missed. This was an especially pressing issue for younger generations, who were born after emancipation had robbed them of their birthright. While Heyward's readings were "wonderfully entertaining," the *News and Courier* wrote, they were also "educational in their scope, and it is hoped that the school children will be able to enjoy hearing her in this recital as well as the grown folks."[17]

The most notable aspect of Heyward's performances was the skill with which she imitated the southern "darkey," though skill was not the word her admirers used. "Mrs. Heyward impersonates her characters in an easy natural manner," commented the *Charleston Evening Post* in 1924. The closeness she shared with her subjects represented the source of her purported authenticity, eliminating the need for acting. Like most of her fellow female performers, Heyward did not don the burnt cork mask that was the hallmark of the minstrel tradition or otherwise attempt to appear black. Despite—and perhaps to some extent because of—this lack of artifice, Heyward seemed to embody the southern "darkey" to white spectators. She performed with "a complete absence of affectation," concluded one reporter.[18]

As word of Heyward's readings spread, she was invited to perform by groups all over South Carolina, North Carolina, Virginia, Georgia, and Florida. In 1923, the Victor Talking Machine Company welcomed her to its Camden, New Jersey, studio to make records so that future generations might learn about the soon-to-be-extinct "darkey." Non-Charlestonians were fascinated by the history she brought to life. In fact, Heyward owed much of her publishing success to an editor at Neale Publishing Company in New York, who had run across "What Mauma Thinks of Freedom" in a magazine in 1905.[19]

Many who congregated to hear her readings in Charleston were white tourists. Heyward regularly entertained visitors in the lobbies of the

Francis Marion and Fort Sumter hotels. An announcement for one Fort Sumter Hotel performance entreated the public in general to attend, but sought to entice "particularly those who are sojourning in Charleston for a short time only." "Visitors coming to Charleston for the first time," it continued, "will be delighted by the 'gullah' stories told by Mrs. Heyward and with her perfect rendition of the dialect of the coast negroes."[20]

Locals were confident, too, that Heyward's shows would help northern audiences grasp an important truth. "Many years ago a distorted description of Southern slavery fanned the flames of great hate," wrote an author from nearby Walterboro. Heyward's performances, he held, provided a necessary corrective to this warped view of the Old South by recreating "an almost forgotten atmosphere of personal loyalty and feudal affection which once bound slave to master."[21]

* * * *

THE MOST ACCLAIMED wardens of the whitewashed soundscape of slavery rose to prominence at the same time Janie Heyward was enjoying her popularity. Founded in the fall of 1922, the Society for the Preservation of Spirituals (SPS) included Heyward's son DuBose and Sam Stoney, as well as scions of other prominent Lowcountry families, such as the Balls, Ravenels, Draytons, Porchers, Smythes, Pinckneys, Grimkés, and Hugers. Reared on plantations but now residing in Charleston, these homesick writers, lawyers, and bankers started meeting at each other's homes to sing the Gullah spirituals they had loved as children. Initially little more than a private social club, the SPS quickly evolved into an organization that focused on performing and preserving spirituals for the broader public.[22]

Although the forty-seven founding members of the SPS had been born after the Civil War, most of them met the essential requirements of being the "descendants of plantation owners and slave owners" and "reared under the plantation traditions." These membership restrictions— combined with a stipulation that the members could not be trained singers—made the SPS "perhaps the most unique society in existence," ventured the *Savannah Press* after a 1926 performance. "You either lived on a plantation or you didn't, and you can't use political influence or money or good looks or any other handy asset to turn that trick for you." This plantation pedigree, in turn, established the group's authority on slave spirituals and its right to preserve them for future generations. Without even a hint of self-consciousness, these descendants of white slaveholders believed they were the appropriate guardians of this remnant of slave culture.[23]

From its beginnings, the group insisted that it was not a minstrel troupe. Modern scholarship on blackface minstrelsy emphasizes how the wildly popular art form afforded white performers and their often urban, working-class audiences a way to cross racial boundaries and safely explore fantasies about African American people and their culture. Yet like Janie Heyward, the SPS did not black up. Although the singers followed the blackface tradition of appropriating African American culture, they avoided the gaudy costumes and buffoonery that had characterized minstrelsy since the early nineteenth century. The SPS sang the songs of the enslaved but dressed like the masters and mistresses of the Old South. These elite Charleston men and women never let audiences forget where they stood in the city's racial and social pecking order.[24]

Within two weeks of the society's first show at a home on the Battery, however, there was concern that the troupe's energetic performances "might be mistaken for a burlesque on the religious practice of the negroes, or the catch-penny mimicry of the familiar 'black-face comedian,'" as SPS secretary Arthur J. Stoney stated at the group's next meeting. Stoney recommended that to prevent any such misunderstanding, members do away with the ecstatic and rhythmic movements they had copied from blacks—the stomping and clapping that were essential accompaniments to Gullah spirituals—and simply sing. His suggestion did not go over well with his fellow spiritualists. "It was apparent from the glances directed at their Secretary," Stoney reported in the minutes of the meeting, "that they reserved the right to shake, rattle and roll, when they got good and ready." The society decided, instead, to begin each performance with an explanation that the intent was not to lampoon spirituals but rather to preserve them as relics of southern folklore.[25]

The SPS felt an obligation to do this important cultural work because, it believed, blacks themselves were not doing so. Fears over the future of slave spirituals had a long history. As early as 1868, an article in *Lippincott's Magazine of Literature* observed that emancipation was resulting in "the rapid disuse of a class of songs long popular with negro slaves." White abolitionists such as Thomas Wentworth Higginson, Charles Pickard

Members of the all-white Society for the Preservation of Spiritu-als singing, clapping, and stomping in the Gullah style at a show, ca. 1955.

Ware, and Lucy McKim Garrison tried to keep the tradition alive, pub-lishing several collections of slave spirituals, including those sung in the Lowcountry. So, too, did black students—many of whom were former slaves—at Fisk University, in Nashville, Tennessee. In 1871, the Fisk Ju-bilee Singers embarked upon a multiyear tour throughout the North and Europe, performing spirituals to raise money for their financially distressed institution. They succeeded and, in the process, provided their white audiences with their first exposure to slave spirituals. One of the original Jubilee Singers was Benjamin M. Holmes, the Charleston-born slave who, as we saw in the prelude, had read the Emancipation Procla-mation to his fellow prisoners in a pen in his hometown's slave-trading district.[26]

By the turn of the century, educational initiatives, transportation im-provements, and demographic changes threatened the spirituals tradition, even on the isolated Sea Islands. As thousands of rural African Americans left for cities north and south (including Charleston) during the Great Migration, some lost touch with the music and culture of their ancestors. Meanwhile, rising literacy rates increased demand for printed hymnals in black churches, some of which preferred to deposit reminders of slavery—like spirituals—in the dustbin of history. "There would be no negro spirituals today," concluded black tenor Ernest Johnson in 1929, "if it was not for the whites, who were responsible for their preservation, as the negro was desirous of forgetting everything associated with his slave days."[27]

This was a gross overstatement. Spirituals remained important in the lives of many African Americans and a key part of the black singer's repertoire well into the twentieth century. Reminiscing about growing up in Charleston in the 1920s and 1930s, College of Charleston professor Eugene C. Hunt noted the role that spirituals had played in his family. Hunt's fellow Avery Normal Institute students also regularly performed spirituals in this period. Future civil rights leader Septima Poinsette Clark, who attended Avery from 1912 to 1916, recalled that the school choir sang spirituals for American Missionary Association trustees every time they visited the school, though at the time she, personally, disliked the songs because she did not appreciate their history. Avery students also raised money for the school by singing spirituals for white audiences.[28]

The SPS's fear over the fate of black spirituals also reflected anxiety over the rumored passing of the old-time "darkey." Both "the primitive negro" and his spirituals were fast dying out, one SPS admirer observed in 1930, ruined by "the canker of 'civilization.'" But, according to this view, the country black untainted by excessive education had not yet entirely disappeared, which provided concerned whites an opportunity. Having grown up on area plantations, SPS members believed that they enjoyed an intimate familiarity with former slaves and their descendants, as well as with Gullah language and culture. "Often it was not until going off to college that the strong influence on their pronunciation of English was diminished," insisted the son of an early SPS leader. The society's Committee on Expeditions built upon these foundations by staying in regular contact with both white and black acquaintances in the surrounding countryside and setting up trips to plantations and churches where traditional black singing still occurred. Interracial tutorials, these trips took on the air of ethnographic expeditions, as SPS members ventured to remote locales to observe "natives" singing spirituals firsthand. After outings, a Committee on Research and Preservation documented each spiritual's origin and history to create a record for future generations. The group took pride in the fact that the songs it performed were indigenous and exclusive to the Charleston area.[29]

The plantation excursions arranged by the SPS often occurred at night and, when possible, on evenings with a full moon. Certainly, there was a practical benefit to a full moon, since the light made it easier to see the assembled group perform. But a full moon also helped create the ambiance the preservationists hoped to find. Katherine C. Hutson, chair of the Committee on Research and Preservation, let readers of the *News and Courier* into this enchanted world in an article she published in 1929:

> *Imagine . . . yourself on a plantation in Coastal Carolina on a summer evening . . . and as you stand, wrapt in the witchery of the night, there steals from somewhere in the shadows a low wailing song. . . . The plaintive song increases in volume as new voices take up the melody and the tom-tom beats are gradually interspersed with the rhythmic staccato of hand clapping . . . and gradually, as one stirring from a dream, we realize that we have come upon a plantation praise house, the place where spirituals are born. Could any one fail to thrill at such a disclosure?*[30]

Early on, the SPS attempted to re-create this thrill for its own pleasure and for small groups in private homes or at charitable functions around the city. By the mid-1920s, the society's crowds and ambitions had expanded, and in the auditoriums where it performed, the SPS used elaborate stage scenery to evoke an antebellum plantation at nighttime. The group employed portable lights, some outfitted with blue bulbs that gave the impression of moonlight, and surrounded the singers with cuttings from azaleas, palms, and, of course, live oaks draped with Spanish moss. Male singers donned "tuxedos and broad, bow ties of the cavalier days and the women, Southern belles up to the southern tradition of beauty," appeared in crinoline dresses. "One could shut one's eyes and fancy the old plantation cabins, in dim light with dusky figures gathered in a circle, creating a native music out of Bible stories and prayers and a simple faith," enthused the *Savannah Morning News*.[31]

The songs themselves began in a "slow, wailing manner," with one singer giving the first line of each verse and the rest of the chorus then joining in. As the spirituals built to a crescendo, the group clapped, stomped, and cried out "spontaneous ejaculations toward the end of the measure, such as 'Oh, Lord,' or 'Come own.'" SPS members gave themselves over to "an orgy of religion," according to one observer. Crowds often joined in, seizing the opportunity to experiment with playing black themselves. "Before the concert was half over the audience was beating out the rhythms and was almost singing with them," wrote the Savannah correspondent. "Another half hour and everyone would have been shouting." Performances typically included over a dozen songs and consisted of two halves and an intermission, though audience members did not always leave their seats during the break. While the singers rested halfway through a 1924 show at Charleston High School, Janie Heyward took the stage to entertain with her Gullah readings.[32]

The letters that admirers wrote to the society make it clear that many fell under just the kind of spell Katherine C. Hutson hoped to achieve. "There is something about the singing of these old melodies by our own people," one Charlestonian wrote to the SPS in 1931, "which always appeals to me and arouses in me a feeling of personal gratitude for the pleasure they give me." Philip Hewitt-Myring, the group's perennial fan and cheerleader, believed it was the performers' unique love for, and knowledge of, the songs that combined to move even those who, like himself, had not been raised under plantation conditions. A Greenville lawyer marveled at the white troupe's capacity to accurately reproduce black music. "The concert your society gave was different—nothing like it that I have heard—except the old-time darkey himself," he wrote SPS president Harold "Dick" Reeves in 1928.[33]

Many doubted that African Americans themselves could do as well. According to the *News and Courier*, educational advances and "cultivated singing" hindered blacks' own ability to perform spirituals in an authentic manner, even if they did still embrace the songs. Hewitt-Myring held that black spiritualists sang "not as darkies on a plantation but as paid performers on a stage." The SPS, he contended, avoided this problem. The white troupe was so "absolutely faithful" in its concerts, insisted Matthew Page Andrews, a white historian from Baltimore, that it was more authentic than a black group could ever be. "It seemed to me," noted Andrews after a 1927 show, "that the acting was perfection itself, because there was no semblance of acting, and no self-consciousness.

In my opinion, the negroes themselves could not do it so well before an audience; they would feel they were on parade." Like so many others, these white reviewers failed to see the irony in arguing that cultivated white singers could perform black spirituals authentically while cultivated black singers could not. So, too, did SPS members themselves.[34]

By preserving and performing Gullah spirituals, the SPS not only offered a tribute to the romance and grandeur of the world built by their slaveholding ancestors; they also embodied the ethos to which those forebears had aspired. Just as the Old South planter claimed to provide for the material and spiritual needs of his inferior and uncivilized black family, SPS members posited themselves as the protectors of a unique musical legacy of a people who seemed bound and determined to forget it. Eventually, the SPS expanded its purview. By 1927, when it created a Committee on Charity, the SPS determined that all of the profits it earned from performances should be used to relieve the "suffering and distress of the old time Negro." From that point on, society members donated money to needy individuals as well as to organizations, such as the Charleston County Tuberculosis Association, which treated black patients, thus maintaining a paternalistic, but hardly inconsequential, charitable program for local African Americans.[35]

As its popularity increased, the group's claims to a special connection with spirituals also grew. In 1931, the SPS published *The Carolina Low-Country*, a collection that included over four dozen spirituals, as well as nine essays on plantation music and culture. The society thereby staked its claim of ownership of the songs, though the decision to release a book had not been made lightly. Throughout the late 1920s, SPS members had wrestled with the possible consequences of publishing and recording Gullah spirituals. They worried that a permanent record of the songs, either oral or written, might subject the material to the damaging forces of commercialism and the corrupting voices of the uninitiated. This fear was one of the major reasons the group created an auxiliary junior spirituals society for members' children in 1929, hoping to safeguard not simply the songs but also "the 'word of mouth' method of learning." With *The Carolina Low-Country*, and the recording of spirituals in and around Charleston beginning in 1936, the SPS overcame these anxieties and sided with the necessity of preservation. It thereby established itself as the national authority on, and a leading repository of, Gullah spirituals.[36]

Many certainly saw the SPS as an assemblage of experts. The group regularly received letters from individuals seeking information on spirituals. Inspired by a feature story about the SPS in *Etude* magazine, for example, one Indiana woman asked for help with a presentation on spirituals she was slated to deliver to her women's club. The successful 1927–28 Broadway run of the theatrical version of DuBose Heyward's novel *Porgy* also elicited inquiries. As a founding member of the SPS, Heyward and his wife, Dorothy, with whom he had adapted the novel for the stage, made sure that the play's program acknowledged the society "for furnishing words and music of spirituals incorporated" into *Porgy*. After the publication of *The Carolina Low-Country* a few years later, still more individuals—from academics to the Girl Scouts—wrote for permission to use songs in their own publications. Asking that proper acknowledgment be given to the group, the SPS always obliged.[37]

* * * *

FOR ALL OF their "sympathetic understanding" of the music they cherished, in the words of Alfred Huger, an early SPS president, society members completely failed to appreciate the meaning that slaves had attached to spirituals. Enslaved Americans composed four basic types of spirituals—freedom songs, alerting songs, protest songs, and slave auction songs—all of which spoke to the challenges and torment of bondage. Slave spirituals at their core were statements of "protest and resistance," as black theologian Howard Thurman once argued. W.E.B. Du Bois called them songs of unhappiness, "of trouble and exile, of strife and hiding." Former bondpeople stressed the way spirituals provided shelter from the storm of slavery. In the late 1930s, eighty-three-year-old Charlestonian Affie Singleton, who had been raised on an Ashley River plantation, said that "the masters and mistresses used to beat the slaves . . . so that at night they would resort to singing spirituals." Another ex-bondperson recollected that "rough treatment . . . made them put greater expression into their songs." Inspired by Old Testament stories of deliverance, slaves had drawn parallels between their own condition and those of Moses, Joshua, Daniel, and Noah. Escape from such oppression was a common theme. Frederick Douglass recalled that the Canaan about which he sang as a slave was not the heaven of his religion, but the North. The Lowcountry slave spirituals repertoire included many songs that captured this affinity between biblical deliverance and freedom from slavery, as the SPS's *The Carolina Low-Country* attests.[38]

Yet the SPS interpreted spirituals differently. "The Society for the Preservation of Spirituals is anxious to correct the erroneous, yet general impression that the Spirituals were 'slave music' or the 'music of bondage sung by a race in their oppression or degradation,'" wrote member Caroline Pinckney Rutledge. "The life of the plantation negro of our coastal section prior to the War Between the States, as attested by those few living today, was a happy one. They were well housed, well clothed and well fed, and were as free from care as irresponsible children." In fact, the SPS insisted that the spiritual was an African rather than a slave song, and thus oppression accounted neither for its existence nor its meaning.[39]

A common error, Robert Gordon wrote in the essay he contributed to *The Carolina Low-Country*, was that the slave "created a large body of spirituals bewailing his position." Gordon conceded that the idea of spiritual slavery—the oppression caused by sin and temptation— permeated the songs, and that the slave may have, at times, imbued them with multiple meanings. But, he concluded, the "total number of cases . . . in which we can be certain that he refers to physical and not to spiritual slavery can be counted on the fingers." Other society members who wrote essays for the collection emphasized the slave's comfort and good cheer—his access to plentiful rations and frequent banjo playing, for example—to prove that spirituals were devoid of any inherent critiques. DuBose Heyward offered the only essay in *The Carolina Low-Country* that departed from this bowdlerized vision of plantation life, dismissing the image of the faithful and contented slave as "the creation of a defensive South." In the end, however, Heyward made it clear that he, too, believed that "it is likely that here in the Carolina Low-Country . . . the rural Negro experienced a higher state of physical and moral well being than at any other period in his history."[40]

This, of course, was far from a novel vision of the Old South. But Charleston's white spirituals singers invoked these images in a new way; they were living, breathing, and singing advertisements for the plantation legend. "I couldn't help but think as I sat there that this was just as it was long ago," New York conductor and composer Walter Damrosch commented after a 1935 SPS show. "The men in stocks and the pretty women in crinolines and hoop-skirts. It was very grand." What's more, the SPS made sure that its audiences did not miss its message about spirituals and the culture in which they were created. During a 1927 show in Columbia, SPS president Alfred Huger paused to explicate the meaning of the group's songs throughout the program. He defined spirituals as "the reaction of the Christian religion upon primitive Negroes not long transplanted," but he rejected the misconception that their tone and message bespoke "the hardships endured under slavery." According to SPS executive secretary Katherine Hutson, "the minor mode and the longing and sadness expressed in the words" of spirituals, which included songs such as "Chillun Ob Duh Wilduhness Moan Fuh Bread" and "Gwine Res' From All Muh Labuh," did not reflect "the outcrying of an oppressed people." Slave spirituals, she concluded, "were not originally or even generally the expression of the negroes longing for freedom."[41]

To the SPS, Gullah spirituals were manifestations of religious belief—a fair reading of the songs, to be sure. In addition to being lamentations over slavery, spirituals *were* a product of Christian devotion, sung in the service of strengthening believers and bolstering their faith. Indeed, this was one of the reasons SPS members found the songs so appealing. Former SPS president Alfred Huger, for example, gained great comfort from spirituals in the waning years of his life, which he spent in Tryon, North Carolina, because of fragile health. After hearing the SPS on an NBC radio broadcast in 1936, Huger wrote the group a letter of thanks. He struggled to articulate how much joy the performance had brought him. Sensing that death was not far off, Huger was grateful for the songs and looked forward to the day when "the religious philosophy of our beautiful Negro Spirituals [will] be proven, in their original, unregimented form, to be the real and eternal spirit of Truth."[42]

The solace he and his colleagues found in slave spirituals was an important part of their affection for the genre, and it should be not dismissed. Just because white spiritualists—and their white audiences, for that matter—did not endure slavery did not mean that their appreciation of the songs was insincere. A history of personal bondage was not a prerequisite for valuing the slave spiritual as an art form or as a vehicle of Christian devotion.

The problem was that, to the SPS, the songs were expressions of religious belief and little more. Local whites, for their part, never questioned the society's interpretation of the spirituals it performed. In fact, influential voices—like *News and Courier* editor William Watts Ball—echoed the SPS's take. In 1947, Ball published a column that took issue with renowned black singer Marian Anderson's interpretation of spirituals as, in Ball's words, "the dirge of a people in bondage, a melancholy music to be sung in sorrow." Nothing could be further from the truth, he insisted. "As thoughtful Southerners know, the indigenous spiritual is anything but sad. It is a paean of joy, a song in praise of the Living God, a description of comforts of the Hereafter," Ball concluded.[43]

A lack of sources makes black responses to the SPS more difficult to gauge, though a few things are certain. In Jim Crow South Carolina, whites could easily lay claim to what they insisted was a genuine memory of slavery with little fear of being challenged. Largely excluded from the public sphere, African Americans lacked the power to stop white singers from appropriating the sounds of slavery for themselves. Moreover, the SPS sang and stomped, above all, for the pleasure of whites. Few black Charlestonians, even those who might have been curious, ever saw an SPS show. In the midst of planning a free concert at the Academy of Music in 1931, for instance, the SPS discussed the possibility that some blacks might attend and wondered how they should be accommodated. The group determined to simply follow the Academy's custom of placing African American patrons in a separate gallery, but it decided not to advertise the fact that blacks would be allowed at the show in the local papers. Instead, each SPS member was instructed "to inform his family servants to pass the word among their friends that they would be admitted." The SPS spread the news of the free show, in other words, to those black Charlestonians least likely, or able, to take issue with its peculiar brand of cultural appropriation.[44]

SPS members, meanwhile, insisted that African Americans appreciated their work. In 1929, Alfred Huger claimed that "the colored people . . . have complimented the society" for its "able re-production" of Gullah spirituals, and one black schoolteacher in Spartanburg did go on record as a supporter of the society's musical efforts. After attending a performance at a local theater, which she enjoyed "even in the far reaches of the balcony," she wrote a letter to the *Spartanburg Herald* praising the group for taking spirituals seriously. Because many whites used the songs to mock blacks, she argued, the younger generation wanted to forget them. She thanked the society for its efforts to keep slave spirituals alive.[45]

White Charlestonians—and, by the mid-1920s, white tourists—found SPS concerts irresistible. Indeed, in addition to seeing the many historical sites in and around the city, visitors expected to catch an SPS show and were disappointed if they did not. In the spring of 1929, the editors of the *News and Courier* thanked the SPS for a recent performance, well attended by both Charlestonians and tourists. But, as the tourist season was just picking up, and more people would soon be in town, the paper hoped the society would arrange additional shows. The SPS owed that much to the city.[46]

The admiration of visitors such as Matthew Page Andrews, Philip Hewitt-Myring, and Walter Damrosch was amply reported by the press, but plenty of others responded similarly to the SPS. "A Yankee, who appreciates your work," for example, wrote to the society and included a substantial donation. In thanking the northerner, one SPS member remarked that such generosity made him feel "that the war between the States was a mistake of the mind and not of the heart," thus framing the gesture—and their mutual appreciation of slave spirituals—as proof of sectional reconciliation.[47]

During its early years, the SPS performed primarily in Charleston and nearby towns in South Carolina and Georgia. By the late 1920s, appreciative Yankees had spread the word about the group up north. Invitations from northern dignitaries and musical organizations poured in. At the behest of the Massachusetts governor and the Boston mayor, the SPS traveled to Boston in 1929 to entertain the National Federation of Music Clubs at its annual conference. The singers gave three Boston-area concerts and then capped off the tour with a performance at the du Pont estate in Wilmington, Delaware, on its way home. The next year, Philadelphia welcomed the SPS, as did the exclusive Thursday Evening Club in New York City. In early 1935, President Franklin Delano Roosevelt, First Lady Eleanor, and two hundred of their guests enjoyed an SPS performance in the East Room of the White House. Radio shows complemented these tours, providing a way for even more non-Charlestonians and non-southerners to hear the SPS sing. After its 1936 NBC broadcast, the society received letters of thanks from fans as far away as Pittsburgh and Chicago.[48]

Northerners who saw the group perform in person were especially effusive. In New York, the Thursday Evening Club was swept off its feet.

The Society for the Preservation of Spirituals performed up and down the East Coast in the interwar period.

The Society for the Preservation of Spirituals

of Charleston, South Carolina

Singing for

THE THURSDAY EVENING CLUB

in New York City

Thursday Evening, January 9th, 1930

The SPS was proud to learn from one audience member, Mrs. Woodrow Wilson, that another in the crowd, composer Walter Damrosch, could barely contain his enthusiasm. Delegates to the National Federation of Music Clubs meeting in Boston were impressed with the how the spiritualists sang "with the utter abandon of the negro." In nearby Salem, this abandon affected even the most reserved of concertgoers. Three elderly women who sat through the first few songs "rather formally, bearing a dignified New England manner," eventually became "infected with the contagion" of the music. All agreed that the SPS knew its craft well. A reporter for the *Boston Transcript* painted the picture for his readers: "Imagine, for example, the old song which Miss Jenkins and Mrs. Hutson learned from their mammy nurse, sung by a perfectly groomed vocale debutante!" The scene was at once a study in contrasts—here was the beautiful southern lady channeling the dark-skinned domestic slave—and a testament to the power of mimicry. It was also a testament to the lady's key role in linking past and present, in perpetuating her memory of slavery.[49]

Back home in Charleston, the value of these trips north was obvious to boosters eager to attract tourist dollars. If the slave-made mansions and gardens provided the foundation for creating Historic Charleston, it was the sounds of slavery—as interpreted by the descendants of Lowcountry slaveholders—that made it complete. The *News and Courier* published a laudatory editorial thanking the SPS for a marketing windfall that was hard to match. On the eve of the Boston trip, the Charleston Chamber of Commerce bombarded southern and northern newspapers with publicity stills of society members in their antebellum dress. The chamber had an Associated Press photographer tag along on the trip to New York and Philadelphia to capture and syndicate the society's successes in real time. The SPS may even have attracted some buyers for surrounding plantations. Shortly after the prominent New York lawyer Victor Morawetz and his wife, Marjorie, sponsored the SPS concert at the Thursday Evening Club, they bought Fenwick Hall on Johns Island. Five years later, the socialites hosted the SPS for a private concert at their plantation.[50]

* * * *

NOT SURPRISINGLY, THE Society for the Preservation of Spirituals had competition in interwar Charleston. As we have seen, Avery Normal Institute students gave black spirituals recitals on a regular basis during these years. The Plantation Melody Singers and the Southern Home Spirituals—both founded in the mid-1920s by elite white women who ran in the same social circles as SPS members—did as well. Although significantly smaller than the SPS, these troupes took similar pride in their pedigrees.

The Plantation Melody Singers was formed by a dozen or so women who hoped "to reproduce the tender memories and deep affection" between masters and their slaves. Led by Lydia C. Ball, the group counted several other Balls, a few Ravenels, and a least one Legare and LaBruce as members. The Plantation Melody Singers began as an all-female group, but eventually it expanded to include several men. The Southern Home Spirituals was created by three former members of the Plantation Melody Singers—Maria Ravenel Gaillard, Mrs. William Seabrook, and Mrs. William Wayne—and seven other leading Charleston ladies. The *Evening Post* reported that "the singers, with one or two exceptions, were from the old plantations in this vicinity, and were thoroughly familiar with the old time negro prayer meeting spirituals."[51]

Although the Plantation Melody Singers and Southern Home Spirituals boasted the same plantation lineage as the SPS, their appearance on stage was decidedly different. The Society for the Preservation of Spirituals may have sung, clapped, and stomped like slaves, but they dressed like southern cavaliers and belles. The Gullah impersonators making up the other two groups went much further in their racial masquerade; they tried not only to sing like slaves but also to look like them. Each member of the Plantation Melody Singers portrayed a black type, reported the *Evening Post*. There were "dignified old maumas, with snowy kerchief and turban and apron," and "young girls with gay plaid ginghams and bright ornaments.... There were one or two of the less sober type of African ... women who wore no head cloth over their unruly locks, no stiffly starched apron over their gaudy dresses. And there were gangling colored youths in pathetic garments of nondescript character." In addition to this racial cross-dressing—a feature that was central to the minstrel tradition—both the Plantation Melody Singers and the Southern Home Spirituals members wore blackface.[52]

The content of Plantation Melody Singers and Southern Home Spirituals shows also had much more in common with minstrelsy than the SPS's more restrained performances. Balancing their rendition of spirituals with storytelling and character skits, the Southern Home Spirituals treated their audiences to something closer to a variety show than a concert. The Plantation Melody Singers took things even further. Wrote the *Evening Post* of a 1927 performance in Kingstree, South Carolina, "The curtain went up upon a semicircle of Charleston folk, twelve in number, dressed in each small detail to represent the negro of yesterday." At the time, most audiences would have associated this arrangement with minstrelsy, especially when they got a look at the singers' garish costumes and heard their characters' names: Jinnie, Nippy, Tildy Polite, Roxy, Galsy, Primus, Pigeon, Cumsee, and Old Uncle Noah. Finally, the routines performed by several of these characters evoked precisely the same response from their white audiences as did blackface minstrels. During a 1928 concert at Rock Hill, South Carolina, the young boy Primus "evoked peals of laughter with his assumed simplicity."[53]

This was not the sort of reaction that the SPS intended to elicit from its audiences. In 1929, SPS president Alfred Huger told a Boston audience that "the society was in dead earnestness in its efforts to preserve and continue the singing of the spirituals and did not do it in a mood to make fun of colored people." The SPS did, however, frequently share the stage with Gullah storyteller and SPS member Dick Reeves, whose readings tended to leave audiences in stitches.[54]

The Plantation Melody Singers and Southern Home Spirituals maintained busy schedules in the Charleston area throughout the late 1920s and early 1930s, and, like the SPS, they sang for both locals and tourists. Yet the Plantation Melody Singers and Southern Home Spirituals did not represent the SPS's stiffest competition in interwar Charleston, as an intriguing episode suggests. On January 15, 1936, SPS executive secretary Katherine Hutson wrote to inform the steering committee of the popular Charleston Azalea Festival that members had recently voted to accept its invitation to perform one evening during the upcoming celebration. "This of course," she continued, "is with the understanding that there will be no other group singing Spirituals in connection with the Azalea Festival."[55]

The SPS was referring to the Plantation Echoes—a group that, by means of its all-black membership, represented a potent challenge to the SPS's claim to authenticity. Since the advent of the Azalea Festival in 1934, the Plantation Echoes had enjoyed a prime-time evening slot in the entertainment lineup. Founded in 1933, the Echoes included fifty black field hands from Wadmalaw Island, several of whom were ex-slaves. The idea to create the group originated with Rosa Wilson, owner of Fairlawn Plantation, on which the singers lived. Alarmed by the plight of her tenants at the height of the Depression—several tied their crumbling shoes together with string—Wilson observed how they found solace in singing spirituals at their weekly religious meetings. She took comfort in knowing that "in these trying times there lived a people among us whose faith lifted them above material things" and determined to help the field hands find a way to earn money from their musical talents.[56]

Financing the endeavor with the sale of two pigs, Wilson arranged for the Plantation Echoes, as she dubbed the group, to debut a three-act show of singing and dancing at the Academy of Music on April 7, 1933. Their first public appearance attracted more than one thousand spectators. For the rest of the decade, the Echoes performed under the directorship of Wilson, offering multiple winter and spring concerts in Charleston and the surrounding area before mixed-race audiences. Eventually, the group was featured in national magazines, such as *Etude* and *National Geographic*, recorded by the Library of Congress, and invited on multiple occasions to participate in the National Folk Festival in Washington, D.C.[57]

Caesar Roper and Sam Simmons, former slaves and members of the Plantation Echoes, an all-black Gullah spirituals group. The Echoes undermined the Society for the Preservation of Spirituals' claims to authenticity. From My Privilege, *published by Rosa Wilson, 1934.*

At times, SPS members actively promoted the Echoes' work. DuBose Heyward arranged for a private Echoes performance for George Gershwin, who visited Charleston in 1933 to hear authentic black singing so he could compose the music for *Porgy and Bess.* "As far as I know nothing of this nature has been attempted before," Heyward later said of the Echoes' show. "There is an electrifying quality to the 'shouting' and the performers' ability to shift from one time to another in perfect unison is a revelation." Coming from an SPS co-founder, this was quite a compliment. But the prospect of performing alongside such an electric show appears to have been too much for Heyward's fellow SPS members, especially when it was staged by a black group. Ultimately, the SPS removed itself from the 1936 Azalea Festival lineup.[58]

Not all of white Charleston shared the SPS's fears about black rivals. Mayor Burnet Rhett Maybank was such a big fan of *Heaven Bound*—a morality play featuring spirituals that was staged by several black Charleston churches in the 1930s—that he requested it be performed every year during the spring tourist season. As the mayor who initiated the Azalea Festival in 1934, both he and the festival steering committee understood the significance of tourism to the municipal economy during the

Depression, a time when the city came dangerously close to bankruptcy. When Congress repealed Prohibition in 1933 but South Carolina kept its no-alcohol law on the books, Maybank announced that tourists' demands trumped state statutes: "We will give...liquor...to them whether it be legal or illegal." Adopting a give-them-what-they-want approach, Maybank and the festival committee clamored to provide tourists with as many glimpses into black life as possible—whether it was through the lens of rice huskers, street criers, the Society for the Preservation of Spirituals, the Plantation Echoes, *Heaven Bound*, plantation field hands, or a sightseeing trip to area plantations led by preservationists. As a writer for *Etude* magazine observed in an article about the Plantation Echoes, Charleston had learned there was "a kind of gold mine" in showcasing the remnants of slave culture. If the SPS felt threatened by these black rivals, city boosters did not mind. The financial benefits outweighed any such concerns.[59]

And tourists did indeed go wild for the African American performers. As we have seen, the black rice huskers who sang spirituals at the 1937 Azalea Festival proved so popular that they extended their run at the Charleston Museum by a week. Rosa Wilson reported that tourists constituted the primary audience at Plantation Echoes shows in the 1930s and left wanting more. "Northerners," she stated, "are very eager about this natural negro scene and even follow us to the plantation day after day." Visitors from New York, Massachusetts, New Jersey, Connecticut, Ohio, Indiana, Georgia, and Northern Ireland took in a 1934 show. *Heaven Bound* also drew a large crowd of white tourists. According to one travel writer of the day, "it is one of those items on the 'must' list" during a trip to Charleston. Folklorist John A. Lomax, who recorded an Echoes show for the Library of Congress, complimented Rosa Wilson for her work in sharing the singers with the rest of the world, especially for letting "the negroes show they come direct from the farm through their style of dress" and their "natural" singing and clapping.[60]

Divining how the Plantation Echoes themselves felt about singing for their admiring audiences is not easy. Rosa Wilson noted that the Plantation Echoes had volunteered their services to a large historical pageant planned for the 1936 Azalea Festival. The director of the pageant, she further stated, "was very much pleased with how the plantation hands responded." Yet Wilson's stewardship of the Echoes must have made it difficult for members to register any discontent, and one tantalizing bit of evidence suggests that not everyone was a willing participant. At the Echoes' 1938 spring concert at Hibernian Hall, a few of the field hands did not perform as they should have. "Several, notably the young bucks," the *News and Courier* reported, "seemed to regard the presentation as a lark," adding that the "more mature performers" sang well. These younger black men apparently did not take to playing the part of the old-time "darkey." This sort of rebellion occurred elsewhere. According to spirituals expert and theologian Howard Thurman, one day in the early 1920s he and his fellow students at historically black Morehouse College sat stone-faced when the spirituals director called out the first line to a song. A contingent of white visitors was present, and they refused to sing spirituals "to delight and amuse white people." The president of the college was humiliated.[61]

* * * *

IN 1934, A New York woman who had vacationed in Charleston since childhood and owned several homes in the city wrote an angry letter to the *News and Courier*. The first annual Azalea Festival had not, in her opinion, been a success. She complained primarily about the crowds that had descended upon Charleston for the festival, trampling hordes that ruined the city's quaint feel and overwhelmed its streets. The commercialization of local charms, including black spiritualists, was also troublesome. It struck her as an "unsuitable dose of Hollywood." "Beauty contests, hucksters' contests, plantation echoes—a profaning of gentle reality for curious and unsympathetic eyes," she wrote. "I am leaving it all, not to come back."[62]

A profaning of gentle reality had been the hallmark of Charleston tourism for years, and along with infrastructure improvements, it had worked. Three hundred thousand tourists traveled to Charleston in 1939, double the number from just three years before and ten times the number who made the trip in the mid-1920s. The New Yorker's consternation, in other words, was not widely shared, and probably reflected dismay that her city had been discovered by the masses as much as anything else.[63]

Those responsible for profaning their city never regretted playing to the desires of the curious traveler, but the spirituals societies, at least, may have been a victim of their own success. The Plantation Melody Singers noted as early as 1933 that ticket sales had declined. Attributing part of the drop to the Depression, Lydia C. Ball, the group's president, also observed that radio stations routinely broadcast spirituals shows, and that the singing of spirituals now occurred well beyond Charleston, having almost become a national pastime. As she stated, "You often hear people say: 'we do not have to go out to hear spirituals[,] we can get all we want at home.'" Ball resigned as Plantation Melody Singers president that year, and the group seems to have dissolved soon after. The Southern Home Spirituals lasted a bit longer, giving its last public concert in 1939. Appropriately, it was broadcast on the radio. The Plantation Echoes stopped performing in 1941.[64]

Even the Society for the Preservation of Spirituals entertained a proposal to disband at the end of the 1930s. The group's biggest concern by this point was not sharing slave spirituals' beauty and uplifting message; rather, it was ensuring that it had sufficient funds to pay for the cocktails members expected at meetings. In the end, the SPS decided to remain together, though the group staged fewer and fewer shows in the decades that followed.[65]

Nevertheless, white Charlestonians' newfound passion for Gullah lived on. Sam Stoney continued to give lectures on and tell stories in the dialect. Fellow SPS member Dick Reeves, who had gained some local renown for reading from a collection of Gullah tales called *The Black Border* during SPS shows, performed both on stage and over the airwaves as a Gullah impersonator in the 1930s and 1940s. According to the account of one white listener, Reeves's renditions of the Gullah tales were so convincing that a neighbor's black servant who had been listening announced, "It's just like a nigguh!" And while the Southern Home Spirituals stopped performing at the end of the 1930s, its founder and leader, Maria Ravenel Gaillard, did not. She continued to dress up as a slave and offer a program of Gullah readings and impersonations.[66]

What's more, the sanitized memory of slavery promoted by Charleston's spirituals troupes and performers remained alive and well, seeping through the crevices of the city's tourism landscape like the fog of Philip Hewitt-Myring's London. Local preservationists and tourism boosters increasingly made room for the Old South in Charleston's historical narrative. Influenced by the wild popularity of *Gone with the Wind*, tourist brochures from the period evoked the antebellum grandeur of the region, featuring hoop-skirted southern belles on the cover. Several visitor guides even offered passing commentary on Gullah people and their culture. SPS member Herbert Ravenel Sass summed up these changes in a 1947 *Saturday Evening Post* article. "Charleston has become for thousands the visible affirmation of the most glamorous of all folk legends in America—the legend of the plantation civilization of the Old South," he wrote. "A single morning spent wandering through its older streets, a single afternoon at one of the great plantations . . . prove that there was at least one region . . . where the Old South really was in many ways the handsome Old South of the legend."[67]

Sass appropriately credited Charleston's sights and spectacles for perpetuating this moonlight-and-magnolia vision of antebellum southern life. But white spirituals troupes and Gullah raconteurs—and, to a lesser extent, the black performers of the Plantation Echoes—provided the soundtrack for the tourist experience in Charleston. In the process, they repackaged the area's Old South past into the comforting commodity that locals would peddle for decades to come.

8

We Don't Go in
for Slave Horrors

ON JULY 24, 1924, CHARLESTON REAL ESTATE BROKER
Sidney S. Riggs wrote to historian Frederic Bancroft, who lived in
Washington, D.C., about a new venture he had in mind. "We have recently
completed two . . . modern hotels in this City," Riggs informed Bancroft:
the Fort Sumter, at the Battery, and the Francis Marion, across from
Marion Square. "As we are able to take care of TOURISTS next season,
I am thinking of putting the Old Slave Mart in such shape that visitors
would be able to get some idea of how it looked in former days," he explained. "I would welcome any suggestion from you as to this."[1]

Bancroft was uniquely qualified to evaluate this unusual proposal.
Since the late nineteenth century, the Columbia University–trained scholar
had made regular pilgrimages to the South to conduct research for what
he hoped would be the definitive study of the region before, during, and
after the Civil War. Although Bancroft never completed his magnum opus,
these southern tours—which included at least six visits to Charleston—
provided ample grist for his pathbreaking *Slave Trading in the Old South*
(1931).[2]

Bancroft and Riggs had been exchanging letters about the Old Slave
Mart for several years. Riggs had a ten-year lease on the property, which was
located in the heart of the city's former slave-trading district. In the 1850s
and early 1860s, Riggs's father, John, had been a prominent Charleston
slave broker, regularly selling enslaved men, women, and children at
the slave-auction complex originally called Ryan's Mart. A half century
later, son Sidney had renovated a portion of that complex, which
fronted Chalmers Street, transforming the Old Slave Mart, as it came to
be known, from a two-story black tenement into a storage garage. Now, the

Charleston realtor wondered whether he might turn a profit by restoring the building to the way it looked when men like his father had built fortunes buying and selling human chattel. Having spent a good deal of time over the past few decades inspecting what remained of Charleston's slave-trading district, including the 6 Chalmers Street property, Bancroft liked Riggs's plan a great deal. He admitted, however, that he had no sense of whether it was practical. "Personally," Bancroft added, "I should like to see it done and should be glad to assist in any way in my power."[3]

Notwithstanding Bancroft's offer, Riggs never followed through with his plan. This is not surprising. By the mid-1920s, Charleston's tourism boosters, preservationists, and entertainers were well on their way toward learning how to appease visitors' desires to see sights and hear sounds associated with slavery and the Old South in a way that was palatable to local sensibilities. But topics such as the slave trade remained taboo.

* * * *

FEW THINGS TROUBLED white southerners more than the notion that their ancestors had actively engaged in the sale of men, women, and children and facilitated the destruction of families. So they tried to distance their region from human trafficking whenever possible. Sometimes this simply involved stating unequivocally that the practice had been foisted upon them by outsiders. In a critical 1885 review of a new edition of *Uncle Tom's Cabin*, for instance, Frank Dawson's *News and Courier* maintained that "the slaveholders at the North sold their slaves to the Southern people and then turned Abolitionists; that Northern ships owned by Northern men carried on the slave trade; and that Northern slave-dealing was carried on as late as seven or eight years before the outbreak of the Confederate war." Almost a half century later, Society for the Preservation of Spirituals president Alfred Huger said much the same thing. "The South stands absolved of immediate responsibility for establishing the institution of slavery," he wrote in his essay for the group's 1931 book, *The Carolina Low-Country*. "Indisputable colonial records show that again and again the South protested against the traffic."[4]

In other moments, white southerners traded stories intended to demonstrate that unlike their unscrupulous and hypocritical countrymen to the North, antebellum planters did everything they could to humanize the slave trade. In 1890, W.W. Legare, a Georgia professor with deep roots in Charleston, wrote the *News and Courier* about a telling event that he claimed had taken place decades earlier. At some point before the Civil War, a relative of antislavery senator Charles Sumner—later revealed to be the abolitionist's brother, Albert—wanted to sell some enslaved people belonging to his wife's estate in Charleston. Ignoring the pleas of a slave who preferred to be auctioned off together with the rest of his family, Albert instead sold just him to a trader. "As soon as the outrageous act of this satellite of the 'higher law' became known" in Charleston, Legare reported, "he was visited by a committee of gentlemen, who forced him to sell the negro at home, and then gave him twenty-four hours to leave the city." Albert's actions, claimed *News and Courier* editor James Hemphill, were "denounced by Southern people as monstrous." This self-serving tale continued to circulate among elite Charlestonians for decades.[5]

White southerners also frequently scapegoated slave dealers as social pariahs who neither came from the Old South nor were accepted by its inhabitants. The lowly reputation of slave dealers reflected selective amnesia about the men who had devoted their lives to buying and selling human beings—a purposeful forgetting that is readily apparent in obituaries and biographies published in the late nineteenth and early twentieth centuries. When Charleston slave trader Ziba B. Oakes died in 1871, for instance, his *Charleston Courier* obituary was front-page news. The newspaper reported that Oakes had made his money "in the Commission and Auction business," but it failed to mention that much of that business had involved buying and selling people, or that Oakes had once owned Ryan's Mart. The same was true of the obituaries of Oakes's colleague John S. Riggs Jr. and a handful of other prominent slave dealers, including Alonzo J. White, John E. Bowers, T. Savage Heyward, and Louis D. DeSaussure. This pattern of deliberate omission extended beyond newspaper death notices. For instance, the *Cyclopedia of Eminent and Representative Men of the Carolinas of the Nineteenth Century*, a biographical compendium that Edward McCrady helped produce, scrubbed clean the records of two leading South Carolina slave dealers: Riggs and John Springs III.[6]

White Charlestonians' selective amnesia about the slave trade often centered on the Old Slave Mart. As we have seen, visitor guidebooks raised doubts about the authenticity of the Chalmers Street site. In fact, Cornelius Irvine Walker's take on the Old Slave Mart in his 1911 *Guide to*

After the Civil War, white Charlestonians displayed historical amnesia about leading slave traders, such as Louis D. DeSaussure, and slave-auction sites, such as Ryan's Mart.

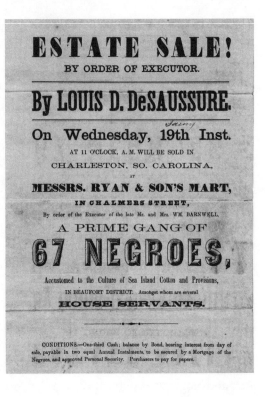

ESTATE SALE!
BY ORDER OF EXECUTOR.

By LOUIS D. DeSAUSSURE.

On Wednesday, 19th Inst.

AT 11 O'CLOCK, A. M. WILL BE SOLD IN
CHARLESTON, SO. CAROLINA,
AT
MESSRS. RYAN & SON'S MART,
IN CHALMERS STREET,
By order of the Executor of the late Mr. and Mrs. WM. BARNWELL,

A PRIME GANG OF

67 NEGROES,

Accustomed to the Culture of Sea Island Cotton and Provisions,
IN BEAUFORT DISTRICT. Amongst whom are several
HOUSE SERVANTS.

CONDITIONS—One-third Cash; balance by Bond, bearing interest from day of sale, payable in two equal Annual Instalments, to be secured by a Mortgage of the Negroes, and approved Personal Security. Purchasers to pay for papers.

Charleston, S.C. proved remarkably influential, parroted not only by later guidebook writers but also by local newspapers, preservationists, and tourism officials. The *News and Courier* maintained in 1930 that the only thing certain about the Old Slave Mart "is that the establishment was never officially designated as an official general slave market, for no record of there ever having been such has ever been located." The paper's editor, William Watts Ball, found reassurance in the notion that Charleston did not have a city-sponsored slave market, explaining, "It does not appear that there existed sufficient buying and selling of slaves in the city to have warranted the establishment of any institution for the purpose." Ten years later, Florence S. Milligan, a member of the Historical Commission of Charleston (HCC), objected to comments about the Old Slave Mart made by a Gray Line tour guide, whose accent suggested he was not a local. Milligan noted numerous factual errors in the guide's presentation, including the claim that slaves had been sold at the Old Slave Mart, which had been reopened as a museum by Miriam B. Wilson just two years earlier. "Is it not wrong to assert that that Chalmers Street building was a slave market?" she wrote in her report. "I know it's always done, but I've been told that it was never so used."[7]

Milligan's colleague, HCC secretary Mary A. Sparkman, knew better. Notes that she compiled for the HCC in 1936 included nine typescript pages about Ryan's Mart, Ryan's Jail (the four-story brick barracoon that was part of the complex), and the slave trade more generally. Yet Sparkman, too, dissembled in describing the Old Slave Mart. Her 1952 tour guide training manual, which provided the foundation of the city's official manual until the mid-1970s, made a point of stating that the Old Slave Mart had no official standing. "Our greatest historians and recognized authorities on recorded history are unanimously agreed that Charleston NEVER had a slave market," Sparkman wrote. "New Orleans had one, but Charleston never did." Like Walker, Sparkman and the Historical Commission did not want city guides to in any way suggest that Charleston sanctioned the slave trade by establishing a city-run market. Human trafficking had the imprimatur of New Orleans's municipal government, Sparkman suggested, but visitors to Charleston needed to know that the trade had been strictly the business of private individuals there. Hence, she concluded, "Ryan's Mart was merely another slave broker's office, not the only one, in Charleston." Ironically, then, in Sparkman's attempt to prove that the slave trade had no official status in Charleston, the HCC secretary inadvertently demonstrated its ubiquity. Careful readers of Sparkman's guide would understand that the buying and selling of human chattel was actually an everyday feature of commercial life in the city. Still, decades after Walker and his Lost Cause colleagues wrote slave-trading out of Charleston's history—indeed, well into the 1970s—city boosters steadfastly perpetuated this whitewashed narrative.[8]

* * * *

NO ONE IN early-twentieth-century America did more to ferret out information about the slave trade, or to expose white Charlestonians' proclivity for forgetting about it, than Frederic Bancroft. Born in 1860 in Galesburg, Illinois, a town reputed to have been an Underground Railroad depot, Bancroft had learned to hate slavery as a child. While an undergraduate at Knox College, he gave public orations praising abolitionists John Brown and William Lloyd Garrison. His early interest in slavery contributed to his decision to focus on the American South as a graduate student at the Columbia School of Political Science, where he enrolled in 1882. Two decades later, Bancroft—whose wealthy older brother enabled him to enjoy the life of a gentleman scholar—set out to write a history of the South in the antebellum and Civil War eras.[9]

Historian Frederic Bancroft (left) visited Charleston many times to do research for his pathbreaking Slave Trading in the Old South *(1931), which challenged white orthodoxy on the subject.*

Merritt. M. *cor. Main & Square, Galesburg, Ill.*

This project took Bancroft back to Charleston, a city he had first visited in 1887. What stands out most in Bancroft's observations from this trip and several others he made to the city in the early 1900s is his fidelity to more than just written sources. Bancroft believed the only way to get a complete picture of the past was to combine the archival work of a historian with techniques more closely associated today with cultural anthropology and investigative journalism. He not only visited libraries and sought out plantation records; Bancroft also immersed himself in his surroundings, hoping to understand the region's past from the perspective of its present residents. He wrote lengthy descriptions of the streets, buildings, and wharves he saw on his visits to Charleston, as well as of the behaviors and practices of its citizenry. And Bancroft struck up conversations with anyone he could—from Confederate veterans and white matrons to former bondpeople—teasing out information on a wide range of topics.[10]

Judging by the conversations he recorded in his southern trip diaries as well as his correspondence with Charlestonians, Bancroft had a knack for disguising his own beliefs on sensitive issues. During his 1902 visit, he regularly dined with Floride Cunningham, a pleasant and talkative white southerner whom Bancroft judged to be at least sixty years old. Despite his own antislavery convictions, he had little difficulty getting Cunningham to talk about slavery, her ancestors, and other topics related to the southern past. Cunningham, for instance, bragged that "her family always gave men Sat. afternoon, & women did not go to the fields at all." Five years later, Bancroft met with attorney Langdon Cheves, a descendant of two established Lowcountry families, at his home near the Ashley River. Although Cheves was more interested in discussing Reconstruction than earlier periods, Bancroft convinced the elite Charlestonian to share his family's plantation books and answer questions about the Old South down to the most minor detail, including the turnover rate for overseers and the way that slaves' shoe sizes were determined.[11]

Bancroft also had numerous conversations with Edward McCrady. The two historians spent most of their time talking about the American Revolution, secession, and the Civil War—all of which McCrady freely addressed. But when Bancroft raised the issue of human trafficking in Charleston, McCrady "seemed disagreeable & showed [a] nervous manner." Despite McCrady's discomfort, Bancroft pressed him for information about the various slave-dealing locales in the city, as well as the reputation of specific slave traders, such as partners Thomas Farr Capers and T. Savage Heyward. McCrady responded that he did not know their family backgrounds, though he insisted that they were auctioneers who sold sizable estates, which inevitably included enslaved laborers. As Bancroft later explained in *Slave Trading in the Old South*, this strategy of explaining away human trafficking as the incidental by-product of the larger social role that auctioneers performed—settling estates—had a long history. It was commonplace before the war and had become a sacrosanct tradition since then.[12]

Bancroft found a few white Charlestonians more forthcoming. A secessionist who claimed to have taken part in firing on Fort Sumter told him that thousands of enslaved people were sold out of Charleston and that members of the best families were professional traders. W. Mulbern, a wholesale grocer with a business on East Bay Street, informed Bancroft in 1902 that "aristocrats did not hesitate to deal slaves [and] make money on it." When their conversation turned to the city's slave trade, Mulbern added, "Better leave [it] out; it wouldn't look well" to "our children." Five years later, Bancroft returned to Charleston and spoke with T.W. Bacot, an attorney and brother-in-law of Edward McCrady. Unlike McCrady, Bacot displayed few misgivings about discussing human trafficking. He introduced Bancroft at the Charleston Library Society, helped him search for old slave advertisements, and advised him on how to determine the price of slaves auctioned off at equity court sales.[13]

Bancroft obtained even more information about the slave trade from his conversations with former slaves. In 1922, he bragged to a fellow historian about his "nearly 40 years' experience" eliciting "historical evidence out of ex-slaves." During an earlier trip to Charleston, Bancroft had recorded a lengthy conversation with William Washington and his wife, whom he met in a rubbish-filled yard a few doors down on Queen Street from Ryan's Jail. Both freedpeople said that they had witnessed slave auctions in Charleston, and Mrs. Washington added that she had, in fact, been sold multiple times. "Were many children sold in this region?" Bancroft inquired. "Dey sell 'em like de hawk take de little chickens, dah," replied Mrs. Washington, gesturing at some baby chickens in the yard. "Deh sen' de chilluns out in de stree an' yo' nevah see'm agin. . . . De specahlatahs pick up de chilluns, like yo' picu up dese chickens, till dey gits a drove & dey driv 'em in de public big road." The Washingtons also described the punishment, including whippings with cowhide, switches, and straps, that the enslaved suffered at the hands of their masters.[14]

Stories such as these enthralled Bancroft so much that midway through his spring 1902 trip to the South he decided that he wanted to write a book focusing squarely on the domestic slave trade. He believed this volume would "wholly demolish the amiable traditions" that conveyed a false impression of southern slavery. Progressive-era historians tended to accept slaveholders' paternalist claims at face value and characterize the institution as benevolent and civilizing. As a result, they de-emphasized the extent of the internal slave trade, argued that slave families were rarely broken up at auction, and underscored the lowly status of professional slave traders. Bancroft was especially critical of Ulrich B. Phillips, the Georgia-born professor whose portrait of slavery set the tone for southern historiography in the first half of the twentieth century. Indeed, after W.E.B. Du Bois wrote a scathing review of Phillips's *American Negro Slavery* (1918), Bancroft sent him a letter of praise. Three days later, Bancroft told another historian that he would unleash "a most deadly array of facts" against the southern scholar in his forthcoming volume on the domestic slave trade.[15]

Bancroft continued to gather those facts in as discreet a fashion as possible over the next decade. In April 1922, not long after a trip to

Charleston, he penned a note to the proprietor of the garage in the Old Slave Mart. "For historical purposes . . . I should like to know, in what year the negro tenements were removed from the old Slave Mart and when it was made into a garage." Then, in deliberately vague fashion, he added, "I wish to make a note to a chapter that I have written about Charleston in the 'fifties." This letter eventually found its way into the hands of Sidney S. Riggs, the son of slave broker John S. Riggs and Old Slave Mart leaseholder.[16]

Sidney Riggs proved to be a goldmine of information. He passed along details about the dimensions of, and changes made to, the Old Slave Mart as well as evidence relating to other sites associated with slavery. Riggs also put Bancroft in touch with individuals who had witnessed auctions at the Old Slave Mart. M.F. Kennedy, who as a young boy had attended several sales, confirmed that they took place from a long, three-foot-high black table, upon which the slave to be sold and auctioneer were perched. The crowd of prospective buyers stood to the west of the table, examining the human chattel put before them. Female slaves' bodies were "partly exposed near the waist line as an exhibition no doubt of robustness," the white Charlestonian told Bancroft.[17]

In his quest for information, Bancroft also struck up an extended correspondence with Theodore D. Jervey Jr., a wealthy lawyer, newspaper editor, and historian who had a unique take on slavery. Unlike many white Charlestonians, Jervey had his doubts about the peculiar institution. He was perfectly willing to admit that it conferred important benefits, functioning as an effective means of racial control, instructing slaves in important trades and skills, and cultivating close ties between master and bondman. Yet Jervey also believed that slavery had had a disastrous impact on the South because it contributed to the rapid increase in the number of African Americans there.[18]

Jervey's unorthodox perspective on slavery helps explain Bancroft's unusually forthright letters to the Charlestonian. In contrast to the way he approached most other southern whites, Bancroft did not disguise his desire to explore—and explode—the South's cherished myths about the slave trade when writing Jervey. By the early 1920s, Bancroft had become particularly interested in documenting the life and reputation of Thomas N. Gadsden, the scion of an old Charleston family that included Colonel James Gadsden, the U.S. minister who negotiated the Gadsden

Purchase. Bancroft had secured newspaper advertisements demonstrating that Thomas N. Gadsden was one of Charleston's leading slave brokers from the 1830s through the 1850s, and he (correctly) suspected that Thomas was the brother of James Gadsden and two prominent ministers in Charleston. "To have a slave-trader in a family where there were several distinguished brothers, two of whom were clergymen, is rather shocking to the universally believed tradition that slave-traders were always hated," he wrote Jervey in 1920.[19]

Bancroft included a detailed portrait of Thomas N. Gadsden in his seminal 1931 study *Slave Trading in the Old South*, which featured an entire chapter on human trafficking in Charleston. This work broke new ground on a variety of fronts. A sharp departure from the scholarly consensus on the domestic slave trade, it was among the first histories to incorporate slave testimony. For decades, *Slave Trading in the Old South* stood as the definitive study of the domestic slave trade, anticipating arguments about the commercial and exploitive nature of southern slavery that are widely accepted by historians today.[20]

Amazingly, Jervey managed to convince his fellow members of the Charleston Library Society Book Committee to purchase a copy of Bancroft's book. We do not know precisely what the Charlestonian thought of Bancroft's history, though a note Jervey wrote about the promotional circular for the book provides a clue. "After gazing at the illustration which accompanied your circular," he wrote Bancroft, "I realize that it would be impossible for scholarship to present a more hideous picture of the 'Old South.'" Referring to Eyre Crowe's depiction of a slave auction near the Old Exchange Building (see the second image in the prelude), which was reproduced in *Slave Trading in the Old South*, Jervey was repelled by "the ferocious Southern types," yearning to buy one of the African Americans up for sale. "There will be much to learn" in your book, he told Bancroft.[21]

No doubt there was, though not everyone in Charleston welcomed its lessons. William Watts Ball, the editor of the *News and Courier*, penned a lengthy and overwhelmingly negative review of *Slave Trading in the Old South*. A conservative from a wealthy Upcountry family, Ball had little patience for Bancroft's thinly veiled moral outrage. Indeed, he subscribed to the notion that as practiced in the Old South slavery was more humane than anywhere else, noting the longevity of the enslaved there when compared to other regions with slavery. White southerners knew the real history of slavery in the South, Ball insisted, regardless of what primary evidence or statistics might suggest to a northern scholar. And if the stories passed over dinner tables were not enough to reassure his readers, Ball offered up the work of Ulrich B. Phillips, whose "great book" on American slavery "has been so fully, adequately and justly written . . . that nothing substantially modifying the final verdict is likely to be produced by another man."[22]

Ball's review infuriated Bancroft. He had no problem with criticism; in fact, Bancroft claimed to welcome it, if only to give him an excuse to write a preface to a second edition. Ball's *News and Courier* review, however, was no such refutation. The Charleston editor "denied not one of my assertions, but changed the subject to *slavery*, and proceeded accordingly," Bancroft told Jervey. Ball lauded Phillips's *American Negro Slavery*, "but neither he nor anyone else has undertaken to answer my criticisms and ridicule of Phillips."[23]

* * * *

FREDERIC BANCROFT WAS not alone in his quest to preserve the memories of former slaves. As we saw in chapter 5, black schools, churches, clubs, and families kept alive a countermemory in the segregated spaces of Jim Crow Charleston. Local whites occasionally lent a hand, too. In the 1920s, Leonarda J. Aimar compiled a book of stories told by ex-slaves who worked for her family. She also recorded the reminiscences of William Pinckney, a former bondman who spoke with remarkable openness about the discipline and sale of slaves in the city. Intimately familiar with the Work House, Pinckney told Aimar that individuals sent to the "sugar house" could be beaten, whipped, placed in the stocks, or forced to walk the treadmill.[24]

Such candor, however, was rare in the segregated South, at least in racially mixed company. Faced with the strictures of Jim Crow culture, ex-slaves often put a positive spin on life before the Civil War when they spoke with white southerners for fear that talking honestly might bring significant social or economic repercussions. As Martin Jackson, a former bondman from Texas interviewed as part of the Federal Writers'

Project (FWP), put the matter: "Lots of old slaves closes the door before they tell the truth about their days of slavery. When the door is open, they tell how kind their masters was and how rosy it all was."[25]

This candor problem has been highlighted by scholars as one of the chief challenges in using the thousands of FWP interviews to reconstruct life in the Old South, and for good reason. But when the interviews are approached as artifacts of historical memory—as reflections not simply of what happened in the past but of how historical memories are shaped over the course of time and by the demands of the present—the candor problem no longer appears so problematic. On the contrary, when examined alongside documents produced by regional, state, and national offices, FWP interviews underscore the high stakes and contested nature of the memory of slavery more than seventy years after its abolition.[26]

A Works Progress Administration (WPA) program created in 1935, the FWP launched its ambitious campaign to interview former slaves in more than a dozen southern and border states in the spring of 1937. The initial goal of the FWP had been to hire unemployed writers to assemble and author a single, multivolume guidebook for the United States. (The FWP eventually settled on producing a series of state and local guidebooks— like the South Carolina guide discussed in chapter 6—rather than a single national guide.) When the mostly black writers hired to make sure that African American history and culture were included in WPA guidebooks began fanning out across the South in 1936, a handful of them took it upon themselves to record the memories of ex-slaves. Early the following year, the Florida Writers' Project forwarded some of these stories to the national headquarters in Washington, D.C., where they captured the imagination of FWP folklore editor John A. Lomax. A Texas folklorist with a passion for black material, Lomax would record the Plantation Echoes for the Library of Congress later that year. He immediately recognized the value of these ex-slave interviews, too. So did Negro Affairs editor Sterling A. Brown and associate director George Cronyn.[27]

In the first week of April 1937, Cronyn instructed southern FWP offices to begin the process of identifying and interviewing former bondpeople. He then distributed a questionnaire that John Lomax had designed for interviewers. These questions, which functioned as an interview script for FWP employees, were far from perfect. Some were leading, others presumptuous. As a whole, however, the questionnaire touched on a range of salient and provocative topics—from slaves' quarters, clothing, work, and religious beliefs to the sale, discipline, and resistance of the enslaved. As Lomax explained in the questionnaire's preface, "The main purpose of these detailed and homely questions is to get the Negro interested in talking about the days of slavery. If he will talk freely, he should be encouraged to say what he pleases without reference to the questions."[28]

Even a cursory examination of the FWP interviews in the Charleston area, however, indicates that many of the ex-slaves who spoke with white writers did not talk freely; instead, they told their interviewers what they thought they would want to hear. According to an account written by interviewer Jessie A. Butler, Abbey Mishow, a former bondwoman from Georgetown County who had lost her mother at a young age, characterized her owners as loving, substitute parents. "As she mentioned the name of the old 'missus,' and enumerated the names of her erstwhile owners," the white writer reported, "Abbey's old, wrinkled, black face softened with memories and her voice became gentle as she told of the care and kindness she had received." Amos Gadsden, who had lived with his owners on St. Philip Street in Charleston, also emphasized his kindly mistress in his conversation with Martha S. Pinckney. "I never got a slap from my mistress; I was treated like a white person," he explained.[29]

These responses not only reflected former slaves' understanding of racial etiquette in the Jim Crow South; they also bespoke the economic realities of elderly African Americans living at the tail end of the Great Depression. After eighty-year-old John Hamilton answered white writer Gyland H. Hamlin's question in expected fashion—"Yassuh, ole Maussa treat us good"—he explained that he depended "on de w'ite folks" for help. "You gimme a nickel or dime?" asked Hamilton at the end of the conversation, having held up his part of the implicit bargain. "T'ank you, suh. T'ank you kin'ly," he responded, once Hamlin followed through on his end.[30]

The slaves who spoke to Augustus Ladson—the only black FWP employee who interviewed a significant number of bondpeople in Charleston—painted a much different picture. Prince Smith, an ex-slave from Wadmalaw Island, informed Ladson that many of the slaves who worked on nearby plantations were forced to labor in the cotton fields seven days a week and were subjected to severe lashings if they failed to finish their work quota. Even Smith's owner, whom he judged a gentle-man who treated his slaves well, employed a system of punishment that today would meet any reasonable definition of torture. Elijah Green, the former slave who said he had dug the grave of John C. Calhoun in his youth, relayed an equally unvarnished portrait of slavery to Ladson. A lifelong resident of Charleston, Green was a well-known figure in the interwar period. When Green spoke with Ladson, he echoed William Pinckney's comments about the Work House and the punishment of slaves. Being caught with a pencil and paper was treated as a major offense—"you might as well had kill your master or missus." The elderly ex-slave also described Thomas Ryan, the former proprietor of the Old Slave Mart, as cruel. "He'd lick his slaves to death," claimed Green.[31]

Such bleak portraits of antebellum slavery were unsettling to many of the FWP directors in the South. The national office had clearly stipu-lated at the outset of the project that writers "should not censor any ma-terial collected, regardless of its nature." This directive, however, was not always followed. Scholars have unearthed evidence that interviews recorded in at least four states—Mississippi, Texas, Georgia, and Virginia—were revised at either the state or national level, often softening their portrait of slavery as a result. Officials in South Carolina did not go this far, but correspondence between the state FWP office in Columbia and the dis-trict office in Charleston reveals that white employees sought to discour-age the collection of interviews that were overly critical of slavery in favor of those that offered a more positive take.[32]

Just one month into the program, Charleston district director Chal-mers Murray wrote to South Carolina director Mabel Montgomery about two stories recorded in Beaufort by Chlotilde R. Martin. Murray had decided not to forward the accounts because they contained "appar-ent falsehoods" that "are utterly unfair to the pre-war south." Murray informed his superior that "we have discussed this subject several times in the office, and it is the unanimous opinion of the Charleston staff that stories of this kind are of little value." An Edisto Island–born journalist, Murray had a deep interest in Gullah lore and culture, which was re-flected in many of his publications, including his novel *Here Come Joe Mungin*. Yet Murray did not think that former slaves who had survived into the 1930s were reliable sources about life in the Old South since most of them had been just children before the war, and "negroes are greatly given to fabrication." Thus, Murray concluded that "the ex-slaves are not telling their own experiences in many instances—they are merely repeating what some one else told them about slavery times." One can easily spot "the propaganda behind most of their statements," he asserted.[33]

Murray detailed this so-called propaganda in a letter he sent to Martin, the interviewer. "It is apparent in reading your recent stories that the narrators have little if any regard for the truth, and do their best to paint slavery days in the darkest colors," he told Martin, who, like Murray, was a white, college-educated journalist. Although Murray cautioned against censorship, he did "not think it wise to take down just any statement an ex-slave might make regarding a controversial subject like slavery." Complaining that Martin's interviewees "have evidently no sense of moral values," Murray observed that their claims that the enslaved were issued starvation rations and inadequate clothing flatly contradicted evidence that had been culled from plantation records. "Spend some time in finding out about the reputation of the persons you propose to interview," he advised. "When you actually interview the person, use all powers at your command to glean the truth from him." It is not clear whether Martin heeded Murray's suggestions, and there is no record that she interviewed another subject. Regardless, Murray eventually forwarded the two narratives he had originally held up, presumably after getting word from Montgomery that the Washington office steadfastly opposed any censorship at the local and state levels.[34]

The controversy over what to do with the material coming out of the Charleston FWP office did not end there. In June 1937, Montgomery, who also believed that African Americans were predisposed to fabrication, wrote Murray about a story that black interviewer Augustus Ladson had sent state Negro FWP supervisor Elise Jenkins. In it, ex-slave Susan Hamilton asserted that enslaved women were given very little time to recover after childbirth. "Dey deliver de baby 'bout eight in de mornin' an' twelve had too be back to work," the former bondwoman had told Ladson. Montgomery inquired whether Murray, as Charleston district director, could pay a visit to Hamilton and re-interview her, pretending that he had not read Ladson's account. She wanted to see if Hamilton would repeat the story, noting that if she did "it probably is true" and warranted

```
S-260-264-N                                              Page I
Project #1885                                           No.Words:1195        233
Augustus Ladson
Charleston,S.C.                        3904.

                           EX-SLAVE 101 YEARS OF AGE

                     HAS NEVER SHAKEN HANDS SINCE 1863

                      Was On Knees Scrubbing when Freedom Gun Fired
                      -------------------------------------------

            I'm a hund'ed an' one years old now,son.De only one livin' in my crowd
     frum de days I wus a slave.Mr.Fuller,my master,who was president of the Firs'
     National Bank,owned de fambly of us except my father.There were eight men an'
     women with five girls an' six boys workin' for him.Most o' them wus hired out.
     De house in which we stayed is still dere with de cisterns an' slave  quarters.
     I always go to see de old home which is on St.Phillip Street.

            My ma had t'ree boys an' t'ree girls who did well at their work.Hope
     Mikell,my eldest bredder,an' James wus de shoemaker.William Fuller,son of our
     master,wus de bricklayer.Margurite an' Casharine wus de maids an'I look at de
     children.

            My pa b'long to a man on Edisto Island.Frum what he said,his master was
     very mean. Pa real name wus Adam Collins but he took his master' name;he wus de
     coachman.Pa did supin one day en his master whipped him.De next day which wus
     Monday,pa carry him 'bout four miles frum home in de woods an' give him de same
     'mount of lickin' he wus given on Sunday.He tied him to a tree an' unhitched de
     horse so it couldn't git tie-up an' kill e self.Pa den gone to de landin' an'
     cetch a boat dat wus comin' to Charleston wood fa'm products.He permitted  by his (was)
     master to go to town on errands,which helped him to go on de boat without bein'
     question'.W'en he got here he gone on de water-front an' ax for a job on a ship
     so he could git to de North.He got de job an' sail' wood de ship.Dey search de
     island up an' down for him wood houndogs en w'en it wus t'ought he wus drowned ,
```

Ex-slave Susan Hamilton spoke of slavery's cruelties in her conversation with Augustus Ladson, a black Federal Writers' Project interviewer.

being forwarded to Washington. Although the national FWP office had instructed them to send all stories "as is," Montgomery added that in her "opinion this statement needed verification."[35]

A few days later, Murray responded that he, too, had grave concerns about Hamilton's statement regarding the treatment of enslaved mothers in the antebellum South. "It is my opinion that she made up a great part of the tale out of the whole cloth, apparently being glad of the opportunity to give vent to her bitterness," he wrote. Once again, Murray juxta-

Project #-1655
Jessie A. Butler
Charleston, S. C.

390431   Approx. 1739 Words 226

INTERVIEW WITH EX-SLAVE

On July 6th, I interviewed Susan Hamlin, ex-slave,
at 17 Henrietta street, Charleston, S. C. She was sitting
just inside of the front door, on a step leading up to the
porch, and upon hearing me inquire for her she assumed
that I was from the Welfare office, from which she had received aid prior to its closing. I did not correct this
impression, and at no time did she suspect that the object
of my visit was to get the story of her experience as a
slave. During our conversation she mentioned her age.
"Why that's very interesting, Susan," I told her, "If you
are that old you probably remember the Civil War and
slavery days." "Yes Ma'am, I been a slave myself," she
said, and told me the following story:

        "I kin remember some things like it was yesterday,
but I is 104 years old now, and age is starting to get me,
I can't remember everything like I use to. I getting old,
old, you know I is old when I been a grown woman when the
Civil War broke out. I was hired out then, to a Mr.
McDonald, who lived on Atlantic street, and I remembers
when de first shot was fired, and the shells went right
over de city. I got seven dollars a month for looking
after children, not taking them out, you understand, just
minding them. I did not get the money, Mausa got it."
    "Don't you think that was fair?" I asked. "If you were
fed and clothed by him, shouldn't he be paid for your
work?" "Course it been fair," she answered, "I belong

*Suspicious of what Hamilton told Ladson, Federal Writers'
Project staff sent Jessie Butler, a white woman, to re-interview her
in hopes of eliciting a more positive spin on slavery.*

posed ex-slave testimony against more trustworthy white sources—this
time William E. Woodward's 1936 *A New American History.* "You may
recall that he points out the fact that most of the stories about cruel and
inhuman treatment of slaves were sheer propaganda," he wrote Montgomery. Murray agreed that Hamilton should be interviewed again,
though not by him, as Montgomery had requested, but rather by a white
woman.[36]

One week later, Murray forwarded to the Columbia FWP office the first of two interviews that white FWP interviewer Jessie A. Butler conducted with Susan Hamilton. "It is a remarkable story—in fact one of the best of its kind that has been turned in so far," he told Montgomery. "It is doubly remarkable because it flatly contradicts almost all of the statements in the article filed by the negro worker Ladson." Murray was right on one front. Ladson and Butler agreed on a few basic facts, but as a whole their accounts are a study in contrasts. Ladson's narrative portrays slavery as characterized by exploitation and suffering. Hamilton told him that her brother was her master's illegitimate son. She also related the story of a hot-tempered washerwoman named Clory, who was savagely beaten after throwing her mistress out of the laundry for criticizing her work. The trauma of the auction block was ever present. "All time, night an' day, you could hear men an' women screamin' to de tip of dere voices as either ma, pa, sister, or brother wus take without any warnin' an' sell," she informed Ladson.[37]

In her interview with Butler, however, Hamilton made a point of avoiding generalizations about slavery, while at the same time describing her personal experiences in neutral, even positive, terms. Many of her comments focused on her owner, Edward Fuller, who barely appeared in Ladson's account. "Seem like Mr. Fuller just git his slaves so he could be good to dem," she told Butler. There is no mention in the Butler interview of a relationship (forced, coerced, or otherwise) between Fuller and her mother, or of Clory being whipped. Hamilton even implied that the pain suffered by mothers who lost children to the slave trade was exaggerated. "Sometimes chillen were sold away from dey parents. De Mausua would come and say 'Where Jennie,' tell um to put clothes on dat baby, I want um. He sell de baby and de ma scream and holler, you know how dey carry on."[38]

What is noteworthy about Butler's interview is neither that Murray judged it one of the best so far (after all, he had been looking for less macabre memories of slavery) nor that it contradicted so much of what Ladson had recorded. It is, rather, that Murray could have read it and still come to the conclusion that Ladson was the only one who had acted unprofessionally. According to Butler's narrative, Hamilton appears to have offered a damning account of her conversation with Ladson, suggesting that he shaped the ex-slave's responses to suit his own ends. "A man come here about a month ago, say he from de Government, and dey send him to find out 'bout slavery," she said. "He ask me all kind of questions. He ask me dis and he ask me dat, didn't de white people do dis and did dey do dat." Hamilton informed Butler that she had readily accommodated Ladson—giving him "most a book"—yet he had given her only a dime in return. Butler's narrative convinced Murray that the black FWP writer had not only asked Hamilton "leading questions" but also "literally put the words in her mouth." Fortunately, Murray concluded, Butler had been "perfectly fair in the way in which she put her questions."[39]

Butler's narrative, in fact, demonstrates quite the opposite. When Butler first visited Hamilton at her Henrietta Street home, the former slave assumed that her white visitor was from the recently closed welfare office, from which she had been receiving support. In an attempt to conceal her true reason for being there, and thereby, in her mind, to elicit more candid testimony, Butler chose not to disabuse Hamilton of this misconception. Yet this subterfuge surely undermined any possibility of gleaning the truth. In an era when few black southerners felt comfortable talking openly (or, at least, negatively) about slavery when among whites, Butler compounded the problem by giving Hamilton economic incentive not to say anything that might upset her white guest. Then, there were Butler's questions. Hired out as a nursemaid, Hamilton had had to give her monthly earnings to her master. "Don't you think that was fair?" Butler asked early in the conversation. "If you were fed and clothed by him, shouldn't he be paid for your work?" Well primed, the elderly ex-slave replied, "Course it been fair. . . . I belong to him and he got to get something to take care of me." Butler lobbed such leading questions again and again over the course of the interview. "Were most of the masters kind?" she asked. "Did they take good care of the slaves when their babies were born?" No doubt an expert in this Jim Crow give-and-take, Hamilton told Butler (and Murray and Montgomery) just what they wanted to hear.[40]

Still, despite their reservations, Murray and Montgomery failed to censor Augustus Ladson's work. When John Lomax visited the Columbia FWP office in July 1937, the same week he recorded the Plantation Echoes in Charleston, Montgomery shared Ladson's interview as well as Butler's with the folklore editor. Lomax suggested that she send both accounts to FWP director Henry G. Alsberg along with all her correspondence with

Murray on the issue. Alsberg's exact response to the materials Montgomery forwarded him is uncertain, but we do know that they did not induce him to disregard either narrative. Instead, both interviews with Susan Hamilton appear in the final FWP ex-slave narratives collection, which were processed and preserved by the Library of Congress's Writers' Project.[41]

Inadvertently, then, Murray and Montgomery have done scholars of historical memory a great service. By commissioning separate interviews with the same former bondwoman, one conducted by a black and the other by a white writer, they provide a clear example of how memory is rarely, if ever, an unmediated window in the past, but rather is something that is shaped by the concerns of the present. More generally, the FWP ex-slave narrative program—in both Charleston and the rest of the South—ensured the survival of thousands of individual stories of slavery, many of which, like the material collected by Frederic Bancroft, posed a fundamental challenge to the dominant narrative about slavery in the early twentieth century. "Whether the narrators relate what they saw and thought and felt, what they imagine, or what they have thought and felt about slavery since, now we know *why* they thought and felt as they did," wrote Benjamin A. Botkin, who succeeded John Lomax as FWP folklore editor, in the introduction to the Library of Congress collection. "To the white myth of slavery must be added the slaves' own folklore and folk-say of slavery."[42]

* * * *

FEW TOURISTS WHO ventured to Charleston in the interwar period would have had such intimate conversations with former slaves. But countless visitors were fascinated by the notion that the quaint buildings they found in the historic district had once played host to auctions of enslaved men, women, and children. While many white Charlestonians were unsettled by this interest, local businesses saw no reason not to capitalize off this darker portion of their city's past. As we saw in chapter 6, merchants sold counterfeit slave badges and postcards of buildings associated (accurately or not) with slavery and the slave trade. The Old Slave Mart was marketed as a must-see attraction. In 1924, Furchgott's Department Store purchased a full-page advertisement in the *Charleston Evening Post* that included short summaries of the sites that visitors to Charleston could see before taking a break at its King Street outlet. The Chalmers Street slave market was the first point of interest the advertisement featured, locating it in the top left-hand corner of the ad. These souvenirs and advertisements worked. In the early twentieth century, a steady stream of tourists re-created the 1865 pilgrimages of abolitionists who had combed the city's slave-trading district in search of relics. One 1920s postcard observed that the Old Slave Mart "attracts thousands of visitors annually."[43]

Miriam Bellangee Wilson knew this perhaps better than anyone. Born in Hamilton, Ohio, in 1878, Wilson grew up poor after her father, James, a Union Army veteran and railroad agent, died when she was just fourteen months old. As a young woman, she took night classes at Toledo University and dreamed of becoming a physician. The need to support her invalid mother, however, forced Wilson to pursue other opportunities, including skippering boats on the Great Lakes, running a tea room in Kansas City, and working for state and federal employment agencies in Toledo. In June 1920, Wilson took a temporary position in Columbia, South Carolina, to investigate employment conditions there. She completed her work by the end of the year and then decided to take a Christmas vacation with a few friends in Charleston. She never left. "The charm of the South appealed to my southern blood," explained Wilson, whose paternal grandparents had lived in Virginia.[44]

The newcomer soon became active in Charleston's burgeoning tourism industry. Working for the Chamber of Commerce, Wilson helped lure snowbirds who might stop off as they traveled home from Florida and produced a popular city map and walking tour guidebook. In 1926, she founded Colonial Belle Goodies, a confectionery that made traditional sweets and delicacies, including peach leather, benne wafers, pralines, and monkey meat cakes. At first, Wilson operated her shop on a shoestring budget, but over time she turned Colonial Belle Goodies into a modest success, shipping her confections across the globe and attracting prominent customers, including automobile magnate Henry Ford. She sold her treats at a variety of locations around the city, including the Anchorage, an antiques shop that she and a partner opened in "an olde pirate house" at 38 Queen Street.[45]

The former Ryan's Mart became the Old Slave Mart Museum in 1938. It was the first, and for much of the twentieth century the only, slavery museum in the United States.

Just a block away from the Anchorage lay the Old Slave Mart. Over the years, Wilson had observed scores of visitors meandering along its cobblestone street, stopping and staring at the rundown building. Although native whites often disputed the property's slave-trading history, Wilson researched the site and became convinced that it had, in fact, been a part of the city's antebellum slave market. By the mid-1930s, she had decided to purchase the 6 Chalmers Street property and turn it into a museum focusing on American slavery. After scraping together $300 for a down payment and spending several months restoring the space, Wilson, at the age of fifty-nine, formally opened the Old Slave Mart Museum (OSMM) for business on February 21, 1938. From 1938 until 1959, this institution, owned and operated by a northern transplant, did more to shape Charleston tourists' understanding of slavery than any other site.[46]

As the first—and, for much of the twentieth century, the only—museum in the United States focused on the history and culture of enslaved Americans, the OSMM was located in what Wilson and her successors marketed as the last remaining building in Charleston where slaves had been sold. Wilson turned the first floor of the building into a gift shop. She also moved her Colonial Belle Goodies operation there, packaging, selling, and shipping confections, which she now advertised as being based on slave recipes. The dark, drab second floor housed the OSMM

Miriam B. Wilson, an Ohio native who relocated to Charleston and opened the Old Slave Mart Museum, displayed slave-made artifacts on the second floor. Although some white Charlestonians questioned her aims, Wilson toed the local white line on slavery.

exhibits, which featured slave-made arts and crafts as well as several in-terview stalls, where, Wilson claimed, prospective buyers had examined human chattel.[47]

Until Wilson's death in 1959, the OSMM was virtually a one-woman show. "Miss Wilson," wrote Mark Harris, a *Negro Digest* reporter who visited in 1950, is "curator, chief ticket-taker, and sole lecturer at the Mu-seum." She was a "mousy little lady," with large eyeglasses that made her appear like a small owl, recalled an acquaintance from the 1950s. Ini-tially, Wilson offered her lecture each hour between nine and six and charged twenty-five cents for admission. By the 1950s, she had cut back the OSMM's hours of operation and increased the entrance fee to fifty cents. Wilson estimated that more than 10,000 people from across the world toured the OSMM annually.[48]

Wilson typically kept the OSMM open for nine months a year, clos-ing her doors only in the hot and humid summer months when tourist visits slowed. She spent many summers devouring books and manu-scripts relating to slavery at universities and libraries, including Yale, Harvard, and the University of North Carolina. Wilson filled dozens of notebooks with excerpts from newspapers, city publications, and scholarly monographs. The OSMM curator also devoted several summers to scouring the southern countryside in search of slave-made arts and crafts. These expeditions took her to every corner of the South, from Virginia to Texas, Kentucky to Georgia. Wilson enlisted local newspapers to publicize her search, and she claimed that she took advantage of the fact that a few slaveholders and former bondpeople were still alive to verify that the items she had acquired were, in fact, authentic. Eventually, Wilson added handmade bricks, tools, bedspreads, cover lids, rice-fanning baskets, furniture, quilts, copper pans, and slave badges to the OSMM collection.[49]

At a time when women involved in preservation and historical tourism faced significant obstacles, Wilson struggled more than most. While cultural elites like Susan Pringle Frost and Nell Pringle put their family names and resources on the line as they restored and preserved historic homes in Charleston, Wilson, a northerner who lived alone in a one-room apartment, had to keep her museum solvent without any sort of safety net. Initially, she used the approximately $2,500 a year she collected in admissions fees to cover her monthly mortgage and other expenses, purchase artifacts, and provide assistance to elderly black residents. Even after Wilson paid off her building note in 1945, the museum's finances remained tight.[50]

Wilson labored in vain to gain external support for the OSMM and related projects, applying unsuccessfully for fellowships from the Guggenheim and Rockefeller foundations, the Rosenwald Fund, the Blue Ridge Cultural Center, and the Eugene F. Saxton Memorial Trust. Still, Wilson was resourceful. Well into her sixties, she made her own display cases, crafted museum labels, and even installed an electrical system and fluorescent lighting. To bolster interest in the OSMM, Wilson advertised in local newspapers and on radio broadcasts, hosted performers, such as Gullah impersonator Maria Ravenel Gaillard, sold flowers, and offered handwriting analysis services. She also produced postcards of the OSMM, including one that featured a picture of Elijah Green, the ex-slave who had been interviewed by FWP writer Augustus Ladson and who sat in front of the museum each day telling stories of bondage until he died in 1945.[51]

Wilson worked hard not only to keep the OSMM afloat for two decades but also to defend it against local detractors. Early on, her interest

Former slave Elijah Green, interviewed by Augustus Ladson for the Federal Writers' Project, was a constant fixture at the Old Slave Mart Museum until he died in 1945.

in, and queries about, the sensitive subject of slavery ruffled white Charlestonians' feathers, particularly because "a Yankee was doing the asking." The OSMM seemed to threaten the idealized image of the Old South promoted by boosters, preservationists, and groups like the SPS. Locals questioned the authenticity of Wilson's site throughout her tenure. Some spread "slanderous tales" about Wilson and her museum. According to the most outlandish, Wilson "used to go out and buy raw meat from a butcher shop so that she could smear the blood on the floor and show it to tourists as the 'blood of the slaves'!"[52]

* * * *

TRUTH BE TOLD, Wilson's critics had little to fear. She did spend a great deal of time authenticating her claim that the building at 6 Chalmers Street had once been used for human trafficking by scrupulously compiling information about the property. Yet this research did not lead the northern transplant to construct a museum that emphasized the exploitative sides of slavery. Indeed, by the time she opened the doors to the OSMM in 1938, Wilson had abandoned her early misgivings about slavery and embraced the local party line.[53]

"When I went to Charleston I was just as ignorant as any other Northerner," Wilson told a Virginia reporter in the 1950s. The daughter of a decorated Union veteran, she had grown up in Ohio reading stories such as *Uncle Tom's Cabin*. And Wilson took great pride in her family's anti-slavery sentiments. She boasted that her paternal grandfather, Robert Wilson, had not only left Virginia for Ohio because of his deep opposition to the institution of slavery but thereafter was active in the Underground Railroad. Although Wilson never disavowed her antislavery heritage, she became sympathetic to the white southern perspective while living in Charleston. Her transformation was so complete, Wilson told a reporter in 1948, that around town "she is called a 'Yamdankee' rather than a 'DamYankee' because of her intense love and sympathy for the South."[54]

Wilson's newfound perspective was not a crass accommodation to popular opinion, nor was she simply catering to tourists' tastes. Instead, by the time Wilson purchased the Old Slave Mart in 1937, she had become a true believer. Perhaps the most important factor in Wilson's conversion was her trips to nearby plantations and conversations with their former owners. In 1927, she visited Mullet Hall Plantation on Johns Island with a senior member of the Legare family, which had owned it for generations. Highlighting the struggles of the former planter class in a letter to her mother, Wilson emphasized how enjoyable this veritable trip back into the past had been, especially when she observed the reunion between Mrs. Legare and "her old servants and plantation hands." Wilson noted that "they were all so delighted to see their Ol' Missis, and she them." Decades later, she attributed her strong interest in history to such early interactions with elderly white southerners. They "had grown up on plantations and had been through the War Between the States and its aftermath," she explained in 1956. "The stories they told stirred my imagination and still linger."[55]

Little wonder that when she opened her museum Wilson underscored the challenges that plantation masters and mistresses faced, while also embracing the trope of the faithful slave so ubiquitous in elite Charleston circles. One of the stalls on the second floor of her museum featured replicas of two slaves, Aunt Cylla and Uncle Pink, who would not abandon their owners during the Civil War. Wilson also dedicated the third edition of *Slave Days*, the published version of her museum tour that she sold as a pamphlet, to "the memory of the loyal faithful negroes who, during and after the war between the states remained faithful to their former owners." And like the Society for the Preservation of Spirituals and other white spirituals groups, Wilson had a paternalistic understanding of her work at the OSMM. "When one sees the beautiful things that they did during slavery, and how these crafts have been lost, it is a shame to deprive posterity of this knowledge," she wrote in 1950.[56]

Wilson found scholarly validation for these nostalgic memories in the academic works that she pored over in the 1930s and 1940s. She was particularly enamored with the scholarship of Ulrich B. Phillips. Wilson urged OSMM visitors to read the southern historian's work, and her own *Slave Days* pamphlet drew on it extensively. In 1951, she made a pilgrimage to New Haven to examine the slave manuscript collection that Phillips had bequeathed to Yale University, calling the trip "the most enjoyable six weeks I have ever spent." Two years later, Wilson received a letter from an Air Force captain stationed in Puerto Rico, requesting to borrow a copy of Phillips's *American Negro Slavery*, no doubt a reflection of the emphasis she put on the book in her OSMM tour. Wilson even gave Phillips the last word on slavery in her tour pamphlet, quoting the final paragraph of *American Negro Slavery* at the end of *Slave Days*.[57]

Influenced by Phillips's work and the reminiscences of local planters, she downplayed local participation in human trafficking, despite her insistence that her building had once been part of a slave-auction complex. In the 1946 edition of *Slave Days*, Wilson held that "in some sections of the South there was very little speculating in slaves." Slave purchases in these areas did not reflect a desire to profit from a trade in human flesh, she insisted, but rather the need to replace a labor force depleted by disease or to settle estates. "Research shows that in many sections it was a matter of pride with the planters never to buy or sell a slave," Wilson wrote. "In fact, there are numerous records showing no slaves bought or sold within one hundred years." Wilson made it clear what part of the South she meant, once telling a Tennessee reporter that slave auctions "were seldom held in Charleston because owners did not like the idea of selling their slaves."[58]

Wilson tried to soften the slave trade's sharpest edges, too. The 1956 edition of *Slave Days* included a copy of a handbill advertising the 1852 sale of twenty-five enslaved laborers, twelve of whom were under the age of ten. Yet Wilson tempered this message with a caption stating that the slaves were sold together as families. Wilson also strove to undercut the idea that slavery itself was inhumane, arguing that the horrors of the institution, at least as practiced in the Old South, have "been greatly overstated."[59]

Wilson even went so far as to try to discredit visual evidence that testified to slavery's cruelty. "Pictures showing Negro drivers (sub-overseers) with whips in their hands do not necessarily mean that whips were for use on Negroes," she declared in *Slave Days*. Wilson was convinced that there had to be alternative explanations for the scars that the survivors of slavery carried on their backs. "The fact has been established," she held, "that where the underground railway prevailed, the Negroes themselves would cause injuries to rouse the sympathy of those who were helping them to escape." When Grace and Knickerbacker Davis, writers from Germantown, Pennsylvania, toured the OSMM in early 1941, Wilson told them that the scars were "the remains of tribal tattooing inflicted before transportation to America."[60]

More generally, Wilson cast slavery as a labor system that rewarded the enslaved with the gift of civilization. Planters may have enjoyed the fruits of their slaves' labor, but they reciprocated by providing food, shelter, and housing for their charges. The artifacts that she displayed in the OSMM reinforced this narrative, offering tangible evidence of the lessons slavery had taught. So, too, did the emphasis that Wilson put on slaveholder manumission, which she suggested was far more prevalent in the Old South than the sale of slaves. And her portrayal of emancipation and Reconstruction only bolstered her message. To her mind, "the crime against the Negro was *not* that he became our slave, for they had always known slavery in some form. . . . The crime against the Negro was turning them loose without proper guidance." In other words, the true tragedy to Wilson was that the Civil War and its aftermath had interrupted the civilizing process inaugurated under slavery before its work was complete.[61]

Wilson believed that by teaching Americans about the black past, the OSMM could help rectify the social problems of the present. "My museum was founded for the purpose of saving specimens of all the crafts that the Negroes became proficient in doing during Ante-bellum days," she wrote the president of the Tuskegee Institute after touring the Alabama school in 1948. "The lecture I give is to try to bring about a better understanding between the two races, so that we can be mutually helpful to each other." Wilson deemed the average white person ignorant of the challenges blacks faced, while she thought that others sought to exploit African Americans or were misguided by sentimentalism. And blacks, to her mind, were apt to view the enslaved past with embarrassment. In contrast, Wilson insisted that she approached the race question from a practical perspective—much like the Tuskegee Institute's founder, Booker T. Washington.[62]

Wilson, in fact, was a strong proponent of Washington, whom she called "the greatest leader the Negroes ever had." She displayed a picture of Washington, who had died in 1915, in the OSMM and praised his accommodationist program as an invaluable alternative to the civil rights agitation of the postwar era, which she steadfastly opposed. In her 1946 *Slave Days* pamphlet, she maintained that "the Negroes who are following his teachings are accomplishing much more for the race" than those working for equal rights. Wilson's civilizing interpretation of slavery dovetailed with Washington's emphasis on gradual change, industrial education, and black self-help. By highlighting the great strides made by the enslaved, the museum operator believed she was helping black and white Americans to see what was possible in the Jim Crow South.[63]

Tourists from across the country appear to have appreciated Wilson's lessons, writing her letters of thanks for what she taught them about slavery. "We felt as though we were transferred to another (more exciting) world," effused a New Jersey housewife after visiting the OSMM with her family in 1952. "I feel the Old South thrills everyone but no one can realize just how thrilling it must have been until they hear you."[64]

Not every visitor, however, was pleased by what they saw and heard at the OSMM. One spring evening in the late 1930s or early 1940s, sociologist Katharine Du Pre Lumpkin stumbled upon Wilson's museum while strolling through town. Although a native Georgian and the daughter of a Confederate veteran, Lumpkin had come to reject the Lost Cause mythology upon which she had been reared. Peeking inside the heavy door of the OSMM, Lumpkin was struck by the place's incongruity with its past. As she wrote in her 1947 autobiography, "What once had seen the buying and selling of slaves now welcomed the visitor to a tidy, almost gay souvenir shop selling candy and postcards and knickknacks." Lumpkin was not able to tour the museum—it was closed for the day—but she was put off by Wilson's brief description of her approach to the slave past.

Noticing the stairs that led to the second floor, where the museum's collection was located, Lumpkin asked what she would find up there. Wilson replied sharply, "only pleasant reminders. We don't go in for slave horrors."[65]

A few years later, *Negro Digest* writer Mark Harris wrote a sarcastic send-up of what he had learned on his 1950 visit to the OSMM. Although this Jewish New Yorker found Wilson charming and expressed appreciation for her preservation efforts, he laid bare myriad misgivings about her characterization of slavery. Clear-eyed visitors "may not agree that slave-owners met their responsibilities to their slaves with 'kindness and courage,'" Harris maintained. "They may doubt her judgment that the crime against Negroes was not that they were enslaved but they were too hastily freed," and "they may flinch at her assertion that the Federal ban on slave-importation in 1808 was a positive evil." But "these are small points," Harris concluded with his tongue firmly planted in his cheek. "When in Charleston do as Charleston does! You'll get along better that way."[66]

As if to head off such critiques, Wilson made a point of highlighting the popularity of the OSMM among African Americans. Black educators who had visited the museum "all speak highly of the work I am doing," she claimed in 1941. Thirteen years later, Avery graduate Ethelyn M. Parker told Wilson that the OSMM "really has a wonderful future." Yet Parker added, "most of my people do not relish the idea of carrying on the slavery idea."[67]

However much other African Americans shared this disinterest, some black South Carolinians did, in fact, visit the OSMM. In April 1956, seventy undergraduates and two teachers from historically black Morris College in Sumter made a trip to Wilson's museum, when it hosted a special exhibit of watercolors depicting slave handicrafts. Millicent Brown, the daughter of the Charleston NAACP chapter president, took regular field trips to Wilson's museum while she was a student at all-black A.B. Rhett Elementary School in the 1950s. Reflecting back on these experiences a half century later, Brown was struck by how little she learned. The museum was a mishmash of artifacts displayed in glass cases. And Wilson did not seem to take much interest in providing context for what Brown and her classmates were seeing. The little that Wilson did say about slavery, Brown recalled, left the impression that she was not sympathetic to the experiences of the enslaved or their descendants.[68]

* * * *

WILSON SPENT A good portion of the late 1940s and 1950s working on a historical novel that she believed would spread the OSMM's message about slavery throughout the United States. According to her notes, "Oogah" would follow the rise and fall of an African prince who, after being captured by slave traders and brought to the Old South, thrived on a southern plantation only to struggle when he and his family were freed without sufficient guidance. Yet Wilson's work at the OSMM afforded her little time to write, and she died on July 8, 1959, before she could complete her novel. She remained an outspoken opponent of civil rights to the end.[69]

Wilson bequeathed the OSMM collection and the 6 Chalmers Street property to the Charleston Museum, which declined both. The OSMM and its contents ultimately ended up in the hands of Wilson's good friend Louise Alston Graves and her sister Judith Wragg Chase. Though born in New Jersey and Georgia, respectively, the sisters—who came from several old-line Charleston families and counted DuBose Heyward a cousin—settled in Charleston in the mid-twentieth century. Graves and Chase thought the OSMM was a treasure that must be preserved. Fearing that it might be torn down, they made arrangements to lease the building and reopened the museum in November 1960. Several years later, the sisters bought the building and its contents.[70]

Graves and Chase made minor improvements to the OSMM, but tried to stick closely to Wilson's vision. "Whatever we do, however, we don't plan to stray from Miss Wilson's original objectives," Chase told a reporter. A few years after taking over the museum, Chase explained what this fidelity looked like. In a 1963 letter lobbying the city to install a sign pointing the way to the OSMM, she informed the chairman of Charleston's Commission on Streets that "since tourists to the South are always interested in the subject of slavery, whether we like it or not, we feel we are doing the South a favor by presenting the History of Slavery in an objective way. Day in and day out we help to correct erroneous and uncomplimentary ideas gained from such books as 'Uncle Tom's Cabin' and to give our visitors a more tolerant viewpoint of the problems that beset the South during Slavery."[71]

While Graves and Chase kept Wilson's mission alive, another segment of Charleston began deploying the black past in a significantly different fashion. Just weeks after Judith Chase wrote these words, in fact, civil rights protesters launched the Charleston Movement to contest the racial barriers that African Americans faced in the city more than a century after emancipation. In the process, they not only cast off the Jim Crow veil that had concealed black memories of slavery for decades, but also enlisted those memories in their new fight for freedom.

Part IV

CIVIL RIGHTS
ERA
AND
BEYOND

9

We Shall
Overcome

IN EARLY JUNE 1963, A SERIES OF NAACP-ORGANIZED boycotts, marches, and sit-ins punctured Charleston's preferred atmosphere of genteel calm. Hundreds of African Americans, mostly students, participated in the Charleston Movement, demanding the desegregation of public schools and public accommodations, fair employment, and the creation of a biracial committee to tackle future problems. By early July, arrests totaled over five hundred, though violence remained at bay. Democratic Mayor J. Palmer Gaillard Jr. and the police chief made sure of it, hoping to prevent another Birmingham, where just two months earlier vicious attacks on protesters by police dogs and firehoses had led to international outrage. On July 7, NAACP national director Roy Wilkins spoke before a capacity crowd at Emanuel A.M.E. Church, a base of operations for the protests, observing that while segregation in Charleston may have been "peaceful and graceful," it mattered little. "Castor oil tastes as bad with a little orange juice as with nothing at all."[1]

Events came to a head on July 16, when a crowd of five hundred gathered outside the *News and Courier* offices at the corner of King and Columbus streets to denounce editor Thomas "Tom" R. Waring Jr.'s hardline position against desegregation. Having assumed the editorial reins of the *News and Courier* from his uncle William Watts Ball in 1951, Waring had led the chorus of white resistance to the black freedom struggle in the Lowcountry for more than a decade.

Asked at one point by the police to stop the singing of freedom songs during their vigil outside the newspaper office, the activists refused. As they confronted one of the most formidable figures of white supremacy in the city, Charleston Movement participants were loath to give up the songs that had proved a potent source of inspiration and camaraderie throughout their campaign. Since the beginning of the protests in June, activists had sung freedom songs—including old slave spirituals—as the police hauled them off to jail. Lindy Cooper, a liberal, white Charleston teenager who watched the demonstrations that summer, remembered witnessing arrests after a boycott of King Street stores. Protesters started drumming on the sides of the paddy wagon and then sang "Come En Go Wid Me." Cooper knew the Gullah spiritual as one the Society for the Preservation of Spirituals liked to perform. But the King Street protesters altered the song to fit their circumstances: "They were saying instead of 'if you want to go to heaven, come and go with me' it was 'if you want your freedom, stay off King Street.'"[2]

This political use of slave spirituals was not new. Back in 1945, when more than one thousand workers at Charleston's American Tobacco Company Cigar Factory went on strike, they, too, looked to the slave past as a source of power. Led by Lucille Simmons, a black laborer with a captivating alto voice, the striking workers sang "I Will Overcome," based, in part, on a Lowcountry slave spiritual known as both "Many Thousand Gone" and "No More Auction Block." In the face of police harassment and company intransigence, the workers found the song a source of hope and, along the way, crafted new verses—"we will win our rights," "we will win this fight," "we will overcome"—that gave the song greater collective and political meaning. "Someone would say, boy I don't know how we are going to make it," striker Stephen P. Graham remembered, "but 'We'll overcome someday.'" By the time the Charleston Movement brought America's Most Historic City to its knees in 1963, a slightly altered version of the tobacco workers' song, "We Shall Overcome," had emerged as the unofficial anthem of the civil rights movement, its redemptive message ringing out from protest lines, Freedom Rides, and jail cells throughout the South.[3]

During Jim Crow, the public memory of slavery in Charleston had been a white one—constructed on concert stages, in tourism guidebooks, and at sites like the Old Slave Mart Museum. As the civil rights movement gained momentum in the postwar period, African American activists in the city and surrounding Sea Islands pushed their own memories of the peculiar institution into the public sphere for the first time in decades. Their aim was, in a sense, simple: they hoped to make the Lowcountry's history more accurate and inclusive. But the African American determination to remember slavery was about more than just a desire to overcome historical amnesia. It was about finding a usable past. Activists harnessed the memory of slavery to animate their fight against Jim Crow, transforming memory into a source of power.

* * * *

THE 1945 TOBACCO workers strike signaled a new day in Charleston, as in the rest of the South. The walkout was an early indication of how rising black expectations in the post–World War II era would shatter the foundations of Jim Crow. Over the next decade, the black assault on the racial status quo became a mass movement. Galvanized by the NAACP's victory in the 1954 *Brown v. Board of Education* decision, which ordered the desegregation of public schools, activists all over the region took aim at the system of racial apartheid that white southerners had imposed in the late nineteenth century. In places like Birmingham, peaceful protesters took to the streets to demand the integration of public facilities, the hiring of African Americans, and the end to discriminatory voting measures.[4]

The backlash at every turn was daunting. White southerners countered the court order to desegregate with a program of massive resistance, instituting creative compliance plans that allowed for minimal, token integration while threatening black parents who dared to push the issue too much. Other forms of reprisal were more malicious. Despite being dedicated to the moral and strategic advantages of nonviolence, civil rights protesters were hauled off to jail, confronted by angry mobs, assaulted with rocks and brickbats, and, sometimes, murdered for their activism.[5]

Still, black southerners and sympathetic whites triumphed, to a degree. If true economic justice remained elusive—and structural racism more difficult to eradicate—the victories were nevertheless real. Pushed by activists, Congress passed the Civil Rights Act in 1964, which outlawed segregation in public accommodations and employment, and the Voting Rights Act in 1965, which swept away the discriminatory measures whites had long used to disenfranchise black southerners. By the mid-1960s, life in the South had been fundamentally altered.[6]

In America's Most Historic City, the 1963 Charleston Movement represented the culmination of local civil rights agitation, building not just on the earlier tobacco workers strike but also on a series of direct action campaigns in 1960 and 1962. By September 1963, the Charleston Movement had won some important victories, such as the establishment of the biracial committee, a promise of equal employment opportunities, and the desegregation of restrooms and water fountains. In keeping with his cautious stance throughout the Charleston Movement, Mayor Gaillard, descended from an old-line Huguenot family, accepted the outcome but never voiced eager support for the protesters' goals. Meanwhile, as the Charleston Movement wound down, a federal district judge ruled in favor of several NAACP plaintiffs and ordered the desegregation of Charleston city schools—nine years after the *Brown* decision. On September 3, 1963, four formerly all-white schools became the first in the state of South Carolina to open their doors to black students.[7]

In challenging Jim Crow, black Charlestonians challenged the myth of interracial harmony that whites had nurtured since imposing segregation—and even before. No group had better epitomized this myth—or had done more to perpetuate it—than the Society for the Preservation of Spirituals (SPS). In some ways, the SPS carried on much as it had before, despite the racial unrest roiling Charleston, continuing to perform several times a year. The society maintained its charity program for needy blacks as well, though in 1958 SPS treasurer Henry B. Smythe noted that the society was currently helping only one person, a fact he called "rather ridiculous" given that philanthropy was one of the group's primary concerns. His fellow spiritualists took heed. By the end of the year, the society had come to the aid of five individuals.[8]

Part of the problem in allocating sufficient money for its welfare fund seems to have resulted from another long-standing tradition: treating practices as parties. In 1968, the society's liquid refreshment expenses totaled $529, while its charity expenses equaled $535, prompting another round of soul-searching. The evidence of declining interest that emerged in the prewar years reappeared in the 1950s and 1960s. One solution was a change in the group's cocktail policy. In 1965, it voted to serve drinks as soon as everyone arrived at meetings, rather than after practice had concluded, in the hopes "that this might result in more prompt attendance, and more enthusiastic singing."[9]

Yet the SPS's records from this era reveal uneasiness over more than just lackluster attendance. Concerns about the assault on segregation permeated the group's meetings, correspondence, and activities. While SPS members had fretted over the disappearance of old-time "darkeys" for decades, in the post-*Brown* South these anxieties reached new heights. One member who requested money for a charity case pointed out that the recipient was from a family of "faithful negroes" and a "relict of the Old Regime," not someone who sympathized with the calls for a new racial order.[10]

Desegregation and the civil rights movement began to challenge the commonly held understanding of the society's singing and preservation work, too. By 1956, the changed landscape inspired an acknowledgment, at least by one white Charlestonian, that some observers might find the SPS problematic. That year, a CBS radio producer wrote to John M. Rivers, a Charleston contact, to inquire if he knew of any Lowcountry folk music that could be featured on the network. Rivers recommended the SPS but admitted that "with all of the to do about segregation, there is some question as to whether or not this kind of music or entertainment would be acceptable to your show." Still, he maintained, the group was unique and "probably more than any other one thing represents the direct affection which the white people of lower South Carolina held and hold for the Negroes in whom they are interested."[11]

African Americans, for their part, began to publicly criticize groups like the SPS. In 1959, a Jacksonville, Florida, newspaper ran a piece about an upcoming SPS concert in the city but predicted that if the NAACP had its way, spirituals would "become extinct as the dodo bird." Since the 1940s, the civil rights organization had sought to improve the way that Hollywood and the emerging television industry portrayed African Americans. This campaign targeted characters, such as Amos and Andy, that reinforced negative stereotypes, as well as stories and songs that used black dialect. The paper regretted that the NAACP was encouraging African Americans to turn their backs on their past and suggested that it was because spirituals were associated with slavery that blacks wanted nothing to do with them. SPS members and like-minded Charlestonians agreed that it was the duty of whites to preserve what blacks would just as soon forget. Artist Elizabeth O'Neill Verner argued in a forceful letter to the *News and Courier* in 1960 that "the colored people do not appreciate their heritage"—specifically, slave spirituals—but fortunately their white friends did.[12]

By the early 1960s, many whites took it for granted that civil rights activists frowned upon the SPS and similar performers. A woman who handled arrangements for a 1960 SPS concert in Cheraw, a small town near the North Carolina border, reported to the group that she had "exploited the fact that the N.A.A.C.P. disapproves of your efforts" in the publicity materials for the performance. "You might bear this in mind in future efforts," she offered, "because I discovered that a number of people who attended on Saturday were there partially because they are so irritated at the N.A.A.C.P." SPS members, however, were more inclined to see African American criticism as a threat rather than as an unintended boon. In November 1963, on the heels of the Charleston Movement, society officers felt uneasy enough about the "racial situation and our concerts" to meet with Mayor Gaillard, *News and Courier* editor Tom Waring, and Emmett Robinson, head of the Footlight Players Workshop, where the SPS gave its annual spring performances. "All three gentlemen agreed the concerts should be continued," SPS president Dr. John A. Siegling reported.[13]

The racial situation caused headaches in other ways, too. In 1968, the SPS was asked to appear in a documentary on the arts in South Carolina produced by the state Arts Commission. After learning that the commission hoped to acquire federal money to pay for the filming, the society voted to invite one of the producers to a practice, but only "after having checked . . . to determine that there would be no integration problem," presumably believing that the federally funded project might invite unwanted scrutiny into its unusual form of cultural preservation or its whites-only membership. But filmmakers were the least of the group's worries. By 1968, the society feared that protests, even violence, might disrupt its shows. That spring, SPS president Siegling requested that police periodically cruise the box offices before two concerts, one at the Footlight Players Workshop in Charleston and another at a theater in Spartanburg, where the society was slated to perform.[14]

It is entirely plausible, as the Jacksonville newspaper contended, that the black opponents of the SPS wanted to forget spirituals and slavery. As we have seen, some educated, urbanized African Americans rejected spirituals in favor of more formal forms of worship. Moreover, by the late 1960s, when the SPS felt compelled to turn to the police, the rise of the Black Power movement may have cast a pall on the spiritual among more radical civil rights activists, who viewed the genre as antiquated and indebted to a passive model of black resistance. But the recollections of white folk musician and civil rights activist Guy Carawan point to another possibility. Carawan noted that for some younger activists in groups like the Student Nonviolent Coordinating Committee, being exposed to spirituals during these years was a revelation. It was the first time, he said, that they had heard "songs from the days of slavery that sang of freedom in their own way. They began to realize how much of their heritage had not been passed on to them." The threats to the tranquillity of SPS shows in 1968, in other words, may have come from black civil rights activists who, newly attuned to the history of slave spirituals, objected to the appropriation of spirituals by whites.[15]

* * * *

GUY CARAWAN HIMSELF played a somewhat surprising role in helping movement participants adapt Lowcountry spirituals to the context of the civil rights struggle. Born and raised in Los Angeles, Carawan was an outsider to the spirituals tradition, though he did have deep roots in the South, even in Charleston. Carawan's mother, Henrietta Aiken Kelly Carawan, hailed from a prominent Charleston family. Her aunt and namesake, Henrietta Aiken Kelly, founded the Charleston Female Seminary, the Poppenheim sisters' alma mater. As a child, the younger Henrietta grew up attending St. Philip's Church and always considered herself a "proud 'Charlestonian blueblood.'" There is no evidence that she had any special interest in spirituals that she passed on to her son, but Guy's southern heritage (his father was from North Carolina) stirred his curiosity about the folkways of the region.[16]

Carawan came of age in the folk music worlds of the West Coast and New York City. As an undergraduate at Occidental College in Los Angeles, he was exposed to folk music, and he later read about Gullah culture while pursuing his master's degree in sociology at UCLA. During his years on the West Coast in the 1950s, he first heard the most famous song to which Lowcountry blacks helped give rise: "We Shall Overcome." Carawan learned the song from folk singer Frank Hamilton, who had picked it up from Pete Seeger, who had gotten it from Zilphia Horton, the music director of the Highlander Folk School, a training ground for civil rights activists located near Monteagle, Tennessee. Zilphia, for her part, first heard the song in its earlier form, "We Will Overcome," from two Charleston tobacco workers—Anna Lee Bonneau and Evelyn Risher. Not long after the Charleston strike concluded, Bonneau and Risher attended a workshop on union organizing at Highlander, sharing the song with Zilphia and other workshop participants.[17]

By the end of the 1950s, Carawan's appreciation for Lowcountry music had deepened. In 1959, he became Highlander's music director, replacing Zilphia after her death. That July, Carawan helped lead a workshop on developing community leadership. Fifty participants, including fifteen from the South Carolina Sea Islands, learned strategies for solving problems in their hometowns. "And such a week of singing I've never heard in my life," Carawan reported. "Old style spiritual singing by the older folks and more modern gospel singing by the younger ones."[18]

On the evening of July 31, the final night of the workshop, police raided Highlander as part of a campaign to shut down the school for allegedly fomenting communist subversion. For an hour and a half, as the police searched the premises, the group sang spirituals, including "We Shall Overcome," adding a new verse, "We are not afraid." Carawan, Septima Clark (the Charleston-born activist then serving as Highlander's director of education), and two others were arrested on bogus alcohol charges (Grundy County was dry). Clark occupied a cell next to Carawan's in the county jail. Through the walls, Carawan heard Clark, who had overcome her adolescent antipathy for slave spirituals, singing "Michael Row the Boat Ashore," a Sea Island slave spiritual. The song "made me feel better," he wrote to Pete Seeger and others after the ordeal. "I shortly fell asleep to it and woke up the next morning well rested in spite of the lumpy hard springs."[19]

Later that year, Carawan took up temporary residency on Johns Island to help Clark with her Citizenship School program. Founded in 1957 by Clark and Esau Jenkins, a Johns Island activist who had also trained at Highlander, Citizenship Schools helped illiterate blacks learn to read and write so that they could pass South Carolina's literacy test and register to vote. Carawan's involvement with Citizenship Schools and his friendship with Jenkins, especially, afforded him unusual access to the Sea Island black community. As Carawan noted, Jenkins was "the most loved and respected 'grass roots'" leader in the area—the "Moses of his people." Connecting with such a prominent local, who himself appreciated the

In 1959, white folk musician Guy Carawan (playing guitar) went to Johns Island, where he worked to preserve Gullah spirituals. He saw the songs as an untapped resource in the fight against segregation.

music of the Sea Islands, proved profoundly important to Carawan. Jenkins was instrumental in facilitating the folk singer's exposure to the local corpus of slave spirituals. Along with Sea Island women like Alice Wine and Bessie Jones, Jenkins became a bridge between the songs' quasi-private use in the African American community and their public use within the civil rights movement.[20]

In fact, at Jenkins's invitation, Carawan became the first white person to ever attend the special Christmas service at Moving Star Hall. Congregants gathered at this hybrid communal center, benevolent society, and interdenominational praise house to hear preaching and to shout—a fusion of song, dance, and polyrhythmic percussion that dated back to the ring shout of the enslaved. At the Christmas Watch Meeting, attendees shouted from midnight on Christmas Eve to dawn. What he heard during that 1959 service was "rich and exciting," Carawan and his wife, Candie, later wrote, and "it brought him back year after year." It also convinced Carawan that spirituals should occupy a prominent place in Citizenship Schools. He incorporated the songs into the curriculum, adding a singing component to the end of every class in early 1960. Carawan then inaugurated a special spirituals concert to conclude each Citizenship School session.[21]

According to Carawan, some black Johns Islanders needed help in appreciating the importance of the old slave spirituals, a claim that was not without some merit. The social and demographic forces that had conspired to endanger spirituals since emancipation had accelerated in the post–World War II years, with greater educational and economic opportunities pushing younger blacks away from Gullah culture, if not off the island altogether, and a suburban boom bringing in whites and more urbanized blacks from the city. Although spirituals singing still occurred at praise houses like Moving Star Hall and, on occasion, at other black churches, younger black islanders were not enthusiastic about the shouting at either place. "Why waste time with something that you aren't gonna get anything out of at all?" asked Black Power activist William "Bill" Saunders, who grew up going to Moving Star Hall. "You gonna be looking forward to when you die, and man, you hungry now." Saunders and his peers were drawn to contemporary musical styles like soul, rhythm and blues, and gospel. Carawan found that even some older residents had started to back away from spirituals, appearing self-conscious when singing in front of more-educated blacks and whites, like folklorist Alan Lomax, son of John Lomax, who celebrated their performances.[22]

Carawan observed that Gullah spirituals singers were genuinely moved to learn that others appreciated their music. They needed no one, however, to tell them what the songs meant, a fact that Carawan understood. When Citizenship School students sang spirituals such as "Been in the Storm So Long," they shared personal testimonies about how the songs had helped them "overcome their many hardships." Esau Jenkins explained why older islanders sang spirituals in similar terms: "They're giving praise to the great Supreme Being who . . . stood by them in the past days from slavery up to the present. . . . Those songs are the ones that made them happy, made them go through those hard days." In addition to the important psychological function spirituals performed in the daily lives of Johns Islanders, Jenkins and Carawan both predicted, correctly, that the songs might bring more students into the Citizenship Schools.[23]

Carawan made the case for spirituals as weapons in the struggle for civil rights beyond Johns Island, too. The sit-in movement was raging throughout the South, and at his urging, spirituals became a part of the body of freedom songs that activists sang in the service of their cause. In 1960, Guy Carawan introduced "We Shall Overcome" to members of the Student Nonviolent Coordinating Committee (SNCC) at their founding meeting in Raleigh, North Carolina. Carawan also taught movement activists "Keep Your Eyes on the Prize," a variation of "Keep Your Hand on the Plow," which he had learned from Alice Wine, a Moving Star Hall singer, during his visit to Johns Island in 1959. Given their focus on liberation and deliverance, spirituals seemed to Carawan valuable tools of protest at this moment of intense social activism. "So many great old spirituals that express hatred of oppression and a longing for freedom were being left out of this growing freedom movement," Carawan held. Since activists "were not taking advantage of what their heritage had to offer," he made it his mission to help them do so.[24]

A visit to Nashville, which was embroiled in a three-month sit-in campaign in the spring of 1960, encapsulated the challenges inherent in Carawan's effort. "The first time I remember any change in our songs was when Guy came down from Highlander," C.T. Vivian, an African American ministerial student and organizer, later said. Carawan introduced "Follow the Drinking Gourd," and "he gave some background on it and boom, that began to make sense. And little by little, spiritual after spiritual after spiritual began to appear with new words and changes." Activists like Vivian were initially unsure of the utility of the songs and ambivalent about the message they conveyed. Carawan observed that some Fisk University students were embarrassed to sing and clap in the "rural free swinging style." The Fisk Jubilee Singers, with which students would have been familiar, sang in a more formal, concert style, without the shouting and stomping that characterized the singing of spirituals in the Lowcountry. But there was also reluctance to sing what were, as Carawan appreciated, "very personal songs about salvation." Activists, in other words, had to break down the division between the sacred and the secular and connect the songs to the aims of the freedom struggle. As Vivian remembered, "I don't think we had ever thought of spirituals as movement material."[25]

According to Vivian, many movement participants gradually warmed to the idea, removing the spiritual from the past and learning to adapt it to the challenges they faced. Bernice Johnson Reagon, a black SNCC activist and founding member of the Freedom Singers group that toured the country in support of the movement, explained this new approach to the songs. She recalled the first time she sang an old tune—"Over My Head I See Trouble in the Air"—at a mass meeting by exchanging the word "trouble" for the word "freedom." Reagon then realized that "these songs were mine and I could use them for what I needed." In Charleston, as we have seen, protesters used the songs for what they needed, too, altering lyrics to suit the context of their local fight against segregation.[26]

Still, pockets of resistance remained. After their marriage in 1961, Guy and Candie Carawan sponsored several music workshops for SNCC and Southern Christian Leadership Conference activists. Candie, whom Guy met during the 1960 Nashville sit-ins, was not a musician herself. But she was a skilled writer and SNCC organizer who became Guy's chief collaborator in sharing music with movement participants. In May 1964, the couple organized the Sing for Freedom Festival and Workshop in Atlanta. The Carawans had invited the Georgia-based Sea Island Singers, led by Bessie Jones, to perform at the workshop. They hoped the assembled activists would see the virtues of using the Sea Island Singers' slave spirituals as they protested segregation in their communities. But Josh Dunson, who covered the event for the folk magazine *Broadside*, reported that several attendees balked at the material. As Jones and her group shared spirituals and told "old slave stories," whispers of Uncle Tomism rippled throughout the group. The discussion became heated. One rural woman complained that she was there to learn new songs, not ones she heard at home. Charles Sherrod, who had played a key role in organizing the 1961–62 Albany Movement in Georgia, argued that slave songs had no place at a freedom workshop. Many of the younger activists, Dunson wrote, preferred newer gospel songs and were "ashamed of the 'down home' and 'old time' music."[27]

Bessie Jones shot back. She insisted on the historical and contemporary importance of slave spirituals, making the case that they were "the only place where we could say that we did not like slavery, say it for ourselves to hear." Rather than viewing the songs as manifestations of degradation, Jones pushed workshop participants to see them as instruments of critique and survival—as the method by which the enslaved safely protested their condition and focused on their ultimate deliverance. Workshop participant Reagon, for her part, told the Carawans that hearing the Sea Island Singers changed her life.[28]

* * * *

THE CARAWANS BELIEVED so fervently in the importance of preserving and promoting indigenous black music on Johns Island that they moved there in 1963. The couple also continued to nurture appreciation for spirituals beyond Johns Island, and their partnership with Esau Jenkins remained central to their efforts. Working closely with Jenkins, they took the Moving Star Hall Singers on the road to perform at folk festivals in Los Angeles, San Francisco, and Newport, Rhode Island.[29]

During their time on Johns Island, the Carawans undertook two other major projects to promote Gullah spirituals and culture. First, they partnered with Jenkins to organize a series of folk festivals. Guy hoped the Sea Island Folk Festival for Community Development, inaugurated in the fall of 1963, would promote a revival of spirituals and provide financial support for groups like the Moving Star Hall Singers. Carawan also envisioned the festivals as a way to meet certain "psychological needs" among blacks who had been "conditioned to be ashamed of the way they express themselves." He wanted, in short, to instill pride in and through slave spirituals. Carawan was careful to position the folk festivals in such a way that local whites might attend, too. He well understood that most white Charlestonians would not go to a "straight political meeting" and publicly insisted that the festivals had "nothing to do with the civil rights question." Yet he saw the festivals, pitched correctly, as an opportunity to facilitate white contact with, and maybe even interest in, the civil rights movement.[30]

Among a small group of liberal white Charlestonians, Carawan's strategy worked. Lindy Cooper saw a newspaper ad about one of the festivals and decided to attend with some friends. "We came out to hear the music, not really expecting what all we got," she recalled. "We had been the bunch of Southerners who had their heads stuck in the sand about the civil rights situation." Hearing the music in this particular setting, learning afterward at the Carawans' home how to shout from the likes of Bessie Jones, and simply being in a racially mixed audience—all of these contributed to a new "awareness" on Cooper's part. Few white festivalgoers

Guy Carawan and Esau Jenkins inaugurated the Sea Island Folk Festival in the mid-1960s to promote spirituals and broaden the appeal of the civil rights movement.

likely experienced such a racial awakening, but Carawan at least succeeded in getting them there. He estimated that 40 percent of the seven-hundred-person audience at one of the early festivals was white. Other folk artists came, too. Alan Lomax, who attended in 1963, claimed that he saw more good folk singers at the Sea Island Folk Festival than he had at the Newport Folk Festival earlier that summer.[31]

One group Lomax did not see was the Society for the Preservation of Spirituals. Lomax himself seems to have appreciated the preservation efforts of the SPS. Guy Carawan, by contrast, was critical. He invited the SPS to attend the Sea Island Folk Festivals, but they refused. "They can say they're interested in this material, but they didn't want the black people to sing [it] publicly or to be heard," he later remembered. Only the SPS "could do it." Whether or not the SPS wanted black spirituals singers to remain silent in public is an open question, but it is clear that the group continued to avoid events that included black spirituals troupes. In 1969, the SPS declined an invitation from the National Folk Festival in Knoxville, Tennessee, because the Moving Star Hall Singers were scheduled to perform.[32]

The Carawans' second major endeavor on Johns Island was researching and writing *Ain't You Got a Right to the Tree of Life*, an eclectic collection published by Simon and Schuster in 1966. In addition to a preface by Alan Lomax and an introduction written by the Carawans, the book includes oral histories, transcriptions of spirituals, and photographs. The Carawans intended the work as a tribute to black folk culture and their friends on the island, especially to Jenkins. Most of the text consists of native Johns Islanders explaining their customs, especially how they relished "shouting for a better day" at Moving Star Hall, and telling family histories.[33]

Interspersed throughout the book, the spirituals root these descriptions and reminiscences in the hardships of the slave past. Indeed, black memories of slavery underpin the entire work. The interviewees did not mince words about the peculiar institution, and the Carawans did not attempt to gloss over what they said. For example, Reverend G.C. Brown, pastor at Wesley Methodist, told the couple that his father, a slave in the foothills of South Carolina, left trails of blood in the winter snow before he got his first pair of shoes at age fourteen. Betsy Pinckney remembered that her grandfather had been sold away from her grandmother. "Yes sir! They sell my father's daddy," she stated in a frank description of the heartless business of slave trading, "sell him for money." Pinckney also related a story about how her father's master knocked him down a flight of stairs for leaving finger marks on shoes he had polished. When the war started, her father "ran off with the Yankees." A reframing of Lowcountry slave spirituals, *Ain't You Got a Right to the Tree of Life* disputed the idealized version of slavery that generations of white Charlestonians had constructed.[34]

Critics generally praised *Ain't You Got a Right to the Tree of Life*. The *New York Times* congratulated the Carawans for their achievement, while city dailies all over the country, including several in the South, ran positive reviews. The Charleston press was less enthusiastic. Longtime newspaper columnist Jack Leland found the book "delightful and touching," but he took the Carawans to task for several minor factual mistakes, which, he suggested, cast doubt on the book's larger critique of white supremacy, past and present. "It is a pity that glaring errors in fact make one wonder about the 'truth' the author is touted as telling in a 'new way,'" Leland concluded.[35]

Julius Lester, an African American musician and folklorist who was a friend of the Carawans, also criticized the project. "To understand the music of a people," Lester wrote in *Sing Out!* magazine, "it is necessary to understand their lives, to intimately know their lives." When dealing with folk culture, "the most precious raw material available," the question of who did the interpretation was, for Lester, crucial. "A diamond," he remarked, "cannot be cut with a nail file." As Lester saw it, the Carawans, because they were white, were incapable of hewing such a valuable gem.[36]

By design, *Ain't You Got a Right to the Tree of Life* downplayed the central part the couple played in emphasizing the importance of spirituals. And as we have seen, many African Americans were open to the Carawans' aims. In part as a result of the Carawans' work, C.T. Vivian, Bernice Johnson Reagon, and the SNCC Freedom Singers, among others, claimed ownership of the spirituals tradition, challenging both black hostility to the genre and the proprietary stance and interpretive bent of white spirituals groups like the SPS. Bill Saunders, who had initially told the Carawans that singing spirituals seemed a waste of time, changed his mind after *Ain't You Got a Right to the Tree of Life* was published. "I have gone through many changes since we were last together," he wrote in a letter to the couple. "Most of the feelings that I had about the Negro music and background have left me, and I feel now that we do have something to feel proud of."[37]

But the Carawans could hardly fade into the background altogether given their conviction, which animated Guy in particular, that blacks "were not taking advantage of what their heritage had to offer." By the time the book was published, the sands beneath the Carawans' feet had begun to shift. Julius Lester's *Sing Out!* review was indicative of the change. Black nationalism and opposition to white involvement in the civil rights movement increasingly affected views of the Carawans' efforts, as the paternalistic undertones of their work, which had always been present, became too much for some to bear. Summarizing the tenor of the times, Candie later remarked that "you almost had to criticize any white people that were taking a serious interest in black culture." In fact, in 1965, the year before *Ain't You Got a Right to the Tree of Life* appeared, the Carawans left Johns Island for New York, no longer comfortable living among the people whose songs they treasured.[38]

* * * *

FORMERLY CONFINED TO black churches or appropriated by white groups like the Society for the Preservation of Spirituals, spirituals singing during the civil rights era resuscitated a memory of slavery that had long existed in the shadows. As spirituals singers of the civil rights era discovered, publicly engaging the history of slavery paid political dividends. Newly empowered African Americans attempted to revive and reshape the public memory of the peculiar institution in other ways—and in other venues—as well. A logical choice was to ensure that Charleston-area public schools taught black students about slavery. (The prospect of teaching white students the same lessons, it seems, was never raised during these years.)

Negro History Week represented an important annual focal point for studying the black past. In the 1950s, black public schools, such as Burke High School in downtown Charleston—which had been the only public high school for blacks in the city until Avery became public in 1947—and Haut Gap High School on Johns Island, observed Negro History Week annually. Private organizations offered educational programs, too. In the late 1950s, the Charleston chapter of the Links, Inc., a national black women's organization, sponsored a six-week course in black history at the Coming Street YWCA, an African American branch of the organization, for middle-school students. Eighty-three students completed the class in 1958.[39]

That year, African American attorney and NAACP counsel John H. Wrighten wrote to the *News and Courier* to express his gratitude to the Links for this important initiative. "I have been wondering for some time now," he added, "why Negro history is not being taught in the Negro Schools." Soon after, Wrighten attempted to persuade the Charleston city school board to include African American history in the curriculum at black schools. An Avery graduate who had unsuccessfully tried to desegregate the College of Charleston and the University of South Carolina Law School (a law school was opened at South Carolina State in Orangeburg as a result of the latter effort), Wrighten submitted the request on behalf of black parent-teacher associations in the city.[40]

He received a polite but equivocal response to the idea. The school board stated that it had no objections to the teaching of black history in black schools, and it agreed to green light an African American history course when a suitable textbook—one based on "historically authenticated material"—could be identified. When, over a year later, no acceptable book had been found, the school board authorized a committee of black teachers to devise their own study guide to be used in regular history courses. The teachers presented "A Study Outline on the Contributions of the Negro to the United States" at a board meeting in July 1959, but board members objected to the outline, claiming that it contained "generalizations and comments not sufficiently authenticated." The school board let the matter die and, when Wrighten inquired about the proposal's status in 1962, the superintendent reported that it was still investigating the issue.[41]

Meanwhile, black families, churches, and teachers continued to do what they could. By the mid-1960s, they had an unexpected new ally: Old Slave Mart Museum co-owner Judith Wragg Chase. Chase and her sister, Louise Alston Graves, had worked hard to keep the slavery museum afloat after taking over in November 1960. The sisters had difficulty gaining much support from the local community, however. "The early 1960s was a bad time to raise money for black heritage projects," Chase later explained. "What money was available was all going for civil rights."[42]

Graves was the OSMM director and oversaw day-to-day operations, but the museum was really Judith Wragg Chase's show. A woman of boundless energy, she curated the OSMM's collection, administered its library and educational outreach program, and led fund-raising initiatives. Like Miriam Wilson before her, Chase believed that the OSMM's distinctive contributions extended beyond the realms of historic preservation and education. "In spite of marches, sit-ins, and racial tensions," she wrote in 1970, the OSMM "has not only survived during the past ten years, but has played an important role in promoting inter-racial harmony and has won the respect and admiration of both Blacks and Whites all over the country, as well as in its own community."[43]

Although Chase was faithful to what she called Wilson's "tolerant" approach to slavery, she broke with her predecessor on the relationship between the museum and the civil rights movement. Chase posited the OSMM as a complement, rather than an alternative, to the struggle for integration. A New Deal Democrat and fan of John F. Kennedy, Chase was drawn into the civil rights crusade in the 1960s. One of her early initiatives was to recruit both black and white members to the board of trustees for the Miriam B. Wilson Foundation, the nonprofit she and Graves had created to oversee the OSMM. In 1967, Chase took a public stand against the decision of Charleston's white YWCA branch to dis-affiliate from the national organization because of its integration policy, among other issues. Two years later, she helped to build a new, interracial YWCA of Greater Charleston, serving as its first vice president and on its inaugural board of directors. In recognition of Chase's commitment to working for equality and justice, a black fraternity awarded her its 1973 outstanding citizenship award.[44]

Chief among Chase's civic contributions, according to the fraternity, were her efforts as curator and education director of the OSMM. Miriam Wilson had always hoped to attract black visitors to the slavery museum, but Chase went much further. Early on, she recognized that some Afri-can Americans were uncomfortable venturing into the predominantly white neighborhood where the museum was located. So she determined "to take the museum to them." By the mid-1960s, Chase was regularly lecturing on African American history and culture to black clubs, churches, and PTA groups. Demand for her lectures in the African Amer-ican community proved so high, in fact, that she began offering a free eight-week course in black history, in part to prepare others to teach sim-ilar courses.[45]

Chase sought to stimulate interest in African American history and culture in local black schools, too. In 1963, she founded an annual art con-test for African American high school students and arranged to have the winners' work put on display at the OSMM. Chase also compiled biblio-graphies and produced audio and visual resources on African and Afri-can American history and culture for black schools and libraries. She reported in 1973 that a slide-rental program she had developed had been embraced by colleges and universities across the United States. Chase's 1971 study of African and African American art, *Afro-American Art and Craft*, was similarly popular among college instructors teaching African American art in the early 1970s.[46]

By that point, the Charleston County School Board, which oversaw instruction in the city and surrounding areas, had finally acknowledged that such topics were worthy of study. In 1970, the board approved a black history syllabus—six years after the desegregation of its schools and more than a decade after John H. Wrighten began lobbying for add-ing black history to the curriculum. Under the provisions of the federal

Ethnic Heritage Studies Act of 1972, the county school board hired Elizabeth Alston, an African American history teacher, as ethnic studies coordinator.[47]

* * * *

LIKE MOST WHITE southerners, white Charlestonians fought school desegregation tooth and nail. For years, they actively resisted the *Brown v. Board of Education* decision. In 1960, the Charleston city school board rejected the applications of fifteen black students seeking admission to white schools because their best interests would be "seriously harmed." Only when some of their parents won a federal lawsuit—and only when the Charleston Movement gave white Charlestonians a glimpse of the disorder that would continue to grip their city if they remained hostile to school desegregation—did officials relent. On September 3, 1963, eleven African American students began the new academic year at formerly all-white schools. Three bomb threats were phoned in that day to Rivers High School, where Millicent Brown—whose grade school field trips to the Old Slave Mart Museum had been such a disappointment— had enrolled. In subsequent school years, white Charlestonians took advantage of a statewide program that provided tuition dollars to attend private schools. By 1967, black students represented more than 86 percent of students in Charleston city schools.[48]

African American students in desegregated schools began advocating for the importance of studying the black past. Their increasing assertiveness tracked with national developments within the Black Power movement as well as within the black student movement to which it helped give rise. Forged at historically black colleges before spreading to formerly all-white institutions, the student movement attacked, among other things, curricula too beholden to white norms and narratives. In Charleston, black students' concerns were met with genuine hostility, even violence, especially in those suburban schools that remained mostly white. Just across the Ashley River in Charleston's western suburbs—where increasing numbers of middle-class African American families moved from the peninsula in the 1970s—black students at St. Andrews High School called for an improvement to what they dismissively called their "Black history supplement." It was "one big joke," they said in early 1972, as the white teachers "don't know and don't care" about the subject and sometimes called on black students to teach it themselves.[49]

Campus traditions at athletic events exacerbated this neglect of black history. At St. Andrews, students waved the Confederate battle flag and sang "Dixie," practices black students loathed. When the school refused to address their concerns, they boycotted classes. Their white classmates responded by flying Confederate flags emblazoned with the letters "KKK." At James Island High School, the observance of Negro History Week in the winter of 1972 led to a well-orchestrated attack on black students. As they arrived at school on the morning of February 15, the white students, some armed with pistols, threw rocks and bricks as their parents looked on.[50]

Black students at Charleston colleges fought similar battles. Desegregated in 1966, the Citadel struggled to respond to its black students' demands to diversify its curriculum and confront its complicated history. The defense of slavery and the Civil War, after all, were central to the college's identity. Founded as a response to the Vesey conspiracy, the school had long bragged that its cadets had fired the opening salvo of the conflict when they shot at a Union supply ship headed to Fort Sumter in January 1861, three months before General P.G.T. Beauregard's fateful assault on the fort. "Dixie" was the unofficial fight song of the college, and the Confederate battle flag, waved at athletic competitions, held deep symbolic meaning for students and alumni.[51]

The *Brigadier*, the student newspaper, explored the racial climate on campus in several 1970 articles. As the spring semester came to a close, the editors raised the question of whether a black history course, or an entire black studies program, should be created. Its willingness to entertain the idea contrasted with that of the *News and Courier* editorial board, which in 1969 deemed black studies the kind of revisionist history favored by totalitarian regimes like Soviet Russia and Nazi Germany. The *Brigadier*, by contrast, suggested that such a program might "eradicate inter-racial misunderstandings which thrive on prejudicial ignorance" and invited campus members to weigh in on the issue. African American cadets supported the proposal, as they felt current faculty soft-pedaled subjects like slavery. One black cadet remembered how difficult it had been for him to challenge a history professor's benign interpretation

African American cadets at the newly desegregated Citadel objected to their fellow students' flying the Confederate flag at football games.

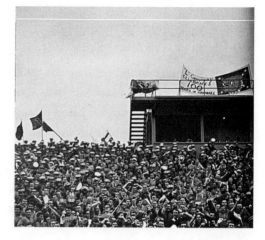

of the institution, especially because he was the only African American student in the class.[52]

The following academic year, African American cadets went on the offensive, moving beyond the call for black studies. Members of the newly founded Afro-American Studies Club (AASC) took aim at the college's traditions, shining a bright light on how the school's particular memory of slavery informed campus culture. After asking, to no avail, that the administration forbid the flying of the Confederate battle flag at football games, the AASC decided in the fall of 1971 to counter this symbol with its own. When the Citadel put its first points on the scoreboard at the Illinois State football game, white cadets, per usual, waved the battle flag. Black cadets responded by raising an "anti-flag flag" they had made; it showed a black fist crushing a Confederate battle flag.[53]

This incident pushed Citadel administrators to ban the use of the flag at games, but they failed to fully understand black cadets' criticisms of college traditions. In a report issued in 1972, Citadel officials summarized the most common grievances of the typical black cadet: racist insults went unpunished, American history courses ignored black contributions to the past, and the "Confederate Legend" dominated campus culture. Concluding that it was impossible to determine the legitimacy of these complaints, administrators offered several observations to guide future campus policies. The Confederate Legend, most importantly, was "an integral part of The Citadel's heritage." Conceding that the battle flag was "inappropriate for a football standard," the report nevertheless insisted that "the school should explain that the Confederate States of America stood for more than slavery and that the Confederate battle flag is not the official emblem of white supremacy." No cadet, white or black, should reject the heritage of his college by presuming to judge the past, it insisted. Indeed, Citadel officials blamed the discord on campus on this very habit: "The current preoccupation with the influence of slavery is responsible for the extreme unpopularity of anything associated with the Confederacy." The report endorsed the request that history professors examine the role of African Americans in the past, but only on one condition—that they do so "without distorting their subject."[54]

Many white Citadel students responded more angrily to their black classmates' grievances. After the 1971 Illinois State game, a group of white cadets vandalized the AASC president's dorm room. To make their point, they suspended a noose from the ceiling, dangling a doll in the loop. The flag ban elicited a slate of articles in and letters to the *Brigadier*, with most writers condemning the administration's decision as a violation of a sacred campus tradition.[55]

Only a handful of white cadets publicly sympathized with the black cadets' position on campus symbols. Preston Mitchell, class of 1974, wrote to the *Brigadier* after a basketball game against Midlands Tech to criticize what he saw as deliberately provocative behavior on the part of the Citadel Regimental Band. The band continually played "Dixie" during the game, Mitchell observed. Each time, the tempo got faster, and the cadets whistled louder and stomped their feet harder. The band seemed intent on harassing the almost exclusively black Midlands basketball players and cheerleaders. Mitchell pleaded with Citadel students to see that from a black person's perspective "Dixie" represented white supremacy and the KKK. Mitchell did not believe that the playing of the song should be dropped as a Citadel tradition, but he felt it needed to be kept "in its proper perspective." A plea to silence "Dixie" would likely have been ignored anyway. The administration's halfhearted commitment to placating black students was fading, and by the end of the decade, cadets were again waving the Confederate battle flag at athletic events.[56]

* * * *

THE LATE 1960s and early 1970s marked a turning point in the political fortunes of black Charlestonians. The freedom struggle had ebbed
since the 1963 Charleston Movement, but in 1969 picket lines and marches
once again rattled the city as a new fight over labor rights erupted. Tensions over low pay and discriminatory employment policies had been
simmering for several years between the Medical College of South Carolina Hospital and the Charleston County Hospital, on the one hand, and
their predominantly black female workers, on the other. On March 20,
after administrators fired twelve union leaders from the Medical College
hospital, over four hundred employees of both hospitals went on strike.
Thousands of local protesters, as well as the Southern Christian Leadership Conference (SCLC), rallied to the workers' cause, while the hospitals
dug in their heels. It was, according to the *New York Times*, "the country's
tensest civil rights struggle." In late April, the South Carolina governor
ordered five thousand National Guard troops to patrol Charleston and
announced a dusk-to-dawn curfew.[57]

Hospital workers drew parallels between their current condition and
antebellum slavery. At a protest held in front of the Old Slave Mart Museum, one picketer held a sign that read, "In Memory of the Old Slave
Tradition, Consult Dr. McCord," a reference to Dr. William McCord,
the president of the Medical College of South Carolina who refused to
meet with the workers' union and portrayed the strikers as children. The
specter of Denmark Vesey, in particular, hung over the hundred-day
walkout, his spirit seeming to animate the hospital workers' own insurrection. As they marched through the streets, strikers and their allies
shouted "Remember Denmark Vesey!"—the same cry that Frederick Douglass had employed to recruit African American soldiers during the Civil
War. In early May, SCLC president Ralph Abernathy told a crowd of
three thousand that he planned to preach against economic injustice at
the "hanging tree" on Ashley Avenue, where local myth held that Vesey
had been executed. Even whites thought of the famous rebel. To the
News and Courier—which, unsurprisingly, had little patience with the
strikers—the "eerie silence" of the nightly curfew called to mind the curfew imposed in the wake of Vesey's thwarted slave rebellion. Alice Ca-
baniss, a liberal Charleston poet, captured the tense events of the summer
in verse, writing, "Merchants lounge in doorways / cursing ease, grouping

angrily / . . . patrolling windows, / counting guardsmen going by. / . . . Denmark Vesey smiles / with pleasure from another century."[58]

Police arrested nine hundred demonstrators before a settlement, which produced modest victories for hospital workers, was reached in the summer of 1969. The resolution was far from perfect, but the mass mobilization was a watershed, creating a larger space for working-class black Charlestonians within the local civil rights movement. It was a call to arms for a broad-based coalition of black activists who drew on nonviolent direct action as well as the militancy of Black Power. Among these were Mary Moultrie, the union president, Bill Saunders, the Johns Island activist, and Robert Ford, a young SCLC organizer.[59]

Two years later, James J. French translated this growing power into a new newspaper, the *Chronicle*, that spoke to the local black community. The *Chronicle* served as a vehicle to galvanize support of black political candidates and to expose ongoing problems of discrimination, though French did make room for a variety of voices, including a conservative white columnist. Significantly, *Chronicle* stories on contemporary issues were intertwined with article after article on black history, which focused overwhelmingly on slavery and resistance to it.

The *Chronicle*'s discussions of slavery supported a vision of activism indebted to Black Power. The first of a four-part series in the fall of 1972 titled "Revolt Against Slavery," for example, noted that very few history books concentrated on slavery's inhumanity, but fewer still detailed those who fought the institution. There were bondpeople, however, "who fought back. They fought back against enormous odds and they often lost, but they did not passively accept their chains. They resisted—sometimes to the death." The interpretation of slavery that permeated the pages of the *Chronicle* was certainly unvarnished, as were the characterizations of how slaves had responded. "The stories of Nat Turner, Denmark Vesey, and Toussaint L'Ouverture—men who stood up in the midst of the overwhelming machinery of slavery and fought for their freedom," the paper stated, "their heritage lives today with young Black militants like Stokely Carmichael, H. Rap Brown, Eldridge Cleaver, and Ron Karenga." The newspaper hoped its memory of slavery would provide black Charlestonians with a usable past to inspire their fight against injustice.[60]

For many local African Americans, in fact, Denmark Vesey—the city's

original black militant—represented the most potent symbol of this usable past, his example of resistance waiting to be harnessed for the contemporary political moment. Striking hospital workers, of course, had
already invoked Vesey as inspiration during their walkout in 1969. In the
spring of 1975, several African American residents suggested that it was
time for Vesey to be more widely known. Charleston, they argued, should
somehow memorialize the insurrectionist. The campaign began when
Reverend Matthew D. McCollom, president of the state NAACP, and
civil rights attorney Arthur C. McFarland, one of nine students who in
1964 had desegregated a local Catholic high school, suggested renaming
a city school after Vesey. McFarland argued that renaming several predominantly black schools—Burke High School, for example, would become Septima Clark High School; Charleston High School would
become Robert Smalls High School; and Columbus Street Elementary
would become Denmark Vesey Elementary School—would give black
children "a sense of history—of how Black people began as slaves in this
city and country and how we have steadily achieved despite overwhelming discrimination and oppression."[61]

McCollom and McFarland's effort inspired other ideas for memorializing Vesey. In October 1975, the city council voted to rename the Municipal Auditorium, completed in 1968, in honor of Mayor J. Palmer
Gaillard Jr., whose administration had overseen construction of the fa-
cility and who had recently announced his retirement from office. Robert Ford, a former SCLC staffer and hospital strike organizer now vying
for a seat on the city council, countered that the auditorium should be
named for Vesey instead. Ford framed his proposal as a way for the city
to render black citizens just compensation. In constructing the massive
structure, the Gaillard administration had razed entire blocks, forcing a
number of black businesses and churches to relocate to other parts of the
city and displacing seven hundred poor, mostly black Charlestonians
from their homes.[62]

Finally, in December, several African American citizens urged the
city to erect a statue of Vesey. One of these was Reverend Frederick
Douglass Dawson, a minister at Calvary Baptist Church, an NAACP
leader, and one of the parents who had successfully sued to desegregate
Charleston's public schools. Dawson envisioned a Vesey statue, situated
in front of the newly rechristened Gaillard Municipal Auditorium, as a

natural complement to another project he had in mind: renaming King Street in honor of Martin Luther King Jr. Dawson made his case for both before the city council. "I think it's about time council members and citizens of Charleston show some respect for our Black heroes and heritage," he proclaimed. City and state leaders had not just ignored men like Vesey. They had fashioned a commemorative landscape that was an affront to black citizens. As he observed, "They have statues of slave holder John Calhoun in the downtown area and Ben Tillman stands on the lawn of the State House in Columbia." Putting up a statue of Vesey would represent a step toward rectifying this "intolerable situation." Bobby Isaac, an African American reporter for the *News and Courier*, threw his support behind the statue idea, too, arguing that a public square or park would be an ideal site. "As a Black Charleston resident," he wrote, "I feel personally slighted because of the gross absence of any significant Black historical marker in this city, which has for so long prided itself for its rich and colorful history."[63]

As Isaac pointed out, Vesey's "invisible landmarks," such as Emanuel A.M.E. Church and the Citadel, "today quietly haunt the city he had plotted to take." Isaac, Dawson, Ford, McFarland, McCollom, and others felt it was time to give Vesey a visible landmark—one that would finally acknowledge how the memory of his conspiracy shaped, and continued to shape, life in Charleston. Initial responses to their proposals were not encouraging. The school board did not adopt the recommendation to rename black schools. The city council, understandably, did not entertain the request to rename the auditorium for the second time in as many months. Council members referred the other suggestions they received to committee. Reactions by and in the white press were cool. The *Evening Post* chided African Americans for trying to turn Vesey into a hero, while a letter writer to the *News and Courier* worried that "cluttering up" the area around Gaillard Municipal Auditorium with a statue to a former slave would hinder downtown revitalization. Tom Hamrick, a conservative white journalist who wrote a weekly column in the *Chronicle*, was the most hostile critic, arguing that Vesey was "a would-be killer who wanted to convert Charleston into a blood inferno." Hamrick speculated that no one could have been less popular among white Charlestonians than Vesey, not even Adolf Hitler.[64]

Hamrick may well have been right, but as of December 9, 1975, the

Vesey memorializers had a distinct advantage. Municipal elections held that day transformed Charleston, ushering in a new political order. This new order was in many ways the product of the 1969 hospital strike, which had increased black voter registration among the working class and elevated a cohort of younger, more militant black leaders who challenged the conservative black establishment and its accommodation of local white Democrats. A Justice Department ruling helped, too. In February 1975, federal officials had ordered the city to switch from at-large to single-member districts, which promised to improve black representation on the city council.[65]

That promise bore fruit. The December 9 elections produced a twelve-member council, evenly divided among white and black members, one of whom was Robert Ford. Along with Bill Saunders, Ford typified the new breed of black activist in the city. Born in New Orleans, Ford had relocated to Charleston in 1969 to help with the hospital workers strike. Through this grassroots activism, Ford hoped to take power away from the "soft-speaking, Uncle Tom Folks." To that end, he ran for city council in the 1975 municipal elections, and in the mayoral contest he backed George Fuller, an African American candidate who ran as an independent, rather than the white Democratic nominee, Joseph "Joe" P. Riley Jr.[66]

Fuller lost the mayor's race to Riley, a thirty-two-year-old racial progressive. A local boy from an Irish Catholic family who grew up south of Broad, Riley had graduated from the Citadel, earned a law degree from the University of South Carolina, and been elected to the General Assembly in 1968. Despite his conservative upbringing, Riley broke ranks on race and helped to forge a new Democratic Party in the process. Riley came on the political scene amid a massive political realignment in the United States, as southern opponents of integration, led by South Carolina's Senator Strom Thurmond, bolted the Democratic fold for the Republican Party in the 1960s and 1970s. Gradually, the term "Solid South" took on a new meaning, with Republicans holding sway across the region by the turn of the century. Cities like Charleston bucked this trend, however, since its sizable population of newly enfranchised black voters flocked to the Democrats.[67]

After the hospital strike and the narrow reelection victory of Mayor Gaillard in 1971, Riley had pleaded with his fellow Democrat to reach out to black Charlestonians and represent their needs. Three years later, he joined with black representative and SCLC member Robert Woods to introduce a bill in the General Assembly to create a statewide Martin Luther King Jr. Day. Riley may not have been a civil rights activist, but his commitment to the welfare of black citizens was genuine, in addition to being politically savvy. In the 1975 mayoral contest, Riley earned the votes of both wealthy white Charlestonians and recently empowered African Americans, Robert Ford notwithstanding. Riley and his new interracial coalition would dominate Charleston politics for the next forty years.[68]

Emboldened by the historic election, the new mayor and the city council still tread carefully when it came to the proposal to memorialize Vesey. In fact, in early 1976 Mayor Riley suggested commissioning a portrait of Martin Luther King Jr. to hang in City Hall instead. But black activists responded that honoring a Charleston or South Carolina native was more appropriate, and that Vesey had already emerged as the preferred choice of any commemorative effort. Riley agreed. On Robert Ford's recommendation, the council commissioned a portrait of Vesey to hang inside the cavernous lobby of Gaillard Municipal Auditorium.[69]

Painted by Dorothy B. Wright, an art teacher at C.A. Brown High School, the portrait showed Vesey from behind, preaching to congregants of the African Church. Wright's composition nodded to his role as a minister while also providing a convenient way around the fact that there are no known images of his face. The city paid $175 for the work and unveiled it on August 9, 1976, at a ceremony attended by 250 people. Various local dignitaries spoke at the event, including Reverend Frank M. Reid Jr., an A.M.E. bishop, and Mayor Riley, who hailed the occasion as proof that his administration would ensure that "parts of history heretofore forgotten are remembered."[70]

But if Councilman Ford, Mayor Riley, and other proponents of the portrait thought their tribute, tucked away inside the auditorium, would not incite controversy, they miscalculated. Many white Charlestonians were outraged that an image of a man they considered a criminal now hung in a civic space, even if it was located behind closed doors rather than in a public park. Shirley J. Holcombe, a Republican running for the state House of Representatives, summarized how many of her constitu-

Denmark Vesey Talking to His People, *by Dorothy B. Wright.*
Black Charlestonians memorialized Vesey with this painting,
hung in Gaillard Municipal Auditorium in 1976. About five weeks
after it was installed, the tribute was stolen.

ents felt in language that echoed Tom Hamrick. Holcombe declared, "If
Vesey qualifies for such an honor, we should also hang the portraits of
Hitler, Attila the Hun, Herod the murderer of babies, and the PLO mur-
derers of the Israeli athletes at Munich."[71]

The primary problem was Vesey's alleged methods. *News and Courier*
columnist Frank Gilbreth Jr., better known by his pen name Ashley
Cooper, admitted that slavery may have been immoral, but it was the law
of the land. An insurrection that would have resulted in the slaughter of
white Charlestonians, as he and other critics contended, was simply inex-
cusable. The evolutionary change in race relations that had characterized
the twentieth century, the *Evening Post* editorialized, was far preferable
to such a violent overthrow, which was doomed to futility anyhow. In
recent years, Ashley Cooper claimed, southern whites had "bent over
backwards to purge themselves of prejudices and to change their ways of
life to accommodate the rights and feelings of blacks." Given their change
of heart, they would never propose a project that was as insulting to the
black community as the Vesey portrait was to the white. They would
not, for example, contend that statues of Robert E. Lee or Jefferson Davis

be installed in Hampton Park, a popular gathering spot for black Charlestonians since its desegregation a decade earlier.[72]

Cooper's estimation of how willingly whites had changed their racial views was generous, to put it mildly, but his remark about Hampton Park reveals an important truth: for many white Charlestonians, the Vesey painting hit close to home. Gaillard Municipal Auditorium, after all, was mostly an elite white civic domain. White patrons would now mingle under a portrait of Vesey before and after every performance they attended. But opponents did not so much object to the location of the painting as to its subject, wondering why Ford and his ilk could not find a better candidate for commemoration. There were plenty of distinguished black men and women from Charleston, they contended. Choosing a man of "evil" made no sense.[73]

Portrait proponents vigorously countered the detractors. To Robert Ford and Reverend Frank M. Reid Jr., who delivered the keynote at the dedication ceremony, Vesey's plan to kill whites so that he and his co-conspirators could set sail for Haiti did not make him a racist, as whites charged, nor was he "a wild-eyed monster." He was a Moses, a freedom fighter sent by God to liberate his people. Vesey defenders also pointed out that slaves had no other alternative but violent rebellion. If men like Vesey and Robert Smalls "did not struggle for what is morally and legally right, then there would be no thirteen Blacks in the S. C. House of Representatives, or Blacks on the school board," declared the *Chronicle*. To think that "natural events" and white benevolence would have ended slavery was "hogwash." For centuries, Americans had committed acts of violence and laid down their lives for causes they held dear. Vesey was no different.[74]

White Charlestonians, Vesey defenders noted, knew this well. They had installed statues and named parks in honor of Revolutionary and Confederate fighters—most of whom had been slaveholders—all over the city. How ridiculous it was, the *Chronicle* declared, for the pot to now be calling the kettle black. To Bill Saunders, this hypocrisy was galling. He bristled at the fact that whites wanted to tell African Americans who to celebrate when blacks had walked by these tributes to white oppressors for decades, largely keeping their opinions to themselves.[75]

None of those who emphasized the inconsistency of white Charlestonians regarding commemoration went so far as to argue that white memorials should be removed. Rather, supporters of the Vesey painting wanted city spaces to be more representative and inclusive. Whites could honor their heroes; African Americans could celebrate theirs.

* * * *

THE WAR OF words that played out after the Vesey painting dedication did not mark the end of the story. Sometime in the late afternoon or evening of Friday, September 17, 1976, about five weeks after it had been installed, the portrait was stolen. The thief or thieves ripped the painting off the wall, leaving four large holes behind. Charlestonians learned of the incident in a brief article relegated to the bottom of Section C of the Sunday *News and Courier*. A $200 reward was offered for the painting's return. Mayor Riley insisted that a replacement would be commissioned if it were not given back. Black activists chided the white press, faulting it for inciting the robbery. As they pointed out, moreover, white newspapers had devoted copious space to attacking Vesey during the previous months but had buried the story detailing the portrait's theft. Sunday night, an anonymous caller informed the *News and Courier* that the painting had been returned to Gaillard. A reporter followed up on the tip and found it lying against an auditorium door. Although the police took fingerprints from the portrait and investigated the crime, they never made an arrest.[76]

The city reinstalled the Vesey painting in Gaillard Municipal Auditorium, hanging it higher up the wall to stave off another theft. But it never replaced the plaque that had accompanied the original painting, which had also gone missing. This plaque paid honor to Denmark Vesey, calling him a "lover of freedom" and "enemy of oppression" who "planned a major slave revolt." In its absence, Gaillard visitors were left to their own devices to figure out the identity and significance of the black preacher depicted in Wright's portrait.[77]

This incident simultaneously highlighted what had changed in Charleston over the last two decades and what remained the same. The city now had a liberal white mayor who not only owed his election to the black community but was also committed enough to memorializing Charleston's African American history that he made sure a portrait of Denmark Vesey would hang in its most prominent auditorium. For this and other acts of racial reconciliation, in fact, Riley earned the derisive nickname "Little Black Joe." Yet the dogged fight conservative whites launched against this single commemorative gesture—symbolically significant as it was—laid bare the deep divisions over the public memory of slavery that persisted throughout the civil rights era and beyond.[78]

10

Segregating
the Past

By the time of the Vesey portrait controversy and theft, Charleston's powerful cadre of preservationists and tourism boosters had stepped up their efforts to remove most traces of slavery from the city. This was a campaign that dated back to World War II, when inscribing white memory into the built landscape became fully institutionalized. In 1941, a committee associated with the Carolina Art Association conducted an architectural survey of Charleston, the first inventory of buildings in the city and one of the first studies of its kind in the nation. The committee tapped Helen Gardner McCormack, a Charlestonian serving as the director of the Valentine Museum in Richmond, to conduct the survey. Beginning in January 1941, McCormack crisscrossed the peninsula, on foot and by car, and by the end of the year she had identified over eleven hundred private dwellings, public buildings, churches, and other sites deemed worthy of preservation. In December 1944, the survey results were published in book form. *This Is Charleston: A Survey of the Architectural Heritage of a Unique American City* included photographs of 572 of the structures identified as important.[1]

The survey and book did not just catalogue the buildings worthy of preservation, as these structures represented so much more. Frederick Law Olmsted Jr., who served as an adviser for the project, came to appreciate this fact during a trip to Charleston. "Whatever else the Committee is concerned with it is very centrally concerned with some intangible values peculiar to Charleston," observed the son of the famous landscape architect. "They are . . . characteristic of certain physical aspects of Charleston and definitely associated with certain kinds of old physical objects and conditions." As it set out to map the cityscape, the committee mapped a landscape of memory that embodied its peculiar values—a landscape of memory that made those values tangible. Old physical objects encapsulated elite Charlestonians' sense of themselves, past and present.[2]

Indeed, the survey methodology was rooted almost entirely in the personal memories and assessments of the individuals who constituted the committee. Helen Gardner McCormack relied on Albert Simons—an architect, head of the city's Board of Architectural Review, and SPS member—who gave her his notes and files, as well as on watercolorist Alice Ravenel Huger Smith, who led her on private tours. Alice "took her car and chauffeur," McCormack explained, "and we drove around and she pointed out things that she remembered that she thought were important. That was extremely helpful." Alice's own sense of what was historically significant had been shaped by her paternal grandmother and her father. Eliza C.M. Huger Smith had regaled her granddaughter with the exploits of Charlestonians dating back to the colonial period. Alice's father, Daniel, an author, antiquarian, and Civil War veteran, had led her as a child on walking tours of the city and area plantations in his search for sites associated with prominent Charlestonians. "We would visit hero after hero," she said. "We would meet famous soldiers and sailors, lawyers, judges, captains of industry and delightful old ladies, and many young ones, too, for he had so many stories to tell us that history became real." Alice valued this "historical training," as she called it, as did McCormack.[3]

This Is Charleston failed to acknowledge that enslaved laborers had constructed or lived and worked in the buildings it listed. The book included photographs of just two sites that explicitly evoked the history of slavery, though the link was not made clear. Slave quarters at 45 Queen Street were described using the popular euphemism "servants' quarters." The Old Slave Mart Museum, which Miriam Wilson had opened as a museum three years before the architectural survey, was labeled simply "6 Chalmers Street. Ante Bellum. Notable."[4]

This Is Charleston became the go-to guide for educated visitors as well as for preservationists and municipal officials. But that was not all. Several committee members decided that Charleston needed a new preservation society, establishing the Historic Charleston Foundation (HCF) in 1947. The HCF bought historic properties, eventually pioneering a revolving fund that was regularly replenished to finance future purchases. The properties, in turn, were rehabilitated for modern use.[5]

One of the HCF's most important and long-lasting projects underwrote this scheme: a springtime series of private home tours inaugurated in 1948 that continues to this day (under the name Festival of Houses and Gardens). For out-of-towners, especially, the tours offered an exciting glimpse into the private, mysterious domains of wealthy Charlestonians, something promoters emphasized. Home-tour patrons could be forgiven for assuming that Charleston had been populated mainly by the prosperous families of merchants and planters in the colonial and antebellum eras. Even ghosts, several said to still haunt grand old homes, occupied a more conspicuous place in the foundation's tour narratives than "servants."[6]

The historical vision of these preservationists lived on in other ways as well, informing Charleston's first attempt to improve the tourist experience in the postwar years. At the request of the city, the Historical Commission of Charleston (HCC) designed a tour guide licensing program in the early 1950s so that guides would possess "authentic, factual and interesting historical data." The program, a series of classes at a local vocational college that culminated in an exam, operated under the supervision of HCC secretary Mary A. Sparkman and Helen Gardner McCormack. Sparkman possessed a formidable knowledge of local history, having served as the secretary of the HCC since its founding in 1933. During her tenure in office, she had personally conducted much of the research necessary for the commission's projects—research that became the basis of the information that prospective guides had to master to obtain licenses. Helen Gardner McCormack was also a logical choice. As head researcher for the 1941 architectural survey, few people could have known more about the streets of Charleston.[7]

Black history largely lay beyond the scope of this licensing program. The 1954 exam, for instance, contained sixty questions, but just one that tested knowledge of black life in the city: "The most modern school for negroes in the city is _____ on _____ Street." This query, of course, reflected what guides were taught. Totaling more than 150 pages, an early version of the study manual for prospective tour guides devoted only a handful of pages to black sites, black history, and black culture. (The city's flowers, by contrast, merited twelve.) An entry for "Negroes," located in the "miscellaneous data" section at the end of the manual, informed guides that they needed to know "something about what has been done and is being done for the negroes in the city"—thus the question about the modern school built for black students. The HCC's tour-guide material from these years did include more information about the Old Slave Mart and the city's slave trade than did most Charleston tour guidebooks from the same period. But, as we saw in chapter 8, Sparkman and her collaborators attempted to distance Charleston from slave trading by stating that the building had no official, municipal standing.[8]

Sparkman and McCormack's material was updated in 1973 by Marguerite C. Steedman, a United Daughters of the Confederacy member hired by the city council to teach a revised instructional course for tour guides. Steedman's revisions were not interpretive in nature, as she was not sympathetic to those calling for a reassessment of the southern past in the wake of the civil rights movement. In 1979, for example, Steedman blamed a recent dustup over the flying of the Confederate flag at the statehouse in Columbia on new, revised textbooks "written and published elsewhere," as well as on the popularity of the television miniseries *Roots*, which she called "a piece of warmed-over Abolitionist propaganda if there ever was one." Steedman lamented that too many southerners could not distinguish between such propaganda and true history.[9]

The longevity and influence of the city's licensing program speak to a larger point. To a remarkable degree, the consolidation of white memory after World War II rested on an expanded, more formalized tourism industry. This more formalized tourism industry, in turn, rested on the work—and recollections—of a handful of leading white Charlestonians. Tourists who hired a licensed guide to lead them through the historic district; those who ventured out on their own with a copy of *This Is Charleston* in hand; those who patronized the annual home-tours festival— all of these visitors navigated a landscape constructed out of a chain of elite personal remembrances.

Artist Elizabeth O'Neill Verner, who, despite her modest background, collaborated in forging this landscape with her romanticized drawings of the city, effectively explained this peculiar dynamic. As Verner wrote in 1941, the year the architectural survey was conducted, "I think people have time to remember better in Charleston than in most places. Perhaps it is easier to remember here where the generations are all known to each other and linked up, for by the time one has reached the half-century mark, a Charlestonian is likely to have known five generations of any family." And what that Charlestonian learned from those earlier generations mattered. As it passed from Daniel Elliott Huger Smith to Alice Ravenel Huger Smith to Helen Gardner McCormack to tour guides to tourists, individual memory became public memory.[10]

* * * *

AN INFAMOUS INCIDENT in 1961—sparked by the highest-profile tourist event in the city since the 1901–2 Exposition—captured Charleston's stubborn commitment to this narrow approach to the past. That April, one hundred years after the Confederacy launched its war to save slavery at Fort Sumter, the city staged an elaborate commemoration of the fateful assault. Fifty years earlier, Charleston had let the Fort Sumter semi-centennial pass without public ceremony, an accommodation to sectional reconciliation and, perhaps, fiscal challenges. By 1961, many locals believed that a Civil War anniversary commemoration was not only fitting but also potentially profitable. The Fort Sumter National Monument, which had been operated by the National Park Service since 1948, had already become an established tourist stop, attracting more than fifty thousand visitors in 1960. With national publications predicting that the centennial could draw twenty million people to Civil War sites and spectacles, Charleston boosters unleashed an unprecedented publicity campaign. "Even if it lost the war," ventured the *News and Courier*, "the South is bound to emerge victorious from the centennial, in terms of tourist dollars, at least."[11]

Yet Charleston's Jim Crow policies threatened to jeopardize those tourist dollars. The Civil War Centennial Commission (CWCC), a federal body created by the Eisenhower administration to coordinate commemorative activities, had decided to hold its fourth national assembly in Charleston during the Fort Sumter anniversary in April. The site selected to host the meeting was the segregated Francis Marion Hotel, a choice that did not sit well with the New Jersey delegation, which included African American Madaline Williams. Its protests, however, proved unsuccessful. CWCC executive director Karl Betts insisted that the matter was outside his commission's jurisdiction. After consulting with the Francis Marion, Mayor J. Palmer Gaillard Jr. reported that neither Williams nor any other African American delegate would be permitted to stay in or to dine at the hotel, a widely publicized stand that earned Gaillard letters of praise from across the South.[12]

In response to the Jim Crow accommodations, centennial delegations from four states—New Jersey, New York, Illinois, and California—proposed boycotting the assembly. With the controversy grabbing national headlines, President John F. Kennedy intervened. On March 14, he urged the CWCC to ensure that all guests attending the meeting were treated equally. By the end of the month, Kennedy aides and Emory University historian Bell Wiley, a self-described southern liberal who sat on the CWCC executive committee, had forged a compromise: the national assembly would be moved from the segregated Francis Marion in downtown Charleston to an integrated U.S. naval station outside the city.[13]

Local whites took the news in stride. The chairman of South Carolina's state centennial commission announced that regardless of where the national meeting was held, his group would neither alter its commemorative program nor "participate in any integrated social functions." Charleston newspapers ran articles highlighting the naval station's austere accommodations, how few delegates had signed up to stay there, and the fact that the station's remote location would prevent its occupants from attending the important commemorative events downtown.[14]

Despite the national uproar, Charleston's Fort Sumter commemoration went on as planned. White fears about civil rights activists picketing at the Francis Marion failed to materialize, though the NAACP did stage a late-night protest rally at Emanuel A.M.E. Church, which was attended by Madaline Williams and a white New Jersey delegate. At that April 11 gathering, a 1,200-person crowd endorsed a statement that denounced any glorification of the Confederacy, "for it was founded on the principle of slavery." But their sentiments were drowned out by the city's Lost Cause party.[15]

Visitors packed area hotels. Local entertainers, including the Society for the Preservation of Spirituals and Gullah raconteur Dick Reeves, offered special performances for southern delegations, which gathered for separate, segregated meetings at the Fort Sumter and Francis Marion hotels. Not even heavy rains and a tornado that touched down in the area on April 12—the anniversary of the first shot fired at Fort

Sumter—could dampen the city's spirits. That afternoon, a crowd of 65,000 turned out for an enormous parade that snaked through the center of the city. Confederate flags and hats were everywhere. In the evening, tens of thousands watched a reenactment of the bombardment of Fort Sumter. On the Battery, "Confederate gentlemen and belles danced and whooped it up" to "Dixie" and "Tara's Theme" from *Gone with the Wind*.[16]

Unsurprisingly, Charleston's Fort Sumter centennial made little room for slavery. For six nights, the Citadel football stadium hosted a historical pageant that dramatized the city's past. "The Charleston Story" featured a cast of five hundred, including more than one hundred principals who depicted both real and historical figures, such as King Charles II and P.G.T. Beauregard, as well as symbolic types, including a plantation owner, a pirate's ransom victim, and a war bond saleswoman. Only a handful of characters represented Charleston's black residents. The pageant did not address slavery, though it made explicit reference to other forms of bound labor, such as indentured servitude. Slavery did not merit much comment at other centennial events either, with the exception of the standard Lost Cause talking points. During a performance at the Fort Sumter Hotel, Dick Reeves told about two hundred delegates that it was an appropriate moment "for the people of the South to remember the loyalty of many Negroes during the Civil War."[17]

Viewed through a national lens, the Fort Sumter commemoration promised to lay bare sectional fault lines over how the nation remembered the Civil War—fault lines that seemed far more potent in light of emerging civil rights challenges to Jim Crow. The negative publicity garnered by the Charleston controversy, in fact, led Congress to cut CWCC funding.[18]

Locally, however, the centennial taught a different lesson. White Charlestonians regarded the Fort Sumter commemoration as "a great success," in Mayor Gaillard's words. Asked by a *News and Courier* reporter if the ruckus over Williams had disturbed the festivities, he left little room for doubt. "No sir," Gaillard replied. "As far as I personally am concerned, it didn't even exist." Charleston tourism operators were similarly upbeat about the positive impact of the centennial. In October, the superintendent of Fort Sumter reported that 60,492 people had visited the site in the first nine months of 1961—almost 9,000 more than the total number of visitors in all of 1960.[19]

D 70252 NATURE'S MIRROR, MAGNOLIA-ON-THE-ASHLEY, CHARLESTON, S. C.   COPR. DETROIT PUBLISHING CO.

Change came slowly to Charleston's historical tourism industry.
Well into the 1970s, plantation owners marketed their sites as
enchanting gardens guaranteed to delight nature lovers.

The Fort Sumter centennial anticipated how the historical tourism industry approached the topic of slavery over the next few decades. What visitors heard when they toured the city or ventured out to area plantations in the 1960s and 1970s was not much different than what they had heard a half century earlier. Although the civil rights movement was transforming Charleston, as it was the rest of the country, change came slowly in the city's most important industry. This had something to do with how deeply entrenched the whitewashed memory of slavery, in fact, was. But it also reflected a fundamental indifference to visitors who might prefer a more inclusive and accurate interpretation of the city's past. In this way, the Madaline Williams affair was an apt metaphor: Charleston tourism officials did not imagine black tourists—or white tourists interested in black history, for that matter—as a part of the traveling public.

The *Negro Motorist Green Book*, a travel guide published from 1936 to 1964, provides one window into the anemic black tourism market in this period. Produced by an African American couple in Harlem, the *Green Book* helped black motorists negotiate the inhospitable environment they encountered when they took to the roads, with state-by-state entries listing hotels, restaurants, and taxi companies that were friendly to African American travelers. In the 1950s and 1960s, the *Green Book* never included more than five boardinghouses or hotels for black visitors to Charleston. Dining establishments in the city numbered between one and three, depending on the year, though the final edition of the *Green Book* published for 1963–64 included none. In theory, travel was an easier proposition for African Americans after the passage of the Civil Rights Act in 1964, which outlawed the segregation of public accommodations. In reality, the desegregation of facilities was fitful and protracted. Well into the 1970s, black travelers confronted hotels and restaurants as inhospitable as the Francis Marion had been to Madaline Williams.[20]

But black interest in travel was on the rise. In 1972, *Time* magazine announced that African Americans—with better incomes, increased access to credit, and a growing sense of comfort as legal and social barriers to travel fell away—represented "the new jet setters." The 1970s also saw the emergence of African American heritage travel, a niche market that focused on the black past. This market arose from a confluence of forces and events: the black nationalist focus on the cultural and historical legacies of Africa; the popular interest in history inspired by the national Bicentennial celebration; and the new appeal of genealogy after the publication of Alex Haley's *Roots* in 1976 and the airing of the television miniseries based on the book in 1977. Indeed, the impact of *Roots* on the black consciousness has been called "catalytic" and "virtually incalculable." It not only removed the shame many African Americans felt about their slave past but also, by encouraging blacks to learn about their family history and reconnect with their cousins, spurred a black family reunion movement.[21]

South Carolina and Charleston boosters failed to embrace this emerging market, though they certainly appreciated the importance of travel to the economy. Domestic tourism in the United States blossomed during the 1960s, with expenditures related to travel doubling during the decade. South Carolina officials worked hard to capture some of these dollars, kicking off an ambitious national advertising campaign in 1968, the first large-scale effort to lure midwestern, New England, and Canadian travelers to the state's sunny clime. In 1970, the director of the state tourism commission proudly announced that travel was South Carolina's fastest-growing industry. The Charleston Chamber of Commerce also reported an uptick in tourist business, a development that was facilitated by major infrastructure improvements, including the completion of Interstate 26, which linked the city to the federal interstate highway system, and new bridges spanning the Ashley and Cooper rivers, which increased north–south travel along Highway 17. In 1968, Charleston County officials created a tourism commission to handle the influx of visitors, which by the early 1970s exceeded 1.3 million people and brought in more than $50 million annually. Yet the state's big promotional campaign that year targeted magazines such as *National Geographic, Better Homes and Gardens, Holiday,* and *Southern Living,* not *Ebony* and *Jet.* Tourism boosters were also much more likely to look beyond American borders for new business than to the untapped African American market. In 1969, the state tourism commission sent a group of thirty South Carolinians, including eight Charlestonians, on a ten-day trip to South America to tout the state's attractions.[22]

Even if boosters had actively courted black tourists, there was no guarantee that Charleston's attractions would enthrall. A white *New York Times* reporter who traveled there in 1970 understood the difference perspective could make. He admitted that he found the area's sites and history intriguing. "Yet, how does a black man see that same history?" he wondered. "How does a tour of Charleston's Slave Market strike his soul? Does Henry Middleton's 'benevolent sway' over more than 1,000 slaves conjure up sweet pictures in his mind? Does he see the same ghosts I do, or far more sinister ones?"[23]

The two sisters who ran the Old Slave Mart Museum (OSMM) were arguably the only tourism operators in Charleston during these years who attempted to find out. After reopening the OSMM in 1960, Judith Wragg Chase and Louise Alston Graves made modest improvements. In addition to Chase's outreach efforts in the black community, they produced new promotional materials, rearranged some of Wilson's exhibits, and added displays of African and Caribbean art. Chase and Graves did not change the museum's basic organization, devoting the first floor to a gift shop and the second floor to the exhibit gallery. Nor did they update the museum's poor lighting, rickety display cases, or handwritten signs—elements that gave the museum an amateurish feel and that Chase insisted were rooted in tourists' preferences, making "them feel they have been transported to the slavery period." Whether in spite or because of these homey features, Chase and Graves managed to revive the OSMM's fortunes. In Miriam Wilson's last year, fewer than two thousand people toured the museum. By the late 1960s, the OSMM was attracting thirty thousand visitors a year, collecting enough in entrance fees to enable Graves and Chase to hire several senior citizens and, on occasion, college students to assist them.[24]

The sisters hoped that these numbers would be bolstered by a wave of black tourism unleashed by civil rights victories. "Integration of public accommodations has greatly increased Negro tourism," Chase argued in a 1970 promotional flyer, but South Carolina "has done little to capture this market." The tricentennial anniversary of the state, which South Carolinians celebrated that year, seemed the ideal time to begin such efforts. "Tourists can, and do, choose between South Carolina and other states when they want to see the Ante-Bellum South recaptured," she said, but if they want to visit a museum devoted to African American cultural contributions, they have no choice. "The Old Slave Market Museum is unique," Chase argued.[25]

She was right. More than three decades after Miriam Wilson founded the OSMM, it was still the nation's only slavery museum. Yet Chase's desire to turn the OSMM into a major draw for African American visitors remained unfulfilled. Although some black Charlestonians viewed it as a valuable historical site, many ignored the museum. A small number of African American tourists continued to stop by the OSMM, as they had since it opened in 1938. Up until the time that Chase and Graves closed down the museum in 1987 because of rising costs, however, white and Asian tourists, who came from as far away as Europe and Japan, outnumbered black visitors.[26]

African Americans may have been put off by how Chase and Graves presented slavery. To be fair, the sisters distanced themselves from a few of Wilson's interpretations. For instance, they continued to sell copies of her *Slave Days* pamphlet in the OSMM, but also posted a sign announcing, "The present operators of the Old Slave Mart Museum are in no way responsible for the opinions expressed in this booklet by the author, Miss Wilson. Written over twenty years ago, its value lies in the interesting facts of history that it presents." Still, the sisters stayed true to Wilson's overall vision for the OSMM, which involved underlining the gains made, and artwork produced, by the enslaved, while downplaying slavery's brutality. "We don't emphasize the whips-and-chains aspect of the past," Chase insisted, "since we feel this is a museum of cultural rather than political history. But through the years, we've had to walk a chalk line to keep both blacks and whites satisfied."[27]

This delicate balancing act had mixed results. A few cheered it. United Daughters of the Confederacy member Marguerite C. Steedman viewed the OSMM as a rejoinder to those who might criticize the plantation South. "Visitors, seeking fetters, chains, and whips, must be disappointed to find a gift shop on the ground floor and innocent handcrafts upstairs," she wrote in the *News and Courier* in 1978. Franz Auerbach certainly had been. On his 1969 OSMM tour, the South African Jewish teacher was shocked to discover a museum that "gloss[ed] over the Middle Passage" and "whitewash[ed]" slavery. "When I made some remarks to the lady at the gift shop about the horrors of slavery," Auerbach later wrote, "she argued that in general the slaves had been well looked after, and had been happy." Some African American visitors were disturbed by the fact that the OSMM's gift shop sold reproductions of slave advertisements to "well-to-do white tourists."[28]

* * * *

THE BLACK HERITAGE tourism market that Chase and Graves envisioned finally emerged in the mid-1980s. By this point, Charleston was a hot spot of southern tourism, with three million visitors spending over $400 million in the city annually. Since taking office in 1975, Mayor Joe Riley had worked hard to revitalize downtown Charleston, countering the suburban flight that plagued twentieth-century American cities by fostering economic and cultural development. First, he helped establish Spoleto Festival USA, one-half of an international arts festival (the other half was hosted in Spoleto, Italy) that brought musicians, dancers, thespians, and thousands of tourists to Charleston for two weeks each spring. Second, Riley led the campaign to build a massive hotel and conference center in the heart of the city. After a protracted battle with preservationists, the $85 million project opened in 1986. The center was a commercial boon, spawning the transformation of King Street into a high-end shopping district and providing a considerable boost to a tourism industry that by the 1980s provided more jobs in Charleston than any other industry.[29]

In the face of criticism that these initiatives—especially Spoleto—meant little to the city's black residents, not to mention the emerging black tourism market, the Riley administration worked with members of the African American arts community to create the Moja Arts Festival in 1984. This annual fall festival featured African, Caribbean, and African American arts and culture. Four years later, Riley arranged for the city to purchase the OSMM from Chase and Graves. The aging sisters had been trying to sell both the building and its collection since the late 1970s. After the College of Charleston, the Charleston Museum, and the Smithsonian Institution declined to buy the OSMM, they turned to the city, mobilizing portions of the black community to lobby the mayor's office. Riley, who viewed the OSMM as "a real treasure," said he was willing to go "digging in the back of the safe" to find the funds to save it. One year after Chase and Graves closed the OSMM in January 1987, the city paid $200,000 for the 6 Chalmers Street building, though it chose not to buy the collection contained within. It would take almost two decades, however, for Charleston to reopen the OSMM.[30]

In the meantime, a handful of black Charlestonians continued diversifying the city's historical narrative. In 1983, husband and wife team Robert Small and Alada Shinault-Small had established Living History Tours. A Charleston native, Shinault-Small knew firsthand that most existing tour companies failed to do justice to African American history. Having obtained her tour guide license in 1982, she worked for one such company before she and her husband ventured out on their own. While Shinault-Small was able to incorporate black history into the tours she gave for the earlier company, she felt hamstrung. "I wanted to do it in my way," she said, "without the constraints of an employer."[31]

The other pioneer in the heritage market was Alphonso Brown, a band teacher who grew up in nearby Rantowles. Having long enjoyed entertaining visiting friends and family with his own tours of downtown Charleston, Brown decided in 1985 to become a licensed tour guide. But Brown, in contrast to Robert Small and Alada Shinault-Small, did not initially focus on black history and culture. He vividly recalled an early tour with several white women from the North who, at the end, asked, "What about the black people in Charleston? Didn't they do anything?" Brown realized his narrative was too narrow. "When I got my license," he explained, "I just did what they did," meaning he mimicked the white tour guides who dominated the city's tourism industry. Although he attended

Alphonso Brown, owner of Gullah Tours, was a pioneer in the black heritage tourism market. His patrons heard a narrative of Charleston's past that was ignored on most traditional tours.

segregated schools and the historically black South Carolina State University, Brown had not learned to see the history of the Lowcountry from the perspective of African Americans. Only after his interaction with curious white tourists did Brown realize his black heritage might be a marketable commodity. Founding Gullah Tours as the main competitor to Living History, he bought a van in which to transport tourists around the city.[32]

Brown's anecdote about the birth of Gullah Tours reveals a significant point about black heritage tourism in Charleston. Just as northern white tourists pushed Charlestonians to uncover traces of the slave past in the early twentieth century, so, too, did they encourage African American tourism purveyors to tell a fuller story decades later. Small and Shinault-Small estimated that only twenty percent of the people who took their tours in the early years were African American. Black tourists, they recalled, tended to look for a jazz club when they came to Charleston, not realizing they could visit historic sites that were connected to black history. Brown's experience was similar. "You didn't have that many black tourists at that time." African American visitors came to see "family and friends rather than being a tourist, and so you had mostly whites." And they were the ones, Brown said, who motivated him and the tourism industry more generally to change. "It was a *demand* from the tourists . . . White tourists demanded the full story . . . These tourists are not crazy. They know we had slaves here. I mean, this is Charleston." (As late as

2015, in fact, Brown reported that his clientele was still predominantly white.) International visitors played a role in effecting this transformation as well. "We have an especially large number of foreign visitors who are curious to know anything about the particularly American, and Southern, aspects of 'The Peculiar Institution' of slavery," explained OSMM owner Judith Chase in the mid-1980s.[33]

These early black heritage entrepreneurs based their tour narratives on a number of sources. Brown, for example, consulted the collections at the Charleston County Public Library and the recently established Avery Research Center for African American History and Culture, located in the old Avery Normal Institute building. At Mount Zion A.M.E. Church, where he was the choir director, he talked with the older congregants, the descendants of slaves. "And oh, they talk. They tell you things. They tell you *things*," Brown once said. In this way, individual memories became public memory within the African American heritage market, just as white memories had within the city's tourism industry in earlier decades.[34]

A more surprising influence on Brown was the Society for the Preservation of Spirituals. As the new millennium approached, the SPS limped along, its all-white membership and antebellum costumes increasingly seeming out of touch, if not offensive. In fact, after a 1995 show, the group retired from performing in public. Several years before that, however, Alphonso Brown had attended an SPS concert. He was amazed. Grateful that the SPS was "preserving that style of music to make sure that we would always have it with us," Brown decided to do his part, too. In 1993, he organized what became an annual "Camp Meeting" performance of Gullah spirituals by the Mt. Zion Spiritual Singers for the Piccolo Spoleto Festival, an offshoot of Spoleto Festival USA. Two decades later, in the spring of 2012, Brown brought the SPS—by then much reduced in size, at about a dozen members, and no longer sporting its Old South outfits—together with the Mt. Zion Spiritual Singers and a Stanford University a cappella group. For the first time since its founding in 1922, the SPS performed with black spirituals singers.[35]

As of 1985, black heritage guides like Brown also had access to a revised version of the study manual for tour guides. Local historian Robert P. Stockton spearheaded the update, which did not stray greatly from the Eurocentric focus of earlier versions. In a nod to the changing times, however, the tourism commission appointed one of its members, Elizabeth Alston, to write a new chapter called "Black Charlestonians." Alston had introduced black history to the Charleston County school system in the 1970s and, as a recognized authority on local black history, regularly gave lectures at African American churches and organizations.[36]

Alston's "Black Charlestonians" was representative of the early black heritage tourism industry in Charleston more generally. It was a necessary, and mostly accurate, revision of a narrative that had failed to do justice to the history of African Americans and slavery. Alston's material appeared as a separate chapter located near the end of the study manual, however. One consequence of segregating this material from the traditional narrative was that the revised manual, taken as a whole, gave the impression that slavery and black history existed outside of Charleston history, that it was somehow separate from, and less important than, its "real," white past. The 1985 tour guide manual both reflected and nurtured a segregation of the past that came to define the city's tourism industry well into the 2000s.

Yet rewriting the narrative and remapping the cityscape in ways that recognized African American history and slavery were hardly inconsequential. While tourists had long found glimpses of the slave past at the OSMM and in King Street antiques shops that peddled slave badges, this new vision of Charleston's past was more revolutionary in scope. Elizabeth Alston's chapter for prospective tour guides underscored the centrality of slavery to Charleston from its founding in 1670, outlining, for example, the slave code that governed their mobility and punishment. She also detailed the long history of slave revolts in the area, including the Stono Rebellion and the plot planned by Vesey, who, "more than anything... wanted to secure the freedom of his people." Alston recounted stories about slave runaways during the Civil War, the Massachusetts 54th, and the Slavery Is Dead parade. No existing guidebooks contained this perspective on the history of slavery in the Lowcountry or on the sectional conflict, though Alston's occasionally limp prose softened the impact of her corrective. "The Vesey plot," she wrote, "caused the enactment of laws to control Blacks." Whether or not she intended to—and she may have, given that she was writing at the request of the city—Alston made her material more palatable with such grammatical constructions, subtly absolving white Charlestonians of their actions.[37]

Given their clientele—visitors who actually sought out tours about the black past—African American heritage guides had little need to be so careful. The owners of Living History immersed visitors in the antebellum and wartime black experience. As he drove around the Sea Islands, Robert Small assumed the persona of a private in the Massachusetts 54th Regiment as well as Jemmy, the slave who led the Stono Rebellion. Alada Shinault-Small portrayed a free black woman who served the Union Army as a cook and spy. Small and Shinault-Small visited sites not typically included in more traditional tours of the city, such as Emanuel A.M.E. Church, and deferred to the interests of tourists in plotting routes, incorporating places they wanted to see. Some asked to see Avery, some the alleged Denmark Vesey home, still others the Old Slave Mart Museum. Other African American heritage guides, including two newcomers—Sandra Campbell, founder of Tourrific Tours, and Al Miller, founder of Sites and Insights—visited these sites in the course of their tours, too. All of these guides also discussed topics (the Vesey conspiracy, Reconstruction) long ignored by more traditional walking, carriage, and bus tour companies. Black heritage guides, in sum, were more inclined to address the often ugly realities of the city's past. "I don't believe in sugarcoating history," remarked Al Miller on a 2009 tour. "History's history."[38]

Even when black heritage guides covered much of the same geographical and historical ground as other guides, their viewpoint was fundamentally different. Alphonso Brown typically drove his Gullah Tours van down to the Battery. Rather than focusing tourists' attention on Fort Sumter in the middle of Charleston Harbor, Brown pointed out Sullivan's Island, just to the left. He invoked historian Peter Wood's observation that this disembarkation location for enslaved Africans "was our Ellis Island," before discussing the pest house where Africans were kept in quarantine prior to being transported into Charleston to be sold. Brown thus shifted the historical lens from the luxury of planter life and the military spectacle of the bombardment of Fort Sumter to the tragic realities of the Middle Passage and the auction block.[39]

Brown also offered an alternative view of the city's antebellum homes. Many guides took tourists past the Miles Brewton House, which Susan

While many tour guides emphasized the stateliness of the Miles Brewton House, black heritage guides focused on the imposing system of spikes on the fence. These chevaux-de-frise *were intended to guard against slave insurrection.*

Pringle Frost and her sisters had saved in the early twentieth century. Like these early preservationists, modern tour guides emphasized the home's architectural significance, noting that it is an outstanding example of a Charleston double house. Brown, however, drew attention to the house's iron fence and its imposing *chevaux-de-frise*, installed out of fear of slave insurrection. Throughout his tours, Brown issued thinly veiled criticisms of real estate agents and tour guides who used euphemisms such as "carriage houses," "dependencies," or "servants' quarters" to describe the dwellings where slaves lived. Passing by the Calhoun Monument in Marion Square, Brown remarked, "If John C. Calhoun had his way right now, blacks would still probably be in slavery."[40]

Despite their more inclusive historical vision, black heritage tour guides at times ventured beyond the historical record in their desire to challenge the silences and erasures of the traditional tour narrative. For instance, on a 2009 tour Al Miller told of how slaveholders blindfolded their slaves and then forced them to have sex with multiple partners. Enslaved women, he argued, thus did not know who impregnated them, making it easier for their owners to break up families at the auction block. Although there is no evidence of this kind of charade, Miller's story nevertheless served an understandable purpose. He wanted to drive home how slavery rested on a perverse foundation of the profit motive and sexual violence.[41]

Black heritage guides also routinely took tourists by the house at 56 Bull Street, claiming it had been the home of Denmark Vesey, who, in fact, did live on that street. Informed in 2009 that experts had concluded the house was constructed after Vesey's death, Tourrific Tours guide Sandra Campbell responded that the home had a historical plaque on it—a National Historic Landmark plaque installed in 1976—which gave it "some legality, some validity." The unwillingness of Campbell and other black heritage guides to relinquish the idea that Vesey slept behind those very walls spoke to the absences in the city's commemorative landscape. As Vesey biographer Douglas Egerton observed, "Imagine living in Charleston, growing up in South Carolina, and all the sites you see have ignored the fact that this was a slave city." You would be "desperate to find some physical connection to the past."[42]

* * * *

TWO DECADES AFTER these African American guides and the city had begun to rewrite Charleston's tourism narrative, the larger impact of such efforts beyond the black heritage market remained uncertain. The city's tour guide licensing program itself provided one indication. In the early 2000s, Sandra Campbell volunteered to judge the demonstration tours of prospective guides. On one occasion, none of the hopefuls identified any sites related to African American history. Scolding the group for its narrow focus, she was dismayed to find that several people who later had to go through the certification process again failed to incorporate black history into their second demonstration tour. "You can't give a history of Charleston without a history of the slave labor that helped build it," Campbell remarked.[43]

What Sandra Campbell meant, of course, was that tour guides should not leave the history of slavery out of the history of Charleston. Yet plenty of them did. The certification process, in other words, could accomplish only so much. Controlling what guides said once they were out in the streets of Charleston was hardly a tenable or even desirable option, and despite access to solid information about the black past in the revised study manual, many gave no sense that African Americans—enslaved or free—had ever played a prominent role in the city.

Efforts to diversify the stories told by tourism operators did not always succeed. An Old South Carriage Company tour guide in 2008 explained that all eighteenth-century Charleston residents were either English or French Huguenots, neglecting the city's black majority.

Wearing the company's trademark Confederate gray costume, an Old South Carriage Company guide, for example, began a tour in 2008 with a discussion of the city's early demographics. In the eighteenth century, she said, the largest minority group in Charleston was the French Huguenots, who comprised about 15 percent of the city's population. The other 85 percent, she explained, were English. Left unmentioned were the facts that by the early 1700s free and enslaved African Americans represented more than half of Charleston's population, while the surrounding countryside had an even higher ratio of black to white residents.[44]

But it was impossible for this guide to sidestep slavery altogether. Passing the home of Nathaniel Russell, a Rhode Island merchant who moved to Charleston in 1765 and engaged in the African slave trade, she began a series of questions that amounted to a preemptive strike on tourists who might associate the city with slavery. "Which state do you think imported the most slaves in the United States?" she asked. Answer: "Rhode Island." "Who did Lincoln ask to lead the Union army at the start of the war?" Answer: "Robert E. Lee." This line of questioning functioned like a Lost Cause catechism. How could the South be held culpable for slavery when northern states like Rhode Island profited from the slave trade? If the Union offered such a high position to Lee, was it any different than the Confederacy, which he served for the duration of the war? "So let's not get into this," she pleaded. "This was just a southern thing."[45]

Other guides during the same years suggested that slavery in Charleston and the surrounding Lowcountry was little more than a residential program for needy wards. On a 2012 walking tour of the city, one Kansas history buff was disappointed by his guide, who contrasted South Carolina's supposedly gentle approach to slavery with the supposedly harsher version practiced in Deep South states like Mississippi and Texas. Other guides juxtaposed Charleston's urban form of slavery with bondage on plantations, whether in Deep South states or closer to home. By paying particular attention to the liberties enjoyed by some Charleston slaves—the opportunity to earn money, to purchase their freedom, and to live apart from their masters—these tours effectively minimized slavery's inhumanity by associating it first and foremost with freedom rather than bondage. Moonlight and magnolias, meanwhile, often accompanied denial and deflection. The Old South Carriage Company guide painted a portrait of antebellum Charleston by reminding the passengers that "this was the Scarlett O'Hara time."[46]

The tenacity of this whitewashed narrative bothered black heritage guides like Alphonso Brown, but they also recognized it as an opportunity. "Keep in mind that the less you mention about slavery, and don't use the word *slavery*," Brown wryly announced at one gathering of tour guides, "the more that is going to fill my bus up, because people want to hear it." His assessment may have been partly true. Brown's business was thriving by the first decade of the twenty-first century—"ask my tax man," he liked to say. Still, the carriage, bus, and walking tour guides who told visitors little to nothing about the history of black Charlestonians were hardly lacking for customers. Millions of tourists traveled to Charleston every year, providing a steady stream of history seekers who were happy to pay for tours cast in the more traditional mold. According to the College of Charleston's Office of Tourism Analysis, in fact, history represented the number one reason tourists chose to visit Charleston.[47]

For many of these history lovers, journeying back in time was a form of entertainment, not edification, particularly if the lessons conveyed disconcerting truths about the American past. Sandra Campbell remembered a white couple that had hired her to drive them around the peninsula and then out to Middleton Place on the Ashley River. Apparently unaware that Campbell incorporated slavery into her city tour, the husband objected when she observed that the first white settlers to Charleston brought enslaved Africans with them. " 'I don't think we want the city tour,' " he announced to Campbell, " 'Let's just to go the plantation.' " The irony of asking to visit a plantation to avoid slavery was lost on him, though perhaps with good reason. He had been taught to view plantations as sites of romance and gentility—as gardens, as they were often advertised. While Middleton Place actually featured reenactors performing slave trades such as blacksmithing, on the day of this tour the reenactors were all white. Their race, and the nature of their work—it was skilled and not performed under the watchful eye of a mock overseer—put the tourist at ease.[48]

African American heritage guides were not alone in appreciating that slavery might ruffle some tourists' feathers. Jack Thomson, a white native of Miami who relocated to Charleston in the 1960s, started leading Civil War walking tours in 1987. The popular guide made a point of discussing slavery, but broached the subject cautiously. "Is it okay to talk about slaves?" Thomson asked as a 2009 tour made its way toward the Old Slave Mart Museum. When pressed about this query, the guide admitted that some tourists grew anxious when slavery or race came up, in which case he changed the subject. Given the green light to proceed, however, Thomson launched into an awkward routine whereby he assumed the role of a slave dealer and asked a member of the tour whether he was in the market for a slave.[49]

Black tourists were sometimes reluctant to confront Charleston's slave past, too. Sandra Campbell occasionally encountered resistance among her African American patrons when she brought up slavery. During one tour, a group of black teenagers became upset when she described the slave quarters behind a home located south of Broad. Their parents tried to diffuse the situation, but the youngsters said, " 'No, we don't want to hear that,' " Campbell recalled, continuing, "They didn't want to hear it because they didn't want to hear about the enslavement of their ancestors. They just thought it was cruel treatment, and they became angry." This response is an important reminder that the act of remembering slavery can cause pain—for some, even shame. Although African Americans have overwhelmingly championed forthright memories of slavery, not all of them have embraced opportunities to hear or bring to light stories that evoke sorrow and anguish.[50]

* * * *

AS CHARLESTON TOUR guides struggled over whether and how to incorporate slavery into their narratives in the 1990s and early 2000s, local historic sites also began to broach the subject. The Avery Research Center for African American History and Culture paved the way. Housed at the former Avery Normal Institute and owned by the College of Charleston, the black museum and archive opened its doors in 1990. Under the direction of Marvin Dulaney, a historian of black America who was hired as director in 1994, Avery started sponsoring public programs and exhibitions that drew attention to the history and culture of enslaved people.[51]

The National Park Service (NPS) also revamped its approach to slavery and African American history at its Charleston properties. At the local level, these efforts were led by Michael Allen, who in 1980 accepted a summer internship at Fort Sumter National Monument before his junior year at South Carolina State University. As the only African American giving tours that summer, Allen faced a bevy of questions from the park's predominately white visitors. " 'Why are you here? What history are you going to tell us?' " he recalled them asking. Having studied African American history at South Carolina State, Allen was troubled by the scant attention that was paid to slavery in the Fort Sumter museum and bookstore and by the park's brochure and official tour guide script. Allen decided to stay and work to reform the site from within. In 1982, he took a full-time position as an NPS ranger with the self-proclaimed mission to change how its properties addressed the black past.[52]

Allen began by developing temporary exhibits on figures such as escaped slave Robert Smalls. Eventually, he built up enough support and momentum that he was able to make deeper, more lasting changes. Allen was instrumental in shaping the permanent exhibit at the Fort Sumter National Monument Visitor Education Center in Liberty Square. A stark break from the NPS's prior interpretative approach—which focused squarely on the military history of the island fort—the exhibit, unveiled in 2002, framed the fort within the context of the rise and fall of slavery in the Lowcountry and the political crisis engendered by South Carolina planters. Allen and NPS colleagues worked with Avery's Marvin Du-laney and community members to put up a plaque commemorating Sullivan Island's role in the transatlantic slave trade at Fort Moultrie National Monument in 1999 and to open an "African Passages" exhibit there a decade later. In 2008, that NPS site also became the site of A Bench by the Road, a slave memorial inspired by Toni Morrison. Twenty years earlier, the black novelist had given an interview about her Pulitzer Prize–winning novel *Beloved*, in which she observed that "there is no place you or I can go, to think about [slavery]. . . . There is no suitable memorial or plaque or wreath. . . . There's no small bench by the road." Inspired by Morrison's remarks, the Toni Morrison Society worked with the NPS to install A Bench by the Road in a quiet corner of the Fort Moultrie grounds.[53]

Michael Allen and several NPS colleagues also took the unprecedented step of reaching out to other historic sites in Charleston to help them revise their exhibitions and programs. They worried that the progress they were making at the NPS would be overshadowed by the taint of area plantations' and homes' gloss on the topic of slavery. Allen and company, for instance, consulted with the Historic Charleston Foundation (HCF), which in 1995 acquired the Aiken-Rhett House in order to better illuminate the African American experience, especially slavery. When he toured emancipated Charleston in the spring of 1865, Henry Ward Beecher had twice visited this downtown property, once to interview its owner, former governor William Aiken Jr., and a second time to interview his former slaves. More than a century later, in 1996, the HCF opened the Aiken-Rhett House with an eye toward communicating the experiences of the latter. This well-preserved urban plantation complex—which includes not only the big house but also the kitchen, stables, and slave quarters where the enslaved worked and lived—offers an unparalleled window into slavery in the city.[54]

The historic plantations outside Charleston were slower to embrace change. Although many of these sites had been operated in a more professional manner since the 1970s—with regular house tours led by docents, for example—they had not made significant interpretive advances in terms of discussing slavery. Visitors to Magnolia Plantation, for instance, were treated to an introductory film suggesting that if you had to live life as a slave, then Magnolia "was a dream come true." Most of the plantation's

In the early 2000s, Charleston-area plantations began restoring their slave cabins. They also inaugurated black history tours, which nevertheless remained separate from those of the big house.

volunteer guides avoided slavery entirely. When a journalist touring Magnolia in the mid-1990s asked his white guide about slavery there, she directed him to the slave cabin near the parking lot, adding, " 'It's really neat.' " On the outside stood a marker that read: "This cabin offered its inhabitants more room and far greater comfort than did most of the one room, dirt floored pioneer cabins typifying those of the frontiers at the time."[55]

Charleston's historic plantations began complicating the stories they told about slavery at the turn of the twenty-first century. Drayton Hall offered tours of its slave cemetery, while docents integrated discussions of slave life and work into the main house tour. Boone Hall restored its long-neglected slave cabins, and Middleton Place did the same with Eliza's House, a freedman's cabin named for a former resident. Middleton also started collecting oral histories from the descendants of African Americans who had labored on the plantation. In 2005, the plantation installed a permanent exhibit on slavery in Eliza's House, which features a wall that lists the names of more than 2,600 enslaved people who had lived at Middleton family homes and plantations. "It's one of those things that really affects people, probably more than anything here," observed Middleton Place vice president Tracey Todd, who compared the wall to the Vietnam Memorial.[56]

By the late 2000s, all the major plantations in the area had created specific tours that address slave history and culture. When a plan to restore Magnolia's five slave cabins was announced in early 2006, Taylor Drayton Nelson—a descendant of the original owners and the site's director—said, "Interpreting African-American history at plantation sites is something that's becoming essential to do across the country. . . . We're trying to tell stories out here beyond the stories of men who built gardens and did grand political things. There are other stories to tell." Local plantation operators also realized that those stories sold. "There were times in our history where people didn't want to hear the slaves['] story," said Middleton's Todd in 2008. "I think, basically, we've gotten to the point now where the market demands it."[57]

These slavery tours could not have been more different from what tourists heard and saw in the main houses in most Charleston-area plantations and house museums. On Magnolia's From Slavery to Freedom tour, which debuted in March 2009, visitors listened to a twenty-five-minute talk on African American history from the colonial period until the civil rights era as they sat near the plantation's five slave cabins, hundreds of yards from the big house. The guide then encouraged visitors to wander through the cabins, which had been restored to re-create five distinct moments in African American life at the plantation—1850, 1870, 1900, 1926, and 1969. *New York Times* reporter Jim Rutenberg judged the tour a "powerful . . . reminder of the brutal condition of the slaves" that "offered vivid sugar-free descriptions of slave life." Designed by D. J. Tucker, a Canadian who had a master's degree in history from the College of Charleston, the tour was rooted in modern scholarship rather than in white family lore. Tucker and his fellow interpreters discussed the Middle Passage and distinctive elements of Lowcountry slavery, such as the task system, paying particular attention to black achievements and contributions.[58]

Still, what was conspicuously absent on slave history tours at area plantations was a forthright discussion of the violence and coercion that were endemic to plantation life. In this way, these tours did not break from the pattern set by Miriam Wilson at the OSMM in the 1930s and perpetuated under Graves and Chase. The market may have demanded slavery tours, but only tours that went so far.[59]

The mostly white visitors who took these slavery tours reacted in different ways. Many were shocked by what they heard; others were angered or saddened. A few even insisted that the refusal of these tours to spend much time on the suffering of slaves on Lowcountry plantations amounted to whitewashing. Denial abounded, too. Some northern tourists balked at the suggestion that merchants from Rhode Island had once played a central role in the transatlantic slave trade, while southern tourists often disputed the contributions made by the enslaved. In 2011, Magnolia interpreter Preston Cooley recounted that some "angry white people" on his tour remarked that "those Africans were heathens, that they were not smart, and that all this stuff we're peddling is nothing but clap trap."[60]

The new black heritage tours began to attract more African American visitors to Charleston plantations, which was no small development. Black tourists had long been reluctant to venture out to such sites. According to the interpreters at Magnolia, when the From Slavery to Freedom tour first opened in 2009, there was a good deal of skepticism by African Americans, who assumed that the Draytons were simply trying to make themselves feel better. But the Magnolia guides reported that most black visitors were impressed by the restored cabins and the tour, and many were emotionally overwhelmed by the experience. Preston Cooley described African Americans who came up to him with tears in their eyes and thanked him for "finally telling the truth about their ancestors." Although whites still represented the vast majority of visitors to area plantations, black visitors to Magnolia had surged upward by more than 30 percent as of 2015, largely fueled by the From Slavery to Freedom tour.[61]

The new presence of African Americans, however, unsettled some. In 2014, a Magnolia guide described an incident in which a truck flying a Confederate flag drove slowly by the slave cabins while she talked to a group that included some African Americans. Someone in the vehicle shouted, "All of y'all are going to be our slaves again. The South will rise again!" On another occasion, a tour guide from the city walked by a group headed toward the From Slavery to Freedom tour and quipped,

"Don't work these slaves too hard." To its credit, Magnolia banned the guide from the property.[62]

Despite the growing popularity of these slave cabin tours, well into the twenty-first century they remained on the margins of the plantation tourism experience. When Jim Rutenberg first toured Magnolia Plantation in May 2009, for example, he completely missed the fact that a slave history tour was also offered. He was embarrassed, he later wrote, to learn about it only while on a second visit a month later. Rutenberg's experience is not surprising. At Magnolia, Middleton, and Boone Hall, tours that focused on the slave experience were separate from tours of the primary attraction—the big house—which continued to dwell on the home's architecture, antiques, and white owners. More inclusive than they once were, the plantations surrounding Charleston separated white and black history, enabling visitors to avoid confronting slavery if they wanted to.[63]

Even properties that sought to integrate slavery into their main house tours did not always live up to their inclusive ideal. On one October 2005 tour of the Aiken-Rhett House, a docent highlighted the experiences of the men, women, and children who lived in the slave quarters behind the mansion. But on a second tour, taken the following day, a different guide lingered for most of the tour in the stately rooms of the mansion, reminiscing about the glorious days when elite Charlestonians "danced the night away." As a guide from the Nathaniel Russell House, another HCF property, observed in 2009, older docents who had been leading tours for decades had difficulty incorporating the new emphasis on slavery into their presentations. Despite explicit instructions, he explained, "they will not call the servants 'slaves.'" The inclusiveness of a particular house tour, then, was largely dependent upon the docent visitors were assigned. In the early 2000s, the Aiken-Rhett House shifted to self-guided tours facilitated by handheld audio devices for all but the largest tour groups. While this change theoretically precluded the moonlight-and-magnolias approach of old-timers, the independence the devices afforded—visitors could pick and choose which parts of the property to view—still provided an opening for the ongoing segregation of Charleston's past.[64]

Much the same was true in the streets, vans, and carriages of Charleston. A handful of traditional tour guides (those, that is, who did not necessarily bill themselves as African American heritage guides) did a superb job of integrating the black and white narratives of the city's history. Yet such guides were few and far between. Tourists who arrived knowing that they wanted to learn about the city's black past had to "deliberately seek it out," in Sandra Campbell's words. The majority of tour guides—whether on foot, behind the wheel, or at the reins of a carriage—interpreted and disseminated one of two discrete narratives about the city's past. A half century after Charleston rid itself of separate water fountains, hotels, and restaurants for blacks and whites, in the city's central industry segregation ruled.[65]

Conclusion

Denmark Vesey's Garden

IN THE FALL OF 2010, A GROUP CALLED THE CONFED-
erate Heritage Trust announced that on December 20 it would hold a
Secession Gala in Gaillard Municipal Auditorium. For $100 a ticket,
Confederate enthusiasts could attend a costume ball to celebrate South
Carolina's decision to secede from the Union one hundred and fifty years
earlier. In the weeks leading up to the ball, Jeff Antley, the organizer,
proposed that it was a commemoration of the brave men who "stood up
for their self-government and their rights under law." The event, he insisted, "has nothing to do with slavery."[1]

Once word got out about the ball, and especially about the Trust's
declaration that the event—and the act of secession—had no connection
to slavery, it attracted a chorus of ridicule from national pundits and
comedy programs, including *The Daily Show with Jon Stewart*. Civil rights
groups took the Secession Gala more seriously. The NAACP announced
that it would lead a day of demonstrations. "It's amazing to me how history can be rewritten to be what you wanted it to be rather than what
happened," South Carolina state chapter president Lonnie Randolph observed. "You couldn't pay the folks in Charleston to hold a Holocaust
gala, could you?"[2]

The NAACP protest began with an organizational meeting at
Emanuel A.M.E. Church. Inside the church basement—just beyond a
vestibule that houses a small sculpture of four black children commemorating Denmark Vesey's planned rebellion—the group listened to a few
inspirational words and planned its route. The protesters, mostly black,
but some white, then made their way down Calhoun Street to picket in
front of the Francis Marion Hotel, one of the official hotels for gala

guests and the locus of the centennial segregation controversy a half century earlier. They carried signs that read, "It's Not About Heritage" and "South Carolina Suffers from a Confederacy of the Mind." Charleston NAACP chapter president Dot Scott minced no words about why they were there. "Celebration in the form that they are doing at Gaillard," she explained as she made the long picket loop in front of the hotel, "it's just not acceptable." Scott made it clear that the NAACP had no quibble with the commemoration of secession. It was the festivities—the dinner, the dancing, the clinking of mint julep glasses, all mixed with a hearty dose of denial—that were inappropriate.[3]

Later that evening, several hundred revelers, dozens decked out like cavalier planters and southern belles, gathered for the gala at the auditorium, located across the street from Emanuel A.M.E. Escaping the chilly winter air and the cold stares of protesters, they walked briskly into the hulking midcentury structure, passing by the controversial portrait of Denmark Vesey. The mood inside was festive and defiant. Asked why they had paid the $100 price of admission, attendees spoke of the bravery and sacrifice of their ancestors. Many connected secession to the Tea Party movement, insisting that its leaders were fighting for the same thing that their Confederate ancestors had fought for one hundred and fifty years before: smaller government and lower taxes.[4]

After a cocktail hour, the guests watched a reenactment of the 1860 secession convention staged by a cast that included several state and local politicians. Glenn McConnell, state senator and senate president pro tempore, played the role of convention president D.F. Jamison. After McConnell (as Jamison) declared South Carolina an independent nation, the delegates led the audience in a rousing rendition of "Dixie." Outside at the NAACP's candlelight vigil, one NAACP leader reminded the world of what it all meant: "Slavery is what you defend when you have a party, a celebration, get drunk, holler loud, act like a rebel, and talk about how you're celebrating your heritage. No matter how you dress it up, it is still slavery."[5]

The gala-goers mostly shrugged their shoulders at the hoopla. One guest even welcomed the protesters. "They actually helped ticket sales," argued Harry B. "Chip" Limehouse, a state representative and secession convention reenactor. "We'd like to thank them," he added. "Without them, we wouldn't have made budget."[6]

Limehouse was on to something, for the Secession Gala was not as grand as anticipated. The Confederate Heritage Trust had made five hundred gala tickets available to the public, but it managed to sell only about four hundred, despite heavy publicity. What's more, just three hundred or so people actually attended the ball, and a handful of them were journalists and scholars who were there to cover the story, rather than toast secession. It was a far cry from the more than sixty thousand people who flooded the city during the centennial back in 1961.[7]

Nor was the Secession Gala widely embraced by local officials or media outlets. Many prominent South Carolina voices joined the NAACP in decrying the event. Just days before the gala, the *Post and Courier*—the city's main paper since the *Evening Post* and the *News and Courier* combined in 1991—printed an op-ed by its former executive editor explaining how slavery was the central issue that drove South Carolinians out of the Union. Robert Rosen, president of the Fort Sumter–Fort Moultrie Historical Trust, which coordinated Charleston's official Civil War sesquicentennial observances, disavowed the Secession Gala. "The Trust believes that slavery was an abomination and therefore cannot celebrate a political event which the participants themselves believed was designed to continue the institution of slavery," Rosen declared in a statement. The *State*, the leading newspaper in the South Carolina capital, published two editorials that similarly railed against a celebration of secession. And although several politicians performed in the play reenacting the secession vote, Mayor Joe Riley denounced the gala affair. He emphasized that the ball was a private event that had not received any assistance or encouragement from the city.[8]

The morning of the gala, in fact, Mayor Riley dedicated a historical marker at the former location of Institute Hall, where the Ordinance of Secession was signed in December 1860, before a crowd of about one hundred people. In his remarks, Riley stated unequivocally that "the cause of this disastrous secession was an expressed need to protect the inhumane and immoral institution of slavery." This was too much for one member of the crowd, who yelled "You're a liar!" echoing South Carolina congressman Joe Wilson's infamous outburst during a 2009 speech by Barack Obama. This lone voice of dissent was overshadowed by the approval of the majority of those in attendance, and the ceremony proceeded without further incident.[9]

The events of December 20, 2010, are an apt symbol of how Charlestonians remembered slavery nearly a century and a half after its abolition. As shaped and promoted by black activists, scholars, and city hall, Charleston's public presentation of slavery was not nearly as whitewashed as it had been even fifty years before, when locals marked the centennial of the Civil War. In 1961, the sectional tension over segregation that erupted in advance of the celebration—and that resulted in southern delegations seceding from the national convention—recalled the conflict that had begun in Charleston a century earlier. By 2010, a commemoration of the Civil War driven by the tenets of the Lost Cause was inconceivable. Still, defenders of whitewashed memories of the peculiar institution, though not as numerous or vocal as before, had not altogether retreated from the scene. Charleston's Civil War sesquicentennial offered concrete signs that the capital of American slavery was inching its way toward a full reckoning with its past, even if not everyone welcomed the move.

* * * *

MAYOR RILEY'S MARKER dedication, rather than the Secession Gala, was a bellwether for Charleston's official Civil War sesquicentennial commemoration. Over the next four years, the Fort Sumter–Fort Moultrie Historical Trust brought together a wide range of figures, including National Park rangers, city officials, Civil War historians, and members of Confederate heritage groups, to stage a commemoration that was sober, reflective, and inclusive. Led by Robert Rosen, an attorney and historian as well as president of the Trust, this coalition took the city's centennial as a blueprint for what not to do.[10]

The most prominent part of the commemoration was a weeklong series of events in mid-April 2011 marking the anniversary of the firing on Fort Sumter. It was a study in contrasts with the celebration held fifty years before. While the Fort Sumter centennial drew comparisons to a raucous football game, the centerpiece of the sesquicentennial in 2011, held in White Point Garden, seemed at once a summer concert and a funeral observance. The program comprised slave spirituals, Civil War tunes, and classical compositions as well as brief remarks by nationally renowned historians and local politicians. The audience of roughly one thousand people—including a handful of reenactors—listened quietly for most of the evening. Even when urged to sing and clap along, they remained reserved. The only departure from this pattern came when the performers on stage struck up "Dixie." Enthusiastic shouts and more spirited applause briefly filled the air, evoking the 1961 commemoration held at the same location. The solemn atmosphere quickly returned as the band transitioned to the "Battle Hymn of the Republic."[11]

The substance of the 2011 Fort Sumter commemoration also bore little similarity to the centennial commemoration. Rather than focusing primarily on military maneuvers, the events emphasized the war's broader social and political context. The speakers at White Point Garden, for example, stressed that slavery had sparked the conflict, that African Americans had played a key role in the war, and that the most significant outcome of the conflict was emancipation. Nodding to Emancipation Day celebrations of the late nineteenth century, Mayor Riley read selections from Abraham Lincoln as the orchestra played Aaron Copland's "Lincoln Portrait." And while the crowd that gathered to watch the performance that night was overwhelmingly white, the area's racial diversity was a central feature of the program. Still directed by Gullah Tours operator Alphonso Brown, the Mt. Zion Spiritual Singers sang. Columbia University historian Barbara Jeanne Fields, granddaughter of Mamie Garvin Fields, who had enjoyed Fourth of July commemorations on the same spot, addressed the crowd. Even the reenactors who participated— members of the Palmetto Battalion and 54th Massachusetts Regiment— reflected this spirit of inclusivity. White Confederate and black Union soldiers marched in and stood together as a combined company.

Later sesquicentennial events continued to highlight the role of slavery and the participation of African Americans in the conflict. On the anniversary of Robert Smalls's dramatic May 1862 escape from Charleston aboard the *Planter*, the city dedicated two Smalls memorials—an interpretative plaque at Waterfront Park and a historical marker on East Bay Street in front of the Historic Charleston Foundation—and held a panel discussion on Smalls's legacy. The following summer, Charleston marked the anniversary of the Union assault on Fort Wagner, which was led by the Massachusetts 54th, with living history demonstrations, a screening of *Glory*, a public forum at the Dock Street Theatre, and the dedication of a marker to the black regiment at the Battery, which looks out toward the spot where Fort Wagner once stood. Finally, on April 19, 2015, a small group gathered in Hampton Park to commemorate the first Decoration Day ceremony that former slaves had held at the Martyrs of the Race Course cemetery one hundred and fifty years earlier. The program on that gray and breezy afternoon included brief remarks by historian David Blight, who was responsible for rediscovering the momentous event, Clementa Pinckney, a pastor at Emanuel A.M.E. Church, and Citadel chaplain Joel Harris. That a black representative of Denmark Vesey's former church and a white representative of the military academy founded in the wake of his failed insurrection came together to pay their respects to the Union fallen underscored how much had changed in Charleston.[12]

Yet the sesquicentennial commemoration was not without its critics. The staff at the Confederate Museum, operated by a local United Daughters of the Confederacy chapter, complained about the emphasis on race in the speeches given at White Point Garden during the Fort Sumter program. So, too, did a local conservative talk radio host, who was disappointed that Mayor Riley and his fellow speakers repeatedly brought up the issue of slavery.

Meanwhile, the *Charleston Mercury* struck a defensive pose throughout much of the four-year Civil War commemoration. The conservative bimonthly had been revived in 2000 by Charles W. Waring III, a publisher who came from a long line of local journalists, including his great-grandfather Thomas R. Waring, who edited the *Charleston Evening Post*, and his great-uncle Tom R. Waring Jr., who edited the *Charleston News and Courier* during the tumultuous years of the civil rights movement. Unlike the Rhetts' *Mercury*, which never bothered to deny that slavery was the issue that precipitated the war, Charles Waring's version of the paper announced in its special Civil War sesquicentennial magazine that it intended to contest "the simplistic notion that the War was 'over slavery,'" a notion that was foisted upon the South by "partisan Northern historians" after the conflict and that persists to the present. Waring admitted that slavery played a role in the conflict, and he even commissioned a series of columns on the peculiar institution written by African American journalist Herb Frazier. On the whole, however, his paper's sesquicentennial coverage emphasized that slavery was a national, rather than a southern, problem. Like many of his Lost Cause forebears, Waring was more concerned with drawing attention to the moral failings of antebellum northerners—who had "no urge to liberate the slaves"—than with probing the motivations of Confederate leaders. And when it came to what brought on the Civil War, he called for an end to "the need to ride the broken down horses of single causality and vilification of the South."[13]

On one occasion, opposition to the commemoration's interpretative bent took the form of action, not words. In June 2012, vandals struck the Robert Smalls marker on East Bay Street, just one month after its installation. Under the cover of darkness, someone ripped the marker from its pole, which was embedded in the promenade several feet above the street. "I know a car didn't hit it up there," National Park Service ranger Michael Allen remarked after the incident. "Whatever happened to it was done on purpose." Staff at the Historic Charleston Foundation suspected the culprit or culprits had hitched a truck to the pole to loosen it from its concrete moorings. City workers reinstalled the marker a month later.[14]

* * * *

BY THE 150TH anniversary of the Civil War, a confluence of factors—black political empowerment and activism, growing support from city hall, tourist demands, and new leadership at numerous historic sites, among others—helped make black history, and especially the history of slavery, a more central part of the tourist experience in Charleston and the city's self-image. Of course, the peculiar institution had been a component of a visit to the city since 1865. But by the second decade of the twenty-first century, this dark chapter had become not only a more prominent feature in Charleston's self-presentation—it was a topic that the city finally began treating in an honest and forthright manner.

The Old Slave Mart Museum, which the city reopened in 2007, emerged as a leader in this revisionary process. Unlike the museum's first two iterations, or any other tourist attractions in the area for that matter, the new OSMM focuses primarily on the city's role in America's domestic slave trade. The museum draws visitors' attention to the unique nature of the 6 Chalmers Street site when they first arrive, informing them in a large sign in the orientation area that "in the mid-1850s, slave traders came to this place to buy and sell African Americans—an interstate trade that brought wealth to Charleston, the state and the region." The OSMM's small permanent exhibit features objects, such as whips and shackles, and audiovisual effects, such as the sounds of an auctioneer's call, that bring human trafficking to life. Visitors remark on the emotional impact of learning about the slave trade in a place where it was once conducted. Robert Norman, an African American from Chicago, felt excitement to "stand in the spot where people were sold into slavery," but he also felt anger at what "they had to go through."[15]

Eight years later, as the sesquicentennial wound down, the Charleston County Parks and Recreation Commission began welcoming visitors to McLeod Plantation, a former Sea Island cotton planation and Freedman's Bureau headquarters that places African Americans' experiences during slavery and its aftermath at the center of its exhibits. "The story of McLeod Plantation is a tale of tragedy and transcendence," reads the plantation's welcoming sign. "Through generations of enslavement, a brutal war and the challenges of building lives amidst institutional inequality and oppression, African-Americans asserted their humanity while white plantation owners struggled to maintain power and wealth." Tour guides focus on the grueling labor required to grow Sea Island cotton and direct visitors toward "transition row"—a series of cabins that housed slaves and later free African Americans. The main house, built in 1855, is an afterthought at McLeod. At the end of the outdoor tour, guides inform visitors that they can wander through the home if they wish.[16]

One of the more unusual initiatives of recent years is the Slave Dwelling Project, which was created by Joseph McGill, an African American Civil War reenactor from nearby Kingstree. McGill worked as a park ranger at Fort Sumter and Fort Moultrie from the late 1980s to the mid-1990s. Tony Horwitz had featured him in his 1998 *Confederates in the Attic*—McGill was the ranger on duty when the author toured Fort Sumter—which in turn led to McGill's appearance in a History Channel documentary about reenactors and the controversies over Confederate monuments and the Confederate flag. In *The Unfinished Civil War* (2001), McGill portrayed a black soldier in the Massachusetts 54th. During production, the filmmaker suggested adding a little "spice" to the documentary. McGill mentioned an idea he had been entertaining: spending the night in a slave cabin. The filmmaker was game, and so McGill arranged to sleep in a Boone Hall slave cabin for a night. "The floor was very hard, and the bugs were terrible," McGill recalled. "I am not sure 'spooky' is the word, but the thought did run through my head of all those who had tried to escape."[17]

Nearly a decade later, McGill consulted on the restoration of the 1850s slave cabins at Magnolia in his capacity as a program officer with the National Trust for Historic Preservation. On March 8, 2010, McGill slept in a newly restored cabin at Magnolia, and the Slave Dwelling Project was born. Within a year, he had spent the night in cabins at a half dozen other plantations, including McLeod Plantation and Hobcaw Barony in Georgetown. Initially, McGill chose sites in or near Charleston and the Lowcountry, but over time he ventured farther from home. By 2017, he had slept at over ninety sites, including several outside the South. Since not all of the structures he visits necessarily qualified as cabins, he chooses the more capacious "dwelling" to describe them.[18]

McGill's primary goal is to encourage the preservation of the old buildings. Although some owners are already on board with preservation, others are not, or lack the resources to make repairs, and the dwellings on their properties have deteriorated. McGill suggests that owners contact the local press to cover his visit, with the aim of raising awareness about preservation and potentially attracting tourist dollars to help defray costs. McGill is not a purist, however. He does not insist that slave dwellings have to be restored to the way they used to be. This approach is impractical, he argues, since many structures were repurposed decades ago as garages, storage sheds, or apartments. He cannot demand that a dwelling be turned into a museum. If an owner needs rental income to keep a structure intact, so be it. "All I ask is that we preserve and interpret them," declares McGill. Interpretation—"telling the whole story" about how the structures were originally used and not just talking about the big house— is more important to him.[19]

But telling the whole story can make for an uncomfortable experience, and it is this vexing reality that motivates McGill, too. "The point I am trying to make in this," he says of the project, "is that we should not be ashamed of our ancestors." Shining a bright light on the conditions in which slaves lived is one way to emphasize their resiliency. Yet even McGill has his limits when it comes to such confrontations. Terry James, a black friend and fellow Civil War reenactor from Florence, occasionally joins McGill for overnight stays at South Carolina slave dwellings. On

James's second stay, he brought two pairs of slave shackles. James wanted to sleep in shackles to simulate the experience slaves endured on ships during the Middle Passage. James offered the second pair to McGill. He declined, noting, "That's too much for me."[20]

As McGill has labored to draw attention to the places in which slaves ate and slept, community activists, scholars, and municipal authorities have worked to reframe the city's public history and refashion its public spaces. In 2011, for example, the Historic Charleston Foundation issued a revised training manual for aspiring tour guides. Although the new version builds on earlier editions of the manual—and thus does not entirely overcome earlier evasions on Civil War causation or the segregation of white and black history—it is vastly improved. Written by local historians, essays such as "Plantation Life," "Charleston, South Carolina: The Site of Slavery," and "A Century of Hardships and Progress" provide prospective guides with a wealth of well-researched material on black history in Charleston. The streets and squares of the city, moreover, are now home to more than a dozen historical markers that memorialize the black freedom struggle from the antebellum period through the civil rights era. In addition to the Institute Hall and Robert Smalls markers, today there are plaques commemorating the first Decoration Day in Hampton Park, the East Bay Street home of white abolitionists Sarah and Angelina Grimké, the 1945–46 Cigar Factory Workers Strike, and the 1969 Hospital Workers Strike, among others.[21]

Most recently, on March 10, 2016, a "slave auctions" historical marker was unveiled in front of the Old Exchange Building at East Bay and Gillon streets. Sponsored by the Old Exchange Building and the Friends of the Old Exchange, the plaque highlights the fact that "Charleston was one of the largest slave trading cities in the U.S.," pointing out its role in both transatlantic and domestic trafficking. As one scholar noted at the dedication, the plaque was the start, not the end, of Charleston's rethinking of its enslaved past. "At a mere 150 words, it can merely nod at a much bigger story," he said. "It's up to us as Charlestonians to tell the bigger story." Joseph McGill, who also spoke at the unveiling, agreed. Much more needs to be done to rewrite "the mint julep, watered-down, hoopskirt version of the story that we've gotten for too long."[22]

As of 2020, that bigger, un-watered-down story will be on display in Charleston at the International African American Museum. Proposed by Mayor Joe Riley in 2000, the museum will document the black past in America from the transatlantic slave trade to the present. As Riley argued in making his case for the project, "African American history has been slow to be taught for a lot of reasons and, of course, slavery was not discussed because it was a source of shame and embarrassment for people of all races. But if we do not understand and present our past, we are shortchanging ourselves and future generations." The $75 million museum, to be funded equally by private donors and local and state governments, will be located on the former site of Gadsden's Wharf on the Cooper River, where an estimated one hundred thousand slaves were offloaded into the city to be sold.[23]

* * * *

PERHAPS THE MOST telling embodiment of the changing culture of Charleston—and of the small but still vocal group of holdouts who resist it—is the monument to Denmark Vesey. Erected in 2014 in a secluded grove in Hampton Park, the statue was the brainchild of Henry Darby, an African American teacher. Though a Charlestonian, Darby had not learned about Vesey until 1971, his freshman year at Morris College, a historically black college in Sumter. Darby's ignorance was not entirely unusual. Black Charlestonians had nurtured stories about Vesey's plot well into the twentieth century, and they succeeded in memorializing him with the portrait at Gaillard Municipal Auditorium back in 1976 after proposals for a statue fell on deaf ears. But not every black Charlestonian knew Vesey's story, and even some who did may have pretended otherwise. In 1999, two elderly members of Vesey's Emanuel A.M.E. Church told a *New York Times* reporter that they grew up having never heard of the black revolutionary. "I don't know whether our parents, or even our grandparents, knew who he was," said one octogenarian. "But if they did, they were afraid to talk about it."[24]

Henry Darby hoped to change that. One day in the mid-1990s, as he walked through the peninsula, he pondered the absence of monuments commemorating the black past and hatched his plan to memorialize Vesey with a statue. In 1996, Darby recruited several members of the local black academic community to help him spearhead the project, among them historians Bernard Powers, Donald West, and Marvin Dulaney, and Avery Research Center curator Curtis Franks. Naming their group the Spirit of Freedom Monument Committee (SFMC), they approached the city with the Vesey memorial idea. To the SFMC, Marion Square seemed the best place for a public monument to Vesey. Not only is it centrally located, but it is also home to the original Citadel (since converted into a hotel). Although Mayor Riley supported the proposal, the final decision to place the memorial in Marion Square belonged to neither him nor the city council. Two nineteenth-century militias—the Washington Light Infantry, which has close historical ties to the Citadel, and the Sumter Guard, Edward McCrady's old Redeemer rifle club—own Marion Square and lease it to the city of Charleston for public use.[25]

Vesey's modern fate was, to a large extent, in their hands, and they were not eager to inscribe the revolutionary's actions in stone in their square. Indeed, they made sure it did not happen. The militias' public explanation for rejecting the proposal revolved around a practical concern. Marion Square was undergoing a multimillion-dollar renovation financed by the city (an extensive plan that included, among other alterations, the removal of the fence surrounding the Calhoun Monument). The Washington Light Infantry argued that no new monuments should be constructed until the redesign was complete. But when the SFMC and the militias met to discuss the Vesey plan, it was an ideological objection that loomed largest. Behind closed doors, the militias charged that Vesey was a criminal who should not be memorialized. As a compromise, militia members proposed a monument to slavery as well as to Native Americans, one that could include Vesey but only as a part of a much broader commemoration of oppression. Interpreting this alternative as an attempt "to blunt the impact of Vesey," according to College of Charleston historian and committee member Bernard Powers, the SFMC declined the offer and decided to find a new location for the memorial.[26]

By 2000, the committee had settled on Hampton Park. While the park does not attract the same volume of tourist traffic as does Marion Square, it has important symbolic ties to Vesey and the black community's century-and-a-half-long struggle to publicly recognize slavery. Located adjacent to the current campus of the Citadel, where the college moved in 1922, Hampton Park was, of course, home to the original memorial to slavery in Charleston, the Martyrs of the Race Course cemetery. There is also a personal tie to Vesey that has not been widely recognized: the Grove, a neighboring plantation once owned by Vesey's master, Joseph

Vesey, was carved from the same estate as the Washington Race Course, which became Hampton Park. Joseph Vesey, and perhaps even Denmark himself, may have walked those grounds two hundred years earlier.[27]

The same year the SFMC selected its Hampton Park site, it won approval from the city's Arts and History Commission for its design and secured $25,000 from the city council to go toward the statue. Additional appropriations from the city—as well as private donations—would follow. Still, the path from approving the plans to erecting the monument was hardly smooth. Critics spoke out, giving public voice to the militias' private objections. The lone member of the Arts and History Commission to vote against the project, for example, denounced Vesey and his co-conspirators' alleged methods. Commission member Charles W. Waring III, publisher of the reincarnated *Charleston Mercury*, said he would support a more general monument to those who fought for their freedom, Vesey included, but insisted that he could not support one for Vesey alone. "Is it appropriate to massacre individuals," Waring asked, "or to slowly win one's freedom through the process? That's what it boils down to."[28]

When another memorial commemorating oppression was proposed for Marion Square in the mid-1990s, however, locals voiced little opposition at all. The Holocaust Memorial, installed in the square by the Charleston Jewish Federation in 1999, pays tribute to victims of the World War II genocide and to survivors who moved to South Carolina. The largest monument in a Charleston city park, covering 6,000 square feet, it is a testament to the cooperation of the Washington Light Infantry, the Sumter Guard, the city of Charleston, and the Charleston Jewish Federation. The Holocaust Memorial elicited no major protest or controversy. (The proposal for the memorial was approved, in fact, before the Marion Square redesign plan had been fully finalized.) Most letters to the *Post and Courier* were supportive, citing the need to remember lest the tragedy happen again. Said a Charleston Jewish Federation member: "I have an issue with people who see the Holocaust as simply a Jewish issue. It's a watershed in human history. It shows the power a state can wield against its own citizens." A plaque installed on the monument itself echoes these comments, proclaiming that "we remember the Holocaust to alert ourselves to the dangers of prejudice, to express our outrage at the scourge of racism, and to warn the world that racism can lead to genocide."[29]

The Vesey Monument seemed to the SFMC a natural complement to the Holocaust Memorial. Indeed, this affinity was one of the reasons the committee pushed to erect its monument when and where it did. In floating its idea for a Vesey memorial as the Holocaust Memorial was under way, committee members wanted to "develop a kind of intellectual synergy between the two," as Bernard Powers recalled. By recognizing the horrors of both slavery and genocide, Marion Square would become a place to contemplate the "inherent humanity . . . of all people" as well as "the depths to which human depravity can sink." The name of their organization—the Spirit of Freedom Monument Committee—was chosen to evoke this broad vision of the long struggle against injustice.[30]

The challenges the committee faced in pushing this vision were perhaps no better captured than by the Boston architect hired to design the Holocaust Memorial. "Charleston is a paradise," he stated when asked about the project. "That was my impression when I visited it for the first time." How, he wondered, could he design a memorial "for something that ghastly in a place that represents the best of what the human experience has to offer? Bringing those two things together was a crisis for me." The architect's observation epitomized the very erasure the SFMC hoped to combat—the idea that there was no ghastly history in Charleston. It also highlighted an odd reality about public memory in the city and in America more generally. If the Holocaust is easily invoked for the purposes of drawing universal moral lessons, the same is not true for American slavery. For some, it is just too close to home. "Jewish history," as Henry Darby remarked, "does not remind white America of a black past." By erecting the Holocaust Memorial in Marion Square, yet rejecting the Vesey Monument in the same location, Charlestonians denounced racism abroad while overlooking a long history of it in their own backyard.[31]

After the Holocaust Memorial was installed, writer Jamaica Kincaid tried to point out this commemorative sleight of hand during a visit to Charleston. In town to speak at a gardening conference, Kincaid had noticed the jarring juxtaposition between the new Holocaust Memorial and the Calhoun Monument in Marion Square. Abandoning the presentation she had planned to give at the gathering, Kincaid instead discussed the green space at the heart of the peninsula. She remarked to her

Prevented from erecting a Denmark Vesey monument in Marion Square, black activists installed one in Hampton Park in 2014 after a nearly twenty-year campaign.

audience that it must be difficult for local blacks to walk by the Calhoun Monument. "Then I said," she later wrote, "that John Caldwell Calhoun was not altogether so far removed from Adolf Hitler; that these two men seem to be more in the same universe than not." The chairman and founder of the organization, who had invited Kincaid to speak, scolded her for her remarks: "I had done something unforgivable—I had introduced race and politics into the garden."[32]

Race and politics had always been there, of course, just as they had always been in the garden named for the Redeemer Wade Hampton, where the Martyrs of the Race Course cemetery had once stood. In Hampton Park—as in Marion Square, White Point Garden, and the numerous plantation "gardens" surrounding the city—race and politics had been entangled with the azaleas, live oaks, and crape myrtles for decades, often choking off black memories of the past.

But in the winter of 2014, almost twenty years after Henry Darby conceived his plan, Hampton Park became home to the Denmark Vesey Monument. On February 15, at a ceremony attended by hundreds, the Spirit of Freedom Monument Committee dedicated the memorial in a serene spot located in the center of the park. Executed by Ed Dwight, a black sculptor from Colorado, the monument features a defiant Vesey, standing tall while holding a carpenter's bag in one hand and a Bible in the other. The text on the base tells the story of Vesey's life and thwarted insurrection. Frustrated by "his inability to legally free his wife and children," a new South Carolina law that made the "emancipation of slaves nearly impossible," and "municipal authorities' repeated attacks on the AME Church," Vesey determined that "rebellion was necessary to obtain liberty," it explains.[33]

Not long after the monument was installed, Curtis Franks, Avery curator and SFMC member, reflected on its meaning. "It's one thing for people to say when you look at the African presence in North America, Charleston is a must see." Yet it was quite another for visitors to search the city in vain for any reminders of the black past, as they had done for decades. Now there was "visible recognition," Franks noted, of the slave presence in Charleston. Said Bernard Powers, "The monument changes the landscape by now offering a counterpoint to those other monuments to white supremacy . . . that populate Charleston's streets."[34]

By the time that counterpoint went up in 2014, the opposition to the monument had been largely silenced, at least publicly. No one showed up to protest the dedication of the statue, and the city received just a handful of complaints about it. The monument to white Charleston's great bogeyman failed to generate the animosity that the proposal to build it had elicited even a decade before, for much had happened since then. Charleston was becoming a different city—not easily, to be sure, but different all the same. Nearly one hundred and fifty years after former slaves constructed their short-lived cemetery in Hampton Park to commemorate the martyrs who died fighting to end slavery, the martyr who had haunted Charleston since 1822 was reborn in bronze and stone. Peering through the grove of live oaks that surrounds him, Denmark Vesey now stands watch over his garden.[35]

Afterword

The Saving Grace of the Emanuel Nine?

NINE HOURS BEFORE DYLANN ROOF'S MURDEROUS RAMpage at Emanuel A.M.E. Church, we were sitting in the Broad Street office of Joe Riley. It was June 17, 2015, and the mayor was just six months away from retiring after a forty-year tenure. We had arranged a meeting with him—our first—to hear his reflections on the strides Charleston had made in confronting its complicated history. Looking back at the cooperation between the city government and local activists on this score, Riley was proud. He was especially pleased that the International African American Museum might soon be a reality. The Charleston City and Charleston County councils had allocated $25 million toward the total price tag of $75 million for the museum. "We have a duty," the mayor argued, "to honor those who were brought here, enslaved, and helped build our country."[1]

After our meeting with Riley, as the two of us headed off to the archives to complete the research for this book, we discussed our own sense of hopefulness. Back in 2005, when we moved to Charleston for what ended up being a two-year stay, we rarely encountered the black past on the many house, walking, and carriage tours we took. But, as we have suggested, the pace of change in Charleston has been notable since we left in 2007. Indeed, as we strolled through Charleston during that 2015 research foray, we overheard several tour guides talking about the region's history of slavery. One even mentioned plantation overseers and slave drivers, topics that were virtually unspeakable a mere decade earlier.

The following morning, we awoke to the news of the Emanuel massacre. Like the rest of the nation, we struggled to understand Roof's unimaginable actions. One thing, however, became immediately clear: the history lessons Roof internalized about black history—and slavery, in particular—were not the ones that black and like-minded white Charlestonians have worked so hard to impart to locals and tourists in recent years.

After the massacre, many Americans saw the selfies Roof had posted on his website, unsettling images that show him holding the Confederate flag. Less newsworthy, though just as important, were those of Roof at the Charleston-area sites he visited in the months before the murders. Roof captured himself standing next to the Sullivan's Island historical marker commemorating a place where African slaves entered America "under extreme conditions of human bondage and degradation." In the sands nearby, he inscribed a numeric code used by white supremacists to proclaim fealty to their cause and to Adolf Hitler, and then took a photo of it, too. Roof posed for pictures at Magnolia Plantation, Boone Hall, and the newly opened McLeod Plantation, perhaps the best site to visit for an honest, unvarnished account of slavery. At each plantation, he made a point of touring the slave cabins. In fact, the selfie he took at the restored Boone Hall slave street, where he stood next to two slave mannequins, he later identified as his favorite. Roof told the psychiatrist assigned to evaluate his mental competency for his federal trial that it was funny people might think the mannequins were his slaves. He snapped the shot, he stated, "to be offensive."[2]

Roof's trips did nothing to change his historical misconceptions. Undertaken to prepare himself mentally, as he put it, they appear to have functioned instead as a perverse form of tourism porn, pumping him up for his self-appointed mission to kill the Emanuel worshippers. As he stood at a terminus of the Middle Passage, as he wandered through the fields and cabins to which the enslaved were consigned for life, he did not see evidence of slavery's inhumanity. He saw evidence of white dominance. Roof sought, and found, historical justification for a return to white supremacy.[3]

Roof's historical pilgrimages raise troubling questions about the efficacy of correcting a flawed understanding of the past. What does it mean when, in the year 2015, someone can so blithely ignore unvarnished memories of slavery and embrace whitewashed ones to justify killing black people? Does it matter that African Americans—along with progressive whites—have succeeded in resurrecting a more truthful memory of slavery

*Emanuel A.M.E. Church,
June 19, 2015, two days
after white supremacist
Dylann Roof murdered
nine parishioners there.*

when a domestic terrorist insists they are lying? If, with a computer and Internet access, a white supremacist like Roof can both find and perpetuate retrograde history to try to start a race war, does the Vesey Monument or a better training manual for tour guides make a difference?

There can be no doubt that Roof's rampage sparked a much-needed national conversation about the meaning of Confederate symbols that still dot the American landscape. Just days after the attack, Alabama governor Robert Bentley took steps to disassociate his state from its secessionist past, ordering four Confederate banners to be taken down in Montgomery. In South Carolina, Governor Nikki Haley altered her stance on the Confederate battle flag that flew at the state capitol and called for its removal. So, too, did Glenn McConnell, the former South Carolina legislator and Confederate enthusiast who in 2000 had brokered a deal that removed the flag from the top of the capitol but kept it on statehouse grounds.[4]

President Barack Obama joined the chorus calling for change in a moving eulogy for one of the Emanuel massacre's nine victims: Reverend Clementa Pinckney. Just two months earlier, the Emanuel A.M.E. pastor, who was also a state senator, had offered a similarly moving homily at the 150th anniversary commemoration of the first Decoration Day in Hampton Park. Invoking the biblical story of King David and his son Absalom, who had died fighting his father in battle, Pinckney had issued a call for Americans to begin to heal their own divided houses. That same generous, reconciliationist spirit was on display on the evening of June 17, when a Pinckney-led Bible study group at Emanuel so warmly welcomed the young white man determined to kill.[5]

On June 26, President Obama flew to Charleston to pay his respects to the slain pastor. Six thousand people, including First Lady Michelle Obama, Vice President Joe Biden, House Speaker John Boehner, Governor Nikki Haley, and former secretary of state Hillary Rodham Clinton, packed a College of Charleston auditorium just blocks from Emanuel A.M.E. Church—Mother Emanuel, as Americans learned it was called. Millions more across the globe watched on television and Internet broadcasts. Adopting the cadence of a revivalist, Obama delivered a soaring eulogy that situated the massacre within the context of black America's long freedom struggle and the violence and recrimination that it has elicited. He spoke poetically of the special place that African American houses of worship like Emanuel have played in this campaign: "Over the course of centuries, black churches served as 'hush harbors' where slaves could worship in safety; praise houses where their free descendants could gather and shout hallelujah; rest stops for the weary along the Underground Railroad; bunkers for the foot soldiers of the Civil Rights Movement." Appealing to the memory of Denmark Vesey, Obama proclaimed, "There's no better example of this tradition than Mother Emanuel, a church built by blacks seeking liberty, burned to the ground because its founder sought to end slavery, only to rise up again, a Phoenix from these ashes."

The president structured much of his eulogy around the Christian idea of grace, which allowed him to ruminate on what the nation had learned as a result of the massacre. Americans, black and white, Republican and Democrat, appeared at long last to be opening their eyes to the fact that the Confederate flag is "a reminder of systemic oppression and racial subjugation," he insisted. Obama called on South Carolina to remove the flag from the capitol grounds, not as "an act of political correctness" but rather as "an acknowledgment that the cause for which [Confederates] fought—the cause of slavery—was wrong, the imposition of Jim Crow after the Civil War, the resistance to civil rights for all people was wrong."

Taking down the flag, he declared, "would be one step in an honest accounting of America's history; a modest but meaningful balm for so many unhealed wounds."[6]

Two weeks later, South Carolina applied that modest balm. President Obama's eloquent plea, combined with a national outcry and the support of newfound converts like Governor Haley, helped to sway many of the flag's conservative defenders in the South Carolina General Assembly, which voted overwhelmingly to take it down. On July 10, 2015, South Carolina removed the Confederate battle flag that had flown at the capitol since the early 1960s, when segregationist legislators had hoisted it atop the statehouse dome in the heat of the civil rights movement. "South Carolina taking down the confederate flag—a signal of good will and healing, and a meaningful step towards a better future," tweeted President Obama.[7]

Activists across the country also set their sights on Confederate and proslavery symbols. While some protesters attacked Confederate monuments with graffiti, other opponents of Confederate and proslavery memorialization took a more formal and potentially permanent approach. From Tennessee to Texas, grassroots groups, universities, and lawmakers reconsidered the prominent location of Confederate statues in their communities, opting to take down tributes to Robert E. Lee, Jefferson Davis, P.G.T. Beauregard, and Nathan Bedford Forrest.[8]

Students at several northern universities pushed their institutions to rethink the honors they had bestowed upon prominent racists. At Yale, they demanded that the university rechristen Calhoun College, an undergraduate residential college named for John C. Calhoun, class of 1804. In February 2017, the university announced its decision to rename the college after alumna Grace Murray Hopper, a pathbreaking computer scientist and naval officer. "John C. Calhoun's principles, his legacy as an ardent supporter of slavery as a positive good," explained Yale president Peter Salovey, "are at odds with this university."[9]

As the nation approached the two-year anniversary of the Emanuel massacre, some southern towns and cities—especially those with active progressive and African American communities—continued to revisit the future of their Confederate memorials. New Orleans, which had voted in late 2015 to take down its four monuments to the Confederacy and white supremacy, was the most prominent example. After a protracted legal struggle and threats of violence against a contractor hired to do the job, the city removed the first monument in the early morning hours of April 24, 2017. Under the cover of darkness, and wearing helmets, flak jackets, and masks to protect them from retribution, workers dismantled the Battle of Liberty Place obelisk, which honored the Redeemer vigilantes who had led a bloody 1874 coup against Louisiana's biracial Reconstruction government. Over the next few weeks, monument supporters from across the country descended upon New Orleans. They held vigils at the remaining memorials, waving Confederate flags and openly brandishing firearms. Monument opponents, including members of the Take 'Em Down NOLA Coalition, a local grassroots organization that had been working to rid the city of all public testaments to white supremacy, staged demonstrations of their own. As tensions mounted, and New Orleans police tried to keep the peace, the city steadily toppled the remaining memorials. First went the Jefferson Davis monument in Mid-City, then the P.G.T. Beauregard statue in City Park. Finally, on Friday, May 19, with a large crowd watching and mostly cheering the workers on, the towering Robert E. Lee monument, which sat in Lee Circle, a prominent roundabout in the heart of the city, came down.[10]

That afternoon, New Orleans mayor Mitch Landrieu, who had pushed for removal since the Emanuel massacre, gave a compelling defense of his hometown's actions. Any conversation about New Orleans's Confederate monuments, he suggested at the outset, had to begin with a forthright reckoning with the place of slavery in the city's history. Although New Orleans was once "a port where hundreds of thousands of souls were brought, sold and shipped up the Mississippi River," the city had not installed a single memorial testifying to this fact. This gaping hole in New Orleans's commemorative landscape, the Democratic mayor continued, amounts to "historical malfeasance, a lie by omission." The city's Confederate monuments only exacerbated the lie. The statues to Lee, Davis, and Beauregard "are not just stone and metal," he declared, "they are not just innocent remembrances of a benign history." Instead, these monuments obscured New Orleans's commitment to slavery and promoted a "fictional, sanitized" vision of the Confederacy that fought to defend the institution. Mayor Landrieu's words were widely lauded across the country.[11]

The momentum for removal intensified that summer. In May and then again in July 2017, the Ku Klux Klan and other white supremacist groups gathered in defense of the Robert E. Lee monument in Charlottesville, Virginia, which city officials had decided to remove. This crusade to keep the Lee monument standing came to a head in August at the "Unite the Right" rally, a terrifying two-day demonstration led by the Klan, neo-Nazis, and other white supremacists. One demonstrator plowed his car into a crowd of counterprotesters, killing one and injuring nineteen others. In response, calls to bring down Confederate statues sounded out from California to Florida. In sixteen states, monuments were either removed—often at night, with no advance notice given—designated for removal, covered, or, in some cases, vandalized. Outside of Phoenix, Arizona, the Jefferson Davis Highway Memorial was tarred and feathered. In Durham, North Carolina, protesters threw a rope around the neck of a statue of a Confederate soldier that stood in front of the old Durham County courthouse and pulled it from its pedestal. One hundred and fifty-two years after the Confederacy lost its war to defend slavery, the fallen soldier—a heap of deflated, twisted metal—lay prostrate in defeat.[12]

* * * *

AND YET.

Have Americans truly turned a corner? Despite all of the attention to symbols and the memories they evoke in the wake of the Emanuel massacre, it's not clear that we have. Between the summer of 2015 and the summer of 2017, more than eighty public Confederate symbols were renamed or removed. But that leaves more than fourteen hundred monuments, schools, counties, holidays, and military bases across the country that still honor the Confederacy and its defenders. Some communities have even added Confederate tributes. After the University of Louisville dismantled its Confederate monument in late 2016, for instance, the small Kentucky town of Bradenburg, about fifty miles away, took the memorial and installed it in a city park. More than four hundred people, nearly all of whom supported the monument, attended the dedication ceremony. Asked whether he thought putting up the memorial might be controversial, Bradenburg's mayor Ronnie Joyner replied, "I never looked at this statue as a black versus white thing or that it had a link to slavery or anything like that." Joyner viewed it simply as a tribute to Confederate soldiers.[13]

Significantly, Charleston itself has seen fewer changes in its commemorative landscape than have other parts of the country—and fewer changes, frankly, than we would have predicted. In the week following the Emanuel massacre, the Citadel Board of Visitors voted 9–3 to remove the Confederate Naval Jack that hangs in the university's Summerall Chapel. But South Carolina's Heritage Act, which was passed in 2000 as part of the bargain that moved the Confederate flag from atop the capitol building, makes the General Assembly the ultimate arbiter of any changes to, including the removal of, historic memorials. When Citadel officials requested that the General Assembly amend the Heritage Act to allow them to take down the Naval Jack, the Republican speaker of the house declined. Some Democratic lawmakers and a group of Citadel alumni who started the #TakeItDownNow campaign have refused to take no for an answer, but they have yet to make discernible progress.[14]

Although Charleston designated a portion of Calhoun Street as Mother Emanuel Way Memorial District, it has no plans to change the name of the street to Emanuel Avenue, as some have suggested, or to tear down the Calhoun Monument or any Confederate monuments in the city, as the NAACP and other local activists have demanded. New mayor John Tecklenburg did announce in the summer of 2017 that the city planned to add contextualizing plaques that explain the problematic histories of the memorials. John Calhoun "was an advocate for slavery," said the mayor, who suggested a properly contextualized Calhoun Monument would underscore that fact. It is unclear, however, if the state Heritage Act would permit such plaques. There is also evidence, albeit inconclusive, that someone tried to vandalize the Denmark Vesey Monument in the spring of 2017 by prying the statue from its base.[15]

Moreover, the backlash engendered by the attack on pro-Confederate symbols reveals a deep reservoir of resistance across the South and beyond. New Orleans's lengthy campaign to take down its Confederate memorials sparked protests, calls for a boycott of the city, and threats of violence. Charlottesville's decision to remove its Robert E. Lee statue led to armed conflict and death. In some states, conservatives mobilized against activists in the liberal cities and college towns most likely to

Standing atop his pedestal, John C. Calhoun towers over Charleston, including Emanuel A.M.E. Church, whose steeple is visible on the right.

demand action, attempting to tie their hands. State legislators in Virginia and Mississippi, for example, tried but failed to strengthen existing laws prohibiting the removal or modification of monuments, while those in North Carolina and Alabama adopted new statutes preventing any such changes. After the Lee statue was toppled in New Orleans, Karl Oliver, a Mississippi Republican state representative, wrote on Facebook that city officials "should be lynched." He later apologized for his incendiary choice of words and deleted the post, though not before two fellow Republican members of the legislature had liked it. The ongoing affinity for Confederate symbols is not confined to the South. According to Dewey Barber, the owner of a Confederate memorabilia store in Georgia, 20 percent of his sales in recent years have been to northern customers. Barber also noted that while the Emanuel massacre was a tragedy, it had been a boon for his business, with sales of Confederate flags spiking after the shootings. Sales surged again at Barber's shop as well as at a similar store in Pennsylvania after the Charlottesville episode in 2017.[16]

The most troubling chapter in the post-Emanuel story has centered around a powerful set of protagonists: President Donald Trump and his supporters, some of whom are avowed white nationalists. Although Trump agreed with the decision to remove the Confederate flag from the South Carolina statehouse grounds in 2015, a handful of backers repeatedly unfurled Confederate banners—some with his name printed on them—at campaign events in 2016. After his election in November, Trump's fans turned even more enthusiastically to the flag, displaying it at rallies from Virginia to Oregon, Florida to Colorado.[17]

The New York native fully entered the fray in August 2017. The white supremacists who organized the Charlottesville demonstrations to defend the city's Robert E. Lee monument that spring and summer made clear their allegiances—both to the racist function of Confederate monuments and to President Trump. "What brings us together," announced Richard Spencer, the leader of the first demonstration in May, "is that we are white, we are a people, we will not be replaced." At the August "Unite the Right" rally, which was kicked off by a nighttime march of Ku Klux Klan and neo-Nazi protesters bearing tiki torches, former KKK imperial wizard David Duke said that he and his fellow white supremacists were "going to fulfill the promises of Donald Trump" to "take our country back." The death of counterprotester Heather Heyer at the hands of the homicidal white supremacist who hit her with his car prompted President Trump to denounce the conflict. But he pointedly attributed the events to "hatred, bigotry and violence on many sides."[18]

Unwilling to draw a distinction between right-wing forces claiming to act in his name—many of whom were armed to the teeth—and their left-wing opponents, Trump served up a mealy-mouthed statement that spread the blame evenly and did not take a firm stand against white supremacy. Prominent white nationalists, meanwhile, interpreted his comments as support for their efforts. Responding to bipartisan pressure to offer a less equivocal condemnation, Trump did so in prepared remarks two days later, only to revert to his earlier sentiments several times in the coming weeks. After declaring that "there were very fine people on both sides" in Charlottesville and tweeting that it was "sad to see the history and culture of our great country being ripped apart with the removal of our beautiful statues and monuments," a defiant Trump doubled down at a Phoenix rally in late August. As an enthusiastic crowd of supporters cheered, Trump charged the "dishonest" media with mischaracterizing his role in the Charlottesville unrest. "The only people giving a platform to these hate groups," he insisted, "is the media itself, and the fake news." Alluding to the push to rid the landscape of Confederate iconography, Trump concluded: "And yes, by the way, they are trying to take away our history and our heritage. You see that."[19]

When the Confederate flag shows up at Republican rallies, when Confederate monument critics are killed in the streets, when even the president of the United States sees Confederate symbols as benign signifiers of American heritage, it's reasonable to wonder if some people will ever change their thinking about the enslaved past. True, not all the evidence on this point is so menacing. In her address to the 2016 Democratic National Convention, First Lady Michelle Obama—whose enslaved ancestors lived on a Lowcountry plantation near Georgetown, about an hour north of Charleston—argued that the story of America is a "story of generations of people who felt the lash of bondage, the shame of servitude, the sting of segregation." But, she continued, those generations "kept on striving and hoping and doing what needed to be done so that today I wake up every morning in a house that was built by slaves." The next day, Fox News host Bill O'Reilly countered that the "slaves that worked there were well-fed and had decent lodgings." O'Reilly may not have underscored his claim with a gun, but as a television commentator with millions of viewers and fans, he spread it far and wide.[20]

Invoking the lash of bondage and the sting of servitude, Michelle Obama emphasized the resiliency of those who had come before her and helped pave the way for the first African American president and first lady. For her, the memory of slavery is deeply personal. For some white Americans who, like O'Reilly, promote whitewashed memories of slavery, the issue is personal, too, particularly if they are descended from slaveholders or Confederate soldiers. These whites object to how unvarnished memories of slavery can be used to implicate their ancestors and, by extension, themselves.

They have a point. We should not be expected to reject our ancestors for their moral failings. And we certainly should not be held responsible for their actions. This does not give us license, however, to turn a blind eye to our forebears' flaws or the complexity of the world in which they lived. We can pay respects to our ancestors without slipping into outright reverence for them, especially when that reverence leads to, in Mayor Landrieu's apt words, historical malfeasance. More important, while it is unfair to ask white Americans today to accept blame for the sin of slavery, it is entirely reasonable to ask that they understand how its memory and legacies continue to shape the daily experiences of whites and African Americans in very different ways.

The issue is not just personal, then—it is political. When it comes to a topic like slavery, getting the past right is important in and of itself. But what is also at stake in remembering slavery honestly is our approach to race and inequality today. And on this front, the partisan divide is clear. Polling data reveal that Republicans are less likely than Democrats and independents to support the removal of Confederate flags and monuments from public spaces, to cite slavery as the primary reason for the Civil War, and to say that schools should teach children that slavery was the conflict's main cause. Meanwhile, nearly six in ten white Republicans believe that too much attention is paid to race today, compared to 42 percent of white independents and 21 percent of white Democrats. Although almost half of white Democrats and a third of white independents say that their race has made it easier for them to be successful in life, only 17 percent of white Republicans believe their race has proven an asset. Before the 2016 election, four out of five supporters of Donald Trump said that whites face just as much discrimination as do African Americans.[21]

It is hardly a coincidence that whitewashed memories of slavery, the Confederacy, and the Civil War find more fertile ground on the political right than on the left. These ideas, after all, have long reinforced reactionary positions. A century ago, the Lost Cause provided the intellectual and emotional foundation for segregationist laws and customs. Today, the enduring misunderstandings born from Lost Cause mythology make it easier to oppose policies and programs that would redress the legacies of slavery and Jim Crow—from affirmative action and more progressive taxation to criminal justice reform and reparations.

In his stirring eulogy to Reverend Clementa Pinckney in 2015, President Barack Obama predicted that the saving grace of the Emanuel massacre might be "an honest accounting of America's history." We should hope so. On its own, of course, such an accounting will not heal our racial divide, and it certainly will not eradicate the racial barriers that continue to plague this country more than a century and a half after emancipation. But it would be a start.

The persistence of racial inequality in America—whether in the form of police brutality, school segregation, mass incarceration, or wealth disparities—reflects, to some degree, the persistence of our divided historical memory. Was slavery really all that bad? Was it really all that important to our nation? The answers to these questions matter. As Charleston proves better than any American city, the memory of slavery has always been fraught and contested ground. If a national consensus about our original sin finally seems within our reach, grasping it will not be easy. And the fact that it took the murder of nine people to inch us closer is a national disgrace.

Acknowledgments

What began as spirited discussions about the many historical tours we took in Charleston from 2005 to 2007 eventually became this book. We have incurred numerous debts along the way. For encouragement of our project in its early stages, we would like to thank David Blight, Tom Brown, Doug Egerton, Bo Moore, Bernie Powers, and Stephanie Yuhl.

A dedicated and extremely knowledgeable group of archivists and librarians in South Carolina provided assistance both on the ground and from afar. At the University of South Caroliniana Library in Columbia, we'd like to thank Robin Copp and Graham Duncan. In Charleston, we are particularly grateful to Nic Butler and Katie Gray at the Charleston County Public Library; Molly Inabinett and Celeste Wiley at the South Carolina Historical Society; David Goble and Tessa Updike at the Citadel; Karen Emmons at the Historic Charleston Foundation; Jennifer McCormick and Jennifer Scheetz at the Charleston Museum; Susan Welsch at the City of Charleston Records Management Division; Sonya Howard at the Charleston County School District Records and Archives; and Becca Heister at the Gibbes Museum of Art.

At the College of Charleston, we thank Barrye Brown, Georgette Mayo, Sherman Pyatt, Aaron Spelbring, and Deborah Wright of the Avery Research Center; Mary Jo Fairchild and Harlan Greene of Special Collections; and Dean of Libraries John White. Harlan deserves a special thanks. As every historian of Charleston and the Lowcountry knows, Harlan is an invaluable resource. We are so grateful for his expertise and generosity.

We also appreciate the work of the research assistants who tracked down sources, among other tasks, over the years: Christina Butler in Charleston; Neal Polhemus in Columbia; Hana Crawford in New York City; Tony Petersen in Boston; Katie Labor in Washington, D.C.; and graduate students Stephanie

Strejan-Hamblen and Harley Hall here at Fresno State. Thanks to the numerous individuals who shared sources and helpful leads: Mary Battle, Edwin Breeden, Lisa Bryant, Nic Butler, Marvin Dulaney, Kevin Eberle, Doug Egerton, Jared Farmer, Curtis Franks, Herb Frazier, Amy Gerald, Harlan Greene, Stephen Hoffius, Joan Marie Johnson, Keith Knapp, Katie Knowles, Simon Lewis, Jeffrey Moosios, Greg O'Malley, Susan Pearson, Katherine Saunders Pemberton, Adam Rothman, Kerry Taylor, Susan Millar Williams, and Stephanie Yuhl.

In Charleston, Kerry Taylor also provided free lodging and good company on many research trips. Mary Jo and Bill Potter graciously allowed us to stay in the home of the late John Zeigler as we tied up loose ends on the manuscript. In Chapel Hill, Hilary Edwards and John Lithgow played host to several research forays. Ben and Ana Solky welcomed Ethan in Boston. In Charlottesville, Bill Van Norman and Esther Poveda housed Ethan for three days during a critical trip to explore the Old Slave Mart Museum Papers, owned by Acacia Historical Arts International. Thank you to Marilyn and the late George Hertel, who safeguarded that collection in their home for many years, for allowing a total stranger to sit in their basement and comb through boxes of unprocessed documents.

Many scholars read and commented on conference papers, chapters, or the whole manuscript: Bruce Baker, Matthew Brown, Tom Brown, Fitz Brundage, Nic Butler, Catherine Clinton, Lori Clune, Peter Coclanis, Karen Cox, Bobby Donaldson, Doug Egerton, Steve Estes, Harlan Greene, Jacquelyn Hall, Brad Jones, Mitch Kachun, Mike Kramer, Jackson Kytle, Anne Marshall, Scott Poole, and Bernie Powers. We appreciate the gift of your time and your criticisms. Our book is much better as a result.

Our colleagues in the history department at Fresno State cheered us on, and Provost Lynnette Zelezny, Dean Michelle DenBeste, and the College of Social Sciences provided the financial support that funded our research. The Interlibrary Loan Department at Madden Library cheerfully fielded our requests for material held elsewhere.

Manisha Sinha introduced us to our agent, Roz Foster. We are grateful to Manisha for this act of generosity. Roz helped us see our manuscript in a new way and demonstrated remarkable patience as we reshaped it. Our editor at The New Press, Marc Favreau, has a sharp eye for what a manuscript needs, and what it can do without. He greatly improved our book. Maury Botton expertly guided us through the production process. Copyeditor April Martinez saved us from many errors, big and small. Bob Schwarz of Shearwater Indexing quickly put together an excellent index of the book.

Finally, our biggest debt is to our family. Josi Kytle, Tari Prinster, and Martha Lou Roberts flew to California to watch our girls while we visited archives, attended conferences, and, on occasion, took a few days for ourselves. Jackson Kytle and Ron Roberts have been a constant source of encouragement and support. We dedicate this book to Hazel and Eloise, who have grown up alongside it.

List of Abbreviations

ACACIA HISTORICAL ARTS INTERNATIONAL, CHARLOTTESVILLE, VA

OSMMP   Old Slave Mart Museum Papers

AVERY RESEARCH CENTER, CHARLESTON, SC (ARC)

AJMP   Albertha Johnston Murray Papers
ELDP   Edmund Lee Drago Papers
MGFP   Mamie E. Garvin Fields Papers
OSMMC   Old Slave Mart Museum Collection
PWLSCP   Phillis Wheatley Literary and Social Club Papers
SNFP   Sandra N. Fowler Papers
SPCP   Septima Poinsette Clark Papers
WMDP   W. Marvin Dulaney Papers
YWCAR   YWCA of Greater Charleston, Inc. Records

CHARLESTON COUNTY PUBLIC LIBRARY, CHARLESTON, SC (CCPL)

HICTG   Historic Information for Charleston Tour Guides, 1964–85
RAFC   Records of the Azalea Festival Committee, 1934–52
RHCC   Records of the Historical Commission of Charleston, 1933–56
RSPMC   Records of the Society for the Preservation of Manners and Customs of the South Carolina Low Country
SCR   South Carolina Room

CHARLESTON COUNTY SCHOOL DISTRICT ARCHIVES, CHARLESTON, SC (CCSDA)

CHARLESTON LIBRARY SOCIETY, CHARLESTON, SC (CLS)
CLSR   Charleston Library Society Records

CHARLESTON MUSEUM, CHARLESTON, SC (CM)
CGTC   Charleston Guidebooks and Tourism Collection
SCC   South Carolina Collection

CITADEL ARCHIVES, CHARLESTON, SC (CAR)

CITY OF CHARLESTON RECORDS, CHARLESTON, SC (CCR)

COLLEGE OF CHARLESTON, SPECIAL COLLECTIONS, CHARLESTON, SC (COC)
COCA   College of Charleston Archives
FAPP   Frederick A. Porcher Papers
OSMMPCC Old Slave Mart Museum Papers

HISTORIC CHARLESTON FOUNDATION, CHARLESTON, SC (HCF)
MCAHCF   Margaretta Childs Archives

HOUGHTON LIBRARY, HARVARD UNIVERSITY, CAMBRIDGE, MA
MOLLUS   Military Order of the Loyal Legion of the United States Commandery of the State of Massachusetts Civil War Collection, 1724–1933

LIBRARY OF CONGRESS, WASHINGTON, DC
AFC   Archives of Folk Culture, American Folklife Center
BTWP   Booker T. Washington Papers

LOWCOUNTRY DIGITAL LIBRARY, LCDL.LIBRARY.COFC.EDU/ (LDL)
ANIOHP   Avery Normal Institute Oral History Project
HFS   Holloway Family Scrapbook

LCDHI	Lowcountry Digital History Initiative
MCALDL	Margaretta Childs Archives
SCOHC	South Carolina Oral History Collection

MAGNOLIA PLANTATION ARCHIVES, CHARLESTON, SC (MPA)

MASSACHUSETTS HISTORICAL SOCIETY, BOSTON, MA

AFP	Amory Family Papers
CFAP	Charles Francis Adams II Papers

MOORLAND-SPINGARN RESEARCH CENTER, HOWARD UNIVERSITY, WASHINGTON, DC

AGP	Archibald H. Grimké Papers

NATIONAL ARCHIVES AND RECORDS ADMINISTRATION, COLLEGE PARK, MD

RG69	Record Group 69, PI 57, Records of the Federal Writers' Project, Records of the Works Progress Administration

RARE BOOKS AND MANUSCRIPTS LIBRARY, COLUMBIA UNIVERSITY, NEW YORK, NY

FBP	Frederic Bancroft Papers

STUART A. ROSE MANUSCRIPT, ARCHIVES, AND RARE BOOK LIBRARY, EMORY UNIVERSITY, ATLANTA, GA

BIWP	Bell Irvin Wiley Papers

DAVID M. RUBENSTEIN RARE BOOK AND MANUSCRIPT LIBRARY, DUKE UNIVERSITY, DURHAM, NC

ALTP	Augustin Louis Taveau Papers
FWDP	Francis Warrington Dawson Family Papers
PMBC	Louisa Bouknight Poppenheim and Mary Barnett Correspondence

SCHOMBURG CENTER FOR RESEARCH IN BLACK CULTURE, NEW YORK PUBLIC LIBRARY, NEW YORK, NY

TGB	The Green Book, digitalcollections.nypl.org/collections /the-green-book#/?tab=about

SOUTH CAROLINA HISTORICAL SOCIETY, COLLEGE OF CHARLESTON, CHARLESTON, SC (SCHS)

AASP	Agatha Aimar Simmons Papers
ASP	Albert Simons Papers
DFP	DeSaussure Family Papers
DMFP	Doar-Middleton Families Papers
EAHP	Edwin A. Harleston Papers
EMP	Edward McCrady Jr. Papers
HGMP	Helen Gardner McCormack Papers
JBP	John Bennett Papers
JSHP	Jane Screven Heyward Papers
LMAR	Ladies' Memorial Association Records
SASCR	Survivors' Association of the State of South Carolina Records
SFJR	Schirmer Family Journals and Registers
SGSP	Samuel G. Stoney Papers
SPSP	Society for the Preservation of Spirituals Papers
TJFP	Theodore Dehon Jervey Family Papers

SOUTH CAROLINIANA LIBRARY, UNIVERSITY OF SOUTH CAROLINA, COLUMBIA, SC (SCL)

BGFP	Ball and Gilchrist Families Papers, 1746–1999
FWPSCL	Federal Writers' Project, 1936, WPA Federal Writers' Project Papers, library.sc.edu/digital/collections/wpafwp.html
MASS	Mary Amarinthia Snowden Scrapbook, Mary Amarinthia Yates Snowden Papers

SOUTHERN FOLKLIFE COLLECTION, WILSON LIBRARY, UNIVERSITY OF NORTH CAROLINA AT CHAPEL HILL, CHAPEL HILL, NC

GCCC	Guy and Candie Carawan Collection

SOUTHERN HISTORICAL COLLECTION, WILSON LIBRARY, UNIVERSITY OF NORTH CAROLINA AT CHAPEL HILL, CHAPEL HILL, NC (SHC)

HEP   Habersham Elliott Papers
NRMP   Nathaniel Russell Middleton Papers
SCIS   South Carolina Inter-State and West Indian Exposition
             Company Papers
SOHP   Southern Oral History Program
WPMP   William Porcher Miles Papers

PUBLISHED PAPERS

PJCC   Wilson, Clyde N., et al., eds., *The Papers of John C.*
           Calhoun (28 vols., Columbia, SC: University of South
           Carolina Press, 1959–2003).
ASCA   Rawick, George P., *The American Slave: A Composite*
           Autobiography, Series One (Westport, CT: Greenwood
           Press, 1972).

JOURNALS

AQ   *American Quarterly*
CWH   *Civil War History*
JAAH   *Journal of African American History*
JAH   *Journal of American History*
JCWE   *Journal of the Civil War Era*
JNH   *Journal of Negro History*
JSH   *Journal of Southern History*
PSCHA   *Proceedings of the South Carolina Historical Association*
SCHM   *South Carolina Historical Magazine*
SCHGM   *South Carolina Historical and Genealogical Magazine*
WMQ   *William and Mary Quarterly*

Newspapers and Periodicals

AC	*Atlanta Constitution*
ADC	*Augusta Daily Constitutionalist*
AI	*Anderson Intelligencer*
AM	*Atlantic Monthly*
AT	*Avery Tiger*
BDA	*Boston Daily Advertiser*
BDJ	*Boston Daily Journal*
BET	*Boston Evening Transcript*
BS	*Baltimore Sun*
CC	*Charleston Courier*
CCP	*Charleston City Paper*
CDN	*Charleston Daily News*
CDR	*Charleston Daily Republican*
CEP	*Charleston Evening Post*
CHR	*Chronicle*
CM	*Charleston Mercury*
CNC	*Charleston News and Courier*
CPC	*Charleston Post and Courier*
CR	*Christian Recorder*
FLN	*Frank Leslie's Newspaper*
FP	*Free Press*
GNR	*Greensboro News and Record*
HW	*Harper's Weekly*
IND	*Independent*
INF	*Indianapolis Freeman*
KC	*Keowee Courier*
LAT	*Los Angeles Times*
LDCN	*Lowell Daily Citizen and News*
LIB	*Liberator*
MSL	*Milwaukee Sentinel*
NASS	*National Anti-Slavery Standard*
NOTP	*New Orleans Times-Picayune*
NYA	*New York Age*
NYF	*New York Freeman*
NYRB	*New York Review of Books*

NYT	*New York Times*
NYTR	*New-York Tribune*
PHP	*Philadelphia Press*
SCLE	*South Carolina Leader*
SMN	*Savannah Morning News*
SP	*Southern Patriot*
WP	*Washington Post*

Notes

INTRODUCTION

1. Dylann Roof, manifesto posted on personal website, lastrhodesian.com, reproduced in "Here's What Appears to Be Dylann Roof's Racist Manifesto," *Mother Jones*, June 20, 2105; Herb Frazier, Bernard E. Powers Jr., Marjory Wentworth, *We Are Charleston: Tragedy and Triumph at Mother Emanuel* (New York: Harper Collins, 2016), 1–3; Edward Ball, "The Mind of Dylann Roof," *NYRB*, Mar. 23, 2017, p.12.

2. Glenn Smith, Jennifer Berry Hawes, Abigail Darlington, "Testimony Shows Dylann Roof Scouted Emanuel AME Church for Months Before Mass Shooting," *CPC*, Dec. 13, 2016; Edward Ball, "United States v. Dylann Roof," *NYRB*, Mar. 9, 2017, p. 6; Associated Press, "Charleston Shooting Trial: Dylann Roof Had List of Other Local Black Churches," *Guardian*, Dec. 12, 2016; Dana Ford, "What We Know about Dylann Roof as Told in Photographs," *CNN*, June 24, 2015, cnn.com/2015/06/23/us/dylann-roof-photographs/.

3. Robert McClendon, "Mitch Landrieu Invokes 'Public Nuisance' Ordinance for Confederate Monuments," *NOTP*, July 9, 2015; Campbell Robertson, Monica Davey, and Julie Bosman, "Calls to Drop Confederate Emblems Spread Nationwide," *NYT*, June 23, 2015; Richard Fausset and Alan Blinder, "South Carolina Settles Its Decades-Old Dispute Over a Confederate Flag," *NYT*, July 9, 2015.

4. Melissa Boughton, "Confederate Monument a Focus of Debate After Graffiti Appears," *CPC*, June 21, 2015; Peter Holley, "'Black Lives Matter' Graffiti Appears on Confederate Memorials Across the U.S.," *WP*, June 23, 2015; Dave Munday, "Vandal Quotes President Barack Obama with Spray Paint on Confederate Memorial Statue," *CPC*, July 10, 2015; John C. Calhoun, "Remarks on Receiving Abolition Petitions (Revised Report)," in *PJCC*, 13: 395; "Tracking Vandalism of Confederate Monuments in 2015," kurtluther.com/confederate/.

5. Southern Poverty Law Center, "Mapping Hate: Pro-Confederate Battle Flag Rallies Across America," Dec. 3, 2015, splcenter.org/hatewatch/2015/07/16/mapping-hate-pro-confederate -battle-flag-rallies-across-america; Southern Poverty Law Center, "Whose Heritage? Public Symbols of the Confederacy," Apr. 21, 2016, splcenter.org/20160421/whose-heritage -public-symbols-confederacy; Christopher Ingraham, "All 173 Confederate Flag Rallies Since the Charleston Massacre, Mapped," *WP*, Aug. 17, 2015; Walter C. Jones, "Georgia Legislator Introduces Pro-Confederate Bills to Combat 'Cultural Terrorism,'" *Online Athens/Athens Banner Herald*, Jan. 29, 2016, onlineathens.com/breaking-news/2016-01-28 /georgia-legislator-introduces-pro-confederate-bills-combat-cultural.

6. Greg LaRose, "Contractor Working on Confederate Monuments Project Quits after Death Threats," *NOTP*, Jan. 14, 2016; Sheryl Gay Stolberg and Brian M. Rosenthal, "Man Charged after White Nationalist Rally in Charlottesville Ends in Deadly Violence," *NYT*, Aug. 12, 2017; Tom Grubisich and Elizabeth Bowers, "How Charleston's Next Mayor Can Help the City Erase Its Stubborn Color Line," *CCP*, Oct. 22, 2015.

7. The home was built either by Dr. Anthony V. Toomer or by his son, Dr. Henry V. Toomer. Jonathan H. Poston, *The Buildings of Charleston: A Guide to the City's Architecture* (Columbia: University of South Carolina Press, 1997), 591. Dr. Henry V. Toomer owned nine slaves in 1850. U.S. Bureau of the Census, *1850 United States Census, Slave Schedule, Parishes of St. Philip and St. Michael, Charleston, South Carolina*, ancestry.com.

8. W. Fitzhugh Brundage, "No Deed But Memory," introduction to *Where These Memories Grow: History, Memory, and Southern Identity*, ed. W. Fitzhugh Brundage (Chapel Hill: University of North Carolina Press, 2000), 6; Jonathan Scott Holloway, *Jim Crow Wisdom: Memory and Identity in Black America since 1940* (Chapel Hill: University of North Carolina Press, 2013), 9.

9. See, for example, "The Flag of Truce," *CNC*, Dec. 21, 1892; and "Most Interesting Reunion," *CNC*, Apr. 28, 1899.

10. Melinda Patience, Brittany Watson, and Bing Pan, "2015 Charleston Area Visitor Intercept Survey Report," Apr. 26, 2016, charlestoncvb.com/travel/login/research/2015_Visitor _Intercept_Report.pdf; Ashley Heffernan, "Charleston Ranked No. 1 for 5th Year in a Row," *Charleston Business*, Oct. 20, 2015, charlestonbusiness.com/news/hospitality-and -tourism/67984/; "The Best Small Cities in the U.S.," *Condé Nast Traveler*, Oct. 18, 2016, cntraveler.com/galleries/2015-10-08/top-small-cities-in-the-us-readers-choice-awards.

11. Roof, manifesto. Scholars have long assumed that most of the enslaved brought to Charleston as part of the transatlantic trade were briefly quarantined at the Sullivan's Island pest house. New research by historian Nicholas Butler, however, suggests that only a tiny fraction of the slaves imported through the city spent time in the island's pest house. Nicholas Butler, "The Pest House on Sullivan's Island: A Brief History," PowerPoint presentation, June 2017, in authors' possession.

12. Kenneth M. Stampp, *The Peculiar Institution: Slavery in the Ante-Bellum South* (New York: Random House, 1956), 3; Calhoun, "Remarks on Receiving Abolition Petitions," 392.

13. We have many excellent studies on the memory of slavery and the Civil War in the fifty years after Appomattox, as well as on the memory of slavery at historic sites and plantations today, but few works bridge this chronological divide. See, for example, David W. Blight, *Race and Reunion: The Civil War in American Memory* (Cambridge, MA: Belknap Press of Harvard University Press, 2001); Caroline E. Janney, *Remembering the Civil War: Reunion and the Limits of Reconciliation* (Chapel Hill: University of North Carolina Press, 2013); James Oliver Horton and Lois E. Horton, eds., *Slavery and Public History: The Tough Stuff of American Memory* (New York: The New Press, 2006); Jennifer L. Eichstedt and Stephen Small, *Representations of Slavery: Race and Ideology in Southern Plantation Museums* (Washington, DC: Smithsonian Books, 2002); and Karen L. Cox, *Destination Dixie: Tourism and Southern History* (Gainesville: University Press of Florida, 2012). On black memory as countermemory, see Bruce E. Baker, *What Reconstruction Meant: Historical Memory in the American South* (Charlottesville: University of Virginia Press, 2007); Robert J. Cook, *Troubled Commemoration: The American Civil War Centennial, 1961–1965* (Baton Rouge: Lousiana State University Press, 2007); and K. Stephen Prince, "Remembering Robert Charles: Violence and Memory in Jim Crow New Orleans," *JSH* 83 (May 2017): 297–328.

14. W. Fitzhugh Brundage, "Contentious and Collected: Memory's Future in Southern History," *JSH* 75 (Aug. 2009): 754–55; Jeffrey K. Olick, "Collective Memory: The Two Cultures," *Sociological Theory* 17 (Nov. 1999): 333–48. For a study of Charleston that skillfully traces the roots of collective memory in personal remembrances during the interwar years, see Stephanie E. Yuhl, *The Making of Historic Charleston: A Golden Haze of Memory* (Chapel Hill: University of North Carolina Press, 2005).

15. James W. Loewen, introduction to *The Confederate and Neo-Confederate Reader*, ed. James W. Loewen and Edward H. Sebesta (Jackson: University Press of Mississippi, 2010), 8–11.

16. Pew Research Center, "Civil War at 150: Still Relevant, Still Divisive," Apr. 8, 2011, people-press.org/2011/04/08/civil-war-at-150-still-relevant-still-divisive/; Lynn Vavreck, "Measuring Donald Trump's Supporters for Intolerance," *NYT*, Feb. 23, 2016.

PRELUDE: SLAVERY'S CAPITAL

1. Elihu Burritt, *Peace Papers for the People* (London: Charles Gilpin, [1851]), 40–41.

2. Peter H. Wood, *Black Majority: Negroes in Colonial South Carolina from 1670 through the Stono Rebellion* (New York: Knopf, 1974), xiv, 13–34 (quote 25); Walter J. Fraser Jr., *Charleston! Charleston! The History of a Southern City* (Columbia: University of South Carolina Press, 1989), 1–5; Robert Olwell, *Masters, Slaves, and Subjects: The Culture of Power in the South Carolina Low Country, 1740–1790* (Ithaca, NY: Cornell University Press, 1998), 5; Philip D. Morgan, *Slave Counterpoint: Black Culture in the Eighteenth-Century Chesapeake and Lowcountry* (Chapel Hill: University of North Carolina Press, 1998), 1–2.

3. Wood, *Black Majority*, 144–50; Philip D. Morgan, "Black Life in Eighteenth-Century Charleston," in *Colonial Southern Slavery*, vol. 3, *Articles on American Slavery*, ed. Paul Finkleman (NY: Garland, 1989), 306; Peter A. Coclanis, *The Shadow of a Dream: Economic Life and Death in the South Carolina Low Country, 1670–1920* (New York: Oxford University Press, 1989), 115; Bernard E. Powers Jr., *Black Charlestonians: A Social History, 1822–1885* (Fayetteville: University of Arkansas Press, 1994), 58–59, 267; Michael P. Johnson, "Charleston, SC, Slavery in," in *Dictionary of Afro-American Slavery, Updated, with a New Introduction and Bibliography*, ed. Randall M. Miller and John David Smith (Westport, CT: Praeger, 1997), 97.

4. Morgan, "Black Life in Eighteenth-Century Charleston," 306–7; Morgan, *Slave Counterpoint*, 32–33, 95–97, 195; Coclanis, *Shadow of a Dream*, 30 ("Bowling ally" quote), 112, 115; Ira Berlin, *Many Thousands Gone: The First Two Centuries of Slavery in North America* (Cambridge, MA: Belknap Press of Harvard University Press, 1998), 142–44; Fraser, *Charleston! Charleston!*, 55; Wood, *Black Majority*, 169–71.

5. Wood, *Black Majority*, 218–19; Olwell, *Masters, Slaves, and Subjects*, 48; *South-Carolina Gazette*, Aug. 27, 1772; Fredrika Bremer, *The Homes of the New World: Impressions of America*, translated by Mary Howitt (New York: Harper & Brothers, 1853), 1: 264.

6. Berlin, *Many Thousands Gone*, 143–44; Morgan, *Slave Counterpoint*, 36–37; Coclanis, *Shadow of a Dream*, 42; Charles William Janson, *The Stranger in America* (London: Albion Press, 1807), 358; Peter McCandless, *Slavery, Disease, and Suffering in the Southern Lowcountry* (New York: Cambridge University Press, 2011), 45–46, 126–30; St. Julien R. Childs, contrib., "A Letter Written in 1711 by Mary Stafford to Her Kinswoman in England," *SCHM* 81 (Jan. 1980): 4.

7. Kenneth Morgan, *Slavery and the British Empire: From Africa to America* (New York: Oxford University Press, 2007), 12. According to the Trans-Atlantic Slave Trade Database, which compiles statistics for *documented* slave voyages, 149,429 enslaved laborers disembarked in Charleston, out of a total of 308,025 slaves brought to mainland North America, which means that the city accounted for 49 percent of the documented traffic. Since the database includes only 80 percent of the *total* number of slaves who were transported in the transatlantic trade, it estimates that, in fact, 210,447 slaves came through South Carolina and Georgia, out of approximately 388,747 people forcibly transported to what became the United States. Because Charleston was responsible for 90 percent of the documented traffic to South Carolina and Georgia, we estimate that roughly 189,000 people disembarked there. Trans-Atlantic Slave Trade Database, slavevoyages.org/voyage/search. See also Gregory E. O'Malley, "Slavery's Converging Ground: Charleston's Slave Trade as the Black Heart of the Lowcountry," *WMQ* 74 (Apr. 2017): 273–74; Gregory E. O'Malley, *Final Passages: The Intercolonial Slave Trade of British North America, 1619–1807* (Chapel Hill: University of North Carolina Press, 2014), 3, 7, 188–90; David Richardson, "The British Slave Trade to Colonial South Carolina," *Slavery and Abolition* 12 (Dec. 1991): 125–72; and James A. McMillan, *The Final Victims: Foreign Slave Trade to North America, 1783–1810* (Columbia: University of South Carolina Press, 2004), 18–48, 110–11. W. Robert Higgins, "Charleston: Terminus and Entrepôt of the Colonial Slave Trade," in *The African Diaspora: Interpretive Essays*, ed. Martin L. Kilson and Robert I. Rotberg (Cambridge, MA: Harvard University Press, 1976): 114–31; Daniel C. Littlefield, "Charleston and Internal Slave Redistribution," *SCHM* 87 (Apr. 1986): 93–105; Kenneth Morgan, "Slave Sales in Colonial Charleston," *English Historical Review* 113 (Sept. 1998): 905–27; Wood, *Black Majority*, xvi; Sean M. Kelley, *The Voyage of the Slave Ship Hare: A Journey into Captivity from Sierra Leone to South Carolina* (Chapel Hill: University of North Carolina Press, 2016), 132–35; Michael D. Thompson, *Working on the Dock of the Bay: Labor and Enterprise in an Antebellum Southern Port* (Columbia: University of South Carolina Press, 2015), 168*n*2; Olwell, *Masters, Slaves, and Subjects*, 166–67; Morgan, *Slave Counterpoint*, 76.

8. Berlin, *Many Thousands Gone*, 162–74; Peter Kolchin, *American Slavery, 1619–1877* (New York: Hill and Wang: 2003), 48; Margaret Washington Creel, *"A Peculiar People": Slave Religion and Community-Culture Among the Gullahs* (New York: New York University Press, 1988), esp. 96–99; M. Alpah Bah, "Gullah," in *The South Carolina Encyclopedia*, ed. Walter Edgar (Columbia: University of South Carolina Press, 2006), 411–12.

9. Olwell, *Masters, Slaves, and Subjects*, 33–36 (Pringle quote 35); Nicholas Michael Butler, "Robert Pringle," in *South Carolina Encyclopedia*, 757; O'Malley, "Slavery's Converging Ground," 289; Coclanis, *Shadow of a Dream*, 48–135; Berlin, *Many Thousands Gone*, 148–49; Morgan, "Slave Sales in Colonial Charleston," 907; Fraser, *Charleston! Charleston!*, 111–12.

10. Fraser, *Charleston! Charleston!*, 121–22, 128–31; Berlin, *Many Thousands Gone*, 151; Mark Antony De Wolfe Howe, ed., "The Journal of Josiah Quincy, Junior, 1773," *Massachusetts Historical Society Proceedings* 49 (1915–1916): 444–45; Coclanis, *Shadow of a Dream*, 90; Olwell, *Masters, Slaves, and Subjects*, 34–35.

11. Olwell, *Masters, Slaves, and Subjects*, 28–32; McMillan, *Final Victims*, 7; Christopher Leslie Brown, *Moral Capital: Foundations of British Abolitionism* (Chapel Hill: University of North Carolina Press, 2006), 144; Pauline Maier, *American Scripture: Making the Declaration of Independence* (New York: Random House, 1997), 146–47; Joseph Kelley, *America's Longest Siege: Charleston, Slavery, and the Slow March to War* (New York: Overlook, 2013), 110–26; Richard Beeman, *Plain, Honest Men: The Making of the American Constitution* (New York: Random House, 2009), 315–29 (quote 324).

12. McMillan, *Final Victims*, 46–48; Patrick S. Brady, "The Slave Trade and Sectionalism in South Carolina, 1787–1808," *JSH* 38 (Nov. 1972): 601–20; Lacy K. Ford, *Deliver Us from Evil: The Slavery Question in the Old South* (New York: Oxford University Press, 2009), 82–103; O'Malley, *Final Passages*, 264–81; Adam Rothman, *Slave Country: American Expansion and the Origins of the Deep South* (Cambridge, MA: Harvard University Press, 2005), 85–86; Janson, *Stranger in America*, 356; Berlin, *Many Thousands Gone*, 309–10.

13. Steven Deyle, *Carry Me Back: The Domestic Slave Trade in American Life* (New York: Oxford University Press, 2005), 283–96; Walter Johnson, *Soul by Soul: Life Inside the*

Antebellum Slave Market (Cambridge, MA: Harvard University Press, 1999), 5–7; Michael Tadman, *Speculators and Slaves: Masters, Traders, and Slaves in the Old South* (Madison: University of Wisconsin Press, 1996), 12, 55–57; Frederic Bancroft, *Slave Trading in the Old South* (1931; repr., Columbia: University of South Carolina Press, 1996), 173; Michael P. Johnson and James L. Roark, *Black Masters: A Free Family of Color in the Old South* (New York: Norton, 1984), 177–78.

14. Bancroft, *Slave Trading in the Old South*, 165–69; Ebenezer Carter Tracy, *Memoir of the Life of Jeremiah Evarts, ESQ.* (Boston: Crocker and Brewster, 1845), 114–15; "Valuable Property By J. Simmons Bee," *City Gazette*, Mar. 12, 1818; R.C. Lehmann, ed., *Memories of Half a Century: A Record of Friendships* (London: Smith, Edler & Co., 1908), 314.

15. Bancroft, *Slave Trading in the Old South*, 169–96; Edmund L. Drago and Ralph Melnick, "The Old Slave Mart Museum, Charleston, South Carolina: Rediscovering the Past," *CWH* 27 (June 1981): 140–43; Maurie D. McInnis, *Slaves Waiting for Sale: Abolitionist Art and the American Slave Trade* (Chicago: University of Chicago Press, 2011), 121–25; "Proceedings of Council," *CC*, Dec. 27, 1856; "Proceedings of Council," *CC*, July 10, 1856; *CC*, July 2, 1856.

16. Fraser, *Charleston! Charleston!*, 194–98, 229–31; George C. Rogers Jr., *Charleston in the Age of the Pinckneys* (Norman: University of Oklahoma Press, 1969), 114; John Radford, "The Charleston Planters in 1860," *SCHM* 77 (Oct. 1976): 227–35; Michael P. Johnson, "Planters and Patriarchy: Charleston, 1800–1860," *JSH* 46 (Feb. 1980): 45–72; Alston Deas, contrib., "A Ball in Charleston," *SCHM* 75 (Jan. 1974): 49.

17. Charles Joyner, *Down by the Riverside: A South Carolina Slave Community, 25th Anniversary Edition* (Urbana: University of Illinois Press, 2009), 19; Richard C. Wade, *Slavery in the City: The South, 1820–1860* (New York: Oxford University Press, 1964), 20. While 25 percent of southern white families owned slaves, more than 75 percent of white families in Charleston and more than 50 percent of white families in South Carolina were slaveholding. Manisha Sinha, *The Counterrevolution of Slavery: Politics and Ideology in Antebellum South Carolina* (Chapel Hill: University of North Carolina Press, 2000), 12; Otto H. Olsen, "Historians and the Extent of Slave Ownership in the Southern United States," *CWH* 18 (June 1972): 101–16.

18. Wood, *Black Majority*, 308–26.

19. Douglas R. Egerton, *He Shall Go Out Free: The Lives of Denmark Vesey, Revised and Updated Edition* (Lanham, MD: Rowman and Littlefield, 2004), 75–202; Ford, *Deliver Us from Evil*, 181–85, 207–37; Francis Asbury Mood, *Methodism in Charleston: A Narrative of the Chief Events Relating to the Rise and Progress of the Methodist Episcopal Church in Charleston, S.C.* (Nashville: Stevenson & J.E. Evans for the Methodist Episcopal Church, South, 1859), 133; Powers, *Black Charlestonians*, 21; Douglas R. Egerton and Robert L. Paquette, introduction to their *The Denmark Vesey Affair: A Documentary History* (Gainesville: University Press of Florida, 2017), xxi. This narrative has been challenged by Michael P. Johnson, who contends that Vesey and his colleagues were, in fact, the victims of a conspiracy cooked up by Mayor James Hamilton Jr., among others, who wanted to undermine South Carolina's overly paternalistic governor, advance their careers, and shut down the African Church. Johnson's argument, though provocative, is ultimately unconvincing. Michael P. Johnson, "Denmark Vesey and His Co-Conspirators," *WMQ* 58 (Oct. 2001): 917–76; Michael P. Johnson, "Reading Evidence," *WMQ* 59 (Jan. 2002): 193–202; Jon Wiener, "Denmark Vesey: A New Verdict," *Nation*, Feb. 21, 2002; Egerton and Paquette, introduction, xxii–xiv; Egerton, *He Shall Go Out Free*, 233–51; Douglas L. Egerton, "Of Facts and Fables: New Light on the Denmark Vesey Affair," *SCHM* 104 (Jan. 2004): 8–35; Robert L. Paquette, "From Rebellion to Revisionism: The Continuing Debate about the Denmark Vesey Affair,"

Journal of the Historical Society 4 (Fall 2004): 291–334; Robert Tinkler, *James Hamilton of South Carolina* (Baton Rouge: Louisiana State University, 2004), 43–44n31.

20. Egerton, *He Shall Go Out Free*, 200–221; Ford, *Deliver Us from Evil*, 269–96; Fraser, *Charleston! Charleston!*, 202–3, 219; Maurie D. McInnis, *The Politics of Taste in Antebellum Charleston* (Chapel Hill: University of North Carolina Press, 2005), 72–82; *CC*, Jan. 7, 1830; William H. Buckley, *The Citadel and the South Carolina Corps of Cadets* (Charleston: Arcadia Publishing, 2004), 9–10. Many accounts of the Vesey affair suggest that the African Church was burned to the ground, but advertisements that we have uncovered indicate that it was actually torn down, no doubt at the insistence of the city. Afterward, church trustees tried to sell off "All the LUMBER" that "comprised the . . . Church." *SP*, Aug. 16, 1822; *CC*, Aug. 14, 1822. See also Mood, *Methodism in Charleston*, 133, which states that the African Church was "demolished" by order of "the authorities."

21. McInnis, *Politics of Taste*, 86–87; "City Accounts," *CC*, Sept. 1, 1806; *CC*, June 3, 1856.

22. McInnis, *Politics of Taste*, 223–30; "Military Hall, Wentworth-street," *CC*, June 27, 1847; *CC*, Feb. 6, 1850; *CC*, July 3, 1850; Nicholas Butler, emails to Ethan J. Kytle, June 25, 2017 and Aug. 7, 2107; John J. Navin, "A New England Yankee Discovers Southern History," in *Becoming Southern Writers: Essays in Honor of Charles Joyner*, ed. Orville Vernon Burton and Eldred E. Prince Jr. (Columbia: University of South Carolina Press, 2016), 184–91; James Redpath, *The Roving Editor: Or, Talks with Slaves in the Southern States* (New York: A.B. Burdick, 1859), 51–54; Laura M. Towne, *The Letters and Diary of Laura M. Towne*, ed. Rupert Sargent Holland (1912; repr., New York: Negro University Press, 1969), 160–61; Norrece T. Jones Jr., *Born a Child of Freedom, Yet a Slave: Mechanisms of Control and Strategies of Resistance in Antebellum South Carolina* (Hanover, NH: Wesleyan University Press, 1990), 76–78; Karl Bernhard, *Travels through North America, During the Years 1825 and 1826 in Two Volumes* (Philadelphia: Care, Lea & Carey, 1828), 2: 9–10; Fraser, *Charleston! Charleston!*, 203; Wade, *Slavery in the Cities*, 95–96.

23. McInnis, *Politics of Taste*, 180–81; Sam Aleckson, *Before the War, and After the Union: An Autobiography* (Boston: Gold Mind Publishing, 1929), 32–33; Abiel Abbot, journal, Nov. 11, 1818, in "The Abiel Abbot Journals: A Yankee Preacher in Charleston Society, 1818–1827," ed. John Hammond Moore, *SCHM* 68 (Apr. 1967): 59.

24. Wade, *Slavery in the Cities*, 55–72, 99; Salley E. Hadden, *Slave Patrols: Law and Violence in Virginia and the Carolinas* (Cambridge, MA: Harvard University Press, 2001), 57–58; Fraser, *Charleston! Charleston!*, 203–4, 238; "Reminiscences of Charleston, S.C., 1830–1832," *Monthly Religious Magazine* 25 (Feb. 1861): 113. See also Thomas Coffin Amory travel diary, 1843, Vol. 58, AFP; and Ivan D. Steen, "Charleston in the 1850's: As Described by British Travelers," *SCHM* 71 (Jan. 1970): 42–44. "Charleston Neck Work House," *LIB*, Aug. 3, 1849; "Office Comm's Cross Roads, Charleston Neck, Jan. 28, 1848," *SP*, Jan. 29, 1848; "Proceedings of the Council," *CC*, Feb. 21, 1856; Powers, *Black Charlestonians*, 9–35.

25. Harlan Greene, Harry S. Hutchins Jr., and Brian E. Hutchins, *Slave Badges and the Slave-Hire System in Charleston, South Carolina, 1783–1865* (Jefferson, NC: McFarland and Co., 2004), 1–66; Harlan Greene and Harry S. Hutchins Jr., "Slave Hire Badges—The 2014 Update," *North South Trader's Civil War* 38 (2014): 69–71.

26. Ford, *Deliver Us from Evil*, 279–80, 282–83; Daniel Walker Howe, *What Hath God Wrought: The Transformation of America, 1815–1848* (New York: Oxford University Press, 2007), 395–403; Sinha, *Counterrevolution of Slavery*, 33–61.

27. William H. Freehling, *Prelude to Civil War: The Nullification Controversy in South Carolina, 1816–1836* (New York: Oxford University Press, 1965), 255–59 (quote 257); Howe, *What Hath God Wrought*, 404–10; Sinha, *Counterrevolution of Slavery*, 33–61.

28. "Incendiary Publications," *SP*, July 30, 1835; "Incendiary Publications," *CC*, July 30, 1835; "Attack on the Post Office," *CC*, July 31, 1835; *CC*, July 31, 1835; *SP*, July 30, 1835; Ford, *Deliver Us from Evil*, 482–85; Richard R. John, *Spreading the News: The American Postal System from Franklin to Morse* (Cambridge, MA: Harvard University Press, 1995), 257–80; Howe, *What Hath God Wrought*, 428–30.

29. James Silk Buckingham, *The Slave States of America, in Two Volumes* (London: Fisher, Son, and Co., 1842), 1: 54–55; Robert Bunch, quoted in Christopher Dickey, *Our Man in Charleston: Britain's Secret Agent in the Civil War South* (New York: Broadway Books, 2015), 19.

30. Howe, *What Hath God Wrought*, 512–15, 609–11; Ford, *Deliver Us from Evil*, 500–503; Daniel Wirls, "'The Only Mode of Avoiding Everlasting Debate': The Overlooked Senate Gag Rule for Antislavery Politicians," *Journal of the Early Republic* 27 (Spring 2007): 115–38; William W. Freehling, *The Road to Disunion*, vol. 1, *Secessionists at Bay, 1776–1854* (New York: Oxford University Press, 1990), 308–52; George C. Rable, "Slavery, Politics, and the South: The Gag Rule as a Case Study," *Capitol Studies* 3 (Fall 1975): 69–87.

31. John C. Calhoun, "Further Remarks in Debate of His Fifth Resolution," in *PJCC*, 14: 84; James Henry Hammond, *Two Letters on Southern Slavery, Addressed to Thomas Clarkson, Esq.* (Columbia: Allen, McCarter, & Co., 1845), 42–43; Ford, *Deliver Us from Evil*, 505–16.

32. Ford, *Deliver Us from Evil*, 257–62, 524–27, 498–99 (quote 260).

33. Calhoun, "Further Remarks," 84; John C. Calhoun, "Speech on Abolition Petitions," in *PJCC*, 13: 105.

34. Dickey, *Our Man in Charleston*, 45–46; *The Pro-Slavery Argument, as Maintained by the Most Distinguished Writers of the Southern States* (Charleston: Walker, Richards, & Co., 1852); Kelley, *America's Longest Siege*, 266–67; Robert N. Rosen, *Confederate Charleston: Illustrated History of the City and the People during the Civil War* (Columbia: University of South Carolina Press, 1994), 19; Edward J. Pringle, *Slavery in the Southern States by a Carolinian* (Cambridge, MA: John Bartlett, 1852), 8–9; Richard N. Côté, *Mary's World: Love, War, and Family Ties in Nineteenth-century Charleston* (Mt. Pleasant, SC: Corinthian Books, 2001), 144–47; William W. Freehling, *The Road to Disunion*, vol. 2, *Secessionists Triumphant, 1854–1861* (New York: Oxford University Press, 2007), 54–56; "Proceedings of Council," *CC*, Jan. 10, 1856; Michael Tadman, "The Interregional Slave Trade in the History and Myth-Making of the U.S. South," in *The Chattel Principle: Internal Slave Trades in the Americas*, ed. Walter Johnson (New Haven: Yale University Press, 2004), 135.

35. Eric H. Walther, *The Fire-Eaters* (Baton Rouge: Louisiana State University Press, 1992), 2, 125–26, 138–49.

36. Robert Bunch, quoted in Dickey, *Our Man in Charleston*, 125; "A Committee of Safety," *CM*, Dec. 13, 1859; "To the Public," *CC*, Dec. 15, 1859; "Committee of Safety," *CC*, Dec. 15, 1859; "Citizens of Charleston!" *CC*, Dec. 6, 1859; Steven A. Channing, *Crisis of Fear: Secession in South Carolina* (New York: Simon and Schuster, 1970), 34, 37–38; William C. Davis, *Rhett: The Turbulent Life and Times of a Fire-Eater* (Columbia: University of South Carolina Press, 2001), 384–85; Freehling, *Road to Disunion*, vol. 2, 294–306; Rosen, *Confederate Charleston*, 32–34; Robert Barnwell Rhett Sr., quoted in Charles Edward Cauthen, *South Carolina Goes to War, 1860–1865* (Chapel Hill: University of North Carolina Press, 1950), 18n12.

37. Michael P. Johnson and James L. Roark, eds., *No Chariot Let Down: Charleston's Free People of Color on the Eve of the Civil War* (Chapel Hill: University of North Carolina Press, 1984), 8–9, 147 (Johnson quote).

38. Circular, Robert N. Gourdin, Chairman of the Executive Committee of "the 1860 Association" to R.F.W. Allston, Nov. 19, 1860, in Broadsides, Digital Collections, SCL; Channing, *Crisis of Fear*, 255–56; Stephanie McCurry, *Confederate Reckoning: Power and Politics in the Civil War South* (Cambridge, MA: Harvard University Press, 2010), 43–46; Freehling,

Road to Disunion, vol. 2, 388–94; William Kauffman Scarborough, *Masters of the Big House: Elite Slaveholders of the Mid-Nineteenth-Century South* (Baton Rouge: Louisiana State University Press, 2003), 287; James D.B. DeBow, *The Interest of the Southern Non-Slaveholder* (1860), reprinted in *Southern Pamphlets on Secession, November 1860–April 1861,* ed. Jon L. Wakelyn (Chapel Hill: University of North Carolina Press, 1996), 84.

39. John Townsend, quoted in Sinha, *Counterrevolution of Slavery,* 233; Southern-Rights Lady, quoted in William L. Barney, *The Road to Secession: A New Perspective on the Old South* (New York: Praeger, 1972), 186.

40. Sinha, *Counterrevolution of Slavery,* 233–37; McCurry, *Confederate Reckoning,* 46–49; "Our Barnwell Correspondence," *CM,* Nov. 21, 1860.

41. Sinha, *Counterrevolution of Slavery,* 237–44; Freehling, *Road to Disunion,* vol. 2, 395–423.

42. *Declaration of the Immediate Causes which Induce and Justify the Secession of South Carolina from the Federal Union; and the Ordinance of Secession* (Charleston: Evans & Cogswell, 1860), 7–8; Thomas Jefferson Withers, quoted in Ulysses Robert Brooks, *South Carolina Bench and Bar* (Columbia: The State Company, 1908), 1: 148; "What Shall the South Carolina Legislature Do," *CM,* Nov. 3, 1860.

43. William Gilmore Simms, quoted in David Moltke-Hansen, "When History Failed: William Gilmore Simms's Artistic Negotiation of the Civil War's Consequences," in *William Gilmore Simms's Unfinished Civil War: Consequences for a Southern Man of Letters,* ed. David Moltke-Hansen (Columbia: University of South Carolina Press, 2012), 11; Charles B. Dew, *Apostles of Disunion: Southern Secession Commissioners and the Causes of the Civil War* (Charlottesville: University of Virginia Press, 2001), 38–39, 74–81.

44. Bruce Levine, *The Fall of the House of Dixie: The Civil War and the Social Revolution that Transformed the South* (New York: Random House, 2013), 43–44 ("the right of property" quote 44); Alexander Stephens, quoted in Dew, *Apostles of Disunion,* 14.

45. Maury Klein, *Days of Defiance: Sumter, Secession, and the Coming of the Civil War* (New York: Knopf, 1997), 408–11; Adam Goodheart, *1861: The Civil War Awakening* (New York: Knopf, 2011), 4–15, 136–66; David Detzer, *Allegiance: Fort Sumter, Charleston, and the Beginning of the Civil War* (New York: Harcourt, 2001), 254–59; Freehling, *Road to Disunion,* vol. 2, 520–21.

46. Mary Boykin Chesnut, diary, Apr. 12, 1861, in *Mary Chesnut's Civil War,* ed. C. Vann Woodward (New Haven: Yale University Press, 1981), 46–47; Mary Boykin Chesnut, diary, [Apr. 12, 1861], in *The Private Mary Chesnut: The Unpublished Civil War Diaries,* ed. C. Vann Woodward and Elisabeth Muhlenfeld (New York: Oxford University Press, 1984), 59; Detzer, *Allegiance,* 272–73; Fraser, *Charleston! Charleston!,* 250–51; Rosen, *Confederate Charleston,* 68–72.

47. William Howard Russell, *My Diary North and South in Two Volumes* (Boston: T.O.P. Burnham, 1863), 1: 98–99, 110; Fraser, *Charleston! Charleston!,* 251; Klein, *Days of Defiance,* 416–30.

48. Russell, *My Diary North and South,* 1: 110.

49. "Reminiscences of Charleston, S.C, 1830–1832," 113; Fraser, *Charleston! Charleston!,* 252–55.

50. "The Faithful Negro," *CC,* June 20, 1861; "A Loyal Slave," *CC,* Aug. 13, 1862; "A Faithful Slave," *CC,* Dec. 2, 1862; "Dr. North's Treatment in a Yankee Prison—A Faithful Negro," *CC,* Feb. 28, 1863; South Carolina slaves, interviewed, 1861, in *Slave Testimony: Two Centuries of Letters, Speeches, Interviews, and Autobiographies,* ed. John W. Blassingame (Baton Rouge: Louisiana University Press, 1977), 360; Louis Manigault, Manigault Plantation Journal, May 1861–May 1862, p. 23, Digital Collections, SHC; Chesnut, diary, Apr. 13, 1861, in *Mary Chesnut's Civil War,* 48.

51. "Escaped Union Prisoners of War to the Provost Marshal General of the Department of the South," Dec. 7, 1864, in *Freedom: A Documentary History of Emancipation, 1861–1867*, ser. 1, vol. 1, *The Destruction of Slavery*, ed. Ira Berlin et al. (New York: Cambridge University Press, 1985), 810; Benjamin Quarles, *The Negro in the Civil War* (Boston: Little, Brown, 1953), 269–70; Benjamin M. Holmes, interview, 1872, in *Slave Testimony*, 618–20.

52. McCurry, *Confederate Reckoning*, 244–45; Okon Edet Uya, *From Slavery to Public Service: Robert Smalls, 1839–1915* (New York: Oxford University Press, 1971), 12–21; Philip Dray, *Capitol Men: The Epic Story of Reconstruction through the Lives of the First Black Congressmen* (New York: Houghton Mifflin, 2008), 1–10; Andrew Billingsley, *Yearning to Breathe Free: Robert Smalls of South Carolina and His Families* (Columbia: University of South Carolina Press, 2007), 51–61 (quote 59), 75.

53. South Carolina slaves, interviewed, 1861, in *Slave Testimony*, 359; *LIB*, Jan. 9, 1863; *Douglass' Monthly* 5 (Feb. 1863): 798; Wilbert L. Jenkins, *Seizing the New Day: African Americans in Post–Civil War Charleston* (Bloomington: Indiana University Press, 1998), 24–25; Powers, *Black Charlestonians,* 67; Fraser, *Charleston! Charleston!*, 258–59; Johnson Hagood, *Memoirs of the War in Charleston* (Columbia: The State Co., 1910), 1: 71; Yael A. Sternhell, *Routes of War: The World of Movement in the Confederate South* (Cambridge, MA: Harvard University Press, 2012), 129–30.

54. Dickson D. Bruce, *Archibald Grimké: Portrait of a Black Independent* (Baton Rouge: Louisiana State University Press, 1993), 1–15.

55. Kelley, *America's Longest Siege*, 15–17, 306–10; Fraser, *Charleston! Charleston!*, 264–67; Rosen, *Confederate Charleston*, 119–40; Alva C. Roach, *The Prisoner of War, and How Treated* (Indianapolis: Railroad City Publishing, 1865), 137; Willard W. Glazier, *The Capture, the Prison Pen, and the Escape, Giving an Account of Prison Life in the South* (Albany, NY: S.R. Gray, 1865), 141.

56. Fraser, *Charleston! Charleston!*, 267–68; *CM*, Jan. 16, 1865; *CM*, Jan. 17, 1865; *CM*, Jan. 19, 1865.

57. Fraser, *Charleston! Charleston!*, 268–69.

1. THE YEAR OF JUBILEE

1. Berwick [James Redpath], "The Fall of Charleston," *NYTR*, Mar. 2, 1865. James Redpath often reported using the pen name "Berwick," taken from the Scottish town in which he was born. John McKigivigan, *Forgotten Firebrand: James Redpath and the Making of Nineteenth-Century America* (Ithaca: Cornell University Press, 2008), 2, 9, 98. Theodore Cuyler, "A Trip to Fort Sumter, and the Doomed City," *LIB*, May 5, 1865; Kane O'Donnell, "Charleston. Details of the Evacuation and Occupation," *PHP*, Mar. 3, 1865; Walter J. Fraser Jr., *Charleston! Charleston! The History of a Southern City* (Columbia: University of South Carolina Press, 1989), 268; E. Milby Burton, *The Siege of Charleston, 1861–1865* (Columbia: University of South Carolina Press, 1982), 320–21; Noah Andre Trudeau, *Like Men of War: Black Troops in the Civil War, 1862–1865* (Boston: Little, Brown, 1998), 356–57; John C. Gray to John C. Ropes, Feb. 24, 1865, in *War Letters, 1862–1865, of John Chipman Gray and John Codman Ropes* (Boston: Riverside Press for the Massachusetts Historical Society, 1927), 459; Benjamin Quarles, *The Negro in the Civil War* (Boston: Little, Brown, 1953), 325–27; Frank [Frances] A. Rollin, *Life and Public Services of Martin R. Delany, Sub-Assistant Commissioner Bureau Relief of Refugees, Freedmen, and of Abandoned Lands, and Late Major 104th U.S. Colored Troops* (1968; repr., New York: Arno Press, 1969), 198–99; C.H. Corey to Nathan Bishop, Feb. 20, 1865, in *IND*, Mar. 16, 1865.

2. Redpath, "Fall of Charleston"; Charles Carleton Coffin, *The Boys of '61; or, Four Years of Fighting* (Boston: Estes and Lauriat, 1884), 481; O'Donnell, "Charleston"; Charles Barnard Fox, *Record of the Service of the Fifty-Fifth Regiment of Massachusetts Infantry* (Cambridge, MA: Press of John Wilson and Son, 1868), 58–59; Trudeau, *Like Men of War*, 356–58; J.H.W.N. Collins, letter to the editor, *CR*, Apr. 15, 1865; Luis F. Emilio, *History of the Fifty-Fourth Regiment of Massachusetts Volunteer Infantry, 1863–1865* (Boston: Boston Book Co., 1894), 283–84.

3. Leon Litwack, *Been in the Storm So Long: The Aftermath of Slavery* (New York: Random House, 1979), 310–16; Henry W. Ravenel, journal, June 14, 1865, in *The Private Journal of Henry William Ravenel, 1859–1887*, ed. Arney R. Childs (Columbia: University of South Carolina Press, 1947), 244; "The South As It Is," *Nation* 1 (Dec. 28, 1865): 82–83; Bernard E. Powers Jr., *Black Charlestonians: A Social History, 1822–1885* (Fayetteville: University of Arkansas Press, 1994), 101.

4. Henry Ward Beecher, "Narrative of His Trip to South Carolina," *IND*, May 11, 1865; Douglas R. Egerton, *The Wars of Reconstruction: The Brief, Violent History of America's Most Progressive Era* (New York: Bloomsbury, 2014), 81; Redpath, "Fall of Charleston"; James Lynch, letter to the editor, *CR*, Mar. 18, 1865; Powers, *Black Charlestonians*, 69–70, 75; "Recruiting," *NAAS*, Mar. 18, 1865; "Recruiting," *CC*, Mar. 1, 1865; "Recruiting," *CC*, Mar. 10, 1865; James Redpath, "The Work at Charleston," *Freedmen's Record* 1 (Oct. 1865): 157; "From Charleston!" *ADC*, Mar. 9, 1865; Dickson D. Bruce, *Archibald Grimké: Portrait of a Black Independent* (Baton Rouge: Louisiana State University Press, 1993), 16.

5. William C. Nell, quoted in Mitch Kachun, *Festivals of Freedom: Memory and Meaning in African American Emancipation Celebrations, 1908–1915* (Amherst: University of Massachusetts Press, 2003), 261n4.

6. James Redpath, "From South Carolina. Grand Procession of Colored Loyalists," *NYTR*, Apr. 4, 1865; "Affairs at Charleston," *NYT*, Mar. 30, 1865; "Affairs in Charleston," *NYT*, Apr. 4, 1865; "Freedmen's Jubilee," *CC*, Mar. 22, 1865; Carole Emberton, *Beyond Redemption: Race, Violence, and the American South after the Civil War* (Chicago: University of Chicago Press, 2013), 15; Kathleen Ann Clark, *Defining Moments: African American Commemoration and Political Culture* (Chapel Hill: University of North Carolina Press, 2005), 35.

7. "Freedmen's Jubilee"; Redpath, "From South Carolina," Apr. 4, 1865; "Affairs in Charleston"; "Letter from Charleston, South Carolina," *Newark Daily Advertiser*, Apr. 13, 1865; Clark, *Defining Moments*, 34–38; Bruce E. Baker, *What Reconstruction Meant: Historical Memory in the American South* (Charlottesville: University of Virginia Press, 2007), 28–29; Litwack, *Been in the Storm So Long*, 177–78; Mark Auslander, "Touching the Past: Materializing Time in Traumatic 'Living History' Reenactments," *Signs and Society* 1 (Spring 2013): 161–83; "A Taxable Citizen in Ward No. 4 to the Honorable the City Council," *SP*, Sept. 19, 1835; Richard C. Wade, *Slavery in the Cities: The South, 1820–1860* (New York: Oxford University Press, 1964), 169–71; Winthrop D. Jordan, "Familial Politics: Thomas Paine and the Killing of the King, 1776," *JAH* 60 (Sept. 1973): 306–8; Albert J. Von Frank, *The Trials of Anthony Burns: Freedom and Slavery in Emerson's Boston* (Cambridge, MA: Harvard University Press, 1998), 209; Bruce Laurie, *Beyond Garrison: Antislavery and Social Reform* (New York: Cambridge University Press, 2005), 241.

8. "Affairs in Charleston."

9. H.M. Gallaher, "The Cradle of Treason," *IND*, May 4, 1865; "The Oath of Allegiance in Charleston," *NYT*, Mar. 30, 1865; "The Bombardment of Charleston," *LIB*, Mar. 10, 1865.

10. Cuyler, "Trip to Fort Sumter." During and after the war, commentators referred to Charleston interchangeably as "the cradle of secession," "the cradle of the confederacy," and "the cradle of the rebellion," which is what minister Theodore Cuyler called it. See, for example, "Charleston at Bay," *Edgefield Advertiser*, Aug. 12, 1863; and "The Flag of Truce," *CNC*, Dec. 21, 1892.

11. "1861–1865, The Old Flag on Fort Sumter Once More," *New York World*, Apr. 21, 1865; Wendell Phillips Garrison and Francis Garrison, *William Lloyd Garrison, 1805–1879: The Story of His Life Told by His Children* (Boston: Houghton Mifflin, 1889), 4: 135–36; "Off for Charleston!" *LIB*, Apr. 7, 1865; George T. Garrison to Daniel Eldredge, Feb. 18, 1895, MOLLUS; Henry Mayer, *All on Fire: William Lloyd Garrison and the Abolition of Slavery* (New York: Norton, 1998), 577.

12. Elizabeth Hyde Botume, *First Days amongst the Contrabands* (Boston: Lee and Shepard, 1892), 172; "Fort Sumter," *NYT*, Apr. 18, 1865; James Redpath, "From Charleston," *NYTR*, Apr. 18, 1865; James Redpath, "From Charleston," *NYTR*, Apr. 20, 1865; "Fort Sumter," *CC*, Apr. 15, 1865; "Sumpter [*sic*]. The Flag Again Floating Over Its Ruins," *PHP*, Apr. 18, 1865; Esther Hill Hawks, diary, Apr. 14, 1865, in *A Woman Doctor's Civil War: Esther Hill Hawks' Diary*, ed. Gerald Schwartz (Columbia: University of South Carolina Press, 1984), 130.

13. Theodore Tilton, "The Excursion to Fort Sumter," *IND*, Apr. 27, 1865; "1861–1865, The Old Flag"; "Fort Sumter," *NYT*; Gallaher, "Cradle of Treason"; William A. Spicer, *The Flag Replaced on Sumter: A Personal Narrative* (Providence, RI: Providence Press Company, 1885), 41–43, 51–52; [Justus Clement French], *The Trip of the Steamer Oceanus to Fort Sumter and Charleston, S.C.* (Brooklyn: "The Union" Steam Printing House, 1865), 43–81 (Beecher quotes 67, 58); Cuyler, "Trip to Fort Sumter"; "Fort Sumter," *CC*.

14. "The Fort Sumter Celebration," *NYT*, Apr. 20, 1865; Spicer, *Flag Replaced on Sumter*, 56–57; "Banquet in Charleston," *LIB*, May 12, 1865.

15. Cuyler, "Trip to Fort Sumter"; James Redpath, "From South Carolina. Our Martyr and His Mourners," *NYTR*, May 13, 1865; Maria Middleton Doar to Maria H. Middleton, Apr. 14, 1865, Folder 8, Box 161, DMFP.

16. Emma Holmes, diary, May 1, 1865, in *The Diary of Miss Emma Holmes, 1861–1866*, ed. John F. Marszalek (Baton Rouge: Louisiana State University Press, 1979), 441–42.

17. Caroline R. Ravenel to Isabella Middleton Smith, Mar. 31, 1865, in *Mason Smith Family Letters*, ed. Daniel E. Huger Smith et al. (Columbia: University of South Carolina, 1950), 188; Mrs. J.J. Pringle Smith to Mrs. William Mason Smith, Mar. 23, [1865], in *Mason Smith Family Letters*, 179; "From South Carolina," *Richmond Whig*, Mar. 31, 1865; "Late from Charleston," *ADC*, Apr. 6, 1865; "Trade[?] in Charleston," *ADC*, Apr. 20, 1865; "Served Him Right for Staying There," *Tri-Weekly (Newberry, SC) Herald*, Apr. 6, 1865; LeConte, diary, Apr. 13, 1865, in *When the Word Ended: The Diary of Emma LeConte*, ed. Earl Schenck Miers (1957; repr., Lincoln: University of Nebraska Press, 1987), 85; "Favors," *Columbia Phoenix*, Mar. 21, 1865.

18. LeConte, diary, July 5, 1865, p.115. The various editions of the *New-York Tribune* alone had a combined circulation of more than 200,000. Adam-Max Tuchinsky, *Horace Greeley's New-York Tribune: Civil War-Era Socialism and the Crisis of Free Labor* (Ithaca, NY: Cornell University Press, 2009), 145–46.

19. Teresa Barnett, *Sacred Relics: Pieces of the Past in Nineteenth-Century America* (Chicago: University of Chicago Press, 2013), 21–23, 50–105; Joan E. Cashin, "Trophies of War: Material Culture in the Civil War Era," *JCWE* 1 (Sept. 2011): 339–67; Megan Kate Nelson, *Ruin Nation: Destruction and the American Civil War* (Athens: University of Georgia Press, 2012), 154–57, 229–32; Brian Matthew Jordan, *Marching Home: Union Veterans and Their Unending Civil War* (New York: Liveright, 2015), 95–97; Jennifer R. Bridge, "Tourist Attractions,

Souvenirs, and Civil War Memory in Chicago, 1861–1915" (Ph.D. diss., Loyola University of Chicago, 2009), esp. 24–84.

20. Tilton, "Excursion to Fort Sumter"; Redpath, "Fall of Charleston." Institute Hall burned down during the Charleston fire of 1861.

21. Redpath, "Fall of Charleston"; Charles C. Coffin, "The Slave Mart," *NYT*, Mar. 6, 1865; O'Donnell, "Charleston"; Kane O'Donnell, "Charleston. Loyalty of the Irish and German Residents," *PHP*, Mar. 30, 1865; Gallaher, "Cradle of Treason"; Edmund L. Drago, ed., *Broke by War: Letters of a Slave Trader* (Columbia: University of South Carolina Press, 1991), 1–2, 5–11; "Various Items," *Springfield Republican*, Mar. 13, 1865; Edmund L. Drago and Ralph Melnick, "The Old Slave Mart Museum, Charleston, South Carolina: Rediscovering the Past," *CWH* 27 (June 1981): 138–54; Steven Deyle, *Carry Me Back: The Domestic Slave Trade in American Life* (New York: Oxford University Press, 2005), 204–5.

22. "Curiosities of the Charleston Slave Market," *Providence Evening Press*, Mar. 31, 1865; "Various Items"; "News and Miscellaneous Items," *BET*, Mar. 17, 1865; O'Donnell, "Charleston. Loyalty of the Irish."

23. "The Steps to the Slave Block of Charleston," *BDA*, Mar. 6, 1865; "An Immense Meeting in Music Hall," *LIB*, Mar. 17, 1865; "A Memorable Scene," *NAAS,* Mar. 18, 1865; Drago, ed., *Broke by War*, 3; Ethan J. Kytle, *Romantic Reformers and the Antislavery Struggle in the Civil War Era* (New York: Cambridge University Press, 2014), 29–71; Garrison and Garrison, *William Lloyd Garrison*, 4: 135; William Lloyd Garrison to Jacob Horton, Mar. 17, 1865, in *The Letters of William Lloyd Garrison*, vol. 5, *Let the Oppressed Go Free, 1861–1867*, ed. Walter M. Merrill (Cambridge, MA: Belknap Press of Harvard University Press, 1979), 262–63; "City and Vicinity," *LDCN*, Mar. 15, 1865; "Lowell Freedmen's Aid Society," *LDCN*, Mar. 16, 1865; "City and County," *Worcester Aegis*, Mar. 20, 1865; Z.E. Stone, "George Thompson, the English Philanthropist in Lowell," in *Contributions of the Old Residents' Historical Association, Lowell, Mass.* (Lowell, MA: Old Residents' Historical Association, 1883), 131–32.

24. A.P. Putnam, "Abolitionists in Charleston," *IND*, Apr. 27, 1865; Laura M. Towne, *The Letters and Diary of Laura M. Towne*, ed. Rupert Sargent Holland (1912; repr., New York: Negro University Press, 1969), 160–61.

25. Gallaher, "Cradle of Treason"; James Redpath, "The Excursion to Charleston," *NYTR*, Apr. 22, 1865. Clinckscales and Boozer was, in fact, the name of an auction firm. *CC*, Sept. 13, 1862.

26. Beecher, "Narrative of His Trip."

27. Putnam, "Abolitionists in Charleston"; "Yankees in Charleston," *Lowell Daily Courier*, Apr. 27, 1865; Beecher, "Narrative of His Trip"; Redpath, "Excursion to Charleston"; Cuyler, "Trip to Fort Sumter"; Theodore L. Cuyler, "Etchings at Fort Sumter," *IND*, Apr. 27, 1865; Mayer, *All on Fire*, 582; French, *Trip of the Steamer Oceanus*, 96.

28. Hawks, diary, Apr. 15, 1865, pp. 131–33; French, *Trip of the Steamer Oceanus*, 96–112; Elizabeth G. Rice, "A Yankee Teacher in the South," *Century Magazine* 62 (May 1901): 151; Powers, *Black Charlestonians*, 70–71, 165, 172; Fraser, *Charleston! Charleston!*, 212–13; "Another Great Rejoicing!" *CC*, Apr. 17, 1865; Redpath, "Excursion to Charleston"; Cuyler, "Etchings"; Putnam, "Abolitionists in Charleston"; Cuyler, "Trip to Fort Sumter."

29. Beecher, "Narrative of His Trip"; Tilton, "Excursion to Fort Sumter"; William Lloyd Garrison to his wife, Apr. 15, 1865, in Garrison and Garrison, *William Lloyd Garrison*, 4: 140; George T. Garrison, diary extract, Apr. 17, 1865, MOLLUS.

30. James Redpath, "Eye and Ear Notes: May-Day in Charleston, S.C.," *The Youth's Companion*, June 1, 1865; "Decoration Day," *Cincinnati Daily Gazette*, June 16, 1869; David W. Blight, *Race and Reunion: The Civil War in American Memory* (Cambridge, MA: Belknap Press of Harvard University Press, 2001), 68–70.

31. Randy J. Sparks, "Gentleman's Sport: Horse Racing in Antebellum Charleston," *SCHM* 93 (Jan. 1992): 20–30; George C. Rogers Jr., *Charleston in the Age of the Pinckneys* (Norman: University of Oklahoma Press, 1969), 114; Charles Fraser, *Reminiscences of Charleston* (Charleston: John Russell, 1854), 61–63; Kevin R. Eberle, *A History of Charleston's Hampton Park* (Charleston: History Press, 2012), 30–38.

32. Lonnie R. Speer, *Portals of Hell: Military Prisons of the Civil War* (Lincoln: University of Nebraska Press, 1997), 214–15, 334; Robert H. Kellogg, *Life and Death in Rebel Prisons* (Hartford, CT: L. Stebbins, 1865), 290–94; Warren Lee Goss, *The Soldier's Story of His Captivity at Andersonville, Belle Isle, and Other Rebel Prisons* (Boston: Lee and Shepard, 1867), 187–96; Samuel S. Boggs, *Eighteen Months a Prisoner Under the Rebel Flag* (Lovington, IL: S.S. Boggs, 1887), 46–47.

33. "The Charleston Race-Course Prisoners," *BDA*, Aug. 11, 1865; A.P. Putnam, "More About Charleston," *IND*, May 4, 1865; Charles W. Sanders Jr., *While in the Hands of the Enemy: Military Prisons of the Civil War* (Baton Rouge: Louisiana State University Press, 2005), 226–27; Speer, *Portals of Hell*, 213–14; William Marvel, *Andersonville: The Last Depot* (Chapel Hill: University of North Carolina Press, 1994), 198–203; "Charleston, S.C.," *The Student and Schoolmate: An Illustrated Monthly for All Our Boys and Girls* 17 (Mar. 1866): 98; James Redpath, "Eye and Ear Notes: May-Day in Charleston Again," *The Youth's Companion*, June 8, 1865; A.O. Abbott, *Prison Life in the South* (New York: Harper & Brothers, 1865), 126; Beecher, "Narrative of His Trip."

34. William B. Hesseltine, *Civil War Prisons: A Study in War Psychology* (Columbus: Ohio State University Press, 1930), 155; Putnam, "More About Charleston"; James Redpath, "From South Carolina. Monument to the Martyrs of the Race-Course," *NYTR*, Apr. 8, 1865.

35. McKivigivan, *Forgotten Firebrand*, x, 105–8; James Redpath, *The Roving Editor: Or, Talks with Slaves in Southern States* (New York: A.B. Burdick, 1859), 50; Hawks, diary, Apr. 6, 1865, p. 126.

36. Redpath, "From South Carolina," Apr. 8, 1865; "Decoration Day."

37. Redpath, "From South Carolina," Apr. 8, 1865; Morse, "Unofficial Memorial Day," 117; "Memorial to the Loyal People of South Carolina," *CC*, Mar. 28, 1865; "From Charleston," *ADC*, Apr. 5, 1865; James Redpath, "Honor to Our Martyrs," *NYTR*, May 13, 1865.

38. Marilyn Richardson, "Taken from Life: Edward M. Bannister, Edmonia Lewis, and the Memorialization of the Fifty-Fourth Massachusetts Regiment," in *Hope & Glory: Essays on the Legacy of the Fifty-Fourth Massachusetts Regiment*, ed. Martin H. Blatt, Thomas J. Brown, and Donald Yacovone (Boston: University of Massachusetts Press in association with the Massachusetts Historical Society, 2001), 94–95; Frances D. Gage to Francis George Shaw, Sept. 6, 1863, in *Memorial R.G.S.* (Cambridge, MA: University Press, 1864), 153–55; Emilio, *History of the Fifty-Fourth Regiment*, 228–30; Virginia Matze Adams, ed., *On the Altar of Freedom: A Black Soldier's Civil War Letters from the Front* (Amherst: University of Massachusetts Press, 1991), 66; Blight, *Race and Reunion*, 155–56.

39. "Our Charleston Correspondence," *NYT*, May 14, 1865; "The Martyrs of the Race Course," *CC*, May 2, 1865; Henry O. Marcy, "First Memorial Day May 1, 1865," clipping from unidentified Boston or Cambridge newspaper, [May 29], 1923 (Concord Free Public Library, Concord, MA); Quartermaster General's Office, *Roll of Honor: Names of Soldiers Who, In Defence of the American Union, Suffered Martyrdom in the Prison Pens Throughout the South* (Washington, DC: Government Printing Office, 1868), 14: 238; Redpath, "Honor to Our Martyrs"; Redpath, "Eye and Ear Notes," June 1, 1865; James Redpath, "A Defense of General Hatch," *NAAS*, July 22, 1865; James Redpath, "The Work at Charleston," *Freedmen's Record* 1 (Oct. 1865): 157; Hawks, diary, Apr. 8 and May 1, 1865, pp. 128, 137–38.

40. "Martyrs of the Race Course"; Redpath, "Honor to Our Martyrs"; "Scenes of the Reconstructed South," *IND*, Feb. 22, 1866; Blight, *Race and Reunion*, 65.

41. Hawks, diary, May 1, 1865, p. 137; Douglas R. Egerton, *He Shall Go Out Free: The Lives of Denmark Vesey, Revised and Updated Edition* (Lanham, MD: Rowman & Littlefield, 2004), 188–91.

42. "Our Charleston Correspondence"; "Martyrs of the Race Course"; Hawks, diary, May 1, 1865, p. 138; Earl Marble, "Origin of Memorial Day," *New England Magazine* 32 (June 1905): 470; "Decoration Day"; Redpath, "Honor to Our Martyrs."

43. Mrs. Francis J. Porcher [Abby Louisa Porcher] to Anna Mason Smith, July 29, [1865], in *Mason Smith Family Letters*, 227; Johnathan H. Poston, *The Buildings of Charleston: A Guide to the City's Architecture* (Columbia: University of South Carolina Press, 1997), 223; Henry William DeSaussure to his father, June 12, 1865, Folder 22, Box 121, DFP.

44. William Middleton to his sister in Philadelphia, n.d., quoted in Robert N. Rosen, *Confederate Charleston: Illustrated History of the City and the People during the Civil War* (Columbia: University of South Carolina, 1994), 142; DeSaussure to his father, June 12, 1865; Henry W. Ravenel to Augustin L. Taveau, June 27, 1865, Box 3, ALTP; Henry W. Ravenel, Apr. 30, 1865, May 30, 1865, in *The Private Journal of Henry William Ravenel, 1859–1887*, ed. Arney Robinson Childs (Columbia: University of South Carolina Press, 1947), 228.

45. Augustin L. Taveau, letter to editor, *NYTR*, June 10, 1865, and Louis Manigault's comments on it, in Louis Manigault, Manigault Plantation Journal, [June 1865], p. 39, Digital Collections, SHC; Eugene D. Genovese, *Roll, Jordan, Roll: The World the Slaves Made* (New York: Random House, 1974), 111–12.

46. Carl Schurz, quoted in Joseph H. Mahaffey, ed., "Carl Schurz's Letters from the South," *Georgia Historical Quarterly* 35 (Sept. 1951): 235–36; Affy to Amie, Sept. 5, 1865, quoted in Powers, *Black Charlestonians*, 227.

47. Redpath, "Defense of General Hatch"; James Redpath, "General Hatch Again," *NAAS*, July 29, 1865; "The Situation," *New York Herald*, July 13, 1865; "Eighty-ninth Anniversary," *CC*, July 6, 1865; "Fourth of July Celebration," *CC*, July 10, 1865; "Charleston Correspondence," *CR*, July 15, 1865; "From Charleston," *NYT*, July 12, 1865.

48. Katchun, *Festivals of Freedom*, 54–96; "Emancipation Celebration," *CR*, Aug. 26, 1865; Litwack, *Been in the Storm So Long*, 426–30; Joel Williamson, *After Slavery: The Negro in South Carolina During Reconstruction, 1861–1877* (Chapel Hill: University of North Carolina Press, 1965), 249–52.

49. "Letter from Charleston, S.C.," *Christian Advocate*, Jan. 18, 1866; "The Day We Celebrate," *SCLE*, Jan. 6, 1866; Botume, *First Days amongst the Contrabands*, 204–6; Powers, *Black Charlestonians*, 194; "Speech of Gen. Saxton," *SCLE*, Jan. 13, 1866.

50. "Letter from Charleston, S.C."

51. Jacob F. Schirmer, diary, Jan. 1, 1866, SFJR; "Glory, Hallelujah!" *CDN*, Jan. 3, 1866. See also "Affairs About Home," *SCLE*, Jan. 13, 1866.

2. Reconstructing Charleston in the Shadow of Slavery

1. Walter Edgar, *South Carolina: A History* (Columbia: University of South Carolina Press, 1998), 383–84; "Incidents of the Convention," *CM*, Jan. 15, 1868; "The Convention," *CDN*, Jan. 15, 1868; "The Great South. The South Carolina Problem; The Epoch of Transition," *Scribner's Monthly* 8 (June 1874): 147; *Appleton's Illustrated Hand-book of American Cities; Composing the Principal Cities in the United States and Canada, with outlines of*

Through Routes, and Railway Maps (New York: D. Appleton and Co., 1876), 133; Richard L. Hume and Jerry B. Gough, *Blacks, Carpetbaggers, and Scalawags: The Constitutional Conventions of Radical Reconstruction* (Baton Rouge: Louisiana State University Press, 2008), 435n9.

2. "The Convention," Jan. 15, 1865; "Reconstruction Convention," *CC,* Jan. 15, 1868; Hume and Gough, *Blacks, Carpetbaggers, and Scalawags,* 169.

3. David Golightly Harris, journal, Jan. 13, 1868, in *Piedmont Farmer: The Journals of David Golightly Harris, 1855–1870,* ed. Philip N. Racine (Knoxville: University of Tennessee Press, 1990), 456; "The Convention," *CDN,* Jan. 14, 1868; "The Convention," Jan. 15, 1865.

4. "The Great Ring-Streaked and Striped Negro Convention," *CM,* Jan. 15, 1868; "Incidents of the Convention," *CM,* Jan. 15, 1868; "Desecration of the Gray," *CM,* Jan. 15, 1868.

5. "The Great Ring-Streaked and Striped Negro Convention"; "Sketches of the Delegates to the Great Ringed-Streaked-and-Striped, The Delegates from Sumter [Number One]," *CM,* Jan. 15, 1868; "Sketches of the Delegates to the Great Ringed-Streaked-and-Striped, The Greenville Delegation [Number Two]," *CM,* Jan. 16, 1868; "Incidents of the Great Ringed-Streaked-and-Striped-Convention," *CM,* Feb. 1, 1868; "Incidents of the Great Ringed-Streaked-and-Striped-Convention," *CM,* Feb. 4, 1868; "Incidents of the Great Ringed-Streaked-and-Striped-Convention," *CM,* Feb. 20, 1868; "Sketches of the Delegates to the Great Ringed-Streaked-and-Striped, The Edgefield Delegation [Concluded]," *CM,* Feb. 3, 1868; "The Great-Ring-Streaked-and Striped. Comments By a 'Looker On,'" *CM,* Jan. 20, 1868.

6. *Proceedings of the Constitutional Convention of South Carolina, held at Charleston, S.C., beginning January 14th and ending March 17th, 1868* (Charleston: Denny and Perry, 1868), 16; Hume and Gough, *Blacks, Carpetbaggers, and Scalawags,* Appendix C, Delegate Biographical Data, n.p.; Richard Zuczek, *State of Rebellion: Reconstruction in South Carolina* (Columbia: University of South Carolina, 1996), 48.

7. Emma Holmes, diary, June 10, 1865, in *The Diary of Miss Emma Holmes, 1861–1866,* ed. John F. Marszalek (Baton Rouge: Louisiana State University Press, 1979), 451; Eric Foner, *Reconstruction: America's Unfinished Revolution, 1863–1877* (New York: Harper & Row, 1988), 183; "Interview Between the South Carolina Delegation and President Johnson," *BET,* June 26, 1865; Hyman Rubin III, *South Carolina Scalawags* (Columbia: University of South Carolina Press, 2006), 3–4; Francis Butler Simkins and Robert Hilliard Woody, *South Carolina During Reconstruction* (Chapel Hill: University of North Carolina Press, 1932), 32–34.

8. Edgar, *South Carolina,* 383–84; *Acts of the General Assembly of the State of South Carolina, Passed at the Sessions of 1864–65* (Columbia: Julian A. Selby, Printer to the State, 1866), 292; Simkins and Woody, *South Carolina During Reconstruction,* 48–51; Joel Williamson, *After Slavery: The Negro in South Carolina During Reconstruction, 1861–1877* (Chapel Hill: University of North Carolina Press, 1965), 74–79; Bernard E. Powers Jr., *Black Charlestonians: A Social History, 1822–1885* (Fayetteville: University of Arkansas Press, 1994), 80–82; William C. Hine, "Frustration, Factionalism, and Defeat: Black Political Leadership in Reconstruction Charleston, 1865–1877" (Ph.D. diss., Kent State University, 1979), 30–32.

9. Williamson, *After Slavery,* 73–74; Edmund Rhett, quoted in Zuczek, *State of Rebellion,* 15.

10. Richard H. Abbott, *For Free Press and Equal Rights: Republican Newspapers in the Reconstruction South,* ed. John W. Quist (Athens: University of Georgia Press, 2004), 32–33; Walter J. Fraser Jr., *Charleston! Charleston! The History of a Southern City* (Columbia: University of South Carolina Press, 1989), 277; "Loyalty and the Planters," *SCLE,* Dec. 16, 1865; "Servants in South Carolina," *SCLE,* Dec. 16, 1865; Thomas David Russell, "Sale Day in Antebellum South Carolina: Slavery, Law, Economy, and Court-Supervised Sales" (Ph.D. diss.,

Stanford University, 1993), 1; Steven Deyle, *Carry Me Back: The Domestic Slave Trade in American Life* (New York: Oxford University Press, 2005), 168–69.

11. Fraser, *Charleston! Charleston!*, 279; Simkins and Woody, *South Carolina During Reconstruction*, 57; Rubin, *South Carolina Scalawags*, 6; Dan T. Carter, *When the War Was Over: The Failure of Self-Reconstruction in the South, 1865–1867* (Baton Rouge: Louisiana State University Press, 1985), 230–31; "Secession Gleams," *SCLE*, Jan. 6, 1866; "Secession Gleams," *SCLE*, Jan. 13, 1866.

12. "South Carolina," *NYT*, May 20, 1866.

13. "Colour and Race," *CM*, Jan. 30, 1868; "Negro Schools and Negro Homesteads," *CM*, Apr. 2, 1868; "The South Vindicated," *CM*, Apr. 2, 1868.

14. "Wade Hampton on the Crisis," *CC*, Oct. 10, 1866.

15. Robert K. Ackerman, *Wade Hampton III* (Columbia: University of South Carolina Press, 2007), xi; Rod Andrew Jr., *Wade Hampton: Confederate Warrior to Southern Redeemer* (Chapel Hill: University of North Carolina Press, 2008), 16–17; "Wade Hampton on the Crisis," *CC*, Oct. 10, 1866.

16. "Speech of General Wade Hampton," *CC*, Mar. 23, 1867; Ackerman, *Wade Hampton*, 109–10; Thomas Holt, *Black over White: Negro Political Leadership in South Carolina during Reconstruction* (Urbana: University of Illinois Press, 1977), 29; "Mass Meeting in Columbia," *SCLE*, Mar. 23, 1867. For national coverage of this speech, see "The Charleston Negroes," *Albany Evening Journal*, Mar. 27, 1867; and "Reconstruction According to Wade Hampton and the Negroes," *NYTR*, Mar. 29, 1867.

17. "The Northern Press," *CDN*, Mar. 27, 1867; "A Black Man's View of the Situation," *CC*, Mar. 21, 1867; Herbert Ravenel Sass, *Outspoken: 150 Years of the* News and Courier (Columbia: University of South Carolina Press, 1953), 35; "The Colored Race and the Ballot," *CC*, Mar. 26, 1867; "Legislature of South Carolina," *CC*, Dec. 19, 1859; Steven A. Channing, *Crisis of Fear: Secession in South Carolina* (New York: Simon and Schuster, 1970), 16. On the moral capital of opposition to slavery, see Christopher Brown, *Moral Capital: Foundations of British Abolitionism* (Chapel Hill: University of North Carolina Press, 2006), esp. 451–62.

18. Abbot, *For Free Press and Equal Rights*, 83; "Wade Hampton," *Charleston Advocate*, Mar. 23, 1867; "Public Meeting," *CC*, Mar. 22, 1867.

19. Hume and Gough, *Blacks, Carpetbaggers, and Scalawags*, 161, Appendix C, n.p.; Edgar, *South Carolina*, 385–86.

20. "An Act to provide for the more efficient Government of the Rebel States," Mar. 2, 1867, in *Statutes at Large*, 39th Cong., 2d sess., 14: 429, memory.loc.gov/cgi-bin/ampage?collId=llsl&fileName=014/llsl014.db&recNum=460; Foner, *Reconstruction*, 276–77; *Proceedings of the Constitutional Convention*, 218.

21. James M. Banner Jr., "The Problem of South Carolina," in *The Hofstader Aegis: A Memorial*, ed. Stanley M. Elkins and Eric L. McKitrick (New York: Knopf, 1974), 60–93; Hume and Gough, *Blacks, Carpetbaggers, and Scalawags*, 168–69; William W. Freehling, *The Road to Disunion*, vol. 1, *Secessionists at Bay, 1776–1854* (New York: Oxford University Press, 1990), 220–23; Manisha Sinha, *The Counterrevolution of Slavery: Politics and Ideology in Antebellum South Carolina* (Chapel Hill: University of North Carolina Press, 2000), 12–14.

22. *Proceedings of the Constitutional Convention*, 455, 874–75; Cole Blease Graham Jr., *The South Carolina State Constitution* (New York: Oxford University Press, 2011), 30–32; Simkins and Woody, *South Carolina During Reconstruction*, 96–98.

23. *Proceedings of the Constitutional Convention*, 824–27, 830–31, 834–35; Benjamin Ginsberg, *Moses of South Carolina: A Jewish Scalawag during Radical Reconstruction* (Baltimore: Johns Hopkins University Press, 2010), 79–81; Leon Litwack, *Been in the Storm*

So Long: The Aftermath of Slavery (New York: Random House, 1979), 456, 467, 471; Williamson, *After Slavery*, 206–7; Powers, *Black Charlestonians*, 205–6; Douglas R. Egerton, *The Wars of Reconstruction: The Brief, Violent History of America's Most Progressive Era* (New York: Bloomsbury, 2014), 8–9; Philip Dray, *Capitol Men: The Epic Story of Reconstruction through the Lives of the First Black Congressmen* (New York: Houghton Mifflin, 2008), 40–41.

24. *Proceedings of the Constitutional Convention*, 198–99, 227–29; Rubin, *South Carolina Scalawags*, 18–19, 29.

25. *Proceedings of the Constitutional Convention*, 219, 226–27; Hume and Gough, *Blacks, Carpetbaggers, and Scalawags*, 172.

26. *Proceedings of the Constitutional Convention*, 231.

27. Ibid., 237–38, 243, 249; Hume and Gough, *Blacks, Carpetbaggers, and Scalawags*, 173; Lamson, *Glorious Failure*, 52. This measure was later deemed an unconstitutional violation of the obligation of contracts. Simkins and Woody, *South Carolina During Reconstruction*, 100.

28. Benjamin F. Perry, quoted in Lou Faulkner Williams, *The Great South Carolina Ku Klux Klan Trials, 1871–1872* (Athens: University of Georgia Press, 1996), 8; *Proceedings of the Constitutional Convention*, 27–29; Dray, *Capitol Men*, 42–43; Peggy Lamson, *The Glorious Failure: Black Congressman Robert Brown Elliott and the Reconstruction in South Carolina* (New York: Norton, 1973), 48–49.

29. "Sketches of the Delegates . . . [Number One]"; "Sketches of the Delegates . . . [Number Two]"; "Sketches of the Delegates to the Great Ringed-Streaked-and-Striped, The Beaufort Delegation [Number Twenty-Six]," *CM*, Feb. 20, 1868.

30. "Sketches of the Delegates to the Great Ringed-Streaked-and-Striped, The Abbeville Delegation [Number Five]," *CM*, Jan. 20, 1868; "Negro Schools and Negro Homesteads."

31. Edgar, *South Carolina*, 386–88; Fraser, *Charleston! Charleston!*, 287–89; Powers, *Black Charlestonians*, 90; Hine, "Frustration, Factionalism," 132–52.

32. Robert B. Rhett Jr., "A Farewell to the Subscribers of the Charleston Mercury," [late 1868], SCHS; William C. Davis, *Rhett: The Turbulent Life and Times of a Fire-eater* (Columbia: University of South Carolina Press, 2001), 556–57, 665n19.

33. Henry L. Swint, ed., *Dear Ones at Home: Letters from Contraband Camps* (Nashville: Vanderbilt University Press, 1966), 180; "Scenes in the Reconstructed South," *IND*, Feb. 22, 1866; "Martyrs of the Race-Course," *HW*, May 18, 1867; "Charleston, S.C.," *The Student and Schoolmate: An Illustrated Monthly for All Our Boys and Girls* 17 (Mar. 1866): 98; Quartermaster General's Office, *Roll of Honor: Names of Soldiers Who Died in Defense of the Union, Interred in the National Cemeteries* (Washington, DC: Government Printing Office, 1871), 17: 7; Caroline Janney, *Remembering the Civil War: Reunion and the Limits of Reconciliation* (Chapel Hill: University of North Carolina Press, 2013), 98–99; Maurie D. McInnis, *The Politics of Taste in Antebellum Charleston* (Chapel Hill: University of North Carolina Press, 2005), 223–24; "A Federal Memorial Meeting," *CDN*, June 1, 1868; A.J. Willard, "At Charleston, South Carolina," in Frank Moore, *Memorial Ceremonies at the Graves of Our Soldiers: Saturday, May 30, 1868* (Washington, DC:, n.p., 1869), 101–109.

34. "Decoration of the Graves of Federal Dead," *CDN*, May 31, 1869; "Honors the Nation's Dead: The Celebration at Charleston," *South Carolina Weekly Republican*, June 5, 1869; *Memorial Ceremonies on the Occasion of Decorating the Graves of the Federal Dead at Magnolia Cemetery, May 29th, 1869* (Charleston: Republican Job Office, 1869), 3; "The Union Dead," *CDN*, May 31, 1870; "Decoration of the Graves of the Federal Dead," *CC*, May 31, 1870.

35. *Memorial Ceremonies on the Occasion of Decorating the Graves*, 6–7; "Union Dead"; "Decoration of the Graves of the Federal Dead."

36. "Honors to the Federal Dead," *CC*, June 1, 1868; "A National Cemetery in South Carolina," *NYTR*, July 17, 1869; "A National Cemetery," *CDN*, Aug. 25, 1869; *Roll of Honor*, 17: 7; John R. Neff, *Honoring the Civil War Dead: Commemoration and the Problem of Reconciliation* (Lawrence: University Press of Kansas, 2005), 138; Mark Hughes, *Bivouac of the Dead* (Westminster, MD: Heritage Books, 2008), 240; Willard, "At Charleston, South Carolina," 101; "Jottings About the State," *CDN*, Jan. 27, 1873; "Memorial Day," *CNC*, May 11, 1875; "Emancipation Day," *CNC*, Jan. 9, 1877; "South Carolina Society," *AM* 39 (June 1877): 683.

37. Bruce E. Baker, *What Reconstruction Meant: Historical Memory in the American South* (Charlottesville: University of Virginia Press, 2008), 77–78; "Emancipation Celebration," *CDN*, Jan. 3, 1871; Wilbert L. Jenkins, *Seizing the New Day: African Americans in Post–Civil War Charleston* (Bloomington: Indiana University Press, 1998), 134; "Mayor's Office," *CC*, May 20, 1843.

38. "Emancipation Day," *FLN*, Feb. 3, 1877; "Emancipation Day," *CNC*, Jan. 2, 1874; "A Humiliating Spectacle," *Orangeburg Times*, Jan. 22, 1874; "The Emancipation Celebration," *CDN*, Jan. 3, 1871; "Emancipation Day," *CDN*, Jan. 2, 1872; "The Glorious Fourth," *CDN*, July 5, 1872; "The Day of Jubilee," *CDN*, Jan. 2, 1873; "Independence Day," *CNC*, July 5, 1873; "The Fourth in the City," *CNC*, July 6, 1874; "Emancipation Day," *CNC*, Jan. 2, 1875; "The Fourth in the City," *CNC*, July 5, 1876; "Emancipation Day," *CNC*, Jan. 9, 1877; Adam Rothman, "'This Special Picnic': The Fourth of July in Charleston, South Carolina, 1865–1900," May 1995, unpublished paper in authors' possession, 16; Kathleen Ann Clark, *Defining Moments: African American Commemoration and Political Culture in the South, 1863–1913* (Chapel Hill: University of North Carolina Press, 2005), 126–27; Steven Hahn, *A Nation Under Our Feet: Black Political Struggles in the Rural South from Slavery to the Great Migration* (Cambridge, MA: Belknap Press of Harvard University Press, 2003), 265–313.

39. "The Glorious Fourth," *CDN*, July 5, 1872.

40. "The Day of Jubilee"; "Independence Day," *CNC*, July 6, 1873; "The Fourth in the City," *CNC*, July 6, 1874; "The Fourth in the City," *CNC*, July 5, 1876; "The Glorious Fourth"; Shane White and Graham White, *The Sounds of Slavery: Discovering African American History Through Songs, Sermons, and Speech* (Boston: Beacon Press, 2005), 111–14, 171–72; Lawrence W. Levine, *Black Culture and Black Consciousness: Afro-American Folk Thought from Slavery to Freedom* (New York: Oxford University Press, 1977), 16–17, 37–38, 164–65; Rothman, "'This Special Picnic,'" 18–19; Jeffery Strickland, "African-American Public Rituals on the Fourth of July and Citizenship in South Carolina during Reconstruction," *Citizenship Studies* 10 (Feb. 2006): 106–8.

41. "The Observance of the Glorious Fourth," *CDN*, July 5, 1871; "The Glorious Fourth"; Holt, *Black over White*, 54; "Humiliating Spectacle"; *CDR*, July 5, 1870, quoted in Jeffery G. Strickland, "Ethnicity and Race in the Urban South: German Immigrants and African-Americans in Charleston, South Carolina, during Reconstruction" (Ph.D. diss., Florida State University, 2003), 146n77; "The Emancipation Celebration," *CDN*, Jan. 3, 1871.

42. Frances Ellen Watkins Harper, "Affairs in South Carolina," in *A Brighter Coming Day: A Frances Ellen Watkins Harper Reader*, ed. Frances Smith Foster (New York: Feminist Press at the City University of New York, 1990), 124; *CC*, Sept. 3, 1869.

43. N.R. Middleton to his daughter, July 6, [ca. 1866], Folder 29, Box 2, NRMP; Jenkins, *Seizing the Day*, 40; "The Fourth of July," *CDN*, July 9, 1866.

44. "South Carolina," *NYT*, Jan. 7, 1867; Jenkins, *Seizing the Day*, 107; "City Affairs," *CC*, July 5, 1869; "The Fourth," *CC*, July 6, 1869.

45. Jacob F. Schirmer, diary, July 4, [1866], July 4, 1867, July 4, [1871], July 4, [1872], Jan. 1, 1870, Jan. 1, 1872, SFJR.

46. "Mills House," Charleston, SC, Minutes, May 14, 1866, p. 1, LMAR; Janney, *Remembering the Civil War*, 92–95; Gaines M. Foster, *Ghosts of the Confederacy: Defeat, the Lost Cause, and the Emergence of the New South, 1865–1913* (New York: Oxford University Press, 1988), 38–39, 44, 220n23; Alice A. Gaillard Palmer, "South Carolina, Ladies' Memorial Association of Charleston, South Carolina," in *History of the Confederate Memorial Associations of the South* (New Orleans: Graham Press, 1904), 241; *A Brief History of the Ladies' Memorial Association of Charleston, S.C.* (Charleston: H. P. Cooke & Co., 1880), 5; "Celebration of the Sixteenth of June, in Memory of the Confederate Dead," *CDN*, June 18, 1866; "South Carolina," *NYT*, July 14, 1866.

47. "Survivors' Association of Charleston District," *CDN*, Nov. 2, 1866; "The Survivors' Association," *CM*, Nov. 23, 1866; "The Survivors' Association—No. 2," *CM*, Nov. 29, 1866; "Survivors' Association—No. 3," *CM*, Dec. 4, 1866; Fraser, *Charleston! Charleston!*, 279; Janney, *Remembering the Civil War*, 96–97.

48. "Gen. Sickles' Report," *CDN*, Dec. 7, 1866; "Ladies' Memorial Association," *CC*, June 6, 1867; "Semicentennial Celebration in Charleston," *Confederate Veteran* 24 (July 1916): 326–27; Minutes, n.d., pp. 14, 26, 67–68, LMAR; *Brief History of the Ladies' Memorial Association*, 9; Thomas J. Brown, *Civil War Canon: Sites of Confederate Memory in South Carolina* (Chapel Hill: University of North Carolina Press, 2015), 69–71; Janney, *Remembering the Civil War*, 97–98.

49. *Confederate Memorial Day at Charleston, S.C., . . .* (Charleston: William G. Mazyck, Printers, 1871); "The Survivors' Association," *KC*, Oct. 8, 1869; "Survivor's Association of Charleston District," *CC*, Nov. 11, 1869; "The Survivors of the War," *CDN*, Nov. 19, 1869; "The State Survivors' Association," *AI*, Nov. 25, 1869; Janney, *Remembering the Civil War*, 140; Sam Jones to [Edward McCrady Jr.], Mar. 21, 1871, Folder 6, SASCR; David W. Blight, *Race and Reunion: The Civil War in American Memory* (Cambridge, MA: Belknap Press of Harvard University Press, 2001), 261.

50. Edward A. Pollard, *The Lost Cause; A New Southern History of the War of the Confederates* (New York: E.B. Treat & Co., 1866); Blight, *Race and Reunion*, 258–59, 273–74; Janney, *Remembering the Civil War*, 136–37; Alan T. Nolan, "The Anatomy of a Myth," in *The Myth of the Lost Cause and Civil War History*, ed. Gary W. Gallagher and Alan T. Nolan (Bloomington, Indiana University Press, 2000), 11–34.

51. John Hammond Moore, ed., *The Juhl Letters to the* Charleston Courier: *A View of the South, 1865–1871* (Athens: University of Georgia Press, 1974), 21; [John Bell Hood], address to South Carolina Survivors' Association, [Dec. 12, 1872], Folder 13, SASCR; Blight, *Race and Reunion*, 2; "Address of Rev. Dr. Bachman Before the Ladies' Association to Commemorate the Confederate Dead," *CDN*, May 17, 1866.

52. "Memorial Celebration," *CDN*, May 11, 1871; *Confederate Memorial Day*, 8, 17, 22; Edger, *South Carolina*, 422–23.

53. Blight, *Race and Reunion*, 79–80; Janney, *Remembering the Civil War*, 148–53.

54. John S. Preston, untitled address, [Nov. 10], 1870, Folder 12, SASCR; "The State Survivors' Association," *CDN*, Nov. 12, 1870; Charles B. Dew, *Apostles of Disunion: Southern Secession Commissioners and the Causes of the Civil War* (Charlottesville: University of Virginia Press, 2001), 68–75.

55. Davis, *Rhett*, 556–57, 570, 586, 665n19; William C. Davis, ed., *A Fire-Eater Remembers: The Confederate Memoir of Robert Barnwell Rhett* (Columbia: University of South Carolina Press, 2000), xvii, 13, 16, 111n24 (Rhett quote).

56. George Lipsitz, *Time Passages: Collective Memory and American Popular Culture* (Minneapolis: University of Minnesota Press, 1990), 213; Yael Zerubavel, *Recovered Roots:*

Collective Memory and the Making of Israeli National Tradition (Chicago: University of Chicago Press, 1995), 10; Baker, *What Reconstruction Meant*, 8–10; Thavolia Glymph, "'Liberty Dearly Bought': The Making of Civil War Memory in Afro-American Communities in the South," in *Time Longer Than Rope: A Century of African American Activism, 1850–1950*, ed. Charles M. Payne and Adam Green (New York: New York University Press, 2003), 116.

57. Blight, *Race and Reunion*, 51–52, 102–3; Janney, *Remembering the Civil War*, 126–32; Mark Wahlgren Summers, *The Ordeal of the Reunion: A New History of Reconstruction* (Chapel Hill: University of North Carolina Press, 2014), 357–58, 450n29; Stephen Budiansky, *The Bloody Shirt: Terror after the Civil War* (New York: Viking, 2008), 2–3.

58. R.W.E., letter to the editor, *FP*, Apr. 11, 1868; "Taxation Without Representation Is Tyranny," *FP*, Apr. 11, 1868; "How Radicalism Is Bolstered Up," *CDN*, Aug. 24, 1868; "A Radical Campaign Document," *CDN*, Aug. 24, 1868.

59. "The Custom House War," *CC*, July 29, 1869; Hine, "Frustration, Factionalism," 146; "Speech of Hon. A.J. Ransier," *CDN*, Supplement, Oct. 8, 1870; Simkins and Woody, *South Carolina During Reconstruction*, 447–48.

60. "Speech of Hon. A.J. Ransier"; "Public Meetings," *FP*, Apr. 5, 1868; Abbot, *For Free Press and Equal Rights*, 83.

61. Fraser, *Charleston! Charleston!*, 291–92 (quote 292).

62. "The Parrot Cry of the Ring," *CNC*, Oct. 23, 1874; *CDN*, Oct. 14, 1870.

63. Sass, *Outspoken*, 40; "Parrot Cry of the Ring"; "A Ring Lie Nailed—Georgetown Solid for Green and Delany," *CNC*, Nov. 2, 1874; "The New Alliance," *CNC*, Nov. 7, 1874; "Burying the Dead Past," *CNC*, Nov. 11, 1874.

64. "Who Brought Negroes to Charleston and Sold Them as Slaves," *CM*, Oct. 10, 1868; "Phases of State History," *CNC*, May 20, 1876.

65. "The Party of Revolution," *CC*, Aug. 19, 1868; James Oakes, *Freedom National: The Destruction of Slavery in the United States, 1861–1865* (New York: Norton, 2012), 483–85; Carter, *When the War Was Over*, 84–85.

66. Charles Reagan Wilson, "Foreword" to *Vale of Tears: New Essays in Religion and Reconstruction*, ed. Edward J. Blum and W. Scott Poole (Macon, GA: Mercer University Press, 2005), vii; Carole Emberton, *Beyond Redemption: Race, Violence, and the American South after the Civil War* (Chicago: University of Chicago Press, 2013), 14; Edmund L. Drago, *Hurrah for Hampton! Black Shirts in South Carolina During Reconstruction* (Fayetteville: University Press of Arkansas, 1999), 7–13; Zuczek, *State of Rebellion*, 174–80.

67. Benjamin Perry, "Who Freed the Slaves?" *CNC*, Sept. 27, 1876.

68. "Hampton at Chester," *CNC*, Oct. 17, 1876; "The Summerville Precinct Democratic Club," *CNC*, Sept. 19, 1876.

69. Zuczek, *State of Rebellion*, 174–75, 190–97; Edgar, *South Carolina*, 402–6; Drago, *Hurrah for Hampton*, 43.

70. Foner, *Reconstruction*, 580–82; Zuczek, *State of Rebellion*, 197–201; Fraser, *Charleston! Charleston!*, 300–301; Edgar, *South Carolina*, 405–9.

71. "State Politics," *CNC*, Aug. 10, 1880.

72. "Emancipation Day," *CNC*, Jan. 9, 1877; "Emancipation Day," *FLN*, Feb. 3, 1877; "Emancipation Day in Charleston, South Carolina," *FLN*, Feb. 10, 1877; "All Africa Was Here," *CNC*, Jan. 3, 1892.

73. "A Hampton Fourth of July," *CNC*, July 5, 1877; "Too-la-loo," *Winnsboro News and Herald*, July 7, 1877; "The Glorious Fourth," *CNC*, July 5, 1878; "The Colored Celebrants," *CNC*, July 5, 1879; "The Fifth for the Fourth," *CNC*, July 6, 1880; "'The Fourth' Under a Cloud," *CNC*, July 5, 1881; "The Colored Troops," *CNC*, July 5, 1881; "The Glorious Fourth," *CEP*, July 3, 1897; George Tindall, *South Carolina Negroes, 1877–1900* (Columbia: University of South Carolina Press, 1952), 286–88; "A Fin De Siecle Fourth," *CNC*, July 5, 1895; "Now for 'Glorious Fourth,'" *CNC*, July 4, 1906; Rothman, "'This Special Picnic,'" 25.

74. See "Decoration Day at Beaufort," *CNC*, June 11, 1880; and "At Hampstead Mall," *CNC*, Jan. 2, 1889.

3. SETTING JIM CROW IN STONE

1. *CNC*, Sept. 3 and 4, 1886; "The Earthquake, 1886," in *City of Charleston Year Book—1886* (Charleston: Walker, Evans, and Cogswell, 1886), Appendix; Susan Millar Williams and Stephen G. Hoffius, *Upheaval in Charleston: Earthquake and Murder on the Eve of Jim Crow* (Athens: University of Georgia Press, 2011), esp. 1–16, 53; Kenneth E. Peters, "Earthquakes," in *The South Carolina Encyclopedia*, ed. Walter Edgar (Columbia: University of South Carolina Press, 2006), 281; "Out of the Depths," *CNC*, Oct. 12, 1884; "Keep Off the Citadel Green," *CNC*, Oct. 19, 1888.

2. "A Day of Gloom," *CNC*, Sept. 3, 1886; "Life in the Camps," *CNC*, Sept. 10, 1886.

3. Williams and Hoffius, *Upheaval in Charleston*, 138, 166, 184; "Here, There and Everywhere," *CNC*, Sept. 10, 1886; "Other Places," *CNC*, Sept. 6, 1886; *A History of the Calhoun Monument at Charleston, S.C.* (Charleston: Lucas Richardson, 1888), 36.

4. John C. Calhoun to Floride Calhoun, Oct. 1, 1807, in *PJCC*, 1: 38; Richard Hofstader, *The American Political Tradition and the Men Who Made It* (New York: Knopf, 1948), 94; George C. Rogers Jr., *Charleston in the Age of the Pinckneys* (Norman: University of Oklahoma Press, 1969), 167–68; Daniel Walker Howe, *What Hath God Wrought: The Transformation of America, 1815–1848* (New York: Oxford University Press, 2007), 204; John Niven, *John C. Calhoun and the Price of the Union: A Biography* (Baton Rouge: Louisiana State University, 1988), xv, 157, 344 ("cast iron man" quote); Fredrika Bremer, *The Homes of the New World: Impressions of America*, translated by Mary Howitt (New York: Harper & Brothers, 1853), 1: 305.

5. Thomas J. Brown, "The Monumental Legacy of Calhoun," in *Memory of the Civil War in American Culture*, ed. Alice Fahs and Joan Waugh (Chapel Hill: University of North Carolina Press, 2008), 132–33; William W. Freehling, *The Road to Disunion*, vol. 1, *Secessionists at Bay, 1776–1854* (New York: Oxford University Press, 1990), 272–75.

6. Irving Bartlett, *John C. Calhoun: A Biography* (New York: Norton, 1993), 17, 27, 61, 217–28; Kelly, *America's Longest Siege*, 173–74; John C. Calhoun to A[ugustin] S. Clayton and Others, Athens, Ga., Aug. 5, 1836, in *PJCC*, 13: 263; John C. Calhoun, "Remarks on Receiving Abolition Petitions (Revised Report)," in *PJCC*, 13: 395; Lacy K. Ford, *Deliver Us from Evil: The Slavery Question in the Old South* (New York: Oxford University Press, 2009), 496–504; Manisha Sinha, *The Counterrevolution of Slavery: Politics and Ideology in Antebellum South Carolina* (Chapel Hill: University of North Carolina Press, 2000), esp. 84–117; John C. Calhoun, "Speech on the Slavery Question," in *PJCC*, 27: 198.

7. Maurie D. McInnis, *The Politics of Taste in Antebellum Charleston* (Chapel Hill: University of North Carolina Press, 2005), 151–56, 352n82; Richard P. Wunder, *Hiram Powers: Vermont Sculptor, 1805–1873,* vol. 2, *Catalogue of Works* (Newark: University of Delaware Press, 1991), 115, 198; Charles Capper, *Margaret Fuller: An American Romantic Life*, vol. 2, *The Public Years* (New York: Oxford University Press, 2007), 503–12; Thomas J. Brown, *Civil War Canon: Sites of Confederate Memory in South Carolina* (Chapel Hill: University of North Carolina Press, 2015), 41–44.

8. "Narrative of the Funeral Honors Paid to the Hon. J.C. Calhoun, at Charleston, S.C.," in *The Carolina Tribute to Calhoun*, ed. John Peyre Thomas (Columbia: Richard L. Bryan, 1857), 65–66; "Mr. Calhoun's Last Speech," *CC*, May 15, 1850; *CC*, May 15, 1850; *CC*,

May 16, 1850; McInnis, *Politics of Taste*, 154; J[ohn] C. Calhoun [Jr.] to Governor W[hitemarsh] B. Seabrook, Apr. 19, 1850, in *PJCC*, 27: 259; "Postscript, April–August, 1850," in *PJCC*, 27: 253; John Stillwell Jenkins, *The Life of John Caldwell Calhoun* (Auburn and Buffalo: John E. Beardsley, 1850), 444–45; "Grave of Calhoun," *CNC*, Mar. 25, 1880; Brown, *Civil War Canon*, 40–41.

9. "An Ordinance," *CC*, Oct. 28, 1850; "Arrival of the James Adger," *NYT*, Mar. 23, 1854; "Honorable N.P. Tallmadge on Spiritual Matters," *CC*, May 31, 1853; "Spiritual Manifestations," *CC*, May 31, 1853; "The Ghostology Business," *CC*, June 1, 1853; Brown, *Civil War Canon*, 39–41.

10. "South-Carolina Mourns for her Dead," *CC*, Apr. 27, 1850; "Obsequies of Mr. Calhoun," *CM*, Apr. 27, 1850; "Narrative of the Funeral Honors," 78–82; Walter J. Fraser Jr., *Charleston! Charleston! The History of a Southern City* (Columbia: University of South Carolina Press, 1989), 228; Rogers, *Charleston in the Age of the Pinckneys*, 167–68; McInnis, *Politics of Taste*, 153–54; Brown, "Monumental Legacy," 133.

11. Bremer, *Homes of the New World*, 1: 305; Elijah Green, in *ASCA*, 2(2): 196; "Dug Grave for Calhoun," newspaper clipping, [Jan. 5, 1940], OSMMP. See also Henry Brown, in *ASCA*, 2(1): 125.

12. James Redpath, "The Fall of Charleston," *NYTR*, Mar. 2, 1865; "The Dark Iconoclast," *HW*, Mar. 25, 1865, 178; Edmund L. Drago, ed., *Broke by War: Letters of a Slave Trader* (Columbia: University of South Carolina Press, 1991), 25n6.

13. "Calhoun's Grave," *NYT*, May 7, 1865; Henry Ward Beecher, "Narrative of His Trip to South Carolina," *IND*, May 11, 1865; *New York World*, Apr. 25, 1865; William M. Meigs, *The Life of John Caldwell Calhoun* (1917; reprint, New York: Da Capo Press, 1970), 2: 466.

14. "The Great Carolinian," *CNC*, Apr. 26, 1887; "Carolina to Calhoun," *CNC*, Nov. 15, 1884; Philip N. Racine, ed., *Gentlemen Merchants: A Charleston Family's Odyssey, 1828–1870* (Knoxville: University of Tennessee Press, 2008), xiii–xxii; Mary Ringhold Spencer, "John C. Calhoun: Post Mortem," *Emory University Quarterly* 11 (June 1955): 98–102; John N. Gregg, "Exhumation of the Body of John C. Calhoun 1863," *SCHM* 57 (Jan. 1956): 57–58; "The Reinterment of John C. Calhoun," *CDN*, Apr. 10, 1871.

15. "Carolina to Calhoun"; "Calhoun's Remains," *NYT*, Nov. 22, 1884; "The Bones of John C. Calhoun," *Rochester Democrat and Chronicle*, Nov. 23, 1884; "A Joint Resolution Appropriating Funds for the Construction and Erection of a Sarcophagus for the Remains of John C. Calhoun," in the *Acts and Joint Resolutions of the General Assembly of the State of South Carolina, Passed at the Regular Session of 1883* (Columbia: Charles A. Calvo Jr., State Printer, 1884), 661; "The Grave of Calhoun," *CNC*, Nov. 15, 1884.

16. Brown, *Civil War Canon*, 45–63; *History of the Calhoun Monument*; "Narrative of the Funeral Honors," 65–66; "The Calhoun Monument," *CNC* (Supplement), Apr. 29, 1882; "Proceedings of the Council," *CC*, July 10, 1854.

17. William Gilmore Simms, "Charleston, The Palmetto City," *Harper's New Monthly Magazine* 15 (June 1857): 12; Brown, "Monumental Legacy," 138; "The Calhoun Monument," *CNC* (Supplement); John P. Radford, "Race, Residence and Ideology: Charleston, South Carolina in the Mid-nineteenth Century," *Journal of Historical Geography* 4 (Oct. 1976): 333–34; Fraser, *Charleston! Charleston!*, 228–29.

18. *History of the Calhoun Monument*, 14.

19. McInnis, *Politics of Taste*, 155–58; "Postscript, April–August, 1850," 253–54; Brown, "Monumental Legacy," 133–34, 142; Anna Wells Rutledge, *Artists in the Life of the Charleston: Through Colony and State, From Restoration to Reconstruction* (Philadelphia: American Philosophical Society, 1949), 146; Anna Wells Rutledge, *Catalogue of Paintings and Sculpture in Council Chamber, City Hall, Charleston, South Carolina* (Charleston: The City Council of Charleston, ca. 1943), 33; Harlan Greene, "Charleston or Bust!" *Charleston*

Magazine, Apr. 2011, charlestonmag.com/features/charleston_or_bust. The Mills bust, which had been removed from City Hall by Charleston's first Republican mayor, Gilbert Pillsbury, was returned in 1931 by Thomas E. Miller.

20. *History of the Calhoun Monument*, 28–29, 32, 36; "The Calhoun Monument," *CNC*, June 16, 1885; "Placed on the Pedestal," *CNC*, Feb. 17, 1887; "The Calhoun Monument," *CNC*, Feb. 15, 1887.

21. Brown, *Civil War Canon*, 81–82; "Calhoun's Wife," *CEP*, Dec. 15, 1894; "Thanksgiving Day," *CNC*, Nov. 29, 1895; "'He Wife's' Turn Next," *CNC*, Nov. 29, 1895. Three of the four allegorical figures were to echo the motto from Powers's sculpture of Calhoun—"Truth, Justice, and the Constitution"—a motto that Powers indicated was chosen by the senator himself. McInnis, *Politics of Taste*, 152.

22. Minutes, n.d., p.26, LMAR; "Thirty Years After," *CNC*, July 21, 1891; "The Memory of Manassas," *CNC*, July 22, 1891; "The Ripley Monument," *CNC*, Apr. 2, 1893; "Survivor's Association of Charleston County," *CNC*, Apr. 3, 1893; Robert N. Rosen, *Confederate Charleston: Illustrated History of the City and the People during the Civil War* (Columbia: University of South Carolina, 1994), 161; Alexander Baring, *My Recollections, 1848–1931* (Santa Barbara, CA: Schauer Printing, 1933), 27–28.

23. Kirk Savage, *Standing Soldiers, Kneeling Slaves: Race, War, and Monument in Nineteenth-Century America* (Princeton, NJ: Princeton University Press, 1997), 129; Thomas J. Brown, *The Public Art of Civil War Commemoration: A Brief History with Documents* (Boston: Bedford Books, 2004), 5.

24. Archibald H. Grimké, "John Caldwell Calhoun," 31–32, 12, Folder 334, Box 18, AGP; Dickson D. Bruce, *Archibald Grimké: Portrait of a Black Independent* (Baton Rouge: Louisiana State University Press, 1993), 18–49.

25. "At Washington," *Huntsville Gazette*, Apr. 30, 1887; Joan Waugh, *U.S. Grant: American Hero, American Myth* (Chapel Hill: University of North Carolina Press, 2009), 279.

26. Mamie Garvin Fields with Karen Fields, *Lemon Swamp and Other Places: A Carolina Memoir* (New York: Free Press, 1983), 57; W. Fitzhugh Brundage, "Meta Warrick's 1907 'Negro Tableaux' and (Re)Presenting African American Historical Memory," *JAH* 89 (Mar. 2003): 1369.

27. Fraser, *Charleston! Charleston!*, 308; Charles J. Holden, *In the Great Maelstrom: Conservatives in Post–Civil War South Carolina* (Columbia: University of South Carolina Press, 2002), 51–57; Walter Edgar, *South Carolina: A History* (Columbia: University of South Carolina Press, 1998), 414–15; Hyman S. Rubin III, "Eight Box Law," in *South Carolina Encyclopedia*, 292; C. Vann Woodward, *The Strange Career of Jim Crow* (1955; repr., New York: Oxford University Press, 2002), 32–33.

28. "Calhoun Unveiled," *CNC*, Apr. 27, 1887; "A Tribute to Calhoun," *NYT*, Apr. 27, 1887; "Unveiling of His Statue," *BS*, Apr. 27, 1887; "Doing Honor to Calhoun," *NYTR*, Apr. 27, 1887; "The Earthquaked City," *NYF*, May 7, 1887.

29. "Calhoun Unveiled"; "The Great Carolinian," *CNC*, Apr. 26, 1887; "The Calhoun Monument," *St. Louis Post-Dispatch*, Apr. 22, 1887; Robert K. Ackerman, *Wade Hampton III* (Columbia: University of South Carolina Press, 2007), 199; Eric Foner, *Reconstruction: America's Unfinished Revolution, 1863–1877* (New York: Harper & Row, 1988), 524–25; Nicholas Lemann, *Redemption: The Last Battle of the Civil War* (New York: Farrar, Straus, and Giroux, 2006), 67–69, 104–34, 180–81.

30. "Calhoun Unveiled"; L.Q.C. Lamar, "Oration on the Life, Character and Public Services of the Hon. John C. Calhoun, Delivered before the Ladies' Calhoun Monument Association and the Public," in *History of the Calhoun Monument*, 102–4.

31. "Doing Honor to Calhoun"; "A Tribute to Calhoun"; Henry S. Holmes, diary, Dec. 2, 1895, pp. 16, 20, CLS.

32. "Charleston News," *NYF,* May 28, 1887.

33. Ibid.; "All Around Town," *CNC,* June 2, 1887; "The Calhoun Monument," *CNC,* Oct. 31, 1895; "The New Monument," *CNC,* Dec. 15, 1895; "A Picture in Bronze," *CNC,* June 10, 1896; "All Around Town," *CNC,* Dec. 2, 1895; "Backward Glances," *CNC,* Dec. 2, 1945; "The Calhoun Monuments," *HW,* Apr. 3, 1897; Brown, "Monumental Legacy," 148; Williams and Hoffius, *Upheaval in Charleston,* 183; "The City by the Sea," *Augusta Chronicle,* Mar. 8, 1890; Holmes, diary, Dec. 2, 1895, p. 20.

34. "All About Town," *CNC,* Feb. 12, 1888; "A Vandal's Work," *CNC,* Sept. 5, 1893; Walter J. Fraser Jr., *Lowcountry Hurricanes: Three Centuries of Storms at Sea and Ashore* (Athens: University of Georgia Press, 2006), 179–82.

35. "Calhoun's Wife," *CEP,* Dec. 15, 1894; "The Dangerous Toy Pistol," *CNC,* Dec. 14, 1894; "Caught the Little Rascals," *CNC,* Dec. 15, 1894.

36. "Arrival of the New Statue," *CNC,* June 9, 1896; "Thanksgiving Day," *CNC,* Nov. 29, 1895; "The Calhoun Monument," Oct. 31, 1895; " 'He Wife's' Turn Next"; "Under the Post's Eyes," *CEP,* Dec. 3, 1895; "Pythian Castle Hall," *CEP,* Aug. 6, 1896; "Sold As Old Metal," *CEP,* Aug. 8, 1896; Brown, *Civil War Canon,* 85–86.

37. "Arrival of the New Statue"; "Completing the Monument," *CNC,* June 11, 1896; "Work on the Monument," *CNC,* June 12, 1896; "Calhoun on Top," *CEP,* June 27, 1896; "Elevating Calhoun," *CNC,* June 28, 1896; "John C. Calhoun's Statue," *NYT,* June 3, 1896; "The Calhoun Monuments," *HW,* Apr. 2, 1897. The first monument was between 48 feet and 59 feet high, while the second is 115 feet tall. "In Memory of Calhoun," *Boston Daily Globe,* Apr. 26, 1887; "Unveiling of His Statue," *BS,* Apr. 27, 1887; "The Great Carolinian," *CNC,* Apr. 26, 1887; Conservation Solutions, Inc., "John C. Calhoun Monument Conservation—Marion Square," conservationsolutionsinc.com/projects/view/374/john-c-calhoun-monument-conservation-marion-square.

38. "Appendix to the History of the Calhoun Monument, Published in 1888" [1898], 2, off-print, Calhoun Pamphlet #5 ½, Published Materials Division, SCL; "The Calhoun Monument," *CNC,* Nov. 17, 1889; Henry S. Holmes, diary, Dec. 2, 1895, p. 21; "All Around Town," *CNC,* Dec. 2, 1895.

39. " 'He Wife's' Turn Next"; Brown, "Monumental Legacy," 148.

40. Edmund L. Drago, *Initiative, Paternalism, and Race Relations: Charleston's Avery Normal Institute* (Athens: University of Georgia Press, 1990), 6; Fields, *Lemon Swamp,* 57.

41. Karen Fields, "What One Cannot Remember Mistakenly," in *History and Memory in African-American Culture,* ed. Genevieve Fabre and Robert O'Meally (New York: Oxford University Press, 1994), 156–58; "Carolina to Calhoun"; "A Cantankerous Crank," *CNC,* May 19, 1887; Timothy Messer-Kruse, *The Haymarket Conspiracy: Transatlantic Anarchist Networks* (Urbana: University of Illinois Press, 2012), 100–105.

42. "Concerning Chalk Marks," *CNC,* Dec. 2, 1894; "Calhoun's Wife," *CEP,* Dec. 15, 1894; *Year Book, 1894, City of Charleston, So. Ca.* (Charleston: Walker, Evans, and Cogswell, 1895), 195; Brown, "Monumental Legacy," 156n57.

43. Brown, *Civil War Canon,* 84–85; Anne E. Marshall, "The 1906 *Uncle Tom's Cabin* Law and the Politics of Race and Memory in Early-Twentieth-Century Kentucky," *JCWE* 1 (Sept. 2011): 377; Savage, *Standing Soldiers, Kneeling Slaves,* 7.

44. Daniel Ravenel, Historical Commission of Charleston, to Mayor and Aldermen of the City of Charleston, June 24, 1946, in *Year Book, 1945: City of Charleston, South Carolina* (Charleston: Walker, Evans, and Cogswell, 1948), 167; Historical Commission of Charleston, Minutes, Nov. 18, 1937, Mar. 31, 1938, Dec. 30, 1938, Feb. 2, 1939, Nov. 7, 1939, Feb. 15, 1945, Sept. 25, 1947, Box 2, RHCC; *City of Charleston Year Book, 1939* (Charleston: Walker, Evans, and Cogswell, 1941), 148; Lucille A. Williams, interview by Edmund L. Drago, Sept. 25, 1984, Folder 69, Box 3, ELDP; Drago, *Initiative, Paternalism, and Race Relations,* 6, 187.

45. Michael Perman, *Struggle for Mastery: Disfranchisement in the South, 1888–1898* (Chapel Hill: University of North Carolina Press, 2001), esp. 91–115; Fraser, *Charleston! Charleston!*, 336.

46. Fields, *Lemon Swamp*, 57; "South Carolina's Condition," *Savannah Tribune*, Apr. 7, 1894.

4. CRADLE OF THE LOST CAUSE

1. "The Survivors' Association," *CNC*, Apr. 13, 1886; "Charleston's Ex-Confeds.," *CNC*, Oct. 8, 1889; "Charleston's Veterans," *CNC*, Apr. 13, 1891; *A Brief History of the Ladies' Memorial Association of Charleston, S.C.* (Charleston: H. P. Cooke & Co., 1880); "Memorial Day in Charleston," *CEP*, May 10, 1897. The Citadel, which had been occupied by federal troops from 1865 until 1879, was reopened in 1882 after a lengthy campaign on the part of alumni. Alexander Macaulay, *Marching in Step: Masculinity, Citizenship, and The Citadel in Post-World War II America* (Athens: University of Georgia Press, 2009), 12–13.

2. " 'Camp Sumter,' " *CNC*, May 19, 1893; "Fall In, Veterans," *CNC*, Feb. 2, 1893; "The Survivors' Association," *CNC*, July 14, 1893; "The Confederate Veterans," *CNC*, Aug. 3, 1893; "The Sons of Veterans," *CNC*, Nov. 14, 1894; "The Sons of Veterans," *CNC*, June 15, 1896; "The Daughters of the Confederacy," *CNC*, Oct. 28, 1894; "Letters from the People," *CNC*, Nov. 11, 1894; Belinda Friedman Gergel, "Irene Goldsmith Kohn: An Assimilated 'New South' Daughter and Jewish Women's Activism in Early Twentieth-Century South Carolina," in *South Carolina Women: Their Lives and Times*, ed. Marjorie Julian Spruill, Valinda W. Littlefield, and Joan Marie Johnson (Athens: University of Georgia Press, 2010), 2: 198; W. Scott Poole, *Never Surrender: Confederate Memory and Conservatism in the South Carolina Upcountry* (Athens: University of Georgia Press, 2004), 185–86.

3. "Veterans in Convention," *CNC*, May 11, 1899; *Minutes of the Ninth Annual Meeting and Reunion of the United Confederate Veterans, Held in the City of Charleston, S.C.* (New Orleans: Hopkins' Printing Office, 1900), 11–18; "Colonel Cornelius Irvine Walker," in *Confederate Military History*, vol. 5, *South Carolina*, ed. Ellison Capers (Atlanta: Confederate Publishing Company, 1899), 887–89; "The Thompson Auditorium," *CEP*, Mar. 3, 1899; "Confederates at Charleston," *Idaho Statesman*, May 11, 1899; *CNC*, Feb. 9, 1900; *CEP*, Apr. 8, 1905; "Confederate Museum Puzzle," *CNC*, Apr. 20, 1910; Walter H. Page to Horace E. Scudder, Mar. 18, 1899, in *The Training of an American: The Earlier Life and Letters of Walter H. Page, 1855–1913*, ed. Burton J. Hendrick (Boston: Houghton Mifflin, 1928), 396.

4. Thomas J. Brown, *Civil War Canon: Sites of Confederate Memory in South Carolina* (Chapel Hill: University of North Carolina Press, 2015), 11–18, 69–70; "Confederate Home Honors Soldiers," *CNC*, Jan. 16, 1939, in MASS; Christine Blanton, "Life of Mary Amarinthia Snowden," *Preservation Progress* 37 (Fall 1994): 7–11; Edmund L. Drago, *Confederate Phoenix: Rebel Children and their Families in South Carolina* (New York: Fordham University Press, 2010), 106–7.

5. "A Wanton Lie," *CNC*, Jan. 26, 1885; Louise Anderson Allen, *A Bluestocking in Charleston: The Life and Career of Laura Bragg* (Columbia: University of South Carolina Press, 2001), 61–62; John Bennett, "Reminiscences of Charleston," [1920], n.p. Folder 1, Box 143, JBP; "Memorial Day," *CNC*, May 3, 1889.

6. Scholars of Civil War memory have focused primarily on cities such as Richmond, Atlanta, and New Orleans and states such as Virginia, Georgia, Kentucky, and Louisiana, rather than Charleston. Charles Reagan Wilson, *Baptized in Blood: The Religion of the Lost*

Cause, 1865–1920 (Athens: University of Georgia Press, 1980); Gaines Foster, *Ghosts of the Confederacy: Defeat, the Lost Cause, and the Emergence of the New South, 1865–1913* (New York: Oxford University Press, 1985); Caroline E. Janney, *Burying the Dead But Not the Past: Ladies' Memorial Associations & the Lost Cause* (Chapel Hill: University of North Carolina Press, 2008); Anne E. Marshall, *Creating a Confederate Kentucky: The Lost Cause and Civil War Memory in a Border State* (Chapel Hill: University of North Carolina Press, 2010); William A. Link, *Atlanta, Cradle of the New South: Race and Remembering in the Civil War's Aftermath* (Chapel Hill: University of North Carolina Press, 2013). Exceptions to this rule are Poole, *Never Surrender* and Brown, *Civil War Canon.*

7. E. Culpeppper Clark, *Francis Warrington Dawson and the Politics of Restoration South Carolina, 1874–1889* (Tuscaloosa: University of Alabama Press, 1980), 9–33; Frank Dawson to his mother, Oct. 26, 1867, Box 6, FWDP.

8. Dale B.J. Randall, *Joseph Conrad and Warrington Dawson: The Record of a Friendship* (Durham, NC: Duke University Press, 1968), 9; Carl R. Osthaus, *Partisans of the Southern Press: Editorial Spokesmen of the Nineteenth Century* (Lexington: University Press of Kentucky, 1994), 159–60; *N.W. Ayer & Son's American Newspaper Annual* (Philadelphia: N.W. Ayer & Son, 1880), 328, 337, 656, 1273; Patricia G. McNeely, Debbra Reddin van Tuyll, and Henry H. Schulte, *Knights of the Quill: Confederate Correspondents and their Civil War Reporting* (West Lafayette, IN: Purdue University Press, 2010), 136–38; Clark, *Francis Warrington Dawson*, 30; Robert Hilliard Woody, *Republican Newspapers of South Carolina* (Charlottesville, VA: Historical Publishing, 1936), 52.

9. Clark, *Francis Warrington Dawson*, 13–23; "James C. Hemphill," *National Cyclopaedia of American Biography* (New York: James T. White & Co., 1895), 2: 29–30; "News and Courier to Lose Its Editor," *CEP*, Jan. 10, 1910; "Mr Hemphill Guest of Honor," *CNC*, Feb. 11, 1910; "How the Palmetto State Aided at the Unveiling," *CNC*, May 31, 1890; "Let the Good Work Go On," *CNC*, Aug. 11, 1898.

10. "Two Stories of Brave Men," *CNC*, Jan. 23, 1880; "No More 'A Nameless Hero,'" *CNC*, Feb. 6, 1880; "An Undying Principle," *CNC*, Dec. 30, 1886; Don H. Doyle, *New Men, New Cities, New South: Atlanta, Nashville, Charleston, Mobile, 1860–1910* (Chapel Hill: University of North Carolina Press, 1990), 159–88, 237; "The New South Nonsense," *CNC*, May 8, 1893.

11. "For the Sake of the Truth of History," *CNC*, June 25, 1885; "Gen. Lee on the Object of the War," *CNC*, May 5, 1885.

12. "The Objects of the Confederate War—What Were They?" *CNC*, June 25, 1885; James D.B. DeBow, *The Interest in Slavery of the Southern Non-Slaveholder* (Charleston: Evans & Cogswell, 1860), 3–4.

13. Link, *Atlanta*, 138–42; Harold E. Davis, *Henry Grady's New South: Atlanta, A Brave & Beautiful City* (Tuscaloosa: University of Alabama Press, 1990), 134; "Mr. Davis and the South," *AC*, Jan. 24, 1882.

14. "Mr. Davis and his Maligners," *CNC*, Feb. 4, 1882; "Contemporaries in a Muddle," *AC*, Feb. 8, 1882.

15. "The War and Slavery," *CNC*, Feb. 18, 1882.

16. "Lincoln and Louisianans," *CNC*, July 12, 1894. See also "President Polk on the War," *CNC*, July 29, 1891; and "What Lincoln Fought for," *CNC*, Aug. 3, 1891.

17. Charles J. Holden, *In the Great Maelstrom: Conservatives in Post–Civil War South Carolina* (Columbia: University of South Carolina Press, 2002), 64–65; "An Active, Useful Life," *CNC*, Nov. 2, 1903; Vernon W. Crane, "Edward McCrady," *Dictionary of American Biography*, vol. 12 (New York: Charles Scribner's Sons, 1933), 1–2; Foster, *Ghosts of the Confederacy*, 49–62; Richard Starnes, "Forever Faithful: The Southern Historical Society and Confederate Historical Memory," *Southern Cultures* 2 (Winter 1996): 177–94.

18. Edward McCrady Jr., "Address of Colonel Edward McCrady, Jr. Before Company A (Gregg's Regiment), First S.C. Volunteers, at the Reunion at Williston, Barnwell County, S.C., 14th July, 1882," in *South Carolina Historical Society Papers* 16 (1888): 246–47.

19. David W. Blight, *Race and Reunion: The Civil War in American Memory* (Cambridge, MA: Belknap Press of Harvard University Press, 2001), 259; "Heroes of the South," *CNC*, May 11, 1900; "The State Survivors' Association," *CC*, Nov. 19, 1869; "One Day for Beauregard," *CNC*, Apr. 8, 1893; Brown, *Civil War Canon*, 112–13; William Lee White and Charles Denny Runion, eds., *Great Things Are Expected of Us: The Letters of Colonel C. Irvine Walker, 10th South Carolina Infantry* (Knoxville: University of Tennessee Press, 2009), xix–xx; C. Irvine Walker, *Guide to Charleston, S.C., with Brief History of the City and Map Thereof* (Charleston: Walker, Evans, and Cogswell, 1919).

20. "Heroes of the South," *CNC*, May 11, 1900. Newspaper references to Stephens in this period regularly mentioned his "cornerstone" speech. See, for example, "Death of Alexander H. Stephens," *Wisconsin State Journal*, Mar. 13, 1883.

21. McCrady, "Address of Colonel Edward McCrady," 246–52.

22. "Evangelist Varley's Offence and Defence," *CNC*, Apr. 9, 1885; "The Sin of Slavery," *CNC*, Apr. 27, 1885. In response to a Camden insurrection scare, South Carolina did, in fact, ban the interstate slave trade in 1816. But state planters never considered abolishing slavery itself, and the controversial ban on the interstate slave trade lasted just three years. Lacy K. Ford, *Deliver Us from Evil: The Slavery Question in the Old South* (New York: Oxford University Press, 2009), 189–92.

23. "Many Hear Col Robert E. Lee," *CNC*, Jan. 20, 1909; Foster, *Ghosts of the Confederacy*, 121, 249n1; "A Lee, of Virginia," *CNC*, Jan. 22, 1909; *Keystone* 10 (Feb. 1909): 12.

24. "The Freedmen as Farmers," *CNC*, Aug. 20, 1873.

25. "The W.L.I. Anniversary," *CNC*, Feb. 24, 1879; Paul R. Begley, "Hugh Smith Thompson," in *The South Carolina Encyclopedia*, ed. Walter Edgar (Columbia: University of South Carolina Press, 2006), 958.

26. "The Vesey Insurrection," *CNC*, Dec. 13, 1885; Frank Dawson to his father, June 13, 1865, Box 6, FWDP; Clark, *Francis Warrington Dawson*, 182.

27. "A Century of Charleston," *CNC*, Jan. 1, 1901; "The Good Old Days of Slavery," *CNC*, Apr. 30, 1890.

28. "What the South Fought For and the Results of the War," *CEP*, Apr. 28, 1905; Edward McCrady Jr., *The History of South Carolina in the Revolution, 1775–1780* (New York: Mac-Millan Co., 1901), 296–97.

29. Holden, *In the Great Maelstrom*, 38, 48; Frederick A. Porcher, undated lecture, pp. 8–9, 11 Folder 2, Box 3, FAPP; Samuel Gaillard Stoney, ed., "The Memoirs of Frederick Adolphus Porcher," *SCHGM* 46 (Oct. 1945): 200; Stephanie McCurry, *Confederate Reckoning: Power and Politics in the Civil War South* (Cambridge, MA: Harvard University Press, 2010), 244–45.

30. Blight, *Race and Reunion*, 222–29, 284–91; Grace Elizabeth Hale, *Making Whiteness: The Culture of Segregation in the South, 1890–1940* (New York: Pantheon Books, 1998), 52–59; K. Stephen Prince, *Stories of the South: Race and the Reconstruction of Southern Identity, 1865–1915* (Chapel Hill: University of North Carolina Press, 2014), 137–52; Micki McElya, *Clinging to Mammy: The Faithful Slave in Twentieth-Century America* (Cambridge, MA: Harvard University Press, 2007), 116–59; "Thousands Coming In," *CEP*, May 10, 1899; "A Great Reunion," *BS*, May 11, 1899; W.M. Grier, "A True and Faithful Slave," *CNC*, May 5, 1899; Walter Duncan, " 'Uncle Jimmie,' Faithful Friend: Devotion and Loyalty Recalled by Death of Aiken Negro," *CNC*, Apr. 20, 1919.

31. [Alexander S. Salley], Secretary of the Historical Commission of South Carolina, to Louisa B. Poppenheim, Feb. 28, 1909, Box 2, PMBC; "Canonized Murder," *CNC*, Oct. 28, 1900; "John Brown and Mrs Stowe," *CNC*, Nov. 3, 1900.

32. "Harriet Beecher Stowe Again," *CC*, Sept. 28, 1869; "New Books," *CNC*, Sept. 27, 1885; Mary Esther Huger, "A Short, Simple Account of the Causes of the Civil War," [1897–1898], p. 11, Folder 10, Box 1, HEP.

33. Bruce E. Baker, *What Reconstruction Meant: Historical Memory in the American South* (Charlottesville: University of Virginia Press, 2008), 21–43; "Slavery and Southern Hospitality," *CNC*, Sept. 19, 1907.

34. "What the South Fought For"; "Senator Tillman's Speech," *CNC*, Mar. 5, 1903; Stephen Kantrowitz, *Ben Tillman and the Reconstruction of White Supremacy* (Chapel Hill: University of North Carolina Press, 2000), 156–97, 280–81.

35. W. Fitzhugh Brundage, *Lynching in the New South: Georgia and Virginia, 1880–1930* (Urbana: University of Illinois Press, 1993), 82–84; "Provocation for Lynching," *CEP*, Apr. 26, 1899.

36. "Distinguished Publicist Here," *CEP*, Dec. 22, 1902; "An Honored Guest," *CNC*, Dec. 24, 1902; Charles Francis Adams II, "The Ethics of Secession," in his *Studies Military and Diplomatic, 1775–1865* (New York: Macmillan Company, 1911), 203–31; Blight, *Race and Reunion*, 359–60.

37. "The Pious Fraud Theory," *CNC*, Dec. 25, 1902; *CEP*, Dec. 27, 1902; "The Ethics of Secession," *Boston Herald*, Dec. 27, 1902; *CNC*, Dec. 28, 1902; *CEP*, Dec. 30, 1902; Edward McCrady Jr. to Charles Francis Adams II, Sept. 10, 1902, Folder 15, Box 8, Reel 25, CFAP; Charles Francis Adams II to Edward McCrady Jr., Sept. 16, 1902, EMP.

38. Theodore Barker, "Address of Maj. Theo. G. Barker, delivered at a meeting of Camp Moultrie, Sons of Confederate Veterans, held on the evening of May 8th, 1895," Folder 13, Box 291, TJFP.

39. James M. McPherson, "Long-Legged Yankee Lies: The Lost Cause Textbook Crusade," in his *This Mighty Scourge: Perspectives on the Civil War* (New York: Oxford University Press, 2007), 97; "The Old Soldiers Must Go," *CNC*, Dec. 12, 1890.

40. Huger, "A Short, Simple Account," 1; "Heroes of the South," *CNC*, May 11, 1900.

41. Caroline E. Janney, *Remembering the Civil War: Reunion and the Limits of Reconciliation* (Chapel Hill: University of North Carolina Press, 2013), 134, 183–85; Karen L. Cox, *Dixie's Daughters: The United Daughters of the Confederacy and the Preservation of Confederate Culture* (Gainesville: University Press of Florida, 2003), 2; Blight, *Race and Reunion*, 272–84; McPherson, "Long-Legged Yankee Lies," 97–98; Foster, *Ghosts of the Confederacy*, 116–19; Fred Arthur Bailey, "The Textbooks of the 'Lost Cause': Censorship and the Creation of Southern State Histories," *Georgia Historical Quarterly* 75 (Fall 1991): 507–33; Herman Hattaway, "Clio's Southern Soldiers: The United Confederate Veterans and History," *Louisiana History: The Journal of the Louisiana Historical Society* 12 (Summer 1971): 213–42; "In the Interest of History," *CNC*, Jan. 4, 1903.

42. Hattaway, "Clio's Southern Soldiers," 218–19; Wilson, *Baptized in Blood*, 55–56; Dewitt Boyd Stone Jr., "Stephen Dill Lee," in *South Carolina Encyclopedia*, 545; Joan Marie Johnson, *Southern Ladies, New Women: Race, Region, and Clubwomen in South Carolina, 1890–1930* (Gainesville: University Press of Florida, 2004), 10–11, 24–59; Drago, *Confederate Phoenix*, 226–27; Joan Marie Johnson, ed., *Southern Women at Vassar: The Poppenheim Family Letters, 1882–1916* (Columbia: University of South Carolina Press, 2002), 1–4; Sidney R. Bland, "Promoting Tradition, Embracing Change: The Poppenheim Sisters of Charleston," in *Searching for a Place: Women in the South Across Four Centuries*, ed. Thomas H. Appleton Jr. and Angela Boswell (Columbia: University of Missouri Press, 2003), 182–89; "The W.L.I.

Veterans," *CNC*, Apr. 10, 1885; "A City in Mourning," *CNC*, Dec. 12, 1889; Mary B. Poppenheim, *Report of the Committee of Education: United Daughters of the Confederacy, Made at Savannah, Georgia, November 13, 1914* (Raleigh: Edwards & Broughton, 1914), 9; *Minutes of the Eleventh Annual Meeting of the United Daughters of the Confederacy, Held in St. Louis, MO., October 4–8, 1904* (Nashville: Press of Foster & Webb, 1905), 197–99; "Editorial," *Keystone* 11 (June 1900): 3.

43. *Minutes of the Fourth Annual Meeting of the United Daughters of the Confederacy, Held in Baltimore, Maryland, November 10–12, 1897* (Nashville: Press of Foster & Webb, 1898), 37; Mary B. Poppenheim et al., *The History of the United Daughters of the Confederacy* (Richmond: Garrett and Massie, 1925), 135; Mary B. Poppenheim, "Daughters of the Confederacy," *Keystone* 7 (Dec. 1899): 9.

44. "The Eighth Annual Convention of the South Carolina Division, U.D.C.," *Keystone* 5 (Dec. 1903): 7; "An Account of the Ninth Annual Convention of the South Carolina Division, U.D.C., held November 29th to December 1st, 1904," *Keystone* 6 (Jan. 1905): 11; *Keystone* 7 (Dec. 1905): 15; *Keystone* 6 (Mar. 1905): 10; "In the Interest of History"; "Historical Programs," *Keystone* 11 (Nov. 1909): 9.

45. "United Daughters of the Confederacy, State Division of South Carolina," *Keystone* 5 (May 1904): 6; "Extract from the Report of Miss Rebecca Alston to the Daughters of the Confederacy," *Keystone* 1 (June 1899): 11–12; "The Daughters of the Confederacy," *Keystone* 8 (Jan. 1900): 5; "Daughters of the Confederacy. Charleston Chapter," *Keystone* 10 (Mar. 1900): 10.

46. *Keystone* 6 (Mar. 1905): 10; "List of Books which Are Commended for Southern Libraries," *Keystone* 9 (Apr. 1908): 11–13.

47. "Notable Work of the Women," *CNC*, Feb. 7, 1904; Wilson, *Baptized in Blood*, 126; "List of Books which Are Commended for Southern Libraries," *Keystone* 9 (Apr. 1908): 11–13; Edward Eggleston, *A History of the United States and Its People* (New York: D. Appleton and Co., 1888), 310.

48. *Keystone* 7 (Dec. 1905): 15; *CEP*, Feb. 22, 1905; "Change of School Books," *CEP*, Sept. 25, 1907; Waddy Thompson, *A History of the United States* (Boston: D.C. Heath & Co., 1904), 341–43.

49. Cox, *Dixie's Daughters*, 90; Poppenheim, *Report on the Committee of Education*, 10; *Minutes of the Twenty-Third Annual Convention of the United Daughters of the Confederacy, held in Dallas, Texas, November 8 to 11, 1916* (Raleigh, NC: Edwards & Broughton, 1917), 69–70.

50. Bruce E. Baker, "Mary Chevillette Simms Oliphant," in *South Carolina Encyclopedia*, 682; Baker, *What Reconstruction Meant*, 168; "School Books Are Adopted for State," *CNC*, June 23, 1917; "Various Factors in Selection of Books," *CNC*, June 24, 1917; William Gilmore Simms, *The History of South Carolina*, revised and updated by Mary C. Simms Oliphant (Columbia: State Company, Printers, 1917), 239, 255.

51. Amy L. Heyse, "Teachers of the Lost Cause: The United Daughters of the Confederacy and the Rhetoric of Their Catechisms" (Ph.D. diss., University of Maryland, 2006), 33–37, 175–77, 261–63, 274–75, 296–97, 310–11.

52. Minutes, June 3, 1915, p. 208, and "Report of the President of the Ladies' Memorial Association, Charleston, S.C, June 5, 1916" in Minutes, June 5, 1916, p.3 [after p. 223], both in LMAR; Blight, *Race and Reunion*, 70–71; "Mrs. Videau Marion Legare Beckwith," in *Lineage Book: National Society of the Daughters of the American Revolution* (Washington, DC: National Society of the Daughters of the American Revolution, 1915), 40: 279.

53. "Flower-Strewn Graves," *New York Evening Post*, May 14, 1867; "A Yankee Custom Borrowed By Rebels," *Cincinnati Daily Gazette*, May 17, 1867; Janney, *Remembering the Civil*

War, 98–99; "Honors to the Dead," *NYT*, June 5, 1868; "Commemoration Day," *Cincinnati Daily Gazette*, May 31, 1869; "The Origins of Decoration Day," *Burlington Free Press*, June 3, 1881; "The First Decoration Day," *Boston Herald*, June 1, 1899; John Redpath, letter to the editor, *NYT*, May 27, 1916.

54. Charles J. Holden, "'Is Our Love for Wade Hampton Foolishness?' South Carolina and the Lost Cause," in *The Myth of the Lost Cause and Civil War History*, ed. Gary W. Gallagher and Alan T. Nolan (Bloomington, Indiana University Press, 2000), 60–61, 67–74; Clyde Breese, *How Grand a Flame: A Chronicle of a Plantation Family, 1831–1947* (Chapel Hill: Algonquin Books of Chapel Hill, 1992), 166; Rod Andrew Jr., *Wade Hampton: Confederate Warrior to Southern Redeemer* (Chapel Hill: University of North Carolina Press, 2008), 323–27.

55. "Memorial Exercises," *CNC*, Apr. 11, 1902; "Charleston's Tribute," *CNC*, Apr. 13, 1902; "Many Eloquent Tributes," *CNC*, Apr. 14, 1902; "Let Charleston Honor Hampton," *CNC*, Apr. 13, 1902; "Monuments to Hampton," *CNC*, Apr. 18, 1902; "Our Own Hampton Monument," *CNC*, Apr. 18, 1902; "Erect It On Citadel Square," *CNC*, Apr. 18, 1902; Baker, *What Reconstruction Meant*, 39–40.

56. *Year Book, 1903, City of Charleston, So. Ca.* (Charleston: Daggett Printing Co., 1904), 144; Kevin R. Eberle, *A History of Charleston's Hampton Park* (Charleston: History Press, 2012), 75; John P. Radford, "Race, Residence and Ideology: Charleston, South Carolina in the Mid-nineteenth Century," *Journal of Historical Geography* 2 (Oct. 1976): 333–46; Fraser, *Charleston! Charleston!*, 338; Mamie Garvin Fields with Karen Fields, *Lemon Swamp and Other Places: A Carolina Memoir* (New York: Free Press 1983), 57. An obelisk in honor of Wade Hampton was also installed in Marion Square in 1912. "Shaft of Granite in Hero's Memory," *CEP*, Mar. 29, 1912. The segregation of Hampton Park was by custom rather than law, despite early appeals to formally ban African Americans from the park. "Hampton Park for Whites," *CEP*, Sept. 29, 1903; "The Negroes and the Parks," *CEP*, Oct. 3, 1903; "Separate Park for the Negroes," *CEP*, Oct. 7, 1903.

5. Black Memory in the Ivory City

1. T. Cuyler Smith, "The Charleston Exposition," *IND*, Jan. 16, 1902.

2. "Things of Beauty," *The Exposition,* Oct. 1901; "The West Indian Building," *CNC*, Oct. 4, 1901.

3. W.D. Parsons, "Charleston and the Exposition with Impressions of the South," *Inter-State Journal: An Illustrated Monthly of the Connecticut Valley* 4–5 (Mar.–Apr. 1902): n.p.; "Charleston and Her 'West Indian Exposition,'" *American Monthly Review of Reviews* 25 (Jan. 1902): 60; "A Trip to Hampton Park," *CNC*, Aug. 14, 1903; Moses P. Handy, ed., *The Official Directory of the World's Columbian Exposition, May 1st to October 30th, 1893: A Reference Book* (Chicago: W.B. Conkey Co., 1893), 203–4; "Making an Exposition," *CNC*, July 28, 1901; Bradford Lee Gilbert to Booker T. Washington, June 4, 1901, in the *Booker T. Washington Papers*, vol. 6, *1901–1902*, ed. Louis R. Harlan and Raymond Smock (Urbana: University of Illinois Press, 1977), 145.

4. "The Negro Group Will Be Removed," *CEP*, Nov. 8, 1901.

5. Thomas E. Miller to Booker T. Washington, Oct. 12, 1901, Container 187, Reel 187, BTWP; "A $1,000 Gift," *Cleveland Gazette*, Feb. 8, 1902.

6. "Charleston and Its Exposition," *NYT*, Dec. 1, 1901.

7. Miller to Washington, Oct. 12, 1901. Reports on Washington's opinion about the controversy are conflicting. "Mr. Washington's Lecture," *CNC*, Sept. 13, 1901; "A Leader of His

People," *CNC*, Sept. 12, 1901; "Negro Group Will Be Removed"; "Offensive Statue Removed," *AC*, Nov. 12, 1901; "Negroes Protest Against a Statue" *AC*, Nov. 2, 1901; "The Group of Negro Life in the South," *NYTR*, Nov. 3, 1901.

8. "Rev. O.D. Robinson, D.D.," in Horace Talbert, *The Sons of Allen: Together with a Sketch of the Rise and Progress of Wilberforce University, Wilberforce, Ohio* (Xenia, OH: Aldine Press, 1906), 176–77; Bernard E. Powers Jr., *Black Charlestonians: A Social History, 1822–1885* (Fayetteville: University of Arkansas Press, 1994), 206; "The West Indian Show," *Colored American* 9 (June 29, 1901): 8; "Charleston Notes," *Savannah Tribune*, Aug. 17, 1901; "Negroes Protest Against Statue"; J.C. Hemphill, "A Short History of the South Carolina Inter-state and West Indian Exposition," in *Year Book, 1902: City of Charleston, So. Ca.* (Charleston: Walker, Evans, and Cogswell, 1903), 139.

9. *CNC*, Oct. 24, 1901; "A Veritable Work of Art," *CNC*, Oct. 25, 1901; *KC*, Nov. 13, 1901; "The Negro Group," *CEP*, Nov. 7, 1901 (*Macon Telegraph* quote).

10. "The Negro Group," *The Exposition*, Nov. 1901.

11. Hemphill, "A Short History," 107, 139; Nathan Cardon, "The South's 'New Negroes' and African American Visions of Progress at the Atlanta and Nashville International Expositions, 1895–1897," *JSH* 80 (May 2014): 318; Bruce G. Harvey, " 'Struggles and Triumphs' Revisited: Charleston's West Indian Exposition and the Development of Urban Progressivism," *PSCHA* (1988): 91; "Condensed Statement of Debits and Credits," June 11, 1902, Folder 1, Volume 1, SCIS; Bruce G. Harvey, *World's Fairs in a Southern Accent: Atlanta, Nashville, and Charleston, 1895–1902* (Knoxville: University of Tennessee Press, 2014).

12. *Year Book, 1903, City of Charleston, So. Ca.* (Charleston: Daggett Printing Co., 1904), 146; Hemphill, "A Short History," 171; "That Exposition Statuary, Again," *CNC*, July 27, 1906; "Now for Hampton Park," *CNC*, Sept. 10, 1903; "A Trip to Hampton Park," *CNC*, Aug, 14, 1903; "With Paint and Shellac," *CNC*, Nov. 2, 1904; "Out at Hampton Park," *CNC*, Aug. 9, 1906; *Year Book, 1904, City of Charleston, So. Ca.* (Charleston: Lucas and Richardson Co., 1905), 207; Kevin R. Eberle, *A History of Charleston's Hampton Park* (Charleston: History Press, 2012), 75; John P. Radford, "Race, Residence and Ideology: Charleston, South Carolina in the Mid-Nineteenth Century," *Journal of Historical Geography* 2 (Oct. 1976): 333–46; Walter J. Fraser Jr., *Charleston! Charleston! The History of a Southern City* (Columbia: University of South Carolina Press, 1989), 338.

13. "The Negro's Best Friends," *CNC*, Jan. 2, 1901; William C. Hine, "Thomas E. Miller and the Early Years of South Carolina State University," *Carologue: Bulletin of the South Carolina Historical Society* 12 (Winter 1992): 11–12; Bruce E. Baker, *What Reconstruction Meant: Historical Memory in the American South* (Charlottesville: University of Virginia Press, 2009), 81; George Tindall, *South Carolina Negroes, 1877–1900* (Columbia: University of South Carolina Press, 1952), 81, 83–84.

14. "Live and Work for the Future," *CNC*, Jan. 2, 1901; Henry H. Lesesne, "Martin Witherspoon Gary," in *The South Carolina Encyclopedia*, ed. Walter Edgar (Columbia: University of South Carolina Press, 2006), 361.

15. "They Enjoyed It Immensely," *CNC*, Jan. 2, 1902; "Negro Day at Exposition," *CNC*, Jan. 2, 1902.

16. "Negro Day at Exposition." On the changing nature of Emancipation Day celebrations, see Kathleen Ann Clark, *Defining Moments: African American Commemoration and Political Culture in the South, 1863–1913* (Chapel Hill: University of North Carolina Press, 2005), 188–228; and Mitch Kachun, *Festivals of Freedom: Memory and Meaning in African American Emancipation Celebrations, 1808–1915* (Amherst: University of Massachusetts Press, 2003), 177–82.

17. "Negro Day at Exposition." Miller failed to acknowledge in his speech the memorial to Robert Gould Shaw and the Massachusetts 54th Regiment, erected in Boston Common in

1897, which did recognize black soldiers. Savage, *Standing Soldiers, Kneeling Slaves*, 193–208.

18. "Negro Day at Exposition." On the Fort Mill monument, see Savage, *Standing Soldiers, Kneeling Slaves*, 155–61.

19. "Honor to Faithful Slaves," *AI*, May 27, 1896; Savage, *Standing Soldiers, Kneeling Slaves*, 160 (quote).

20. *MSL*, Aug. 7, 1895; "A Monument to the Southern Slave," *CNC*, July 16, 1895. The *Tribune*'s remarks were reported in "Personal Mention," *MSL*, July 28, 1895.

21. "Monument to Southern Slaves," *INF*, Aug. 3, 1895.

22. "Negro Day at Exposition."

23. "A Monument to the Southern Slave"; "A Confederate Monument to the Negro," *CNC*, June 21, 1907; Micki McElya, *Clinging to Mammy: The Faithful Slave in Twentieth-Century America* (Cambridge, MA, Harvard University Press, 2007), 116–59.

24. "Negro Day at Exposition."

25. Savage, *Standing Soldiers, Kneeling Slaves*, 161; W. Fitzhugh Brundage, "Meta Warrick's 1907 'Negro Tableaux' and (Re)Presenting African American Historical Memory," *JAH* 89 (Mar. 2003): 1388; Anne E. Marshall, "The 1906 *Uncle Tom's Cabin* Law and the Politics of Race and Memory in Early-Twentieth-Century Kentucky," *JCWE* 1 (Sept. 2011): 387; Angelina Ray Johnston and Robinson Wise, "Commemorating Faithful Slaves, Mammies, and Black Confederates," *Commemorative Landscapes of North Carolina*, University of North Carolina Library, docsouth.unc.edu/commland/features/essays/ray_wise.

26. Miller to Washington, Oct. 12, 1901.

27. "The State's Survey," *State*, Jan. 4, 1901; Coleman L. Blease, quoted in Hine, "Thomas E. Miller and the Early Years," 12; Ernest McPherson Lander Jr., *A History of South Carolina, 1865–1960*, 2nd ed. (Columbia: University of South Carolina Press, 1970), 154.

28. Thomas J. Jackson to J.H. Holloway, Sept. 23, 1901; G.S. Dickerton to J.H. Holloway, July 23, 1905; James E. Davis to J.H. Holloway, Mar. 25, 1907; Arthur L. Macbeth to J.H. Holloway, June 12, 1907; Thomas J. Colloway to J.H. Holloway, [ca. 1908]; and "Century Fellowship Society," all in HFS; Harlan Greene and Jessica Lancia, "The Holloway Scrapbook: The Legacy of a Charleston Family," *SCHM* 111 (Jan.–Apr. 2010): 5–33.

29. J.H. Holloway, letter to the editor, *CNC*, May 26, 1907; "Century Fellowship Society"; J.H. Holloway to Theodore Jervey, July 26, 1907, Folder 2, Box 481, TJFP.

30. Greene and Lancia, "Holloway Scrapbook," 22–33; James H. Holloway to Theodore Jervey, n.d., in HFS; Charlene Gunnells, "Desecration Reparations: Graves Found at College Site to Be Honored," *CPC*, Jan. 25, 2001; Charlene Gunnells, "College Construction Uncovers 4 Cemeteries: C of C Plans to Commemorate Burial Site," *CPC*, Mar. 24, 2001.

31. Tindall, *South Carolina Negroes*, 286–88; W. Fitzhugh Brundage, *The Southern Past: A Clash of Race and Memory* (Cambridge, MA: Belknap Press of Harvard University Press, 2005), 72–73; "The Glorious Fourth," *CEP*, July 3, 1897; "Negro Day at Exposition"; "Birth of 1905 Is Quietly Kept," *CEP*, Jan. 2, 1905; "Now for 'Glorious Fourth,'" *CNC*, July 4, 1906; Savage, *Standing Soldiers, Kneeling Slaves*, 180–208; Charles Johnson Jr., *African American Soldiers in the National Guard: Recruitment and Deployment during Peacetime and War* (Westport, CT: Greenwood Press, 1992), 76–78; Roger D. Cunningham, "'They Are as Proud of Their Uniform as Any Who Serve in Virginia': African American Participation in the Virginia Volunteers, 1872–1899," in *Brothers to the Buffalo Soldiers: Perspectives on the African American Militia and Volunteers, 1865–1917*, ed. Bruce A. Glasrud (Columbia: University of Missouri Press, 2011), 63–64.

32. "A Hampton Fourth of July," *CNC*, July 5, 1877; "Colored People and the Fourth," *CNC*, July 3, 1878; *Revised Ordinances of the City of Charleston, South Carolina* (Charleston: Walker, Evans, and Cogswell, 1903), 309; Adam Rothman, "'This Special Picnic': The Fourth of July in Charleston, South Carolina, 1865–1900," May 1995, unpublished paper in authors' possession, 28–30.

33. "'The Fourth' Under a Cloud," *CNC*, July 5, 1881; "The Colored People," *CNC*, July 5, 1882; "The Colored Troops," *CNC*, Jan. 3, 1882; "Emancipation Day," *CNC*, Jan. 2, 1884; "A Happy New Year To All," *CNC*, Jan. 1, 1887; "Emancipation Day," *CNC*, Jan. 2, 1883; "The First Day of the New Year," *CNC*, Jan. 2, 1886; "All Africa Was Here," *CNC*, Jan. 3, 1892; "Celebrated in Divisions," *The Freeman*, Jan. 19, 1895; "Celebrated Emancipation Day," *CNC*, Jan. 2, 1913; "Emancipation Day Observed By Negroes," *CNC*, Jan. 2, 1919; "Charleston News Gleaned in a Day," *State*, Jan. 2, 1920.

34. "The Fourth of July," *CNC*, July 5, 1883; Susan Millar Williams and Stephen G. Hoffius, *Upheaval in Charleston: Earthquake and Murder on the Eve of Jim Crow* (Athens: University of Georgia Press, 2011), 216; "The Day That Never Dies," *CNC*, July 6, 1886; "Too-la-loo," *CNC*, July 1, 1887; "The Fourth in the City," *CNC*, July 5, 1887; "A Little Mixed on History," *CNC*, July 5, 1887; "The Day We Celebrate," *CNC*, July 4, 1888; "A Phenomenal Fourth," *CNC*, July 5, 1888; "The Fourth at St. Andrew's," *CNC*, July 5, 1888; "The Day We Celebrate," *CNC*, July 4, 1892; "The Nation's Birthday," *CNC*, July 5, 1892; "A Fin De Siecle Fourth," *CNC*, July 5, 1895; "Independence Day in Charleston," *CEP*, July 5, 1897; "The Birthday of Uncle Sam," *CEP*, July 4, 1899; "Gave Up the Day to Celebration," *CEP*, July 4, 1905; "Quiet Celebration of Fourth," *CNC*, July 5, 1913.

35. "The Same Old Fourth," *CNC*, July 5, 1890; "More or Less Glorious," *CNC*, July 5, 1900; Mamie Garvin Fields with Karen Fields, *Lemon Swamp and Other Places: A Carolina Memoir* (New York: Free Press, 1983), 55–57.

36. "Emancipation Day," *CNC*, Dec. 31, 1909; "Emancipation Day Observed By Negroes"; "Emancipation Day," *CEP*, Jan. 1, 1920; "Charleston News Gleaned in a Day"; "Emancipation Day Is Observed Here," *CNC*, Jan. 2, 1921; "Tempus Fugit in Charleston," *CEP*, Jan. 1, 1942; "Parade to Mark Emancipation Day," *CNC*, Jan. 1, 1958; Baker, *What Reconstruction Meant*, 84; Fields, *Lemon Swamp*, 227–29.

37. Dickson D. Bruce, *Archibald Grimké: Portrait of a Black Independent* (Baton Rouge: Louisiana State University Press, 1993), 67–82, 88–90, 93–200; Douglas R. Egerton, *He Shall Go Out Free: The Lives of Denmark Vesey, Revised and Updated Edition* (Lanham, MD: Rowman & Littlefield, 2004), 3–4n1, 240–41, 253–54; Archibald H. Grimké, *Right on the Scaffold, or the Martyrs of 1822, American Negro Academy: Occasional Papers No 7* (Washington, DC: American Negro Academy, 1901), n.p., gutenberg.org/files/31290/31290-h /31290-h.htm. Grimké may also have heard details about the Vesey episode from his aunt Angelina, who was a teenager living in Charleston during the trial and execution.

38. Baker, *What Reconstruction Meant*, 70. Baker was writing here about the countermemory of Reconstruction, but his insight about how memory functioned in the Jim Crow South applies equally well to black memories of slavery.

39. "A Negro to His People," *CNC*, Nov. 19, 1905; Club Minutes, 1924, Folder 3, Box 1; Club Minutes, 1931, 1932, Folder 4, Box 1, and Jenatte Keeble Cox, "A History—by Administrations—of the Phillis Wheatley Literary and Social Club," Folder 3, Box 1, all in PWLSCP; Joan Marie Johnson, "'Drill into us ... the Rebel Tradition': The Contest over Southern Identity in Black and White Women's Clubs, 1898–1930," *JSH* 66 (Aug. 2000): 548–52; Georgette Mayo, "Susan Dart Butler and Ethel Martin Bolden: South Carolina's Pioneer African American Librarians," in *South Carolina Women: Their Lives and Times*, ed. Marjorie Julian Spruill, Valinda W. Littlefield, and Joan Marie Johnson (Athens: University of Georgia Press, 2012), 158–61.

40. Michael Fultz, "Charleston, 1919–1920: The Final Battle in the Emergence of the South's Urban African American Teaching Corps," *Journal of Urban History* 27 (July 2001): 636–49; Fields, *Lemon Swamp*, 44–45; Peter F. Lau, *Democracy Rising: South Carolina and the*

Fight for Black Equality Since 1865 (Lexington: University of Kentucky Press, 2006), 33–48; R. Scott Baker, *Paradoxes of Desegregation: African American Struggles for Educational Equity in Charleston, South Carolina, 1926–1972* (Columbia: University of South Carolina Press, 2006), 105.

41. Fields, *Lemon Swamp*, 208; Mamie Garvin Fields, fifth grade history lesson plans, Folder 1, Box 2, MGFP; Harry F. Estill, *The Beginner's History of Our Country* (Dallas: Southern Publishing Co., 1904); *Report of the Historical Committee, Eleventh Annual Reunion Convention of the United Sons of Confederate Veterans, New Orleans, LA, April 25–27, 1906* (Nashville: Brandon Printing Co., 1907), 175, 214; Baker, *Paradoxes of Desegregation*, 1, 14–15.

42. Edmund L. Drago, *Initiative, Paternalism, and Race Relations: Charleston's Avery Normal Institute* (Athens: University of Georgia Press, 1990), 110, 126–27; Fields, *Lemon Swamp*, 40–45, 53–55; Katherine Mellen Charron, *Freedom's Teacher: The Life of Septima Clark* (Chapel Hill: University of North Carolina Press, 2009), 42.

43. Drago, *Initiative, Paternalism, and Race Relations*, 110–11; Johnson "'Drill into Us . . . the Rebel Tradition,'" 557; Joseph Hoffman, interview by Edmund L. Drago and Eugene C. Hunt, Sept. 25, 1980, and Oct. 9, 1980, ANIOHP.

44. Drago, *Initiative, Paternalism, and Race Relations*, 145–48, 169–70, 182, 229–30, 252; Edmund L. Drago, notes on an interview with Eugene C. Hunt, Dec. 4, 1985; Edmund L. Drago, notes on an interview with Dr. Leroy Anderson; and Sadie Green Oglesby, interview by Edmund L. Drago, Sept. 14, 1980, all in Folder 69, Box 3, ELDP; Michael Graves, interview by Edmund L. Drago, Mar. 7, 1985, ANIOHP; "Lincoln Legacy," *AT*, Jan. 1948.

45. Drago, *Initiative, Paternalism, and Race Relations*, 229, 252; C.W. Birnie, "Education of the Negro in Charleston, South Carolina, Prior to the Civil War," *JNH* 12 (Jan. 1927): 13–21; Brundage, *Southern Past*, 155–77; "Negro History Week Observed at Avery," *AT*, Feb. 1932; "Why We Celebrate Negro History Week," *AT*, Feb. 1941; Louise Wright, "Avery Celebrates Negro History Week," *AT*, Feb. 1947.

46. Cynthia McCottry-Smith, "Slavery Through Avery Eyes," *Avery Messenger* 6 (Spring 2008): 10; Gwendolyn A. Simmons, quoted in "The Effects of Slavery," *Avery Messenger* 6 (Spring 2008): 11.

47. "Library of Avery Normal Institute," n.d., Folder 77, Box 4; Alphonso William Hoursey, "A Follow-up Survey of Graduates of Avery Institute, Charleston, South Carolina, For Years 1930–1940" (master's thesis, University of Michigan, 1941), 17, Folder 7, Box 1; Mrs. Charlotte DeBerry Tracy, interview by Edmund L. Drago, Nov. 24, 1938, Folder 69, Box 3; and Julia Brogdon Purnell, interview by Edmund L. Drago, Nov. 13, 1987, Folder 70, Box 3, all in ELDP; Drago, *Initiative, Paternalism, and Race Relations*, 230–31.

48. Felder Hutchinson, quoted in "The Effects of Slavery," 11; Simmons, quoted in "The Effects of Slavery," 11.

49. Tracy, interview; Drago, *Initiative, Paternalism, and Race Relations*, 128–38; Charron, *Freedom's Teacher*, 43–44; Fields, *Lemon Swamp*, 227.

50. Charron, *Freedom's Teacher*, 70 (quote); Drago, notes on an interview with Dr. Leroy Anderson; Brundage, *Southern Past*, 140.

51. Drago, *Initiative, Paternalism, and Race Relations*, 160; "Dr. John A. McFall," *CNC*, July 24, 1954; Sonya Fordham, "A Conversation with Edward Ball," in Edward Ball, *Slaves in the Family* (New York: Farrar, Straus, and Giroux, 2001), 513–14.

52. Walter Johnson, *River of Dark Dreams: Slavery and Empire in the Cotton Kingdom* (Cambridge, MA: Harvard University Press 2013), 216; Drago, notes on an interview with Dr. Leroy Anderson; Drago, notes on an interview with Eugene C. Hunt.

53. Edwin A. Harleston to [Elise Forrest], [late 1919 or early 1920], Folder 6, Box 61, EAHP; Susan V. Donaldson, "Charleston's Racial Politics of Historical Preservation: The Case of

Edwin Harleston," in *Renaissance in Charleston: Art and Life in the Carolina Lowcountry, 1900–1940*, ed. Harlan Greene and James M. Hutchisson (Athens: University of Georgia Press, 2003), 189; Program, Lincoln-Douglass Memorial Meeting of the Charleston Branch of the NAACP at Zion Presbyterian Church, Feb. 13, 1919, Folder 11, Box 62, EAPH.

54. Augustus Ladson, "Attempted Insurrection in 1822: Thirty-Five Hung on Oak Tree in Ashley Avenue," 2, FWPSCL; W.E.B. Du Bois, "The Perfect Vacation," *The Crisis* 40 (Aug. 1931): 279; "Ashley Avenue Oak Is Part of Charleston's History," *CNC*, Dec. 28, 1964; "Study Leader Says S.C. Steeped in Black History," *CNC*, July 19, 1969; John A. Alston, "Oak Giveaway Is Popular," *CNC*, Aug. 23, 1973; David Robertson, *Denmark Vesey: The Buried Story of America's Largest Slave Rebellion and the Man Who Led It* (Knopf: New York, 1999), 129–30.

55. Henry Brown, in *ASCA*, 2(1): 123; Susan Hamilton, in *ASCA*, 2(2): 234; Grace and Knickerbacker Davis, "'Thenceforward, and Forever Free,'" *Forward*, magazine clipping, [1941 or 1942], 12, OSMMP; Frederic Bancroft, *Slave Trading in the Old South* (1931; repr., Columbia: University of South Carolina Press, 1996), 171n11; Frederic Bancroft to Sidney S. Riggs, June 19, 1922, and Sidney S. Riggs to Frederic Bancroft, June 28, 1922, both in Box 89, FBP; Robert P. Stockton, letter to the editor, *CPC*, Apr. 9, 1988; Trip DuBard, "Slave Museum's Fate Remains Up in the Air," *Marietta Daily Journal*, Apr. 9, 1987.

56. "An Old-Time Negro Slave-Holder," *CNC*, May 21, 1907; "Negro Slaveholders in Charleston," *CNC*, May 18, 1907; "As to Negro Slaveholders," *CNC*, May 29, 1907; "Negroes Owned Slaves," *NYT*, May 23, 1907; "Colored Slave Owners," *NYT*, May 26, 1907; Stratton Lawrence, "'Terrorist' or 'Freedom Fighter'? Efforts to Honor Denmark Vesey Running into Financial, Historical Obstacles," *CCP*, Apr. 26, 2006.

57. "The Negro as a Slaveholder," *CNC*, May 26, 1907; Greene and Lancia, "Holloway Scrapbook," 11.

58. "'Negro Slaveholders,'" *CNC*, May 25, 1907; Drago, *Initiative, Paternalism, and Race Relations*, 56. Although the *News and Courier* identified the correspondent as L.L. Dart, the biographical details referred to in the letter suggest strongly that it was written by John L. Dart.

59. Marcellus Forrest, interview by Edmund L. Drago, Eugene C. Hunt, and Margaretta P. Childs, Feb. 12, 1981, ANIOHP.

60. Septima Poinsette Clark, *Echo in My Soul* (New York: E.P. Dutton, 1962), 41; Septima Poinsette Clark, interview by Jacquelyn Dowd Hall, transcript, July 25, 1976, SOHP; Peter Poinsette, interview by Edmund L. Drago and Eugene C. Hunt, Mar. 31, 1981, ANIOHP; Charron, *Freedom's Teacher*, 19–24.

61. "The 'Fourth of July' in Charleston 50 Years Ago," *CNC*, July 4, 1926; "Concert by Plantation Melody Singers," *CEP*, Feb. 26, 1927. For more on the Plantation Melody Singers, see chapter 7.

62. Brundage, *Southern Past*, 221.

6. AMERICA'S MOST HISTORIC CITY

1. George F. Durgin, "Visions and Impressions of the Southland," *Zion's Herald*, Mar. 21, 1906; "In Memoriam," *Bostonia* 8 (July 1907): 25; *CNC*, Feb. 17, 1906.

2. Durgin, "Visions and Impressions of the Southland." Like so many tourists then and today, Durgin appears to have mistaken the City Market for Charleston's slave-trading district.

3. Henry James, *The American Scene: Together with Three Essays from 'Portraits of Places'* (1907; reprint, New York: Charles Scribner's Sons, 1946), 418.

4. James, *American Scene*, 418; Thomas J. Brown, *Civil War Canon: Sites of Confederate Memory in South Carolina* (Chapel Hill: University of North Carolina Press, 2015), 168–70; Reiko Hillyer, *Designing Dixie: Tourism, Memory, and Urban Space in the New South* (Charlottesville: University of Virginia Press, 2015), 5.

5. Nina Silber, *The Romance of Reunion: Northerners and the South, 1865–1900* (Chapel Hill: University of North Carolina Press, 1993), 66–92; Rebecca Cawood McIntyre, *Souvenirs of the Old South: Northern Tourism and Southern Mythology* (Gainesville: University Press of Florida, 2011); W. Fitzhugh Brundage, *The Southern Past: A Clash of Race and Memory* (Cambridge, MA: Belknap Press of Harvard University Press, 2005), 183–90; Hillyer, *Designing Dixie*, 27–32.

6. McIntyre, *Souvenirs of the Old South*, 39; Michael Grunwald, *The Swamp: The Everglades, Florida, and the Politics of Paradise* (New York: Simon and Schuster, 2006), 103–4; Hillyer, *Designing Dixie*, 80–87; Constance Woolson, "Up the Ashley and Cooper," *Harper's Monthly* 52 (Dec. 1875): 2; Silber, *Romance of Reunion*, 72–73.

7. Edward King, *The Great South: A Record of Journeys* (Hartford, CT: American Publishing Co., 1875), 441; Oliver Bell Bunce, "Charleston and Its Suburbs," in *Picturesque America*, ed. William Cullen Bryant (New York: Appleton, 1872), 1: 199.

8. Woolson, "Up the Ashley and Cooper," 22–23; King, *The Great South*, 451; Bunce, "Charleston and Its Suburbs," 208; McIntyre, *Souvenirs of the Old South*, 89–92; Silber, *Romance of Reunion*, 76–78.

9. Dona Brown, *Inventing New England: Regional Tourism in the Nineteenth Century* (Washington, DC: Smithsonian Institution Press, 1995), 8–9; Woolson, "Up the Ashley and Cooper," 7; Bunce, "Charleston and Its Suburbs," 208.

10. Bunce, "Charleston and Its Suburbs," 203, 208; Mary Pinckney Battle, "Confronting Slavery in Historic Charleston: Changing Tourism Narratives in the Twenty-First Century" (Ph.D. diss., Emory University, 2013), 77; King, *The Great South*, 430, 435, 443; McIntyre, *Souvenirs of the Old South*, 104.

11. McIntyre, *Souvenirs of the Old South*, 103; Silber, *Romance of Reunion*, 77; Bunce, "Charleston and Its Suburbs," 205.

12. James Clayton Prentiss, *The Charleston City Guide* (Charleston: J.W. Delano, 1872), n.p., 11, 57; Arthur Mazyck, *Guide to Charleston* (Charleston: Walker, Evans, and Cogswell, 1875); *Guide to Charleston* (Charleston: Walker, Evans, and Cogswell, 1884). Prentiss himself appears not to have been a local, but the guide's prefatory material indicates that he wrote the book at the behest of Charlestonians and also consulted local authorities and libraries for information.

13. Susan Millar Williams and Stephen G. Hoffius, *Upheaval in Charleston: Earthquake and Murder on the Eve of Jim Crow* (Athens: University of Georgia Press, 2011), 143–44, 184–90; "The Proposed Fall Festival and Excursion," *CNC*, July 29, 1887; " 'Expecting Company,' " *CNC*, Sept. 23, 1887; Don H. Doyle, *New Men, New Cities, New South: Atlanta, Nashville, Charleston, Mobile, 1860–1910* (Chapel Hill: University of North Carolina Press, 1990), 171.

14. "The Young Men's Meeting," *CNC*, June 3, 1888; " 'Enlisted for the War,' " *CNC*, Aug. 7, 1888; Doyle, *New Men, New Cities, New South*, 170–71, 175; "A Good Town for Hotels," *CNC*, Jan. 2, 1901; Stephen Kantrowitz, *Ben Tillman and the Reconstruction of White Supremacy* (Chapel Hill: University of North Carolina Press, 2000), 181–97.

15. "Reunion Work Started," *CNC*, Aug. 9, 1898; Doyle, *New Men, New Cities, New South*, 178–79; J.C. Hemphill, "A Short History of the South Carolina Inter-State and West Indian Exposition," in *City of Charleston Yearbook—1902* (Charleston: Daggett Printing Co., 1903), 139, 149.

16. James, *American Scene*, 405, 416, 420.

17. Harlan Greene, Harry S. Hutchins Jr., and Brian E. Hutchins, *Slave Badges and the Slave-Hire System in Charleston, South Carolina, 1783–1865* (Jefferson, NC: McFarland and Co., 2004); Harlan Greene and Harry S. Hutchins Jr., "Slave Hire Badges—The 2014 Update," *North South Trader's Civil War* 38 (2014): 64–71.

18. "All Around Town," *CNC*, Sept. 10, 1889; "Souvenirs of Slavery," *CNC*, Sept. 11, 1889; *CEP*, Nov. 21, 1895.

19. D.E. Huger Smith, *A Charlestonian's Recollections, 1846–1913* (Charleston: Carolina Art Association, 1950), 64; Alice R. Huger Smith, "Daniel Elliott Huger Smith," *South Carolina Historical and Genealogical Magazine* 33 (Oct. 1932): 316–18.

20. Harlan Greene, *Mr. Skylark: John Bennett and the Charleston Renaissance* (Athens: University of Georgia Press, 2001); John Bennett, "'Slave Tags' for Tourists," *CNC*, May 3, 1903.

21. John Bennett, quoted in Greene, *Mr. Skylark*, 92; Bennett, "'Slave Tags' for Tourists." According to Harlan Greene, Harry S. Hutchins Jr., and Brian E. Hutchins, who have written the only book-length study of Charleston's slave-badge system, just one of the many badges described by Bennett was authentic. Greene, Hutchins Jr., and Hutchins, *Slave Badges*, 3.

22. Bennett, "'Slave Tags' for Tourists."

23. Ibid.

24. "Central Market and the Buzzards, Charleston, S.C.," postcard, n.d.; "Old Slave Market," postcard, n.d.; and "The Old Market, Charleston, S.C.," postcard, [sent in 1918], all in authors' possession; Vachel Lindsay, quoted in Dennis Camp, "Uncle Boy: A Biography of Vachel Lindsay" (unpublished), ch. 17, p. 11, vachellindsay.org/UncleBoy/uncle_boy_17 .pdf; David S. Shields, *Southern Provisions: The Creation and Revival of a Cuisine* (Chicago: University of Chicago Press, 2015), 167–68; "Old Slave Market, Charleston, S.C.," postcard, [sent in 1921], and "Old Slave Market, Chalmers St., Charleston, S.C.," postcard, both in authors' possession; "Old Slave Market, Chalmers St., Charleston, S.C.," [sent in 1929], Box 1, Folder 1, OSMMC. To avoid confusion, we refer to the Chalmers Street building as Ryan's Mart or the Old Slave Mart, but not the Old Slave Market.

25. [C. Irvine Walker], *Guide to Charleston, S.C. with Brief History of City* (Charleston: Walker, Evans, and Cogswell, 1911), 48, SCR. Walker is identified as the author of a later edition of this guide. See C. Irvine Walker, *Guide to Charleston, S.C., with Brief History of the City and Map Thereof* (Charleston: Walker, Evans, and Cogswell, 1919). Edmund L. Drago and Ralph Melnick, "The Old Slave Mart Museum, Charleston, South Carolina: Rediscovering the Past," *CWH* 27 (June 1981): 144–51; Stephanie E. Yuhl, "Hidden in Plain Sight: Centering the Domestic Slave Trade in American Public History," *JSH* 79 (Aug. 2013): 598.

26. Benjamin G. Cloyd, *Haunted by Atrocity: Civil War Prisons in American Memory* (Baton Rouge: Louisiana State University Press, 2010), 76–78 (quote 78).

27. "Race Gleanings," *INF*, Aug. 27, 1890.

28. "An Historic Southern City," *Colored American* 9 (Oct. 12, 1901): 4.

29. William D. Crum, "The Negro at the Charleston Exposition," *Voice of the Negro* 1 (1904): 335; "The Negro at the Exposition," *CNC*, Apr. 29, 1902 (*New York Age* quote).

30. Alphonso Brown, *A Gullah Guide to Charleston: Walking Through Black History* (Charleston: History Press, 2008), 19–20; Mamie Garvin Fields with Karen Fields, *Lemon Swamp and Other Places: A Carolina Memoir* (New York: Free Press, 1985), 31; "The Cradle of Secession," *INF*, Feb. 11, 1905.

31. "The Cradle of Secession."

32. "The Grimkés in Charleston," *NYA*, June 21, 1906; "Progress in Charleston, S.C.," *NYA*, July 5, 1906; "Entertained their Guests," *CNC*, June 22, 1906; "Entertained their Guests," *CNC*, June 30, 1906, clipping, Folder 729, Box 36, AGP; Fields, *Lemon Swamp*, 31; Katherine Mellen Charron, *Freedom's Teacher: The Life of Septima Clark* (Chapel Hill:

University of North Carolina Press, 2009), 85–86; Peter F. Lau, *Democracy Rising: South Carolina and the Fight for Black Equality Since 1865* (Lexington: University of Kentucky Press, 2006), 33–35.

33. W.E.B. Du Bois, "Editorial," *The Crisis* (Apr. 1917): 269–70.

34. "Tourist Season Sure to Be Heavy," *CNC*, Dec. 15, 1919; Stephanie E. Yuhl, *A Golden Haze of Memory: The Making of Historic Charleston* (Chapel Hill: University of North Carolina Press, 2005), 161, 165; Tammy Ingram, *Dixie Highway: Road Building and the Making of the Modern South, 1900–1930* (Chapel Hill: University of North Carolina Press, 2014); Brundage, *Southern Past*, 193; "An Achievement and an Augury," *CNC*, Aug. 8, 1929; Robert Lee Frank, "The Economic Impact of Tourism in Charleston, South Carolina, 1970" (master's thesis, University of South Carolina, 1964), 36.

35. Yuhl, *Golden Haze of Memory*, 162 (Stoney quote), 164; "Francis Marion Hotel to Open Today," *CNC*, Feb. 7, 1924; Sidney S. Riggs to Frederic Bancroft, July 24, 1924, Box 89, FBP.

36. Yuhl, *Golden Haze of Memory*, 24, 28.

37. Ibid., 27, 30–32; Stephanie E. Yuhl, "Rich and Tender Remembering," in *Where These Memories Grow: History, Memory, and Southern Identity*, ed. W. Fitzhugh Brundage (Chapel Hill: University of North Carolina Press, 2000), 234.

38. George A. Devlin, *South Carolina and Black Migration, 1865–1904: In Search of the Promised Land* (New York: Garland, 1989), 224–87; Louise Anderson Allen, *A Bluestocking in Charleston: The Life and Career of Laura Bragg* (Columbia: University of South Carolina Press, 2001), 80; unnamed source, quoted in Walter J. Fraser Jr., *Charleston! Charleston! The History of a Southern City* (Columbia: University of South Carolina Press, 1989), 373; Alston Deas, "Ancient Beauty of Once Neglected Buildings in Lower City Regained," *CNC*, Dec. 17, 1928; Yuhl, *Golden Haze of Memory*, 31, 45–50.

39. "As to Landmarks," *CNC*, May 13, 1928; Yuhl, *Golden Haze of Memory*, 43, 166.

40. Fraser, *Charleston! Charleston!*, 374; Yuhl, *Golden Haze of Memory*, 165; "City Challenged on Its History," *CNC*, Mar. 1, 1927; "Sends Reply to Fredericksburg," *CNC*, Mar. 3, 1927; "Williamsburg Cites Its History," *CNC*, Apr. 7, 1927.

41. Yuhl, *Golden Haze of Memory*, 28 (Frost quote), 43.

42. Yuhl, "Rich and Tender Remembering," 230; Yuhl, *Golden Haze of Memory*, 45; Brundage, *Southern Past*, 201–3; Josephine Rhett Bacot, "Notable Old Homes in Charleston," *CNC*, Mar. 19, 1905.

43. "Sumter Semi-Centennial To-Day," *CNC*, Apr. 12, 1911; Brown, *Civil War Canon*, 171–73; William Oliver Stevens, *Charleston: Historic City of Gardens* (New York: Dodd, Mead, and Co., 1939), 284–89.

44. Minutes, Mar. 2, 1937, RSPMC; Brown, *Civil War Canon*, 166–67; "Star's Dress to Be Shown," *CEP*, Jan. 29, 1940; "Small Girls in Scarlett's Day," *CEP*, Feb. 1, 1940; Yuhl, *Golden Haze of Memory*, 173.

45. Yuhl, "Rich and Tender Remembering," 230, 234; Radio Play Scripts, 1935, Box 1, and Nov. 21, 1935 Minutes, Box 2, both in RHCC.

46. "Tour of Historic Charleston," 1940, and "A Tour of Old Charleston," Nov. 8, 1940, both in Annual Reports, 1936–1956, Box 1, RHCC.

47. Yuhl, *Golden Haze of Memory*, 45; *Picturesque Charleston* (Charleston: Walker, Evans, and Cogswell, 1930), 3, COC.

48. Samuel Gaillard Stoney, *Charleston: Azaleas and Bricks* (Boston: Houghton Mifflin, 1939), 9.

49. Thomas Petigru Lesesne, *Landmarks of Charleston, Including an Incomparable Stroll* (1932; reprint, Richmond: Garrett & Massie, 1939), 63–64; Frank B. Gilbreth, "Thomas Petigru Lesene," in *Outspoken: 150 Years of the* News and Courier, by Herbert Ravenel Sass (Columbia: University of South Carolina Press, 1953), 102–6.

50. *South Carolina: The WPA Guide to the Palmetto State* (1941; reprint, Columbia: University of South Carolina Press, 1988), v–xi, 37, 487–88; Jerrold Hirsch, *Portrait of America: A Cultural History of the Federal Writers' Project* (Chapel Hill: University of North Carolina Press, 2003), 41–102, 107–39; Alice Ravenel Huger Smith, narrative by Herbert Ravenel Sass, *A Carolina Rice Plantation of the Fifties* (New York: William Morrow, 1936); Augustine T. Smythe, Herbert Ravenel Sass, Alfred Huger et al., eds., *The Carolina Low-Country* (New York: Macmillan, 1931); Lauren Rebecca Sklaroff, *Black Culture and the New Deal: The Quest for Civil Rights in the Roosevelt Era* (Chapel Hill: University of North Carolina Press, 2009), 89–106; Sharon Ann Musher, *Democratic Art: The New Deal's Influence on American Culture* (Chicago: University of Chicago Press, 2015), 122–26.

51. Jody H. Graichen, "Reinterpreting South Carolina History: The South Carolina Negro Writers' Project, 1936–1937" (master's thesis, University of South Carolina, 2005), 1–19. The draft essays are in FWPSCL.

52. Augustus Ladson, "Attempted Insurrection in 1822: Thirty-Five Hung on Oak Tree in Ashley Avenue," 2; "Slavery of the Negro in South Carolina," 5; and Robert L. Nelson, "Early Negro Life in South Carolina Low-Country," 6, all in FWPSCL.

53. "Negro Contributions to South Carolina," 2; "Slavery of the Negro in South Carolina," 4; and "The Negro's Adjustment to Slavery and His Development Under Slavery Regime," 1, all in FWPSCL.

54. "The Stono Insurrection, 1739, Charles Town, South Carolina," 1–3; Hattie Mobley, "Denmark Vesey"; and Ladson, "Attempted Insurrection in 1822," all in FWPSCL; Graichen, "Reinterpreting South Carolina History," 18–19.

55. Miriam B. Wilson, *Street Strolls Around Charleston: Giving the History, Legends, Traditions* (n.p., 1930), 42, Box 3, CGTC; Miriam B. Wilson, *Street Strolls around Charleston, South Carolina*, 3rd ed. (Charleston: Miriam Bellangee Wilson, 1942), 29, COC; "Charleston Welcomes You" (Charleston: Walker, Evans, and Cogswell, 1938), Box 2, CGTC.

56. Stoney, *Charleston: Azaleas and Bricks*, 9; Yuhl, *Golden Haze of Memory*, 75–83; Elizabeth O'Neill Verner, "Spiritual of the Low Country," *CNC*, Jan. 11, 1925.

57. Harlan Greene and James M. Hutchisson, "The Charleston Renaissance Considered," introduction to their *Renaissance in Charleston: Art and Life in the Carolina Lowcountry, 1900–1940* (Athens: University of Georgia Press, 2003), 1–18; Yuhl, *Golden Haze of Memory*, 14–15, 90–91; Melissa L. Cooper, *Making Gullah: A History of Sapelo Islanders, Race, and the American Imagination* (Chapel Hill: University of North Carolina Press, 2017), 19–29. Although the term "Charleston Renaissance" did not come into regular use until relatively recently, it was occasionally used in the 1920s. See "Literature—and Less," *NOTP*, Sept. 28, 1924.

58. Langston Hughes, quoted in Nathan Miller, *New World Coming: The 1920s and the Making of Modern America* (Boston: Da Capo Press, 2004), 221; Arnold Shaw, *The Jazz Age: Popular Music in the 1920s* (New York: Oxford University Press, 1987), 92; Todd Decker, *Show Boat: Performing Race in an American Musical* (New York: Oxford University Press, 2013), 19–20; Jill Watts, *Mae West: An Icon in Black and White* (New York: Oxford University Press, 2001), 68; Sieglinde Lemke, *Primitivist Modernism: Black Culture and the Origins of Transatlantic Modernism* (New York: Oxford University Press, 1998), 66–70, 136; Brown, *Civil War Canon*, 177, 183; Robert L. Dorman, *Revolt of the Provinces: The Regionalist Movement in America, 1920–1945* (Chapel Hill: University of North Carolina Press, 1993), xi–xii.

59. Alice Ravenel Huger Smith, "Reminiscences," in *Alice Ravenel Huger Smith: An Artist, a Place, and a Time*, by Martha R. Severens (Charleston: Carolina Art Association, 1993), 67–69, 80–83, 94–95, 97; Yuhl, *Golden Haze of Memory*, 60–70; Smith, *A Carolina Rice Plantation of the Fifties*.

60. Yuhl, *Golden Haze of Memory*, 65–66, 70–73 (quote 73); Smith, *A Carolina Rice Planta-tion of the Fifties*; "Atlantic St. Art Studios," *CEP*, Apr. 21, 1928.

61. DuBose Heyward, *Porgy* (New York: George H. Doran, 1925), 11–12; James M. Hutchis-son, *DuBose Heyward: A Charleston Gentleman and the World of Porgy and Bess* (Jackson: University Press of Mississippi, 2000), 6–10.

62. Heyward, *Porgy*, 11–12, 115; Hutchisson, *DuBose Heyward*, 60–65; Ellen Noonan, *The Strange Career of Porgy and Bess: Race, Culture, and America's Most Famous Opera* (Chapel Hill: University of North Carolina Press, 2012), 18–25; Yuhl, *Golden Haze of Memory*, 114–25.

63. DuBose Heyward, "The Negro in the Low-Country," in *The Carolina Low-Country*, 181; Dorothy Heyward, "Denmark Vesey—Whose Life Was a 'True Thriller,'" *New York Star*, Oct. 31, 1948; Brooks Atkinson, "'Set My People Free,'" *NYT*, Nov. 14, 1948.

64. David Robertson, *Denmark Vesey: The Buried Story of America's Largest Slave Rebellion and the Man Who Led It* (New York: Knopf, 1999), 127; Brundage, *Southern Past*, 220; Miriam B. Wilson, *Street Strolls around Charleston, South Carolina*, 2nd ed. (Charleston: Miriam Bellangee Wilson, 1937), 15; Stoney, *Charleston: Azaleas and Bricks*, 9; "Charleston Expects Book Possibilities Via Gershwin's 'Porgy,'" *Variety*, Aug. 7, 1935, pp. 1, 60.

65. Peter A. Coclanis, *The Shadow of a Dream: Economic Life and Death in the South Caro-lina Low Country* (New York: Oxford University Press, 1989), 15; Yuhl, *Golden Haze of Memory*, 177; "Romantic Charleston," Elliman, Huyler, and Mullally, Inc. brochure, n.d., CGTC.

66. Albert Simons to J.H. Dingle, city engineer, May 6, 1933, ASP; Yuhl, *Golden Haze of Memory*, 43–45, 256n146.

67. Yuhl, *Golden Haze of Memory*, 184; "Negroes to Husk Rice at Museum," *CNC*, Mar. 15, 1937; "Rice Show Draws Many to Museum," *CNC*, Mar. 21, 1937.

68. Catherine Cocks, *Doing the Town: The Rise of Urban Tourism in the United States, 1850–1915* (Berkeley: University of California Press, 2001), 175, 176, 189; Anthony J. Stanonis, *Creating the Big Easy: New Orleans and the Emergence of Modern Tourism, 1918–1945* (Ath-ens: University of Georgia Press, 2006), 224–25, 228, 230.

69. "Rice Huskers Recall Congo to Woman Explorer of Wilds," *CNC*, Mar. 26, 1937.

7. THE SOUNDS OF SLAVERY

1. Philip Hewitt-Myring to [Charles H. Drayton], n.d., Minute Book 1929, SPSP.

2. Philip Hewitt-Myring, "A Bachelor Editor and a Borrowed Boy See the Circus," *Pitts-burgh Press*, May 6, 1928; Philip Hewitt-Myring, "Charleston's Urbanity, Its Harmony, Dignity, Charm Win Englishman's Affection," *CNC*, Apr. 8, 1928; Philip Hewitt-Myring, "Whole World of Art Richer by Spirituals' Preservation," *CNC*, Apr. 6, 1928, May Martin Scrapbook I, 1924–1929 (May), SPSP.

3. Society for the Preservation of Spirituals (SPS) Program for Thursday Evening Club, in New York City, Jan. 9, 1930, and Alfred Huger to Dr. Cornelia Brant, Aug. 22, 1931, both in SPSP; Stephanie E. Yuhl, *A Golden Haze of Memory: The Making of Historic Charleston* (Chapel Hill: University of North Carolina Press, 2005), 133–35; Edward Ball, *Slaves in the Family* (New York: Ballantine Books, 1998), 389; M.A. De Wolfe Howe, "The Song of Charleston," *AM* 46 (July 1930): 109.

4. *CPC*, Sept. 19, 2003; Herbert Ravenel Sass, *Outspoken: 150 Years of the* News and Courier (Columbia: University of South Carolina Press, 1953), 58, 62; Charles J. Holden, *In the Great Maelstrom: Conservatives in Post–Civil War South Carolina* (Columbia: University of South Carolina Press, 2002), 87–110.

5. Howe, "Song of Charleston," 108–9, 111.

6. Harlan Greene, *Mr. Skylark: John Bennett and the Charleston Renaissance* (Athens: University of Georgia Press, 2001), 102–3; John Bennett to his family, Oct. 17, 1937, Folder 14, Box 142, JBP.

7. John Bennett, quoted in Greene, *Mr. Skylark*, 70.

8. Greene, *Mr. Skylark*, 94–95, 104–5, 132, 238.

9. Charles Joyner, *Down by the Riverside: A South Carolina Slave Community, 25th Anniversary Edition* (Urbana: University of Illinois Press, 2009), esp. 196–224; Greene, *Mr. Skylark*, 104, 118; Shane White and Graham White, *The Sounds of Slavery: Discovering African American History through Songs, Sermons, and Speech* (Boston: Beacon, 2005), 85–88; Edward King, *The Great South: A Record of Journeys* (Hartford, CT: American Publishing Co., 1875), 429; John Bennett, "Gullah: A Negro Patois," *South Atlantic Quarterly* 8 (Jan. 1909): 39–52. This was the second half of a two-part article, which may have been the first scholarly analysis of the Gullah language. See also John Bennett, "Gullah: A Negro Patois," *South Atlantic Quarterly* 8 (Oct. 1908): 332–47.

10. "Old Negro Songs," *CEP*, Feb. 10, 1903; "Our Plantations Songs," *CEP*, Feb. 11, 1903; "Women's Clubs Meet," *CNC*, Feb. 10, 1903; Greene, *Mr. Skylark*, 49–64, 101–4, 106–16.

11. "Women's Clubs Met," *CNC*, Feb. 20, 1908; "Brilliant Meeting of the Club Women," *CEP*, Feb. 20, 1908; "A Lady Protests," *CEP*, Feb. 20, 1908; "Another Protest," *CEP*, Feb. 21, 1908; "Mr. Bennett's Lecture," *CEP*, Feb. 21, 1908; Kitty Ravenel, "John Bennett's Legends Caused Uproar in 1908," *CNC*, Feb. 10, 1946; Greene, *Mr. Skylark*, 104, 122–26, 238–39; Yuhl, *Golden Haze of Memory*, 125; "To Broadcast from WJZ," *CEP*, Apr. 3, 1930; "Lectures on Gullah Stories," *CEP*, July 25, 1933; "S.G. Will Speak in Savannah," *CEP*, Apr. 4, 1935; "Stoney Is Speaker in Lecture Series," *CEP*, Apr. 30, 1943; "Stoney Is Speaker," *CEP*, Jan. 28, 1944; William S. Pollitzer to Samuel G. Stoney, Apr. 11, 1952, and Samuel G. Stoney Jr. to William S. Pollitzer, Apr. 23, 1952, both in SGSP.

12. James M. Hutchisson, *DuBose Heyward: A Charleston Gentleman and the World of Porgy and Bess* (Jackson: University Press of Mississippi, 2000), 22; Dorothy Heyward, quoted in Ellen Noonan, *The Strange Career of Porgy and Bess: Race, Culture, and America's Most Famous Opera* (Chapel Hill: University of North Carolina Press, 2012), 26; Yuhl, *Golden Haze of Memory*, 124–25; "Spirituals Not Printed," *CEP*, Apr. 14, 1928.

13. "Society Notice," *CEP*, Oct. 29, 1912; "King's Daughters to Conduct Charming Tea Room," *CNC*, Nov. 14, 1912; Hutchisson, *DuBose Heyward*, 1, 4–8, 18, 19; Harlan Greene, "Charleston Childhood: The First Years of DuBose Heyward," *SCHM* 83 (Apr. 1982): 154–67.

14. David W. Blight, *Race and Reunion: The Civil War in American Memory* (Cambridge, MA: Belknap Press of Harvard University Press, 2001), 221–31; Micki McElya, *Clinging to Mammy: The Faithful Slave in Twentieth-Century America* (Cambridge, MA: Harvard University Press, 2007), 38–73; Grace Elizabeth Hale, *Making Whiteness: The Culture of Segregation in the South, 1890–1940* (New York: Vintage, 1998), 88, 98.

15. "Recital at Georgetown," *CEP*, Apr. 6, 1923; Program Introduction, n.d., Gullah Notebook #2; "The First Trolley Car," n.d., Gullah Notebook #1; and "What Mauma Thinks of Freedom," n.d., Gullah Notebook #2, all in Box 37, JSHP.

16. Program Introduction, n.d., Gullah Notebook #2, Box 37, and "Foreword," n.d., Gullah Notebook #6, both in JSHP.

17. "Mrs. Heyward's Reading," *CEP*, Jan. 13, 1922; "Gullah Dialect Recital Planned," *CNC*, Nov. 25, 1922.

18. "Reading by Mrs. Heyward," *CEP*, Dec. 29, 1924; clipping, *CNC*, Mar. 26, 1925, and unidentified newspaper clipping, n.d., both in Box 38, JSHP; McElya, *Clinging to Mammy*, 66–73.

19. Clippings file, Box 38, JSHP; "Dialect Reading," *CEP*, Apr. 12, 1922; "Gullah Dialect Recital Planned," *CNC*, Nov. 25, 1922; "Mrs. Heyward's Dialect Reading," *CEP*, Dec. 4, 1922; "'Gullah' Stories Please Auditors," *State*, May 17, 1922; "Mrs. Heyward's Dialect Reading," *CEP*, Dec. 4, 1922; "Mrs. Heyward's Book," *CEP*, Oct. 18, 1905.

20. "Reading by Mrs. Heyward," *CEP*, Mar. 27, 1926; Greene, *Mr. Skylark*, 299n39; Scrapbook, Box 38, JSHP.

21. Clipping, *CNC*, Mar. 26, 1925, Box 38, JSHP; E.T.H. Shaffer, "The Work of Mrs. Janie Screven Heyward," *State,* Dec. 10, 1922.

22. Executive Secretary to Mrs. Edwina Kellenberger, July 30, 1930, [John A. Siegling] to Myra Wofford Elmers, Aug. 8, 1960, both in SPSP; SPS Program for Thursday Evening Club; "Preservation Society Tour," *CEP*, Apr. 4, 1941; Yuhl, *Golden Haze of Memory*, 133–35; Ball, *Slaves in the Family*, 389. The group was occasionally called the Society for the Preservation of Negro Spirituals.

23. Alfred Huger to Mrs. Humbert Barton Powell, Oct. 10, 1929; Alfred Huger to Dr. Cornelia Brant, Aug. 22, 1931; and Constitution [ca. 1924], all in SPSP; Executive Secretary to Mrs. Edwina Kellenberger; "The Song of Charleston," *AM* 46 (July 1930): 109; Yuhl, *Golden Haze of Memory*, 133–35; "Spirituals Win Savannah," *CEP*, Feb. 15, 1926 (*Savannah Press* quote).

24. Eric Lott, *Love & Theft: Blackface Minstrelsy and the American Working Class* (New York: Oxford University Press, 1993), 6; Yuhl, *Golden Haze of Memory*, 130–31.

25. Minutes, May 14, 1923, Minute Book 1923, SPSP; Yuhl, *Golden Haze of Memory*, 144; "Fine Rendering of Spirituals," *CNC*, Apr. 1, 1924, May Martin Scrapbook I, 1924–1929 (May), SPSP.

26. Christian McWhirter, *Battle Hymns: The Power and Popularity of Music during the Civil War* (Chapel Hill: University of North Carolina Press, 2014), 177–82 (*Lippincott's* quote 177); William Francis Allen, Charles Pickard Ware, and Lucy McKim Garrison, eds., *Slave Songs of the United States* (1867, repr., Toronto: Dover Publications, 1995); Thomas Wentworth Higginson, "Negro Spirituals," *AM* 10 (June 1867): 685–94; Andrew Ward, *Dark Midnight When I Rise: The Story of the Jubilee Singers Who Introduced the World to the Music of Black America* (New York: Farrar, Straus, and Giroux, 2000); Toni P. Anderson, *"Tell Them We Are Singing for Jesus": The Original Fisk Jubilee Singers and Christian Reconstruction, 1871–1878* (Macon, GA: Mercer University Press, 2010); Eric Bernard Grant, "'Message in the Music': Spirituals and the Cultural Politics of Race and Nation, 1871 to 1945" (Ph.D. diss., Yale University, 2005), 4–49.

27. Eric Sean Crawford, "The Penn School's Education Curriculum: Its Effects on the St. Helena Songs," *Journal of African American Studies* 17 (2013): 348–69; Guy and Candie Carawan, *Ain't You Got a Right to the Tree of Life? The People of Johns Island, South Carolina—Their Faces, Their Words and Their Songs* (New York: Simon and Schuster, 1966), 9; Yuhl, *Golden Haze of Memory*, 134–35; Executive Secretary to Mrs. Edwina Kellenberger; "History of Negro Spirituals," *Nashua (NH) Telegraph*, Nov. 14, 1929.

28. Edmund L. Drago, notes on an interview with Eugene C. Hunt, Dec. 4, 1985, ELDP; Edmund L. Drago, *Initiative, Paternalism, and Race Relations: Charleston's Avery Normal Institute* (Athens: University of Georgia Press, 1990), 3–4, 111–12, 141, 145–47, 155–56, 164–66; Septima Clark, interview by Peter Wood, Feb. 3 and 4, 1981, Folder 11, Box 1, SPCP; Katherine Mellen Charron, *Freedom's Teacher: The Life of Septima Clark* (Chapel Hill: University of North Carolina Press, 2009), 371n89; "Negro Spirituals at Avery," *CEP*, Mar. 30, 1925; "Negro Spirituals at Hotel," *CEP*, Feb. 23, 1926; "To Sing Spirituals," *CEP*, Feb. 2, 1928; "Spirituals Concert," *CEP*, Mar. 24, 1939.

29. DuBose Heyward, "The Negro in the Low-Country," in *The Carolina Low-Country*, ed. Augustine T. Smythe, Herbert Ravenel Sass, Alfred Huger, et al. (New York: Macmillan,

1931), 185–86; "An Appreciation," *Augusta Chronicle*, Mar. 3, 1930, May Martin Scrapbook, II 1930 (Feb.–Mar.), SPSP; John Arthur Siegling Jr., preface, *Gullah Lyrics to Carolina Low Country Spirituals* (Charleston: Society for the Preservation of Spirituals, 2007), n.p.; Crawford, "The Negro Spiritual of Saint Helena Island," 41; Minutes, Feb. 21, 1924, Minute Book 1924–1925, SPSP; Barbara L. Bellows, *A Talent for Living: Josephine Pinckney and the Charleston Literary Tradition* (Baton Rouge: Louisiana State University Press, 2006), 70–71; Yuhl, *Golden Haze of Memory*, 136–37; Minutes, Feb. 1, 1924, Minute Book 1924–1925, and song information cards, undated, Programs, 1930–1935, both in SPSP.

30. Katherine C. Hutson, "Slave Spirituals in Native Form," *CNC*, Feb. 15, 1929, Alice Burkette Scrapbook IV, 1923–1961, and Minutes, Feb. 21, 1924, Minute Book 1924–1925, both in SPSP.

31. Executive Secretary to Mrs. Edwina Kellenberger; Harold Stone "Dick" Reeves, interview by Joan Ball, Mar. 24, 1971, SCOHC; "Many Features for Festival," *CNC*, May 2, 1923; Yuhl, *Golden Haze of Memory*, 132, 142; "Fine Rendering of Spirituals"; [Katherine Hutson] to Mr. Graham [Winthrop College, Rock Hill, SC], Jan. 21, 1937; R.L.C., "Spirituals Singing by Society of Charleston Is Highly Complimented," *Augusta Chronicle*, Mar. 3, 1930, May Martin Scrapbook II 1930 (Feb.–March); and "Southern Voices Sing Spirituals," *Boston Post*, June 16, 1929, May Martin Scrapbook I, 1924–1929 (June), all in SPSP; *SMN*, Feb. 17, 1924, quoted in Grant, " 'Message in the Music,' " 135.

32. "Fine Rendering of Spirituals"; Executive Secretary to Miss Florence Gerald, July 26, 1930, SPSP; "Give Concert of Spirituals," *Boston Herald*, June 17, 1929, May Martin Scrapbook I 1929 (June); *SMN*, quoted in Grant, " 'Message in the Music,' " 135.

33. Nathan B. Barnwell to Alfred Huger, Feb. 21, 1931, SPSP; Hewitt-Myring, "Whole World of Art Richer by Spirituals' Preservation"; "A High Quality of Publicity," *CNC*, Jan. 13, 1930; "Greenville Man Impressed," newspaper clipping, [1928], Alice Burkette Scrapbook IV, 1923–1961.

34. "Singing Spirituals," *CNC*, n.d., May Martin Scrapbook I, 1924–1929 (May); Hewitt-Myring, "Whole World of Art Richer by Spirituals' Preservation"; "Historian Lauds Spirituals Here," *CNC*, Nov. 26, 1927.

35. Yuhl, *Golden Haze of Memory*, 140–42, 242n79; Minutes, May 4, 1927, Minute Book 1926–1927, SPSP.

36. Minutes, Jan. 14, Oct. 2, Oct. 16, and Dec. 8, 1929, Minute Book 1929, SPSP; "Spirituals Not Printed," *CEP,* Apr. 14, 1928, May Martin Scrapbook I, 1924–1929 (May); Minutes, Jan. 6, 1926, Minute Book 1926–1927.

37. Mrs. Winifred T. Hunt to the SPS, Feb. 9, 1931; Mrs. Lucile Francis to the SPS, Feb. 24, 1931; Mary W. Cahn to Mr. Alfred Huger, Oct. 3, 1929, Minute Book 1929; Minutes, Jan. 14, 1936, Minute Book 1936; Minutes, June 25, 1937, Minute Book 1937; and Minutes, Mar. 4, 1940, Minute Book 1940, all in SPSP; "Spirituals Not Printed"; Noonan, *Strange Career*, 73–80.

38. Alfred Huger to T.E. Oertel, Mar. 7, 1930, Minute Book 1930, SPSP; Josephine Wright, "Songs of Remembrance," *JAAH* 9 (Fall 2006): 413–24; Howard Thurman, *Deep River and the Negro Spiritual Speaks of Life and Death* (Richmond, IN: Friends United Press, 1975), 3; Lawrence W. Levine, *Black Culture and Black Consciousness: Afro-American Folk Thought from Slavery to Freedom* (New York: Oxford University Press, 1977), 51; Joyner, *Down by the Riverside*, 163–69; W.E.B. Du Bois, *The Souls of Black Folk* (1903; reprint, New York: Bantam Books, 1989), 182; P. Sterling Stuckey, "Afterword: Frederick Douglass and W.E.B. Du Bois on the Consciousness of the Enslaved," *JAAH* 91 (Fall 2006): 451–58; McWhirter, *Battle Hymns*, 149–52; Robert L. Nelson, "Research on the Negro Spirituals," FWPSCL (Affie Singleton and ex-bondperson quotes); Frederick Douglass, *My Bondage and My Freedom*

(New York: Miller, Orton, and Mulligan, 1855), 278; Smythe et al., eds., *Carolina Low-Country*, 229–327.

39. Iain Anderson, "Reworking Images of a Southern Past: The Commemoration of Slave Music after the Civil War," *Studies in Popular Culture* 19 (Oct. 1996): 176–77 (quote 176); "Evening of Pure Delight," *CEP*, Feb. 21, 1927.

40. Robert W. Gordon, "The Negro Spiritual," in *Carolina Low-Country*, 216–17; Herbert Ravenel Sass, "The Low-Country," in *Carolina Low-Country*, 5; Heyward, "The Negro in the Low-Country," 171, 182.

41. Yuhl, *Golden Haze of Memory*, 143, 147; "Walter Damrosch Thrilled By Concert of Spirituals," *CNC*, Apr. 22, 1935; "Evening of Pure Delight"; [Katherine Hutson], performance notes on 11 Gibes Street stationery, n.d., SPSP. For the titles, lyrics, and music of the spirituals collected and performed by the SPS, see *Carolina Low-Country*, 223–327; and *Gullah Lyrics to the Carolina Low Country Spirituals*.

42. Alfred Huger to Louis T. Parker, Apr. 15, 1936, SPSP; "Death Claims Alfred Huger," *CEP*, May 18, 1938; Bellows, *Talent for Living*, 72–73.

43. "Bad Public Relations," *CNC*, Apr. 1, 1947.

44. Minutes, Dec. 8, 1931, Minute Book 1931, SPSP; Yuhl, *Golden Haze of Memory*, 151.

45. "Southern Voices Sing Spirituals"; "The Negroes Appreciate the Spirituals," *Spartanburg Herald*, [Apr. 1928], Alice Burkette Scrapbook IV, 1923–1961.

46. "Another Concert Asked For," *CNC*, Apr. 1, 1929.

47. Unsigned letter to A. Jermain Slocum, Nov. 7, 1929, Minute Book 1929, SPSP; Yuhl, *Golden Haze of Memory*, 145.

48. "Our Spirituals in Boston," *CNC*, Mar. 18, 1929, May Martin Scrapbook I, 1924–1929 (May); Minutes, Oct. 2, 1929, Minute Book 1929; Minutes, May 12, 1936, Minute Book 1936; and "Program Tonight Dedicates WCSC," *CNC*, May 8, 1939, May Martin Scrapbook II 1930 (Apr.–Dec.), all in SPSP.

49. "Spirituals Applause Is Led by Damrosch in New York," *CNC*, Jan. 30, 1930, May Martin Scrapbook II 1930 (Jan.), SPSP; "Give Concert of Spirituals"; "Spirituals Are Hailed," *CEP*, June 17, 1929, May Martin Scrapbook I 1929 (June), A.H.M., "Spirituals with a Different Flavor," *Boston Transcript*, June 18, 1929, May Martin Scrapbook I, 1929 (June), both in SPSP.

50. "A High Quality of Publicity"; "Spiritual Group to Leave Today," *CNC*, Jan. 8, 1930; "To Give Concert in New York City," *CNC*, Nov. 8, 1929; "Announce Tree Property Deals," *CNC*, Apr. 5, 1930; "Walter Damrosch Thrilled By Concert of Spirituals"; Yuhl, *Golden Haze of Memory*, 146, 149–50.

51. "To Sing Tonight," *CEP*, Feb. 14, 1925; "Melody Singers Praised," *CEP*, May 15, 1926; "Melody Singers at High School," *CNC*, Nov. 30, 1926; "Splendid Concert by Plantation Singers," *CEP*, Feb. 19, 1927; Original PMS, North Charleston Boy Scouts Benefit Concert Program, June 19, 1928, in "PMS, Lydia C. Ball," Bound Volume, Volume 25, BGFP; "To Sing Tonight," *CEP*, Feb. 14, 1925; Lydia C. Ball, to [PMS], [ca. Apr. 1933], in "PMS, Lydia C. Ball"; Edward Ball, Descendants of Elias Ball I of South Carolina, in his *Slaves in the Family*; Society for the Preservation of Spirituals Active Members Season 1929–1930, Membership Information, SPSP; "Southern Home Spirituals on December 10," *CEP*, Nov. 27, 1926; "Spirituals Most Entertaining," *CEP*, Dec. 11, 1926.

52. "Southern Voices Sing Spirituals"; "Melody Singers to Appear in Concert," *CEP*, Feb. 18, 1926; "Delightful Evening of Negro Spirituals," *State*, May 24, 1928; "PMS Delight Kingstree Folk," *CEP*, May 5, 1927; "Melody Singers to Give Concert," *CNC*, Feb. 20, 1927; "Recital Here Tuesday," *CNC*, Feb. 25, 1927; Michael Rogin, *Blackface, White Noise: Jewish Immigrants in the Hollywood Melting Pot* (Berkeley and Los Angeles: University of California Press, 1996), 30; "Southern Home Spirituals Enjoyed," *CEP*, Feb. 18, 1927.

53. "Southern Home Spirituals to Sing," *CEP*, Nov. 22, 1926; "Spirituals Most Entertaining"; "Southern Home Spirituals Enjoyed"; "Enjoyable Concert by Home Spirituals," *CEP*, Mar. 25, 1927; "Concert to Be Given Saturday Evening," *CEP*, Apr. 14, 1928; "Delightful Evening of Negro Spirituals"; "PMS Delight Kingstree Folk"; "Fine Concert by Melody Singers," *CEP*, Dec. 4, 1926; "Concert at Winthrop by Melody Singers," *CEP*, Feb. 16, 1926.

54. "Southern Voices Sing Spirituals"; "Singing of Spirituals Enjoyed at Ft. Moultrie," *CEP*, Jan. 27, 1927; Alfred Huger to Louis T. Parker, Apr. 15, 1936, SPSP.

55. "PMS Concert," *CEP*, Nov. 27, 1926; "Home Spirituals Concert Enjoyed," *CEP*, Nov. 19, 1927; "Discussions of Business," *CEP*, June 6, 1928; "200 Travelers to Meet Here," *CEP*, May 9, 1929; "Music Board Opens Session," *CEP*, Apr. 7, 1930; "Bandmasters' Bill Endorsed," *CEP*, Apr. 9, 1930; "Concert by Melody Singers," *CEP*, Feb. 9, 1927; "To Sing Tonight," *CEP*, Feb. 14, 1925; Lydia C. Ball, to [PMS], [ca. Apr. 1933]; Katherine Hutson to H.M Pace, Jan. 15, 1936, SPSP.

56. "Negro Programs Will Be Offered," *CNC*, Mar. 5, 1934; "Azalea Festival Programs," *CNC*, Mar. 11, 1934; Program, Second Annual Azalea Festival, Mar. 20–29, 1935, RAFC; "Field Hands Put on Show," *CEP*, Mar. 24, 1934; "'Plantation Echoes,'" *CEP*, Mar. 26, 1935; Rosa Warren Wilson, Hibernian Hall, Charleston, SC, July 13, 1937, John A. Lomax Southern States Collection, 1937, AFC.

57. Virginia E. Tupper, "Plantation Echoes," *Etude* (Mar. 1937): 153–54, 204; Rosa Warren Wilson, *My Privilege: A Romance of America's Most Historic City, Charleston, South Carolina* (Charleston: Walker, Evans, and Cogswell, 1934), 35; "Hard Times Bring Music Discovery," *CNC*, Mar. 3, 1937; "'Plantation Echoes' Is Presented Again," *CNC*, Apr. 7, 1940; "'Plantation Echoes,' with Gullah Natives at Academy Next Friday," *CEP*, Apr. 1, 1933; "Capacity House Enjoys 'Echoes,'" *CEP*, Apr. 8, 1933; "'Plantation Echoes' at Academy Friday," *CEP*, Jan. 13, 1934; "'Plantation Echoes' Show," *CEP*, Mar. 21, 1934; "'Plantation Echoes,'" *CEP*, Apr. 17, 1934; "Plantation Echoes Concert Will Be Given at John's Island, Feb. 1," *CEP*, Jan. 29, 1935; "Wadmalaw Island Negroes to Present Program at Hibernian Hall," *CNC*, Mar. 3, 1939; "'Plantation Echoes,' Is Presented Again," *CNC*, Apr. 7, 1940.

58. "Plantation Songs Billed on Friday," *CNC*, Apr. 2, 1933; "Plantation Songs May Be in Film," *CNC*, May 14, 1933; Tupper, "Plantation Echoes," 153; "'Plantation Echoes,' Is Presented Again"; "'Plantation Echoes' to Be Given Twice," *CNC*, Mar. 27, 1938; DuBose Heyward, "Porgy and Bess Return on Wings of Song," *Stage* 13 (Oct. 1935): 25–28; "George Gershwin Concludes Visit," *CEP*, Dec. 6, 1933; Noonan, *Strange Career*, 176–78. The SPS eventually claimed that it backed out of the festival, which was postponed to April owing to a meningitis scare, because it was "too late for our best interest" to reschedule its concert. The SPS did, however, give a concert—which was broadcast nationally by the NBC radio network—the night before the rescheduled Azalea Festival began. H.M. Pace to W. Elliott Hutson, Mar. 5, 1936, SPSP; Minutes, Mar. 4 and 5, 1936, Steering Committee of the Azalea Festival, RACF; "Azalea Festival Postponed; Date Now Set for April 15," *CNC*, Mar. 6, 1936; Minutes, Mar. 10, 1936, Minute Book 1936, SPSP; John B. Rogers to Major Henry Church, Mar. 9, 1936, and John B. Rogers to Mr. H.J. O'Neill, Mar. 17, 1936, Azalea Festival Correspondence, RAFC; Mrs. Eding Whaley [Rosa] Wilson to My Dear Sir, Mar. 9, 1936, Correspondence, General, RAFC; Third Annual Azalea Festival Schedule, Apr. 15–21, 1936, RAFC.

59. William Oliver Stevens, *Charleston: Historic City of Gardens* (New York: Dodd, Mead, and Co., 1939), 317; "Emmanuel A.M.E. Church," *CEP*, Apr. 1, 1933; "'Heaven Bound,'" *CEP*, May 9, 1933; "'Heaven Bound,'" *CEP*, Mar. 23, 1935; "To Render 'Heaven Bound,'" *CEP*, Apr. 29, 1935; Walter J. Fraser Jr., *Charleston! Charleston! The History of a Southern City* (Columbia: University of South Carolina Press, 1989), 377–78, 380 (Burnet

Rhett Maybank quote); "Azalea Festival Programs," *CNC*, Mar. 11, 1934; Tupper, "Plantation Echoes," 153.

60. Mrs. Eding Whaley [Rosa] Wilson to My Dear Sir, Mar. 9, 1936; " 'Plantation Echoes,' " *CEP*, Apr. 17, 1934; Stevens, *Charleston: Historic City of Gardens*, 319; E.E.G. Younge to Henry J. O'Neill, Mar. 26, 1936, Correspondence, General, RAFC; " 'Plantation Echoes' to Be Given Twice."

61. Mrs. Eding Whaley [Rosa] Wilson to My Dear Sir, Mar. 9, 1936; " 'Plantation Echoes' Heard by 300 Here," *CNC*, Apr. 1, 1938; Thurman, *Deep River*, 4.

62. "A Plea for Charleston," *CNC*, Apr. 4, 1934.

63. Robert Lee Frank, "The Economic Impact of Tourism in Charleston, South Carolina, 1970" (master's thesis, University of South Carolina, 1972), 35.

64. Lydia C. Ball, to [PMS], [ca. Apr. 1933]; "Summerville Benefit Scheduled Today," *CNC*, Apr. 7, 1934; "Mrs. Maria R. Galliard and the Southern Home Spirituals Present 'The Trouble I've Seen,' " *CEP*, Oct. 14, 1939; "Sojourners Begin Convention Today," *CNC*, May 22, 1941.

65. Minutes, Jan. 17, 1938, Sept. 28, 1939, and Mar. 4, 1940, Minute Book 1938–1940; and Minutes, Jan. 16 and Nov. 24, 1941, Minute Book 1941, all in SPSP.

66. "Stoney Is Speaker in Lecture Series," *CEP*, Apr. 30, 1943; "Slavery, Secession, Figure in Addresses Given Here," *CEP*, Nov. 9, 1940; "Gives Program of Spirituals," *State,* Feb. 9, 1927; "Dick Reeves Among Singers Expected with Spirituals Group Next Saturday," *State*, Feb. 27, 1932; "Program for Convention," *CEP*, Apr. 26, 1941; "Mrs. Maria Gaillard to Perform in Gullah," *CEP*, Mar. 29, 1938; "Gullah Readings by Mrs. Gaillard," *CEP*, Apr. 16, 1940.

67. "Charleston, South Carolina," n.d.; "Charleston, South Carolina, America's Most Historic City," n.d.; and Anthony Harrigan, "Charleston: The Place and the People," n.d., all in Box 5, CGTC; "Charleston . . . City of Charm," n.d., Box 1, CGTC; Herbert Ravenel Sass, quoted in W. Fitzhugh Brundage, *The Southern Past: A Clash of Race and Memory* (Cambridge, MA: Belknap Press of Harvard University Press, 2005), 183.

8. WE DON'T GO IN FOR SLAVE HORRORS

1. Sidney S. Riggs to Frederic Bancroft, July 24, 1924, Box 89, FBP.

2. Jacob E. Cooke, *Frederic Bancroft: Historian* (Norman: University of Oklahoma Press, 1957), 36–37, 69–75; Frederic Bancroft, Diaries of Southern Trips, Box 92, FBP; Frederic Bancroft to the Jailor, Magazine Street, Apr. 27, 1922, Box 89, FBP.

3. *CC*, Dec. 27, 1862; Sidney S. Riggs to Frederic Bancroft, May 31, 1922, and Frederic Bancroft to Sidney S. Riggs, Aug. 28, 1924, both in Box 89, FBP; Frederic Bancroft, *Slave Trading in the Old South* (1931; repr., Columbia: University of South Carolina Press, 1996).

4. "New Books," *CNC*, Sept. 27, 1885; Alfred Huger, "The Story of the Low-Country," in Augustine T. Smythe, Herbert Ravenel Sass, Alfred Huger et al., eds., *The Carolina Low-Country* (New York: Macmillan, 1931), 114.

5. "Notes and Queries," *CNC*, Apr. 20, 1890; "Sumner at the Auction Block," *CNC*, Apr. 30, 1890; "The Good Old Days of Slavery," *CNC*, Apr. 30, 1890; "Sumner at the Auction Block," *CNC*, Sept. 5, 1890; Frederic Bancroft, notes on interview with Mr. Ball, Southern Trip Notes, Vol. 8, 1907, Southern Trip, Charleston, Mar. 1907, n.p., Box 92; Frederic Bancroft to Anna [Anne] S. Deas, Apr. 17, 1911, Box 17; and Anne S. Deas to Frederic Bancroft, Apr. 19, 1911, Box 38, all in FBP; Cooke, *Frederic Bancroft*, 4, 7–9.

6. Michael Tadman, "The Reputation of the Slave Trader in Southern History and the Social Memory of the South," *American Nineteenth Century History* 8 (Sept. 2007): 247–71; Michael Tadman, "The Hidden History of Slave Trading in Antebellum South Carolina: John Springs III and Other 'Gentlemen Dealing in Slaves,'" *SCHM* 97 (Jan. 1996): 6–29; Michael Tadman, "The Interregional Slave Trade in History and Myth-Making of the U.S. South," in *The Chattel Principle: Internal Slave Trades in the Americas*, ed. Walter Johnson (New Haven: Yale University Press, 2014), 138–39; "Death of Z.B. Oakes," *CC*, May 27, 1871; "Mr. John S. Riggs," *CNC*, Feb. 4, 1899; "John S. Riggs," *CEP*, Feb. 4, 1899; Edmund L. Drago, ed., *Broke by War: Letters of a Slave Trader* (Columbia: University of South Carolina Press, 1991), 6, 11; Steven Deyle, *Carry Me Back: The Domestic Slave Trade in American Life* (New York: Oxford University Press, 2005), 279–80; Michael Tadman, *Speculators and Slaves: Masters, Traders, and Slaves in the Old South* (Madison: University of Wisconsin Press, 1996), 55, 192–93; Bancroft, *Slave Trading in the Old South*, 190–91; "Mr. Alonzo J. White," *CNC*, July 2, 1885; "Death of Capt. John E. Bowers," *CNC*, Sept. 18, 1888; "Mr. T. Savage Heyward," *CEP*, July 11, 1901; "Louis D. DeSaussure," *CNC*, June 21, 1888; *CM*, July 10, 1863; *CM*, May 20, 1863; Edward McCrady et al., eds., *Cyclopedia of Eminent and Representative Men of the Carolinas of the Nineteenth Century* (Madison: Brant and Fuller, 1892), 2: 480–82.

7. "Do You Know Your Charleston?" *CNC*, Dec. 30, 1930; [C. Irvine Walker], *Guide to Charleston, S.C. with Brief History of the City and Map Thereof* (Charleston: Walker, Evans, and Cogswell, 1911), 48, SCR; Thomas Petigru Lesesne, *Landmarks of Charleston, Including an Incomparable Stroll* (1932; repr., Richmond: Garrett & Massie, 1939), 64; Minutes, Jan. 25, 1940, Rough Minutes/Agendas 1940 Folder, Box 2, RHCC.

8. Mary A. Sparkman, Guidebook Notes to Historic Charleston, 1936, CLS; Robert Behre, "Early Notes Paved Way for Charleston Guides," *CPC*, Dec. 26, 2011; [Mary A. Sparkman], Tour Guide Class Material, 1952, Guidebooks, Tourism Box 1, SCC; Mary A. Sparkman, "Lectures for Guides of Historic Charleston," 1964, n.p., HICTG; "Information for Guides of Historic Charleston" (Charleston, 1975), 113–14, HICTG; Stephanie E. Yuhl, "Hidden in Plain Sight: Centering the Domestic Slave Trade in American Public History," *JSH* 79 (Aug. 2013): 606–7. Helen Gardner McCormack used the same explanation in her Charleston tours. Helen Gardner McCormack, "Tour of Historic Charleston," n.d., HGMP. Despite Sparkman's arguments to the contrary, New Orleans's slave trade closely resembled Charleston's. Both cities had slave-trading districts (New Orleans, in fact, had two), and much of the trade in those districts was conducted in large, public (though not municipally operated) auction spaces. Bancroft, *Slave Trading in the Old South*, 312, 319–20, 333–34; Walter Johnson, *Soul by Soul: Life Inside the Antebellum Slave Market* (Cambridge, MA: Harvard University Press, 1999), 2–3.

9. Cooke, *Frederic Bancroft*, 3–8, 19–26, 33–56, 69.

10. Frederic Bancroft to the Jailor, Magazine Street; Frederic Bancroft, Second Trip Diary, 1887, Diaries of Southern Trips, Box 92; and Frederic Bancroft to André Beydon, July 10, 1909, Box 13, all in FBP; Cooke, *Frederic Bancroft*, 70–73, 104–5.

11. Cooke, *Frederic Bancroft*, 72–73; Frederic Bancroft, notes on interview with Floride Cunningham, Southern Trip, 1902, Vol. II, p. 114, and Frederic Bancroft, notes on interview with Langdon Cheves, Southern Trip, 1907, Vol. VIII, p. 771, both in Box 92, FBP.

12. Frederic Bancroft, notes on interview with Edward McCrady, Southern Trip, 1902, Vol. I, pp. 54–55, Box 92, FBP; *CC*, Nov. 22, 1853; "Dissolution of Co-Partnership," *CC*, Nov. 15, 1861; Bancroft, *Slave Trading in the Old South*, 170, 190–91, 377–78.

13. Frederic Bancroft, notes on slave dealers and respectability, Southern Trip, 1902, Vol. II, n.p., p. 118, and Frederic Bancroft, notes on interview with T.W. Bacot, Southern Trip, 1907, Vol. VIII, n.p., both in Box 92, FBP.

14. Frederic Bancroft to Theodore D. Jervey, Jan. 19, 1922, Box 140, FBP; John David Smith, *Slavery, Race, and American History: Historical Conflict, Trends, and Method, 1866–1953* (New York: Routledge, 1999), 172n17; Frederic Bancroft, interview with "Uncle" William Washington and his wife, Apr. 13, 1902, Southern Trip, 1902, Vol. II, n.p., pp. 104–6, Box 92, FBP.

15. Frederic Bancroft to Carl Schurz, May 14, 1902, Box 26, FBP; Michael Tadman, introduction to Bancroft, *Slave Trading*, xv, xxii–xxv, xxix–xxxii; Cooke, *Frederic Bancroft*, 9–10, 119–21; Smith, *Race, Slavery, and American History*, 33–43; Ulrich B. Phillips, *American Negro Slavery: A Survey of the Supply, Employment and Control of Negro Labor as Determined by the Plantation Regime* (New York: D. Appleton and Co., 1918), 200; W.E.B. Du Bois, review of *American Negro Slavery*, by Ulrich B. Phillips, *American Political Science Review* 12 (Nov. 1918): 722–26; Frederic Bancroft to W.E.B. Du Bois, Dec. 11, 1918, Box 140, and Frederic Bancroft to James Ford Rhodes, Dec. 14, 1918, Box 143, both in FPB.

16. Frederic Bancroft to Proprietor of the Garage in the "Old Slave Mart," Apr. 29, 1922, and Sidney S. Riggs to Frederic Bancroft, May 31, 1922, both in Box 89, FBP.

17. Sidney S. Riggs to Frederic Bancroft, June 28, 1922; Sidney S. Riggs to Frederic Bancroft, July 31, 1922; Sidney S. Riggs to Frederic Bancroft, Aug. 12, 1922; Sidney S. Riggs to Frederic Bancroft, Aug. 15, 1922; Sidney S. Riggs to Frederic Bancroft, May 31, 1922; and M.F. Kennedy to Frederick Bancroft, Aug. 12, 1922, all in Box 89, FBP.

18. Charles J. Holden, *In the Great Maelstrom: Conservatives in Post–Civil War South Carolina* (Columbia: University of South Carolina Press, 2002), 67–86; Theodore Jervey, "The Readjustment of the Negroes to the Social System of the Sixties: From the Standpoint of the Negroes," 5, Folder 2, Box 261, TJFP; Theodore Jervey, *The Slave Trade: Slavery and Color* (1925; repr., New York: Negro Universities Press, 1969), 4, 54, 49–50.

19. Frederic Bancroft to Theodore Jervey, Mar. 31, 1923, Folder 12; Frederic Bancroft to Theodore Jervey, Apr. 24, 1923, Folder 12; Frederic Bancroft to Theodore Jervey, July 26, 1920, Folder 1; and Frederic Bancroft to Theodore Jervey, Aug. 2, 1920, Folder 10, all in Box 248, TJFP.

20. Bancroft, *Slave Trading in the Old South*, xxii–xxxviii, 168.

21. Frederic Bancroft to Theodore Jervey, Jan. 8, [1931], and Frederic Bancroft to Theodore Jervey, Oct. 10, 1931, both in Folder 20, Box 248, TJFP; Theodore Jervey to Frederic Bancroft, Sept. 26, 1931, Box 49, FBP; Accession Records, 1907–1934, Sept. 8, 1931, CLSR; Bancroft, *Slave Trading in the Old South*, insert between pp. 168 and 169.

22. William Watts Ball, "Bancroft Writes of Slave Trading in the Old South," *CNC*, Mar. 15, 1931; Holden, *In the Great Maelstrom*, 87–101.

23. Frederic Bancroft to Theodore Jervey, July 21, 1931, and Frederic Bancroft to Theodore Jervey, Oct. 10, 1931, both in Folder 20, Box 248, TJFP.

24. Leonarda J. Aimar, "Stories Collected from Slaves," and William Pinckney, interview, Oct. 16, 1917, both in Folder 12, Box 603, AASP.

25. Martin Jackson, in *ASCA*, 4(2): 189; John Blassingame, introduction to his *Slave Testimony: Two Centuries of Letters, Speeches, Interviews, and Autobiographies* (Baton Rouge: Louisiana State University Press, 1977), xlv; Henry Bennett to Mrs. Warton, Feb. 21, 1941, Folder, "Ex-Slave Correspondence," Box 1, Entry 21, RG69.

26. Blassingame, introduction, xlii–lvi; Norman R. Yetman, "Ex-Slave Interviews and the Historiography of Slavery," *AQ* 36 (Summer 1984): 186–89; Marie Jenkins Schwartz, "The WPA Narratives as Historical Sources," in *The Oxford Handbook of the African American Slave Narrative*, ed. John Ernest (New York: Oxford University Press, 2014), 89–92; Sharon Ann Musher, "The Other Slave Narratives: The Works Progress Administration Interviews," in the *Oxford Handbook*, 106–14; Jerrold Hirsh, *Portrait of America: A Cultural History of* *the Federal Writers' Project* (Chapel Hill: University of North Carolina Press, 2003), 152–53; Stephanie J. Shaw, "Using the WPA Ex-Slave Narratives to Study the Impact of the Great Depression," *JSH* 69 (Aug. 2003): 623–58; Catherine A. Stewart, *Long Past Slavery: Representing Race in the Federal Writers' Project* (Chapel Hill: University of North Carolina Press, 2016).

27. Norman R. Yetman, "The Background of the Slave Narrative Collection," *AQ* 19 (Autumn 1967): 534–53; Sharon Ann Musher, *Democratic Art: The New Deal's Influence on American Culture* (Chicago: University of Chicago Press, 2015), 122–24; Paul Gardullo, "'No Deed But Memory': Slavery in the American Cultural Imagination, 1909–1939" (Ph.D. diss., George Washington University, 2006), 88–113.

28. George Cronyn to Mabel Montgomery, Apr. 2, 1937, Folder, "South Carolina, July 1937– Feb. 1938," Box 47, Entry 13, RG69; "Slave Narratives: A Folk History of Slavery in the United States From Interviews with Former Slaves" (Washington, DC: Library of Congress, 1941), ix–xxii (quote xx); Extracts from State Correspondence of George Cronyn, Apr. 14, 1937, Folder, "Ex-Slaves," Box 1, Entry 21, RG69; Gardullo, "'No Deed But Memory,'" 114–15; Yetman, "Background of the Slave Narrative Collection," 550.

29. Abbey Mishow, in *ASCA*, 3(3): 198–99; Amos Gadsden, in *ASCA*, 2(2): 91–92.

30. John Hamilton, in *ASCA*, 2(2): 221–22.

31. Dave White, in *ASCA*, 3(4): 194–95; Laura L. Middleton and Augustus Ladson to [Franklin Delano Roosevelt], July 8, 1937, Folder, "South Carolina Employment," Box 42, Entry 1, RG69; Prince Smith, in *ASCA*, 3(4): 117–18; Elijah Green, in *ASCA*, 2(2): 196– 97; "Dug Grave for Calhoun," *CNC*, Jan. 5, 1940; Elizabeth O'Neill Verner, *Mellowed by Time: A Charleston Notebook*, 3rd ed. (Columbia: Bostick and Thornley, 1953), 56.

32. "Supplementary Instructions #9-E to American Guide Manual, Folklore: Stories from Ex-Slaves, Apr. 22, 1937," in "Slave Narratives," xx; Sharon Ann Musher, "Contesting 'The Way the Almighty Wants It': Crafting Memories of Ex-Slaves in the Slave Narrative Collection," *AQ* 53 (Mar. 2001): 1–2; Blassingame, introduction, xlix–l; Gardullo, "'No Deed But Memory,'" 122–23.

33. Chalmers Murray to Mabel Montgomery, May 19, 1937, Folder, "South Carolina Folklore," Box 2, Entry 22, and Mabel Montgomery to Henry G. Alsberg, Jan. 30, 1936, Folder, "South Carolina 'M'–'N'," Box 43, Entry 1, both in RG69; Charles Spencer, *Edisto Island, 1861–2006: Ruin, Recovery and Rebirth* (Charleston: History Press, 2008), 165–66.

34. Chalmers Murray to Chlotilde Martin, May 20, 1937, Folder, "South Carolina Folklore," Box 2, Entry 22, RG69; "Chlotilde Martin, Former Reporter, Dies in Beaufort," *CEP*, Nov. 19, 1991; John Lomax to Mabel Montgomery, May 26, 1937, Folder, "South Carolina Folklore," Box 2, Entry 22, RG69.

35. Mabel Montgomery to Chalmers Murray, June 28, 1937, Folder, "South Carolina," Box 1, Entry 21, and Mabel Montgomery to John Lomax, May 21, 1937, Folder, "South Carolina Folklore," Box 2, Entry 22, both in RG69; Susan Hamilton, in *ASCA*, 2 (2): 236.

36. Chalmers Murray to Mabel Montgomery, July 1, 1937, Folder, "South Carolina," Box 1, Entry 21, RG69.

37. Chalmers Murray to Mabel Montgomery, July 8, 1937, Folder, "South Carolina," Box 1, Entry 21, RG69. Jessie A. Butler incorrectly identified Susan Hamilton as Susan Hamlin. Butler claimed that Ladson had mistakenly recorded Susan's surname as Hamilton, but the ex-slave's 1942 obituary reveals that Ladson, rather than Butler, had the correct surname. Jessie A. Butler, note appended to interview with Susan Hamlin [Hamilton], in *ASCA*, 2(2): 232; "Former Slave Passes Away," *CEP*, Jan. 12, 1942; Susan Hamilton, in *ASCA*, 2(2): 233–36.

38. Susan Hamlin [Hamilton], in *ASCA*, 2(2): 226–32.

39. Susan Hamlin [Hamilton], in *ASCA*, 2(2): 228; Murray to Montgomery, July 8, 1937.

40. Susan Hamlin [Hamilton] in *ASCA*, 2(2): 226–27, 229, 231; James West Davidson and Mark Hamilton Lytle, *After the Fact: The Art of Historical Detection*, 4th ed. (Boston: Mc-Graw Hill, 2000), 1: 163–69; Emily West, "Dolly, Lavinia, Maria, and Susan: Enslaved Women in Antebellum South Carolina," in *South Carolina Women: Their Lives and Times*, ed. Marjorie Julian Spruill, Joan Marie Johnson, and Valinda W. Littlefield (Athens: University of Georgia Press, 2009), 1: 137–39.

41. Mabel Montgomery to Henry Alsberg, July 30, 1937, Folder, "South Carolina," Box 1, Entry 21, RG69; Benjamin A. Botkin, introduction to "Slave Narratives," vi–viii; Jerry Mangione, *The Dream and the Deal: The Federal Writers' Project, 1935–1943* (Boston: Little, Brown, 1972), 263; Monty Noam Penkower, *The Federal Writers' Project: A Study in Government Patronage of the Arts* (Urbana: University of Illinois Press, 1977), 232; Ira Berlin, Marc Favreau, and Steven F. Miller, eds., *Remembering Slavery: African Americans Talk About Their Personal Experiences of Slavery and Freedom* (New York: New Press, 1998), xv–xvi.

42. Botkin, introduction, ix.

43. *CEP*, May 6, 1924; "Old Slave Market, Charleston, S.C.," postcard, [sent in 1921], and "Old Slave Market, Chalmers St., Charleston, S.C.," postcard, n.d., both in authors' personal collection.

44. Birth certificate, Miriam Anna Bellangee Wilson; Notarized document about parents, birth, name, and christening of Miriam B. Wilson, n.d.; Miriam B. Wilson to Ethelyn M. Parker, May 15, 1954; Miriam B. Wilson, resume, Oct. 6, 1936; and Miriam B. Wilson, "Personal History," May 10, 1957; all in OSMMP; Judith Wragg Chase, "Miriam Bellangee Wilson—Founder Old Slave Mart Museum," 1, in authors' possession; "Miss Miriam B. Wilson, Founder of Museum, Dies," *CNC*, July 8, 1959.

45. Thomas P. Stoney to Whom it May Concern, Jan. 25, 1925; Miriam B. Wilson, open letter for Tourist and Convention Bureau, Chamber of Commerce, Charleston, SC, n.d.; and Judith Chase Scrapbook, 7, 9, all in OSMMP; "Miss Miriam B. Wilson"; Chase, "Miriam Bellangee Wilson," 2; "News of Food: Old Slave Market in Charleston, S.C., Turned into Shop for Making Delicacies," *NYT*, Sept. 6, 1950; *CEP*, Jan. 4, 1927; Frank Campsall to Miriam B. Wilson, Apr. 9, 1930, OSMMP; Mary Read Lilly, " 'Yankee' Woman Makes Success of Southern Sweets and History," *CEP*, Jan. 28, 1949; *CEP*, Mar. 22, 1927; "Miss Wilson's Colonial Belle Goodies," *CEP*, Apr. 10, 1930.

46. Miriam B. Wilson, *Street Strolls Around Charleston: Giving the History, Legends, Traditions* (n.p., 1930), 42, CGTC; Chase Scrapbook, 5–7, 26; Chase, "Miriam Bellangee Wilson," 2, 4; "Three Pieces of Real Estate Sold," *CEP*, Jan. 13, 1938; *CEP*, Mar. 16, 1938; "Old Slave Market Restored in 1937," *CEP*, Dec. 2, 1941; Contract for sale of OSMM, July 26, 1937, OSMMP; Edmund L. Drago and Ralph Melnick, "The Old Slave Mart Museum, Charleston, South Carolina: Rediscovering the Past," *CWH* 27 (June 1981): 153–54; Stephanie E. Yuhl, "Hidden in Plain Sight: Centering the Domestic Slave Trade in American Public History," *JSH* 79 (Aug. 2013): 601–2. Wilson's museum was initially called the Old Slave Market, but by 1941 she had changed the name to the Old Slave Mart Museum.

47. "Old Slave Market Restored"; promotional flyer, Chase Scrapbook, 2; Old Slave Mart Museum guide leaflet, n.d., CGTC; Theodore Carlisle Landsmark, " 'Haunting Echoes': Histories and Exhibition Strategies for Collecting Nineteenth-Century African American Crafts" (Ph.D. diss., Boston University, 1999), 201; Andrea Burns, *From Storefront to Monument: Tracing the Public History of the Black Museum Movement* (Amherst: University of Massachusetts Press, 2013).

48. Mark Harris, "Best Buy in Charleston," *Negro Digest* 8 (July 1950): 43; Alston Chase, phone interview by Ethan J. Kytle, Nov. 11, 2015; "Old Slave Market Restored in 1937"; Miriam B. Wilson, proposal to Rosenwald Foundation to purchase Ryan's Jail, [1941]; Miriam B. Wilson,

"Project of Miriam Bellangee Wilson," n.d; Miriam B. Wilson to editors, *American Magazine*, [after Feb. 1940]; Miriam B. Wilson to Carl Van Vechten, Sept. 10, 1951; and Miriam B. Wilson to W.M. Spells, [May 17, 1959], all in OSMMP; Chase, "Miriam Bellangee Wilson," 4; Lib Wiley, "Operator of Charleston's Slave [Mart] Here Seeking Hand-Made Items," newspaper clipping from Lynchburg, VA [1950s], and Martha Carson, "Through Dedicated Friendship: A Life's Work Still Lives," *CEP*, Mar. 1, 1963, both in Chase Scrapbook, 6, 26; *CEP*, Apr. 10, 1939; *CEP*, May 29, 1944.

49. Nell Denney, "Visitor Finds Slave-Made Articles for Museum," newspaper clipping, n.d., Chase Scrapbook 6; "Museum Proprietor Completes Research in African Culture," *CEP*, Nov. 27, 1952; Miriam B. Wilson, application for the Eugene F. Saxton Memorial Trust, 1956; Chase, "Miriam Bellangee Wilson," 1; Miriam B. Wilson to Ruth Reynolds, Mar. 26, 1956; Miriam B. Wilson to Hank Drane, Mar. 13, 1952; Miriam B. Wilson to Mrs. C.L. Amos, May 17, 1953, including handwritten note by Mrs. C.L. Amos; Mrs. Daniel Banks to Miriam B. Wilson, Aug. 26, 1956; Miriam B. Wilson to Eva W. Davis, Aug 25, 1954; Eva W. Davis to Miriam B. Wilson, Sept. 2, 1954; and "She Collects Crafts of the Slave Era," [*Louisville Courier Journal*, Nov. 12, 1949], all in OSMMP; "Girl Scout Activities Reviewed," *CEP*, Mar. 17, 1944; Chase, "Miriam Bellangee Wilson," 3–4; Harris, "Best Buy in Charleston," 43.

50. Yuhl, "Hidden in Plain Sight," 601–2, 605; Yuhl, *Golden Haze of Memory*, 28–38; "Old Slave Market Restored in 1937"; Wilson, proposal to Rosenwald Foundation; Miriam B. Wilson, "Project of Miriam Bellangee Wilson"; Chase, "Miriam Bellangee Wilson," 4; Carson, "Through Dedicated Friendship"; Drago and Melnick, "Old Slave Mart Museum," 153–54; Wilson to Carl Van Vechten; Miriam B. Wilson to George McCue, Oct. 19, 1948, OSMMP; "Furtwangler Buys Old Slave Mart Gift Shop Here," *CEP*, Jan. 27, 1949; Wilson, application for the Eugene F. Saxton Memorial Trust.

51. Wilson, proposal to Rosenwald Foundation; Wilson, application for the Eugene F. Saxton Memorial Trust; "Notification Concerning Fellowship Application," Mar. 14, 1935; W.D. Watherford, president, Blue Ridge, Sept. 2, 1941; Norma S. Thompson, secretary, Rockefeller Foundation, to Miriam B. Wilson, Feb. 19, 1947; Bertha Wilcox Smith to Miriam B. Wilson, June 9, 1956, and Miriam B. Wilson, letter about medical difficulties on trip from St. Louis [after July 16, 1950], all in OSMMP; Chase, "Miriam Bellangee Wilson," 4; "Old Slave Mart Depicts Progress Made by Negroes"; Miriam B. Wilson, WCSC radio interview transcript, Oct. 11, 1939, OSMMP; *CEP*, Mar. 16, 1938; *CEP*, Mar. 20, 1940; "Mrs. Maria Gaillard to Perform in Gullah," *CEP*, Mar. 29, 1938; *CEP*, Mar. 29, 1939; Elijah Green postcard, 1953, University of Maryland, Baltimore County, Digital Collection, contentdm.ad.umbc.edu/cdm/ref/collection/rookscoll/id/67; "109-year-old Negro Dies at Home," *CEP*, May 22, 1945.

52. Carson, "Through Dedicated Friendship"; Chase, "Miriam Bellangee Wilson," 3; Minutes, Jan. 25, 1940, RHCC; "Chalmers Street Market Was Used to Sell Slaves," *CNC*, Sept. 19, 1948; Bartley I. Limehouse, "Charleston's Old Slave Mart Bequeathed to Museum Here," *CNC*, Aug. 5, 1959, in 6 Chalmers Street, Vertical File, SCHS.

53. OSMM brochure, n.d., in Chase Scrapbook, 11; Miriam B. Wilson, *Slave Days: Condensed from Factual Information* [also titled *Condensed History of Slavery*], 3rd ed. (Charleston: Old Slave Mart Museum, 1956), in authors' possession; Wiley, "Operator of Charleston's"; Yuhl, "Hidden in Plain Sight," 607; Theodore C. Landsmark, "Preserving African-American Culture in Spite of Itself," *Avery Review* 1 (Spring 1998): 54–55.

54. Wiley, "Operator of Charleston's"; Chase, "Miriam Bellangee Wilson," 1; Lilly, "'Yankee' Woman"; Miriam B. Wilson, untitled manuscript about Wilson and the Old Slave Mart Museum, n.d., and Miriam B. Wilson, "Childhood Remenicences [*sic*] of the South Sixty Years Ago," [1940s], both in OSMMP; Wilson to Carl Van Vechten; Landsmark, "'Haunting Echoes,'" 191; "South Carolina Museum Owner Is Visitor in City," *Vicksburg Post-Herald*, Aug. 1, 1948, OSMMP.

55. Miriam B. Wilson to Anna Wilson, [ca. 1927]; Miriam B. Wilson, "They Know Us," [1940s]; and "Novelist at Huckleberry for Research," newspaper clipping, July 19, 1956, all in OSMMP.

56. Miriam B. Wilson, *Slave Days* (1956), 11, n.p.; Old Slave Mart Museum Guide Leaflet, [after 1959], p. 7, CGTC; Darlene O'Dell, *Sites of Southern Memory: The Autobiographies of Katharine Du Pre Lumpkin, Lillian Smith, and Pauli Murray* (Charlottesville: University of Virginia Press, 2001), 63–64; Miriam B. Wilson to Ashley Halsey Jr., Sept. 6, 1950, OSMMP.

57. Miriam B. Wilson to Robert J. Kalthoff, [Feb.–Mar. 1953], OSMMP; Wilson, *Slave Days* (1956), 25; Wilson to Carl Van Vechten; "Woman Studying at Yale on Slavery Crafts," *New Haven Register*, Aug. 21, 1961, Chase Scrapbook, 6.

58. Miriam B. Wilson, *Slave Days: Condensed from Factual Information* (Charleston: Old Slave Mart Museum, 1946), 9, Folder 2, Box 1, OSMMC; "Miss Miriam B. Wilson"; Denney, "Visitor Finds Slave-Made Articles"; Miriam B. Wilson, "Highlights of Slavery," n.d., p. 15, OSMM.

59. Wilson, *Slave Days* (1956), n.p.; Grace and Knickerbacker Davis, "'Thenceforward, and Forever Free,'" *Forward*, magazine clipping, [1941 or 1942], 13, and Miriam B. Wilson, notes on OSMM lecture, n.d., both in OSMMP.

60. Wilson, *Slave Days* (1946), 10; Wilson, notes on OSMM lecture; Davis and Davis, "'Thenceforward, and Forever Free,'" 13; Knickerbacker Davis to Miriam B. Wilson, Mar. 16, 1942, OSMMP.

61. Miriam B. Wilson to Robert Taft, May 16, 1950, OSMMP; Wilson, "They Know Us"; Wilson, "Highlights of Slavery," 16, 28–29, 32; Yuhl, "Hidden in Plan Sight," 608; Wilson, *Slave Days* (1946); Wilson, untitled manuscript on the history of slavery, p. 15, OSMMP.

62. Miriam B. Wilson to Dr. Patterson, May 6, 1949, and Miriam B. Wilson, "Suggestions which may help the Negro Race," n.d., both in OSMMP.

63. Wilson, *Slave Days* (1946), 13; Millicent Brown, phone interview by Ethan J. Kytle, July 8, 2015; Landsmark, "'Haunting Echoes,'" 209–16.

64. Wilson, proposal to Rosenwald Foundation; C. Gordon Beacham to Miriam B. Wilson, Aug. 11, 1942; B. Claire Reenstjerna to Miriam B. Wilson, May 5, 1954; Louise Boatwright to Miriam B. Wilson, n.d.; and Doris Pollock to Miriam B. Wilson, Jan. 11, 1952, all in OSMMP.

65. Katharine Du Pre Lumpkin, *The Making of a Southerner* (1947; repr., Athens: University of Georgia Press, 1981), 115; Jacquelyn Dowd Hall, "Open Secrets: Memory, Imagination, and the Refashioning of Southern Identity," *AQ* 50 (1998): 109–24; O'Dell, *Sites of Southern Memory*, 63–64.

66. Harris, "Best Buy in Charleston," 44.

67. Wilson, proposal to Rosenwald Foundation; Miriam B. Wilson to Maggie F. Jones, Jan. 28, 1957, OSMMP; Ethelyn M. Parker to Miriam B. Wilson, June 11, 1954, OSMMP; Biographical Note, "Inventory of the Ethelyn Murray Parker Papers, 1899–1922," avery.cofc.edu/archives/Parker_Ethelyn.html.

68. "Negro Students Visit Display on Slave Art," *CNC*, Apr. 18, 1956; "Old Slave Mart Art Exhibit Depicts Negro Handicrafts," *CNC*, Apr. 10, 1956; Brown, phone interview.

69. Wilson, application for the Eugene F. Saxton Memorial Trust; Miriam B. Wilson, introduction to outline, n.d.; Miriam B. Wilson, "Plan for Work," 1947; Miriam B. Wilson, unpublished letter to the editor of the *NYT*, Oct. 18, 1952; and Miriam B. Wilson to Marion A. Woodson, Apr. 16, 1957, all in OSMMP.

70. "Miss Wilson, Dies at Residence," *CEP*, July 7, 1959; "Miss Miriam B. Wilson"; "'Slave Mart' Bequeathed to Museum," *CEP*, Aug. 5, 1959; Limehouse, "Charleston's Old Slave

Mart Bequeathed"; Board of Trustees Minutes, Charleston Museum, Jan. 1960, CM; Chase, "Miriam Bellangee Wilson," 4; Christine Randall, "Curator Catalogs Collection," *CNC*, Nov. 1, 1978; Judith Wragg Chase to Bernard [Fielding], Mar. 27, 1973, Box 6, YWCAR; Greta Tilley, "Sisters Try to Save Museum," *GNR*, May 18, 1986; Alston Chase, phone interview; "Old Slave Mart Reopening as a Museum Is Announced," *CNC*, Nov. 26, 1960, 6 Chalmers St., Vertical File, CCPL; Louise A. Graves, application, Institute of Museum Services, Department of Health, Education, and Welfare, Mar. 8, 1979, and 6 Chalmers Street, deed of sale, June 12, 1964, both in OSMMPCC; "Old Slave Mart Museum Is Sold," *CEP*, Mar. 31, 1965, Vertical File, CCPL.

71. Chase Scrapbook, 3, 14; "Searching Africa for Art," *CNC*, Feb 24, 1967; Randall, "Curator Catalogs Collection"; Judith Wragg Chase to Fred J. Martschink, May 14, 1963, Old Slave Mart, General Files, CCR.

9. WE SHALL OVERCOME

1. Roy Wilkins, quoted in Stephen O'Neill, "From the Shadow of Slavery: The Civil Rights Years in Charleston" (Ph.D. diss., University of Virginia, 1994), 229. The description of the Charleston Movement that follows is from O'Neill, 223–26, and Millicent Ellison Brown, "Civil Rights Activism in Charleston, South Carolina, 1940–1970" (Ph.D. diss., Florida State University, 1997), 175–92.

2. Lindy Cooper, interview by Guy Carawan, Apr. 1983, Folder 79, GCCC.

3. Shana L. Redmond, *Anthem: Social Movements and the Sound of Solidarity in the African Diaspora* (New York: New York University Press, 2014), 152–69; Thomas Wentworth Higginson, *Army Life in a Black Regiment and Other Writings* (1870; reprint, New York: Penguin, 1997), 169; William Francis Allen, Charles Pickard Ware, Lucy McKim Garrison, eds., *Slave Songs of the United States* (1867; reprint, New York: Dover, 1995), xix, 64; Victor V. Bobetsky, "The Complex Ancestry of 'We Shall Overcome,'" in *We Shall Overcome: Essays on a Great American Song*, ed. Victor Bobetsky (Lanham, MD: Rowan Littlefield, 2014), 4–6; Stephen A. Schneider, *You Can't Padlock an Idea: Rhetorical Education at the Highlander Folk School, 1932–1961* (Columbia: University of South Carolina Press, 2014), 157–59; Lillie May Marsh Doster, interview by Otha Jennifer Dixon, transcript, June 25, 2008, SOHP; Lillie May Marsh (Doster), quoted in Guy and Candie Carawan, *Sing for Freedom: The Story of the Civil Rights Movement through Its Songs* (Bethlehem, PA: Sing Out Corporation, 1992), 238; Stephen P. Graham, quoted in Bernice Johnson Reagon, "Songs of the Civil Rights Movement, 1955–1965: A Study in Culture History" (Ph.D. diss., Howard University, 1975), 74.

4. See, for example, Glenn T. Eskew, *But for Birmingham: The Local and National Movements in the Civil Rights Struggle* (Chapel Hill: University of North Carolina Press, 1997).

5. R. Scott Baker, *Paradoxes of Desegregation: African American Struggles for Educational Equity in Charleston, South Carolina, 1926–1972* (Columbia: University of South Carolina), 127–38; Matthew D. Lassiter and Andrew B. Lewis, eds., *The Moderates' Dilemma: Massive Resistance to School Desegregation in Virginia* (Charlottesville: University of Virginia Press, 1998).

6. Clay Risen, *The Bill of the Century: The Epic Battle for the Civil Rights Act* (New York: Bloomsbury, 2014); Gary May, *Bending Toward Justice: The Voting Rights Act and the Transformation of American Democracy* (New York: Basic Books, 2013).

7. O'Neill, "From the Shadow of Slavery," 198–203, 217–21, 236–40; Brown, "Civil Rights Activism in Charleston, South Carolina, 1940–1970," 88–90, 166–75, 209–212; Jon Hale, "'The Fight Was Instilled in Us': High School Activism and the Civil Rights Movement in Charleston," *SCHM* 114 (Jan. 2013): 4–48; Baker, *Paradoxes of Desegregation*, 154–57.

8. O'Neill, "From the Shadow of Slavery," esp. 6–143; Henry B. Smythe to Mrs. Joseph J. Waring, Mar. 31, 1958, and Minutes, Nov. 7, 1958, Minutes, Executive Committee, both in SPSP.

9. Henry B. Smythe to Dr. John Arthur Siegling, Apr. 23, 1958, SPSP; Minutes, Annual Meeting, 1968, and Minutes, Annual Meeting, Oct. 18, 1965, both in Minutes, Annual Meetings, SPSP.

10. Jennie R. Porcher to John Arthur [Siegling], Apr. 12, 1956, SPSP.

11. John M. Rivers to Mr. Paul Roberts, Sept. 4, 1956, SPSP.

12. "Other Men's Opinions," *Florida Times Union*, n.d., n.p., reprinted in *CNC*, Mar. 19, 1959, Clippings, 1950s–1960s, SPSP; Jenny Woodley, *Art for Equality: The NAACP's Cultural Campaign for Civil Rights* (Lexington: University Press of Kentucky, 2014), 127–89; Elizabeth O'Neill Verner, "Don't Forget Spirituals," *CNC*, Mar. 24, 1960, Clippings, 1950s–1960s, SPSP.

13. Mrs. Henry S. Walker to Mrs. John Siegling, Nov. 26, 1960, and Nov. 4, 1963, Minutes, Executive Committee, both in SPSP.

14. Minutes, Mar. 24, 1968, and Minutes Mar. 19, 1968, both in Minutes, Executive Committee, SPSP.

15. Jeffrey O.G. Ogbar, *Black Power: Radical Politics and African American Identity* (Baltimore: Johns Hopkins University Press, 2004), 111; Kristen Meyers Turner, "Guy and Candie Carawan: Mediating the Music of the Civil Rights Movement" (master's thesis, University of North Carolina at Chapel Hill, 2011), 9; Guy Carawan, quoted in Peter J. Ling, "Developing Freedom Songs: Guy Carawan and the African-American Traditions of the South," *History Workshop Journal* (Autumn 1997): 208.

16. Much of the information that follows about Carawan and his family comes from Peter J. Ling, "Developing Freedom Songs," 198–213; Peter J. Ling, "Spirituals, Freedom Songs, and *Lieux de Memoire*: African-American Music and the Routes of Memory," *Prospects* 24 (October 1999): 213–30; Turner, "Guy and Candie Carawan"; Joe Street, *The Culture War in the Civil Rights Movement* (Gainesville: University Press of Florida, 2007), 15–26; Guy and Candie Carawan, *Ain't You Got a Right to the Tree of Life? The People of Johns Island, South Carolina—Their Faces, Their Words and Their Songs* (New York: Simon and Schuster, 1966); Guy and Candie Carawan, interview by Katherine Mellen Charron, transcript, Nov. 12, 2001, in authors' possession; Guy and Candie Carawan, *Sing for Freedom*, 4; "Henrietta Aiken Kelly and the Post–Civil War Silk Industry," *PSCHA* (May 2014): 13–24; Candie Carawan, emails to Blain Roberts, July 13 and 17, 2014; and Debra Bloom, email to Blain Roberts, July 20, 2014.

17. Pete Seeger, *Where Have All the Flowers Gone? A Musical Autobiography* (Bethlehem, PA: Sing Out, 1993), 32–35; John M. Glen, *Highlander: No Ordinary School, 1932–1962* (Lexington: University Press of Kentucky, 1988), 148; Reagon, "Songs of the Civil Rights Movement, 1955–1965," 76–82; Redmond, *Anthem*, 173–74; Horton, *The Highlander Folk School*, 148; David King Dunaway, *How Can I Keep from Singing: Pete Seeger* (New York: McGraw-Hill, 1981), 222; Pete Seeger and Bob Reiser, *Everybody Says Freedom* (New York: W.W. Norton, 1989), 8; Guy and Candie Carawan, *Sing for Freedom*, 4, 238; Guy and Candie Carawan, eds., *Freedom Is a Constant Struggle: Songs of the Freedom Movement* (New York: Oak Publications, 1968), 138–39; Josh Dunson, *Freedom in the Air: Song Movements of the Sixties* (Westport, CT: Greenwood Press, 1965), 29–30; Robert Rogers Korstad, *Civil Rights Unionism: Tobacco Workers and the Struggle for Democracy in the Mid-Twentieth-Century South* (Chapel Hill: University of North Carolina Press, 2003), 239.

18. Guy Carawan to Pete [Seeger], Moe [Asch], and Irwin [Silber], Aug. 3, 1959, Folder 403, GCCC.

19. "'We Shall Overcome': Origin of Rights Song," *Washington Star*, July 11, 1965; Katherine Mellen Charron, *Freedom's Teacher: The Life of Septima Clark* (Chapel Hill: University

of North Carolina Press, 2009), 269; Allen, Ware, Garrison, *Slave Songs of the United States*, iii, 23–24; Guy Carawan to Pete [Seeger], Moe [Asch], and Irwin [Silber].

20. O'Neill, "From the Shadow of Slavery," 176–77, 181–92; Charron, *Freedom's Teacher*, 216–63; Peter Ling, "Local Leadership in the Early Civil Rights Movement: The South Carolina Citizenship Education Program of the Highlander Folk School," *Journal of American Studies* 29 (Dec. 1995): 399–422; Brown, "Civil Rights Activism in Charleston, South Carolina, 1940–1970," 118–24; Guy Carawan, "The Living Folk Heritage of the Sea Islands," *Sing Out!* (Apr.–May, 1964), 29; Guy and Candie Carawan, interview; Redmond, *Anthem*, 173.

21. Guy and Candie Carawan, *Ain't You Got a Right*, 10; Art Rosenbaum, *The African American Ring Shout Tradition in Coastal Georgia* (Athens: University of Georgia Press, 1998), 1, 48–49; Song Lists, Folder 595, GCCC.

22. Ling, "Developing Freedom Songs," 201; Guy and Candie Carawan, *Ain't You Got a Right*, 9–10, 107 (Saunders quote); Josh Dunson, "Slave Songs at the 'Sing for Freedom,'" typescript of *Broadside* article, May 30, 1964, in Sing for Freedom Festival and Workshop Report, 1964, Folder 158, GCCC; Steve Estes, *Charleston in Black and White: Race and Power in the South after the Civil Rights Movement* (Chapel Hill: University of North Carolina Press, 2015), 28; Carawan, "The Living Folk Heritage of the Sea Islands," 31.

23. Guy Carawan, undated report on Highlander work, Folder 18, Box 7, SPCP; Esau Jenkins, quoted in Guy and Candie Carawan, *Ain't You Got a Right*, 85; Charron, *Freedom's Teacher*, 216–63; Ling, "Developing Freedom Songs," 204; Guy and Candie Carawan, interview.

24. Ling, "Spirituals, Freedom Songs, and *Lieux de Memoire*," 225; Ling, "Developing Freedom Songs," 203, 206 (Carawan quote); John Michael Spencer, *Protest and Praise: Sacred Music of Black Religion* (Minneapolis: Fortress Press, 1990), 83, 85, 104; Turner, "Guy and Candie Carawan," 71. On freedom songs, see Kerran L. Sanger, *"When the Spirit Says Sing!": The Role of Freedom Songs in the Civil Rights Movement* (New York: Garland, 1995); Guy and Candie Carawan, *Sing for Freedom*; Dunson, *Freedom in the Air*; Seeger and Reiser, *Everybody Says Freedom*; T.V. Reed, *The Art of Protest: Culture and Activism from the Civil Rights Movement to the Streets of Seattle* (Minneapolis: University of Minnesota Press, 2005), 1–39; Street, *The Culture War in the Civil Rights Movement*, 15–39; and Reagon, "Songs of the Civil Rights Movement, 1955–1965."

25. Reverend C.T. Vivian, quoted in Guy and Candie Carawan, *Sing for Freedom*, 4; Brian Ward, *Just My Soul Responding: Rhythm and Blues, Black Consciousness, and Race Relations* (Berkeley: University of California Press, 1998), 173–216, 294 (first Guy Carawan quote); Guy and Candie Carawan, interview; Turner, "Guy and Candie Carawan," 23; Guy Carawan, quoted in Seeger and Reiser, *Everybody Says Freedom*, 39.

26. Bernice Johnson Reagon and Reverend C.T. Vivian, quoted in Guy and Candie Carawan, *Sing for Freedom*, 3, 4; Bernice Johnson Reagon, "Since I Laid My Burden Down," in *Hands on the Freedom Plow: Personal Accounts by Women in SNCC*, ed. Faith D. Holsaert et al. (Urbana: University of Illinois Press, 2010), 149; Ward, *Just My Soul Responding*, 294.

27. *Ain't You Got a Right to the Tree of Life* and Kristen Meyers Turner's master's thesis, "Guy and Candie Carawan: Mediating the Music of the Civil Rights Movement," provide the best window into the important and often unrecognized role that Candie Carawan played in helping her husband promote and preserve the music of Johns Island. Dunson, *Freedom in the Air*, 103; Dunson, "Slave Songs at the 'Sing for Freedom.'"

28. Dunson, "Slave Songs at the 'Sing for Freedom'"; Bernice Johnson Reagon to Guy Carawan, Sept. 29, 1987, Folder 158, GCCC.

29. Guy and Candie Carawan, "Sea Islands," Guy and Candie Carawan: A Personal Story Through Site and Sound Website, digitalstudio.ucr.edu/studio_projects/carawan/seaislands4

.html; Ronald D. Cohen, *A History of Folk Music Festivals in the U.S.: Feasts of Musical Celebration* (Lanham, MD: Scarecrow Press, 2008), 62, 70, 86; "John's Island Group to Play in Washington," *CNC*, June 29, 1969; "Folk Festival Launched at Capital Park," *Toledo Blade*, July 27, 1972.

30. Carawan, "The Living Folk Heritage of the Sea Islands," 31; Robert Shelton, "Beneath the Festival's Razzle-Dazzle," *NYT*, Aug. 1, 1965; Guy Carawan, Sing for Freedom Festival and Workshop Statement and Proposal, 1965, Folder 165, GCCC; Barbara J. Stambaugh, "Folk Festival to Mark End of Voter Workshop," unidentified newspaper clipping, Folder 621, GCCC.

31. Cooper, interview; Guy Carawan, Sing for Freedom Festival and Workshop Statement and Proposal, 1965.

32. Alan Lomax, "Folk Singing Is Rediscovered on Island," *CNC*, Jan. 19, 1964, Folder 621, GCCC; Guy and Candie Carawan, interview by John Sundale, "Society for the Preservation of Spirituals," 1979, Digital Library of Appalachia, Warren Wilson College, dla.acaweb.org /cdm/singleitem/collection/Warren/id/2661/rec/8; Minutes, Annual Meeting, 1969, Minutes, Annual Meetings, SPSP.

33. Guy and Candie Carawan, *Ain't You Got a Right*, 9, 85 (Esau Jenkins quote).

34. Ibid., 21–22.

35. Book review of *Ain't You Got a Right to the Tree of Life*, by Guy and Candie Carawan, *NYT*, June 11, 1967; Jack Leland, "Errors of Fact Cloud Report on Negroes of John's Island," *CEP*, Mar. 26, 1967, and Owen Daugh [Jack Leland], "Unfortunate, Glaring Errors Mar Carawan Book on John's Island," *CNC*, Mar. 26, 1967, both in Folder 43, GCCC.

36. Julius Lester, review of *Ain't You Got a Right to the Tree of Life*, by Guy and Candie Carawan, *Sing Out!* 17 (June/July 1967): 41

37. Guy and Candie Carawan, *Ain't You Got a Right*, 10; [William] Bill Saunders and Frankie [?] to Guy and Candie Carawan, June 15, 1967, Folder 43, GCCC.

38. Turner, "Guy and Candie Carawan," 11 (Candie Carawan quote), 54–55.

39. Mary Ancrum, "Negro History Week Observed," *Parvenue*, Mar. 29, 1951, ARC; Haut Gap High School, Johns Island, South Carolina, Negro History Week Program, n.d., Box 1, Folder 4, AJMP; "Negro History to Be Studied," *CEP*, Jan. 11, 1958; "Classes to Be Held in Negro History," *CEP*, Jan. 8, 1959; "Classes in History of Negro to Begin Tomorrow Morning," *CNC*, Jan. 9, 1959, Folder 108, Box 5, ELDP; "83 Students Here Complete Course in Negro History," *CNC*, Feb. 20, 1958.

40. "Negro History," *CNC*, Jan. 16, 1958; John H. Wrighten to Superintendent [Thomas A. Carrere], Jan. 17, 1958, Negro History 1958 Folder, Box 863, CCSDA; Drago, *Initiative, Paternalism, and Race Relations: Charleston's Avery Normal Institute* (Athens: University of Georgia Press, 1990), 231–34; Brown, "Civil Rights Activism in Charleston, South Carolina, 1940–1970," 44–48.

41. [Thomas A. Carrere] to Mr. F.M. Kirk, Jan. 21, 1958; [Thomas A. Carrere] to John H. Wrighten, Feb. 17, 1958; Thomas A. Carrere to Mr. Wilmot J. Fraser, July 14, 1959; John H. Wrighten to Mr. Thomas A. Carrere, Jan. 26, 1962; and Thomas A. Carrere to Mr. John H. Wrighten, Jan. 30, 1962, all in Negro History 1958 Folder, Box 863, CCSDA; "Negro History," *CNC*, July 11, 1959, Scrapbook, District 20, Feb. 1959–Apr. 1960, CCSDA.

42. Alston Chase, phone interview by Ethan J. Kytle, Nov. 18, 2015; "Old Slave Mart Plans to Have Special Preview," *CEP*, Nov. 25, 1960; Judith W. Chase, "Comprehensive Information Relating to the History, Purpose, and Operation of the Old Slave Mart Museum & Library, 1937 through 1985" and 6 Chalmers Street, deed of sale, June 12, 1964, both in OSMMPCC; Christine Randall, "Curator Catalogs Collection," *CNC*, Nov. 1, 1978; Louise A. Graves, application, Institute of Museum Services, Department of Health, Education, and Welfare, Mar. 8, 1979, p.12, OSMMPCC.

43. Alston Chase, phone interview; Chase, "Comprehensive Information," 37, 45; Stephanie E. Yuhl, "Hidden in Plain Sight: Centering the Domestic Slave Trade in American Public History," *JSH* 79 (Aug. 2013): 610–11; OSMM flyer, 1970, in Judith Chase Scrapbook, 3, OSMMP.

44. Greta Tilley, "Sisters Try to Save Museum," *Greensboro News and Record*, May 18, 1986; Alston Chase, phone interview; Chase, "Comprehensive Information," 41; Miriam B. Wilson Foundation, Board of Trustees Meeting Minutes, Mar. 20, 1974, OSMMC; "YWCA Votes to Quit National Organization," *CNC*, May 20, 1967; "New YWCA Organization Forms Here," *CNC*, Mar. 11, 1969; First Board of Directors List, n.d., Administrative Papers, 1970s, Box 6, and Judith Chase to Bernard [Fielding], Mar. 27, 1973, Administrative Papers, 1972, Box 6, both in YWCAR; "King to Be Honored," *CEP*, Jan. 8, 1972; "YWCA Explains National Affiliation," *CEP*, Dec. 14, 1972; Cherisse Jones-Branch, *Crossing the Line: Women's Interracial Activism in South Carolina during and after World War II* (Gainesville: University Press of Florida, 2014), 99–103.

45. Beta Kappa Lambda Chapter of Alpha Phi Alpha, Citizenship Award Statement, Apr. 1, 1973, Administrative Papers, 1972, Box 6, YWCAR; Chase, "Comprehensive Information," 41, 49–50; Graves, application, Institute of Museum Services, 14; Phillis Wheatley Activities Through the Years, Box 2, Programs Folder, PWLSCP; "Museum Curator to Speak at YWCA Meeting," *CEP*; "Church Plans Festival of Arts," *CEP*, Nov. 18, 1965; "March Classes Scheduled at Coming Street 'Y,'" *CEP*, Feb. 25, 1965; Miriam B. Wilson, Board of Trustees Minutes, May 1, 1965, OSMMC; Tilley, "Sisters Try to Save Museum"; Press Release on Judith Wragg Chase, Nov. 1965, Administrative Papers, 1972, Box 6, YWCAR.

46. "Old Slave Mart Begins Art Competition Project," *CEP*, June 6, 1963; Miriam B. Wilson Foundation, Board of Trustees Meeting Minutes, May 1, 1965, OSMMC; Judith Chase to Bernard [Fielding], Mar. 27, 1973; "Afro-American Art Offered at Carolina," *CEP*, Jan. 14, 1972.

47. Sandra Burch, "Emphasis on Minorities," *CEP*, Mar. 19, 1975; Sheryl Brunson, "New Course Emphasizes State's Ethnic History," *CEP*, May 1, 1978; Karen Amrhine, "Bicentennial Committee Seeks to Involve Blacks," *CNC*, June 30, 1973; Office of Education, Department of Health, Education, and Welfare, "Title IX Ethnic Heritage Project Analysis: A Study of Title IX, ESEA, Ethnic Heritage Projects Funded by the U.S. Office of Education, Health, Education and Welfare, July 1, 1974, through June 30, 1975" (June 1975), 13, 56, 58, 59, 60, 61–62, files.eric.ed.gov/fulltext/ED109006.pdf; John David Skrentny, *The Minority Rights Revolution* (Cambridge, MA: Harvard University Press, 2004), 302; Michael Kammen, *Mystic Chords of Memory: The Transformation of Tradition in American Culture* (New York: Vintage, 1993), 616.

48. Baker, *Paradoxes of Desegregation*, 127–77 (quote 145); Doug Pardue, "A Walk that Changed History," *CPC*, Sept. 1, 2013.

49. Martha Biondi, *The Black Revolution on Campus* (Berkeley: University of California Press, 2012); Baker, *Paradoxes of Desegregation*, 172–73; "Black Students 'Outnumbered' in Dispute at St. Andrews High," *CHR*, Jan. 27/Feb. 2, 1972.

50. Jim French, "Schools: Soul of Charleston," *CHR*, Feb. 17–23, 1972; "Parents, Civil Leaders Say James Island Showdown Planned by Whites," *CHR*, Feb. 17–23, 1972; "Students, Cops and Fire Trucks Boxed Us in Says Blacks," *CHR*, Feb. 17–23, 1972.

51. Alex Macaulay, *Marching in Step: Masculinity, Citizenship, and The Citadel in Post–World War II America* (Athens: University of Georgia Press, 2009), 61–86.

52. "Black Cadets Interview: Is The Citadel Biased?" *Brigadier*, Mar. 7, 1970, CAR; "Truth in History," *CNC*, Apr. 7, 1969; "African History," *CNC*, Sept. 22, 1968; "Black Studies . . . ," *Brigadier*, May 1, 1970, CAR; Macaulay, *Marching in Step*, 78.

53. Christopher Lewis, quoted in John M. Coski, *The Confederate Battle Flag: America's Most Embattled Emblem* (Cambridge, MA: Belknap Press of Harvard University Press, 2005), 221.

54. "A Self Study, The Citadel," 1972, chapter seven, 29–30, CAR.

55. Macaulay, *Marching in Step*, 81; Frank Ward, "Tradition or Prejudice?" *Brigadier*, Dec. 8, 1972; John Brasington, "The Flag," *Brigadier*, Nov. 19, 1971; Ralph Towell, "State of the Corps," *Brigadier*, Sept. 29, 1972; and James Gilpatrick, letter to the editor, *Brigadier*, Oct. 5, 1973, all in CAR.

56. Preston Mitchell, letter to the editor, *Brigadier*, Feb. 22, 1974, CAR; Coski, *The Confederate Battle Flag*, 221. The appropriateness of the Confederate battle flag and "Dixie" became an issue at the Citadel again in the late 1980s. K. Michael Prince, *Rally 'Round the Flag, Boys! South Carolina and the Confederate Flag* (Columbia: University of South Carolina Press, 2004), 140; Macaulay, *Marching in Step*, 183–91.

57. O. Jennifer Dixon-McKnight, " 'We Shall Not Always Plant While Others Reap': Black Female Hospital Workers and the Charleston Hospital Strike, 1943–1970" (Ph.D. diss., University of North Carolina at Chapel Hill, 2017); Jewell Charmaine Debnam, "Black Women and the Charleston Hospital Workers' Strike of 1969" (Ph.D. diss., Michigan State University, 2016); Leon Fink and Brian Greenberg, *Upheaval in the Quiet Zone: A History of Hospital Workers' Union, Local 1199* (Urbana: University of Illinois Press, 1989), 129–58; O'Neill, "From the Shadow of Slavery," 252–70; "Arrests in Charleston," *NYT*, Apr. 29, 1969; Walter J. Fraser Jr., *Charleston! Charleston! The History of a Southern City* (Columbia: University of South Carolina Press, 1989), 422.

58. Elaine S. Stanford, "Negotiators Meet in Hospital Strike," *CNC*, March 23, 1969; O'Neill, "From the Shadow of Slavery," 281; David Robertson, *Denmark Vesey: The Buried Story of America's Largest Slave Rebellion and the Man Who Led It* (New York: Knopf, 1999), 129, 117; W.K. Pillow Jr. and Stewart R. King, "Thousands March in Support of Strike," *CNC*, May 12, 1969. On the myth of the hanging tree, see chapter 5. "Curfews Nothing New to City," *CNC*, May 4, 1969; Alice Cabaness [*sic*], "Strike and Curfew," *New South* 24 (Summer 1969): 44.

59. O'Neill, "From the Shadow of Slavery," 253–99; Debnam, "Black Women and the Charleston Hospital Workers' Strike of 1969," 2–26.

60. "Revolt Against Slavery," *CHR*, Sept. 16, 1972; "Revolt Against Slavery," [part 4], *CHR*, Oct. 14, 1972.

61. Bobby Isaac, "Plan to Capture City Failed," *CNC*, May 18, 1975; Arthur C. McFarland, "We Refuse to Allow Denmark, Esau, Septima to Go Unrecognized," *CHR*, Apr. 26, 1975; James L. Felder, *Civil Rights in South Carolina: From Peaceful Protests to Groundbreaking Rulings* (Charleston: History Press, 2012), 18; "McFarland Retires as Municipal Judge," *CPC*, Dec. 23, 2009.

62. Kacy Sackett, "Council Votes to Sell City Airport Property," *CEP*, Oct. 29, 1975; "Robert Ford Rejects Name for Auditorium," *CNC*, Nov. 5, 1975; Robert R. Weyeneth, *Historic Preservation for a Living City: Historic Charleston Foundation, 1947–1967* (Columbia: University of South Carolina Press, 2000), 65.

63. O'Neill, "From the Shadow of Slavery," 228, 238; Clyde Johnson, "Charleston Is Requested to Honor King, Vesey," *CEP*, Dec. 24, 1975; "Asks Renaming of King St.," *CHR*, Dec. 20, 1975; Bobby Isaac, letter to the editor, *CHR*, Nov. 22, 1975.

64. Bobby Isaac, "Plan to Capture City Failed"; "Murderous Mankind," *CEP*, Dec. 9, 1975; Carlton J. Poulnot Sr., letter to the editor, *CNC*, Jan. 14, 1976; Tom Hamrick, "Tom Hamrick Speaks Out," *CHR*, Nov. 15, 1975.

65. O'Neill, "From the Shadow of Slavery," 288–314, esp. 296–99; Fraser, *Charleston! Charleston!*, 408, 428–29; Estes, *Charleston in Black and White*, 44.

66. Barbara S. Williams, "Riley Wins Mayor's Race," *CNC*, Dec. 10, 1975. The previous city council had included thirteen whites and three blacks. O'Neill, "From the Shadow of Slavery," 298, 299 (Ford quote); "Ford Accuses Ministers of Using the Church for Political Gain," *CHR*, Dec. 13, 1975.

67. Brian Hicks, *The Mayor: Joe Riley and the Rise of Charleston* (Charleston: Evening Post Books, 2015), 42–68; Walter Edgar, *South Carolina: A History* (Columbia: University of South Carolina Press, 1998), 545–47.

68. "Ford Accuses Ministers of Using the Church for Political Gain"; O'Neill, "From the Shadow of Slavery," 313; Williams, "Riley Wins Mayor's Race"; Estes, *Charleston in Black and White*, 35–56; Hicks, *The Mayor*, 86–94.

69. Bobby Isaac, "King Portrait Support Growing," *CNC*, May 11, 1976; Ashley Cooper, "Doing the Charleston," *CNC*, May 13, 1976; Clyde Johnson, "Management Study Firm Is Hired by Charleston," *CEP*, March 24, 1976; Karen Greene, "Teacher Communicates with Art," *CEP*, Aug. 22, 1976; Robert Ford, "Says Daily Press Responsible for Theft of Vesey Painting," *CHR*, Sept. 25, 1976.

70. "City Hall to Unveil Portrait of Rebel Slave Leader," *CNC*, Aug. 3, 1976; Mary A. Glass, "Slave's Picture Hung in Auditorium," *CNC*, Aug. 10, 1976; "At Unveiling of Denmark Vesey," *CHR*, Aug. 14, 1976; Greene, "Teacher Communicates with Art."

71. Shirley J. Holcombe, letter to the editor, *CNC*, Aug. 9, 1976.

72. Ashley Cooper, "Doing the Charleston," *CNC*, Aug. 13, 1976; "Black Judges," *CEP*, Aug. 2, 1976.

73. Mr. and Mrs. W. Lester Webb, letter to the editor, *CNC*, Aug. 11, 1976; Eleanor R. Craighill, letter to the editor, *CNC*, Aug. 16, 1976.

74. "At Unveiling of Denmark Vesey"; "Finally—More Judges and Denmark Vesey!" *CHR*, Aug. 7, 1976.

75. "The Vesey Affair," *CHR*, Aug. 21, 1976; William Saunders, letter to the editor, *CEP*, Aug. 21, 1976.

76. Bobby Isaac, "Vesey Painting Missing from Auditorium," Sept. 19, 1976, *CNC*; Ford, "Says Daily Press Responsible for Theft of Vesey Painting"; "Vesey Painting Returned; Blame Laid to Anti-Vesey Editorials in White Press," *CHR*, Sept. 25, 1976; Margaret Locklair, "Investigation Continuing in Painting Theft," *CEP*, Sept. 20, 1976; Edward C. Fennell, "Reporter Finds Vesey Portrait," *CNC*, Sept. 21, 1976; Edward C. Fennell, "Painting Back at Auditorium," *CNC*, Sept. 22, 1976.

77. Sarah Katherine Dykens, "Commemoration and Controversy: The Memorialization of Denmark Vesey in Charleston, South Carolina" (master's thesis, Clemson University, 2015), 68, 72–76 (quote 74); Dottie Ashley, "Dorothy Wright: Artist Honors the Champions of Civil Rights," *CPC*, Sept. 27, 1997.

78. Estes, *Charleston in Black and White*, 56.

10. Segregating the Past

1. Robert R. Weyeneth, *Historic Preservation for a Living City: Historic Charleston Foundation, 1947–1997* (Columbia: University of South Carolina Press, 2000), 23–31; Charles B. Hosmer Jr., *Preservation Comes of Age: From Williamsburg to the National Trust, 1926–1949* (Charlottesville: University of Virginia Press, 1981), 1: 254–73; Samuel Gaillard Stoney, *This Is Charleston: An Architectural Survey of a Unique American City*, 3rd ed. (Charleston: Carolina Art Association, 1964).

2. Frederick Law Olmsted Jr., "Central Considerations," May 1940, Folder 8, Civic Services Committee Papers, MCALDL.

3. Stephanie E. Yuhl, *A Golden Haze of Memory: The Making of Historic Charleston* (Chapel Hill: University of North Carolina Press, 2005), 50–52; Helen Gardner McCormack, quoted in Hosmer, *Preservation Comes of Age*, 1: 261; Alice Ravenel Huger Smith, "Reminiscences," in *Alice Ravenel Huger Smith: An Artist, a Place, and a Time*, by Martha R. Severens (Charleston: Carolina Art Association, 1993), 67–69, 83, 94–95.

4. Stoney, *This Is Charleston*, 3rd ed., 22, 87.

5. Jonathan H. Poston, *The Buildings of Charleston: A Guide to the City's Architecture* (Columbia: University of South Carolina Press, 1997), 8; Weyeneth, *Historic Preservation*, 31–40; Hosmer, *Preservation Comes of Age*, 1: 269–73.

6. Thomas R. Waring, "Charleston Americana," *NYT*, Mar. 6, 1949; Charleston's Historic Houses, Brochures, 1949–1957, Historic Charleston Foundation's Tours of Homes Collection, MCALDL.

7. Minutes, Nov. 29, 1951, and Minutes, Apr. 25, 1951, both in Rough Minutes/Agendas, 1951, Box 2, RHCC; Mary A. Sparkman, Guidebook Notes to Historic Charleston, 1936, CLS; Robert Behre, "Early Notes Paved Way for Charleston Guides," *CPC*, Dec. 26, 2011.

8. Lectures for Guides Examination—1954, Tour Guide Exams, 1954–1956, Box 1, RHCC; Sparkman, "Lectures for Guides of Historic Charleston," 1964, HICTG.

9. "Causes of War," *CPC*, Jan. 8, 1994; Marguerite C. Steedman, letter to the editor, *CEP*, Apr. 21, 1979; [Marguerite C. Steedman], Lectures for Guides (1973), HICTG.

10. Elizabeth O'Neill Verner, *Mellowed by Time: A Charleston Notebook*, 3rd ed. (Columbia: Bostick and Thornley, 1953), 35.

11. Thomas J. Brown, *Civil War Canon: Sites of Confederate Memory in South Carolina* (Chapel Hill: University of North Carolina Press, 2015), 185–91; "Fort Sumter Visitor Rate Sets May Record," *CNC*, June 1, 1960; Kevin Allen, "The Second Battle of Fort Sumter: The Debate over the Politics of Race and Memory at the Opening of America's Civil War Centennial, 1961," *Public Historian* 33 (May 2011): 100; "City Ready for Fort Sumter," *CNC*, Apr. 9, 1961.

12. Everett J. Landers to Karl S. Betts, Feb. 4, 1961, Folder 15, Box 184, BIWP; Robert J. Cook, *Troubled Commemoration: The American Civil War Centennial, 1961–1965* (Baton Rouge: Louisiana State University Press, 2011), 15, 88–94; Mrs. J.G. Matty to J. Palmer Gaillard, Mar. 24, 1961; G.W. Goodman to J. Palmer Gaillard, Mar. 24, [1961]; and Mrs. Willard Steele to J. Palmer Gaillard, Mar. 24, 1961, all in Civil War Centennial Folder, CCR.

13. "Group to Shun Local Pageant," *CNC*, Mar. 10, 1961; Cook, *Troubled Commemoration*, 93–98, 101–7; Jon Wiener, "Civil War, Cold War, Civil Rights: The Civil War Centennial in Context, 1960–1965," in *The Memory of the Civil War in American Culture*, ed. Alice Fahs and Joan Waugh (Chapel Hill: University of North Carolina Press, 2004), 238–41; John F. Kennedy to Ulysses S. Grant III, Mar. 14, 1961, and CWCC Executive Committee, minutes of meeting held Mar. 21, 1961, p. 4, both in Folder 7, Box 84, BIWP; "Centennial Hassel Gains Momentum," *CEP* Mar. 24, 1961; Bell Wiley to Anne Freedgood, Mar. 29, 1961, Folder 2, Box 62, BIWP; Ulysses S. Grant III to J. Palmer Gaillard, Mar. 27, 1961, Civil War Centennial Folder, CCR.

14. "Hollings Says President Can't Dictate to Hotels," *CEP*, Mar. 24, 1961; "Only 50 Request Naval Housing," *CEP*, Mar. 24, 1961; "Naval Base Says Housing to Be Austere," *CNC*, Mar. 26, 1961; Jack Roach, "Long Distance Wires Hum with War Centennial Volleys," *CEP*, Mar. 29, 1961; "Move May Cause Visitors to Miss Events," *CNC*, Mar. 26, 1961.

15. Edmund G. Gass to Bell I. Wiley, Apr. 5, 1961, Folder 26, Box 184, BIWP; Neil Gilbride, "Is Nation Still a House Divided Against Itself? You'd Think So in Charleston," *Greensboro Record*, Apr. 11, 1961; "2 N.J. Centennial Delegates Attend NAACP Meeting," *CNC*, Apr. 12, 1961.

16. "Visitors, Delegates Pouring In," *CNC*, Apr. 11, 1961; "Confederates Start Meeting Ball Rolling," *CEP*, Apr. 11, 1961; "Vicious Tornado Hits James Island Homes," *CEP*, Apr. 12, 1961; "Parade Gets Break as Sun Comes Out," *CNC*, Apr. 13, 1961; Claire McPhail, "The Rocket's Red Glare," *CNC*, Apr. 14, 1961.

17. John B. Rogers Producing Company, "A Proposal for Charleston County and the City of Charleston, South Carolina to Conduct a War of the Confederacy Centennial Commission in 1961," and Official Program, "The Charleston Centennial of the Confederacy Commemoration, 1861–1961," both in CM; "Confederate War Group Wins Yanks with Kindness," *CNC*, Apr. 11, 1961; "Confederates Start Meeting Ball Rolling"; Allen, "Second Battle of Fort Sumter," 104–5.

18. "'Reliving of War' Feared by Byrnes," *NYT*, Apr. 16, 1961; "A Word with Our Readers," *Holiday*, July 1961, p. 25; Cook, *Troubled Commemoration*, 117–19.

19. "Centennial 'Fitting,' Says Mayor," *CNC*, Apr. 14, 1961. The mayor's comments also reflected a dustup between New Jersey delegates and one speaker, Ashley Halsey Jr., who made disparaging remarks about them. Cook, *Troubled Commemoration*, 115–18. "8,050 Visited Fort During May," *CEP*, June 6, 1961; "1961 Visitors to Fort Sumter Already Top '60," *CEP*, Oct. 17, 1961.

20. Michael Ra-Shon Hall, "The Negro Traveller's Guide to a Jim Crow South: Negotiating Racialized Landscapes During a Dark Period in United States Cultural History, 1936–1967," *Postcolonial Studies* 17 (2014): 307–19; Gretchen Sorin, "'Keep Going': African Americans on the Road in the Era of Jim Crow" (Ph.D. diss., University at Albany, State University at New York, 2009), 168–209; 1938–1964 Green Books, TGB; Tammy S. Gordon, "'Take Amtrak to Black History': Marketing Heritage Tourism to African Americans in the 1970s," *Journal of Tourism History* 7 (2015): 56.

21. "Tourism and Minorities" in *Special Studies*, vol. 5 of *Destination USA: Report of the National Tourism Resources Review Commission* (Washington, DC: U.S. Government Printing Office, 1973), 69–83; "The New Jet-Setters," *Time*, June 19, 1972, 88; Gordon, "'Take Amtrak to Black History,'" 55–57; W. Fitzhugh Brundage, *The Southern Past: A Clash of Race and Memory* (Cambridge, MA: Belknap Press of Harvard University Press, 2005), 295–96; Michael Kammen, *Mystic Chords of Memory: The Transformation of Tradition in American Culture* (New York: Vintage, 1993), 642–44.

22. Brundage, *Southern Past*, 309–10; *Domestic Tourism*, vol. 2 of *Destination USA: Report of the National Tourism Resources Review Commission* (Washington, DC: U.S. Government Printing Office, 1973), 11; "S.C. Tourism Group Reveals New Promotion Plan," *State*, Sept. 13, 1968; "Canada Is Major Target in S.C. Tourist Campaign," *CNC*, Feb. 10, 1969; "'Leisure Market' Growing: Fraser," *CNC*, Jan. 21, 1970; Walter J. Fraser Jr., *Charleston! Charleston! The History of a Southern City* (Columbia: University of South Carolina Press, 1989), 412; U.S. Department of Transportation, "Economic Development History of Interstate 26 in South Carolina," fhwa.dot.gov/planning/economic_development/studies /i26sc.cfm; Robert Lee Frank, "The Economic Impact of Tourism in Charleston, South Carolina, 1970" (master's thesis, University of South Carolina, 1964), 106–9; Ben S. Palmer, "Tourism Booming in Charleston," *CNC*, Apr. 19, 1969; W.K. Pillow Jr., "Recreation Officer Works to Make Program Familiar," *CNC*, Feb. 24, 1969; Sharon A. Feaster, "Tourism Business Means $$," *CNC*, Sept. 10, 1972; "Don't Kill the Goose," *CNC*, Nov. 14, 1977; Katharine Mary Sparks, "The Relationship Between Changes in Business Structure and Tourism Growth and Development in Charleston, South Carolina, 1899–1999" (Ph.D. diss., Clemson University, 2012), Appendixes IV and V, 346–48; "Mission Will Explore Tourism Market Potential," *CNC*, Nov. 9, 1969.

23. Barnard Law Collier, "South Carolina: A Yankee View," *NYT*, June 21, 1970.

24. Judith Chase Scrapbook, 3, 14, OSMMP; "Searching Africa for Art," *CNC*, Feb 24, 1967; Judith W. Chase, "Comprehensive Information Relating to the History, Purpose, and Operation of the Old Slave Mart Museum & Library, 1937 through 1985," OSMMP; Louise A. Graves, application, Institute of Museum Services, Department of Health, Education, and Welfare, Mar. 8, 1979, pp. 37, 39, 45, OSMMPCC; Christine Randall, "Curator Catalogs Collection," *CNC*, Nov. 1, 1978; John Michael Vlatch, "Evaluation of the Old Slave Mart Museum, Charleston, South Carolina," Apr. 9, 1979, 3–4, OSMMP; Stephanie E. Yuhl, "Hidden in Plain Sight: Centering the Domestic Slave Trade in American Public History," *JSH* 79 (Aug. 2013): 613–14; Greta Tilley, "Sisters Try to Save Museum," *GNR*, May 18, 1986.

25. Chase, "Comprehensive Information," 37; Yuhl, "Hidden in Plain Slight," 610–11; OSMM flyer, 1970, in Judith Chase Scrapbook, 3.

26. "Grim Reminder of Slavery Preserved," *LAT*, Mar. 23, 1975; Vlatch, "Evaluation of the Old Slave Mart Museum," 10; John Vernelson and Laura Nelson, "Money, Time Force Slave Mart to Close," *CEP*, Feb. 3, 1987; Tilley, "Sisters Try to Save Museum"; Chase, "Comprehensive Information," 46; Graves, application, Institute of Museum Services, 13.

27. OSMM flyer, 6 Chalmers Street, Old Slave Mart Museum Vertical File, CCPL; OSMM sign, n.d., OSMMP; Randall, "Curator Catalogs Collection"; Alston Chase, phone interview by Ethan J. Kytle, Nov. 18, 2015.

28. "Historic Half-Truths," *CNC*, July 28, 1978; Franz E. Auerbach, *No Single Loyalty: Many Strands One Design: A South African Teacher's Life* (New York: Waxman, 2002), 80; Tilley, "Sisters Try to Save Museum."

29. Steve Estes, *Charleston in Black and White: Race and Power in the South after the Civil Rights Movement* (Chapel Hill: University of North Carolina Press, 2015), 57–60; Weyeneth, *Historic Preservation for a Living City*, 92–105; Fraser, *Charleston! Charleston!*, 430–32, 434–37; Brian Hicks, *The Mayor: Joe Riley and the Rise of Charleston* (Charleston: Evening Post Books, 2015), 120–23, 126–28, 133–39, 144–46, 191–92; Sparks, "The Relationship Between Changes in Business Structure," Appendixes IV, V, 347, 349; Roger R. Stough, introduction to "The Report of the Mayor of Charleston's Tourism Management Committee: Recommendations," Feb. 2, 1982, p. 1, Tourism Management Reports File, HCF.

30. Hicks, *The Mayor*, 142, 194–95; Sparks, "The Relationship Between Changes in Business Structure," 272; Colleen K. Reilly, "Staging Charleston: The Spoleto Festival U.S.A." (Ph.D. diss., University of Pittsburgh, 2009), 50–51; Jim Parker, "Officials Have High Hopes for Black Festival," *CNC*, Feb. 1, 1984; Shirley Greene, "Moja Arts Festival to Offer Charleston Look at Black Culture," *CNC/CEP*, Sept. 15, 1984; Frank B. Jarrell, "February Declared Black Arts-History Month," *CNC*, Feb. 2, 1983; Kerri Morgan, "Chas. to Buy Slave Museum for $200,000," *CNC*, Jan. 29, 1988; Judith W. Chase to C.T. Wallace, Chairman, Members of Charleston County Council, Sept. 24, 1984; Sandra N. Fowler to Joseph P. Riley Jr., Aug. 8, 1985; and Judith W. Chase to Joseph P. Riley Jr., Jan. 2, 1986, all in SNFP; Verneslon and Nelson, "Money, Time Force Slave Mart to Close"; "Time's Awasting," *CEP*, Nov. 27, 1987; Yuhl, "Hidden in Plain Sight," 613–20. In 2000, the OSMM collection was purchased by Acacia Historical Arts International, Inc.

31. Marsha White, "Proposed Tours Would Emphasize Black History," *CNC*, Mar. 1, 1983; Dorothy Givens, "Guides Offer Tour of City from a Black Perspective," *CPC*, Nov. 21, 1991; Mary Pinckney Battle, "Confronting Slavery in Historic Charleston: Changing Tourism Narratives in the Twenty-First Century" (Ph.D. diss., Emory University, 2013), 192.

32. Alphonso Brown, interview by Rachel Martin, transcript, June 17, 2008, pp. 7–8, SOHP; Battle, "Confronting Slavery," 186–87; Wevonneda Minis, "Getting the Whole Story," *CPC*, Jan. 20, 1997.

33. Minis, "Getting the Whole Story"; Brown, interview, transcript, pp. 10–12; Adam Parker, "The Whole Story: Lowcountry Historic Sites, Tours Include More About African-American Experience," *CPC*, Nov. 7, 2015; Chase, "Comprehensive Information," 46.

34. Brown, interview, transcript, pp. 8–9, 18; Warren L. Wise, "Gullah Tours Operator Offers a Different Take on Charleston History," *CPC*, July 8, 2013; Battle, "Confronting Slavery," 187–88.

35. Park Dougherty, phone interview by Blain Roberts and Ethan J. Kytle, Dec. 8, 2014; Robert Behre, "Spiritual Society Back in National Spotlight," *CPC*, July 23, 2011; Eric Frazier, "Singers Reproduce Sights, Sounds, Rhythms of Tradition," *CPC*, June 7, 1996.

36. Julia Coaxum, "3 Names to Update Tour Guide Manual," *CNC*, Apr. 26, 1984; Michael Trouche, "City Tourism Group Holds First Meeting," *CNC*, Sept. 21, 1983; Robert Stockton, ed., "Information for Guides of Historic Charleston" (Charleston: Charleston Tourism Commission, ca. 1985), HICTG; "Schools, Hospital to Focus on Black History," *CEP*, Feb. 20, 1981; "Black History Program Planned Here Sunday," *CNC*, Feb. 24, 1983.

37. Elizabeth H. Alston, "Black Charlestonians," in "Information for Guides of Historic Charleston," 481–82. On how grammatical choices can obscure the role of slaveholders in perpetuating slavery, see Ellen Bresler Rockmore, "How Texas Teaches History," *NYT*, Oct. 21, 2015.

38. Minis, "Getting the Whole Story"; Givens, "Guides Offer Tour of City from a Black Perspective"; Al Miller, Sites and Insights Tour, Aug. 13, 2009.

39. Alphonso Brown, Gullah Tours Tour, Apr. 14, 2007.

40. Maurie D. McInnis, *The Politics of Taste in Antebellum Charleston* (Chapel Hill: University of North Carolina Press, 2005), 180–81; Brown, Gullah Tours Tours, Apr. 14, 2007 and Apr. 13, 2009.

41. Miller, Sites and Insights Tour, Aug. 13, 2009; Steven Deyle, *Carry Me Back: The Domestic Slave Trade in American Life* (New York: Oxford University Press, 2005), 47; Michael Tadman, *Speculators and Slaves: Masters, Traders, and Slaves in the Old South* (Madison: University of Wisconsin Press, 1989), 121–29; Gregory D. Smithers, *Slave Breeding: Sex, Violence, and Memory in African American History* (Gainesville: University Press of Florida, 2012), 4–10.

42. Sandra Campbell, interview by Blain Roberts, Aug. 15, 2009, Charleston, SC. Vesey lived on Bull Street, between Pitt and Smith streets, though not in the current structure at 56 Bull Street, which research suggests was built between the 1830s and 1850s—after Denmark Vesey was executed. Vesey's Bull Street home, moreover, was most likely located several houses away from the 56 Bull Street structure. Douglas R. Egerton, *He Shall Go Out Free: The Lives of Denmark Vesey, Revised and Updated Edition* (Lanham, MD: Rowman and Littlefield, 2004), 83*n*18; Sarah Katherine Dykens, "Commemoration and Controversy: The Memorialization of Denmark Vesey in Charleston, South Carolina" (master's thesis, Clemson University, 2015), 35–57; Douglas R. Egerton, interview by Ethan J. Kytle, July 19, 2009, Springfield, IL.

43. Campbell, interview; Jonathan Sanchez, "Downtown Walking Tour Highlights Slave Contributions," *CPC*, Aug. 28, 1997.

44. Carriage Tour, June 21, 2008; Peter H. Wood, *Black Majority: Negroes in Colonial South Carolina from 1670 through the Stono Rebellion* (New York: Knopf, 1974), 147; Philip D. Morgan, *Slave Counterpoint: Black Culture in the Eighteenth-Century Chesapeake and Lowcountry* (Chapel Hill: University of North Carolina Press, 1998), 95.

45. Carriage Tour, June 21, 2008.

46. Scott A. Michie, phone interview by Ethan J. Kytle, Oct. 10, 2013; Kristan Poirot and Shevaun E. Watson, "Memories of Freedom and White Resilience: Place, Tourism, and

Urban Slavery," *Rhetoric Society Quarterly* 45(2): 105–6; Carriage Tour, June 21, 2008; Carriage Tour, Aug. 13, 2009; Van Tour, Aug. 14, 2009.

47. Alphonso Brown, quoted in Battle, "Confronting Slavery," 191; Brown, interview, transcript, pp. 11, 13; Office of Tourism Analysis, College of Charleston, "Estimation of Tourism Economic Impacts in the Charleston Area 2008," in authors' possession.

48. Campbell, interview.

49. Wevonneda Minis, "History Through the Eyes Of...," *CPC*, Jan. 18, 2004; Dorothy Givens, "PBS 'Civil War' Series Attracts Tourists," *CPC*, Oct. 25, 1990; Jack Thomson, Walking Tour, Aug. 15, 2009.

50. Campbell, interview. On African Americans' reluctance to confront the enslaved past, see Jonathan Holloway, *Jim Crow Wisdom: Memory and Identity in Black America since 1940* (Chapel Hill: University of North Carolina Press, 2013), 174–213; and the essays in James Oliver Horton and Lois E. Horton, eds., *Slavery and Public History: The Tough Stuff of American Memory* (New York: The New Press, 2006), especially, John Michael Vlach, "The Last Taboo Subject: Exhibiting Slavery at the Library of Congress," 57–73.

51. Edmund L. Drago, *Charleston's Avery Research Center: From Education and Civil Rights to Preserving the African American Experience* (Charleston: History Press, 2006), 266–85; Stephanie Harvin, "High Style," *CPC*, Sept. 19, 1988; College of Charleston Office of College Relations, "Avery Research Center to Sponsor 'Juneteenth' Celebration," May 31, 1995, WMDP; Herb Frazier, "Children Map Black History," *CPC*, Nov. 10, 1998; "Shout Tradition Lives in Exhibit at Avery Center," *CPC*, May 18, 1995.

52. Michael Allen, interview by Ethan J. Kytle, June 16, 2011, Charleston, SC; Michael Allen, phone interview by Ethan J. Kytle, Jan. 11, 2016; Michael Allen, interview by Rachel Martin, transcript, June 20, 2008, pp. 1–3, SOHP; Paul Bowers, "Michael Allen Brings Together NAACP, Sons of Confederate Veterans," *CCP*, July 6, 2011; Battle, "Confronting Slavery," 204–7.

53. Allen, phone interview by Kytle; Allen, interview by Martin, transcript, pp. 4–7; Battle, "Confronting Slavery," 204–10; Brown, *Civil War Canon*, 198–99; Cathy N. Davidson to the Director of National Park Service, Sept. 26, 1994; Edwin C. Bearss to Cathy N. Davidson, Nov. 18, 1994; and W. Marvin Dulaney to John Tucker, Dec. 13, 1994, all in WMDP; Wood, *Black Majority*, xiv; William R. Ryan, *The World of Thomas Jeremiah: Charles Town on the Eve of the American Revolution* (New York: Oxford University Press, 2010), 111; Wevonneda Minis, "Site Honors Black and White Histories," *CPC*, Feb. 7, 1999; Linda L. Meggett, "New Monument Honors Slaves," *CPC*, July 3, 1999; Jessica Johnson, "Fort Moultrie Seeks Comments on Slave Exhibit," *CPC*, Jan. 24, 2008; David Munday, "Betting on History," *CPC*, Mar. 13, 2009; Toni Morrison, "A Bench by the Road: Beloved," *World: Journal of the Unitarian Universalist Association*, 3 (Jan.–Feb. 1989), 3; Dottie Ashley, " 'Bench by the Road' Tribute to Slaves," *CPC*, July 28, 2008; Ryan Quinn, "Honoring Those Lost," *CPC*, June 12, 2011.

54. Battle, "Confronting Slavery," 203–4, 208–9; Bowers, "Michael Allen Brings Together"; Marvin Dulaney, phone interview by Ethan J. Kytle, Oct. 15, 2013; Weyeneth, *Historic Preservation*, 157–58; Kitty Robinson, interview by Blain Roberts, Aug. 13, 2009, Charleston, SC; "Sale of Historic House Goes On," *CPC*, Dec. 12, 1995.

55. Weyeneth, *Historic Preservation*, 133; Battle, "Confronting Slavery," 17–18, 58, 84–97, 115–16; "Magnolia Plantation House," Tour Guide Notes, n.d., n.p., and "The Magnolia Plantation," n.d., n.p., both in Clippings Binder, MPA; R.J. Lamrose, "The Abusable Past," *Radical History Review*, 57 (1993): 275–76 ("dream come true" quote 275); David K. Shipler, *A Country of Strangers: Blacks and Whites in America* (New York: Knopf, 1997), 165.

56. Deneshia Graham, "Tour Teaches History of Slavery," *CPC*, Nov. 7, 2004; Kyle Stock, "Selling Slavery," *CPC*, July 26, 2008; Bruce Allison, "Youthful Insight," *CPC*, June 11, 2002; Jim Rutenberg, "Dueling Visions of the Old South," *NYT*, Sept. 13, 2009; Drayton Hall Tours, Mar. 21, 2006, Mar. 22, 2006, Mar. 23, 2006, Aug. 16, 2009, and June 21, 2011; Thurston Hatcher, "Slave Cabins May Be Restored," *CPC*, May 4, 1992; David Quick, "How Garden Will Grow at Boone Hall," *CPC*, Apr. 2, 1998; Robert Behre, "A Restoration of History," *CPC*, Mar. 7, 2006; Adam Parker, "Plantation Confronts its History," *CPC*, Sept. 10, 2006; Allyson Bird, "Open to Interpretation," *CPC*, Oct. 20, 2008; Jill L. Norman, "Middleton Place Widening Black Focus," *CNC*, Jan. 25, 1990; Bo Petersen, "Middleton's Slaves Named in New Exhibit," *CPC*, Feb. 1, 2005.

57. Robert Behre, "Gullah Project Is Latest Way Area Presents Black History," *CPC*, Nov. 20, 2006; Stock, "Selling Slavery"; Battle, "Confronting Slavery," 111–17.

58. Battle, "Confronting Slavery," 103, 113–58; From Slavery to Freedom Tours, Magnolia Plantation, Aug. 16, 2009 and June 21, 2011; Rutenberg, "Dueling Visions of the Old South."

59. Battle, "Confronting Slavery," 103, 113–58; From Slavery to Freedom Tours, Aug. 16, 2009 and June 21, 2011; Rutenberg, "Dueling Visions of the Old South"; Holloway, *Jim Crow Wisdom*, 200.

60. Battle, "Confronting Slavery," 128–29 (Preston quote 128); Jennifer Haupt, interview by Ethan J. Kytle, Nov. 11, 2014, Charleston, SC; Caroline Howell, interview by Ethan J. Kytle, Nov. 11, 2014, Charleston, SC.

61. Battle, "Confronting Slavery," 128–29 (Preston quote 128), 138, 138*n*157; Haupt, interview; Howell, interview; Sandra Jackson-Opoku, "Black Charleston: A Blend of History and Southern Charm," *Essence*, May 1, 1985, 24; Norman, "Middleton Place Widening Black Focus"; Parker, "The Whole Story."

62. Haupt, interview; Howell, interview.

63. Rutenberg, "Dueling Visions of the Old South"; House Tour, Boone Hall Plantation, Aug. 15, 2009; House Tour, Middleton Place Plantation, Aug. 16, 2009; House Tour, Magnolia Plantation, Aug. 16, 2009; Brundage, *Southern Past*, 327; Jennifer L. Eichstedt and Stephen Small, *Representations of Slavery: Race and Ideology in Southern Plantation Museums* (Washington, DC: Smithsonian Books, 2002), 170–202.

64. Aiken-Rhett House Tours, Oct. 19 and Oct. 20, 2005; Nathaniel Russell House Tour, Aug. 14, 2009.

65. Campbell, interview.

Conclusion: Denmark Vesey's Garden

1. Robert Behre, "NAACP to Protest Secession Event," *CPC*, Dec. 3, 2010.

2. "The South's Secession Commemoration," *The Daily Show with Jon Stewart*, Dec. 9, 2010; Carl Weinburg, "Nat Turner Rebellion Cotillion," *OAH Magazine of History* 25 (Apr. 2011): 3; Gina Smith, "NAACP Plans Protests as South Celebrates Confederacy," *State*, Dec. 12, 2010; Behre, "NAACP to Protest Secession Event."

3. Dot Scott, interview by Blain Roberts and others, Dec. 20, 2010, Charleston, SC. Other quotes from and descriptions of the Secession Ball and protests are based on observations by Blain Roberts, who attended the events.

4. Manuel Roig-Franzia, "At Charleston's Secession Ball, Divided Opinions on the Spirit of S.C.," *WP*, Dec. 22, 2010; Michael Givens, interview by Blain Roberts, David Usborne, and Edward Pilkington, Dec. 20, 2010, Charleston, SC.

5. Nelson B. Rivers III, Secession Ball protest, Dec. 20, 2010.

6. Roig-Franzia, "At Charleston's Secession Ball, Divided Opinions on the Spirit of S.C."

7. "Ball Draws Celebrators, Protestors," *State*, Dec. 21, 2010; " 'Secession Ball' Marks Start of American Civil War with Champagne and Dancing," *Guardian*, Dec. 21, 2010.

8. R.L. Schreadley, "Slavery Drove the South to Doorstep of Disunion," *CPC*, Dec. 14, 2010; Robert Behre, "President Obama Asked by Mayor Riley to Participate in Area's Observance of Start of Civil War," *CPC*, Dec. 16, 2010; "Civil War Is Nothing to Celebrate," *State*, Dec. 12, 2010; Warren Bolton, "What's There to Celebrate," *State*, Dec. 17, 2010; "South Carolina Secedes: A Four Act Re-Enactment of South Carolina's Secession Convention," program in authors' possession.

9. Robert Behre, "Historical Secession Marker Unveiled, Protests Ongoing," *CPC*, Dec. 20, 2010; Roig-Franzia, "At Charleston's Secession Ball, Divided Opinions on the Spirit of S.C."

10. Bo Moore, interview by Ethan J. Kytle, Apr. 14, 2011, Charleston, SC.

11. The description of the Fort Sumter sesquicentennial and responses to it are based on the observations of Ethan J. Kytle, who attended many of the events. See also "Observing the Sesquicentennial of the Civil War, Charleston, South Carolina, Schedule of Events—April 2011," Program, in authors' possession.

12. Brian Hicks, "Robert Smalls' Legacy Will Be Remembered This Weekend," *CPC*, May 8, 2012; Robert Behre, "Charleston Marking 150th Anniversary of the Civil War's Biggest Local Battle," *CPC*, July 7, 2013. The 54th Massachusetts marker was not completed and installed until late 2015. Robert Behre, "54th Massachusetts Marker Tells Another Side of Civil War Story," *CPC*, Jan. 1, 2016. Our account of the Martyrs of the Race Course ceremony is based on our observations at the event and David W. Blight, "Clementa Pinckney, a Martyr of Reconciliation," *Atlantic*, June 22, 2015.

13. Harris Jordan, "*Charleston Mercury* Past, Present and Future," *CM*, 2012, charleston-mercury.com/index.php/en/news/211-charleston-mercury-past-present-and-future; Charles W. Waring III in *CM Magazine: Sesquicentennial 2011*, vol. 6, no. 2, p. 5; Herb Frazier, "Preparing for the Sesquicentennial: Slavery in Barbados," *CM*, Dec. 14, 2010; Herb Frazier, "Preparing for the Sesquicentennial: Columbus and Slavery in the Caribbean," *CM*, Nov. 30, 2010; Herb Frazier, "Preparing for the Sesquicentennial: Haiti and Slave Revolts," *CM*, Dec. 14, 2010; "Slings and Arrows of the Sesquicentennial: Publisher Defends Newspaper from BBC Smear," *CM*, Apr. 19, 2011; "Myths, History, and Mr. Lincoln's War," *CM*, Dec. 14, 2010; "Slavery, Our Name, and a Visit with the BBC," *CM*, Apr. 7, 2011.

14. Brian Hicks, "Smalls Monument Falls a Month After Dedication," *CPC*, June 22, 2012; Katherine Saunders Pemberton, phone interview by Blain Roberts and Ethan J. Kytle, Sept. 17, 2012; Brian Hicks, "Smalls Marker Back on the Battery," *CPC*, July 19, 2012.

15. Stephanie E. Yuhl, "Hidden in Plain Sight: Centering the Domestic Slave Trade in American Public History," *JSH* 79 (Aug. 2013): 619–21; Herb Frazier, "Hearing the Passions of History," *CM*, June 14, 2011; Edward Rothstein, "Emancipating History," *NYT*, Mar. 11, 2011.

16. Robert Behre, "McLeod Plantation—Opening This Week—Tackles Slavery, Freedom," *CPC*, Apr. 20, 2015; David Slade, "$3.3 M for McLeod; Plantation Purchased the Latest in String of Deals for PRC," *CPC*, Oct. 22, 2010; McLeod Plantation Tour, June 14, 2017.

17. Joseph McGill, interview by Blain Roberts, Sept. 13, 2013, Charleston, SC; The Slave Dwelling Project, slavedwellingproject.org/; Tony Horwitz, *Confederates in the Attic: Dispatches from the Unfinished Civil War* (New York: Pantheon, 1998), 46–48; Jennifer Schuessler, "Confronting Slavery at Long Island's Oldest Estates," *NYT*, Aug. 12, 2015.

18. Wevonneda Minis, "Project Seeks to Save Slave Cabins," *CPC*, May 8, 2010; McGill, interview; Robert Behre, "Report Assesses Conditions of Several S.C. Slave Dwellings," *CPC*, Jan. 10, 2016; The Slave Dwelling Project, slavedwellingproject.org/.

19. McGill, interview; The Slave Dwelling Project, slavedwellingproject.org/; Bruce Smith, "Slave Dwelling Project Works Toward Preservation," *CPC*, Aug. 26, 2013; Behre, "Report Assesses Conditions of Several S.C. Slave Dwellings."

20. Minis, "Project Seeks to Save Slave Cabins"; McGill, interview.

21. Historic Charleston Foundation, ed., *The City of Charleston Tour Guide Training Manual* (Charleston: City of Charleston, 2011), in authors' possession; Derek Legette, "Reclaiming History: Charleston Commemorates Site of First Memorial Day Celebration," *CPC*, June 1, 2010; Ted Mellnik, "The Remarkable History of Charleston's Racial Divide, as Told by the City's Silent Statues," *WP*, Wonkblog, June 24, 2015, washingtonpost.com/news/wonk/wp /2015/06/24/the-remarkable-history-of-charlestons-racial-divide-as-told-by-the-citys-silent -statues/.

22. Robert Behre, "Slave Auction Marker Dedicated Thursday Tells 'A Bigger Story,'" *CPC*, Mar. 10, 2016; "Slave Auctions" Historical Marker Dedication Handout, Mar. 10, 2016, in authors' possession; Robert Behre, "Painting of 1853 Charleston Slave Auction Basis of Old Exchange Building Exhibit," *CPC*, Feb. 11, 2016; Edwin C. Breeden, phone interview by Ethan J. Kytle, Mar. 1, 2016; Edwin C. Breeden, email to Ethan J. Kytle, Mar. 2, 2016.

23. "Worthy Plan for Black History," *CPC*, Jan. 12, 2000, Scattered Site African American Heritage Museum File, HCF; Diane Knich, "Charleston Mayor Joe Riley Expects to Raise $75 Million for the International African American Museum Before He Leaves Office," *CPC*, July 12, 2015.

24. Henry Darby, phone interview by Blain Roberts and Ethan J. Kytle, Feb. 3, 2010; Susan Jacoby, "Weekend Getaways; Beyond Charm in Charleston," *NYT*, May 2, 1999.

25. Darby, phone interview; John P. Thomas, *The History of the South Carolina Military Academy* (Charleston, 1893). The Sumter Guard had dropped the "s" from its name by this point.

26. Ron Menchaca, "Marion Square Redo Under Way," *CPC*, Apr. 6, 2000; Elsa McDowell, "Monument's Future Needs Consideration," *CPC*, Jan. 23, 2001; Darby, phone interview; Curtis Franks, interview by Ethan J. Kytle, Aug. 14, 2009, Charleston, SC; Bernard E. Powers Jr., phone interview by Blain Roberts and Ethan J. Kytle, Feb. 12, 2010.

27. David Slade, "Groundbreaking for Vesey Monument," *CPC*, Feb. 2, 2010; Curtis J. Franks, interview by Daron Lee Calhoun II and Deborah Wright, transcript, May 5, 2104, p. 14, ARC; Douglas R. Egerton and Robert L. Paquette, introduction to their *The Denmark Vesey Affair: A Documentary History* (Gainesville: University Press of Florida, 2017), 5n1; Kevin R. Eberle, *A History of Charleston's Hampton Park* (Charleston: History Press, 2012), 28–31.

28. Slade, "Groundbreaking for Vesey Monument"; Jason Hardin, "Historians to Debate Vesey Legacy, Planned Monument," *CPC*, Mar. 22, 2001.

29. Marsha Guerard, "Memorial to Those Who Perished," *CPC*, Dec. 14, 1995; Robert Behre, "Holocaust Memorial Plan Studied," *CPC*, Mar. 28, 1996; Robert Behre, "Ground Broken at Site, Holocaust Memorial," *CPC*, July 24, 1997; Robert Behre, "Holocaust Memorial Taking Shape," *CPC*, Aug. 17, 1998; "David Popowski: The Holocaust Memorial on Marion Square Has Special Meaning . . . ," *CPC*, May 15, 1999; Robert Behre, "Remembering Holocaust Memorial Dedication Set," *CPC*, June 6, 1999; Plaque, Holocaust Memorial, Marion Square, Charleston, SC.

30. Powers, phone interview.

31. Behre, "Remembering Holocaust Memorial Dedication Set"; Darby, phone interview.

32. Jamaica Kincaid, "Sowers and Reapers: The Unquiet World of a Flower Bed," *New Yorker*, Jan. 22, 2001, pp. 41–42.

33. Adam Parker, "Denmark Vesey Monument Unveiled in Hampton Park Before Hundreds," *CPC*, Feb. 15, 2014; Deborah Wright and Daron Calhoun, "Remember Denmark

Vesey of Charleston," *Avery Messenger* (Summer 2014): 7; Barney Blakeney, "Vesey Monument Unveiled as First to Honor an African American in the Lowcountry," *CHR*, Feb. 19, 2014; Franks, interview by Calhoun and Wright, p. 14; Inscription, Vesey Monument, Hampton Park, Charleston, SC.

34. Wright and Calhoun, "Remember Denmark Vesey of Charleston," 8.

35. Joseph P. Riley Jr., interview by Blain Roberts and Ethan J. Kytle, June 17, 2015, Charleston, SC.

AFTERWORD: THE SAVING GRACE
OF THE EMANUEL NINE?

1. Joseph P. Riley Jr., interview by Blain Roberts and Ethan J. Kytle, June 17, 2015, Charleston, SC.

2. Justin Miller, "Dylann Roof Visited Slave Plantations, Confederate Landmarks," *Daily Beast*, June 20, 2015; Catherine Thompson, "An Annotated Guide to the Charleston Massacre Suspect's Racist Photo Trove," *Talking Points Memo*, June 23, 2015; Neeley Tucker and Peter Holley, "Dylan Roof's Eerie Tour of American Slavery at Its Beginning, Middle, and End," *WP*, July 1, 2015; Edward Ball, "United States v. Dylann Roof," *NYRB*, Mar. 9, 2017, p. 6; Evaluation of Competency to Stand Trial, 18 U.S.C. 4247 (Section 4241), Defendant Dylann Roof, Examiner James C. Ballenger, M.D., Nov. 15, 2016, pp. 32–33, posted on post andcourier.com/church_shooting/newly-released-documents-say-dylann-roof-saw-his-reputation-not/article_c25f720a-35b1-11e7-99fb-fbc1a612bf73.html.

3. Ball, "United States v. Dylann Roof," 6.

4. "As SC Honors Church Victims, Alabama Lowers Its Flags," *NYT*, June 24, 2015; Frances Robles, Richard Fausset, and Michael Barbaro, "Nikki Haley, South Carolina Governor, Calls for Removal of Confederate Battle Flag," *NYT*, June 23, 2015; Cynthia Roldan and Deanna Pan, "Glenn McConnell Backs Removal of Confederate Flag; Civil War Descendants Vow Fight," *CPC*, June 25, 2015.

5. David W. Blight, "Clementa Pinckney, a Martyr of Reconciliation," *Atlantic*, June 22, 2015.

6. Kevin Sack and Gardiner Harris, "President Obama Eulogizes Charleston Pastor as One Who Understood Grace," *NYT*, June 26, 2015; Barack Obama, "Remarks by the President in Eulogy for the Honorable Reverend Clementa Pinckney," June 26, 2015, obamawhitehouse.archives.gov/the-press-office/2015/06/26/remarks-president-eulogy-honorable-reverend-clementa-pinckney; Michiko Kakutani, "Obama's Eulogy, Which Found Its Place in History," *NYT*, July 3, 2015.

7. Alan Blinder and Richard Fausett, "South Carolina House Votes to Remove Confederate Flag," *NYT*, July 9, 2015; Stephanie McCrummen and Elahe Izadi, "Confederate Flag Comes Down on South Carolina's Statehouse Grounds," *WP*, July 10, 2015; Michael Prince, *Rally 'Round the Flag, Boys! South Carolina and the Confederate Flag* (Columbia: University of South Carolina Press, 2004), 45–49.

8. Melissa Boughton, "Confederate Monument a Focus of Debate After Graffiti Appears," *CPC*, June 21, 2015; Peter Holley, "'Black Lives Matter' Graffiti Appears on Confederate Memorials Across the U.S.," *WP*, June 23, 2015; Dave Munday, "Vandal Quotes President Barack Obama with Spray Paint on Confederate Memorial Statue," *CPC*, July 10, 2015; Kurt Luther, "Tracking Vandalism of Confederate Monuments," Aug. 22, 2015, kurtluther.com/confederate/; Campbell Robertson, Monica Davey, and Julie Bosman, "Calls to Drop Confederate Emblems Spread Nationwide," *NYT*, June 23, 2015; Richard Fausset and Alan Blinder, "South Carolina Settles Its Decades-Old Dispute Over a Confederate Flag," *NYT*,

July 9, 2015; Lauren McGaughy, "UT Removes Jefferson Davis Statue," *Houston Chronicle*, Aug. 30, 2015.

9. Noah Remnick, "Yale Grapples with Ties to Slavery in Debate Over a College's Name," *NYT*, Sept. 11, 2015; Emma Peters, "Jefferson Davis Award Discontinued," *Bowdoin Orient*, Oct. 21, 2015, bowdoinorient.com/article/10551; Andy Newman, "At Princeton, Woodrow Wilson, a Heralded Alum, Is Recast as an Intolerant One," *NYT*, Nov. 22, 2015; Noah Remnick, "Yale Will Drop John Calhoun's Name from Building," *NYT*, Feb. 11, 2017.

10. Cleveland Tinker, "County Votes to Offer 'Old Joe' to United Daughters of the Confederacy," *Gainesville Sun*, May 23, 2017; "A Protest in Virginia with Echoes of the Klan," *NYT*, May 17, 2017; Daniel Victor, "New Orleans City Council Votes to Remove Confederate Monuments," *NYT*, Dec. 17, 2015; Christopher Mele, "New Orleans Begins Removing Statues Commemorating the Confederacy," *NYT*, Apr. 24, 2017; Avi Selk, "New Orleans Removes a Tribute to 'the Lost Cause of the Confederacy'—with Snipers Standing By," *WP*, Apr. 24, 2017; Richard Fausset, "Tempers Flare," *NYT*, May 7, 2017; Brentin Mock, "How Robert E. Lee Got Knocked Off His Pedestal," *Atlantic*, May 29, 2017; Campbell Robertson, "New Orleans Removes Beauregard Statue and Subdued Crowd Looks On," *NYT*, May 17, 2017; Campbell Robertson, "From Lofty Perch, New Orleans Monument to Confederacy Comes Down," *NYT*, May 19, 2017; Peter Applebome, "New Orleans Mayor's Message on Race," *NYT*, May 24, 2017.

11. Mitch Landrieu, "We Can't Walk Away from This Truth," *Atlantic*, May 23, 2017.

12. Laura Vozzella, "White Nationalist Richard Spencer Leads Torch-bearing Protesters Defending Lee Statue," *WP*, May 14, 2017; Hawes Spencer and Matt Stevens, "23 Arrested and Tear Gas Deployed after a K.K.K. Rally in Virginia," *NYT*, July 8, 2017; Sheryl Gay Stolberg and Brian M. Rosenthal, "Man Charged after White Nationalist Rally in Charlottesville Ends in Deadly Violence," *NYT*, Aug. 12, 2017; Associated Press, "Confederate Monuments Removed or Vandalized Across the U.S.," *NYT*, Aug. 18, 2017; "Confederate Monuments Are Coming Down Across the U.S. Here's a List," *NYT*, Aug. 22, 2017.

13. Southern Poverty Law Center, "Weekend Read: The State of the Confederacy in 2017," Apr. 28, 2017, splcenter.org/news/2017/04/28/weekend-read-state-confederacy-2017; Southern Poverty Law Center, "Whose Heritage? Public Symbols of the Confederacy," Apr. 21, 2016, splcenter.org/20160421/whose-heritage-public-symbols-confederacy; "Confederate Monuments Are Coming Down"; Jonah Engel Bromwich, "Confederate Monument, Shunned by One Kentucky City, Is Welcomed in Another," *NYT*, May 30, 2017.

14. Robert Behre, "Heritage Act Isn't Likely to Go the Way of the Confederate Flag," *CPC*, July 19, 2015; Jeff Hartsell, "Many Citadel Alumni Urge Flag's Removal," *CPC*, Nov. 14, 2015; Paul Bowers, "Citadel Alumni Renew Pressure to Remove Confederate Flag from Chapel," *CPC*, Sept. 1, 2017.

15. James W. Loewen, "Why Should Charleston Keep Honoring John C. Calhoun?" *CPC*, July 13, 2015; Tom Grubisich and Elizabeth Bowers, "How Charleston's Next Mayor Can Help the City Erase Its Stubborn Color Line," *CCP*, Oct. 22, 2015; "Rename Calhoun Street," *CPC*, July 6, 2015; Diane Knich, "Portion of Calhoun Designated as Mother Emanuel Way Memorial Dist.," *CPC*, Sept. 9, 2015; Robert Behre, "Charleston Looks at Amending—Not Removing—Its Confederate-Era Monuments," *CPC,* Aug. 17, 2017; Abigail Darlington, "Was the Denmark Vesey Monument in Charleston's Hampton Park Vandalized?" *CPC*, May 8, 2017.

16. Applebome, "New Orleans Mayor's"; David A. Graham, "Local Officials Want to Remove Confederate Monuments—But States Won't Let Them," *Atlantic*, Aug. 25, 2017; Antonio Olivo, "After Charlottesville, Va., Democrats See Opening to Change 114-Year-Old Monuments Law," *WP*, Aug. 25, 2017; Morgan Wagner, "Standing Mississippi Law Protects Historical Monuments," WTOK ABC News, May 25, 2017, wtok.com/content/news

/Standing-Mississippi-law-protects-historical-monuments-424437524.html; Lynn Bonner, "What's the Future for NC's Confederate Statues?" *Raleigh News and Observer*, Aug. 14, 2017; Andrew Blake, "Alabama Governor Signs Law Protecting Confederate Monuments from Removal," *Washington Times*, May 27, 2017; Arielle Dreher and Donna Ladd, "State Rep. Karl Oliver Calls for Lynching, Later Apologizes," *Jackson Free Press*, May. 21, 2017; Sarah McCammon, "Feeling Kinship with the South, Northerners Let Their Confederate Flags Fly," *National Public Radio*, May 4, 2017; Chris Kenning, "Confederate Battle Flag Sales Boom after Charlottesville Clash," Aug. 29, 2017, *Reuters*.

17. Nick Corasaniti, "At a Donald Trump Rally, a Confederate Flag Goes Up, and Quickly Comes Down," *NYT*, Aug. 11, 2016; Richard Fausset, "As Trump Rises, So Do Some Hands Waving Confederate Battle Flags," *NYT*, Nov. 18, 2016.

18. Vozzella, "White Nationalist Richard Spencer Leads Torch-bearing Protesters Defending Lee Statue"; Stolberg and Rosenthal, "Man Charged after White Nationalist Rally in Charlottesville Ends in Deadly Violence"; Summer Concepcion, "David Duke: Charlottesville Rally 'Fulfills the Promises of Donald Trump,'" *Talking Points Memo*, Aug. 12, 2017; John Wagner, Jenna Johnson, Robert Costa, and Sari Horwitz, "White House Confronts Backlash Over Trump's Remarks on Charlottesville," *WP*, Aug. 13, 2017.

19. Amy B. Wang, "One Group Loved Trump's Remarks about Charlottesville: White Supremacists," *WP*, Aug. 13, 2017; "Transcript and Video: President Trump Speaks about Charlottesville," *NYT*, Aug. 14, 2017; Michael D. Shear and Maggie Haberman, "Trump Defends Initial Remarks on Charlottesville; Again Blames 'Both Sides,'" *NYT*, Aug. 15, 2017; "Full Text: Trump's Comments on White Supremacists, 'Alt-Left' in Charlottesville," *Politico*, Aug. 15, 2017; Michael D. Shear and Maggie Haberman, "Defiant, Trump Laments Assault on Culture and Revives a Bogus Pershing Story," *NYT*, Aug. 17, 2017; Mark Landler and Maggie Haberman, "At Rally, Trump Blames Media for Country's Deepening Divisions," *NYT*, Aug. 22, 2017; "President Trump Ranted for 77 Minutes in Phoenix. Here's What He Said," *Time*, Aug. 23, 2017.

20. Shailagh Murray, "A Family Tree Rooted in American Soil," *WP*, Oct. 2, 2008; "Transcript: Read Michelle Obama's Full Speech from the 2016 DNC," *WP*, July 26, 2016; Daniel Victor, "Bill O'Reilly Defends Comments about 'Well Fed' Slaves," *NYT*, July 27, 2016.

21. Marist College Institute for Public Opinion, "A Nation Still Divided: The Confederate Flag," McClatchy-Marist Poll, Aug. 6, 2015, maristpoll.marist.edu/wp-content/misc /usapolls/us150722/CivilWar/McClatchy-Marist%20Poll_National%20Release%20 and%20Tables_The%20Confederate%20Flag_August%202015.pdf; Marist College Institute for Public Opinion, untitled poll, Aug. 2017, maristpoll.marist.edu/wp-content/misc /usapolls/us170814_PBS/NPR_PBS%20NewsHour_Marist%20Poll_National%20Na ture%20of%20the%20Sample%20and%20Tables_August%2017,%202017.pdf#page=3; Pew Research Center, "On Views of Race and Inequality, Blacks and Whites Are Worlds Apart," June 27, 2016, pewsocialtrends.org/2016/06/27/on-views-of-race-and-inequality -blacks-and-whites-are-worlds-apart/; PRRI/Brooking Survey, "How Immigration and Concerns about Cultural Change Are Shaping the 2016 Election," June 23, 2016, prri.org /research/prri-brookings-poll-immigration-economy-trade-terrorism-presidential-race/.

Image Credits

Index

About the Authors

ETHAN J. KYTLE and BLAIN ROBERTS are professors of history at California State University, Fresno. Kytle is author of *Romantic Reformers and the Antislavery Struggle in the Civil War Era*. Roberts is author of *Pageants, Parlors, and Pretty Women: Race and Beauty in the Twentieth-Century South*. They live in Fresno, California.

Celebrating 25 Years
of Independent Publishing

Thank you for reading this book published by The New Press. The New Press is a nonprofit, public interest publisher celebrating its twenty-fifth anniversary in 2017. New Press books and authors play a crucial role in sparking conversations about the key political and social issues of our day.

We hope you enjoyed this book and that you will stay in touch with The New Press. Here are a few ways to stay up to date with our books, events, and the issues we cover:

- Sign up at www.thenewpress.com/subscribe to receive updates on New Press authors and issues and to be notified about local events

- Like us on Facebook: www.facebook.com/newpress books

- Follow us on Twitter: www.twitter.com/thenewpress

Please consider buying New Press books for yourself; for friends and family; or to donate to schools, libraries, community centers, prison libraries, and other organizations involved with the issues our authors write about.

The New Press is a 501(c)(3) nonprofit organization. You can also support our work with a tax-deductible gift by visiting www.thenewpress.com/donate.